# The Routledge Handbook of Psychoanalysis in the Social Sciences and Humanities

*The Routledge Handbook of Psychoanalysis in the Social Sciences and Humanities* provides a comprehensive, critical overview of the historical, theoretical and applied forms of psychoanalytical criticism. This path-breaking handbook offers students new ways of understanding the powers and limits of psychoanalysis, and of the social, cultural and political possibilities of psychoanalytic critique.

The book offers students and professionals clear and concise chapters on the development of psychoanalysis, introducing key theories that have influenced debates over the psyche, desire and emotion in the social sciences and humanities. There are substantive chapters on classical Freudian theory, Kleinian and Bionian theory, object relations psychoanalysis, Lacanian and post-Lacanian approaches, feminist psychoanalysis, as well as postmodern trends in psychoanalysis. There is a strong emphasis on interdisciplinary approaches to psychoanalytic critique, with contributions drawing from developments in sociology, politics, history, cultural studies, women's studies and architecture.

**Anthony Elliott** is Director of the Hawke Research Institute and Executive Director of the Hawke EU Centre, where he is Research Professor of Sociology at the University of South Australia. He is Visiting Global Professor of Sociology at Keio University, Japan and Visiting Professor of Sociology at University College Dublin, Ireland. His recent books include *Concepts of the Self* (3rd edition, 2014), *Psychoanalytic Theory: An Introduction* (3rd edition, 2015) and *Identity* (4 volumes, 2015).

**Jeffrey Prager** is a Professor of Sociology at UCLA, former Dean and Training and Supervising Analyst at the New Center for Psychoanalysis in Los Angeles and in private practice in Beverly Hills. His published research is on social repair in post-conflict societies, cross-generational transmission of trauma, and American racism and reparations. He is the author of many books and articles, including the award-winning *Presenting the Past, Psychoanalysis and the Sociology of Misremembering* (Harvard).

# The Routledge Handbook of Psychoanalysis in the Social Sciences and Humanities

*Edited by Anthony Elliott and Jeffrey Prager*

Routledge
Taylor & Francis Group

LONDON AND NEW YORK

First published 2016 by Routledge

2 Park Square, Milton Park, Abingdon, Oxfordshire OX14 4RN
52 Vanderbilt Avenue, New York, NY 10017

*Routledge is an imprint of the Taylor & Francis Group, an informa business*

First issued in paperback 2019

*British Library Cataloguing in Publication Data*
A catalogue record for this book is available from the British Library

*Library of Congress Cataloging-in-Publication Data*
Names: Elliott, Anthony, 1964– editor. | Prager, Jeffrey, 1948– editor.
Title: The Routledge handbook of psychoanalysis in the social sciences and
    humanities / edited by Anthony Elliott and Jeffrey Prager.
Other titles: Handbook of psychoanalysis in the social sciences and humanities
Description: 1 Edition. | New York : Routledge, 2016.
Identifiers: LCCN 2015043666| ISBN 9780415626927 (hardback) |
    ISBN 9781315650821 (ebook)
Subjects: LCSH: Psychoanalysis—History. | Psychoanalysis—Social aspects. |
    Psychoanalysis and culture.
Classification: LCC BF173 .R728 2016 | DDC 150.19/5—dc23
LC record available at http://lccn.loc.gov/2015043666

ISBN: 978-0-415-62692-7 (hbk)
ISBN: 978-0-367-24462-0 (pbk)


Typeset in Bembo
by Apex CoVantage, LLC

# Contents

Contents

# Figures

# Contributors

**Jessica Benjamin** is a supervising faculty member of the New York University Postdoctoral Psychology program in Psychotherapy and Psychoanalysis and at the Stephen Mitchell Center for Relational Studies. She has been part of the relational psychoanalytic movement from its inception, helped to found the relational track at New York University Postdoctoral, the International Association for Relational Psychoanalysis and Psychotherapy and the Mitchell Center for Relational Studies. She is the author of *The Bonds of Love* (1988), *Like Subjects, Love Objects* (1995) and *Shadow of the Other* (1998), and the forthcoming volume *Beyond Doer and Done To: Recognition Theory, Intersubjectivity and the Third*. Her current work considers the importance of acknowledgment with reference not only to clinical practice but also collective, historical trauma.

**Chloe Campbell** is a Research Fellow at the Psychoanalysis Unit, University College London. Her research interests involve mentalizing, epistemic trust and the history of childhood. Recent publications include "Bad Blood Revisited: Attachment and Psychoanalysis" in the *British Journal of Psychotherapy* (with Peter Fonagy, 2015); "Social Science, Parenting and Child Development" in *Why the Social Sciences Matter* (with Pasco Fearon and Lynne Murray, 2015); and "Why Are We Interested in Attachments?" in *The Routledge Handbook of Attachment: Theory* (with Peter Fonagy, Nicolas Lorenzini and Patrick Luyten, 2014).

**David Caudill** is Professor and Arthur M. Goldberg Family Chair in Law at Villanova University, where he teaches expert evidence, sports law and property; he is currently a Senior Fellow at the University of Melbourne Law Faculty in Australia. Professor Caudill is the author of *No Magic Wand: The Idealization of Science in Law* (2006) and *Stories About Science in Law: Literary and Historical Images of Acquired Expertise* (2011). His research and scholarly interests focus on law and science studies, law and literature, and sports and entertainment law.

**Nancy Chodorow**, PhD, is Training and Supervising Analyst, Boston Psychoanalytic Society and Institute; Supervising Analyst, Pittsburgh Psychoanalytic Center; and Faculty, San Francisco Center for Psychoanalysis. She is Lecturer on Psychiatry, Harvard Medical School, Cambridge Health Alliance; and Professor Emerita of Sociology and Clinical Faculty Emerita, University of California, Berkeley. She is in private practice in Cambridge, Massachusetts. Nancy Chodorow's books include *The Power of Feelings: Personal Meaning in Psychoanalysis, Gender, and Culture* (1999) and *Individualizing Gender and Sexuality: Theory and Practice* (2012). Since 2000, she has published extensively on Loewald and the Loewaldian legacy, psychoanalysis and the social sciences, and comparative psychoanalytic theory and technique. In 2004, she named an American independent tradition, intersubjective ego psychology, and she is completing a book on that tradition.

Contributors

**Giuseppe Civitarese,** psychiatrist, PhD, in relational sciences, is a training and supervising analyst in the Italian Psychoanalytic Society (SPI), and an APsaA and IPA member. He lives and is in private practice in Pavia, Italy. He lectures in Italy and internationally and publishes widely on various subjects including the theory of the analytic field, Bion and psychoanalytic criticism. Currently he is the Editor of the *Rivista di Psicoanalisi*, the official journal of the Italian Psychoanalytic Society. Among his latest books are *The Necessary Dream: New Theories and Techniques of Interpretation in Psychoanalysis* (Karnac, London 2014) and *Losing Your Head: Abjection, Aesthetic Conflict, and Psychoanalytic Criticism* (Rowman & Littlefield, New York 2015).

**Elizabeth Danze** is a Fellow of the American Institute of Architects and a Professor at the University of Texas at Austin School of Architecture, where she is the Associate Dean for Graduate Programs and is a Fellow of the Meadows Foundation Centennial Professorship in Architecture. She is a principal with Danze Blood Architects, and her work integrates practice and theory across disciplines by examining the convergence of sociology and psychology with the tangibles of space and construction. Danze is co-editor of *Psychoanalysis and Architecture – The Annual of Psychoanalysis*, Volume 33, and *CENTER 17: Space and Psyche.*

**Muriel Dimen,** PhD, is a psychoanalyst, anthropologist and writer. She is Adjunct Clinical Professor of Psychology, NYU Postdoctoral Program in Psychotherapy and Psychoanalysis, and Editor-in-Chief of *Studies in Gender and Sexuality.* Most recently, she edited *With Culture in Mind.* Her *Sexuality, Intimacy, Power* received the Goethe Award, Canadian Psychological Association. Her current book-length project is *Leaving Dr. O: An Analyst Remembers When Her Analyst Crossed the Line.*

**Anthony Elliott** is Director of the Hawke Research Institute and Executive Director of the Hawke EU Centre, where he is Research Professor of Sociology at the University of South Australia. He is also Visiting Global Professor of Sociology at Keio University, Japan and Visiting Professor of Sociology at University College Dublin, Ireland. Professor Elliott has published extensively on psychoanalysis, including his books *Psychoanalysis in Contexts* (edited with Stephen Frosh, 1995), *Freud 2000* (1998), *Psychoanalysis at Its Limits* (edited with Charles Spezzano, 1999), *Social Theory and Psychoanalysis in Transition* (2nd ed., 1999), *Subject To Ourselves* (2nd ed., 2004), *Social Theory Since Freud* (2004), *The New Individualism* (2nd ed., with Charles Lemert, 2009) *Psychoanalytic Theory: An Introduction* (3rd ed., 2015) and *Identity Troubles* (2016).

**Antonino Ferro** is Training Analyst and President for the Italian Psychoanalytic Society. He is an APsaA and IPA member. He has published several books translated in many languages, the last are *Torments of Soul* (Routledge) and *Rêveries: An Unfettered Mind* (Karnac). In 2007 he was selected to be a recipient of the Mary S. Sigourney Award. He works with children and patients with severe pathologies.

**Matt Ffytche** is Deputy Director of the Centre for Psychoanalytic Studies at the University of Essex and Editor of the journal *Psychoanalysis and History.* Recent publications include *Psychoanalysis in the Age of Totalitarianism*, co-edited with Daniel Pick (Routledge, 2015), and "Freud and the Neocons: The Narrative of a Political Encounter From 1949–2000," in *Psychoanalysis and History* (2013). In 2014 he was recipient of a fellowship from the Independent Social Research Foundation to pursue research into bridging psychoanalytic notions of "projective identification" with sociological analyses of social interaction.

**Peter Fonagy** is Freud Memorial Professor of Psychoanalysis and Head of the Research Department of Clinical, Educational and Health Psychology at University College London, and Chief Executive of the Anna Freud Centre, London. His clinical interests center on issues of early attachment relationships, social cognition, borderline personality disorder and violence. Among his major contributions is the innovative research-based dynamic therapeutic approach mentalization-based treatment, which he developed with colleagues in the UK. He has published over 400 scientific papers and 250 chapters, and has co-authored or co-edited 34 books, most recently *What Works for Whom? A Critical Review of Treatments for Children and Adolescents*, 2nd edition (Guilford Press, 2014) and the *Handbook of Contemporary Psychodynamic Approaches to Psychopathology* (Guilford Press, 2015).

**Rubén Gallo** is the Walter S. Carpenter Jr. Professor in Language, Literature and Civilization of Spain at Princeton University. He is the author of *Freud's Mexico: Into the Wilds of Psychoanalysis* (2010), a cultural history of psychoanalysis and its reception in Mexico. His other publications include *Mexican Modernity: The Avant-Garde and the Technological Revolution* (2005), an essay about the Mexican avant-garde's fascination with machines, and two books about Mexico City's visual culture: *New Tendencies in Mexican Art* (2004) and *The Mexico City Reader* (2004). His most recent book is *Proust's Latin Americans*, published in 2014 by Johns Hopkins University Press. He is a member of the board of the Sigmund Freud Museum in Vienna, and in 2009 he was the Freud-Fulbright Visiting Scholar in Psychoanalysis in Austria. He teaches at Princeton University and lives in New York City.

**Pumla Gobodo-Madikizela** was Professor of Psychology at the University of Cape Town, and currently is Senior Research Professor in trauma, forgiveness and reconciliation at the University of the Free State. She served on the Truth and Reconciliation Commission's Human Rights Violations Committee, and since then her research and public engagement have been concerned with the question of transformation in the aftermath of mass trauma and violence. Her critically acclaimed book, *A Human Being Died That Night: A South African Story of Forgiveness*, won the Alan Paton Award in South Africa and the Christopher Award in the United States. Her other books include *Narrating our Healing: Perspectives on Healing Trauma*, as co-author; as co-editor of *Memory, Narrative and Forgiveness: Perspectives on the Unfinished Journeys of the Past*; and as editor of the forthcoming volume, *Breaking Intergenerational Cycles of Repetition: A Global Dialogue on Historical Trauma and Memory*.

**Max Hernández** is a full member of the British Psychoanalytic Society and founding member of the Peruvian Psychoanalytic Society. Max has been Vice President of the International Psychoanalytical Association and President of the Peruvian Psychoanalytic Society. He lives and practices in Lima, Peru. Amongst his interests are applied psychoanalysis, psychohistory and politics. He served as Executive Secretary to the Peruvian National Accord and has been distinguished as Grand Officer of the Order of the Sun of Peru and Commander of the Order of Isabella the Catholic of Spain. His most recent books are *En los márgenes de nuestra memoria histórica* (*In the Margins of our Historical Memory*) and *Doce años del Acuerdo Nacional* (*Twelve Years of the National Accord*).

**Sean Homer** is the Associate Professor of Literature at American University in Bulgaria. His last two publications are "The Politics of Comradeship: Philosophical Commitment and Construction in Alain Badiou and Slavoj Žižek," in *Badiou and the Political Condition*, edited by Marios Constantinou (Edinburgh: Edinburgh University Press, 2014), and "To Begin at the Beginning

Again: Žižek in Yugoslavia," in *Slavic Review* (2013). Professor Homer's research interests include Lacanian psychoanalysis and cultural theory, as well as Marxist cultural criticism. He has recently published articles on Balkan cinema and is currently working on a book on Slavoj Žižek's politics in relation to the Balkans.

**Adrian Johnston** is a Professor in the Department of Philosophy at the University of New Mexico at Albuquerque and a faculty member at the Emory Psychoanalytic Institute in Atlanta. He is the author of *Time Driven: Metapsychology and the Splitting of the Drive* (2005), *Žižek's Ontology: A Transcendental Materialist Theory of Subjectivity* (2008), *Badiou, Žižek, and Political Transformations: The Cadence of Change* (2009) and *Prolegomena to Any Future Materialism, Volume One: The Outcome of Contemporary French Philosophy* (2013), all published by Northwestern University Press. He is the co-author, with Catherine Malabou, of *Self and Emotional Life: Philosophy, Psychoanalysis, and Neuroscience* (Columbia University Press, 2013). His most recent book is *Adventures in Transcendental Materialism: Dialogues With Contemporary Thinkers* (Edinburgh University Press, 2014). With Todd McGowan and Slavoj Žižek, he is a co-editor of the book series *Diaeresis* at Northwestern University Press.

**Rafael E. López-Corvo** is a Training and Supervising Psychoanalyst IPA, Canadian and Venezuelan Psychoanalytic Societies. His last two publications are "Time Distortion Between 'Conceptual' and 'Pre-conceptual' Traumas," in *Psychoanalytic Review* (2013); and *The Traumatised and Non-traumatised States of the Personality. A Clinical Understanding of Trauma Using Bion's Approach* (Karnac Books: London, 2014). His areas of interests are unconscious alpha function (dreams) and "pre-conceptual traumas."

**Edna O'Shaughnessy** is Distinguished Fellow, Training Analyst and Child Analyst of the British Psychoanalytical Society, and Honorary Consultant to the Fitzjohn's Unit of the Tavistock Clinic. *Inquiries in Psychoanalysis*, a volume of her collected papers, was published in 2014 by Routledge. Edna's main professional interest is in psychoanalysis as a method of inquiry into the mind.

**Caroline Polmear** is a Training and Supervising Analyst of the British Psychoanalytical Society. She works mainly in private practice in London. Two of her recent publications are "The Basic Fault and the Borderline Psychotic Transference," in *Independent Psychoanalysis Today*, edited by P. Williams, J. Keene and S. Dermen (Karnac Books 2012); and "Envy and Gratitude: An Independent View," in *Envy and Gratitude Revisited*, edited by P. Roth and A. Lemma (Karnac and IPA 2008). She has an interest in teaching clinical psychoanalysis and runs clinical workshops for analysts from various European countries.

**Jeffrey Prager** is a Professor of Sociology at UCLA, former Dean and Training and Supervising Analyst at the New Center for Psychoanalysis in Los Angeles and in private practice in Beverly Hills. His published research is on social repair in post-conflict societies, cross-generational transmission of trauma, and American racism and reparations. He is the author of many books and articles, including the award-winning *Presenting the Past, Psychoanalysis and the Sociology of Misremembering* (Harvard).

**Michael Roth** became the 16th president of Wesleyan University in 2007, after having served as Hartley Burr Alexander Professor of Humanities at Scripps College, Associate Director of the Getty Research Institute, and President of the California College of the Arts. At Wesleyan, he has increased grant support for students who receive financial aid and has overseen the launch of the

Allbritton Center for the Study of Public Life, the Shapiro Creative Writing Center, and four new colleges emphasizing interdisciplinary research and cohort building: the College of the Environment, the College of Film and the Moving Image, the College of East Asian Studies and the College of Integrative Sciences. Author and curator (most notably of the exhibition "Sigmund Freud: Conflict and Culture," which opened at the Library of Congress in 1998), Roth describes his scholarly interests as centered on "How people make sense of the past." His fifth book, *Memory, Trauma and History: Essays on Living With the Past* was published in 2012. His most recent book, *Beyond the University: Why Liberal Education Matters*, is a stirring plea for the kind of education that has, since the founding of the nation, cultivated individual freedom, promulgated civic virtue, and instilled hope for the future. He regularly publishes essays, book reviews and commentaries in the national media and scholarly journals. He continues to teach undergraduate courses and through Coursera has offered MOOCs, the most recent being "How to Change the World."

**Margaret Rustin** is a Child, Adolescent and Adult Psychotherapist in private practice. She is Honorary Consultant Psychotherapist at the Tavistock and Portman NHS Foundation Trust, a member of the Association of Child Psychotherapists and of the British Psychoanalytic Council, and a Child Analyst with the British Psychoanalytical Society. Her most recent book is "Young Child Observation," edited jointly with Simonetta Adamo (Karnac, 2014), and most recent paper "The Relevance of Infant Observation for Early Intervention: Containment in Theory and Practice," in *International Journal of Infant Observation and Its Applications* (2014). Her main interests are in the practice and teaching of child analysis and its essential continuity with adult work.

**Michael Rustin** is a Professor of Sociology at the University of East London, a Visiting Professor at the Tavistock Clinic, and an Associate of the British Psychoanalytical Society. He has written extensively on the relations between psychoanalysis, society and culture. Among his books are *The Good Society and the Inner World* (1991); *Reason and Unreason* (2001); *Narratives of Love and Loss: Studies in Modern Children's Fiction* (1987/2001) and *Mirror to Nature: Drama, Psychoanalysis and Society* (2002) (both with Margaret Rustin); *The Inner World of Doctor Who* (with Iain MacRury 2014); and *Social Defences Against Anxiety: Explorations in a Paradigm* (edited with David Armstrong (2015). *Reading Melanie Klein* (with Margaret Rustin) will appear in 2016.

**Andrea Sabbadini**, CPsychol, is a Fellow of the *British Psychoanalytical Society*, the Director of the *European Psychoanalytic Film Festival (epff)*, a Trustee of the Freud Museum, London and a Lecturer at University College, London (UCL). His two latest books are *Moving Images* (Routledge, 2014) and *Boundaries and Bridges* (Karnac, 2014), and his main interest is in the relationship of psychoanalysis to the arts, in particular to cinema.

**Janet Sayers** is Emeritus Professor of Psychoanalytic Psychology at the University of Kent in Canterbury, where she also works as a Clinical Psychologist for the NHS. Her most recent publications include "The Autobiography of Melanie Klein," *Psychoanalysis and History* (2013), and *Art, Psychoanalysis, and Adrian Stokes* (Karnac, in press). Her current research focuses on the work of Virginia Woolf's psychoanalyst brother, Adrian Stephen, and on the sculpture of Barbara Hepworth.

**Stephen Sonnenberg,** MD, in Clinical Professor of Psychiatry and Behavioral Sciences at Baylor College of Medicine, in Houston, Texas, and Fellow-in-Residence at the Humanities Institute at the University of Texas at Austin. At UT–Austin he teaches in the School of Architecture, the Plan II Honors Program in the College of Liberal Arts, and the School of Undergraduate

Studies, all through the lens of the medical humanities. He sees psychoanalysis as simultaneously a healing art and a humanities discipline, and his research focuses on illuminating that perspective through his collaborative teaching activities. Currently, he is working on the book *Teaching Medical Humanities to Undergraduates*. His last two major publications are "Psychoanalysis and the United States Research University," *International Journal of Psychoanalysis* (2011), and with Elizabeth Danze the co-edited book, *CENTER 17: Space & Psyche* (Austin, TX: Center for American Architecture and Design, 2012).

**Ellen Handler Spitz,** PhD, is the Honors College Professor at the University of Maryland (UMBC) and sole author of seven books, the most recent of which are *Illuminating Childhood: Portraits in Fiction, Film, and Drama* (Ann Arbor: University of Michigan Press, 2012) and *Magritte's Labyrinth* (eBook: William Morris, Argo Navis, 2014). Her most recently published articles are "Alison Bechdel's Graphic Memoirs," *Contemporary Psychoanalysis* (2014), "Kris-Crossing," *Brooklyn Rail* (2014) and "The Amherst Belle," *New York Times Book Review* (2014). She writes on the arts and psychology, aesthetics and the cultural lives of children.

**Madelon Sprengnether** is Regents Professor in the Department of English at the University of Minnesota, where she teaches literature and creative writing. She has published widely in the field of feminism and psychoanalysis, most notably as co-editor of *The (M)other Tongue: Essays in Feminist Psychoanalytic Interpretation* and as author of *The Spectral Mother: Freud, Feminism and Psychoanalysis*. She has also published memoir and poetry. Her most recent publications are *Great River Road: Memoir and Memory* and *Near Solstice: Prose Poems*.

**Sverre Varvin** is the Professor at the Oslo and Akershus University College of Applied Sciences and psychoanalyst at the Norwegian Psychoanalytical Society. His last two publications are *Psykoanalysen og kvalitativ forskning. Forskning på narrativer, dialoger og prosess [Psychoanalysis and qualitative research. Research on narratives, dialogues and process]* (2014), *Matrix, Nordisk tidsskrift for psykoterapi.* Volume 31(4) s. 260–281; and Varvin, S., Rosenbaum, B. (2014). Trauma: Depletion and resilience. *Revista Portuguesa Psicoanalise,* Volume 34 (2) s. 6–17. His areas of interests are research on and treatment of severely traumatized patients, transcultural psychoanalysis and developing psychoanalysis in China.

# Acknowledgments

Psychoanalysis, a former professor of ours once claimed, puts the flavor back into your chewing gum! This comment may or may not convince, but it is intriguing. For it captures something of the rawness, intensity and power of psychoanalysis as a method of interpretation in the social sciences and the humanities. Capturing something of the flavor of psychoanalysis is what we have set out to provide with this handbook.

Many people have helped us, directly or indirectly, in the preparation of this book. We would like to thank Gerhard Boomgaarden, Nick Stevenson, Nicola Geraghty, John Cash, Anthony Moran, Stanley Gold, Deborah Maxwell, Debora Silverman, Maria Lymberis and Alexander Stein.

We could not have completed this book without the generous assistance of David Radford, who managed the administrative work associated with the handbook with unstinting determination and professional commitment. We are also grateful to Ross Boyd, Shannon Surridge-McCann, Natasha Biggins, Alyson Claffey and to Apex CoVantage for the skillful copyediting.

Anthony Elliott and Jeffrey Prager
Adelaide and Los Angeles

# Introduction

*Anthony Elliott and Jeffrey Prager*

*The Routledge Handbook of Psychoanalysis in the Social Sciences and Humanities* provides a systematic guide to the leading traditions, trends and trajectories in psychoanalysis. We focus throughout on psychoanalysis as both clinical research and method on the one hand and a body of knowledge applicable to the social sciences and humanities on the other. Part of our motivation for producing this Handbook is a growing awareness that there have been important changes taking place in psychoanalysis in recent years. Theoretical development has always been central to the enterprise of psychoanalysis, but in recent years there has been considerable growth of psychoanalysis as a complex field of theories and clinical approaches. These developments remain typically influenced by Freudian thought, but now also stretch across the most recent thinking in the social sciences and the humanities. Indeed these developments – while far from representing a unified framework for psychoanalysis – have become embedded in both national and regional contexts; throughout this volume, we will examine how various post-Freudian ideas have become embedded and reembedded in psychoanalytic theories and institutions throughout Europe, North America, Mexico and Britain.

From fin-de-siècle Vienna to the 21st century, psychoanalysis has been a powerful theoretical and therapeutic discourse for the critical analysis of our everyday lives, interpersonal relationships, sociality, culture, politics and history. Freud discovered the power of the "repressed unconscious" in the lives of women and men at the historical moment in which faith in science and its twin beacons of objectivity and rationality had moved center stage. While Freud powerfully deconstructed the age-old opposition between reason and passion, he nonetheless remained committed to the principles of scientific truth and the power of rationality to contribute to a better life, at once individual and collective. "Our best hope for the future is that intellect – the scientific spirit, reason – may in the process of time," wrote Freud, "establish a dictatorship in the mental life of man."[1] (Freud 1933, pp. 171–172). The unconscious is an otherness at the core of the self that can be profoundly troubling, but it is one that propels the self forward and drives culture and its various scientific enterprises onward. The shift from Freud's world to our world, however, has witnessed a crisis in reason and claims to knowledge, and where science no longer has an automatically privileged place. Today in a globalizing, culturally cosmopolitan world – where there is a plurality of heterogeneous claims to knowledge – there has been a profound shift away from faith in the idea that humanly engineered progress is guaranteed. On the contrary, the advances of modernity are today increasingly equated with the production of risks, hazards, insecurities and anxieties on an unprecedented scale – at once individual and social. The question of changing climates and global warming, the destructive power of nuclear weapons, forced migration and the veritable explosion in asylum seekers worldwide, overpopulation: these are just some of the broad institutional contours of the early 21st century, a world that appears in large part beyond human mastery and outside of rational control.

But such worldwide metamorphosis is not simply institutional; it is also deeply personal, and hence cuts to the core of psychoanalysis itself. If the notion of scientific progress is an enormous irony – the very gains in scientific knowledge also reveal the profound limits of human understanding – then so in a different sense is the psychic realm of human subjects on which rationalism and reason are founded. The forging of the ego is overdetermined by contradictions: self-consciousness and human reflectiveness provide a means of standing outside our own worlds, but because such constructions of the self are perspectival and thoroughly representational, they threaten at every point to return the human subject to that archaic, undifferentiated realm of the pre-Oedipal (that is, the infant–mother dyad) prior to the instantiation of subjectivity itself. For contemporary psychoanalysis, the self is shot through by an internal fissure, and the name for the experience of it is suffering, anxiety, self-disturbance or the disabling malady of the soul.

In our own time, this has meant the language of psychoanalysis has necessarily changed. The shift is evident in both theoretical and diagnostic terms. From "repression" to "addiction," from "intrapsychic" to "intersubjective," from "self-control" to "self-autonomy": psychoanalysis today is grounded less on the recovery and undoing of the repressed unconscious; instead it is focused on the force field of interpersonal meaning and the cultivation of emotional life engaged with the powers of the passions, affect, fantasy and the imagination. Consequently, the clinical picture of patients entering psychoanalysis today is not that of individuals suffering from disturbances of sexual repression and self-control (although of course such instances do still present themselves), but rather of individuals experiencing an emotional deficit in relation to other people, coupled with a more general estrangement from the self. The language of post-Freudian psychoanalysis that has emerged to comprehend these transformations includes that of "holding," "containing," "intersubjectivity," "the analytic Third," "new maladies of the soul," "radical imagination" and many others.

One aim of *The Routledge Handbook of Psychoanalysis in the Social Sciences and Humanities* is to introduce readers to the growth of psychoanalysis as a field, particularly its rich diversity of development since the founding works of Sigmund Freud. Another aim is to critically examine and review appropriations of psychoanalytic theory in the social sciences and humanities. Why has psychoanalysis proved at once so challenging and vexing to the social sciences and humanities? What is the likely ongoing relevance of psychoanalysis to the academy, as well as broader public debate? These are fundamental questions explored throughout the volume.

## Psychoanalysis and psychoanalytic theories

### Developments in psychoanalytic theories

Dramatic changes in psychoanalytic thought have occurred since Freud first established the foundation for a new science of the mind and implemented a novel practice of therapeutic treatment. By his own example, Freud also succeeded in establishing psychoanalysis as a scientific field always open to the revisiting of earlier formulations and integrating new findings and new thinking into the body of thought. He was a prodigious writer, and his contributions from his earliest writings to his last clearly revealed his own mind at work, as a clinician, problem solver, concept builder and theory maker. He would often return to his earlier writings, not to reject them but to build upon them. He would add sentences and footnotes here and there to previously published works, sometimes even whole sections incorporating his changing way of thinking.

Freud began his career by presenting a topographical model of the mind, a mapping of the psychic interior where the small realm of conscious awareness sits atop a much larger map of largely uncharted terrain, the unconscious. He described the "repression barrier" as a fortress, *almost* impermeable, that sets apart the two realms, largely blocking to awareness access to a whole cauldron of unconscious thoughts, feelings, fantasies, memories, desires and forgotten but nonetheless formative experiences. From this vantage point, Freud characterized therapeutic action as a "talk-therapy" to better access the unconscious, to break down the repression barrier, thereby enabling the energy misdirected in the form of symptom formation to be rechanneled in healthier directions.

As his own thinking and clinical experience developed, Freud's model of the mind itself became more complex. For much of his career, he offered a structural model of psychic activity characterized by an ever-present conflict between id, ego and superego. These were three functions of the mind governed by competing agendas and, therefore, were in perpetual conflict. Here, the therapeutic aim becomes "where id goes, there ego shall be." Never rejecting his topographical model, Freud continued to develop the structural model as an overlay.

In some of his most important essays, Freud attempted to account for the role that others played in psychic development and the constitutive role of those who nourished the psyche for personal psychological development. Following Freud, there came a deepening understanding of the significance of the internalization of others into the psyche, a fuller account of child development attempting to capture how and when these processes took place, and also far greater attention to the dyadic relationship between mother and child. In all respects, the creation of an "object relations" theory of the mind made a person's psychological functioning more complex. It also documented the ways that the therapeutic challenge toward psychic change was more formidable than previously conceived. Most recently, neuroscience brain research, affirming many of Freud's earliest suppositions, has laid heavier emphasis on the plasticity of the brain, psychic impairments now reformulated as possible to treat therapeutically. Psychoanalysis and neuroscience challenge any assertion that the brain is simply hard-wired and immutable. Ironically, Freud's widely dismissed early writing "Project for a Scientific Psychology" (1895) is now seen as surprisingly prescient for its ambition, and sharing similar contemporary efforts to bring together the biology of the brain with the complexity of mental life. The hope for an integrated theory has not waned over the years.

While this is the more or less conventional rendering of the history of psychoanalysis, there is a perhaps more useful way to characterize it, especially for those who seek to employ analytic ideas in other fields in the social sciences and humanities. Psychoanalysts since Freud describe with considerably more depth and subtlety the environment where psychic life becomes constituted. Psychoanalysis now perceives itself not so much as the science of the mind as Freud originally proposed it, where the mind is treated as an isolated object under the watchful and microscopic gaze of analytic scientific and clinical attention. Rather, it perceives itself most broadly as the science of subjectivity: a study of the unique and feeling self, what Christopher Bollas describes as each person's "self-experiencing," or personal idiom. As persuasively as Freud was able to describe the treacherous waters that the young boy has to navigate through this conflictual period of life, he missed similarly complex and more primitive psychic moments between mother and child occurring from actual birth onward. Now these infantile experiences that precede both language and genital sexuality are no longer under-observed or under-theorized. In fact, in many respects they are given pride of place. Where once, with Freud especially, the psychological life of the infant began with the fluorescence of the triangulated Oedipal conflict between ego, mother and father, now psychoanalysis conceptualizes psychology as in formation from birth and manifest in the earliest connection between mother and child. Psychoanalysts now uniformly acknowledge that psychic life does not begin with Oedipus but long before, it is not only male-conceived, and the relationship between son and mother as loving, and father and son as fearful and hating overly simplifies psychic life and interpsychic relationships. The post-Freudian attention to the maternal realm of experience nearly unifies all psychoanalytic thought today. In many respects, the work of Melanie Klein, a child analyst who asserts the presence of powerful fantasies of love, hate, envy and greed initially organized around the infant's earliest experience of the breast, has as central a standing in the field as the original Freudian model.

## New directions in clinical technique

In the consulting room of today, the psychoanalytic relationship is understood, when proper attention is paid to it, as also revealing the pre-Oedipal and pre-linguistic sources of intimate connectedness. Adult intimacy is seen to mimic the earliest forms of social life, between infant and caregiver. It is recovered only as bodily, or sensate, manifestations of this newly created intimate space. The psychoanalytic relationship, thus, is read as more than the development of a shared, verbally forged understanding of the patient's early childhood experiences capturing the Oedipal period and beyond; it is also the re-creation of infantile feelings and sensations that presently express themselves through all five bodily senses. The nature and character of that bond provide clues as to the sources of inhibition or unhappiness creating the need or desire for the analytic relationship in the first place.

Even beyond these developments, the psychoanalytic study of subjectivity has amplified to a more robust understanding of the world around which the individual mind is embedded. Beginning perhaps with Winnicott, who states there is no such thing as a baby without its mother, the position is taken that the development of the self is dependent on an outside world, its nourishing or frustrating qualities, and its accepting or persecutory nature.

It is recognized that the psychic life of the individual has always been inextricably linked to the psychic life of others. Clinically this has meant a more relational understanding of the analytic relationship. Many have now added to the analytic corpus about the deepening interpsychic relationship occurring over time. It can become particularly intense, replete with its own language, grammar, idiom, method of speaking, tone, cadence and so forth unique to that particular twosome. It is a bond between two people whose mutually reflexive understanding, conscious and unconscious, yields greater insight into the needs, desires and inhibitions of the patient and, as importantly, that through shared experience generates in the patient new capacities for healthful living. As intimate experience, it is expected that the analyst, too, necessarily is moved and changes as a result of the relationship. While the language of plasticity is seldom invoked, the malleability of the brain is at the core of therapeutic work.

Contemporary psychoanalysis does not possess a single voice. There remain significant differences between analysts depending on many factors, including the national analytic tradition from which it arose. Nonetheless, modern analysis has succeeded in opening itself up to larger cultural and social issues encouraging interdisciplinary thought and research. Again, traces of these developments are found in Freud himself, as he turned late in his career to topics that included religion, aesthetics, anti-Semitism and "Civilization."

Today psychoanalysis contributes significantly to questions of gender identification and patterns of male domination, inequality and injustice, challenges to an exclusively cognitive-based conception of science, and to political, historical and cultural themes of mourning, loss, and separation. The important psychoanalytic contributions of Nancy Chodorow, Heinz Kohut, Jessica Benjamin, Betty Joseph, Wilfred Bion, Hannah Segal and many others are products of this development and help define, even as it is practiced in the consulting room, a modern expression of psychoanalysis continuous with but moving beyond its earliest formulations.

## Psychoanalysis and the social sciences and humanities

Psychoanalysis, as developed by Sigmund Freud and his followers, has had a major impact upon the humanities and the social sciences. Freud's central discoveries – the unconscious, sexual repression, the Oedipus complex and the like – have been deployed by those working in the social sciences and the humanities to interpret and discuss the self and human subjectivity, gender and sexuality, the family and socialization, language and ideology, as well as the formation of cultural identities and forms of political domination. Notwithstanding this impact, social scientists have long had a difficult and indeed fraught relationship with psychoanalysis. Social scientists and scholars of the humanities have criticized psychoanalytical theory on the grounds of its methodology, epistemology and ontology.

Despite these criticisms, many scholars and intellectuals remain engaged with, and some strongly committed to, the psychoanalytic tradition in order to conceptualize the relation between the individual and society, especially the complex, contradictory ways that human subjects acquire and reshape the ideas, values, symbols, beliefs and emotional dispositions of the wider society. This has been particularly evident over recent decades, in which Freudian themes and psychoanalytic motifs have been used to analyze sexual politics, issues of identity and lifestyle, as well as the debates over modernity, postmodernism and post-humanism.

Some of the major appropriations of psychoanalysis in the humanities and social sciences include:

- several early and influential articulations of psychoanalysis and sociology developed in Europe (particularly as represented in the work of the Frankfurt School of Critical Theory) and North America (especially in the writings of Talcott Parsons);
- structuralist and post-structuralist appropriations of psychoanalysis;
- feminist and postmodern social theory.

### Interdisciplinary articulations: critical theory and North America

In Europe, Herbert Marcuse and Theodor Adorno – leading members of the Frankfurt School of Critical Theory – turned to Freud in order to reconceptualize the relation between self and society. The political motivation prompting this turn to Freud had its roots in Marcuse's and Adorno's attempts to conceptualize the rise of fascism, Nazism and also the spread of bureaucratic capitalism. From Freud's theory of the Oedipus complex, and particularly his theorem concerning the repression of infantile sexuality, Marcuse and Adorno developed the notion of "the authoritarian personality." Driven by a desire for conformity and clear rules, the authoritarian personality was viewed by Marcuse and Adorno as a character type strongly prevalent in the German middle class, a character type who hungered for strong leadership, social order and regulation. Not only in Nazi Germany, however, was this personality type to be found; in the advanced liberal societies of the West, tendencies toward authoritarianism and conformism were increasingly evident. Marcuse thus spoke of the emergence of "one-dimensional man."

Marcuse's radical Freudianism, in particular, won a wide audience in the 1960s – not only in social science circles but also among student activists and sexual liberationists. Arguing that the so-called sexual revolution of the 1960s did not seriously threaten power structures of the established social order, Marcuse sought to show how demands for freedom were routinely rechanneled for commercial interests. The core of his analysis rested upon the distinction he drew between basic and surplus repression. Basic repression he defined as the minimum level of psychological renunciation demanded by the social structure and cultural order. Surplus repression, by contrast, refers to the intensification of self-restraint demanded by asymmetrical relations of power. Marcuse describes the "monogamic-patriarchal" family, for example, as a site of surplus repression. Interestingly, while Marcuse saw signs of surplus repression increasingly everywhere in late capitalist society, he remained remarkably optimistic about the possibilities for social and cultural change.

On the other side of the Atlantic, a different approach to the integration of psychoanalysis and the social sciences was fashioned. The core thematic of this approach concerned social order, socialization and the reproduction of the social system. The grand theorist of American sociology, Talcott Parsons, employed Freudian ideas to understand how basic symbols and values are internalized by human subjects throughout the socialization process. According to Parsons's appropriation of Freud for social theory, the structure of human personality is an outcome of an internalization of desired objects, role relationships, and ethico-cultural values that make up the broader social network. In this approach, it is the linkage of personality structure, the social system and the cultural system that is stressed.

Unlike Marcuse's and Adorno's emphasis on the social manipulation of the unconscious, Parsons finds a kind of pre-established harmony between the individual and society.

## Structuralism and post-structuralism: the psychoanalytic perspective

For many years, the integration of psychoanalysis and social analysis developed by the Frankfurt School was commonly regarded as the most sophisticated and important work in this subfield of modern sociology. From the late 1960s onward, however, the impact of French theory, particularly structuralist and post-structuralist philosophy, became increasingly influential in terms of theorizing the social dimensions of psychoanalysis. The key figure in this connection was Freud's French interpreter, Jacques Lacan. Seeking to rework the core concepts of psychoanalysis in the light of modern linguistics, Lacan argued that the unconscious exemplifies key features of language; as Lacan famously argues, "the unconscious is structured like a language." The subject or "I," according to Lacan, is not self-transparent but is rather located in a system of signification from which identity is fashioned. For Lacan, intersubjectivity is at the center of psychological functioning and its disturbances; distortions or pathologies at the level of the self are, says Lacan, located in "the discourse of the other."

It is perhaps Lacan's essay "The Mirror Stage as Formative of the Function of the I" (1949) that has come to exert the most influence on appropriations of psychoanalysis in many disciplines of the social sciences and humanities. In the essay, Lacan conceptualizes the infant's initial recognition of itself in a mirror or reflecting surface, and of how this generates a sense of identity. Through the mirror, says Lacan, the infant makes an imaginary identification with its reflected image, an identification that the infant reacts to with a sense of jubilation and exhilaration. But the mirror image of the self for Lacan is, in fact, a distortion: the mirror lies. The mirror stage is radically "imaginary," in Lacan's theorization, since the consolingly unified image of selfhood that it generates is diametrically opposed to the bodily fragmentation and lack of coordination of the child. These imaginary traps and distortions are a universal and timeless feature of self-organization, and Lacan sees such illusions as directly feeding into and shaping pathologies of the self in contemporary culture.

Lacan was not especially interested in the social applications of psychoanalysis; it was one of his followers, the French Marxist political philosopher Louis Althusser, who brought Lacanian theory into the center of key debates in sociology. In his important essay "Ideology and Ideological State Apparatuses" (1984[1971]), Althusser analyzed ideology in terms of the process by which individuals come to understand and relate to themselves in a manner that supports dominant class relations. According to Althusser, ideology provides an imaginary identity, an imagined map for locating oneself in the wider social network. Echoing Lacan, Althusser uses the notion of the mirror stage to deconstruct ideology. There is a duplicate mirror structure at the heart of ideology, says Althusser, a structure that grants to the self an ideological mirror in which it can recognize itself and other people. Althusser calls this process "interpellation": the capturing of the individual within the net of received social meanings.

The Lacanian/Althusserian account of the de-centering of the subject has been highly influential in recent sociological theory and has impacted upon debates concerning agency, structure, class, social fragmentation and cultural order. The social-theoretical work of Paul Hirst, Barry Hindess, Stuart Hall, Etienne Bailbar, Pierre Machery, Fredric Jameson and Slavoj Žižek is, in differing ways, indebted to the Lacanian/Althusserian theory of the subject and its ideological subjection.

## Feminism and psychoanalysis

It is not only in studying politics and social change that psychoanalysis has become an important theoretical tool for sociology; in debates concerning gender and sexual politics Freudian ideas have also been incorporated into social theory. In the social science of sexuality, the sociology of the family and especially the social theory of gender transformation, Freudian psychoanalysis has played a vital role in expanding our understanding of the subjective and affective components of human social relationships.

The psychoanalytic perspective made a forceful entry into contemporary feminist sociological theory in Juliet Mitchell's pioneering book *Psychoanalysis and Feminism* (1974). Mitchell deployed Freudian and Lacanian psychoanalytic ideas as a means of connecting a discussion of gender power with an Althusserian/Marxist theory of late capitalist society. Against this theoretical backdrop, she asserted that definitions of masculinity and femininity are framed through linguistic and historical structures – with man as a self-determining, autonomous agent, and woman as a lacking other. Such gender dualism, according to Mitchell, is highly conducive to capitalist social regulation – the split between private and public, the pathologies of the familial life and the like. Mitchell's ideas, while criticized in some feminist sociological circles, had a lasting impact on psychoanalytically oriented feminist sociology. Especially in terms of Lacanian feminist approaches, the writings of authors such as Julia Kristeva, Luce Irigaray, Jacqueline Rose and Judith Butler have significantly influenced sociological debate in recent years.

In the United States, the feminist theories of Nancy Chodorow, Jessica Benjamin and Jane Flax have been influential in contemporary sociology. These feminist authors draw from the psychoanalytic perspective, but instead of turning to Lacan and French psychoanalysis their work selectively incorporates the insights of Freudian and post-Freudian (especially object-relational) theory. In Chodorow's work, it is part of an attempt to understand the psychic components of female and male socialization, especially in terms of the unconscious forces that shape gender roles. In Benjamin's work, psychoanalysis is deployed to rethink the dynamics of domination and submission within the wider frame of gender, society and history. In Flax's discussion of psychoanalysis, feminism and postmodernism, it is primarily a set of philosophical observations about the development of gender relations and the sociology of sexuality and intimacy.

## The Routledge Handbook of Psychoanalysis in the Social Sciences and Humanities

This handbook sets out to provide a reasonably comprehensive account of contemporary psychoanalysis along the twin axes of clinical research and applications in the social sciences and humanities. The first part of the book examines the ways that psychoanalysis has developed as a remarkably complex field and body of ideas. Contrary to those who assume that psychoanalytic ideas begin and end with Freud, these chapters capture the changing theories and evolving concepts within the discipline since his original writings.

Psychoanalysis pioneered a unique scientific research method built upon the case study and continues to produce a steady flow of psychoanalytic research written by practicing analysts. While it remains a source of contention for those who believe that there is only one form of empirical science to which it does not comply, psychoanalytic research is distinctive because those who write about it are simultaneously practitioners of it. This body of work is grounded in clinical engagement pursued by the researcher, where the implications of findings have broader applicability to non-clinicians and non-psychoanalysts.

Part I demonstrates that psychoanalysis has been a remarkably generative discipline. Several chapters here focus on the contributions of specific analysts to the development of the discipline. Matt Ffytche offers an opening chapter on Freud himself and the breakthrough discoveries that created psychoanalysis: the unconscious, repression and transference. The next chapters are devoted to three major figures after Freud: Melanie Klein, Donald Winnicott and Wilfred Bion. Edna O'Shaughnessy, Margaret Rustin, Jeffrey Prager and Rafael López-Corvo examine the post-Freudian progression toward object relations, begun during Freud's own lifetime but extending far beyond it. The object relations theorists represented in this volume are all British psychoanalysts; they share a desire to extend Freud's foundational attention to the workings of the individual psyche by considering the ways in which specific experiences with others shape the human mind. These analysts develop a framework for understanding the way individuals internalize the "other" and the critical role this process plays both for psychic health and, when internalization goes awry, pathology. The French contribution to psychoanalytic theory appears in a chapter by Sean Homer on Jacques Lacan, a thinker who has had a profound, though controversial, impact on the field.

The chapters in Part I on individual analysts are only a sample of major theoretical contributions. To convey the richness of psychoanalysis, three chapters are devoted to conceptual innovations in post-Freudian psychoanalysis that have had significant influence. First, Peter Fonagy and Chloe Campbell explore how attachment theory and mentalization have now become fully integrated into the psychoanalytic framework. Second, Antonino Ferro and Giuseppe Civitarese discuss the important concept of "the analytic field," which draws upon object relations theory while not being limited to it. Third, intersubjectivity has now become a powerful conceptual tool to describe the interpsychic field and the ways that unconscious communication shapes psychological development. Jessica Benjamin's chapter presents both intersubjectivity's German origins and its growing significance for psychoanalysis.

Current developments in the field are also explored in Part I by considering the history of psychoanalysis within specific national contexts. Anthony Elliott tackles the complex theoretical currents on the European continent, with special focus on the French contributions of psychoanalytical theorists such as Julia Kristeva, Cornelius Castoriadis and Jean Laplanche. The particular historical and intellectual forms of American psychoanalysis are characterized by Nancy Chodorow, who pays special attention to the writings of Hans Loewald and other figures in ego psychology. Rubén Gallo captures the rich engagement with psychoanalysis in Mexico, while Caroline Polmear looks at the history of British psychoanalysis in the 20th century.

Part II of the book shifts focus to the social sciences and humanities, and examines how path-breaking social, cultural, literary, philosophical and political thinkers have brought psychoanalysis to the fore in critiques of identity, society, culture, communication, politics and history. Here the humanities and social sciences are revealed as constituted through a deep and lasting engagement with the Freudian and post-Freudian movements, psychoanalytic precepts, psychosocial accounts of identity formation and the shift to engage with the emotional contours of human subjectivity. As a result, the analysis and critique of society and culture comes to denote a mixture of desire, discourse, repression, anxiety, displacement, condensation, considerations of representation and much more.

Michael Roth, Michael Rustin, Adrian Johnston and Madelon Sprengnether take stock of these shifts in the opening chapters of Part II, looking in different ways at how psychoanalysis has informed, shaped and reshaped the disciplines of history, sociology, philosophy and literary studies.

A good deal of the social sciences and the humanities are preoccupied with the question of defining subjectivity and the status of the human subject in social and cultural research. Much of the most radical cultural theory in the humanities certainly keeps definitions of subjectivity in mind, but crucially also looks for new connections – new ways of understanding the relationship – between identity and society, subjectivity and intersubjectivity, selfhood and modern culture. Elizabeth Danze and Stephen Sonnenberg, in examining developments in architecture, find psychoanalysis of continuing importance for engaging with questions of form, spatial consciousness, urban life and intersections in psychic and social interiors.

Andrea Sabbadini reviews cinema and specifically the relationship of film to the mental activities and emotional experiences of spectators, as well as the central concepts of screen memories, primal scenes and free association for the advancement of psychoanalytically informed film studies. Ellen Handler Spitz explores how many new practices in the visual arts have developed through an extraordinary creative dialogue with psychoanalysis. David Caudill considers developments in law and legal theory informed by the resources of psychoanalysis, with special attention devoted to psychoanalytic jurisprudence as a philosophy of law. Janet Sayers interrogates the engagement of psychoanalysis with feminism and gender, highlighting throughout the interrelation of psychic constitution and gender.

Muriel Dimen focuses on human sexuality, considering the forces of libido and lust, eros and energy, in terms of psychoanalytic thought and practice. Pumla Gobodo-Madikizela and Max Hernández consider the role of psychoanalysis in understanding and combatting political repression and issues of reconciliation and social justice. Finally, Sverre Varvin examines the complex, contradictory terrain of trauma in psychoanalysis throughout its history, and asks – suggestively – what makes experience traumatic?

## Note

1  Freud, S., 1933. *New Introductory Lectures On Psychoanalysis*, pp.171–172.

## Reference

Freud, S 1933, 'The acquisition and control of fire', XXII, in J Strachey (ed), *The Standard Edition*, The Hogarth Press, London, pp. 185–197.

# Part I
# Psychoanalysis and psychoanalytic theories

# Sigmund Freud

## Psychoanalysis and the unconscious

*Matt Ffytche*

## The Freudian unconscious

### The unconscious: a foundational concept

Psychoanalysis begins with the unconscious. According to the most substantial reference work on psychoanalytic concepts (Laplanche & Pontalis, 1988, p. 474), it is the "single word" that sums up Freud's discovery. This perception is widely reflected in contemporary academic literature on Freud: the unconscious is the "one idea at the centre of psychoanalysis" (Craib, 1984, p. 21), and "a *sine qua non* for a psychoanalytic theory, marking it out from non-psychoanalytic approaches" (Frosh, 2002, p. 17). But the unconscious has also meant a number of different things to different people. Freud's own conception of it shifted during the course of his career (a factor to be examined in the first part of this chapter). Its meaning has also varied within different clinical traditions of psychoanalysis as they have developed over the course of a century. Yet another shift occurs when the unconscious is taken up in academic work, at a distance from the clinical imperatives of psychoanalysis, leading to a semi-autonomous tradition of the implications of the unconscious within the humanities and social sciences themselves. Such academic accounts of the core concepts have undergone numerous developments and form the basis for much of the material later in this volume. This chapter, on a smaller scale, aims to chart something of all these changes in the foundational status of the unconscious as one moves through Freud's original accounts to more contemporary investigations in the wider intellectual field, acknowledging on the way that some version of the unconscious is significantly involved in almost every later permutation of work influenced by psychoanalysis.

The unconscious was foundational for Freud, first, because the point at which he began to defend a particular view of the unconscious was the point at which something truly psychoanalytic emerged in his work (and psychoanalysis itself became distinguishable from other contemporary psychiatric, neurological and psychological accounts). Second, Freud placed the unconscious at the foundation of the theoretical edifice of psychoanalysis, as one of its cornerstones, alongside the theorization of repression, sexuality and the "Oedipus complex" (1923a, p. 247). However, anyone setting out to delimit the meaning, or function, of the Freudian unconscious meets with a problem acknowledged by various previous writers, that "almost the whole of Freud's writings might be treated as his contribution to a theory of the unconscious" (Cousins, 2005, p. x). If psychoanalysis is a continued working through of the implications of Freud's original assertions, where does the concept begin or end? Nevertheless, at various points in his career, Freud gave very specific definitions of what he meant by the unconscious, how it was to be distinguished from other similar terms circulating in the psychology of his day, and how it contributed to the operations of a "psychic apparatus" – most significant amongst these are *The Interpretation of Dreams* (1900, chap. 7), "Formulations on the Two Principles of Mental Functioning" (1911), "A Note on the Unconscious in Psychoanalysis" (1912), "The Unconscious" (1915), "Repression" (1915) and *The Ego and the Id* (1923b). It is on these accounts, and other summaries given in Freud's *Introductory Lectures* and *New Introductory Lectures*, that I will be drawing here, though it should be borne in mind that many contemporary psychoanalysts and non-psychoanalysts alike now emphasize that the unconscious is ultimately enigmatic and breaks free of Freud's attempt to contain it within a scientific description. For Anthony Elliott, "The discovery of the *mode* of unconscious psychic processes lies at the centre of Freud's most profound contribution to the analysis of human subjectivity" (1999a, p. 14), and yet the unconscious is also an "elusive and unlocatable force" (p. 19); Josh Cohen suggests there is a striking mismatch between the "precision of the vocabulary" Freud employs and "the obscurity of the entity it describes" (2005, p. 24).

If psychoanalysis "begins" with the unconscious, the notion of an unconscious does not begin with Freud. There is now an expanding field of work on the development of various kinds of notions of "unconscious" factors in psychology, taking in the work of late 19th-century figures such as Jean-Martin Charcot, Pierre Janet, Théodore Flournoy and Frederic Myers, among others, as well as earlier versions of the unconscious stemming from Romantic psychology and philosophy. Nevertheless, there are reasons for isolating Freud as the writer of this period who gave the unconscious the most central place within his theory of psychological analysis, and whose version of it had the greater and longer-lasting public impact in the 20th century. We first encounter it as a clinical problem relating to his treatment of hysterical and neurotic patients (Elliott, 1999b, p. 18; Frosh, 2012, p. 37). Later on, Freud explained the concept as "*necessary* because the data of consciousness have a very large number of gaps in them" (Freud, 1915, p. 166), referring to the fact that "our most personal daily experience acquaints us with ideas that come into our head we do not know from where" (pp. 166–167). However, the original gaps to be confronted related to gaps in the memory of hysterical patients, and Freud's first public use of the term *unconscious* was in his report on his treatment of Frau Emmy von N, published in the *Studies on Hysteria* Freud co-wrote with his then mentor, the Viennese medical practitioner Josef Breuer.

Freud and Breuer, in the studies they published in 1895, were following a lead from an earlier case of the 1880s, in which Breuer had treated a young woman, Bertha Pappenheim (known in the case material as "Anna O"). She presented with various symptoms of nervous disorder including anorexia, coughing fits, disturbances of vision, anesthesia and hallucinations. Such "hysterical" phenomena were at this time classified as an elusive nervous disorder and became a focus of medical experimentation with hypnotism in France (research that, according to Freud, even before the time of psychoanalysis, "had tangibly demonstrated the existence and mode of operation of the mental unconscious" (1915, pp. 168–169). Experimenting with the use of hypnosis on Anna O, Breuer discovered that she easily fell into a trance state during which she was able to recall certain disturbing occurrences, each of which had a connection with the emergence of one of her particular symptoms. It appeared that when Anna O, aided by Breuer, had returned these events to conscious memory, there was an experience of emotional release and the symptom disappeared (though see Borch-Jacobsen & Shamdasani, 2012, for a questioning of the accuracy of this account). Somehow, events and associated memories and ideas were being excluded from patients' consciousness, and the inability then to mentally process such material was making them ill. There followed a formal realization "that the patient's manifest mind was not the whole of it, that there lay behind it an *unconscious* mind" (Strachey, 1893–1895, p. xvii). Building on this example, which they further tested on patients in the early 1890s, Breuer and Freud formulated the principle that they aired in their "Preliminary Communication" of 1893, that "hysterics suffer mainly from reminiscences" (p. 7).

Breuer and Freud differed in their assessment of the principle through which memories were withheld from consciousness. For Breuer, the clinical issue had to do with the "hypnoid" state itself – hysterics, due to a weakness of the nerves, were prone to fall into such states in which conscious material might become split off, or dissociated from their conscious minds. But for Freud, it was the content of the material that was key. He saw his patients as putting up an active resistance to ideas and feelings, which they experienced as threatening, usually relating to sexual experiences, and which were pushed away from consciousness. Thus was born Freud's dynamic theory of material driven into and maintained in a state of repression by various active forms of mental resistance. This still forms one of the central motifs of contemporary academic accounts of the unconscious: psychoanalysis concerns "ideas which are radically *unavailable* to thought" (Frosh, 2002, p. 12); "unpalatable thoughts, phantasies, unacceptable memories, ideas and wishes are pushed back into the unconscious, or repressed along with their associated emotions" (Clarke, 2003, p. 64). Correspondingly, the early aim of psychoanalysis became "making conscious what is unconscious, lifting repressions, filling gaps in the memory" (Freud, 1917, p. 435). In doing so the analyst attempts to "remove the preconditions for the formation of symptoms" (p. 435).

Psychoanalysis began with this very specific set of clinical insights. However, from early on Freud supplemented these insights with other kinds of examination of repressed material and its potentially disturbing reemergence into consciousness. He investigated the phenomenon of accidental mistakes in communication (the notorious Freudian slip), as well as the psychical mechanisms at work in jokes; most famously of all he studied the operation and function of dreams, leading to the publication of *The Interpretation of Dreams* in 1900, which many still consider his magnum opus. Freud became interested in dreams as part of a modification of the technique through which he attempted to access unconscious thoughts in neurotic patients. Gradually he replaced hypnosis with a principle of free association, in which the patient was encouraged simply to follow trains of thought, placing no restriction on the material that entered their minds (thus seeking to lower the threshold of mental resistance to unconscious ideas). A fruitful source of such trains of association were the dreams patients recounted in sessions with Freud, and he began experimenting with associations to his own dreams, hoping to uncover "substitutive structures, which will enable us to arrive at what is concealed from view" (1916, p. 113). Freud's study of dreams put the theory of the unconscious on a more general footing – that is, it was no longer restricted to the study of neurotic pathology.

But more than this, as Freud developed his analyses of dreams, they became the "royal road to a knowledge of the unconscious activities of the mind" (1900, p. 608). This is a point that again proliferates in the literature: "Freud's description of dream work is in fact a discussion of the working of the unconscious itself" (Craib, 2001, p. 30); dreams offered a privileged "glimpse of the symbolic productions of the unconscious" (Elliott, 1999b, p. 20).

What was it that Freud discovered? He supposed that the bewildering appearance of dreams, and our difficulties in recounting them, were products of a form of censorship imposed by the conscious ego on the resisted ideas of the unconscious, on the same principle as the resistance already revealed in hysterical patients. The book on dreams thus supported and developed the analysis of the more clinical evidence. However, Freud also learned new things about the operation of unconscious processes. In the daytime, consciousness was generally successful in keeping repressed material out, but at night, in dreams, the guard was lowered and the psyche was able to form a compromise whereby certain repressed ideas could be symbolically represented in visual form. His key thesis was that every dream formed around the nucleus of an unconscious wish or impulse that could gain access to consciousness only in this incomplete and distorted form. Freud reconstructed a specific set of mental processes to account for the distorted appearance of "dream thoughts." The principle mechanisms were displacement (an idea is transferred from its original object onto a substitute) and condensation (two or more ideas are blended to form a more bizarre composite form, which hinders their recognizability). Freud's dream theory is further discussed in Chapter 10 of this volume.

Freud's work on dreams also produced further insights into the nature of the repressed material that made it so unacceptable to consciousness. This concerns Freud's notion of the Oedipus complex, or the sexual and aggressive nature of the thoughts and feelings originally directed toward the parents in childhood, which the mature mind was keen to exclude. This was a thesis that he carried over, a little hesitantly at this point, from his work with neurotic patients into general psychology (his key public assertion of the role of sexual life in the unconscious came in 1905 in the *Three Essays on Sexuality*). As sexuality is being dealt with in a different chapter in this volume, I will not cover it extensively here; however, it is important to note that Freud was convinced of the intimate connection between repression and sexual impulses in mental life (1916, p. 22). This connection was present in Freud's earliest formulations of psychoanalysis, given his original conviction that the "reminiscences" that hysterics suffered from were memories of some kind of sexual trauma. However, as he pursued the investigations of dreaming, he made a crucial shift in his theory. What was at stake was not at root disturbing *memories*, if this implies memories of historical incidents, imposing themselves on a person from without. Rather his concern centered increasingly on disturbing ideas and impulses, the implication being that sexual disturbance was encountered, in the first instance, as an internal problem – not necessarily the traumatic memory of an actual seduction, but as threatening forms of excitation and fantasies that asserted themselves more powerfully than reality. The dynamic aspect of Freud's unconscious needs to be understood in a double sense, then. Not only is there the factor of repression, actively keeping material out of consciousness, but impulses from the unconscious – sexual drives, wishes for omnipotent mastery – are actively pressing to assert themselves in consciousness. Hence, there is the image of people "driven by forces beyond their consciousness or their control" (Craib, 2001, p. 21).

## The structure of the unconscious

By 1915, Freud was in a position to provide several more systematic overviews of the functioning of the unconscious from a psychoanalytic perspective, most significantly in his two metapsychological papers on "The Unconscious" and "Repression," and the slightly earlier "Note on the Unconscious" (1913). It will be useful to go over some of the main points here, especially as they form the basis for many contemporary accounts of the Freudian unconscious in the humanities and social sciences. One of the key distinctions Freud introduces is that between two different kinds of unconscious material: the preconscious and the unconscious proper. The former represents mental material that is "latent and capable of becoming conscious," on the understanding that "a state of consciousness is characteristically very transitory" (1923b, p. 14); therefore ideas, memories and associations are passing into states of latency, or unconsciousness, all the time. However, the unconscious with which psychoanalysis is more concerned represents material for which the transformation into consciousness "is difficult and takes place only subject to a considerable expenditure of effort or possibly never at all" (1933, p. 71). This material is unconscious not just in the descriptive sense, of not being consciously present, but in the dynamic sense as well: "we restrict the term *unconscious* to the dynamically unconscious repressed" (1923b, p. 15).

This tripartite structural division of the psyche into conscious, preconscious and unconscious material is referred to as Freud's first "topography" of the mind (see Clarke, 2003, p. 64; Craib, 2001, pp. 21–22; Frosh, 2012, p. 40).

Freud also approached the unconscious through a hierarchical distinction between different kinds of mental process. The mental functions and judgments known to us from conscious and rational thinking are described by Freud as "secondary processes" and ascribed to the ego (this also includes the functioning of the preconscious), while the unconscious has its own different way of dealing with mental material, known as "primary processes." The ego is secondary (perhaps one of the most significant inversions in Freud's psychology as a whole) because it is the later formation, resting on the surface of an unconscious mind whose operations are more primitive and more historically archaic. When described this way, the unconscious appears not just as a state of certain mental materials (a state of being denied access to consciousness) but as a "mental province" or system (1933, p. 71) with its own internal principles. Some of these principles distinctive of the unconscious have been touched on in relation to dreaming; for instance, the fact that mental associations may be combined according to quite different rules from ordinary thinking, such as condensation and displacement. But in the 1915 paper on the unconscious Freud assembles a more definitive account of the functioning of the "system Ucs." The important features are that the unconscious knows no logical functions – "there are in this system no negation, no doubt, no degrees of certainty" (1915, p. 186), and that the nucleus of the unconscious consists of unorganized "wishful impulses." These impulses, furthermore, "are not ordered temporally, are not altered by the passage of time," neither do they pay any regard to a principle of "reality" (p. 187; Cohen, 2005, pp. 21–25; Frosh, 2002, p. 14). Together these constitute the most significant and recurrent characterizations of the unconscious in classical and contemporary literature, when it is treated as a specific domain of psychical functioning.

Having arrived at this definitive portrait of the nature of the unconscious, it now remains to be said that Freud proceeded to dismantle aspects of this account in his work of the 1920s. One reason was his dissatisfaction with the imprecision of the term *unconscious* – a "quality which can have many meanings" (1923b, p. 18). Another was Freud's increasing awareness that aspects of the ego and its defenses against unconscious material must themselves be unconscious in order for the repression to be successful. In this case, "we have no right to name the mental region that is foreign to the ego 'the system Ucs.,' since the characteristic of being unconscious is not restricted to it" (1933, p. 72). A third factor affecting Freud's revisions to the earlier topography stemmed from his increasing interest in moral life and the question of how external authority was internalized in the individual psyche. In a group of texts from the early 1920s, Freud extended the theoretical framework of psychoanalysis by arguing for the presence of a further psychical component – the "superego" – which included the functions of internal conscience and the idealization of authority figures (which Freud at first called the "ego ideal"). As he developed the concept further, he put forward the idea that the superego was itself bound to destructive and erotic instinctual trends. Thus it, too, had unconscious dimensions, on which Freud based his account of the individual's unconscious need for punishment, or sense of guilt (1933, p. 109), ideas that were to become highly influential in accounts of criminality in the mid-20th-century social sciences.

As a result of such complications, Freud abandoned the description of the unconscious as a system in itself, counterposed to ego-consciousness, and instead made a new tripartite division of the psyche into the ego (the more rationally cognitive part of the mind that accepted and imposed "a reality principle"), the superego (moral and critical functions) and the id (literally the "it"), a new term for the reservoir of uncoordinated instinctual trends. In this "second topography" of the psyche, the id is the inheritor of those aspects of instinctual drives, timelessness and repressed ideas that had formed the basis of Freud's former conception of "the system unconscious": in it "the logical laws of thought do not apply . . . contrary impulses exist side by side, without can-celling each other out" (1933, p. 73); it is the "dark inaccessible part of our personality" (p. 73); it "knows no judgments of value: no good and evil, no morality" (p. 74).

Freud's reorientation of the framework of psychoanalysis around the ego, the id, and the superego came to dominate appropriations of psychoanalysis in the social sciences in particular from the 1930s through to the 1960s. The task of analysis itself now gave equal weight to the unconscious portions of all three agencies. However, it represents a modification of the way in which the description of psychical processes is organized, rather than an entirely new insight into the nature of those processes (although the superego does represent a genuine extension of the theory into the psychology of moral life). In the conflict between the ego and the id one sees repeated the original insight, dating back to the 1890s, concerning a consciousness menaced by aspects of its experience (primarily sexual, but in the later theory increasingly also destructive aspects) that it has tried to exclude, but which find their way back into consciousness as a seem-ingly alien disturbance (an error, a symptom, an ingress of anxiety).

And yet, arguably, a new emphasis does emerge, in the form of a consolidation of a more instinctual framework for thinking about the unconscious per se. Whereas the emphasis in the early work on dreams and jokes fell on the intricate coding and decoding of mental associations, in the later writings there is a greater concern with the irreducible pressure of the drives – the id is a "cauldron full of seething excitations" dominated by an "economic pressure towards the discharge of energy" (1933, pp. 73–74). Aspects of repression are themselves "primal" (primary repression) and originate in psychical defenses, active from infancy onward, against the experi-ence of unwanted levels of internal stimulation. Furthermore, the repressed is itself now merely a part of the id, which is in turn open "to somatic influences." None of this was entirely new – as Strachey observed, the notion of the unconscious as an "economic" problem, to do with main-taining constancy in the experience of levels of excitation in the body, and which emerges most strongly in Freud's postwar essay "Beyond the Pleasure Principle," was a prominent feature of Freud's pre-psychoanalytic thinking about mental operations in the 1890s. But aspects of the late formulations do appear to emphasize the naturalistic basis of social life, giving rise to con-tributions such as John Bowlby's attachment theory, which developed the unconscious within a more overtly biological or ethological framework, as an issue of animal instincts. Even though it must be remembered that Freud characteristically theorizes drives rather than instincts (the former being more variable and volatile translations of aspects of the latter into the medium of symbolic representation), the id is at times presented as the repository for the "vicissitudes of the human species" (1923b, p. 36). Further implications of this shift in perspective emerge in Freud's late writings on human civilization (see Chapter 2 of this volume), in which society lives under the strain of its animal impulses, falling sick, entertaining religious delusions or descending into open warfare.

Although, as we shall see, few contemporary explorations of the Freudian unconscious retain this connection between the unconscious and "the most primitive drives" (Craib, 2001, p. 22) – sexual and destructive – in quite this way, naturalism and hermeneutics have remained two poles of the reception of Freud, both within psychoanalysis and in the social sciences and humanities (the hermeneutic model deriving primarily from the work on dreams). Moreover, the notion of a primary form of repression, or an unconscious, irrational or irrevocably opaque basis on which subjectivity is founded, admits of both kinds of emphases. If the unconscious "can be said to exist as a condition of subjectivity; it is the basis from which consciousness emerges" (Elliott, 1999b, p. 20) – this could be taken as indicating the opaque relation between the psyche and the body, or the obscurity in the way meaning, or self-apprehension, is itself generated in the psyche. It is precisely this kind of ambiguity over what the Freudian theory of the unconscious entails that has allowed it to be so fruitfully mobilized by a number of differing projects in the social sciences and humanities.

## Transference: going beyond structure

There is one other aspect of the unconscious to be considered, which puts a different spin on Freud's model, and this is his account of "transference." Characteristically this is treated separately from the theory of the unconscious because it arose in the context of writings on psychoanalytic technique rather than metapsychology. However, it makes sense to touch on it here, given that it presents a facet of Freud's account that has taken on an ever more significant role, both in post-Freudian clinical work and in the importation of psychoanalytic ideas and methods into the social sciences (although it has made fewer inroads in the humanities). It was first theorized in a postscript to Freud's case study of Dora (1905), in order to describe the way in which Dora had unconsciously transferred an emotional relationship toward her father onto the relation to the analyst, which led to her abrupt termination of the therapeutic encounter. In "The Dynamics of Transference" (1912) he defines transference in terms of unconscious anticipatory ideas (alongside conscious ones) through which prototypes of erotic relations going back to childhood are transferred onto contemporary figures. He compared the formation of these prototypes to "stereotype plates," constantly repeated in a person's life, though not incapable of modification (pp. 99–100).

Though more recent accounts often trace the term back to Freud in this way, they are more usually working with post-Kleinian extensions of what transference and the related issue of "countertransference" is taken to mean (countertransference indicating feelings unconsciously provoked in the analyst in response to material mobilized by the patient). In contemporary work, however, the terms no longer necessarily indicate models of emotional relationship laid down in the deep past, but simply the unconscious transferring of emotional responses from one context to another, or from the inner life of the patient to the analyst.

The important point is that contemporary concepts of transference access the phenomena of unconscious life not through a reconstruction of the full history of a person's psychical life (a project that Freud aimed to realize in case studies such as the Wolfman), or the elaboration of a complete psychical "system," but as a more mobile and complex factor, which has to do with the permeability between conscious life and the strata of emotional conflict perpetually provoking it, or provoked by it. The terms *transference* and *countertransference* have thus come to have a crucial relevance for the social sciences and humanities – particularly in psychosocial studies, but not only here – where they can indicate the creation of a methodological space that acknowledges the experience of oblique emotional and ideational responses, as they arise between researcher and research subject, including such features as a significant part of the data to be processed.

Although this is jumping ahead to consider work on or with the unconscious in the contemporary non-psychoanalytic academic context, it is worth establishing one point before leaving Freud's original account behind. Freud's aim may appear to be that of increasingly differentiating and specifying the nature of unconscious processes in mental life, so as to arrive at as complete an account of its functions as might be obtained of conscious mental processes (Strachey suggested chapter 7 of *The Interpretation of Dreams* showed "what the unconscious was like, how it worked" (Freud, 1915, p. 164). However, the very complexity of the unconscious (certainly in Freud's version of it) as well as the opacity attaching to the notion of unconscious material per se, means that Freud's descriptions are capable of being read antidogmatically, as an expanding set of highly suggestive problems, or forms of methodological and epistemological complication, whose relationships will necessarily be resolved, if at all, by ongoing acts of interpretation. Thus Nancy Chodorow uses Freud's assertion in the *Introductory Lectures* that the ego is not master in its own house, and "must content itself with scanty information of what is going on unconsciously in its mind" (Freud, 1917, p. 285) to introduce a far more open-textured account of Freud's own theoretical frames of reference to unconscious psychical structures: "forces and structures beyond conscious control or even knowledge: sexual and aggressive drives within the id; primary process thinking . . . powerful ideas and wishes that anxiety and repression have removed from consciousness," as well as "conflict, as these wishes and ideas seek recognition" and further "superego pressures" (Chodorow, 1989, pp. 154–155). The metapsychology, then, implies "fragmentation of structure, function, and process," affecting "the everyday subjective experience of the self," rather than providing an integrated account of a psychical "system" (p. 155). By incorporating a principle of unconscious psychical processes, the individual is capable of being approached as more epistemologically complex than would be suggested by a philosophy or psychology of "consciousness," which aimed to make the self systematically knowable. Such an approach may have ethical and political, as well as epistemological benefits to convey.

## Psychoanalytic science: the 1940s–1960s

Before exploring the reworking of Freud's account in contemporary human and social scientific practice, I want to give a brief overview of an intervening phase in the uptake of psychoanalytic models in which the importation of "classical" Freudian concepts typically rendered them in more dogmatic form. This concerns the period from the late 1940s to the early 1960s in which, due to the embracing of psychoanalytic ideas in post–World War II American psychiatry (itself partly the result of the influx of psychoanalysts exiled from Europe during the war), Freudian and neo-Freudian ideas were granted a medical and scientific legitimacy on a much broader scale than had hitherto been achieved.

Psychoanalysis emerged from the war with a greater reach into areas such as sociology, developmental psychology, anthropology, educational theory and moral philosophy, as well as a wider infiltration into nonacademic culture in the form of popular psychologies on the neuroses of modern life. All this was very different from the scandal attached to Freud's theory of the role of infantile sexuality in mental life when it emerged from Vienna 40 years earlier. To dip into one study of psychoanalysis and the social sciences from 1962, which sums up many interactions from the previous decade, one finds that psychoanalysis is now "part of the complex functioning of American Society" (Ruitenbeek, 1962, p. vii) and has "won a welcome both as a therapy and as a tool for inquiry into social and individual behaviour" (p. xxvi). Along the way, Freud, and writers building on his insights such as Karen Horney, Margaret Mead, Erik Erikson, Herbert Marcuse, David Riesman and Erich Fromm, have transformed "cultural anthropology, sociology, social psychology, and even history" (p. xiii) as well as having a marked effect "on the society which these disciplines study" (p. xx). Because of Freud, social scientists influenced by psychoanalysis now concerned themselves with motivational dynamics: "frustration, guilt, aggression, anxiety, repression, projection, displacement, wish fulfilment, defence mechanisms, reaction formation, transference, and insecurity" (p. xvii).

What had been enlisted was not so much Freud's general notion of the unconscious, and certainly not its anti-epistemological connotations. In fact, the *unconscious* as a key term has all but dropped out, its significance displaced by more particular analyses of specific developmental problems: the transition through oral, anal and genital stages with their attendant fixation points; problems in the resolution of the Oedipus complex; and the reemergence of infantile conflicts in response to adult crises. Such concepts were mobilized to address issues ranging from the pressures on the contemporary consumer family, and the social psychology of the Russians, to tackling juvenile delinquency or marketing tobacco.

A classic example of the alliance between academic and psychoanalytic culture is the work of Talcott Parsons, who began his 1950 article "Psychoanalysis and the Social Structure" with an assertion of their basic common frame of reference, the theory of action. Within the social theorization of action, a certain place has to be given to "the individual personality as a system" (p. 371) and psychoanalysis, in this respect, seems to trump the other psychologies. It shows that the behavior and attitudes of others are not enough to account for constructs of typical motivation. "Certain typical elements of structure of the particular personality such as superego content and ways in which the instinctual components are organised are also involved" (p. 375). Without this contribution, "a far cruder level of dynamic interpretation would have to be accepted" (p. 382).

Another significant example of dialogue comes from Theodor Adorno and Max Horkheimer's involvement in *The Authoritarian Personality* (1950). The introduction to this compendium of surveys and qualitative research projects on the genesis of antidemocratic behaviors again argues that the framework of investigation requires a "theory of the total personality" (p. 5). For this theory they also leaned heavily on Freud, drawing from his work an account of the individual as an organization of forces: "primarily *needs* (drives, wishes, emotional impulses)" including "primitive emotional needs" and "needs to avoid punishment" (p. 5), the latter two reflecting Freud's theorization of the id and the superego. Note how the investigators of *The Authoritarian Personality* use an armory of psychoanalytic concepts to predict the presence of specific unconscious structures in the personality of individuals (as opposed to Chodorow's "fragmentation of structure, function and process" quoted at the end of the last section). The index to the volume contains entries for *ambivalence, anxiety, inner conflict* and *superego*, but, interestingly, not *unconscious* itself.

A not dissimilar story emerges when one turns to other academic disciplines in the period – for instance, historical studies such as Erikson's *Young Man Luther*, which uses a quasi-psychoanalytic lens to understand the personality structure of Martin Luther, and the role of conflict within his personal development (though Erikson was sensitive enough to make the case run both ways: Luther's historical example is in turn formative for the Western Protestant culture Freud's work comes to inhabit). Likewise, though theorists such as Lionel Trilling set up the dialogue between Freud and culture in a sophisticated manner, much of the psychoanalytic study of literature pursued in the middle decades of the 20th century now appears reductive in its aims: intent on discovering sexual symbolism, or on relating literary content to neurotic complexes in the personality of the author, which are traced back to scenes of childhood Oedipal conflict (for criticisms, see Wright, 1998 and Ellmann, 1994). This is not to say that the psychoanalysis of literature has not proved to be a fruitful vein, but that the diagnostic approach typical of the mid-century legitimization of psychoanalysis as a medical-psychological discourse (and apparent in both Parsons's and Adorno's approaches) has been overwhelmingly rejected in recent work, which tends to draw more on Lacanian or object relations models.

## The contemporary Freudian unconscious

In this latter part of the chapter I shall stick to works that specifically foreground the unconscious in a quasi-Freudian form, acknowledging at the same time that the classical conception has been displaced, within many contemporary accounts, by versions developed by later psychoanalytic thinkers – primarily the Lacanian "linguistic" unconscious and post-Kleinian notion of unconscious phantasy (covered in Chapters 3, 4, and 8 in this volume). It is perhaps in these currents that the notion of the unconscious was being most creatively rethought during the 1940s and

1950s. However, the Freudian unconscious still provides a crucial reference point. As Jessica Benjamin has argued: "to critique and revise [Freud's] theory . . . is our prerogative, as well as our way of being determined by it" (1995, p. 4).

By far the most significant modification to be taken into account is that which intervened in the models of human and social sciences during the 1970s and 1980s, radically transforming internal debates about the construction of knowledge and having important knock-on effects on the reception of psychoanalytic ideas. These include the impact of feminism, post-colonialism, social constructivism and deconstruction across the human and social sciences, each in their own way opening the fabric of knowledge up to pluralism, and criticizing the epistemological foundations and implicit bias in the social and ethical bases of various academic disciplines. The impact of this shift is commonly voiced in the academic literature on psychoanalysis: "Since the 1990s, partly due to the impact of feminism, the social sciences have begun to change. Traditional models of human rationality, which opposed reason to passion, are being challenged" (Clarke & Hoggett, 2009, p. 1); "psychoanalysis might benefit from accepting the challenge to modernist ideas of subjectivity posed by the deconstructionist formulations of Derrida or by the poststructuralist position of Foucault" (Benjamin, 1995, p. 13). Much of what is to follow concerns the way in which the unconscious has thus been reshaped to integrate with new agendas concerning particularity, complexity, plurality and nuance in the construction of social knowledge and theories of selfhood.

During the same period (roughly the 1970s onward) the position of psychoanalysis in American psychiatry was challenged by a number of factors including the increasing turn toward prescription drugs as the solution to psychological anxiety, and by the growing preference in academic psychology for cognitive and biological models of mental process. This in turn affected the wider cultural image of psychoanalysis as a "scientific" and medically legitimate practice. Critiques by Karl Popper and others from the 1960s onward, leveled at the scientific standards of psychoanalysis, likewise did much to dismantle the capital that had been built up in the postwar period, through which psychoanalysis appeared to grant special technical access to the lesser known aspects of psychological motivation. Ironically, all these challenges to the status of psychoanalysis as a science may have ultimately worked in its favor – as far as the hermeneutic and social sciences are concerned – because it was precisely the retreat from the kind of diagnostic dogmatism alluded to in the last section that paved the way for the re-assimilation of the unconscious into contemporary academia, as the psychology of the particular, the unexpected and the marginal. Introducing the unconscious became one way of asserting provisionality within the very structure of knowledge.

Along with this comes a return to the primacy of the *unconscious*, as opposed to the more specific concern with Oedipal conflict, or developmental pathologies in the formation of the superego. We saw at the beginning of the chapter how often the unconscious is still placed center stage in accounts of psychoanalysis – for writers like Frosh and Craib it is the key idea, the touchstone of psychoanalysis. Here it can be added that in contemporary works this "beginning" with the unconscious is most often at the expense of the specifics of the sexual theory. It was not sexuality, according to Frosh, but the unconscious that was Freud's unwelcome idea (2012, p. 38). Likewise, for Chodorow, sexuality, emotions and the unconscious are threaded together in such a way that no term is any longer centralized:

> People everywhere have emotions that they care about, connections to others, sexual feelings, and senses of self, self-esteem, and gender. People everywhere form a psyche, self, and identity. These are everywhere profoundly affected by unconscious fantasies as well as by conscious perceptions that begin as early as infancy.
>
> *(Chodorow, 1989, p. 4)*

Psychic life is not necessarily governed by unconscious propensities, and sexual feelings are to take their place alongside many other feelings and ideas out of which identity is complexly woven (though compare Elizabeth Wright's suggestion that "psychoanalysis brings out the unconscious aspect of language through its concentration on the relationship between sexuality and social role"; 1998, p. 4).

What strikes one in contemporary cultural and social applications of psychoanalysis, then, is the more general and provisional way in which the idea of the unconscious is formulated. It is "where things happen behind our backs . . . the place, for example, where I first take the decision to fall in love" (Craib, 1989, p. 5); or concerns "the irrational, the "crazy" side of human life" (p. 3). It stands for the existence of "something else . . . something disturbing and tripping-up" (Frosh, 2002, p. 12) or "inconsistencies and incongruity in behaviour" (p. 11). It foregrounds "commonsense ideas such as that people might lie to themselves" (p. 11). First impressions "contain much that eludes our conscious assessment of another person" (Hollway & Jefferson, 2000, p. 46).

One way of understanding these more open-ended and suggestive formulae is that they provide the most plausible general ground for encouraging academics within the human or social sciences to embrace a dialogue with psychoanalytic perspectives: at the very least, one must accept the presence of the *unconscious*. The generality of the approach also concedes the many shifts and divergences in psychoanalytic practice and theorization, such that it is no longer one particular account of psychic processes (and no longer Freud's specific account of its function) that commands assent, but the general principle, into which insights from Freud, Klein, Winnicott, Lacan, Bion and Jung might be variously blended. However, the style of description also reflects moves toward anti-foundationalism or anti-essentialism, such that there is no longer the same drive to combine psychological and sociological models within a total "theory of the person," or in establishing the definitive symbolic interpretation of a text.

On this note one might distinguish two kinds of reaction against the uses of psychoanalysis from the 1950s. One is in the name of greater nuance and greater sensitivity to the diversity of social identities. Such authors draw on the notion of unconscious factors in order to construe data in new and more complex ways. Examples of this might be Wendy Hollway and Tony Jefferson's project to draw on psychoanalytic concepts in order to refine their methodological approach to "something as complex (and hence unquantifiable) as fear" (2000, p. 2), or Ian Craib's statements that without giving up the commitment to rigorous and systematic enquiry, it is also good "to be open to the richness, complexity and unexpectedness of our experience of the world," and that "the meanings in which we live are multi-dimensional" (2001, pp. viii, 24).

The other response, more influenced by deconstruction and post-structuralism, is that which employs the unconscious to complicate epistemological and methodological frameworks per se. For instance, the implication that Josh Cohen draws from Freud's work on dreams is that "every displacement only displaces another displacement," or "the paradox of interpretation is that it's complete only when it runs up against the impossibility of completion" (2005, p. 41). Hermeneutics does not discover an unsupposed object but the absence of its object. Or see Maud Ellmann's argument for the unconscious as an attention to "the echoes and resources of words themselves," through which we can "recognize the otherness of literature, its recalcitrance as well as its susceptibility to theorisation" (1994, p. 3).

It may appear from these examples that uses of the unconscious in the service of method, and in resistance to it, divide between work in the social sciences and in the humanities. Since post-structuralism, however, hermeneutics has led a wider assault on naturalist or essentialist bias in social science (at least to some degree) and this has impacted strongly in the way psychoanalysis is applied. Thus psychosocial studies gives rise as much to "deconstructive" uses of the unconscious as to forms of qualitative research *on* the unconscious. Simon Clarke's framework for empirical research modifies the Freudian unconscious with Freud's notion of the "uncanny," drawing on Alvesson and Skoldberg. Read via the latter, "the unconscious becomes something that does not really exist, but is an ascribed meaning" (Clarke, 2003, p. 72).

There is one further way to think about transformations of the unconscious in contemporary academia, and this is that they represent a genuine rethinking of its implications for particular disciplines far removed from the contexts engaged by Freud's original clinical work – thus a new beginning. It may be that this is happening now not so much, or not just because of anti-foundationalist tendencies, but because it has taken a century to find the most appropriate way of translating psychoanalytic ideas from the clinic into disciplines such as sociology, politics, philosophy, post-colonial studies, gender, film and literary studies (or indeed, for many of these disciplines themselves to be founded). An important factor here is that much of the more transformatory deployment of the unconscious in the last 20 years – and particularly the more complex versions of this – has been via writers who combine a career within a particular academic discipline with some form of clinical psychoanalytic training (this includes Juliet Mitchell, Stephen Frosh, Jessica Benjamin, Nancy Chodorow, Jeff Prager, Josh Cohen and Ian Craib, among others). This is not because such academics are in a position to apply psychoanalytic concepts within their disciplines with a greater degree of self-certainty. The combination has in many cases proved unsettling: in the preface to *Psychoanalysis: A Critical Introduction*, Craib wrote of the difficulties of integrating the theories connected with his life as a psychoanalytic group therapist with teaching the philosophy of social science and social theory to undergraduates (2001, p. vii); Benjamin explains "the position from which I write – that of a psychoanalyst involved from the beginning with feminist thought – is not one that can rely on the well-worn grooves of an established discipline" (1995, p. 1). But it has meant that such writers have had greater sanction to mobilize the theory in more fluid and exploratory ways, having learned firsthand that psychoanalysis, whatever it is, is not the science of certainty, and that this, in conjunction with the anti-essentializing tendencies at work in their own disciplines since the 1960s, has made for reinterpretations of Freudian concepts that are also highly original contributions to the extension of psychoanalysis beyond the clinic in their own right. The unconscious continues to be rethought.

In what follows I will outline a number of recurrent themes and positions on the unconscious that one could find in most areas of contemporary cultural and social writing incorporating psychoanalytic perspectives. Pride of place goes to the repositioning of the unconscious as the negation of reason, which newly centralizes Freud's relevance within the post-structuralist or post-modernist wings of particular academic disciplines: psychoanalysis "challenges the Western view that the distinguishing mark of humanity is reason and rationality" (Frosh, 2002, p. 17); it is "a force that violates common sense" (Cohen, 2005, p. 25). The unconscious "challenges the emphasis in Western thought on the power of reason and rationality, of reflective and conscious control over the self" (Elliott, 1999b, p. 14). As we saw earlier on, Freud's several portraits of the unconscious always accentuated its refusal of, or inaccessibility to, logic. But it was only in the last third of the 20th century that such a "realm of primary negation" (p. 15) might actually cement its role within academic disciplines wanting to begin their work anew from the point of view of a de-centered and un-masterful subject of knowledge.

## Pluralism and the de-centered self

From this point, a number of more particular implications radiate outwards. One of these concerns the direct effects of the challenge to reason and consciousness on the authority of the self. Although for Prager and Rustin, Freud "attempted to stake out a space for individual autonomy and rationality against the many social and individual forces which would (and did) close this down" (1993, p. x), Chodorow argues that "psychoanalysis begins with a radical challenge to traditional notions of the individual self" (1989, p. 154). According to Freud,

> we are not who or what we think we are: we do not know our own centres; in fact, we probably do not have a centre at all. Psychoanalysis radically undermines notions about autonomy, individual choice, will, responsibility and rationality, showing that we do not control our own lives in the most fundamental sense.
>
> *(Chodorow, 1989, p. 154)*

In a similar fashion, Frosh suggests we are spoken by something else:

> This something is not to do with identity, or a "true self" . . . it is rather the precise opposite of this, insisting that there is no such "self" – an insistence that is now a routine legacy of poststructuralism and postmodernism.
>
> *(Frosh, 2010, p. 7)*

In post-structuralist approaches, the challenge to reason and the de-centering of self go hand in hand, and this further affects the way theory is formulated and identity is thought. In the first place, a more pluralistic account of process arises. Earlier I quoted Craib's observation that "the meanings in which we live are multi-dimensional" (2001, p. 24); correspondingly, Craib views psychoanalysis as "a body of ideas with multi-faceted relationships to each other and to the human psyche that is their object" (p. vii). This can be matched by Chodorow's notion of feminist theory as "multiplex," or Benjamin's argument for an "overinclusive" psychoanalysis, "inspired by such theoretical developments outside the psychoanalytic world as deconstruction and poststructuralism" (1995, p. 9). This means "accepting the paradoxes that can arise from an ability to identify with more than one perspective" (p. 10).

For many writers, pluralism of perspective leads directly on to issues of intersubjectivity. This is very obviously the case for Benjamin, who has made intersubjectivity the focus of much of her writing on psychoanalysis, gender and social theory. Chodorow likewise draws on the psycho-analytic writings of Hans Loewald for "a vision of intersubjectivity deeply imbued with multiply tiered ways to understand and experience self and other" (1989, p. 12). For Elliott, too, "the human subject proposed by the theory of the unconscious demonstrates that the psyche is forever thrown off-centre in relation to itself," but this de-centering "allows for a reflexive involvement with the self and others" (1999b, p. 2).

## Psychosocial

These are all examples of a more radical integration of the psychoanalytic theory of the uncon-scious with post-structuralist trends, the goal being to retheorize the nature of subjectivity. It is interesting to compare these projects with psychosocial research oriented more toward eliciting new research tools. According to Clarke and Hoggett,

> psycho-social studies uses psychoanalytic concepts and principles to illuminate core issues within the social sciences. These have recently included the role of loss and mourning in the constitution of community; the nature of identities such as "girl," "white," or "mother"; the experiences of rapid social change, particularly the experiences of the powerless; the negotia-tion of ethical dilemmas by public service professionals.
>
> *(Clarke and Hoggett, 2009, pp. 1–2)*

Psychoanalysis here informs the use of new methodologies, such as "use of free association and biographical interview methods, application of infant observation methodologies to social observation, development of psychoanalytic ethnography/fieldwork; attention to transference-countertransference dynamics in the research process" (Clarke and Hoggett, 2009, p. 2). Significantly, the authors do not themselves foreground the concept of the unconscious, using instead the more Kleinian or object relations term *internal world*: "In psychoanalytic ethnography this world is often hidden, and the transference and countertransference between respondent and researcher thus becomes a way in which the hidden inner world reveals itself" (p. 5). It is a term also favored by Hollway and Jefferson and earlier by Craib, for whom knowledge of the external world is "distorted or coloured by what is going on in the internal world" (2001, p. 197). This seems a different approach from that outlined by Chodorow and Benjamin, with the emphasis more on techniques through which to chart the less accessible, but still concrete, emotional responses of individual research subjects. And yet, for Hollway and Jefferson, "the shared starting-point of all the different schools of psychoanalytic thought is the idea of a dynamic unconscious which defends against anxiety and significantly influences people's actions, lives and relations" (2000, p. 19) – that is to say, despite drawing on Klein for their technical understanding of defense processes, behind this stands a more primary and still recognizably Freudian commitment to the dynamic unconscious. Second, the engagement with defense and anxiety once more reveals inflections caused by post-structuralist trends, which direct focus onto the role of intersubjectivity in research, and encourage reformulations of the epistemological process that, if they don't de-center, at least problematize the role of the enquirer:

> We intend to construe both researcher and researched as anxious, defended subjects, whose mental boundaries are porous where unconscious material is concerned. This means, that both will be subject to projections and introjections of ideas and feelings coming from the other person.
>
> *(2009, p. 45)*

This porosity is an example of the extension of Freud's concept of unconscious transference into the research process. Likewise Clarke and Hoggett place the "reflexive practitioner" at the heart of their project of "researching beneath the surface" (2009, p. 7).

## Radicalism of the unconscious

Another line radiating out from the unconscious in its challenge to Western reason is an association with radicalism. Where Ernst Gellner gave a negative assessment of the unconscious as a form of "systematic interference" with knowledge, for many cultural and social theorists this negativity in fact ensures its critical relevance. Freud's masterpieces "have never lost their power to irritate" (Ellmann, 1994, p. 1); the unconscious is "of its nature, disruptive of everyday and established ways of thinking" and has a "fundamentally unsettling and disturbing quality" (Rustin in Bainbridge et al., 2007, p. 1). With a more forceful articulation, such disruption and provocation easily takes on political dimensions. The unconscious, for Frosh, is "the great revolutionary of everyday life" (2002, p. 14).

The potential for transformation that psychoanalysis offers to the individual (as therapy, self-interpretation or critique) here shifts toward a wider claim about the transformation of social life. If Freud makes unconscious desire "the organizing principle of all human thought, action and social relations" (Elliott, 1999b, p. 13), then this implies that the law of social relations can be "actively reshaped by the creative dynamics of desire itself" (pp. 2–3). Such possibilities were seriously explored in the social and political writings of the psychoanalyst Wilhelm Reich in the 1930s, and by various critical theorists, including Herbert Marcuse, in the 1950s and 1960s. Compared with those attempts at a systematic theory of social transformation, contemporary allusions to the radical dimensions of the unconscious tend to be more incidental and suggestive. The unconscious, for instance, is endowed with continuing shock value, as something "so radically different . . . it was never really accommodated by the twentieth century" (Cousins, 2005, p. ix). Freud's "dynamic" picture of the unconscious, as a pressure exerted by the repressed on consciousness, is extended into an agency of social revolution:

> Psychoanalysis has the capacity to disrupt the complacent acceptance of the status quo by revealing both the disturbance that lies behind it, and the way *nothing* is stable because there is always a pressure towards change, whether this be as a consequence of love or destructiveness.
>
> *(Frosh, 2010, p. 6)*

But it is rarely systematically theorized in this way. Jacqueline Rose's account of Rosa Luxemburg brings a further identification of the unconscious as "something radically unknowable at the core of political life" (Rose, 2014, p. 33). Revolution must partake of uncertainty, spontaneity, the incalculable:

> How could you possibly believe that a revolution can or should be mastered or known in advance if you are in touch with those parts of the mind which the mind itself cannot master and which do not even know themselves?
>
> *(Rose, 2014, p. 49)*

Note how closely these terms of the unknowable and incalculable repeat the many general apprehensions of the unconscious quoted at the beginning of this section as representative of the post-structuralist reception of Freud.

One of the more developed contemporary theorizations of the unconscious as a political force is that proposed by Elliott, drawing on work by Cornelius Castoriadis, which foregrounds its function as an irrepressible principle of creativity and desire. This concept constellates a number of different trends in social and cultural theory. It reconnects the hermeneutic unconscious to Freud's theory of the wish. If "the unconscious is unable to do anything but wish" (Elliott, 1999a, p. 15), it can again represent an insistent, utopian pressure.

But this storehouse of unconscious wishes at the core of the dream theory is also approached more positively than in Freud, as a "realm of dynamic imaginary production" (Elliott, 1999a, p. 15). This pregnant phrase suggests both a new wellspring of human agency, "through which human beings create themselves anew and the potential shape of their society" (p. 4), and intersects with the kinds of theorization of social identity pursued by Benjamin and Chodorow, because "the primary unconscious, as discussed by Freud, is the key psychical mechanism through which human beings establish an imaginary relation with the self, others, received social meanings, and society" (p. 4). This idea of an inherent, radical creativity in the psyche is echoed at many points in the contemporary academic literature: "the unconscious is an intriguing source of creativity that is at work within us without our awareness" (Craib, 2001, p. 30); "this book . . . is an argument for the existence of an irreducible realm of psychological life in which we create unconscious personal meaning in the experiential immediacy of the present (Chodorow, 1999, p. 1); the notion of the unconscious "gives us access to a way of seeing people and the cultures they create as endlessly inventive" (Frosh, 2002, p. 11).

## The other side of the humanities

Elliott's refocusing of the unconscious as a principle of creative imagination illuminates a crucial hinge between psychoanalysis and literary theory: "If the unconscious operates according to the stratagems of rhetoric, this means that psychoanalytic and literary criticism are united by a common object of investigation: the boundless creativity of tropes" (Ellmann, 1994, p. 5). The association of psychoanalysis with literary aesthetics represents one of its oldest and strongest allegiances with a cultural field other than medical psychology. It is rooted in Freud's own attention to literature (his accounts of Oedipus, Hamlet, Dostoevsky and E.T.A. Hoffmann) as well as critical interest from the other side, in Freud's theorization of dreams and modes of symbolic association. Ellmann writes:

> There are more things in literary texts than are dreamt of in Freudian philosophy . . . text and reader each reveal the inadvertent intuitions of the other: and it is out of this exchange that psychoanalytic theory is evolving still, in spite of its practitioners' attempts to petrify its dogma.
>
> *(1994, p. 26)*

She is recalling Soshona Felman's stronger thesis from the 1970s:

> As the unconscious traverses consciousness, a theoretical body of thought always is traversed by its own unconscious, its own "unthought," of which it is not aware, but which it contains in itself as the key condition, of its disruption, as the possibility of its self-subversion.
>
> *(1977, p. 10)*

Some key points follow from this last statement. One is that these suggestions of the proximity between psychoanalysis and literary theory reflect the shift in the center of gravity in the academic reception of psychoanalysis following the hermeneutic turn of the 1970s (including the impact of deconstruction and the post-structuralist analysis of discourse). Certainly, psychoanalytic perspectives on the unconscious may still be applied in a more instrumental fashion in both social and cultural theory. But theorists are now as likely to problematize the framework of psychoanalysis itself – turning the unconscious against it, in order to complicate its own epistemology (Felman's "self-subversion"). The second point is that the foregrounding of indeterminacy, non-closure and the anti-epistemological currents in interpretive work expressed by many of the authors in this section reflect trends that have impacted on psychoanalytic work itself (and have done so, perhaps, via dialogue with academic trends). For many contemporary practitioners, the analyst's chamber is no longer a laboratory for diagnostics, knowledge creation or the final articulation of unconscious meaning. It too is a place of indeterminacy, reinvention and collaborative interpretive work. The consulting room "marks the end of theory as a coherent body of ideas, and the beginning of a creativity that does not depend on theory" (Craib, 2001, p. vii); "psychoanalysis is first and foremost a theory about the creation of personal meaning in the clinical encounter" (Chodorow, 1999, p. 1). The final point is that the unconscious is here represented as situated *between* disciplines: "psychoanalysis points to the unconscious of literature, *literature, in its turn, is the unconscious of psychoanalysis*" (Felman, 1977, p. 10). It is formulations such as this that have most opened up the fabric of the Freudian unconscious to new disciplinary interpretations, in which both sides of the equation undergo transformation.

Another key example of this kind of exchange in the humanities appears in recent continental philosophy. Michel Foucault (in *The Order of Things*) and Jacques Derrida in various works, including *Resistances of Psychoanalysis*, began this task in the 1970s, exploring the relationship between the psychoanalytic unconscious and the restructuring of the human sciences in modernity (Foucault) and between deconstruction and the limits of psychoanalytic thinking (Derrida). Psychoanalysis and philosophy is dealt with at greater length in Chapter 16; what I want to emphasize here is only how often these encounters hinge specifically on the unconscious. Michel Henry's *The Genealogy of Psychoanalysis* and Jacques Rancière's *The Aesthetic Unconscious* provide two versions of this. For the former, "Freudianism holds deep within it what our era most lacks" (Henry, 1993, p. 7), because with the unconscious, which made its appearance felt in Descartes, "simultaneously with and as the exact consequence of the concept of consciousness" (p. 2) points the way beyond the regimes of representation that have dominated Western thought, and toward the affirmation of life defined as immanence and affectivity. Freud is thus placed in a tradition, running through Schopenhauer, which turns its attention to life as "the very soil in which thought grows" (p. 4), and which speaks to thought "as the unconscious" (p. 9). In a similar fashion, Rancière argues, that there is "thought that does not think" (2009, p. 31), and that this unconscious mode of thought had already been identified outside of the clinical domain, its privileged ground being works of art and literature (p. 4). These were already concerned with the "relation between thought and non-thought," or the immanence of logos in pathos, prior to Freud. As with Felman's account of literature and psychoanalysis, what matters is "to point out the relations of complicity and conflict established between the aesthetic unconscious and the Freudian unconscious" (pp. 43–44).

This situating of Freud in a deeper historical context brings us finally to changes in the historiography of the unconscious. Several recent works have taken pains to situate Freud's work either in its social context (Zaretsky, 2004), or as an act of synthesis out of many contemporary intellectual trends (Makari, 2008), or as wrongly mythologized around Freud's individual "genius" at the expense of other contemporary psychologists (Borch-Jacobsen & Shamdasani, 2012). If it is true that Freud himself has been de-centered in recent accounts of the development of the unconscious, it is also true that such renegotiations continue to engage the concept on Freudian turf. For Benjamin, "it is impossible not to be determined by those . . . primary coordinates" (1995, p. 4). Perhaps it is precisely the historical longevity of the concept that has made the unconscious into such a productive opening on the historical, cultural and critical dimensions of modern academic thought. The Freudian unconscious is the work of a century, coincident with the academic constitution of psychology, sociology and literary studies themselves.

What the unconscious signifies today is perhaps more of an open question than it ever was. An extraordinary amount of new research, new acts of conceptualization, are being undertaken at the borderlines between the psychoanalytic and the academic world, and this underlines the continuing currency of the unconscious. For the better part of a century, the non-psychoanalytic world has used Freud to keep reopening the sutures at the margins of consciousness, the margins of the rational, and has made the unconscious part of its own more recent turn to challenge the epistemological frameworks, and disciplinary boundaries, of academic work.

## References

Bainbridge, C, Radstone, S, Rustin, M & Yates, C 2007, *Culture and the unconscious*, Palgrave Macmillan, Houndmills Basingstoke.

Benjamin, J 1995, *Like subjects love objects: essays on recognition and sexual difference*, Yale University Press, New Haven.

Borch-Jacobsen, M & Shamdasani, S 2012, *The Freud files: An inquiry into the history of psychoanalysis*, Cambridge University Press, Cambridge.

Breuer, J & Freud, S 1893, 'On the psychical mechanism of hysterical phenomena: Preliminary communi-cation from studies on hysteria', in J Strachey (ed), *Standard edition of the complete psychological works of Sigmund Freud*, vol. 2, Hogarth, London, pp. 1–17.

Chodorow, N J 1989, *Feminism and psychoanalytic theory*, Yale University Press, New Haven.

Chodorow, N J 1999, *The power of feelings: Personal meaning in psychoanalysis, gender and culture*, Yale University Press, New Haven.

Clarke, S 2003, *Social theory, psychoanalysis and racism*, Palgrave Macmillan, Houndmills Basingstoke.

Clarke, S & Hoggett, P (ed), 2009, *Researching beneath the surface: Psycho-social research methods in practice*, Karnac, London.

Cohen, J 2005, *How to read Freud*, Granta, London.

Cousins, M 2005, 'Introduction', in S Freud, *The unconscious*, Penguin, London, pp. xvi–xx.

Craib, I 1984, *Modern social theory from Parsons to Habermas*, Harvester Wheatsheaf, Brighton.

Craib, I 1989, *Psychoanalysis and social theory: The limits of sociology*, Harvester Wheatsheaf, Hemel Hempstead.

Craib, I 2001, *Psychoanalysis: a critical introduction*, Blackwell, Oxford.

Elliott, A (ed) 1999a, *The Blackwell reader in contemporary social theory*, Blackwell, Oxford.

Elliott, A 1999b, *Social theory and psychoanalysis in transition*, Free Association Books, London.

Ellmann, M 1994, *Psychoanalytic literary criticism*, Longman, Harlow.

Felman, S (ed) 1977, *Literature and psychoanalysis: the question of reading: otherwise*, Johns Hopkins University Press, Baltimore.

Freud, S 1900, 'The interpretation of dreams (first part)', in J Strachey (ed), *Standard edition of the complete psychological works of Sigmund Freud*, vol. 4, Hogarth, London, pp. ix–627.

Freud, S 1912, 'The dynamics of transference', in J Strachey (ed), *Standard edition of the complete psychological works of Sigmund Freud*, vol. 12, Hogarth, London, pp. 97–108.

Freud, S 1915, 'The unconscious', in J Strachey (ed), *Standard edition of the complete psychological works of Sigmund Freud*, vol. 14, Hogarth, London, pp. 159–215.

Freud, S 1916, 'Introductory lectures on psycho-analysis' (Parts I and II), in J Strachey (ed), *Standard edition of the complete psychological works of Sigmund Freud*, vol. 16, Hogarth, London, pp. 9–239.

Freud, S 1917, 'Introductory lectures on psycho-analysis' (Part III), in J Strachey (ed), *Standard edition of the complete psychological works of Sigmund Freud*, vol. 17, Hogarth, London.

Freud, S 1923a, 'Two encyclopedia articles', in J Strachey (ed), *Standard edition of the complete psychological works of Sigmund Freud*, vol. 18, Hogarth, London, pp. 235–259.

Freud, S 1923b, 'The ego and the id', in J Strachey (ed), *Standard edition of the complete psychological works of Sigmund Freud*, vol. 19, Hogarth, London, pp. 12–59.

Freud, S 1933, 'New introductory lectures on psycho-analysis', in J Strachey (ed), *Standard edition of the complete psychological works of Sigmund Freud*, vol. 22, Hogarth, London, pp. 1–184.

Frosh, S 2002, *Key concepts in psychoanalysis*, British Library, London.

Frosh, S 2010, *Psychoanalysis outside the clinic*, Palgrave Macmillan, Basingstoke.

Frosh, S 2012, *Brief introduction to psychoanalytic theory*, Palgrave Macmillan, Basingstoke.

Henry, M 1993, *The genealogy of psychoanalysis*, Stanford University Press, Stanford, CA.

Hollway, W & Jefferson, T 2000, *Doing qualitative research differently: Free association, narrative and the interview method*, Sage, London.

Laplanche, J & Pontalis, J-B 1988, *The language of psychoanalysis*, Karnac, London.

Makari, G 2008, *Revolution in mind: The creation of psychoanalysis*, Duckworth, London.

Parsons, T 1950, 'Psychoanalysis and the social structure', *Psychoanalytic Quarterly*, vol. 19, pp. 371–384.

Prager, J & Rustin, M (eds) 1993, *Psychoanalytic sociology, vol. 1: Social theory*, Edward Elgar, Aldershot.

Rancière, J 2009, *The aesthetic unconscious*, Polity, Cambridge.

Rose, J 2014, 'What more could we want of ourselves!', *London Review of Books*, vol. 33, no. 12, pp. 5–12.

Ruitenbeek, HM (ed) 1962, *Psychoanalysis and social science*, Dutton, New York.

Strachey, J 1893–1895, 'Editor's introduction', in J Strachey (ed), *Standard edition of the complete psychological works of Sigmund Freud*, vol. 2, Hogarth, London, p. xvii.

Wright, E 1998, *Psychoanalytic criticism: A reappraisal* (2nd ed), Polity Press, Cambridge.

Zaretsky, E 2004, *Secrets of the soul: A social and cultural history of psychoanalysis*, Alfred A. Knopf, New York.

# 2

# Kleinian psychoanalysis

*Edna O'Shaughnessy*

Melanie Klein's hypothesis that psychic life occurs in two elemental constellations, a paranoid-schizoid position and a depressive position, introduced into psychoanalysis a new and far-seeing vision. These two constellations offered a new way of understanding an infant's earliest object relations, which Klein saw as the foundation for subsequent further psychic development in the course of life. Moreover, Klein also proposed the hypothesis that in these early paranoid-schizoid and depressive positions will be found the fixation points for neurosis and for psychosis.

The many constituents of both positions are the same, but in different manifestations and connections: love and hate, relations to external objects, relations to internal objects, phantasies (unconscious and conscious), perceptions, introjections and projections, emotions, gratifications, frustrations – all experienced or not with characteristic anxieties and characteristic defenses.

The nature of each position, and the nature of the connections between the two positions, came piecemeal to Melanie Klein in the course of 15 years of work that began in the twenties with the psychoanalysis of small children; older and adult patients were included in her practice a little later. It was this psychoanalytic work that enabled Klein to make a number of psychological observations that kindled new conceptions (Frank, 2009).

Several things are of interest in Klein's conception of the two psychic positions. First, it presupposes a particular view of the link between instincts and objects – a moving away from an instinct theory in which the object had mostly only a secondary role as the means of gratifying the instinct (i.e., instincts seen as essential pleasure seeking) to a general object relations theory in which the relation to the object is as fundamental to the structure and state of the ego as the nature of the instinct itself. It is interesting that both theories – instincts are primarily pleasure seeking through gratification, and instincts are of their nature object seeking – are to be found in Freud's writings. For an excellent discussion of Freud's views see Laplanche and Pontalis (1973, p. 273) in their entry on the "Object." During the 1920s a shift to the overall view of instincts as object seeking was being made not only by Klein but also by others also like Fairbairn, Winnicott and Balint.

Klein's conception of two positions also involves a new and extended view of the nature and role of phantasy in mental life. Klein saw phantasy as an ego activity present from birth – a primal activity of the mind that accompanies and expresses in bodily feelings or (at first) primitive images, and later uses also words, all our mental experience, so contributing to both the structure and state of the inner world as well as the way the outer world is perceived. This accorded to phantasy a different and much enlarged role in mental life that at first was highly controversial. Freud, while positing the existence of some primal phantasies, had conceived of the significance of phantasy life as being mainly the fulfilment of a wish.[1]

Also much expanded in Klein's new thinking was Freud's notion of an inner world. In Klein's view the inner world, by means of projections and introjections, is in continual interaction with external reality, so affecting both the experience of external reality and also installing within the mind a whole world of internalized figures.

But overall, what was most original in Klein's theories was the grouping together of the inner world, external object relations, instincts, phantasies, feelings, anxieties and defenses as elements of a position. "Position" was a new concept that Klein was concerned to distinguish from the older psychoanalytic notions of "phase" or "stage." She writes:

> The term "position" was chosen because though the phenomena involved occur in the first place during early stages of development – they are not confined to these stages but represent specific groupings of anxieties and defences which appear and reappear during the first years of childhood.
>
> *(Klein, 1948, p. 45)*

She is writing here in her preface to the 3rd edition of *The Psychoanalysis of Children*; later she made it clear that in her view these anxieties and defenses appear and reappear throughout life. Moreover, and importantly, the need for psychic working through again and again also recurs throughout life – under pressure and anxiety the depressive position will give way to a more paranoid-schizoid constellation of hostile objects and will need once more to be regained. These two positions take the place of Freud's psychosexual stages, and in this way, the paranoid–schizoid and depressive positions become, in Kleinian theory, the primary modules of development, while psychosexual stages – oral, anal and genital – find a new place as aspects of the two different positions.

We must remember that Freud was alive during this time – and still writing. From his marvelously innovative late phase two new ideas in particular influenced Klein: one was Freud's revised view of anxiety; the other was his final theory of the instincts as a duality of life and death instincts.

For many years Freud maintained the view that anxiety arose from an accumulation of sexual excitation in the absence of "psychical working over," which transformed libido into anxiety. Then in 1926, in *Inhibitions, Symptoms and Anxiety*, Freud revised this view. He unyoked anxiety from sexual excitation and instead saw anxiety as a danger signal to the ego, as "signal anxiety" relating to "anxiety situations" met within the course of life.

A few years later, in *Civilization and its Discontents* (1930), Freud recorded an even more momentous change in his thinking – his final theory of the instincts as a duality of Life and Death Instincts. He wrote,

> I drew the conclusion that besides the instinct to preserve living substance and to join it into ever larger units, there must exist another contrary instinct seeking to dissolve those units and to bring them back to their primeval, inorganic state. That is to say, as well as Eros there was an instinct of death. The phenomena of life could be explained from the concurrent or mutually opposing action of these two instincts.
>
> *(1930, p. 118)*

Freud's new view of anxiety as a signal of danger to the ego, and Freud's revised duality of the instincts as eros and thanatos both enter in to Melanie Klein's account of the paranoid-schizoid and depressive positions.

## The paranoid-schizoid position

This first position is the foundation of all later development. Here in Klein's own words is a description from her paper (1952) "The Emotional Life of the Infant."

> At the beginning of post-natal life the infant experiences anxiety from internal and external sources . . . the working of the death instinct within gives rise to the fear of annihilation. . . . The first external source of anxiety can be found in the experience of birth. . . . It would appear that the pain and discomfort he has suffered, as well as the loss of the intra-uterine state, are felt by him as an attack by hostile forces, i.e. as persecution. Persecutory anxiety, therefore, enters from the beginning into his relation to objects in so far as he is exposed to privations.
>
> *(1952, p. 62)*

She goes on to say:

> That the infant's first experiences of feeding and of his mother's presence initiate an object relation to her . . . the breast, in as much as it is gratifying, is loved and felt to be "good"; in so far as it is a source of frustration, it is hated and felt to be "bad" . . . The various factors which enter into the infant's feelings of being gratified such as the alleviation of hunger, the pleasure of sucking, the freedom from discomfort and tension, *i.e.* from privations, and the experience of being loved – all these are attributed to the bad (persecuting) breast . . . It is characteristic of the emotions of the very young infant that they are of an extreme and powerful nature. The frustrating (bad) object is felt to be a terrifying persecutor, the good breast tends to turn into the "ideal" breast which should fulfill the greedy desire for unlimited, immediate and everlasting gratification.
>
> *(1952, pp. 62–64)*

Klein gives a vivid picture of complex first months after birth – of life and death instincts active in the infant, of projections and introjections, of persecutory anxieties, but also deep gratifications experienced in relation to split and polarized objects, which in this first period are part-objects – the foremost part-object being the feeding breast:

> the infant's first experience of feeding and of his mother's presence initiate an object relation to her . . . This relation is at first a relation to a part-object, for both oral-libidinal and oral-destructive impulses from the beginning of life are directed towards the mother's breast.
>
> *(1952, p. 64)*

There is also the face of the mother, her eyes, her arms and lap, and just as the baby has a mouth, there is mother's mouth, too. These part-objects are experienced in a polarized way – ideal at one extreme, as persecutors at the other extreme – that induce fear and distress, and may arouse anxieties of annihilation. "The breast, in as much as it is gratifying is loved and felt to be 'good'; in so far as it is the source of frustration, it is hated and felt to be 'bad'" (Klein, 1933, p. 32). All these events, whether arising from within (e.g., feelings of hunger) or coming to the baby from outside (e.g., being picked up, kept waiting, being fed), are experienced by the newborn in phantasies.[2]

In all of this Klein emphasizes two things. One is the importance of the introjection of the good object and its establishment in the inner world as the core of the ego. This gives an internal orientation around which the ego can cohere and is the foundation of development. The other is the need for the ego when anxieties become unmanageable to protect itself and employ defenses.

In an important paper, "Notes on Some Schizoid Mechanisms" (1946), Klein gave an account of various schizoid defense mechanisms. She also introduced a new one, which in a later version of the paper (1952) she called "projective identification." In her view, projective is the main defense against anxiety in the paranoid-schizoid position. In unconscious phantasy, unwanted parts of the self and frightening internal figures are split off and projected into objects, in this way constructing the characteristic narcissistic relations of this period where objects are equated with split-off parts of the self.

Klein's notion of projective identification has aroused wide interest. Heimann (1950) was among the first to link it with psychoanalysis and see the analyst's countertransference as coming from the patient's projective identifications – a view now widely accepted and much written about as illuminating the clinical situation. Bion (1959) in a seminal paper extended the concept further. He recognized projective identification, while it can be used in defensive ways, was also a primal and universal mode of communication between human beings.

## Clinical illustration: Molly

Here is a clinical illustration from the analysis of a 12-year-old girl. Molly is responding to the coming reality of the absence of her analyst. Before an impending summer break she made a calendar for the month of August, illustrating it with a drawing of a large tea-garden that she said was hers. Most of the picture is filled by a table in the foreground on which were two tall glasses with huge, highly colored round ice-creams. Molly was denying the coming separation, felt as a separation from her mother, by making herself the owner of the tea-garden – that is, by in phantasy projecting herself into her mother and taking over her possessions, notably the ice-creams, her breasts.

In her first session after the August break, she told me that she had had a dream a few days before returning. In the dream she was standing on the edge of a beach. She had been advised to go out into the sea for a bathe. As she looked at the sea, it seemed cold, and already dark, and was uninviting. So she decided not to try it. Then came a change of scene in the dream. She was in a hip bath, together with another girl, a school friend. Her tummy was very big, she was pregnant. There was a big knob sticking out at one place in her tummy, which she thought must be the baby's head.

I think as the August break was coming to its end and Molly was near to returning to her analysis she could allow reality to intrude into her omnipotent phantasy of being the owner of the tea-garden. The dream shows how Molly is beginning to have some insight into the omnipotence of her phantasies and to understand their purpose: how they save her from the uninviting sea of what she feels to be a cold and dark reality. In the second part of the dream, however, she is a pregnant mother, making a couple with a school friend in a hip bath. While this in some ways is an early fast-forward phantasy of the future – Molly, after all, is a 12-year-old nearing puberty, she is again in a state of projective identification, this time with fertile parents. She has once more in phantasy taken over and become the "owner" – of the parental couple and pregnant mother. However, she understands that her analysis is, as it were, "advising" her to bathe in the reality of who she is and where she is. And indeed, this holiday dream proved to be something of a turning point, a nodal moment in which her anxieties about being small, and young, and by herself feeling excluded in the dark and the cold could be recognized along with her ways of trying to deny reality, internal and external.

## Discussion

Molly's psychic life is, as yet, taking place at the boundary of the paranoid-schizoid and depressive positions. Her drawing and her words communicate her phantasies of the presence of her object, which are still part-objects, a table with two oversize ice-creams on it, while the absence of her analyst is seen in her dream as a frightening and uninviting (she has not been included) sea. In contrast to the uninviting sea, which is dark and cold, the tea-garden is idyllic, bright and warm and at first protects herself from the persecution of the object that abandons her to coldness and darkness by means of a phantasy of projective identification into the object, so that she is the possessor of the tea-garden with its ice-creams.

However, she doesn't maintain this phantasy through the entire break. Near the time of her return to analysis Molly is able to regain and know the reality of what threatens her: the object's absence, being left, being excluded.

### Clinical illustration: John

Here is a contrasting illustration from the analysis of another 12-year-old. John had broken down at his boarding school and left, suffering terrifying experiences. In this emergency he began coming to see me four times a week. So that there would be a little time left to us to try to work about a sudden, too-soon break in treatment, in his 11th session I had to tell him that we would be stopping for a fortnight at Easter.

John had been standing by the window, looking out. When I made this announcement, he swung round to stare at me for a long time, his face wide and disbelieving. The next day he brought with him an exercise book. Nearly filling the first page was a large drawing. He sat down and continued it. It was a drawing of concentric circles. At the center was a small inner circle. Around this small central circle were four surrounding circles that I thought represented his feeling of having his four sessions around him. However, at the top John had drawn a shaft that seemed to have pushed through the circles down into the center, so damaging the smooth alignment of the circles and making a gap in the first ring and shoving each successive ring into the one below it.

I asked John about his drawing. In his customary expressionless speech he told me, "It's of England and France who were once joined. Then a volcano came, and they got separated. The middle bit got sunk, and now they're like this," and he showed me with his pencil how each of the four rings was mismatched at the sunken bit. I spoke to him about how he was making a picture of how we were. He felt he and I, like England and France, were once joined; he had his four sessions around him. But when I told him we would be stopping for 2 weeks at Easter, my words were like a volcano. They went into him and sunk him like a shaft down into his middle.

John was continuing his drawing. I spoke to him saying something along the following lines. I reminded him how he had stared at me, shocked. He could not believe I was this bad going-away-breast, and he tried to volcano it away, out of sight, out of him, but somehow it had got into him. I said he now feels we are not like before: we don't fit round each other anymore.

He was shading the small central circle. He said "There's a fire burning in the middle because it mustn't get out the other side." Yet, in fact, things were getting out: he was farting and making smells, and he turned his drawing over and closely inspected the reverse side of the page to check if anything was coming through. The drawing for John rather than being a representation in

Segal's sense was a symbolic equivalent to his inner state. He felt he should hold in the mess and fear inside him, yet he could not – which added to his distress.

As the session went on he made more drawings. Among these was a circle he said was the moon. He drew four rockets round it, saying, "The rockets are dropping darts of air into the moon, then there will be enough air to live." I understood this circle as a picture of the distant, dead-moon-breast that I had become for him, and that he felt he needed to breathe life into me so then there would be enough air for him to live too. I interpreted to him that his words and his drawings, both of which tell things to me, are the darts of air that bring life again into the analysis. Looking very worried, John again turned his page of drawings over and inspected it to see if the drawings were coming through on the other side, making smells as he touched the marks that showed. I spoke to him about how worried he was that his smells continue to come out and attack me for my Easter going away and spoil his revival of the atmosphere between us that he is trying to do with his talk and drawings.

He began another small drawing. First he drew the earth, then a big moon. He put in the four rockets – not around the moon as before, but near to the earth – saying in a despondent voice, "They're going back now." He drew some irregular shapes, saying, "They're what you see in the evening, if you look up at the moon." I asked him what these things on the moon were. After a long hesitation he answered, "I know what they are now. They're called craters." He was uneasy – the whole atmosphere in the room was different: it had changed from the strange and distant cooperativeness that we had before to discomfort and fear. In a rather long interpretation I spoke about his despair that a cratered breast – as he felt I was now – could not help him or keep him feeling alive.

## Discussion

My language and my technique, I think, both require some preliminary comment. John was among my first patients in the '50s when I was inexperienced in how to talk to patients and in how to write up sessions to record and to convey what happened between analyst and patient. The previous account is a shortened version of an account written long ago in 1964. At that time, many Kleinian analysts interpreted in part-object body language, readily using words like *breast*, *penis* and so forth. This was done on the assumption of the nearness to awareness, most especially in children, of a basic unconscious symbolism, an assumption later found to be mistaken and simplistic, and so the practice stopped. However, I think that there was a to and fro of communication and understanding going on between my patient and myself, even though I was somewhat clumsy and in some ways mistaken.

## *Contrasts*

Molly and John are in profound ways different. As I remarked earlier, Molly is on the boundary of the paranoid-schizoid position, edging forward toward a depressive position. John, as I shall discuss, is in an abnormal form of the paranoid-schizoid position, distressed and ill. The contrasts between them are painful. While both experience anxieties that are persecutory, Molly's situation is one of privation: she feels the threat of losing the presence of the tea-garden with its big ice-creams, and of being instead in an uninviting, cold, dark sea. For John, however, it is a matter of survival, of life and death: either he or his object will be annihilated. Molly's ideal object has to do with food and an everyday place like a tea-garden. There is no sign of feeding in John's world. In his phantasy his ideal object stays wrapped around him wherever he is, at distances smaller and larger. My announcement of the break comes at him like a destructive volcano and smashes his feeling of staying joined with me; he feels sunk and burning in his middle, invaded by a mismatch that he cannot contain, and the mess and debris seep out from the hole of his anus and lodge in his object – the craters he sees in the moon. Molly uses phantasies of projective identification as a defense against the experience of privation and the emotional pains that might be stirred by absence – *she* is the owner of the tea-garden! Yet she is able, as the time nears for returning to her analyst, she is able to dream of, and in this way come in contact with, both her awareness of the uninviting dark cold sea of absence, and also to recognize that her "tea-garden" analyst advises she experience it. I think Molly, from gratifying experiences of feeding and other good early experiences, has installed ideal objects, at this stage pictured as two overlarge ice-creams on a table in a tea-garden, in her inner world. John has no such installation or core to his ego.

With distress and guilt his parents told me his early history. It was not one of gratification. John was a baby who was almost continually crying. Also there was one period when his hunger was not recognized for a while when failing breast-feeding was too long prolonged. A mismatch, we might say. John's world is bleak, a flat place, like his voice that is empty of emotion and far away – there are planetary distances between him and a moon-dead object that he sees has craters in it. About the origin of the craters John was deeply uneasy – did he make the craters? Or was the distant moon of an object like that in itself? This is his uncertainty about where the mismatch between him and his objects starts – is it him? Or is it them?

In the session reported we see him bring and express his need to be wrapped round by the object, ultimately to feel he is inside it, warm, safe and held together. When this feeling is interfered with he is catastrophically persecuted, penetrated by bad, sinking, burning sensations that go all the way through his body and come out the other end as feces and smells. In the session in which I tell him about the Easter interruption he tries to volcano this bad news, this terribly changed object that is not fitting round him, out of himself. He institutes violent psychotic mechanisms – volcanoing the bad object out along with unwanted parts of his mind – especially awareness and feelings. Yet some awareness of his predicament remains in his mind, and he is able to bring this to communicate to me in his next session. During this first period of his analysis he often experienced the room as being full of small hovering fragments; sometimes he felt he was being watched by an expelled eye sitting on the window latch. John's world of an abnormal paranoid-schizoid position of safety inside his object on the one hand and invasive persecutory terrors and on the other is utterly different from Molly's idealized tea-garden and uninviting, cold, dark sea.

## The depressive position

Here is an account, again in Klein's own words, from *Some Theoretical Conclusions Regarding the Emotional Life of the Infant* (1952).

> During the second quarter of the first year certain changes in the infant's intellectual and emotional development become marked . . . The various aspects – loved and hated, good and bad – of the objects come closer together, and these objects are now whole persons . . . All these processes of integration and synthesis cause the conflict between love and hatred to come out in full force. The ensuing depressive anxiety and feeling of guilt alter not only in quantity but also in quality. Ambivalence is now experienced predominantly towards a complete object. Love and hatred have come much closer together and the "good" and "bad" breast, "good" and "bad" mother, cannot be kept as widely separated as in the earlier stage. Although the power of the destructive impulses diminishes, these impulses are felt to be a great danger to the loved object, now perceived as a person.

These steps in integration and synthesis result in a greater capacity of the ego to acknowledge the increasingly poignant psychic reality. The anxiety relating to the internalized mother who is felt to be injured, suffering, in danger of being annihilated or already annihilated and lost forever leads to a stronger identification with the injured object. The identification reinforces both the drive to make reparation and the ego's attempts to inhibit aggressive impulses. The ego again and again makes use of the manic defense (Klein, 1952, p. 71 et seq.).

In Klein's view it is also at this time of the infantile depressive position that the Oedipus complex begins – Klein places it early. The baby, as his perceptions mature and widen, sees that his mother has relations not only with himself, but also with others, especially the father. He senses that the link between mother and father is of a different kind from the link between himself and his mother – Klein presupposes the existence of innate ideas of the genitals of both sexes and of a pleasurable and fertile sexual intercourse. The infant's notions will be imbued with his own desires, phantasies and projections, including primitive forerunners from his first 3 months of life of part-object combinations (e.g., mother's body and psychic receptivity; breast and milk-giving nipple; mother with thinking) – all of which he may equate to "mother with internal penis" at a wordless level of phantasies with images and feelings.

Of particular importance are Oedipal phantasies of parents continually combined in a gratifying intercourse. This combined parental figure arouses painful feelings of jealous exclusion and envious deprivation that impel the infant to attack. In his mind he feels he has injured them with resulting guilt and depressive concern, while the fear that the parents are combined in hostility to him may push him back to a more paranoid position.

In all of this the infant will need the help of his external objects in his struggle with his conflicts of love and hatred, his anxieties and his guilt. Crucial too, will be his own wish to make reparation, which arises from the ego's love for and empathy with its damaged objects. Reparation was another new Kleinian concept with a key place in the resolution of the depressive position – a way of overcoming guilt and despair – and a concept with a general significance for psychoanalysis. In *Civilization and its Discontents* (1930), Freud described humankind's psychic journey from its infantile state to "civilization." He showed how it ends with discontents, unhappiness and suffering under a punishing superego. Klein saw that the psychic journey need not end there: it could continue. If some working through of the depressive position with reparation is achieved, the superego will become less cruel, more of a humanistic conscience, and guilt and depression will significantly lesson. If this development goes well, reparative phantasies will also become part of evolving sexuality.

Intercourse that gives sexual pleasure with a fertile potential to create a child in identification with a parental couple will become an aspiration, a part of the ego ideal, realizable to different degrees in various outcomes of the Oedipal situation – the complexities of which lie outside the reach of this chapter.

## Development from the paranoid-schizoid position to the depressive position

As we have seen, this transition brings big changes. Splitting of the object and the self gives way to an increasing integration of both the object and the self. Object relations are no longer to part-objects, but more to whole persons who are both good and bad, from a self that is also less schizoid and so is then confronted with conflicting feelings of love and hate for the object, which ushers in new feelings of guilt and anxiety about damage done to the object on which the self depends. This is depressive anxiety, which arises from the identification with, and a new feeling of empathy for, the object. Is the object alive and well? Is it injured and in danger from his hatred? Feelings of remorse and love for the object impel him to make what Klein came to call *reparation* to the object, and as time went on reparation took a key place in her conception of the working through of the anxiety and guilt of the depressive position. However, if the guilt and depression of this situation are unmanageable, the ego resorts instead to manic defenses to protect itself from the emotional pain of the state of the object and the self, and also from the harshness of its own superego.

## The two patients

I return now to Molly and John to consider the depressive position in relation to them both. What are the particular problems of each?

Both children in the sessions reported are in the paranoid–schizoid position, yet it is evident that their worlds, external and internal, are vastly different. Both children relate to part-objects. Molly draws two big ice-creams (rather more linkable to Mother's two feeding breasts) on a table in a tea-garden so bringing in ideas of feeding, eating, drinking, and growing – the garden. It is a human, sustaining place. In contrast, John's circles and rockets depict a flat, bleak world of spaces, arrangements in spaces, and distances, vast distances. The one thing having to do with life is air – this makes it possible to survive. All that gets into, or comes out, of John is dangerous and bad: volcanoes, sinking shafts, burning, smells, wind, craters.

Molly's world is split between two: a warm ideal tea-garden with ice-creams and a cold, dark, uninviting sea. John has had to resort to the minute fragmentation and dispersal of hostile, dangerous objects. While Molly has persecutory anxieties about the impending absence of her tea-garden, her fears are of coldness, being in the dark and excluded – the uninviting sea. Against these threats she uses phantasies of projective identification into the tea-garden to make herself the owner of it. For John, however, the impending absence of his object is a catastrophe, a matter of life and death, a question of the survival of his object and himself. This thrusts guilt and a confused sense of responsibility prematurely on him. When he says, "The rockets are dropping darts of air into the moon, then there will be enough air to live," it is not, I think, clear to John, who has to save whom. Do I save him with the four sessions or does he come to them to restore life to me?

There is also the question of psychic movement. Molly leaves for the break with defensive phantasies of possession: the tea-garden is hers; she has no loss of it. Near the time of her return, however, she is able to relinquish her defense of projective identification and be in touch with the absence of the object and also discover from her dream that she experiences absence as an uninviting, cold, dark sea. This is a small bit of important psychic work. John, however, in unmanageable distress has cut himself off emotionally from his psychic situation, which is then experienced as only a somatic one. And he was not able, as he felt he should, to keep the burning mess inside himself; it came out through his anus into his surroundings as wind and smells. In this way his predicament is lost to him.

Bearing in mind what has already been noted, how might we think about Molly and John making the transition from the paranoid–schizoid to the depressive position?

This crucial developmental movement is founded on an integration of formerly split parts of the object and the self. This brings contact with both the love and the hate in the self, and brings also new causes for love and hatred of the object, as well as the experience of a new type of anxiety: depressive anxiety. New feelings of pain and guilt arise from the identification with and empathy for the object, along with a wish to make reparation to the object.

Molly's ice-creams of the tea-garden represent a good feeding part-object that she has internalized and can keep. Molly remembers what she is returning to: it stays as the core of her ego.

John's good object that wraps around him and keeps him safe is not installed as the core of his ego, nor is it retained. Under privation and the anxiety of annihilation, John's experience of it changes; his object becomes a monstrous mismatch that is a terrifying persecutor. All he is left with internally are persecutors from which he must protect himself by fragmenting and expelling them. John also feels a violent hatred that makes shit of his objects. I think his own hatred, which he can't control and keep in, also alarms him enormously. In the end his objects, along with unwanted parts of his self, especially awareness and feelings, are smashed and evacuated either in eye volcanoes or as wind and feces, which leaves him empty and bleak. The retrieval and integration of these fragments and dispersed particles of objects and self would be extraordinarily difficult for John, perhaps achievable only to a minimum extent in some aberrant way.

Molly is more fortunate. She has only the two splits to deal with, and we see already just the beginnings of an integration when she returns to the analysis. We see Molly do some psychic work. She has a significant dream in which she becomes aware that her tea-garden analyst is also an "adviser" telling her to bathe in the cold dark sea and get to know the reality of being "uninvited."

Her problems with herself and her objects are also quite different. There seems a certain over-heatedness in her relations to the ice-creams of the tea-garden, which look overlarge and luscious, and she herself is very possessive. She tends to evade the reality of exclusion and separation from her object by an omnipotent phantasy of projecting herself into the object to make herself the *owner* of the tea-garden, and we also see a defensive Oedipal phantasy in her dream picture, she *is* the couple with the girl in the hip bath and already *has* the pregnancy of a fertile intercourse, in these ways escaping from the conflicts, pains and uncertainties of her Oedipal situation – but it is there, unlike with John where no humans are in sight.

Psychic work comes from the life instinct and John I think is doubly unfortunate. His personality is heavily weighted with death instincts, and furthermore, in external reality his objects have found it difficult to do their psychic work with him, to be in touch with John's physical and emotional state and receive, without being overwhelmed or becoming hostile to him, his transmissions of need, hunger, desperation, hate and love. As he looks at his drawing of the moon breast, as I called it, he was troubled and uneasy about the dark marks he had drawn on it that he called craters. He believes he has marked his objects, and I think he is right. His parents were in reality depressed, anxious and guilty, damaged – though in reality not only by him – they had other serious troubles as well as the troubles of their own personalities. But in John's mind the craters accuse him, and he is made to feel guilty prematurely, long before his ego can manage it.

Molly, we can imagine, will manage the transition to a depressive position. She will be able to find in herself empathy for her objects, based on an identification with them that will become the spur for making reparation to them. I do not think that guilt – for her possessiveness, bossiness, the reversal of roles, which here are her defenses against loss, for her emerging jealousy and envy – will be too persecuting. There would seem to be problems in the area of her sexuality – her relations to her object, and perhaps her objects to her, are a little over-close, too hectic, highly colored, somewhat sexualized, perhaps – and we see her own sexual phantasies with her girl-friend in the hip bath. But these are some of the rather usual troubles of growing up. Molly will need to become more able to bear painful feelings of distance, difference and exclusion and their difficult consequences. Such things are never easy or worked through completely and, as Melanie Klein emphasizes, nor are they ever obtained finally, but won and lost and need to be regained again.

John, however, will need to take a different path. He will not move into the depressive position, but with analytic help will function in an ameliorated though still aberrant paranoid–schizoid position. Along with many schizoid mechanisms and paranoid anxieties that will remain, he will tend to suffer a persecuting guilt about his damaged primary objects and feel he must revitalize them, even that he should be absent and spare them the impact of his presence.

## The role of analysis

Though there are generalizations to be made, one psychoanalysis differs from another, both because analysts are different, but more importantly because by its very nature an analysis offers a place in which the individuality of each patient can emerge. Molly can be helped in an analysis to change and develop further into the depressive position so that she will have more contact with herself and be identified with her objects in a warm and empathic rather than a hectic, possessive way; she will come to be able to know something of the pain of exclusion and difference, rather than use schizoid mechanisms to disown cold, dark experiences of being uninvited. As Klein emphasizes, the depressive position is never achieved finally or fully, but may be lost under pressure to a reversion to a more paranoid–schizoid mode of functioning. But even if not permanent, a working through in analysis lays the foundations when the need arises for working through again.

For John, though analysis will have a different role, it is of no less importance. If this is true – and in practice it turned out that way – that he cannot go along an ordinary trajectory, what is the role of analysis for him? John feels alone; he knows he is paranoid and violent and wrapped up in his objects. His cruel superego passes a judgment on him: alien to the human race. Above all, what mattered to John in treatment was to be *known*, and *known by the analyst without judgment*.

To be known by another may seem minimal, yet it is fundamental. And as time went on and John felt more sure that I survived and had a willing place for him he could allow me to see more. There were crises, of course. And also, as in every analysis, there was sometimes the unexpected, such as a sudden shrewd and truthful observation by John about himself – and indeed, about me and my ways, too.

## Conclusion

Melanie Klein's new constellations, the paranoid–schizoid and depressive positions, her new concepts of projective identification and reparation, her work on psychosis and in child analysis, have all bequeathed to psychoanalysis a legacy that has led to further psychoanalytic explorations. Some of these developments of her theories and practice are in papers by various authors collected in the two volumes of *Melanie Klein To-day* (Spillius, 1988). There is also a valuable bibliography of Kleinian publications from the period 1920–1989 in *The New Dictionary of Kleinian Thought* (Spillius 2011), and there are many other more recent and contemporary Kleinian publications.

In this chapter I have tried to give some account of Klein's contributions to psychoanalysis, and also to provide some idea of a Kleinian way of thinking about patients and psychoanalysis. The interested reader could do no better than turn to the four volumes of Melanie Klein's own writings (1975).

## Notes

1 A good discussion of the differences between Freud's conception and Klein's can be found in Elizabeth Spillius's "Freud and Klein on the Concept of Phantasy" (2001).
2 For an excellent discussion of all this, consult Catalina Bronstein (2001), *Melanie Klein: Beginnings in Kleinian Theory*.

## References

Bion, W 1959, 'Attacks on linking', in *Second thoughts*, Heinemann, London.

Bronstein, C 2001, *Melanie Klein: Beginnings in Kleinian theory* (C Bronstein, ed), Whurr, London.

Frank, C 2009, *Melanie Klein in Berlin: Her first psychoanalyses of children*, Routledge, London.

Freud, S 1926, *Inhibitions, symptoms and anxiety*, Hogarth, London.

Freud, S 1930, *Civilization and its discontents*, Hogarth, London.

Heimann, P 1950, 'On counter-transference', *International Journal of Psychoanalysis*, vol. 31, pp. 81–84.

Klein, M 1933, 'The early development of conscience in the child', in S Lorand (ed), *Psychoanalysis today*, Convici-Friede, New York.

Klein, M 1946, *Notes on some schizoid mechanisms in the writings of Melanie Klein*, vol. 3, Hogarth, London.

Klein, M 1948, *Contributions to psychoanalysis, 1921–1945*, Hogarth, Honolulu, HI.

Klein, M 1952, *Some theoretical conclusions regarding the emotional life of the infant in the writings of Melanie Klein*, vol. 3, Hogarth, London.

Klein, M 1975, *The writings of Melanie Klein*, vols. 1–4, Hogarth, London.

Laplanche, J & Pontalis, J-B 1973, *The language of psycho-analysis*, Hogarth, London.

Spillius, E 1988, *Melanie Klein to-day*, vols. 1–2, Routledge, London.

Spillius, E 2001, 'Freud and Klein on the concept of phantasy', *International Journal of Psychoanalysis*, vol. 82, pp. 361–373.

Spillius, E 2011, *The new dictionary of Kleinian thought*, Routledge, London.

# 3

# Infant Observation

*Margaret Rustin*

Observing the behavior of young children has always played a central role in psychoanalysis: Freud's observation of his grandson's play with the cotton reel is at the heart of one of his best-known papers (Freud, 1920), and the analysis of Little Hans (Freud, 1909) via his father's consultations with Freud was the starting point of child analysis as well as a vital source of Freud's understanding of infantile sexuality. The excitement felt by the early psychoanalysts as the meaning of the behavior of young children became a topic of research expressed the hopes of understanding the early roots of neurotic disorders in adults – of gathering data not of the retrospective variety gleaned in the psychoanalytic treatment of adult patients, but from the study of the contemporaneous events of childhood, of seeing the mind in the making. This work also revealed the much broader potential relevance of psychoanalytic theory for the upbringing and education of children, and in the view of the analysts of the time, the prevention of neurosis.

The idea that the future development of psychoanalysis lay in child analysis led to the encouragement by Freud, Ferenczi and Abraham of the two most significant figures in child analysis in the 20th century: Anna Freud and Melanie Klein. Each of these women based their theories on close observation of children, in both clinical and ordinary life settings. For Anna Freud the residential nursery and school setting provided much to observe (Midgley, 2013); for Melanie Klein (Klein, 1921, 1923), observing her own children was a formative experience. Their conclusions were very different, however. In this chapter, the story is presented of how Klein's work led to the invention of Infant Observation as a disciplined practice within psychoanalytic education and how the experience of observing infants in turn influenced the scope and direction of clinical work in psychoanalysis.

The outstanding group of analysts drawn to Klein's ideas when she settled in London included Susan Isaacs, whose experimental Malting House School, where innovative educational methods had integrated psychoanalytic ideas, provided her with a store of detailed observations of children's development (Isaacs, 1930). As the conflicting theories of Klein and the Viennese group led by Anna Freud gave rise to intense debate in the British Psychoanalytic Society, and ultimately to the formal process of the "Controversial Discussions" (King & Steiner, 1991), the Kleinian group decided to base its presentations at these meetings on clinical evidence, the observations of the consulting room, and to argue for the development of psychoanalytic theory in light of this experience. Isaacs seems to have been an important figure in approaching the debates in this way. This emphasis on the empirical basis for theory is of course a characteristic of British psychoanalysis, as of so much else in British intellectual traditions. As is evident in the published accounts of the Controversial Discussions, this clinically based approach impressed many of those present beyond the convinced group around Klein.

At the end of World War I, huge changes in British society began to take shape, in particular the expansion of the welfare state and the creation of the National Health Service (NHS). While the British Psychoanalytic Society remained outside this new structure, the Tavistock Clinic – which had pioneered the psychotherapeutic treatment of traumatized war veterans after World War I and subsequently developed a range of psychotherapy services including a clinic for children – decided to join the NHS. John Bowlby was the director of the Department of Children and Parents, and he invited Esther Bick to set up psychoanalytic psychotherapy training for child therapists who would be able to offer psychoanalytic treatment to children and adolescents in the new NHS (Dicks, 1970; Rustin, 2009). She was an analysand of Melanie Klein and an experienced child therapist with a background of observational research with Charlotte Bleuler in Vienna.

## Esther Bick's model of Infant Observation

Bick's inspiration was to begin the training of child therapists with an experience of longitudinal, naturalistic observation of babies. At first she thought this would have to take place in day nurseries, but she quickly realized that the observation would be much enriched if the observer could arrange to visit a family with a new baby on a weekly basis, and to continue this for the first 2 years of the baby's life. This became the classical Tavistock model of Infant Observation (Rustin, 2009). The student would visit the family prior to the baby's birth and explain to both parents her wish to observe their baby at a regular time each week while in mother's care, stressing that her purpose was to learn from her observations about the growth and development of babies as part of her training. It was emphasized that it was the ordinary daily life of an infant in the family that was the object of study: the everyday events of feeding, toileting, bathing, playing and sleeping were what the observer hoped to see. If the parents agreed to this, the observer hoped to begin observations as soon after the birth as the mother felt able to welcome a visitor.

Bick wrote a famous account of this method of Infant Observation (Bick, 1964), and in this she outlined her purpose in giving this practice so central a role in the training she developed. She wished it to give her students "some practical experience of infants" to prepare them for clinical work with children in which they would be attuned to the infantile elements in their patient's material. In similar vein, she wrote of students beginning psychotherapy with a child "interviewing the mother" about a child's history, implying how much they would be helped to understand what a mother has to say about a child in emotional difficulties if they had had experience of sustained observation of a mother–infant pair, and could be readily in touch with maternal anxieties in the face of the vulnerabilities of tiny infants. We can note here that the contribution of fathers is at this point marginalized, but nonetheless, when discussing the observer's place in the family home, Bick explicitly referred to needing to take account of both parents in describing the subtle and often awkward or painful process of the observer finding an appropriate position (both in spatial and relational senses) during observational visits. One can see that Bick had in mind the ordinary comings and goings of any family, and the observer's need to be open to the fluidity of who might be present on any particular occasion. Although the central observational emphasis was indeed going to focus on the baby's and mother's experiences, the privileged visitor has to find a way to relate to all the members of the household – even family pets, who can complicate things quite a bit – without, as she put it, "acting out a role" among those whom the family may offer to her, consciously or unconsciously. The observer has to struggle simultaneously with the pressures toward enactment stirred within herself as a consequence of strong feelings and internal infantile disturbance in the face of the encounter with the overwhelming intimacy of mother and baby in the early months.

This emphasis on the privilege accorded to an observer remains a core element in the approach necessary to establish an observation on a good basis. The primary gift is that of the parents in allowing the observer to come into their home. Indeed, many families say that they agreed to an observation because they wished to support the training of people who will later take on professional roles with children – to offer observers the chance to learn to watch and understand babies' development in the contexts of their families.

The guiding principle about the stance of the observers Bick wanted to get across was the importance of resisting acting out a role that involved infantile transference between family members and observer, while being present in the moment as fully as possible, open to perceiving as much as possible. She was also explicit about the risk of an infantile transference from observer to mother (another baby for mother to care for) or from observer to father (e.g., forming a couple that excluded mother). The "free-floating attention" familiar as an injunction about technique in psychoanalytic practice is what Bick wanted observers to achieve. This would give access to adequate remembered detail on the one hand and to the observer's own emotional responses on the other, both those recollected by the observer and those emerging subsequently in the seminar discussion. This, of course, is why from the start she did not want people to take notes during the observation, since such activity would prevent the student from "responding easily to the emotional demands of the mother" – and one should add, of being alive to the moment-by-moment activity of the baby and of the baby's interactions with others.

The vital importance of face-to-face contact between mother and infant is foundational for all later relationships that involve intimacy and understanding. The eyes of the observer and their steady focus on mother and baby are essential for establishing a relationship with each. While in adult analysis the main focus in terms of perceptual apparatus is on what is heard and spoken (though with adults, analysts who have had Infant Observation experience are more likely to note with interest, for example, the patient's behavior on the couch), in Infant Observation and analytic work with children, the visual field is much more central. Hence, anxieties about seeing and being seen are widespread and indeed unavoidable. Observers worry, and those observed often feel similar anxieties, that their looking might not be experienced as kind, interested and open to discovery (staying "in the question") but instead as intrusive, as introducing the evil eye, voyeuristic impulses or eyes green with envy. Looking can involve the eye as an organ of projection rather than receptivity.

The basic instructions given to the observer about how to conduct herself sounded simple but were by no means easy to follow. She was to be friendly and unobtrusive during her visit; not to ask questions or initiate conversation with the mother or others beyond the requirements of respect and civility; not to engage with the infant except by offering very close attention throughout the 1-hour visit; and all the while to be holding in mind as many details of all that took place as possible. After leaving, she was to write as soon as possible a detailed account of all she recalled – the baby's behavior, bodily movements, sounds, direction of gaze, facial expression and so forth. Just as significant were the mother's activity, posture and expression, and conversation with the baby, observer and any others present, including any other children in the family. Events that involved others, which could include contributions from father, siblings, neighbors, grandparents, friends, or indeed any of the other people who might feature in everyday family life from time to time, also needed to be recorded.

These detailed notes would then be discussed in a weekly seminar with a small number of other observers (usually 3–5) with an experienced seminar leader – Bick herself, in the first instance. In the seminar discussion, the emotional response of the observer would be a further element for exploration. Bick herself did not favor the observer including the details of her personal response in the written record, preferring to keep the notes as objective as possible and to focus the observations in the first instance on what she saw. The question of whether observers should write about their own feelings remains debated among infant observers. One solution often adopted is for notes of the seminar discussion during which they are explored to be kept alongside the original observation notes. As the shift in psychoanalytic technique brought about by fresh understanding of countertransference phenomena took hold, including references to emotional response seemed more natural. Thus Bick's method allowed the impact of the observation on the observer and then within the group to emerge in the discussion and to be kept boundaried (avoiding "wild analysis") by the seminar leader. She was preoccupied with the question of objectivity and underlined two matters in elaborating her views on this point.

The first was her warning that observers must bear limitations to their curiosity – the unknowable, the mysterious and the not-yet-known can, she suggested, "intrigue too much." Rather like Bion, in his more or less contemporaneous emphasis on putting up with not-knowing as an essential component in genuine psychoanalytic exploration (for patient and analyst; Bion, 1962), Bick was alert to the need to ally our curiosity about each other, so much stimulated by Infant Observation, with awareness of the risks of intrusiveness and of premature certainties. She was also allergic to anything tending in the direction of wild analysis, or the sloppy assumption that the observer's own emotional response was an infallible guide to the emotional truths in the observed family. Her way of conducting seminars was very much to work toward describing possible hypotheses about states of mind in mother and infant, as evidenced by their interactions, to study both conscious and unconscious communications, reminding everyone that further observations over time were the only proper basis for confirming or refuting the line of interpretation being developed. The infant observer does not offer verbal interpretations as one does in analysis when their validity is tested by the patient's response. The evidence available (just 1 hour of observation each week) is always limited, and Bick emphasized that only repeated observations of similar patterns could be a basis for more confident claims about the relationships taking shape and the internal worlds of the individuals in the family.

The second point Bick made was that she was assuming all observers were in personal analysis throughout their observation. She could thus take it for granted that there was analytic scrutiny of observers' countertransference-like reactions alongside her seminar supervision of the observations. This was consistent with the training function of Infant Observation as she conceived it, when it was undertaken at the beginning of child psychotherapy training, alongside personal analysis five times a week and theoretical and clinical seminars, and preceding supervised clinical work with children.

So we have here Infant Observation conceived as a three-stage process – the observational visit, the writing up of notes and the seminar discussion. To this can be added in most contemporary practice the expectation that observers write a paper on some aspect of their observation at its close toward the end of the infant's second year. In the many psychoanalytic trainings that have taken up Infant Observation as part of their curriculum, the observation is frequently of a 1-year duration and the paper, when required, consequently written on the baby's first year of life. The gradual amassing of very interesting records of such infant observations and their distillation into written papers has produced a remarkable flowering of publications in more recent years. The first books (e.g., Miller et al., 1989) coincided with the growth of interest outside the UK and with the establishment of regular conferences on Infant Observation at the Tavistock Clinic and in Europe. Later came the *International Journal of Infant Observation* and its applications, which covers a broad field of related work (infant and young child observation, links to child development research, clinical applications, etc.). Alongside this expansion of written records came the possibility of research of various kinds (M. J. Rustin, 2006).

## The function of the seminar group

The group studies closely the text of the observation being presented, and in dialogue with the observer attempts to elucidate the conscious and unconscious elements in the emotional interactions in the material. It is the meaning of the behavioral facts that are at the heart of the approach; indeed, a psychoanalytic model of human development that puts meaning in pride of place is the context in which Infant Observation of this sort grew and flourished. In other words, it is the minds of baby, mother and other family members in which the observer is primarily interested. In the case of the baby, at the start of life there is a chance to see the very beginnings of the mind, and especially to observe the fluidity of the mind–body relationship, and to see the nature of the baby's sensuous somatic experiences out of which meaning and thinking can grow. Observers ponder how the family members are feeling, how they experience themselves and each other, and they also learn to wonder at their own responses, to get to know hitherto unfamiliar aspects of their own minds. Unconscious responses to the intimacies of mothers and babies in observers as they feel the impact on them of their exposure to the mother–baby couple, to which they can feel so close and yet simultaneously very much outside, become evident over time. Uncomfortable recognition of personal preconceptions, identifications and prejudices are inevitable. For example, an observer can recognize in themselves an unconscious belief that mothers are only too prone to misunderstand babies, that mothers should be perfectly attuned, a conviction that babies are a threat to a poor displaced toddler with his precariously established sense of self, or a view that fathers do or do not belong in the nursery – or most disturbing of all, that the observer would do a much better job at mothering than the actual mother. Memories of one's own family of origin are stirred, and if observers are already parents themselves, they will find themselves thinking of their own current or recent experiences. Such encounters with our own infantile selves can be very troubling, and the group dynamics within the seminar can sometimes be dramatic. The wisdom and containing capacity of the seminar leader are vital to sustaining the adult identity of the observers and the focus on the task of observation.

## What do we gain from Infant Observation?

### *An observational example*

To take us close to this experience, here is some material from the early weeks of the observation of a mother and her baby. Some observational sequences from 2 days, 8 weeks and 11 weeks are followed by a discussion of their significance. The observer had some previous observational experience, and this is mother's second child, a baby girl named Anna. The mother had welcomed the observation warmly, saying at the first meeting with the observer, "I think it would be good for me. It will help to slow me down and notice more." The observer was invited to visit when Anna was 2 days old. She described the baby as looking "perfectly beautiful" and tenderly swaddled in an old T-shirt of mother's – to provide, as mother explained, the comfort of her smell. She was however disoriented at mother's response to her admiration of the baby:

> I cannot help saying to mother just how beautiful I thought her baby was. Mother smiles and reaches over and tenderly strokes the baby's head with her finger tips, touching her little ears. I say "just look at those little ears, so perfect." Mum sits back, laughs and says "nearly perfect, but she has a stub on one of her little fingers." She then makes a joke about giving birth to a 6 fingered baby and refers to a film about the birth of a "mutant being."

Mother's "glowing tenderness" (the observer's phrase) is here briefly transmuted into something the shocked observer felt to be painfully mocking. She mused that possibly the baby's arrival 2 weeks early had disrupted something in her state of mind. She then observed the baby strain and shudder as mother recounted the story of the birth, her voice rising to a high pitch as her words poured out. But father then arrived, picked up the swaddled and now sleeping baby and handed her to mother, who held her close, stroking her and whispering to her.

When Anna was 8 weeks old, the observer noted a sequence in which the baby's response to mother's shifts of attention is recorded:

> Every now and again mum nuzzles her own nose on Anna's forehead or nose, kissing her. This is the most affectionate I have ever seen her. Then, while mum is talking to a wide-eyed Anna, Anna's mouth muscles begin to move, once, twice and then she produces a full smile whilst staring into mum's eyes. It was amazing to see, and mum cries out in delight. Anna does it again and then a third time. Mum says "Actually this is her first full smile." Mum beams with pleasure. At this point Mum said that Anna likes her looking into her eyes, but that the poor girl has to compete with her mobile phone. Mum says her own eyes are on her phone a lot of the time as she gets emails and uses the internet. She gave some details of this. Anna is now propped up against a pillow and not moulded into the corner of mother's arms. She looks exposed, unsupported and older. As Mum looks at her phone, Anna extends both arms sideways. Mum looks over at her, laughs and says "she's an aeroplane." When Mum speaks, Anna brings her arms back close to her body. Mum laughs again and turns back to her phone. Anna's arms extend out again, suspended in the air. Mum looks over and says "what are you doing, funny bean?" Anna looks at mother, and as her hand goes to touch her, attempts to grasp Mum's finger.

Three weeks later, the observer described the following:

> Mum's two visiting friends, who have come to lunch, prepare to leave. One talks about how broody she feels. There is a lot of fast talk about what is going on at work. Mum places Anna in her bouncy chair in the middle of the large kitchen table. As soon as she is put down she begins to arch her back and looks strained. Mum quickly says "I know you are ready for a feed – just one moment, I'll be back in a minute" and sees her friends to the door. Whilst she is gone, Anna arches her back several times, as though willing herself out of the chair. Her mouth turns downwards, but she does not cry. She turns her head to the side and momentarily becomes quiet and still as she looks out of the window. She remains like this for a while, then turns away from the window, tenses her body and tops her head in a backward position and sees me (the observer). She becomes still again, looking at me, but then fixing her gaze to one side of me.

Mum returns, offers me tea and then comes to sit facing Anna, beaming at her. "What a busy day we are having, aren't we?" Anna stares at her. Her eyes twitch as she looks straight at Mum and then away. Mum offers her little endearments and wiggles her feet. "Are you going to give me a smile, come on, let's have one." Anna looks serious. Then one side of her mouth turns up as though she is going to smile, but she doesn't. As Mum gets up to make tea, Anna's face breaks into a large smile. I can't resist calling Mum back. She quickly returns and Anna's smiling eyes are fixed onto Mum's, bright and shiny. Then just as quickly Anna turns her head away and the smile is gone.

## Discussion

These beautifully observed everyday moments between a fundamentally warm and loving mother and her baby record their ways of coming together and the times at which mother's other preoccupations, whether internally or externally driven, demand of the baby that she turn to her own resources to deal with her feelings. The observer commented in this period that she was greatly impressed by the growing strength in Anna's neck that enabled her to see her mother in a frame with others, to take hold of a wider perspective as she looked around her. She also felt that it was imperative that she herself sit up straight and look at mother and baby together, and that she had to be careful not to leave mother out of her gaze for too long.

It is very striking to note the ways in which we can observe the layers of containment around this baby. The newborn is bundled up warmly in mother's old soft T-shirt, signaling mother's sensitivity to her need to be held together. When mother's emotional availability is punctured by her anxiety about the evidence of imperfection in her baby and her own overwhelming feelings about giving birth, baby shivers and the observer does too. (Here is an instance of the identification with the infant that observers often experience.) But father's arrival repairs the situation, with his confidence that mother and baby belong together, and this was characteristic of this father's generous spirit. He thus contains the mother–baby couple that has briefly become emotionally isolated.

In the observations that followed, the observer felt herself to be required to make a lot of space for mother as well as Anna, and was strongly aware of how much she was depended on. She learned more, over time, about this mother's painful sense of rejection by her own mother and to understand how much the unconscious internal picture of a competitive and rather distant mother–daughter relationship had to be struggled with in order for the new mother–daughter couple to be able to make their own way, not too much shadowed by the "ghosts in the nursery" (Fraiberg, 1980). Anna's capacity to reach out and communicate both vividly and movingly with her mother at times seemed to show how she could contain her mother as well as the more expectable reverse of that. She was one of those babies who help their mother by their life-seeking behavior. The observer also felt that her seminar group helped her to bear the sense of shock and isolation recurrently present in this observation, and at times the disturbing loss of her observational capacities that these emotions brought about, when she would become overidentified with mother or baby to the detriment of the one excluded. In other words, her containment by the group helped her to keep her balance.

This example gives a glimpse of the kind of detail observers seek to record and of the way in which the observer can come to understand the relationship between mother and baby, and something of the individual personality of each, to see the part played by the dynamics of the family in the evolution of the mother–baby relationship and to sense the intricacies of the intergenerational elements in the current situation. The self-observation of the observer's own responses, which were here so acutely felt that they were included in her write-ups, allow both for her reflection on the shifting identifications she feels (with neglected baby, leading to criti-cal thoughts about mother, or with needy mother, leading to getting too drawn into mother's conversation and losing her focus on baby) and for thoughts about the three-person dynamics of observation. Thus the observer learns the value of detailed sequential observation, the humility needed for understanding the complexity and continuously changing nature of family relation-ships, and the discipline of reflection on her own reactions to what she sees.

As Freud and Klein both noted, countertransference experiences in psychoanalysis can be usefully informative but are also a source of risk. In modern clinical practice, we make increased use of countertransference phenomena because of the theoretical advances in understanding con-sequent on Klein's description of projective identification. "Enactment," "role responsiveness" and "the pressures on the analyst" are concepts elaborating this trend. This makes it all the more essential that we have a disciplined approach to giving meaning to the emotions stirred within the analyst, and this may be one reason why Infant Observation has achieved such a widespread take-up as a tool in training psychoanalytic practitioners.

There is an obvious affinity between the interest in studying mother–baby relationships and the early growth of the mind in the infant, and the broad direction of psychoanalytic theoriza-tion in recent decades. Following Bion's and Winnicott's lead as patient and supervisor of Klein, respectively, psychoanalysts have continued to explore early states of mind. Klein's description of infantile anxieties and phantasy life has proved fertile in allowing the understanding of a vast range of clinical problems, particularly in the light of changing clinical populations and contem-porary concern with narcissistic and borderline states. Bion's concepts of containment, maternal reverie, and his theory of thinking, and Winnicott's of the facilitating environment and mater-nal holding, are the background to much current clinical research and practice. Alongside this there is the explosion of academic work building on Bowlby's attachment theory – and strange indeed to keep in mind that Bick and Bowlby were the joint originators of the Tavistock child psychotherapy training! Attachment theory has become a widely influential discourse on early development, with forms of laboratory-based observation linked both to ethological theory and to psychoanalysis among other disciplines (see Chapter 5 in this volume).

## Difficulties that can arise in Infant Observation

Here is a second example of an Infant Observation that highlights some other characteristic preoccupations. This particular example is also recorded on film, as it was part of a BBC series about the work of the Tavistock, "Talking Cure: Mind and Method of the Tavistock Clinic" (Observation Observed). A later film *Observation Observed*, explored this observation in more detail alongside a presentation of the main theoretical ideas of Infant Observation (Rustin & Miller, 2001). The discussion here is based on the observer's presentation in an ordinary Infant Observation seminar.

The young parents had had good support from the wider family in the first turbulent weeks of the baby's life, and the observation was often rather a happy and hopeful experience. The observer delighted in seeing the growth of tenderness and lively play between father and son that matched mother's delight in her baby, which had been evident from the start.

### A visit to baby David

One day when David was 9 months old, the observer arrived as usual and was shown into the parents' bedroom where baby David lay sleeping in his cot. The observer was left there while the parents continued their social chat with two visitors. She was aware of some talk from the next room, somewhat at her expense. They were jokingly asking, what on earth could be the point of watching a sleeping baby? This contrasted with her usual welcome, so she felt rather hurt and excluded from the cheery chat next door. At one point one of the visitors peered at her through the crack of the slightly open door so she herself was a direct object of observation. Baby David was sleeping quite peacefully, but the observer suddenly saw, as he moved his arm, a large scar on the back of his hand, which was clearly a burn. She was horribly shocked and found herself wincing. Although her notes described the baby's apparently untroubled sleep, well wrapped up and surrounded by lovely toys in his cot, the observer found her eyes continually drawn back to this distressing wound. What had happened to him? She spent the whole hour watching the sleeping baby while there was more excited activity next door – chat, laughter, snacks, and talk about her. "They take notes, you know, and before you know it social services are involved!" When it was time to leave and she was making her departure, mother explained that baby David had fallen against a radiator while playing in his walker, and got his hand trapped between walker and radiator. "A big blister came up. He is going to have a scar on his hand," she added quietly. The observer said that it must have been very frightening for both of them, and mother spoke of having to watch him every minute now. Then they said their goodbyes.

In the seminar discussion of this material, the observer was able with relief to express her distress, horror, loneliness and intense identification with the baby. The seminar explored how she felt placed in the position of the accusing social services officials who might arraign the parents for failure to protect the child, and how this was linked to her raw re-experiencing of the child's pain as she winced at the sight of the burn: the child too must have felt angry and terrified at this shock and hurt, and blamed mother for not keeping him safe. We wondered if his long, peaceful sleep that contrasted so sharply with the observer's turbulent thoughts might even be sustained by her silent presence. The observer was particularly struck by how persecuted and humiliated she had felt during the visit by the feeling of being left out and laughed at, and also how stunned she was by her first sight of the burn. It was recognized that in saying nothing at the outset the parents had probably forcibly projected onto her their shock, distress, fear, guilt and shame. Their anxieties about being condemned, even punished, as the reference to social services makes clear, were probably mitigated by their underlying trust in the observer's kindly concern for both their child and themselves.

But she then had to struggle to contain these very painful emotions, on their behalf as well as on her own account. The observer felt she had a quite new understanding of what containment meant and of the nature and consequences of projective identification in real time. This was much more compelling to her as a demonstration of the meaning of these concepts than her current analytic work with her patients: she was a clinical psychologist training in psychotherapy. In clinical sessions she felt less exposed to the full brute force of projections, perhaps partly because she was more prepared for them. Particularly evident was the strain on the observer of the multiple identifications she was holding on to – with mother, father and baby – and her feeling that the emotional task she was being asked to perform for the family was to process in her mind an as yet unassimilable traumatic event. The observer linked the intensity of her reaction to her clinical experience in working with traumatized patients.

## Observation as preparation for clinical work

The awareness of conflicting multiple identifications is particularly crucial for therapists working with children and families and for couple therapists. The trust of both child and parents has to be gained and maintained through a scrupulously even-handed attitude in listening to the many versions of family life that we learn about. The infant observer's frequent struggles to empathize with the conflicting wishes and perspectives of baby, toddler sibling, mother, father, grandmother and whoever else may be part of the baby's familial world is wonderful preparation for the inevitable pressure of the clinical role and for withstanding the impact of familial conflict, and the conflicts inherent in multidisciplinary professional collaboration. In using a student's aptitude for Infant Observation as a guide for suitability for psychoanalytic training, one of the most telling difficulties that emerges is a student's tendency to criticize the parent, overidentify with the baby, and convey subtly (or even not too subtly) in the seminar that he or she would do a much better job as a parent. A clinician in competition with parents is a predictable disaster story, particularly but not only for child therapists, but it is inherent in work with children that those of us with a grievance against parents are drawn to it. Psychoanalysis, more broadly, always carries the risk of an attitude of arrogant superiority to the patient's original family, and with difficult-to-like patients the reverse may operate – that is, an identification with parents worn down by their difficult child.

There are a number of areas in which Infant Observation in conjunction with the development of psychoanalytic theory and technique has influenced clinical practice in the years since Klein's death. Several writers have drawn attention to the creative interaction of Bick's, Winnicott's and Bion's theories (Rustin, 2009; Waddell, 2006) and the interest has spread well beyond the UK (Diem-Wille, 2009; Houzel, 2010; Maiello, 2000). Of particular relevance are the following areas: interventions with parents and babies (Emanuel & Bradley, 2008); work with severely deprived and abused children (Boston & Szur, 1983); work with children and adults on the autistic spectrum (Mitrani, 2001; Reid & Alvarez, 1989; Rhode, 2003); with patients with eating disorders (Williams, 1997); and with patients who are difficult to reach (Joseph, 1989). This list is selective and not by any means exhaustive.

To give a more concrete sense of how the infant observational state-of-mind and observational skills can contribute to clinical work, I have selected three examples.

## Example 1: Esther

Esther is a 9-year-old girl from a very large Orthodox Jewish family growing up in a part of London with a substantial Orthodox community. Esther's difficulties had remained intractable: despite a variety of prior interventions in a child and adolescent mental health clinic, she would not talk to anyone. Psychotherapy was the last resort (as it so often is!). Esther's problems had two dimensions: behaviorally, she had been enuretic and encopretic for many years; in terms of her relationships and emotional life, she was quite depressed and unhappy at home, though she was a very intelligent girl and got on well at school.

When I assessed her, although she did not utter a single word in our first meeting she shocked me by the extent of her extremely thin and lifeless looks. She was able with much encouragement to use the toys I provide for child patients to communicate with me. In play with the animals and little doll figures, the picture was conveyed that everyone was part of a cozy couple except the baby, who remained excluded and was repeatedly accidentally dropped or tossed aside. This vision of a falling, unprotected infant combined in my mind with the striking way in which Esther related to me and my room: she used her large sad eyes to study every detail slowly as she sat completely still on the chair she had selected – the one furthest from mine. I felt in the deep silence as if I were in the presence of a baby whose sole resource was her power of vision. When I managed to encourage her to draw, which she did in a painfully restricted fashion, she produced a complete plan of my room, with each article of furniture, the markings on the carpet, the pictures on the walls and so on. She had recorded the place, but no figures were present. We, the people, were absent. The desolation of her internal world felt palpable.

When we began therapy, she had retreated yet a greater distance, no doubt partly due to a wait for me to free a regular time for her weekly session. She sat motionless and silent for many weeks, unable to investigate her drawer of toys and other materials. I had very little to go on, just the evidence before me of an apparently almost lifeless child and of my own countertransference feelings. There were tiny indications of her way of trying to create a bit of comfort out of the way she sat in the chair, occasional hand movements to hold some strands of hair between her fingers, and her eyes upon me most of the time. I felt terribly rejected and dejected, punished relentlessly for keeping her waiting, but also intensely responsible for keeping alive an infant whose capacity to take hold of life was almost extinguished.

Over many months I spoke about the abandoned baby that she was letting me know about and the need for two of us to find a way to link up to help her. Eventually she began to use paper and pencils while lying on the floor behind two chairs so that she was as hidden from me as possible. She showed me nothing of what she did and tried to take it home with her, which she knew I would not allow. Eventually I was given glimpses of her paper of writing in Hebrew, which I think she believed (correctly) that I did not understand. The importance of not understanding and not being understood as a starting point emerged in this way, and her need to see whether I could contain the painful experience of failing to understand – of being in effect an excluded infant while she and her language constituted a kind of self-enclosed couple, cruelly ignoring me.

The silence of the sessions was finally ended, though Esther's voice when it appeared was a minute whisper, very difficult for her, and requiring me to make excruciating efforts to pick up what she said. I had to strain every sense, every muscle, every theoretical and personal resource to take hold of the crumbs she offered. Just enough to stay alive was what I got. The intensity of this was considerable, and I sometimes felt pretty clear that I was in the presence of a very profound experience of failure to link, or a destruction of links (Bion, 1957).

## Discussion

In the busy household at home, Esther had perhaps competed unsuccessfully with her mother's many other concerns. The seven children in the family included a disabled brother 2 years older and another child born only a year after her. The years of wet sheets and dirty knickers could be thought of as the infant's bitter reproach to the unavailable mother felt to be unable or unwilling to receive her distress, the mother needed to contain the baby's earliest outpourings who had not been found.

The jealousy projected into mother, who was enraged by the teachers' enjoyment of Esther in contrast to her own continuous frustration, was something I came to feel vividly. Helpful to me in sustaining myself in Esther's sessions was the slowed-down rhythms of the infant observer. It became evident how vital it was that I put a great deal of effort into processing what I felt before I spoke. She was a very small and desperately defended creature, clinging to life in an omnipotent impasse. Interesting her in another way of living required tiny spoonfuls of highly digestible interpretation. The practice of nonintervention of infant observation alongside the recording of minute details of the infant's behavior was helpful to me in finding the right pace and in tolerating all the waiting entailed in the apparent absence of response.

### Example 2: Mark

Some of the same disciplines were required in the second case I will describe. Mark is a 13-year-old boy whose rather disturbed mother idealizes psychotherapy and who has proved a very demanding and indeed bullying parent who alarms staff by threats of complaint. He had been seen for just over a year by a colleague who was retiring. She asked me to take him on.

Mark had never spoken to his therapist but in the last weeks of their sessions he had begun to do intricate drawings that the therapist felt were urgent requests for his therapy not to end.

After some initial sessions, when Mark did talk a bit and also drew one very striking picture with a huge bridge at its heart, he then closed down and became silent. He would come from the waiting room looking resentful and hostile and then settle himself at once to sleep, using two chairs in various combinations, never the couch. I spent many months trying to come to a conclusion in my mind about the balance of helplessness, hatred and adolescent contempt in this behavior and the implications for whether or not I should continue the treatment. I would talk a fair bit to Mark while he appeared asleep, since I was convinced that some of the time he was only half-asleep and probably, despite appearances, listening to me. I always made a huge (though regularly unsuccessful) effort at the beginning of sessions to get something going that might keep him awake. A few minutes before the end, I would wake him. So overall, there were limited times when I thought he heard me, though I am sure sometimes I spoke to help myself keep working. When he said anything, it was to reiterate that he did not need to come: he had no problems; other children needed therapy but he didn't; it was his mother's problem that she thought he should come.

Watching him as he slept, one set of thoughts arose from observations of his baby-like state when he was asleep. His nasty expression and the stiff, adolescent challenge of his body posture would melt as he slept. I saw before me a smooth-faced little boy, even a baby, resting his cheek on a curled arm and the soft part of the chair. His handing over of himself to my care and his letting me know in this way that he trusted me to look after him seemed important. The intrusive bad-object me that he was protecting himself from seemed replaced by a benign mother figure watching over her child's sleep. It looked in every way for a while that he was having a rest from exposure to a persecuting object. My countertransference response at these moments was tender and patient, especially since I had had enough uncomfortable contact with his mother to know just what a problem it must be to live with someone so determined to define things for other people as she saw them.

But then a second, much more disturbing set of reflections started to surface. I began to see this apparently blissful state as a suicidal retreat from life, a cutting-off of the sources of vitality and creativity (projected wholesale into me) and a deathly idealization of nothingness. I became alarmed, and my way of talking to Mark became urgent, as I attempted to recall him from what now seemed a mad refusal of nourishment. At the moments when he would be awake, his response to my many attempts to make contact very frequently consisted of "nothing" or "no," and his negativism now seemed formidable and dominating.

One of the things that weighed heavily with me as I struggled with this ego–destructive force in Mark was the very different way in which he now seemed to wake up when I woke him a few minutes before the end of the session. In the early months he had seemed to stir like a child refreshed, a bit bewildered about where he was, but soft and open. I had felt I needed to end the session gently, and to emphasize the element of his depending on me to do the thinking about him. Now the atmosphere was quite different. Mark would open his eyes with a blank gaze, as if to blot me out afresh, and having asked me how much longer we had would turn on his side and defiantly claim to be going to sleep again for the last few minutes. There was nothing to talk about, so he might as well sleep.

For some time I persisted in analyzing the violence of his assault on the potential meaningfulness of his therapy and in trying to put him in touch with the tragedy and risk to himself, which this surrender to cynicism involved. But I also felt concerned that if I simply allowed this to go on endlessly, he would perceive me to be helpless against his omnipotence and his mother's manipulativeness. The realization that his mother had in effect bullied the clinic into taking Mark on as a patient against his will made me think hard about the ethics of the position. I did not have a willing patient, one who had given consent to psychotherapy, but rather he and I seemed to be enacting a corrupted version of what should be happening. Mark was by now 14, and the inappropriateness of this position with an adolescent was stark. I decided I must confront him with my refusal to continue his therapy on the current basis.

I came to conceive the therapeutic impasse as deriving from Mark's unconscious experience of himself as a child lost inside of a picture of me experienced as the idealized or persecutory mother in the transference. This meant he was out of touch with his own sense of agency. I felt my loneliness was akin to that of a mother with no supportive paternal figure helping to regulate the relationship between mother and baby, protecting each from a deadly symbiotic state. My conviction that action was required of me felt linked to the sense of being able to think myself out of the threat of presiding over the death of therapy. I had to assert that therapy was only available if the patient consented. At this point in time he did not, but that left open the possibility that he might at some other time. It was possible to convey this to him quite straightforwardly.

I think the need for the presence of a paternal figure in the internal world, the vital protection for mental health embedded in the facing of the early Oedipal situation, is something that infant observers become sharply aware of. The work of Ron Britton in linking Klein's "depressive position" with the experience of the Oedipal triangle has been widely influential, but I think also shows the influence of Britton's acknowledged interest in infant observation. I think the hypnotic quality of a mother–child dyad that is functioning to prevent development is what I was facing with Mark. I thought he was relieved and astonished that I could put my foot down, as he had assured me that his mother would not allow me to end his therapy.

## Example 3: Jane

Jane was 14½ when I began to see her. She was a very big, awkward girl, adopted together with her younger brother when she was 8. Her early history was grim: chronic early neglect followed by particularly dreadful sexual abuse by her father and others in a pedophile gang. She had been adopted by an older, well-educated couple whose cultural style was about as far from her origins as can be imagined. Adolescence brought with it hostility to her mother, and both parents were also very worried about Jane's lack of friends and poor performance at school and the violent relationship between the siblings.

For a long time, Jane's sessions were filled to overflowing with talk. She had an unending flow of stories, mainly about school life and the minutiae of who was getting on with whom and all the bitchy things people said and did. Sometimes I would hear about family life, in which her mother and brother usually featured as the unreasonable people that she had to put up with. The superficiality and sheer boringness of much of what she said was particularly irritating because of a veneer of psychobabble. Her obvious intelligence was submerged in a relentless focus on what seemed to be the emotionally irrelevant, including a vast involvement with the idea of becoming a witch. Wicca was to be her religion. I survived these weeks by sticking to observation. I pondered her relationship to the couch where she sat, to her long hair that she played with in very intricate ways (sadistic and tender in equal measure), to her clothes and her tooth braces. This activity helped me to keep in mind a person of potential depth. I never looked forward to seeing her, because it truly was a struggle not to protect myself from her empty chatter by some form of emotional evasion. It was very hard work not to drift off. I increased the sessions to twice a week in the hope that this would help me to reach her.

After 16 months a startling change took place. She returned from an Easter break completely silent. This was the fourth holiday break since we began and one term after the start of the twice-a-week rhythm. To my astonishment, I now found the sessions riveting. The silence was full of life and depth, and my mind was happily at work trying to understand her, in contrast to the guilt-inducing boredom of the earlier phase. The observations of her minute activities as she sat silent became much more convincingly meaningful. I could speak about the long-ago, little-girl experiences I now felt in touch with – the neglected child who had only self-comfort to turn to, the hurt and angry child who had missed me in the holiday, the baby who wondered whether there was a mother – I who could understand her and who cared about her.

I came to believe this movement into an authentic psychoanalytic therapy was probably a consequence of my barely withstanding her initial conviction that I would have no real interest in her, like a mother who sees her baby as an emotionally irrelevant arrival, leaving the infant to people in her world as best she can with impoverished sensation-dominated experience. What saved me from simply replicating the initial catastrophe were the twin resources of psychoanalytic theory and an observational focus. It was a very long time before I could make much of what I observed, but I think I was amassing a resource bank that would serve me well as the therapy later developed. The clinical task seemed to be survival as a thinking and feeling being in the face of mindlessness. But I thought that my patient's silence was emotionally genuine – it was the talk that had been our problem.

What occurred following Jane's gradual reentry into a verbal world was very different from what had preceded the 3-month silence. Sessions were no longer full of wearying talk – transference interpretations began to have weight and her dependence on me was overt and acknowledged. Sadly, in the ensuing summer holiday this new openness to feeling vulnerable rather than omnipotent contributed, I think, to her having a nasty accident and breaking her leg very badly. However, she returned determinedly on crutches and we could then explore the vulnerability of her baby-self that she did not feel able to look after very well on her own. When she entered sixth-form (the last 2 years of school), she chose to study history and art history and at last to begin to piece together in her therapy the extraordinarily discrepant fragments of her life.

I hope these three examples show how the experience of infant observation contributed to my work. With Esther, the crucial focus had to be on very early, preverbal, infantile states of body and mind and an intensity of attention on my part that recalled the near-total maternal preoc-cupation needed at the start of a baby's life. With Mark, giving meaning to the months of hostile silence depended on the conjunction of observing the minute details of his bodily posture and expression and scrutinizing the strong feelings evoked in me. In Jane's therapy, the well-known distinction between attending to process and to content was my vital resource. What was alive in a true sense was not the surface agitation (a neglected baby keeping herself going with autoerotic activity), but the baby within her waiting to be found by an object capable of perceiving her desire for contact, and her pain and anger when it was interrupted.

## The contemporary place of Infant Observation in the psychoanalytic community

Infant Observation is well established as a valued discipline in the training of psychoanalytic therapists, in both the child and adult fields (Sternberg, 2005). From this perspective, its influence continues to expand. One can anticipate that gifted clinicians will continue to open up new areas of understanding as they study the intricacies of their work with patients. A large current research project on interventions with moderate to severely depressed adolescents (Midgley et al., 2013) has made it clear that to make contact with many of the patients receiving short-term psycho-analytic psychotherapy, the observational skills of their therapists are fundamental. Verbalization can be minimal in withdrawn adolescents, and behavior of the acting-out variety can be the main form of communication in others. The kind of "ontological" depression repeatedly encountered in these patients seems to have its roots in very early disturbances of the formation of self. Thus, both the techniques of infant observation and the understandings of early development it offers prove highly relevant. Staying with depressed patients is notoriously difficult, and a conviction that being thought about over time is the origin of ego growth is one that infant observers tend to experience as foundational.

The crucial difference in orientation between psychoanalytic infant observation and other forms of observation seems to be better understood than it once was, when some psychoanalysts saw it as ignoring the unconscious and did not distinguish it from laboratory-based child development research (Green, 2000). It remains an important question whether there can be continuing creative dialogue between people investigating the early mental development of children with such very different tools. Such cross-disciplinary discussions might well prove a growing point (Hopkins, 1989).

The scientific silos of modern academic life are not conducive to productive links across disciplines, and Infant Observation has a very small foothold in the university. However, the possibilities of substantial research both using Infant Observation techniques (e.g., Gretton, 2006; Wakelyn, 2012) and on Observation (e.g., comparing cases, studying seminar process, collecting data from groups of cases with similar features, researching cultural differences) are being recognized in doctoral studies and research projects of various kinds (M. J. Rustin, 2006). One of the areas of converging interest may prove to be between neuroscientific attention to the early development of the brain and its necessarily relational functioning (Schore, 2003) and the infant observer's capacity to describe the beginnings of mind as observed in their work.

The observational method is also being adapted and used increasingly with diverse objects of study: observation of neonatal units (Cohen, 2003), the elderly (Davenhill et al., 2003), of institutions (Hinshelwood & Skogstad, 2000), of nursery-aged children (Adamo & Rustin, 2013), and as part of wider research projects in which infant observation is one methodology used in conjunction with others (Urwin & Sternberg, 2012).

The growth of interest and spread of sites of training in observation inevitably bring with them varieties of practice – for example, the widespread form of Infant Observation in France where only one observation is studied in the seminar at any one time rather than the seminar being composed of a small group of peer-observers. The Bick method is sometimes represented as rigid – a similar, and similarly unjustified accusation as that leveled at Klein's technique of child analysis – but it is in truth extraordinary to see what a huge and varied progeny seems to be flourishing, though the classical 2-year observation is indeed a demanding thing to do. In time and mental and emotional energy, it has a capacity to inspire as probably only babies do: watching close-up the growth of a baby grabs people's interest and commitment, and this fact is probably a protection for the future of Infant Observation.

## References

Adamo, S & Rustin, ME 2013, *Young child observation*, Tavistock/Karnac, London.

Bick, E 1964, 'Notes on infant observation in psycho-analytic training', *International Journal of Psychoanalysis*, vol. 45, pp. 558–566.

Bion, WR 1957, 'Attacks on linking', in *Second thoughts*, Heinemann, London, pp. 93–109.

Bion, WR 1962, *Learning from experience*, Heinemann, London.

Boston, M & Szur, R 1983, *Psychotherapy with severely deprived children*, Routledge, London.

Cohen, M 2003, *Sent before my time*, Tavistock/Karnac, London.

Davenhill, R, Balfour, A, Rustin, M, Blanchard, M & Tress, K 2003, 'Looking into later life: Psychoanalytic observation and old age', *Psychodynamic Psychotherapy*, vol. 17, no. 3, pp. 253–266.

Dicks, HV 1970, *50 years of the Tavistock Clinic*, Routledge and Kegan Paul, London.

Diem-Wille, G 2009, *Das Kleinkind und seine Eltern: Perspektiven psychoanaltischer Babybeobachtung* [*Young children and their parents*], Karnac, London, 2014.

Emanuel, L & Bradley, E 2008, *What can the matter be?*, Tavistock/Karnac, London.

Fraiberg, S 1980, *Clinical studies in infant mental health*, Tavistock, London.

Freud, S 1909, 'Analysis of phobia in a five-year-old boy', in J Strachey (ed), *Standard edition of the complete psychological works of Sigmund Freud*, vol. 10, Hogarth, London, pp. 3–149.

Freud, S 1920, 'Beyond the pleasure principle', in J Strachey (ed), *Standard edition of the complete psychological works of Sigmund Freud*, vol. 18, Hogarth, London, pp. 7–64.

Green, A 2000, 'What kind of research for psychoanalysis' and 'Science and science fiction in infant research', in J Sandler, A-M Sandler & R Davies (eds), *Clinical and observational psychoanalytic research: Roots of a controversy*, Karnac, London, pp. 21–26 and 41–72.

Gretton, A 2006, 'An account of a year's work with a mother and her 18 month old son at risk of autism', *International Journal of Infant Observation*, vol. 8, no. 1, pp. 21–34.

Hinshelwood, R & Skogstad, W 2000, *Observing organisations*, Routledge, London.

Hopkins, J 1989, 'Ways of seeing', *Journal of Child Psychotherapy*, vol. 15, no. 2, pp. 33–39.

Houzel, D 2010, 'Infant observation and the receptive mind', *International Journal of Infant Observation*, vol. 13, no. 2, pp. 119–133.

Isaacs, S 1930, *Social development in young children*, Routledge, London.

Joseph, B 1989, *Psychic equilibrium and psychic change: Selected papers of Betty Joseph* (M Feldman & E Spillius, eds), Routledge, London.

King, P & Steiner, R 1991, *The Freud-Klein controversies 1941–45*, Routledge, London.

Klein M 1921, *The development of a child in love, guilt and reparation 1921–45*, Hogarth Press, London.

Klein, M 1923, 'Early analysis', in *Love, guilt and reparation 1921–45*, Hogarth Press, London.

Maiello, S 2000, 'The cultural dimension of early mother–infant interaction and psychic development: An infant observation in South Africa', *International Journal of Infant Observation*, vol. 3, no. 2, pp. 80–92.

Midgley, N 2013, *Reading Anna Freud*, Routledge, London.

Midgley, N, Cregeen, S, Hughes, C & Rustin, Margaret 2013, 'Psychodynamic psychotherapy as a treatment for depression in adolescence', *Psychoanalytic Approaches to Psychopathology*, vol. 22, no. 1, pp. 67–82, Child & Adolescent Psychiatric Clinics of North America.

Miller, L, Rustin, Margaret, Rustin, Michael & Suttleworth, J (eds) 1989, *Closely observed infants*, Duckworth, London.

Mitrani, J 2001, *Ordinary people and extraordinary protections*, Brunner-Routledge, London.

Reid, S & Alvarez, A 1989, *Autism and personality*, Routledge, London.

Rhode, M 2003, 'Sensory aspects of language development in relation to primitive anxieties', *International Journal of Infant Observation*, vol. 6, no. 2, pp. 12–32.

Rustin, ME 2009, 'Esther Bick's legacy of infant observation at the Tavistock', *International Journal of Infant Observation*, vol. 12, no. 1, pp. 29–41.

Rustin, ME & Miller, B 2001, *Observation observed*, A film published by the Tavistock Clinic Foundation, London.

Rustin, MJ 2006, 'Infant observation research: What have we learned so far?' *International Journal of Infant Observation*, vol. 9, no. 1, pp. 35–52.

Schore, J 2003, *Affect dysregulation and disorder of the self*, Norton, New York.

Sternberg, J 2005, *Infant observation at the heart of training*, Karnac, London.

Urwin, C & Sternberg, J (eds) 2012, *Infant observation and research*, Routledge, London.

Waddell, M 2006, 'Infant observation in Britain: A Tavistock approach', *International Journal of Psychoanalysis*, vol. 87, no. 4, pp. 1103–1120.

Wakelyn, J 2012, 'A study of therapeutic observation of an infant in foster care', in C Urwin & J Sternberg (eds), *Infant observation and research*, Routledge, London, pp. 81–92.

Williams, G 1997, *Internal landscapes and foreign bodies: Eating disorders and other pathologies*, Tavistock/Karnac, London.

# 4

# Donald Winnicott and psychoanalysis

*Jeffrey Prager*

Donald Winnicott occupies a place in the same post-Freudian psychoanalytic pantheon as Melanie Klein, Anna Freud, Wilfred Bion, Jacques Lacan, Hans Loewald and Heinz Kohut. Like the others, his contributions have changed psychoanalysis both in theory and in practice. Largely determined by his work as a pediatrician prior to training in psychoanalysis, as he worked both with infants and their mothers and fathers, he advances the view that psychic life and healthy adaptation to social life occurs only in relation to others, what is now commonly described as intersubjectivity. Throughout his analytic career, he describes from many different angles this crucible of mutual engagement between the inner world of a psychological *being-in-formation* and the psychic world of others responsible for the care, nourishment and growth of that person. Winnicott may be seen as a pioneer in the field of psychoanalytic intersubjectivity.

Winnicott's distinctive psychoanalytic vision revolves around two overlapping formulations that have profoundly shaped the nature of post-Freudian psychoanalytic inquiry. First, he pays primary attention not to the psychological structuring of the individual subject in the way that Freud had done, but rather to the joint creation of a unique subjectivity of each person. The psychological experience of being alive does not occur in isolation; for Winnicott, each individual's unique subjectivity is the consequence of the personal engagement of one's mind amongst a rich cauldron of the mind's significant others. By presuming the intersubjective field in this way, Winnicott revisits many of the core presumptions of Freud and early psychoanalysis. What are the internal challenges a person encounters as his or her world moves beyond the dyadic relationship of mother and child and increasingly confronts the reality of a world not entirely organized with him or her at the center? How do feeling-states take more specific form alongside an increased capacity to acknowledge the objective world distinct from the self?

How to describe the psychological challenges faced by the infant, he asks, as he or she moves from feelings of psychological omnipotence toward "psychic integration"? What is the psychological process through which the infant moves from a state of abject dependence to a sense of greater personal autonomy? *What* is the psychological experience, in short, of being alive? Aliveness is first posed with respect to child development. Yet, beyond that, he also considers lifelong challenges to the psychological experience of feeling alive.

Second, by examining the psychological *space* created as a result of the intersubjective relationship forged between mother and child, Winnicott insists that human existence is not two-dimensional, oscillating between an isolated subjective state and objective reality. Rather, *aliveness*, Winnicott claims, is three-dimensional. He poses the question previously unformulated among psychoanalysts: what are the psychic conditions required, by self and by other, for the *space* to be created enabling that growth? Known famously for his statement that there is no such thing as a baby without his mother, Winnicott describes a fully subjectivized relationship, one made uniquely personal, forged between infant and caregiver. For him and many of his followers, understanding ways in which a healthy connection may not occur defines the heart of psychoanalytic inquiry. Without that psychic field being "good enough," human development and psychic growth is compromised. But when this co-created environment is sufficiently established and the infant can continue to grow into his being, a third realm of existence takes form: the *illusionary* realm. Here, Winnicott argues, much of our lives are lived from then on, a psychic space that help us constantly negotiate between internal perception and feeling-states and external realities. This space becomes the critical site throughout life, he argues, where the *perpetual* human task of distinguishing between subjective perception and objective reality becomes negotiated.

Since the creation of this psychic space is seen as essential to personal growth, it is not surprising that Winnicott's ideas have been applied to the therapeutic setting itself. Therapy, after all, is the effort to better understand and alter what went wrong and what continues to impinge on one's sense of being fully alive. Building upon these formulations, it is now taken for granted that for psychological change and growth to occur therapeutically, the consulting room itself requires transformation into an illusionary realm. What is first experienced as "objective space" requires appropriation by the two inhabitants into a unique co-created environment where psychic transformation might occur. Concepts such as the "holding environment" and the "container," the safety and reliability of the relationship – all employed by Winnicott to describe characteristics of the "facilitating environment" – now have become nearly axiomatic features describing the interpsychic conditions that need to obtain between analyst and analysand.

These are the conditions for the patient's unconscious (and the analyst's) to become playfully engaged. When this third realm of experience is actively established, the patient can safely explore his own memory and desire, previously sequestered because of some combination of inhibition and fear of reprobation. The true self, for Winnicott, is one in which a healthy accommodation can be arrived at, satisfying the needs and wants of the person through an engagement with the objective world, now transformed in more full service to the person. In sum, Winnicott describes the goal of treatment as one in which the rigidity of a feeling self and the objectivity and depriving character of external reality gives way to the activation of a realm of experience far more permeable, fluid, shared with others and pleasurable. The individual is freed to move in the *space-in-between* and to act on and in the world as if he or she had created it for one's own pleasure and gratification. The playfulness established in the consulting room yields greater capacity for individuals similarly to engage the rest of the world. What had been psychically blocked cedes to its unblocking; from the shadows emerges a person's "true self."

Yet in drawing upon contemporary case material from a young man who grew up in mainland China, I suggest that Winnicott's description of the healthy person may not be as universal as he supposed. And the capacity of Winnicott's psychological theory to serve as a model for change may be more easily suited to those whose self-formations – analysts and analysands alike – are products of a similar social and political world. Winnicott grew up in the interwar years in England and wrote largely in post–World War II, at a time when the welfare state was dramatically expanding. It was also a time when, especially in the shadows of both Hitler's Germany and Stalin's Soviet Union, the commitment to liberal democratic principles, especially individualism, went largely uncontested in England and in the West more generally. A benign, providing government and a concomitant celebration of the independent and rationally minded citizen defined the spirit of the times and the unique feature of Western democracy.

The historically and politically situated character of Winnicott in particular and psycho-analysis more generally is thrown sharply into relief when one encounters psychoanalytically an individual who has grown up and was shaped according to different commitments and to an alternative vision of the healthy self. Most specifically, the psychic space deemed necessary by Winnicott for playful creativity is a space actively discouraged in totalitarian societies. An alter-native ideal self is posited in these regimes where the feeling self and external reality are to be experienced not as distinct but as identical.

I present this case material to illustrate two major claims. First, Winnicott's concept of psychic space as constitutive of the healthy self represents his own experience of living in a Western, liberal democratic society committed to individual autonomy, individuation and separation. This space-in-between that Winnicott astutely articulates draws upon his own unconscious experi-ence living when and where he did. It emanates from a social world valorizing precisely these ideas of separation and individuation, values embodied in his family, his school, and in his oth-erwise lived experience. In Western democracies, social institutions are organized to help realize these principles. What the China case material documents is the critically important roles that social institutions play – especially those of the political apparatus – in generating the two-dimensional self-in-formation as described by Winnicott. Rather than Winnicott describing a universal feature of human experience, as he implicitly proclaims, I argue he distills in his work the essence of the *Western three-dimensional democratic self* and proclaims it as *natural*. In naturalizing the healthy self as he defines it, Winnicott underestimates the complex environmental features that together collude in the self's formation and in the valorization of individuality. Said differently, Winnicott's "good-enough" mother is the caregiver who has sufficiently internalized culturally and specifically presumptions about individuality, separation and autonomy. And the therapist seeking to similarly provide for his or her patient by helping to establish an environment where playful creativity may occur is similarly assisting the patient to adapt to a specific political world, one very different from China today.

Second, I suggest that psychoanalysis, as it penetrates polities whose political and cultural foundational principles diverge from Western democracies, requires a fuller accounting of the task it has set out for itself. In China, the growth of psychoanalysis is significant, and likely cor-responds with dramatic economic changes that have occurred over the past two decades, with its celebration of entrepreneurship and personal initiative. Currently China might be described as a mixed model of development: deregulating the economic sphere while attempting to maintain tight political control over all other social and cultural institutions in the country. Psychoanalysis, as I argue, is a product of the embrace of a thoroughly democratic conception of the self, where individuation, autonomy and separation are the ultimate standards through which healthiness is evaluated.

Understood in this way, psychoanalysts working in China and other nondemocratic societies must be self-conscious that analytic work faces specific challenges that have not been carefully identified. In replicating a form of treatment as it occurs in democratic societies, the psychoana-lytic movement in China is a subversive one.

Therapy intended to promote the realm of experience enabling playful creativity to occur is more than importing Western mental health treatments to China. It constitutes a political project to reconfigure individuals' understanding of their psychic selves and to promote the idea of unique subjectivities. It is a project of self-transformation: an effort to create the psychic space-in-between in polities whose institutional apparatus attempt to move individuals in a dif-ferent direction.

Psychoanalysis in these instances encourages the creation of a Western, democratic self as a wedge against the efficacy of all social forces being brought to bear to close down this third realm of experience, the illusionary realm.

## Psychological totalitarianism and democratic political work: a case report of Yuzhen

A young man in his late twenties began psychoanalytic treatment with me approximately 18 months ago. He had recently moved to Los Angeles from a large city in southern China in search of a professional degree. He arrived with his wife who was also seeking further training. Their plans are to return together to China upon completion of their education. Yuzhen took advantage of his stay in the West to pursue his own psychoanalysis. Hardly a widespread preoccupation among young Chinese students, his interest stemmed in large measure from his grandfather, an eminent scientist, who himself had a deep and abiding interest in Western psychology, especially psychoanalysis. Yuzhen also believed he might benefit from the treatment. He understood that both his grandparents and their children, including his father, had been profoundly affected psychologically by their experiences in the Cultural Revolution. He was hopeful that his own treatment would enable him not to transmit to his own children the damage it inflicted psychologically on him.

Despite dramatic economic and social changes over the past decades, China remains organized as a totalitarian society. The government is in complete control of the security apparatus and the propaganda machine, effectively penetrating every sphere of social life. Each social institution has the capacity in its own way to regulate individual behavior and to strongly influence beliefs and attitudes. Boundaries between public and private life, when compared to the West, are blurred in profound ways. One's duty to the Communist Party and one's love of the nation and ancestors are promulgated as synonymous. From the first day of school, children learn that the party is responsible for the preservation of the nation. The Chinese flag, having replaced the flag of the Republic of China in 1949, features a yellow star in its center. The star expresses the centrality of the Communist Party for the new China.

Yuzhen describes his life as defined by politicized prohibitions: he remembers the fear he experienced when learning not only that the bust of Mao was required to be on display in every home in China, but that any form of sexual behavior was forbidden under his watchful eye. He recalls being reassured that upon his death he would be reunited in heaven with Karl Marx. He describes the experience of students today completing their PhDs, who are all required, regardless of academic field, to complete courses on Marxism and Chinese socialism. And he describes recently how academics in the finest universities in China are now being asked to swear that they will neither teach Western ideas nor be critical of Chinese Socialism. As I will describe, Yuzhen's psychological difficulties today are manifestations of the politics he and his extended family lived through since the 1949 Socialist Revolution. The totalitarian restructuring of society following the Revolution profoundly shaped the psychology of those subjected to it. Civil society and a stable, secure and safe private realm of sociability largely collapsed. Chinese politics, its impact on the very conception of privacy, and all the twists and turns the totalitarian regime has taken since 1949, I believe, proved to be decisive in Yuzhen's psychological structuring from the time of his birth. His own character and current emotional difficulties are deeply intertwined with China's political formation. Making matters worse for him, throughout his life Yuzhen has been most strongly influenced by the patrilineal side of his family. His entire extended family – his father, his father's parents, and his aunts, uncles and first cousins – all identified as sharply critical of post-Revolutionary China. Time and again, each generation was targeted as among those standing against the unfolding "forces of history." The family's fate during the Cultural Revolution served as the denouement of their status as the regime's opponents. Yuzhen's life was made still more complicated as he was the result of a "mixed marriage." His mother's family, too, suffered tremendously during the Cultural Revolution – but in her case, it was the result of her family, stolid members of the Communist military elite, who were identified by the Red Guard as having become too complacent in their revolutionary fervor and too comfortable in their privileged standing in the country. The fate of her family was even more tragic. Yuzhen's mother was left an orphan. Her father had been killed for his political complacency and his mother committed suicide. And still, Yuzhen's mother and father did not similarly share an oppositional stand toward the Chinese leadership. His father remained critical of the government while his mother, though deeply affected by the loss of her parents, in her quiet way was largely tolerant of the Communist regime. Thus, for Yuzhen, the Cultural Revolution brought him into treatment and, as far as he was concerned, to the source of all of his mental difficulties.

It is worth noting, that Yuzhen's story of his own personal history, as he told it, could not be narrated without him simultaneously locating his family within post-1949 Chinese history. In his mind, family realities were interchangeable with political moments. He described his parents as anti–Red Guard and ambivalent toward the revolutionary program of the Communist Party, while he describes his wife as a "communist." By that, he means that her family was once prominent members of the Communist military elite. Yuzhen, a deeply introspective person, until recently had been content with these politicized descriptions of his own personal history as a way to understand his own psychological challenges.

As his psychoanalyst and as an American, it soon became apparent that I was faced with a unique set of difficulties, which I had not anticipated. From the outset, I knew it would be incumbent on me to familiarize myself as best I could with the "local knowledge" of Chinese society. Yet developing a deeper grounding in Chinese culture – its customs, social practices, cultural values, institutional norms and so forth – did not sufficiently capture the challenges faced. The most formidable obstacle lay in the difficulties posed in applying a *democratically convened* psychoanalysis to an individual psychic formation profoundly shaped by totalitarian presumptions.

In China, a person's self-understanding both normatively and typically mirrors the perception held of it from the state. For most, citizens see themselves in the image projected upon it. For others, like Yuzhen, it operates as a mirror-opposite, its negation. Whether as an affirmation of the state's vision or its repudiation, the creation of the self is largely a response to China's totalitarian ambition. From the Western perspective, individual autonomy and personal privacy in this context are severely compromised. In Yuzhen's case, his mother's and father's different stances toward the Communist government aggravated his difficulties. They were significant in intensifying his internal conflicts. It made our work together more difficult, characterized by his shifting stances toward compliance with state-imposed civic ideals. Competing loyalties and identifications within his nuclear family, mediated through politicized lenses of loyalty and betrayal, were largely indistinguishable from similar struggles he encountered with the outside world and toward public authority.

As we began our work together, Yuzhen was ending a 3-year period of online therapy with a European, non-Freudian therapist. It began in China and continued for a time in the United States after his arrival. At the time we began seeing one another, Yuzhen suffered at times from uncontrollable rage. He has no idea of its origin, either why it began or why, at any given moment, it becomes activated and sometimes acted upon. The consequences, as he now well knows, have been devastating. At times he has physically injured his wife, and he would periodically terrorize or injure his beloved cat and dog. Through his prior therapy, he now understands some of the reasons why his rage is directed toward those whom he loves most, and also toward public figures who are in positions of authority. In adolescence, his rage would be directed most often toward his father but at times it would include others as well, including military or police figures. Soon after our work began, he began to recognize that the feelings of rage toward others paralleled how he imagined his own father's anger directed at him, when his father would become physically abusive.

Yuzhen's personal life history took time to unfold over the first several months of treatment, largely because while telling the story he would oftentimes be flooded with feelings. But in the very telling, his story and the story of post-1949 China – especially its failures – became hopelessly entwined. This was hardly a defense through intellectualization, as I early on had thought, because the various civil tragedies he was recounting were laden with intense and painful emotion. Oftentimes our sessions would end with him either in a fit of fury, as he painstakingly described various events that had transpired since 1949, or tearful, as he reflected on the ways in which the two generations of his family before him were profoundly affected. I learned of the Great Leap Forward, the anti-Rightist campaign, and most notably of the Red Guard and the Cultural Revolution. In each instance, he would situate various members of his family, always thinking in generational terms, in relation to these awful moments. Understanding the long-term and personal consequences for him, he recently concluded that "the Government consumed my parents, my parents consumed me."

Yuzhen also understands strains and conflicts within his own family, now the third generation of survivors of the Cultural Revolution, as a result of political fallout. He speaks both of himself and his wife as part of its lineage. Yuzhen never attempts to understand family dynamics independent of the political circumstances in which they occurred. For Yuzhen, there was hardly a trace of being able to capture conflictual feelings toward his father in personal, Oedipal terms. Yuzhen's father had never found much success in life, despite frequent interventions on his behalf by his eminent father (Yuzhen's grandfather). But Yuzhen had no inkling of ways the shadow of his eminent father might have plagued him as he sought to establish himself independently in the world. As a result, Yuzhen could not understand how his father might simultaneously demand success from him and, at the same time, resent and demean his achievements. In short, no prior emotional groundwork had been done for Yuzhen to understand family rivalries and passions as having their origin in anything more than the result of different forms of accommodation to the political regime. In this same way, he describes his rage at times directed to his wife as a result of his own "mixed marriage," for his wife's family had been part of the Chinese military and not significantly affected by the Cultural Revolution. His parents and grandparents, his wife and her parents, his aunts and uncles embody the fundamental divisions that the Communist victory helped construct for modern China. For him, the Cultural Revolution crystallized and magnified any tensions that had been dormant in post-1949 China and brought them alive and to center stage.

The almost completely porous boundaries between himself, his family and the telling of China's national history have produced in Yuzhen an extremely fragile self. He has never felt entirely safe from his own uncontrollable emotional life, either in his own home or in the outside world. Inside and outside, he is always on the lookout for others threatening him with annihilation. He holds an ever-present fear, sometimes manifest, sometimes latent, of being humiliated. He has suffered periodically from intense panic attacks and feelings of not being able to breathe. He often describes the experience as feeling as though he was about to suffocate. At various times he has a very "full stomach" when he feels that only by swallowing often might the fullness disappear. He pushes on his stomach to help soothe the sensation, but it remains nonetheless a very unpleasant symptom for which he has been unable to find relief.

Fears of humiliation compete with Yuzhen's awareness that he has the capacity to become suddenly overcome with uncontrollable rage. Beginning in middle school, he was a terror in school, and at times was very difficult to control. He was always among the very brightest students; nonetheless, continuing through high school he would often act out toward his teachers, toward public officials and also toward his father. He and his father had an extremely tempestuous relationship. His father would often ridicule him for poor school performance, typically by comparing himself and his superior school achievements to those of Yuzhen. Oftentimes they would fight, resulting in an escalation of the intensity and duration of punishment for Yuzhen, including physical beatings. Sometimes, Yuzhen would respond through compliance and would apply himself harder in school, oftentimes with very positive effect. It was not uncommon for him to find himself among the top two or three students in the class. His father might be mollified for a time, but it would not be long before his father would express disdain, disappointment and disrespect for him. He would often throw Yuzhen out of the house, threaten to disown him, and exact stronger and stronger punishments on him.

Especially during his adolescence, all members of his immediate and extended family perceived Yuzhen as impulsive, mischievous, angry and potentially violent. During times of good humor, he was often referred to as the "little monkey king," which emphasized his more impish, mischievous side. But when his behavior was seen as more dangerous and self-destructive, family meetings were convened where he would be interrogated about his behavior, censured, and reminded of the high standing of the family from which he came. Everyone in the family, including his grandparents, would reiterate their high expectations of him and the disappointment and shame they felt. According to Yuzhen, he was often perceived and condemned for being, in his words, "a kind of Red Guard." Coming from that family who had suffered greatly during the Cultural Revolution, this was an appellation that could not have been more damning or shaming.

Yuzhen's paternal grandparents were victims of the Cultural Revolution during the 1970s (and his great-grandmother on that side of the family nearly starved to death in the late-1950s during the Great Leap Forward). Unlike both his grandmother and grandfather's siblings who all left the Mainland in 1949, they chose to remain in the new China rather than to immigrate to Taiwan, hoping that the vision of Chairman Mao might be realized. His grandmother had watched the Red Guard march in rural China (before 1949) in large numbers and was so moved by their idealism and seemingly pristine purity, she aligned herself with their Revolutionary aspirations. His grandfather, in contrast, at the time courting his wife to be, was from an elite Republic of China military family. In his large immediate family, all of his siblings emigrated to Hong Kong. He, nonetheless, moved by his young wife's idealism, chose to remain in China, in large measure to remain with his wife. His grandparents experienced great disappointments as the Maoist regime developed, and they identified with those in the late 1950s who sought to depose the Chairman. Yuzhen's own ambivalence about traveling abroad to study and an important reason why it was delayed was explained to me because of his sense that his grandparents chose to improve the nation, not to abandon it. He sometimes feared his decision to study abroad was an act of cowardice and was shameful.

Yuzhen's grandfather died about three years ago, though not before filling his grandson with his own disappointments and bitterness toward Chairman Mao and the Revolution. He communicated to his grandson that he is expected to uphold the important legacy of the family by finding a way to better resist the tyranny of the regime. The Chinese nation was now in his sacred trust; his achievements, it was pronounced, need to be on behalf of the nation. Those aspirations should never be compromised by the dictates of the regime. The greatness the grandfather was denied as a result of the Cultural Revolution explicitly came to be expected of Yuzhen. The fate of the family name and its reputation were placed squarely on his shoulders.

Yuzhen's father, the child of this landlord family, similarly suffered, though at the time he was in late teenage years. His removal to the countryside to a work camp with others his own age was likely experienced as less devastating. Still, Yuzhen is filled with stories told by his father of his many humiliations in school before being sent away: being slapped, bullied, forced to publicly apologize for his family's background, denied doctor's care despite a serious illness until all of the children from "peasant" backgrounds were first attended to and so forth. As a result of all of these experiences, he too harbors deep resentment toward the regime for its treatment both of him and of his parents. But, in the end, he married a "Communist," Yuzhen's mother, a young, largely uneducated woman. Her personal history was traumatic as well. As I described, she was an orphan when she married. This marriage was ill-fated from the beginning, and shortly after the birth of Yuzhen, his father began having affairs with other women.

None of these circumstances augured well for Yuzhen's childhood. For as long as he can remember, there was intense conflict between his parents. Yuzhen was subject to sudden outbursts of angry physical abuse by his father, along with frequent pronouncements by his father of disappointment, disdain and diminishment. His mother's behavior was even more erratic and damaging. She demonstrated clearly inappropriate physical closeness to Yuzhen, oftentimes sexually exciting him, only then to mock him for his presumption that he could perform as a man. He suffered serious physical abuse as a young boy as well. His mother's behavior and frequent acts of irresponsibility in the care of her son resulted in Yuzhen, at the age of 7, being removed to the care of his paternal grandparents. He naturally experienced this as a profound loss and missed his mother dearly. These feelings, Yuzhen believed, could never be outwardly expressed for fear that he would be perceived as unappreciative of his grandparents' care, who had themselves already suffered greatly during the Cultural Revolution.

I will return to this clinical vignette later in the chapter. But it is worth reiterating that Yuzhen's story of himself *as he told it* was inextricably bound with the narrative of China's modern national history. As I have suggested, our work began with him holding a very weakened sense of the boundaries that exist between himself as an individual and the compliant (or oppositional) Chinese patriotic citizen, where self-understanding and the ideological understanding of the Chinese Socialist person, from a Western psychoanalytic perspective, are profoundly collapsed. As I have described, Yuzhen has taken an antagonistic stance toward the feeling of external (especially male) authority he needs to protect himself from them. His personal suffering, prior to our work together, was simultaneously a result of the conflicted internalized identifications and loyalties toward his mother and father *and* the absence of a private realm separate from the public sphere where this conflict could be more easily navigated and better circumscribed. Because of the societal intolerance toward Western personal privacy, Yuzhen could find no way to express these conflicts in a socially acceptable way. In short, Yuzhen could not serve the nation and his family name well, as his grandfather had insisted, inside a regime intolerant of public challenges to its undisputed authority. Thus as long as he remained in China, his conflicted psychic life had always been in danger of erupting into some form of antisocial activity. His issues toward authority surely remain, considering his personal history, but the likelihood for extreme forms of acting out has greatly diminished.

My task, as we both have come to understand it, has been to help Yuzhen create less permeable boundaries between his inner world, understood as his own private chamber of historically derived conflictual life and where his feelings reside, and the outside world constantly impinging upon him and encouraging some of those feelings simply to be silenced. The result for him, until now, has been a very limited realm of freedom where meaningful forms of sublimated expression can live. Psychoanalysis promises to help Yuzhen better develop the capacity to know where his inner life ends and the "objective" world begins. In this way, it will be more possible for him to distinguish both real and dangerous infringements on his own person from those outside dangers that simply project or "objectify" internal struggles. The development of this capacity, further, allows for the possibility that he more clearly demarcate his own hopes and aspirations from those imparted upon him by others.

Yuzhen and his wife's decision to study abroad offers him, for the time being, a place and a time, through his analytic work, to create a psychic capacity that, wherever he chooses to settle, will not ultimately generate antisocial and personally destructive behavior. To make this analysis effective, I believe, is not so much my success at bridging Eastern and Western cultures. A successful psychoanalysis depends on the two of us doing political work: confronting the psychic consequences of totalitarianism. By presenting the democratic alternative and being able to construct together a language of understanding based on Western psychoanalysis, the treatment constitutes an insistence on personal freedom in a space where efforts have been specifically intended to eliminate it. In this setting, psychoanalysis is a political project. Its aim is to counter the negative psychological effects that result when the individual comes to understand himself only in terms of those set by the government. In these settings, it is a subversive practice: in attempting to establish (or reestablish) borders between a person's inside and outside, it constitutes a challenge, one person at a time, to counter the totalizing efforts of public and governmental control.

## The precarious place of illusion in the world order

In one of his boldest and most captivating passages in what some regard as his single-most important essay, "Transitional Objects and Transitional Phenomena," Donald Winnicott writes,

> the third part of the life of a human being, a part that we cannot ignore, is an intermediate area of *experiencing*, to which inner reality and external life both contribute. It is an area that is not challenged, because no claim is made on its behalf except that it shall exist as a resting-place for the individual engaged in the **perpetual** *human task of keeping inner and outer reality separate yet interrelated.*
>
> *(Winnicott, 1971, p. 15, my emphasis)*

These sentences are taken from Winnicott's essay on the transitional object, "the first not-me possession," and provides his basis to assert the essential role of "illusion" in personal development: "play, symbolization, art, religion and science." Through these activities – always involving self *and* other – the person strives to overcome the strain of relating inner to outer reality, establishing a workable relationship between subjectivity and the external world. Winnicott describes this as making "progress toward experiencing." This progress, Winnicott insists, "is never completed," and defines the challenge of life for the individual long after being weaned from his or her mother.

This is a remarkable assertion, introducing to psychoanalysis an illusionary realm. While Freud conceived illusion as a neurotic human experience characterized by false belief and delusion, as in religion, Winnicott argues quite the contrary. For him, it is rather a dimension of life to be cultivated and forever maintained. Even beyond it as a description of the human psyche, transitional space describes the *social* realms of symbolization – art, religion, science and vocation – that contribute to human creativity and imagination. It is a space that can only be sustained by individuals capable of investing psychic energy in these realms. For Winnicott, the psychological start of this process begins with the teddy bear. Illusion, he insists, characterizes a person healthy enough to live playfully. Such an achievement requires a world of others that does not impinge too deeply on one's psyche and that enables and encourages the self-discovery of one's own unique "personal idiom". A "not-too-persecutory" psychic world, in Winnicott's terminology, is a prerequisite for self-discovery. For Winnicott, illusionary phenomena are the vehicles through which individuals invest dimensions of the objective world with meaning and significance, and from which they derive their own particular, idiosyncratic pleasures. For him, making this progress over the course of a lifetime means constant personal engagement with a symbolic dimension of life that allows the constant interaction between oneself and the objective world. It enables both the objectification of the inner self and the *subjectification* of the objective world. Transitional objects and transitional space describe a largely unacknowledged third or "intermediate" realm. Parts of the external environment become subjectively infused with significance occupying a psychic space that is neither exclusively one's own nor someone else's. This netherworld, neither self nor other, serves as the resting place for continually navigating one's own reality set up against the world of others and of things.

The mother–infant relationship lays the foundation for the possibility of illusion or imaginary play, the possession of a transitional object and an ongoing creative life. As Winnicott describes, the task of demarcating *between* what is generated from within *and* objective reality requires both (1) the *internalization* of external reality, beginning with one's mother, as good-enough, or not too persecutory and (2) "depends for its qualities on the *existence and aliveness and behavior of the external object*" (Winnicott, 1971, pp. 9–10). Despite the brevity of his statement, Winnicott beautifully captures the psychoanalytic perspective of what makes human beings human: a capacity to reconcile inner impulses with an objective reality or, said differently, of *not* relating to the objective world *as if* its reality is simply a manifestation of one's own subjectivity. Individuals are intended to stand outside of externality while simultaneously being constituted by it. The participation with transitional phenomena, like religion or science, helps some to navigate this terrain, to creatively or symbolically engage both self and other, and thereby to better discover the boundaries that frame inner experience with the outside world. When individuals are able to engage this world spontaneously and authentically, and internalize the pleasures of this experience, creativity – or unique human potential – is realized. Otherwise, false or pseudo-adaptations result. The "false self" enables survival in an unsupportive world (Winnicott, 1965). Through various forms of strategies of compliance, a "true self" is defensively protected and preserved. Yet when this occurs, there is a very real possibility that it may forever exist only in the shadows of one's mind, existing both to oneself and to others as almost thoroughly foreign (see Abraham and Torok, 1994; Prager, 2003).

Unlike Freud (1927), who insists that religion is an illusion to overcome, Winnicott heralds symbolization as the quintessential expression of human activity, a result of the human task of differentiating subjective needs from an already constituted social world. Winnicottian "creativity," as Mari Ruti (2011, p. 143) describes it, "calls for the subject's ability to surrender its habitual psychic boundaries to allow non-habitual modes of thought and being to emerge; in this sense, it is only by relinquishing the ordinary that the extraordinary can be discovered." From this perspective, adaptation and human survival depends on the capacity for illusionary activity. Illusion is generated by the inherent conflict that Freud (1930) so powerfully described in *Civilization and its Discontents*, between the individual desire for happiness (the claims of the individual) and the civilized world demanding of individuals various forms of renunciation of desire (the cultural claims of the group). Freud identifies this inherent conflict in social life as an ever-present battle between eros and thanatos, life forces struggling against the death instinct. In this rendering, illusion is a product of the assertion of thanatal forces seeking to contain and control erotic and life-affirming drives. The Freudian person who has worked through his neurosis no longer holds any illusions.

Yet for Winnicott, illusion does not connote distortion of human impulses. Rather, it serves as *the* vehicle through which human and collective needs reconcile one another. For Winnicott, human civilization *is* the "future of illusion." Writing in the post–World War II mid-century environment of Britain, he was far more sanguine than Freud about the possibility for human gratification to survive inside a restrictive social world. There is no mistaking Freud's pessimism late in his life, having witnessed the capacity for self-destruction during World War I and aware of the build-up toward another world war during the 1930s. Each of their views reflected, in part, the political milieu in which they were working and writing.

But, notably, each had an exclusively Eurocentric orientation of the world, both axiomatically sharing the view that Western democracies constituted the zenith of contemporary civilization. Western societies, for each, established the standard by which healthy human development was measured. But only certain political forms, I argue in contrast, encourage and possibly enable such a compromise formation. Only democratically organized societies lay the groundwork for individuals who are capable of relinquishing and surrendering certain desires to the collectivity, individuals who can coexist with the capacity of "civilization" to acknowledge and enable the fulfillment of idiosyncratic, uniquely personal, wishes. A totalitarian polity is a political formation that, in contrast, cannot respect the demarcation of the individual who stands apart from the larger world in which he or she is embedded. Psychoanalytic premises, in this sense, necessarily clash with totalitarian assumptions.

As a clinician, Winnicott naturally interests himself in those features of one's relationships with others that impinge on an ability to internalize them as good-enough or not too persecutory. He treated both children and adults who, for various reasons, experienced great difficulty in successfully negotiating between oneself and the outside world. As a result, they were unable to playfully engage the world. The outcomes, seen in the consulting room, are individuals incapable of an age-appropriate "spontaneous gesture" (Winnicott, 1965), people not able (to paraphrase Freud) to freely love and/or work. To various degrees, these are individuals incapable of *progressing toward experiencing*. Winnicott's writings focus largely on his contrasting "normal" psychological development with individuals who clinically present various forms of psychopathology. He accounts for various expressions of psychic disturbances through this lens of an internalized *not* good-enough environment, one *too* persecutory, where a person is trapped instead either in the world of "me" *or* of "not-me."

Subsequent psychoanalytic writers inspired by Winnicott, including Masud Khan, Christopher Bollas, Tom Ogden, Wilfred Bion, Jessica Benjamin and others, have attended to various psychoanalytic practices – holding and containing, creating an analytic frame, allowing regression to dependence, thinking and linking made possible – that contribute to reinstating the possibility for illusion. They each attempt to describe the interpsychic conditions, the space-in-between, necessary to encourage in the analysand this third realm of experiencing. Conceived broadly as an emotional or interpsychic corrective, analysands develop the capacity, previously stalled, to internalize a not-too-persecutory external other, now able to move toward creative living.

A parable by Slavoj Žižek captures just how difficult the therapeutic challenge is to transform an internalized bad or persecutory object into one that allows playfulness and trust in the world to reemerge. This, of course, is especially true in environments that are indeed hostile to individual creative development. Žižek tells the story of a man who commits himself to a mental hospital terrified that he is but a piece of grain and likely to be eaten by a chicken. After extensive work with his psychiatrist, the man leaves the hospital believing he is cured. He quickly rushes back, however, fearing once more for his life. When the psychiatrist reminds him that as a result of their work together his conviction grew that he is not a piece of grain and needn't fear for his life, the man responds: "I know I'm not a piece of grain and you know I'm not a piece of grain, but I don't know the chicken knows I'm not a piece of grain." For this man, a too-persecutory external reality makes experiencing, in Winnicott's sense, impossible. The parable draws attention to the contrast between a closed environment, the mental hospital, and a more challenging and frightening world beyond which the individual can exercise little control. But Žižek makes the point here as well that there are external environments that, by definition, are so dangerous to the psychic health of the person that its internalization of others as safe enough is not possible. What Winnicott characterizes as an enhanced ability to embrace one's own "personal pattern," in some social settings, may not be achievable.

Yuzhen's narrative is remarkable because he experiences his private life and public events as hardly distinguishable. His story, as he tells it, illustrates, I believe, the profound collapse for individuals of transitional space in post-1949 Chinese society. Consistent with many trauma-tized patients, he experiences the past, even those family members who lived and died before his birth, as if they coexist with him in the present. What occurred as public humiliations to many members of his family in the past now have been privately internalized as a *presently* threaten-ing world ever-poised to harm and humiliate. The objective world of today is internalized as a hostile one. His psychic reality – riven between rage and fears of humiliation – encapsulates the internalization of a world too persecutory and an inside, as a result, too dead to enable an unfet-tered flourishing of this third dimension of being. "Certain kinds of environments – oppressive or impinging environments," Mari Ruti (2011, p. 142) writes, "elicit psychic compliance. They put individuals on the defensive. And they cause individuals to die inside so as to fend off being violated, exploited or run over by the outside world."

Winnicott's passage introduces into the psychic field still more complexity. What does Win-nicott mean when he asserts here that this third realm of experience "is not challenged" because "no claim is made on its behalf"? Who makes no claim on its behalf? Why is such a claim *naturally* withheld? And is this feature of social life, as Winnicott seems to imply, universal to all humankind? Speaking of the transitional object, with which the third realm gives birth, he makes a similar claim:

> Of the transitional object it can be said that it is a matter of agreement between us and the baby that we will never ask the question: "Did you conceive of this or was it presented to you from without?" The important point is that no position on this point is expected. The question is not to be formulated.
>
> *(Winnicott, 1971, p. 12)*

Winnicott refers to those meaningful others situated outside oneself who embrace illusion, who facilitate playfulness, and who enable the "perpetual human task" of knowing the difference between one's inner world (of feeling, affect, emotion, desire, fantasy; i.e., subjectivity) and the external world (of reality, others, structure, limits, constraints; i.e., objectivity). Only then can transitional space be created and preserved and transitional phenomena be mutually engaged. When that occurs, the true self is able to *go-on-being* without impediment. Good-enough envi-ronments are those that promote a definite relationship between an individual's inner world and an external reality, always open to a fluid interchange between self and outside world, where the boundaries between the two are simultaneously clear, demarcated and sustained. Still, the boundaries, while more or less fixed, are not in place rigidly.

This process cannot occur in isolation. Others, significant in one's life, must also avow this illu-sionary world of the subject as always in creation. The forging of a healthy psychic reality requires external confirmation for it to be treated as real. Contemporary China is an exceptional case, illustrating, from the psychoanalytic perspective, the troubles that result when self and other do not successfully collude with one another to build this third realm of experience. In this sense, my analytic work with Yuzhen provides a unique angle to consider anew the writings of Winnicott.

Winnicott, unknowingly, I believe, prescribes a *special* form of social relationship, a three-dimensional one, that characterizes features of his own society – British parliamentary democracy in the mid-20th century – where private interpersonal relationships are relatively impervious to public intrusion. His formulation provides clear evidence for the particular, culturally specific individual as envisioned by psychoanalysis, not proof that as a descriptive science psychoanalysis is generally applicable around the world. This might be formulated in a different way. As psychoanalysis seeks to expand beyond its culture of origin, it should be acknowledged that the model of the mind, the person's relationship to others and others' relationship to the person are indeed deeply inspired by social conditions prevailing in the West. Its most significant challenge to modern China is the promotion of the ideal of a clear demarcation between the inner life of the individual and the collective life of the nation.

In Britain, like other Western democracies, the boundary between public and private has altered and changed over time. In the now-classic essay *Citizenship and Social Class* – written, ironically, in 1950 – T.H. Marshall characterizes Western societies as having experienced an evolution of rights as guaranteed by the state. He argues that the 18th century is noted for first granting individual rights as in freedom of assembly and expression, the 19th century political rights insuring broad-based voting, and the 20th century social or economic rights. He illustrates the shifting relationship between the state and individuals who constitute it, though noting specifically how the provisions granted by governments to individuals have gradually expanded over time. Stated differently, as the Western state has guaranteed individuals more protections over time, greater intrusiveness of the public realm on private lives has resulted. Nonetheless, despite these kinds of alterations and this movement toward a more encompassing social welfare state, the commitment to a firm boundary between private and public spheres persists. The clear and explicit preservation of the two realms in these democratic societies, while demonstrably permeable over the centuries, is in no respect thoroughly porous.

What Winnicott describes as an intermediate realm of experience, where the question of origins is "not formulated," I suggest, describes a construction particular to Western liberal democratic societies. This experiential realm helps to organize every sphere of social life, reinforcing the distinction between the public and private sphere. (Prager, 1993). Even the mother–child relationship is shaped by the sociopolitical assumptions and values that underlie it. The mother, helping to create and preserve transitional space for her infant, denotes a positive, "natural" commitment to individuation and separation. Ideas of privacy and difference, and an axiomatic belief in idiosyncratic subjectivity are taken for granted. The mother (and others) takes delight in the baby enacting his or her own subjectivity that includes choosing a transitional object and investing it with a special, sacred status. Embodied in the practice of good-enough mothering, in short, is its resonance to ideals and concepts that Western democratic societies cherish. "Not formulating" who "owns" what only occurs when the environment is neither too oppressive nor too impinging.

Even within that subset of Western societies, these conditions oftentimes do not fully obtain, and they contribute to considerable human suffering. Elsewhere, I have argued that the persistence of racism in America, beginning in the 18th century and continuing to this day, has profoundly affected the lives of African Americans. The sense of safety, security and stability as preconditions for the creation of illusionary or transitional space has been severely compromised for many, many generations of people who have been objects of this invidious thought and subsequent behavior. The consequence has been that America has systematically constrained a significant portion of its population from full-blown opportunities to creatively contribute to the nation. A too-persecutory outside world, as I have suggested, has yielded various forms of psychic deadening. Attempting to nourish the *me* and/or defining oneself as oppositional to the *not-me* has foreclosed the possibility for this population to operate in America as fully free, autonomous and separate individuals. American racism has succeeded in creating within African American communities particularly individuals for whom the illusionary realm of experience has been effectively suppressed (Prager, 2014).

The failure to promote transitional space and phenomena are not only defined in the breach, where the necessary conditions for it to occur in Western democracies do not obtain. Other sociopolitical formations today, I argue, self-consciously attempt to create for their members an alternative psychic reality. These are a set of commitments and orientations toward the individual social member that the "not formulated" question instead *be formulated* and uttered explicitly: where does your capacity to live "freely" originate? Who provides you the conditions necessary for you *to be*? In what ways are you beholden to those who established the conditions? I describe this as the totalitarian alternative: a unique social and political arrangement whose goal, among others, is to create a psychic reality for the individual that contends with a Western democratic one. Deference to the state is required, and acknowledgment of the government and party's role in providing what is necessary for survival. This reality largely collapses the differences between public and private, between self and others and, in so doing, devalues the third realm of human experience that Winnicott identified and powerfully endorsed.

## Totalitarianism, boundary impingements and the attack on creative thinking

Totalitarianism is characterized by a unique set of internalized others that, as a rule, *normatively* challenge Winnicott's illusionary realm. It is characterized by an external reality where specific claims *are made* on the potential intermediate *space between*. These impinge on personal efforts to reconcile the strain between one's own need and external reality. They can be experienced either as an oppressive force or a deadening one. What is privileged instead is the task of attempting to reconcile demands imposed from the outside (internalized constraints persecutory in nature) to the tasks of internalized self-regulation (personal desires, tastes, ideals, ambitions). The consequence is a unique form of selfhood, distinct both from democratic societies, from authoritarian ones and purely tyrannical ones.

Political theorists Hannah Arendt (1951) and Michael Walzer (1983) both characterize totalitarianism as a unique form of social and political organization, with specific features that distinguish it from other political forms: liberal democracy, tyranny and authoritarianism. It has had no predecessors prior to the 20th century, because, as Walzer emphasizes, its authority is based upon a mass political movement organized around some messianic vision of the future. As a result of its emergence we are now confronted, Arendt insists, with a set of moral and political considerations unique to our age, ones in which the whole Western tradition of political and moral debate no longer sufficiently inform current ethical and moral questions. The totalitarian option now places freedom and personal responsibility within a new framework of consideration characterized by the foregrounding of objective reality and compliance to it while squeezing back the transitional three-dimensional space co-created by self and others. In necessarily subordinating oneself to a larger purpose and deferring to political agents themselves empowered a result of their relation to the larger social vision, the idea of selfhood is placed against a political backdrop of collective possibilities never before imagined. In its most thorough form, selfhood itself is redefined, the destruction of the unconscious is sought, and the capacity to think creatively as oneself is abrogated.

Arendt describes a unique relation in this form of rule of the present to the past, where memory itself serves as a political instrument of the state to achieve its own popular legitimacy.

The results are individuals who learn never to hold too firm a commitment to any one view of the past or to any one set of heroes: any given narrative can be dramatically and in an instant altered, always dependent on the needs of the movement. Power, dependent on the pursuit of some totalizing vision, requires among its leaders resistance to routinization of authority, accomplished through constant revision of the messianic message. Rule, on behalf of the vision, requires a permanent revolution, Walzer claims; otherwise, it comes to be seen as less than total in its aims.

A recent blogger on social media in the People's Republic of China (PRC) is reportedly to have commented on a changing post-revolutionary China: in the first 30 years or so after the Chinese Revolution, she noted, the expectation was that individuals would turn against members of their family and their neighbors if they demonstrated a failure to be loyal to revolutionary ideals. For the past two decades or so, individuals were expected to promote their own self-regard on behalf of building a new economic order, that is, to act selfishly and to be greedy. What has become of the Chinese soul, this blogger queried? The question might be posed more profoundly, in light of the previous discussion: what has become, since 1949, of Chinese selves? (see Plaenkers, 2010). In the PRC, the Great Leap Forward of the late 1950s, the Cultural Revolution of the mid-1960s and early 1970s, and the Economic Miracle of the present all serve or have served to constrict transitional space, to interfere with individuals' "progress toward experience." The globalization of social media clearly presents a major contemporary challenge to totalitarian political authority. The "Chinese soul" has nearly disappeared, according to this blogger, while the Chinese self has been under sustained attack. The disappearances, it might be said, are the result of the collapse of illusion and transitional space. Psychically speaking, this has been the key victim of the profound transformation occurring in Chinese society since 1949.

Totalitarianism signifies the collapse of the distinction between public and private. There *should be* no realm autonomous from the state. It is a boundary collapse unique in world history. Yet the effect extends beyond the difficulty to experience an inner reality distinct from an all-too-powerful outside world. The failure to know subjectively life as a private person generates, as well, an inadequate capacity to separate past events, even those that occurred in generations prior from one's own, from those of the present day. Life today can only be lived falsely or inauthentically because it fails to escape from the long shadows of the past. With little capacity for creativity, the totalitarian subject today lives in his or her own bodily reality forged in the past, perhaps in the messianic vision of its founders, or in the acquired oppositional stance toward it. This constricted realm of creativity yields an incapacity to experience this day from days that came before, a diminished ability to differentiate between personal indignity suffered now from the public indignities of before, a limited ability to distinguish today's oppressiveness from the coercion and constraint imposed in the past. Time remains continuous with little sense in the here and now of forward progress. People in totalitarian societies continue to live in the past, a traumatic one, and describe it *as if* it were the present.

On a more optimistic note, the aim of this misrecognition is a vehicle to preserve the "true self." For Winnicott, misrecognition succeeds in defending a genuinely harrowing fear, nonrecognition or annihilation. The kernel of spontaneity, or the idiosyncratic personal pattern, while submerged, doesn't die. Rather, in totalitarian societies, it requires a form of conserving, that is, preservation through psychic sequestration. Transitional space serves as a bridge between, as James Gorney (2011) writes in an essay on Lacan and Winnicott, the imaginary and the symbolic; without the bridge, or with an impoverished one, creative symbolization of the human world is stymied. What remains instead is a fantastic conviction of the constancy of the human world and its unchangeability – what I have referred to elsewhere, with respect to the persistence inequality as a consequence of American racism, as a melancholic resignation to the *what is* (Prager, 2014). Nonetheless, for Winnicott and others, these are all defensive forms of self-protection. The possibility remains that the objective world might change to a less persecutory one, enabling the efflorescence of the unique person who lies in waiting. The true self is in hiding until conditions prevail that enable its full and therefore creative expression.

In tyranny, it might be said, there is no protected private realm: everyone and everything is fair game to best serve power and control. In democratic societies the boundaries are often negotiated and modulated but never abandoned, while in authoritarian societies the distinction is harshly enforced: public power and control, on the one side, private freedoms on the other. Authoritarian political rule, in fact, oftentimes depends precisely on the preservation of this rigid boundary between the two spheres. In totalitarianism, no private sphere is exempt, including families, religious institutions, workplaces and schools. The early mother–child relationship reflects these values. Individual autonomy and personal idiosyncrasy are subordinated to values of compliance and obedience. The individual person is expected to self-regulate by defining himself or herself first and foremost as serving the interests of family, state and nation. Significantly, no effort is made to demarcate state from nation – in fact, just the opposite. Selfhood and personal identity themselves are shaped by such proscription – including the fluidity of that which is proscribed – and creates, at least compared to the democratic sociopolitical form, an ahistorical person with little in the present anchoring from one's personal or even generational past.

## Conclusion: two illustrative vignettes

The following are two illustrative vignettes drawn from my sessions with Yuzhen. When he was about to have his last sessions with his European analyst, he didn't speak about it in our session, though I was aware of this impending loss. Instead, he repeated again the traumas and humiliations suffered by his grandparents during the Cultural Revolution. The more he spoke about it, the more he was able to access both fury at the Red Guard as well as his sadness, clearly welling up with tears. When I suggested that part of his sadness and rage in the moment might be expressing his feelings about the loss of his therapist, he stopped, thoroughly confused by my suggestion. Despite his considerable capacity for insight developed during the course of his therapeutic work, the idea that an affective response of anger and sadness may be, for the time being, misapplied to a narrative largely irrelevant to the feelings of the moment, had not occurred to him. Nor did he have a clear sense that "ordinary" or personal events had a place in our work together, only his inability to deal with regulating his private life from affect experienced as too strong or behavior considered antisocial. The boundary-less character of his self-experience, as he had lived it for so long, is now only beginning to take shape.

In a group meeting that Yuzhen attended prior to departing for the United States, he was asked to give a name to the painful stomach symptoms he experiences. Surprisingly, he immediately uttered the words "Red Guard." At that moment, he realized to his horror he had internalized his grandparents' sense of an external evil: the agency for them of brutal suppression, and he came to believe that, especially in extreme periods of stress, his spontaneous swallowing (so as to burp) is his futile effort of expelling the evil in him. The Red Guard is within him, in his words, "fully monsterized," sometimes taking the form of anger at his grandparents for removing him from his mother, sometimes at his mother for abandoning him, sometimes at his father for having too high expectations of him. In the session, he was able to speak the voice of this "little" Red Guard: "the fucking intellectuals, the fucking capitalists, they are forcing me to fail. They want to humiliate me. We have to wipe out all of the adults." In fact, as he was relaying this insight to me, he recalled a moralism he learned at school that came from the Soviet Union: "Don't use the suffering of your generation to cover over your own evil." At the end of this session, Yuzhen recounted a blog of an aged member of the Red Guard who solemnly offered his apology for his behavior during the Cultural Revolution. Yuzhen was powerfully moved by the apology, greatly admiring the man for courageously coming forth as he did. The recognition of past suffering, apology and forgiveness is what he longs for the most. Yuzhen wept profusely as he recounted the story to me. He commented that this was the first time he could recall weeping with a male authority figure witnessing it. And, so, currently Yuzhen remains dominated by an internalized external reality still too persecutory and always ready to humiliate. He was so moved by the apology as it signaled the possibility for the resurrection of personal agency distinct from state domination. For us, our task to is to facilitate, if possible, a new therapeutic reality – a transitional space – so the analysand can better discover his own personal pattern of progressing toward experience.

## References

Abraham, N & Torok, M 1994, *The shell and the kernel*, vol. 1 (N Rand, ed), University of Chicago, Chicago.

Arendt, H 1951, *The origins of totalitarianism*, World, New York.

Freud, S 1927, 'The future of an illusion', in J Strachey (ed), *Standard edition of the complete psychological works of Sigmund Freud*, vol. 21, Hogarth, London, pp. 3–56.

Freud, S 1930, 'Civilization and its discontents', in J Strachey (ed), *Standard edition of the complete psychological works of Sigmund Freud*, vol. 21, Hogarth, London, pp. 57–146.

Gorney, J 2011, 'Winnicott and Lacan: A clinical dialogue', in L Kirschner (ed), *Between Winnicott and Lacan, a clinical engagement*, Routledge, New York, pp. 51–64.

Marshall, TH 1950, *Class, citizenship and social development in citizenship and social class and other essays*, Cambridge University Press, Cambridge.

Plaenkers, T 2010, 'The cultural revolution in the mirror of the soul', in T Plaenkers (ed), *Landscapes of the Chinese soul, the enduring presence of the cultural revolution*, Karnac, London, pp. 83–120.

Prager, J 1993, 'Politics and illusion: A psychoanalytic exploration of nationalism', *Psychoanalysis and contemporary thought*, vol. 16, pp. 561–595.

Prager, J 2003, 'Lost childhood, lost generations: The intergenerational transmission of trauma', *Journal of Human Rights*, vol. 2, no. 2, pp. 173–181.

Prager, J 2014, 'Melancholia and the racial order: A psychosocial analysis of America's enduring racism', in L Chance & J Andrews (eds), *The unhappy divorce of sociology and psychoanalysis, diverse perspectives on the psychosocial*, Palgrave Macmillan, London, pp. 284–316.

Ruti, M 2011, 'Winnicott and Lacan: Living creatively in a postmodern world', in L Kirschner (ed), *Between Winnicott and Lacan: A clinical engagement*, Routledge, New York, pp. 133–150.

Walzer, M 1983, 'On failed totalitarianism', in I Howe (ed), *1984 revisited, totalitarianism in our century*, Harper and Row, New York, pp. 103–121.

Winnicott, D 1965, 'Ego distortion in terms of true and false self', in M.M.R. Khan (ed), *The maturational process and the facilitating environment: Studies in the theory of emotional development*, International Universities Press, New York, pp. 140–152.

Winnicott, D 1971, *Playing and Reality*, Routledge, New York, pp. 1–34.

# 5

# Wilfred Bion and psychoanalysis

*Rafael E. López-Corvo*

In elaborating this chapter I will be more inclined to provide an outlook of Wilfred Bion's main theories, rather than to reflect on the series of mental constructs he produced. I hope that in doing so, I will be able to achieve a greater clarity in his communications. Bion was very demanding about avoiding concepts that were so previously handled that he felt they were contaminated or "saturated," as he preferred, with other misleading meaning.

In the process of describing Bion's contributions I will consider four different periods or *caesuras*:[1]

1   from the time he was a psychiatrist and produced his well-known work on groups;
2   after he became an analyst in 1950 and worked with individual patients, providing several papers about his clinical experience with psychotic patients, which were later published as *Second Thoughts*;
3   after Melanie Klein's death in 1960 when, according to Meltzer, Bion's creativity sprouted and he produced perhaps the most original aspects of his theory, which appeared in five books: *Elements of Psychoanalysis*, *Learning from Experience*, *Transformations*, *Attention and Interpretation* and *The Grid*;
4   his considerations about what he designed as the "Sigma space" ($\Sigma$), intuition and "O."

In addition to Freud and Klein, Bion is possibly the third great contributor to the structural understanding of the working mind. If following Fairbairn we consider Freud's approach as a "psychology of impulses," we could consider Klein's as a "psychology of affects" and Bion's as a "psychology of intuition." However, these are not three separated psychologies, for each one has added to its predecessor.

There is an increasing interest in Bion's work, possibly because of the unquestionable input his work has provided to the clinical comprehension of psychoanalytic theory and practice. Ignoring such contributions could present the danger of being left behind in the continuous evolution of psychoanalysis and psychotherapy. However, we must recognize also the great density and obscurity of some of Bion's prose and concepts, which makes it very difficult for anyone to understand

and validate the useful relevance of his thoughts in everyday practice. I have previously stated that Bion has used

> a holistic and coherent "binocular vision" of the mind, covering a wide spectrum: from the ultra-spiritual to the infra-physic; from the illumination by O to the reproduction of emotions measured inside the rigid squaring of the Grid. If his intention and dedication can be understood as a global conception of the mind, we should also, when understanding his work, conceive it from a holistic approach: one Bion for an act of faith, and at the same time, another for the "mathematization" of the mind, as a defender of contradictions who was able to palpate the certitude in the center of the uncertainty.
>
> *(López-Corvo, 2003, pp. 16–17)*

## Group psychology

The first field of interest Bion investigated was group dynamics (1948). It was produced at the time when he was a psychiatrist and provided him with a well-earned international recognition that strongly influenced the work of intramural psychiatry, group therapy and the creation of thera-peutic communities. I believe that such early interest in the psychology of groups was perhaps an intuitive attempt to provide meaning to his existential experience. I have previously stated:

> Bion grew up among groups, very large groups. From the age of eight at the boarding school, and afterward, at the age of eighteen when enlisted to fight in War World I, he was able to empirically observe and existentially suffer the social behavior and the immediateness of anonymous multitudes.
>
> *(López-Corvo, 2003, p. 5)*

His experience in group therapy started with the British Army during World War II, when at the beginning of the 1940s, at the Northfield Hospital in Birmingham, England, he treated sol-diers suffering from war neurosis. His main innovation was the creation of "self-interpretative" or "leaderless" groups, where the "abstinence law" and "neutrality" of the therapist, similar to individual psychoanalysis, were maintained. He then stated:

> One disadvantage of the group situation is that seeing, say, six to ten people at the same time leads one to suppose that there are six or ten discrete personalities present. In other words, the distinct physiology of the participants is so dominant that one is liable to assume that the personality is similarly bounded by physical appearance.
>
> *(Bion, 1987, p. 298)*

And also: "The group analysis would have to depend on the assessment of the 'gist' of an obtruding emotion. It bears a similarity to psycho-analysis, but it is not the same thing" (Bion, 1974, p. 190).

Bion determined that two different but parallel forces would rule any kind of group in progress. In the first place, there is the reason that originally motivated the creation of that particular group, which will determine the conscious purpose according to reality. At the same time, there is a series of powerful emotions running parallel, which might surface at any given moment and dominate the original intention of the group. The original purpose he referred to as the "sophisticated or working group (W)," while the parallel emotions he named the "basic assumptions" or "ba"). The working group always maintains a contact with reality, recognizes the need to evolve and is capable of working together for a collective aim, away from the control of the basic assumptions. It is dominated by the tendency to deal with conflicts in a rather "scientific" manner (1948, p. 99), and is equivalent to the ego according to Freud's postulates (1911) (1948, p. 143). The working group could last hours or months, depending on the capacity of the group to solve the pressure of the emotions from the latent *ba*, which continuously attempts to dominate the group.

Bion defined *group mentality* according to basic assumptions, as an unconscious consensus of several individuals in a group that will involuntarily neutralize all individual aspirations (1948, p. 59). He distinguished three different kinds of *ba*, depending on which type of emotions dominated the group: (1) "dependence *ba (Dba)*," (2) "fight and flight *ba (Fba)*" and (3) "pairing *ba (Pba)*." Only one *ba* will dominate the group at a given time, while the other two will remain hidden inside a virtual space he referred to as the "proto-mental system (pm)," which he considered as a

> system or matrix where differentiation of physical and mental states began. It contains precursors for emotions present in all basic assumptions including those that remain latent. When any of the basic assumptions become manifest and its feelings predominate in the group, the others that remain latent stay contained within the proto-mental system; for instance, if fight–flight is manifest, dependent and pairing emotions will be latent.
>
> *(López-Corvo, 2003, p. 105)*

The presence of a particular *ba* can be recognized according to the kind of emotions that dominate the group, which act as links that structure the whole group. Guilt and depression, for instance, will dominate the dependent group, while messianic hopes rule the pairing group and anger and hate control the fight-flight (1948, p. 166). In the course of 1 hour, for example, a therapeutic group could be dominated by one or several *ba*, or one *ba* can dominate the group over several months. The communication between members of the group is instantaneous, regardless of cultural differences or incapacity to form symbols, and could be achieved following a mechanism Bion referred to as "valence," or the tendency of an individual to combine with the group, depending on a specific *ba* (1948, pp. 151–152). The dominating *ba* represents what Bion has described as the "establishment," which might be present in any existing social structure. In summary, Bion considered three entities: (1) the individual, (2) the group mentality and (3) the group culture, represented by those aspects of behavior resulting from the conflict between the dominating group mentality and the individual interest. There are also three different kinds of cultures: dependence, fight-flight and pairing (1948, pp. 59–61).

The leadership is established as a consequence of projective identifications always resulting from unconscious needs within the group. Different from the leader of the working group, the *ba* leader has only contact with the internal reality of the specific *ba* (1948, pp. 144–145). I have previously stated:

> The possibility of a member becoming the leader of the group depends on his capacity to instantly and involuntarily (maybe voluntary) combine with every other member of his group, as well as to fulfill the necessary requirements needed to be the leader of such a specific basic assumption (ba). The main difference with the leader of a work group (W) relies on the access this leader has to external reality, whereas the basic assumption leader is confined to his specific assumption.
>
> *(López-Corvo, 2003, p. 105)*

All *ba* have a leader: in the dependence group (*Dba*), the interaction between the group and the leader will be similar to the doctor–patient or teacher–pupil relationship, where ambivalence and feelings of guilt due to greed and depression prevail (Bion, 1948, p. 166). The dynamic in the fight and flight group (*Fba*) will be similar to those present in the army, and the group will search for leaders capable of fulfilling the need either to fight or fly – usually individuals with paranoid traits who defend themselves from internal persecution by projecting the "enemy" outside. Feelings of anger and fear predominate in this *ba*. In the pairing group (*Pba*), the leader could be "nonexistent" or "unborn," and might be identified not with a person, but with a metaphor, an idea or an inanimate object (1948, p. 155). About this group I have previously stated that

> there is the ineluctable paradox that the leader would never be born, that is, the hope must stay in suspense, and it should always remain as such: "pure hope." At the very moment in which is felt that idea or leader can become a reality, feelings of anger and destruction will again predominate.
>
> *(Bion, 1948, pp. 151–152)*

> Under the dominance of this kind of ba, feelings of messianic hope will prevail. These feelings could also be observed outside the therapeutic group, like in religious beliefs or in the aristocracy, and in some sense, assures Bion, in the analytic couple [Ibid, p. 176]. A good example is given by Bion in presentation No. 4 of his Brazilian seminars.
>
> *(López-Corvo, 2003, p. 105)*

## Individual psychology

Bion seldom referred to these concepts about group dynamics after his analytical training, although we could presume they evolved into other ideas. The interaction between the working group and the basic assumptions, for instance, became represented within individual psychology, as the *non-psychotic* and *psychotic* parts of the personality, respectively. Also, it could be deduced that the basic assumptions corresponded to those emotions originated from points of *fixation* associated with the three stages of Freud's psychosexual development: dependence (*Dba*) being equivalent to the oral stage; fight and flight (*Fba*) to the anal stage; and pairing (*Pba*) to the genital stage.

The subject of the "double" was already discussed by Freud (1919), under the name of the "Imaginary Twin." This was his first psychoanalytically oriented article where he attempted to defend Klein's controversial theories on the metapsychology of a pre-genital Oedipus. It was followed by an extensive and paradigmatic study on psychosis, as well as a phenomenological conceptualization of the process of *thinking*, or in his words, of an "apparatus to think thoughts." These clinical articles, published in the 1950s, were later compiled and partially reviewed by Bion in his book *Second Thoughts* (1967). The articles include "Notes on the Theory of Schizophrenia" (1953), "Development of Schizophrenic Thought" (1956), "Differentiation of the Psychotic from the Non-psychotic Personalities" (1957a), "On Arrogance" (1957b), "On Hallucination" (1958), "Attacks on Linking" (1959) and "A Theory of Thinking" (1962b).

### Psychotic and non-psychotic parts of the personality

It is obvious from these publications that Bion, at the beginning of his analytical practice, worked mostly with schizophrenic patients, as was the common clinical trend at that time. Perhaps Bion was then under the influence of a similar confusion of those who believed Klein's concept of "paranoid-schizoid position" was referring specifically to psychosis (Grosskurth, 1986, p. 429), instead of a mechanism present in all individuals. It was a confusion Bion later recognized as he stated:

> I further consider that even in the severe neurotic there is a psychotic personality that has to be dealt with in the same way. [Bion, 1967, p. 42] . . . On this fact, that the ego retains contact with reality, depends the existence of a non-psychotic personality parallel with, but obscured by, the psychotic personality. [Ibid., p. 46] . . . I consider that this holds true for the severe neurotic, in whom I believe there is a psychotic personality concealed by neurosis as the neurotic personality is screened by psychosis in the psychotic.
>
> *(Grosskurth, 1986, p. 429)*

In a similar inquest, Meltzer (1978) pointed out that Bion did not discriminate between the "psychotic part of the personality" and clinical psychoses, because due to Klein's influence he, as many others, envisioned the paranoid-schizoid position as representing the fixation point for schizophrenia. Meltzer also added that it was not clear whether Bion "thinks that this part of the personality is ubiquitous or only present in the person who actually presents a schizophrenic disorder" (1978, p. 26). Several years later in Brazil, Bion remarked jokingly:

> I am amazed how often an analyst seems to think that he can hardly claim his title unless he has treated many schizophrenic patients. From the little I know I find it difficult to believe that so many analysts are treating schizophrenics. Such a claim belongs to the domain, not to the science of psycho-analysis but to fashion. As it is sometimes the fashion to wear feathers in hats, so psycho-analysts wear "psychotics in their hair."
>
> *(1974, pp. 92–93)*

There was a difference in the defense format also. While the non-psychotic part of the personality uses repression, the psychotic part uses projective identifications. Because there is no repression, the unconscious is replaced by a world made of objects similar to dream furniture, in which these individuals dwell. Extension of mechanisms of splitting and projective identification increments the breach between both parts of the personality to such a point that any attempt to reunite them becomes impossible.

The change from the *psychotic* to the *non-psychotic* part of the personality is achieved accordingly with the presence of an epistemological apparatus for thinking Bion referred to as "alpha function," which emulates a digestive system and whose main purpose is, among many other purposes, to convert beta elements into alpha. Alpha function interacts according to the model "container–contained," where the psychotic part could contain the non-psychotic, or vice versa. Behavior will depend on which part contains which and for how long. In the case of clinical psychosis, for instance, the psychotic part contains the non-psychotic almost all of the time; the opposite will occur in a person who displays a kind of "insightful awareness"; this leaves the middle ground for borderline pathology.

The opposite, that is, the change from the *non-psychotic* to the *psychotic* part of the personality is produced following a special sequence Bion referred to as "reversal of alpha function." Following this mechanism, alpha elements "cannibalize" themselves and change back into special kinds of beta elements Bion designated as "bizarre objects," which are always projected and confused with reality. "Ordinary beta" elements represent all forms of sensory perceptions that remain stored in the unconscious waiting for a thinking mind or alpha function to provide them with a meaning. Bizarre objects differ from ordinary beta elements because they contain aspects of the ego and superego. A clinical example I have used somewhere else (López-Corvo, 2014, pp. 52–53) will make these theoretical descriptions more comprehensible:

> While lying on the couch a patient was coherently reasoning over oedipal matters associated to a previous interpretation. Suddenly, she saw a little spider on the ceiling and rushed to the door in total panic. What induced a logically thinking mind to suddenly change into a state of psychosis? Schizophrenic patients are capable of sustaining a conversation with absolute logic and suddenly switch to a delusional system when the matter of argumentation changes to a particular sensitive ground. What happened to this gifted patient's alpha function that up to that instant was totally engaged, and logically discerning about important material? How could such an insignificant, harmless, minuscule spider, produce such an uncontained, abrupt, and violent reaction? Further investigation revealed the little spider was not so "innocent," that it was pregnant with memories from nocturnal sexual games with her siblings, of crawling little fingers over her genitals they referred to as "little spider walking." The spider had become a powerful "absence-presence," a negative space or "minus K," which Bion (1962a) baptized as "a bizarre object." In other words, Bion discriminates between beta elements that result from the accumulation of undigested sensory experiences and those secondary to the digestion of alpha elements:
>
>> we could consider that reversal of alpha-function did in fact affect the ego and therefore did not produce a simple return to beta-elements, but objects which differ in important respects [little spider] from the original beta-elements [sexual game] which have no tincture of the personality adhering to them. The beta-element differs from the bizarre object in that the bizarre object is beta element plus ego and superego traces [the spider's superego accuses!].
>>
>> *(Bion, 1962b, p. 25)*

The spider lost its real characteristics of harmless insignificance once it became the container of the patient's projection, – "beta elements plus ego and superego traces" – acquiring the power of an unyielding monster as it takes place in any bad dream. Every time the external object is enveloped by projected beta elements and thereby loses its true mien, the individual will remain immersed inside a world of projections or "dream furniture," unable to wake up, similar to Plato's description of the men in the Allegory of the Cave (López-Corvo, 2014, pp. 47–48).

On an equal footing with his paper on psychotic and non-psychotic parts of the personality, there were also his articles "Attacks on Linking" (1959) and "A Theory on Thinking" (1962a). The paper "On Arrogance" (1957b) was a warning to psychotherapists acting in the form of arrogance and impatience.

## On thinking

By the end of the 1950s, the world of psychology was dealing with two major models that were parallel and did not interact. On the one hand was Klein's psychoanalytical contribution on affects, and on the other was Piaget's input on cognitive psychology. Both ran their own particular course to great depths. Klein's theory was wrongly conceived as an explanation for the mechanisms of psychosis, and Piaget's considered as a "psychology without emotions." I remember stating in a congress on child psychology in Bello Horizonte (Brazil) that a "marriage" between Klein and Piaget was absolutely indispensable!

In 1962 this missing link was produced when Bion fashioned his theory on thinking (1962a), which he compared to a philosophical theory, because for years philosophers had been concerned with similar inquiries, although his theory was also different because it carried the intention of being used in ordinary psychoanalytical practice, and its hypotheses to be empirically validated by psychoanalysts. Although Bion followed a model based on the digestive apparatus, very similar to Piaget's notion of "assimilation and accommodation," as far as I know they never quoted each other's works.[2]

Bion contemplated the existence of a "thinking apparatus" or "alpha function" that was forced to happen due to the pressure exercised by the presence of thoughts. It could be similar to saying that the need to eat food produced the existence of a stomach. Thinking was then the consequence of two significant constructs: *thoughts* and an *apparatus for thinking*. Depending on the ego's capacity to tolerate frustration and to contain the presence of the absence of the object, Bion considered two possibilities: (1) if tolerance was satisfactory, the absent object-like "no-breast" – or "bad object" – could be transformed into a thought that will induce the creation of an apparatus for thinking, capable of allowing a more feasible toleration of frustration; (2) if the capacity to tolerate frustration was inadequate, the absence of the object – or "bad object" – will pressure the mind toward evasion of frustration and instead of creating a thought, the no-breast will change into a persecutory bad object or beta element[3] that can only be used for evacuation via projective identification. According to Bion, alpha function and the digestive apparatus have common origins, for it is the same one that has originally dealt with sense impressions related to the alimentary canal: milk and affect – or the "good breast" – arrive at the same time (1962a, p. 57). The "swallowed" thought is independent from the existence of an object that has really been put inside the mouth; in this way, the breast or the "thing in itself" is equivalent to the idea in the mind and reciprocally undistinguishable from the thing in itself in the mouth (López-Corvo, 2003). Further, in his systematization of the apparatus for thinking, Bion used the notion of container–contained, a model that became central to the future development of his theory.

Alpha function is active continuously – day and night (Grotstein, 2007) – because it alternates between two disparate dominions: one is *conscious* and voluntary, the other *unconscious* and involuntary; this is why Bion originally referred to alpha function as "dream-work α" (Bion, 1992, p. 73; López-Corvo, 2003, p. 26). They seem to work differently, but interact continuously. The conscious one deals with sensory impressions in the manner I have just explained, digesting raw sensory impressions or beta elements and changing them into alpha elements. However, whenever there are facts that were not properly digested while awake because of low frustration tolerance – in the sense that some "lies" were not adequately dealt with – the unconscious alpha function could elaborate a dream while sleeping, with the purpose of revealing the unexposed truth. In other words, the unconscious alpha function corrects the duties shirked by the conscious alpha function that, in order to avoid frustration, were not dealt with while physically awake; a situation equivalent to what Freud described as "day residue." This is why Bion stated that dreams are not, as some people might think, the consequence of "indigestion," but the opposite: the product of a digestion of whatever might have been left undigested. It is this unconscious form of alpha function that is used by a mother in a state of intuitive "reverie" when attending her baby, or the analyst in a similar fashion when listening to the patient without memory and desire. In other words, analysts attempt to "dream" the patient's discourse using their unconscious alpha function in order to procure O – the ineffable, or the "Form" in Plato's theory – and then use their conscious alpha function to change O into K (knowledge) with the purpose of producing the interpretation. We follow a similar itinerary when we attempt to achieve the meaning of a dream produced by the patient's unconscious alpha function, using the patient's as well as the analyst's conscious alpha function.

For Bion the main purpose of dreaming will be to avoid "frustration intolerance" induced by the facts of reality. "Wish fulfillment" falls into this category, but is not the only method; there are many other possibilities of frustration produced by the limitations of reality. Bion was critical of "primary and secondary process," finding the theory "true, but weak" (1962b, p. 54). He thought that, due to the existence of alpha function, the *unconscious* exercises activities that could be identified with *consciousness* (secondary process), and the opposite, of *consciousness* presenting behavior compatible with *dream* activity (primary process). Dreams during sleep are a product of alpha function (dream-work α); but also, if awake, when consciousness is dominated by the psychotic part of the personality and alpha function is precluded, the individual would be in a state of hallucinosis, where reality and phantasy are not distinguished. In this same direction, the main purpose of dream-work for Bion will not be determined by the need to deceive a censorship, but to evade frustration; and the raison d'être of dream-thoughts as well, would be to modify the reason of frustration. I believe that an essential source of frustration results from the conjoint of actual facts presented by reality and automatically produced emotion from early pre-conceptual traumas triggered by the actual facts. Freud had advised quite early over these matters:

> We have learned that no hysterical symptom can arise from a real experience alone, but that in every case the memory of earlier experiences awakened in association to it plays a part in causing the symptom.
>
> *(Freud, 1896, p. 197)*

Alpha elements congregate as a membrane Bion named as the "contact barrier,"[4] which positions itself between conscious and unconscious – in the preconscious – where it helps to discriminate between being awake and being asleep, being conscious or unconscious, or being or not being receptive to the truth elaborated in dreams. In this last sense, this barrier will preserve the sleeping as Freud originally expressed; a kind of discrimination also carried out by the conscious form of alpha function. However, when this fails, the individuals might think they are absolutely awake, although they could be experiencing a nightmare by being immersed in a world of projective and introjective identifications. It will be very similar to how men were depicted by Plato when living inside the Cave and believing that images projected on a wall represented true reality. Perhaps this mental construct introduced by Bion as the phenomenology of the alpha function could be considered, after Freud, as the "third topography"!

## Container–contained (♀♂)

The model of container–contained[5] is a central instrument Bion used to comprehend the dynamic of a working mind. "It ranks," said Grotstein (2007), "as the best-known and most widely used, both in theory and in technique" (p. 151). The precursor of this model can be observed in Bion's work with groups at the time he was a psychiatrist. He used the feminine sign (♀) for the "container" and masculine (♂) for the "contained," but leaving out any sexual connotation (1970, p. 106), I have previously described the interaction as follows:

> They are linked [container and contained], according to the pleasure principle, to objects or concepts such as vagina–penis, mouth–breast, thinker–idea, or to models such as "evacuation-retention," "remembering-forgetting," etc. (Ibid, p. 29) The preference about when to use this model is similar to the decision of when to "include" or "exclude" something, and related to questions like "what?," "where?," "when?," or why is something included or excluded.
>
> *(López-Corvo, 2003, p. 70)*

For instance, if the psychotic part contains the non-psychotic, the person could behave like a madman, as long as that containment remains, even if the person is not a psychotic individual. Conversely, the non-psychotic could contain the psychotic and the person will act sensibly and logically. By the same token, if an individual contains an idea he or she could become very creative; however, if the idea contains the person he or she could become a fanatic. The mechanism can acquire higher levels of abstraction, for instance, in the situation where a word contains a meaning, or the opposite, where a meaning contains a word.

Bion described three different forms of interaction between container and contained: commensal, symbiotic and parasitic (1962b, p. 91; 1970, p. 95):

1    "Commensal" represents a condition where both container and contained benefit from each other, like an invention that profits from a thinker and vice versa. This experience will enhance alpha function resulting in the capacity to learn from experience and the production of sensible knowledge or +K.
2    "Symbiotic," where one will destroy the other. The word "suspect," for instance, originated from Latin *suspicere*, a compound formed from the prefix "sub-," meaning "under" and *specere*, "to look at." Originally this could have referred to someone's need to search impulsively or look under the bed, for instance. Even though suspect still bears a similar connotation, the original meaning of a compulsive looking-under had disappeared or been contained by the use of the word.
3    Finally the relationship could be "parasitic," where both, ♀ and ♂, would destroy each other, for instance where a relationship dominated by envy and revenge will leave at the end only pain and destruction. Bion had emphasized this condition and refers to it as *withoutness*, a situation completely dominated by envy that can be observed in some borderline pathology, where feelings of fear, envy and hate are projected into the object, preventing any possibility of a commensal type of interaction as well as the production of +K. The end result could be a serious state where the ego "not only is unable to neutralize the wish to die, but removes the wish to live" (1962b, pp. 97–99), something Bion represented as "minus container–contained," ($-♀♂$) or withoutness, meaning an internal object without an exterior. It is an alimentary canal without a body. It is a super-ego that has hardly any of the characteristics of the super-ego as understood in psycho-analysis: it is a "super" ego. It is an envious assertion of moral superiority without any morals. In short it is the resultant of an envious stripping or denudation of all good . . . and will continue this process till $-♀ -♂$ represents hardly more than an empty superiority-inferiority that in turn degenerates to nullity.

*(1962a, p. 97)*

## The links

Bion considered three main "links": hate (H), love (L) and knowledge (K), which summarize all other existing emotions, such as envy, gratitude, depression, sex, guilt and so forth. These represent hypotheses about emotional relationships that take place between human beings (Bion, 1992, pp. 249–250, 262–270). They are like "constant conjunctions"[6] related or not to the senses. If I were to say for instance, "I love coffee," this could be emotions or hypotheses about constant conjunctions of impressions that I could have perceived by the senses, but if I were to say, "I hate my anxiety," this would be different, because anxiety does not carry taste or odor (Bion, 1992, pp. 266–267). Hypochondria, suggested Bion, might correspond to an attempt to set up a link with a psychic quality, when substituting physical sensations with sense information that it is absent in psychic quality. In this sense, Bion suggested that communicating with patients presents similar limitations, because when they refer to their anxiety, we might not know what exactly they are talking about, because anxiety has no physical qualities.

Bion considered the existence of positive as well as negative links (+H, +L, +K and −H, −L, −K) that do not represent opposite emotions, like −L is not equivalent to +H. Bion was extensive in his evaluation of −K but said little about −L and −H. I think positive links are related to truth and negative to lies, which can be used for evacuatory purposes. I think Bion preferred to use "hate" and "love" instead of "aggression" and "libido," as Freud did, because he was not referring to drives or impulses but to emotional links. A simple way to comprehend the difference between positive and negative links is through the use of emotional dynamics present in the transference. For instance, some aggression observed in the transference toward a mother-like internal object that has been projected into the analyst is not a true aggression against the analyst. Instead, it represents false hate or −H aimed at a narcissistic object placed inside the analyst by means of projective identification. Such aggression can also be directed toward an internal object, in ways I have previously described in mechanisms of self-envy (López-Corvo, 1992, 1995). By the same token, love present in the erotic transference is also a false link or −L, since it is not a true emotion honestly linked to the analyst, but consequence also of projective identifications from internal objects narcissistically located in the analyst. These mechanisms represent a form of defense against the incapacity to mourn and contain the loss of the original objects. In other words, false or negative links are hypotheses about unremembered emotional memories.

About minus K (−K) Bion said more, like the dynamic observed in what Bion describes as "reversible perspective," a condition where both, patient and therapist, run in parallel dimensions without ever really communicating with each other, sort of like a "dialogue between the deaf." Minus K also represents the central mechanism present in intellectualization as a form of defense. About this Bion said the following:

> Interpretations are part of K. The anxiety lest transformation in K leads to transformation in O is responsible for the form of resistance in which interpretations appear to be accepted but in fact the acceptance is with the intention of "knowing about" rather than "becoming."
>
> *(1965, p. 160)*

To illustrate I would like to use the case of a patient I have previously referred to:

> A 32 year old patient, the last of three brothers, remembered being sent away when very small to a summer camp. Although he remembers little about the event, feelings appearing in the transference showed that it was a very traumatic experience. He only remembered two situations: that he was always carrying a camera with him, to the point that he was nicknamed "little camera," and that he had a dream where he saw a car with someone inside, that was pushed away by the powerful stream of a nearby river, which in reality was a dry water bed. Motivated by the memory of the camera he searched family albums for pictures and felt rather bewildered after finding nothing. It was then interpreted that the camera he carried had just that purpose, to make sure he would remember nothing, it was a "minus camera," to photograph absences and forgetfulness (−K) as the only means to make sure something was completely forgotten [being sent away] in order to avoid terrible mental pain. He wished not to photograph the presence of the absent breast, or what Bion would refer to as a "minus point": (−.).
>
> *(López-Corvo, 2003, p. 180)*

At a given moment he got curious about the real truth of these memories and decided to visit the summer camp several years later. He found the place very different, invaded by "delinquents," and when he called at the door, two "murderous dogs" appeared. I then said that perhaps the picture he did not wish to take was the invasion of his memories with "murderous violence" because of the impotence he then experienced when sent away; the only picture taken that *remained* was the car with someone inside (his parents? brothers who stayed at home?), which was being carried away, *but not to be ever carried away* (López-Corvo, 2003, p. 180).

## "Mathematization" of the mind

Throughout most of his work, Bion seriously attempted to grant psychoanalysis the status of a scientific deductive system, relying on mathematical constructs taken from Euclidian geometry. He further elaborated what he started during the previous period as the understanding of an "apparatus for thinking," which in addition he referred to as "alpha function" or "alpha space." I believe that most psychoanalysts and psychotherapists face the need to produce, for their own use, a comprehensive and multidimensional model of the working mind, similar to sailors who require numbered coordinates as latitude and longitude to enable them to find their bearings in the unknown immensity of the sea. Psychoanalysts might feel pressed to create a similar instrument to help them find their way in the immensity of an unknown and always changing sea of abstractions, and to journey at ease into all corners of the mind. This, I believe, was perhaps what inspired Bion to conceive the Grid, and what Grotstein (2007) has baptized as "dream ensemble." Bion devoted several works to this endeavor, such as "Elements of Psycho-analysis (1963), "Transformation" (1965), *Two Papers: The Grid and Caesura* (1977) and *Taming Wild Thoughts* (1997). The Grid became the representation of the working mind and its capacity to digest thoughts and change them, from raw sensory impressions to mathematical calculus. In 1965 he stated, "I wish to introduce as a step towards formulations that are precise, communicable without distortions, and more nearly adequate to cover all situations that are basically the same" (Bion, 1965, p. 125). In order to describe what his purpose consisted of, Bion (1992) stated that

> a set of hypotheses which form a deductive system; that is, which is arranged in such a way that from some of the hypotheses as premises, all the other hypotheses logically follow [1992, pp. 2–3] . . . A peculiarity of psychoanalysis is that the scientific deductive system is a series of hypotheses about hypotheses about hypotheses . . . [Ibid., p. 46] [it is] . . . any system of hypotheses in which certain hypotheses occupy a high level in the particular system, and are used as premises from which lower-level hypotheses are deduced. [Ibid., p. 156]

### The Grid

Attempts to conceptualize the mind in order to create a working model that satisfies our enquiries would not be free from greater difficulties, particularly if there was a demand for achieving a "perfect instrument." Bion, for instance, endeavored to produce a complicated system of coordinates he named the "Grid," following instrumentations isomorphic with the concept of analytic geometry invented by Descartes, which permits one to locate positions of a given point on a plane using a pair of numbered axes: vertical ($y$) and horizontal ($x$). The horizontal or $x$-axis, also known as the "axis of uses," depicts the *synchronic* architecture of a working mind and was inspired by Freud's well-known paper "Formulations on the Two Principles of Mental Functioning" (1911). The vertical or $y$-axis, also referred to as the "genetic axis," represents a *diachronic* dimension that is based on the systematic evolution or transformation of thinking from sensual and undetermined experiences, to more sophisticated and abstract forms of conceptualization. The horizontal axis, from column 1 to *n*, operates following dynamics compatible with the container–contained ($♀♂$) model, while the vertical axis, on the other hand, follows the progressive movements of Klein's positions: PS→←D (Bion, 1963, p. 34).

a)   *Horizontal axis:* Bion refers to this function as "schematic" or axis of "uses," representing the "mind" that "contains" thoughts and allows them to evolve (vertical axis). It is considered to be incomplete ( . . . *n*), meaning that eventually it could be expanded. There are six columns in this axis: (1) definitory hypothesis, (2) Ψ (psi), (3) notation, (4) attention, (5) action and (6) *n* . . ., indicating possible addendums. Any statement could be a definitory hypothesis. The interpretation, for instance, stands for a hypothesis that synthesizes the meaning of something, representing facts that are bound by a "constant conjunction." It is also limiting because the statement involved in the hypothesis excludes all other previous assertions. There is always as well a negative element, because if we believe that something *is*, in some way we are also assuming that it might be *not*. In other words, if we say that today is Monday we are also implying that it is not Tuesday.

In classical psychoanalysis, column 2, designated by Bion with Greek letter Ψ, would correspond to defenses in the patient and of countertransference resistance in the analyst. Bléandonu (1994, p. 166) suggested that this column could be related to the *proton pseudos*, a concept used by Freud parodying Aristotle, when he referred to the "first lie" present in a hysterical patient. For columns 3, 4 and 5, Bion used Freud's 1911 article "Formulations on the Two Principles of Mental Functioning." About these columns I have previously stated the following:

*Column 4* refers to what Freud defined as attention, especially to the way in which the analyst's listening takes place, to free floating attention or to the search and discovery of

*Table 5.1* The Grid

| | Definitory Hypothesis 1 | Ψ 2 | Notation 3 | Attention 4 | Inquiry 5 | Action 6 | . . . n |
|---|---|---|---|---|---|---|---|
| **A—β-element** | A1 | A2 | | | | A6 | |
| **B—α-element** | B1 | B2 | B3 | B4 | B5 | B6 | . . . Bn |
| **C** **Dream Thoughts** **Dreams, Myth** | C1 | C2 | C3 | C4 | C5 | C6 | . . . Cn |
| **D** **Pre-conception** | D1 | D2 | D3 | D4 | D5 | D6 | . . . Dn |
| **E** **Conception** | E1 | E2 | E3 | E4 | E5 | E6 | . . . En |
| **F** **Concept** | F1 | F2 | F3 | F4 | F5 | F6 | . . . Fn |
| **G** **Scientific Deductive System** | | G2 | | | | | |
| **H** **Algebraic Calculus** | | | | | | | |

meaning . . . It also refers to the attention given to repetition of previous propositions or constant conjunctions . . . *Column 5* is related to inquiry, curiosity, exploration or discrimination of facts related especially with search for *moral* meaning . . . In the first Grids Bion referred to this column as Oedipus, mainly because of the tenacity with which Oedipus, according to the myth, had "inquired" about the truth (Bion, 1997, p. 10) . . . *Column 6* is related to acting out, in the patient as well as the analyst. According to Bion, the analysis itself could sometimes be also used as a form of acting out.

*(López-Corvo, 2003, pp. 121–122)*

b)   *Vertical axis*: It is formed by *non-saturated* elements ready for a realization[7] or experience, which will thrust these elements to evolve toward a higher level of abstraction. Each stage of this axis is a record of a previous one and a pre-conception of the subsequent stage. Successive growth from A to H implies a difference in degrees of sophistication instead of a difference in functioning, as observed in the horizontal axis (Bion, 1963, p. 87; Bion, 1965, p. 43). These are similar to mechanisms of integration and disintegration described in the Kleinian Ps→←D positions; however, changes between A and H also correspond to mechanisms of container–contained ($♀♂$), where a pre-conception (row D), for instance, is contained in a conception (row E), and this one contained in a concept (row F), and so on. There also exist emotional links, similar to the horizontal axis, like L, H and K elements (Bion, 1963, pp. 34–35). The growth of this axis will hinge on several mechanisms such as: (1) psycho-mechanics, (2) alternation of particularization and generalization (concretization and abstraction), (3) successive saturation, and (4) emotional drives. (Bion, 1963, p. 84). I have previously summarized these mechanisms as follows:

a) *Psycho-mechanic* is described by Bion as a condition that takes place in the relationship that exists between projective identification and the alternation of the paranoid-schizoid and the depressive position, in relation to K. Bion considers that fragmented bits might be capable of providing integration and solutions to problems, that will facilitate the alternation present in PS→←D and also in $♀♂$.

*(López-Corvo, 2003, pp. 126–127)*

In other words, there is a natural tendency toward mental growth, due to the capacity of part objects to consolidate on their own accord and to move toward total objects and the depressive position.

*Particularization and generalization* processes are related to abstraction; that is, to a process by which an element is particularized following a realization or saturation, from where later on a generalization takes place. Naming the process and then remembering it (notation) will prevent the loss of the experience by dispersion or disintegration of its components. *Generalization or abstraction* could be understood as a process by which an unsaturated element becomes saturated . . . *Bion relates emotional impulses to a premonitory state* that would represent more of an emotional condition than an ideational content . . . although similar to a pre-conception, a premonition is also private and unconscious. In other words, emotions are to pre-monitions what ideas are to pre-conceptions (López-Corvo, 2003, pp. 126–127). I believe it is something similar to Freud's theory on "signal theory."

Row A of the vertical axis corresponds to β-elements, which cannot discriminate the *animate* (human) from the *inanimate* (thing), neither the subject from the object nor what is moral from what is scientific. These beta elements also have a capacity for ego's imprisonment and can only be used as projective identifications. The progress from A, or beta elements, to B, or alpha elements, is equivalent to a switch from a *pre-conception* to a *conception* and will be similar to the model of container–contained (♀♂). Bion stated:

> β-elements are intended to denote objects that are unknown and therefore may not even exist. By speaking of α-elements, β-elements and α-function, I intend to make it possible to discuss something, or to talk about it, or think about it before knowing what it is. At the risk of suggesting a meaning, when I wish the sign to represent something of which the meaning is to be an open question, to be answered by the analyst from his own experience, I must explain that the term "β-element" is to cover phenomena that may not reasonably be regarded as thoughts at all.
>
> *(1997, pp. 10–11)*

Row B corresponds to α-elements, the product of α-function. I had previously wondered whether the significance of this function on the whole genetic evolution of thinking in this axis, might not justify it being located at the margin of the Grid. Row C represents a type of thought category that could be articulated in aesthetic terms, usually visual images or pictograms like those use to fabricate dreams, myths or hallucinations. Bion suggested that this category should have a grid of its own (1977, p. 3). Row D stands for pre-conceptions, similar to Kant's concept of *empty thoughts* (1967, p. 111), representing a state of mental expectancy for some kind of experience or realization. It is similar to a baby's expectation of the breast right after birth, or the analyst's anticipation when figuring out the meaning of the manifest content and the structure of the unconscious phantasy in order to produce the interpretation. Bion represents the pre-conception with the following formula: $\Psi(\xi)$, where $\Psi$ represents an incognita, the unknown, while $\xi$ signifies an unsaturated element, which once saturated by knowledge, becomes a conception and will hence correspond to row E, that results from the realization of a pre-conception. In summary, a conception might be considered as a variable that has been replaced by a constant, or as Bion has previously expressed it:

> Row F corresponds to formulations of psychoanalytic and non-psychoanalytic theory, which intend to show scientific observations. Conceptions change into concepts by a process "designed to render it free of those elements that would unfit it to be a tool in the elucidation or expression of truth."
>
> *(1963, p. 24)*

Rows G and H, as well as brief introduction of the use of the Grid, I have previously summarized as follows:

> *Row G* is of little use and must wait until the psychoanalytic scientific deductive system develops. Something similar could be said about *row H*, which also might have to wait until algebraic systems build up. Free floating attention and relaxed unsaturated listening to the patient's material, correspond to D4, that is, "attentive pre-conceptions." The comprehension of this material would imply a movement from D4 (a pre-conception) to a conception or E4. Searching for a confirmation comparing one material with the other would signify a movement towards E3 and E5. Structuring the interpretation, verbalizing impressions, integrating and so on, would correspond to F5. Lastly, when the interpretation is verbalized with the intention of affecting the patient's mind, it could be placed on G6.
>
> *(López-Corvo, 2003, pp. 130–131)*

Rafael E. López-Corvo

Meltzer described how some aspects of the vertical axis operate:

> The "molecules" of psycho-analysis, are seen to be compounded of elements from three
> rows of the grid, B, C and G, that is the sensa, or alpha-elements which have been derived
> from the perception of the emotional experience, the myth or dream thought in which its
> elements are bound, and the passion of the scientific deductive system into which it would
> grow if allowed.
>
> *(1978, p. 67)*

## Sigma space (Σ)

Bion (1992) has distinguished between alpha and beta spaces," where "alpha space" represents the
world of reality as it is perceived by the senses, "namely certain active constellations of thought
that are associated with the discipline of biology and spoken of in those terms" (p. 314).[8] Bion
also referred to the world of sigma (Σ), a space he compared with the *noösphere* described by
Teilhard de Chardin[9] and depicted as the space of the *intuitable* that can be used in order to reach
a close acuity of reality's extreme spectrum of "infra" and the "ultra real." It is subjected to its
own terms and conditions even if these rules were not even known:

> These realities are "intuitable" if the proper apparatus is available . . . The conditions in
> which the intuition operates (intuits) are pellucid and opaque . . . These are [the opacities]
> memory, desire, understanding. All are opacities obstructing "intuition."
>
> *(Bion, 1992, p. 315)*

### *Bion's dilemma: the grid and human intuition*

In summary, the Grid represents the conjunction of two dimensions: the space or synchronicity
(horizontal axis) and time, transformation or diachronicity (vertical axis). Possibly influenced by
Husserl (Levinas, 1963), Bion started to envision the importance of another dimension, that of
*intuition*, a practical instrument to read the elusive unconscious that he categorized as O. The conflict presented to Bion, to conceptualize these three magnitudes on the same plane, was perhaps
similar to Einstein's challenge of integrating velocity with time and space dimensions in order to
produce his theory of relativity.[10] Velocity is the main characteristic of intuition; Sartre (1943)
for instance, stated that "L'intuitionest la présence de la conscience à la chose,"[11] meaning that
the intuition is there already, ahead of the conscious mind. Because of such speed, intuition can
be used in psychoanalytic practice to attempt "reading" the unconscious as reliably as possible,
because the unconscious is an organ that incessantly changes, making it very difficult to grasp.
What might be true at this moment might not be true later on. It is obviously impossible to place
intuition with regard to more actual dimensions such as mental time and space.

If we examine the index of Bion's four last works portraying the main kernel of his theory, we
find that in *Learning from Experience*, published in 1962, neither O nor the Grid was mentioned;
while in "Elements of Psycho-analysis," published in 1963, the Grid was mentioned 9 times and
O was not cited at all. In "Transformation" (1965), O is mentioned 19 times and the Grid 14;
and in *Attention and Interpretation* (1970), O is cited 9 times and the Grid only once. If I were to
speculate about these numbers, I would say that when *Learning from Experience* was published,
these dimensions of O and the Grid were not yet completely systematized as they were later in
"Elements of Psycho-analysis," a work dealing mostly with the evaluation of the horizontal or
synchronic axis, and "Transformation" afterwards, referring to the vertical or diachronic axis. In

his last book, I gather, Bion was becoming aware of the impossibility of introducing intuition as the third dimension of the Grid that then remained as a limping monument, missing a third and indispensable leg to be sustained. His disappointment was already there in 1974, when in Brazil he declared that

> I think it is [the Grid] good enough to know how bad it is, how unsuitable for the task for which I have made it. But even if it inflicts a certain amount of mental pain I hope you can turn it to good account and make a better one.
>
> *(1974, p. 53)*

And in 1980, when asked how difficult the Grid was, he said: "Not for me, only a waste of time because it doesn't really correspond to the facts I am likely to meet."[12]

Is there a possibility of placing intuition within the framework of the Grid? In the first place intuition is related to unconscious thinking or "dream thoughts," which means that there is no intellectual mediation of a manipulated epistemological system, and the benefits of those functions associated with consciousness, like *notation, attention, inquiry* and *action* present in the axis of uses, do not apply. It could either belong to the unidentified territory of $n$, or placed in row C of the vertical axis, as Bion already recommended together with dreams and myths (1992, p. 314). I am differentiating here between intuition as an automatic and involuntary quality of the mind independent of the senses, and O as a conjecture of intuition. It is similar to dream thought, which Bion had placed in row C of the vertical axis, a category he suggested should amount to a grid of its own (1977, p. 3). By means of intuition O evolves, if picked up with an "act of faith" and transformed into K, then it would become substance to manufacture an insightful interpretation. The insight can also act as a kind of turbulence,[13] capable of producing a catastrophic[14] change, once an already established equilibrium moves into a different one. Although it could be understood as a paradox, Bion conceived O at the end as a kind of beta element and located it at the first box (A1) of the Grid; after all, O presents itself as an undigested sensory impression that requires transformation in K. O is like an impression that unconsciously infects the mind and has to be picked up with an act of faith, in order to ascertain the meaning enclosed in the intuited and change it into K. In order for analysts to allow intuition to flow and provide it with significance – as Bion often said – it is indispensable to free themselves from three opacities, *memory, desire and understanding*, as an enduring and continuous discipline. Alpha function is important only if it is "receptive" or an "emitter" of sigma, but it could induce a turbulence if confused with sigma. Intuition represents for Bion an attempt to reach the true core of what is unconscious, because, as he stated, "unconscious could sometimes be replaced by obvious but unobserved" (1992, p. 316).

## "O"

In 1965, Bion stated the following:

> What the absolute facts are cannot ever be known, and these I denote by the sign O. My description is of the facts as they appear now to have been at the time they took place . . . The first question is, What is O, or, to express it in more conventional terms, what was the patient talking *about*?
>
> *(1965, p. 17)*

O was also defined as the "ultimate reality," and following Kant, as "the thing in itself." It is incommensurable, the unknown and absolute fact that takes place in the work of an artist, or in a state of illumination as it is experienced by a religious person. O is continuously becoming, like Heraclitus's river: O of this moment will be completely different from tomorrow's O and once it is known it will be no longer O. It is not a "position," but a possibility, which might be feasible or not. From the perspective of the analyst and using Klein's psychology, O will be like the *intuitive* capacity to perceive the "unconscious phantasy." From the perspective of the patient O would be equivalent to the *insight*; but for both, it is always a sudden revelation of truth. Falsehood cannot be a genuine becoming of O, because O is always the absolute truth of any object. In psychoanalysis any O that is not at the same time common to both patient and analyst, and therefore is not available for the transformation of both of them, must be ignored and considered irrelevant, for it would not be feasible to investigate it in any way (Bion, 1965, p. 48). In relation to O I have previously expressed that,

> Transformation of O into K [knowledge] (O→K) represents the act of structuring the interpretation, but this act will require from the analyst a special stance in order to previously allow transformation of K into O, a condition already present in Freud's "free floating attention," although observing in Bion's notion a greater density that perhaps indicates a connection with Zen Buddhism.
>
> *(López-Corvo, 2003, p. 200)*

O can appear in different forms: as a sensation, an emotion, an image and so on. A clinical vignette will be useful. I remember Tony, a young patient I have previously described (López-Corvo, 2006, pp. 197–201), who consulted because he felt very shy with girls. His parents divorced when he was around 8 years old. He had a brother 4 years his senior, whom he admired and envied because he felt he was like his father: "very at ease with girls." His mother was a very attractive, dominating and seductive woman, and she, together with the absence of his father as an essential object that could have rescued him from the Oedipal ambush, played a determining role in Tony's existence. At a given moment, he remembered my words that if he would let go he could end up seducing even his own mother. I reminded him that I had also stated that it seemed as if he had difficulties differentiating between his mother and the rest of women. At this moment he produced a dream:

> He was at a party with many attractive women. One of them, the most beautiful, approached him and invited him to dance, and while they were dancing they were also kissing and everybody was looking at them. After some time he left her, but another woman, even prettier, came close to ask him to dance also, and the same scene was again repeated. At the end, both women were looking at each other filled with anger, jealousy, and ready to fight for his attention.

He did not give any associations, and I said that there was a great dissimilarity between how he usually performed in front of girls and the dream content. He agreed and added that in the dream, he acted just as he would really like to be in real life. His brother, he said, was very much like the person in the dream. As I was listening to him with my eyes closed,

> I was suddenly invaded by a particular blue color, and I thought it might have represented a dream-like phenomenon, although, later I thought it was a true representation of O. I associated this kind of blue color with the one in a water fountain I had built and painted many years previously with my son, when he was around 8 or 10 years old. I remembered that the experience of building this fountain was very rewarding for both of us. Using this memory

[This was like a process of transformation of O→K], I then said to my patient, that perhaps he was feeling that his father had taught things to his brother that he did not teach to him, and that this made him very angry, inducing complicity with his mother against his father. This was similar to the complicity he could have developed with her against me, like for instance not paying me on time, because he also felt that I, just like his father had not done in the past, was not teaching him anything either. I thought that he wanted me to teach him how to seduce or make love to a woman without being so frightened. He laughed very loudly and added that his father was very good with women, a real Don Juan . . . who had many lovers always looking for him: "Perhaps you are right," he said, "but I wouldn't know how to be like that, I would love to, but I don't know how. You are right, my father never taught me how."

*(López-Corvo, 2006, p. 200)*

## Dreaming the session

Meaning portrayed by the unconscious could best be conceived by intuitive approximation because the language spoken lacks the sincerity and precision of conscious significance. The interpretation of dreams, for instance, and the interpretation of the manifest discourse articulated by the patient using free association, follow opposite paths. In the first we move from the abstract to the concrete, and in the latter we move from the concrete to the abstract. Freudian psychoanalysis tries to reach *repressed* unconscious contents by making them conscious, while the Bionian approach attempts to decipher unconscious messages by using *unconscious* alpha function, similar to how "unconscious messages" are manufactured using unconscious alpha function when physically sleeping.

Bion stated that "psychoanalysts will have to invent and manufacture a way of 'seeing' the other person" (1974, p. 27), for what the person might stand for, or at least close to that possibility, perhaps to be

> as forgetful as we can of the various facts in order that our intuition, however feeble, can have a chance of seeing something, however faint and however obscure, in what the patient is saying to us. We need a kind of mental binocular vision – one eye blind,[15] the other eye with good enough sight . . . How can I put to you that I think you ought to use your intuition, however feeble and however misleading and however dangerous the possible wrong path be?
>
> *(Bion, 1974, pp. 63–64)*

To interpret a dream we use logic based on either deductive or inductive reasoning, moving from the parts to the whole or vice versa; different from the logic used to interpret the manifest discourse. In this case, it would be necessary to "dream the session" (Bion, 1992, p. 120), using mechanisms similar to the logic present in the *unconscious* alpha function, or logic by *transduction*, that moves from the parts to the parts – or details to details – instead of following deductive or inductive logic. Ferro (2009) has referred to this form of instrumentation as "transformation in dreams."

An example could be useful: a young patient often suffering from depressive bouts as a consequence of cruel persecutions and continuous debasing from a primitive superego had started to work selling newspaper subscriptions door to door. Unable to discriminate between the purpose of his work (selling subscriptions) and a deep unconscious need of finding meaning to his existence through the Other's "acceptance" (buying his subscriptions), he often succumbed to "unfair" states of depression whenever he sensed he had failed his superego's selling expectation.

However, he felt that in spite of his ambivalence it was important to continue with his work. I experienced in the countertransference similar feelings of ambivalence about the analysis that he had not yet verbalized. Caught in a maelstrom of feeling depressed because he was not selling and not selling because he felt depressed, he had the following dream: his father and sister came to visit him and brought his dog that went to sleep on his bed, but the dog in the dream was completely different from his dog in real life. He stated that the dream was very similar to what had happened the night before when his father and sister came to visit and did in fact bring his dog, which he had left at his parent's home. The only difference was that his dog was a completely different breed than the dog in the dream. I said that it seemed the dream was about dogs because the rest of the dream was equal to real life. He said he liked his dog better than his family, and could not understand why his dog was different in the dream, as he would never even think of changing him. I said that perhaps the dream was about that quality of faithfulness, about being faithful to his work and not quitting (not changing) even though he often felt like doing so. Similarly, his analysis also brought conflictive issues that induced in him ambivalent feelings about the analysis and thoughts about whether to quit or continue – finding it difficult for him to consider such feelings in the session (projected superego), he then dreamed about them.

Louise is another patient who has been dealing, for some time, with unconscious envious and murderous phantasies related to sibling rivalry toward her younger sister, something that filled her with guilt and persecutory anxiety. At a given moment and after a long silence, she stated that she had nothing to say and that her mind was occupied with other things that had nothing to do with her treatment. I said that everything in her mind had to do with her treatment. She continued:

> I thought of calling my sister to tell her I was leaving, but I changed my mind. I am thinking of cleaning the apartment thoroughly before I leave I had washed the sheets, and taken all the garbage out. I cleaned the refrigerator very carefully and threw away leftovers that were getting rotten. As you can see these are unimportant issues. I did not want to leave the keys with anybody; the concierge told me someone else had left the keys and when they came back, they had found several long-distance calls made from their phone. I am thinking to leave around 2 o'clock. I think I am going to drive myself instead of using my driver. He talks too much about X [a well-known politician who has been accused of corruption and murder].

Considering that her manifest discourse represented internal elements similar to those found in any dream, I interpreted that she did not wish her sister to know and had cleaned her apartment thoroughly "of any trace," trying her best to conceal, from herself and the rest of us, of the presence of an unconscious "murderous child element" that wished to destroy her younger sister by poisoning mother's milk with feces (she cleaned the refrigerator by throwing away spoiled food) because she wanted to have total control and did not want to have any surprises (did not want to leave the keys with anybody because she did not wish to find surprise calls). She wished also to be her own driver, because she feared that I would continuously insist about the existence of a corrupt and murderous "Louise" element in her.

## Notes

1 About *caesura*, Bion stated the following:

> Picasso painted a picture on a piece of glass so that it could be seen on both sides. I suggest that the same thing can be said of the caesura: it depends which way you look at it, which way you are traveling. Psychosomatic disorders, or soma–psychotic – take over the choice – the picture should be recognizably the same whether you look at it from the psychosomatic position, or from the soma–psychotic position.
>
> *(Bion, 1977, p. 306)*

2  I have previously stated the following:

> Similar to Bion, Piaget also used the digestive apparatus as a model to understand the mind. Piaget introduced the existence of two functions: a) Organization, and b) Adaptation. Any living being act implies a certain degree of organization: from a protozoa's simple act of phototropism, to the more complex act of a mathematic calculus. Adaptation entails a dynamic and progressive process that involves also two functions: a) Assimilation and b) Accommodation. Assimilation represents the act of incorporating an external reality inside mental schemata that is already there. Accommodation on the other hand, represents the change that the schemata must suffer in order to assimilate the new experience.
>
> *(López-Corvo, 2003, p. 33)*

3  I will prefer to say a "preconceptual trauma."

4  Bion described another barrier as a "screen of β-elements," representing

> a construct in the phenomenology of the apparatus to think thoughts, structured as an agglomeration of beta-elements placed between the unconscious and consciousness within the mind of psychotic patients or the psychotic part of the personality. It is responsible for a state of confusion similar to dreams, as well as the possibility of massive projections of beta-elements.
>
> *(López-Corvo, 2003, p. 263)*

5  Following Diogenes Laertius, there were at least 10 men in antiquity with the name of Bion; however, he only referred to the biography of Bion (ca. 325–250 B.C.), the "philosopher from Borysthenes" [Olbia], a town located on the north shore of what is now the Dnieper River, in the Ukraine. According to Laertius (Bion, 1925, p. 429), "when referring to a wealthy miser," Bion stated: "He has not acquired fortune; the fortune has acquired him." A statement that on the line of the model of container–contained described by our Bion, it strikes as an uncanny coincidence. After all, as Wilfred Bion often expressed, "truth does not need a thinker"!

6  It is a concept Bion (1967, 1992) borrowed from David Hume, who stated that two elements are constantly conjoined when we infer one from the other not by reason, but from the particular experience that surrounded them, even though we might fail to penetrate inside the logic of such conjunction. However, once the conjunction is established by chance, it will repeat by compulsion (López-Corvo, 2003, pp. 67–68).

7  Bion defined "realization" as an experience with an external fact. See Bion (1965, p. 12).

8  Beta space, on the other hand, was considered like a "multi-dimensional space of thoughts without a thinker." I have considered that beta space corresponds to a "*traumatized state*" and alpha space to a "*non-traumatized state*" (López-Corvo, 2013).

9  A word used by father Pierre Teilhard de Chardin to explain the notion of a "sphere of reflection, of conscious invention, of conscious souls" or "collective mind or conscious," some kind of global trade network, communication, accumulation and exchange of knowledge, related to fields such as economy, "psychic affiliations" and so on. For many, Chardin had predicted what we know today as cyberspace or the Internet.

10  One of the principles involved in the theory of relativity is that if speed were to reach the speed of light, space and time will be affected.

11  "Intuition is the presence of consciousness in the thing."

12  I have previously reviewed Bion's concept of O, and not wanting to repeat myself, I would like to refer the reader to those works: López-Corvo (2003, 2006); also Grotstein (2007).

13  Bion defines turbulence as a state of resistance or mental disturbance associated with change, in relation to communication with others, and most of all, with what might be considered as a psychological growth of great importance (1970, p. 34). It is similar to the way in which a stream of transparent water remains unnoticed, until the moment it finds an obstacle that generates turbulence. The *noumenon* or thing-in-itself remains invisible, unknowable – like the transparent stream of water – that could only be intuited, although it could be known through a realization – or turbulence – with an object, giving then place to a phenomenon (López-Corvo, 2003).

14  Concept based on René Thom's "catastrophe theory" that Bion relates to abrupt changes between two *stable states*, as a theory to explain many situations involving a rapid transformation of behavior from an old system into a new one, like the catastrophic change or injury that a new truth might create on the old one that has not adapted. It is catastrophic in the sense that it is accompanied by feelings of disaster

in the participant and that it is sudden and violent in an almost physical way. Usually occurs when a change that has taken place cannot be contained, following container–contained theory (López-Corvo, 2003).

15 Tiresias, the Greek soothsayer, was blind.

# References

Bion, WR 1948, *Experiences in groups*, vols. 1–4, Tavistock, London.

Bion, WR 1953, 1967, 'Notes on the theory of schizophrenia', in *Second thoughts*, Jason Aronson, New York, pp. 23–35.

Bion, WR 1957a, 'Differentiation of the psychotic from the non-psychotic personalities', *International Journal of Psychoanalysis*, vol. 38, nos. 3–4, pp. 266–275.

Bion, WR 1957b, 1967, 'On arrogance', in *Second thoughts*, Jason Aronson, New York, pp. 86–92.

Bion, WR 1958, 1967, 'On hallucination', in *Second thoughts*, Jason Aronson, New York, pp. 65–85.

Bion, WR 1959, 1967, 'Attacks on linking', in *Second thoughts*, Jason Aronson, New York, pp. 93–109.

Bion, WR 1962a, 1967, 'A theory of thinking', in *Second thoughts*, Jason Aronson, New York, pp. 110–119.

Bion, WR 1962b, *Learning from experience*, Karnac Books, London.

Bion, WR 1963, 1977, 'Elements of psycho-analysis', in *Seven servants*, Jason Aronson, New York.

Bion, WR 1965, 1977, 'Transformations', in *Seven servants*, Jason Aronson, New York, pp. 1–183.

Bion, WR 1967, 1993, *Second thoughts*, Karnac, London.

Bion, WR 1970, 1984, *Attention and interpretation*, Karnac Books, London.

Bion, WR 1974, 'Brazilian lectures', *Rio/Sao Paulo* No. 2, Imago Editora, Rio de Janeiro.

Bion, WR 1977, *Two papers: The Grid and Caesura*, Karnac Books, London.

Bion, WR 1980, *Bion in New York and Sao Paulo*, Karnac Books, London.

Bion, WR 1987, *Clinical seminars and four papers*, Fleetwood Press, Oxford.

Bion, WR 1992, *Cogitations*, Karnac Books, London.

Bion, WR 1997, *Taming wild thoughts*, Karnac Books, London.

Bléandonu, G 1994, *Wilfred Bion: His life and works 1897–1979*, Free Associated Press, London.

Ferro, A 2009, 'Transformations in dreaming and characters in the psychoanalytic field', *International Journal of Psychoanalysis*, vol. 90, pp. 209–230.

Freud, S 1896, 'The aetiology of hysteria', in J Strachey (ed), *Standard edition of the complete psychological works of Sigmund Freud*, vol. 3, Hogarth, London, pp. 191–221.

Freud, S 1911, 'Formulations on the two principles of mental functioning', in J Strachey (ed), *Standard edition of the complete psychological works of Sigmund Freud*, vol. 12, Hogarth, London, pp. 218–226.

Freud, S 1919, 'The uncanny', in J Strachey (ed), *Standard edition of the complete psychological works of Sigmund Freud*, vol. 12, Hogarth, London, pp. 219–256.

Grosskurth, P 1986, *Melanie Klein, her world and her work*, McClelland & Stewart, Toronto.

Grotstein, JS 2007, *A beam of intense darkness: Wilfred Bion's legacy to psychoanalysis*, Karnak Books, London.

Levinas, E 1963, "La trace de l'autre," *Tijdschrift Voor Filosofie*, vol. 25, no. 3, pp. 605–623. Retrieved from http://www.jstor.org/stable/40881053

López-Corvo, RE 1992, 'About interpretation of self-envy', *International Journal of Psychoanalysis*, vol. 73, pp. 719–728.

López-Corvo, RE 1995, *Self-envy, therapy and the divided inner world*, Jason Aronson, New York.

López-Corvo, RE 2003, *The dictionary of the work of W. R. Bion*, Karnac Books, London.

López-Corvo, RE 2006, *Wild thoughts searching for a thinker, a clinical application of W. R. Bion's theories*, Karnac Books, London.

López-Corvo, RE 2013, 'Time distortion between "conceptual" and "preconceptual" traumas', *Psychoanalytic Review*, vol. 100, no. 2, pp. 289–310.

López-Corvo, RE 2014, *The traumatised and non-traumatised states of the personality, a clinical understanding using Bion's approach*, Karnac Books, London.

Meltzer, D 1978, *The Kleinian development part III: The clinical significance of the work of Bion*, Clunie, Perthshire, Scotland.

Sartre, JP 1943, *L'être et le néant*, Gallimard, Paris.

# 6

# Jacques Lacan
## Freud's French interpreter

*Sean Homer*

## Intellectual development

Jacques Lacan was arguably the most original and influential psychoanalyst since Freud. His philosophical and linguistic interpretation of Freud has transformed the practice of psycho-analysis across the globe. He was also, as his biographer Elisabeth Roudinesco (1997[1993]) has pointed out, an arrogant, narcissistic and a deeply divisive figure. Born in 1901, Lacan grew up in a comfortable, middle-class Catholic family and attended the prestigious Catholic school, the Collège Stanislas. He studied medicine at the Paris Medical Faculty, specializing in psychiatry with a particular interest in psychosis. It was through his critique of psychiatry that Lacan was drawn to psychoanalysis. He was also influenced by Surrealism and Salvador Dalí's "paranoid-critical methodology," and published part of his thesis, *Paranoid Psychosis and Its Relations to the Personality* (1931), in Dalí's journal *Minotaure*.

Lacan undertook analysis with Rudolph Loewenstein, at the time the most famous train-ing analyst in the Société Psychanalytique de Paris (SPP), and their relationship would last for 6 years. Lacan's analysis was known to have been very "stormy" and ended rancorously in 1938, although it lasted long enough for Lacan to be accepted as a training analyst within the SPP. In the 1930s Lacan attended Alexandre Kojève's lectures on Hegel's phenomenology and was influenced, like so many of his generation, by the three great Hs: Hegel, Husserl and Heidegger. In 1953 disputes within the SPP came to a head over the question of training and Lacan's use of the variable session (which was invariably shorter than the standard 50-minute hour). A group of prominent analysts including Lacan broke away to form the Société Française de Psychanalyse (SFP). Lacan established his clinical seminar at Sainte-Anne Hospital and for the next 26 years it would become the main platform for the dissemination of his ideas. In September 1953 Lacan delivered a lecture entitled "The Function and Field of Speech and Language in Psychoanalysis" (also known as "The Rome Discourse"), which effectively became the manifesto for the new society. He attacked the deadening effects of the psychoanalytic establishment and called for a "return to Freud," that is to say, a rediscovery of the radicalism of Freud's discovery, the truth of the unconscious. For Lacan, psychoanalysis must return to the study of the symbolic function, and above all speech, as constitutive of the analytic experience and the subject of the unconscious. Psychoanalysis is not about strengthening defense mechanisms or the adaptation of the subject to the reality principle, but the study of unconscious desire. In order to undertake such a return

Lacan drew on the structural anthropology of Claude Lévi-Strauss and the linguistic theories of Ferdinand de Saussure and Roman Jakobson.

After protracted negotiations with the International Psychoanalytical Association (IPA), the SFP was refused membership in 1963 as long as Lacan remained a training analyst of the association. Following his "excommunication," Lacan founded the École Freudienne de Paris (EFP) in 1964, and set out the objectives of the school as providing psychoanalysis a firm scientific basis. In contrast to his previous philosophical renovation of Freud, Lacan now cast himself as an anti-philosopher and the unconscious as that which subverts everything that derives from the Cartesian cogito. The year 1964 marked a crucial shift in Lacan's teaching, as he began to elaborate what we would now recognize as an explicitly Lacanian form of psychoanalysis. The real emerges as the central category and analysis is seen as essentially an encounter with the real that eludes us.

The break with the SFP necessitated Lacan leaving Sainte-Anne and, at the invitation of Louis Althusser, Lacan delivered his seminar at the École Normale Supérieure (ENS) from 1964 to 1969. The move opened up the seminar to a whole new audience of philosophers and student radicals, and it is noticeable that the seminars after 1964 are much less accessible. In the final decade of his life Lacan became increasingly dissatisfied with the use of linguistics to represent the structure of the unconscious, turning to topology and what he called "mathemes" to formalize the logic of the unconscious. He attempted to diagrammatically represent the workings of the unconscious through knots, such as the interlinking circles of the Borromean knot and the endless loop of the Möbius strip. It was as if Lacan was attempting to attain that impossible encounter with the real for which he had so long theorized. His seminars and writings increasingly took on the style of Joyce's *Finnegans Wake*, the subject of one of his last seminars, which Roudinesco describes as the language of psychosis that remains intelligible (just) but utterly untranslatable. As Lacan's health declined, his seminar and clinical practice was reduced ever further to the most rudimentary element of his whole theoretical edifice, silence.

## Key contributions

Lacan's influence has stretched far beyond the realm of the clinic and into an extraordinary range of academic disciplines. In this first section of the chapter, I will focus on his major contributions to the field of psychoanalysis, and in the second section I will explore the broader impact of these ideas within social theory and the humanities.

### The formation of the ego

In 1936 Lacan was unfamiliar with the work of Melanie Klein, but his ideas were running in parallel to developments in Klein's thought. Both Lacan and Klein were attempting nothing less than an internal overhaul of psychoanalytic thinking in opposition to ego-psychology and the model of adaptation being developed by Anna Freud. After Freud's second topography – the ego-id-superego – there were two options open, writes Roudinesco: one was to

> make the ego the product of a gradual differentiation of the id, acting as a representative of reality and charged with containing drives (this was ego-psychology); the other turned its back on any idea of an autonomous ego and studied its genesis in terms of identification.
>
> *(2003, p. 29)*

Lacan took the second route when he presented "The Mirror Stage" at the 14th congress of the IPA at Marienbad in 1936. He came at these ideas through Kojève's philosophy and the experimental psychology of Henri Wallon. Kojève elaborated a reading of Hegel that transformed the "I think" of Cartesian philosophy into "I desire," and suggested a split between the I that desires and the ego as the site of mere representations. Lacan would combine these ideas with Wallon's 1931 "mirror test," whereby an infant placed in front of a mirror gradually comes to distinguish its own body from the reflected image, and "this dialectical operation takes place because of the subject's symbolic comprehension of the imaginary space in which his unity is created" (2003, p. 29).

Lacan never acknowledged his debt to Wallon's work.

According to Lacan, the mirror phase occurs roughly between the ages of 6 and 18 months and corresponds to Freud's stage of primary narcissism. As the infant begins to recognize his/her image in the mirror he/she for the first time becomes aware that his/her body has a total form.

The infant can govern the movements of this image through the movements of its own body and thus experiences pleasure, but this sense of mastery is in contrast to its experience of its own body. While the infant feels his/her body to be fragmented, it is the image that provides him/her with a sense of unification and wholeness. The mirror image, then, anticipates the mastery of the infant's own body and stands in contrast to the feelings of fragmentation the infant experiences. The infant *identifies* with this mirror image. The image is him/herself. At the same time, the image is *alienating*, in the sense that it becomes confused with the self. The image actually comes to take the place of the self. The ego emerges through this process of alienation and fascination with the image, and its function is to maintain the illusion of coherence and mastery. The function of the ego is, in other words, one of *misrecognition (méconnaissance)*, of refusing to accept the truth of fragmentation and alienation. Through the mirror stage Lacan provided an account of the infant's emergent sense of self in relation to an-other. The ego is not the site of a stable identity but of neurosis and aggressivity. This rivalry will form the template for all future relations between subject and other as well as the dialectic between the subject and social institutions.

## The unconscious is structured like a language

In one of his earliest presentations of Freudian psychoanalysis, "Beyond the Reality Principle" (2006[1966]) Lacan observed that the analytical experience exists within language and requires not only a speaking subject but also an interlocutor, an analyst who listens. While the words of the speaking subject may "have no meaning," they will have a meaning to the analyst within the analytic situation. In 1936 Lacan did not yet have the language or vocabulary with which to develop this insight – that psychoanalysis exists within the world of language; this would require an account of the symbolic order and a theory of language. It was from Claude Lévi-Strauss that Lacan derived the notion of a single elementary structure, a process of symbolic exchange, that underlies all kinship and social relations and, more importantly, that this structure remains unconscious to social agents. In other words, what characterizes the human world is the *symbolic function*, a function that mediates all aspects of our lives and experience. Lévi-Strauss also provided Lacan with the initial idea that the unconscious is a space in which the symbolic function achieves autonomy, that is to say, a space where symbols are more real than what they symbolize and where the signifier precedes the signified (Roudinesco, 1997[1993], p. 211).

Lacan combined this conception of the symbolic function with a radical rereading of Saussurian linguistics, derived from the work of the Russian linguist Roman Jakobson, but again mediated through Lévi-Strauss. Lacan interpreted Saussure's bar binding the two halves of the linguistic sign as the bar of Freudian repression, the boundary between consciousness and the unconscious. The bar between signifier and signified represents the separation between signification and meaning; one can never attain the ultimate meaning of the signifier because all we are presented with is another signifier and another in an almost endless chain of signification. In short, Lacan prioritized the now capitalized Signifier over the unobtainable signified. From Jakobson Lacan also took the idea of metaphor and metonymy as functions of substitution and contiguity, respectively, and mapped these onto Freud's unconscious processes of condensation and displacement. Lacan was now in a position to declare that *the unconscious is structured like a language*.

According to Lacan, the unconscious is essentially linguistic in nature and functions *like* a language according to its own rules and grammar; thus we can read the unconscious just as Freud taught us how to read dreams, jokes and slips of the tongue. In one of his few reflections on this famous slogan at the Baltimore conference on "The Languages of Criticism and the Sciences of Man" (1966), Lacan remarked that the statement is tautological in the sense that "the unconscious is structured like a language" simply means that "the unconscious is structured." Psychoanalysis, for Lacan, is not about helping the subject adapt to reality but is fundamentally a relation to truth, and, as truth exists within language, the unconscious would be of no interest if it were not within language and had this relation to truth (2008[2005], p. 29). For Lacan, the unconscious speaks; it speaks the truth about human sexuality and desire. This may not be a truth that we often want to hear, but it is something that *insists* on making itself heard.

## The subject of the unconscious

Following Heidegger, Lacan argues that man dwells within language; indeed, man is not only born into language but is born through language. We are born into a circuit of discourse that marks us before our birth and will continue after our death. To be human we are subjected to this symbolic order, the order of language; we cannot escape it, although its structure escapes us. The subject is constituted in the symbolic realm of language but always as a divided subject, split between the subject of enunciation and the subject of the utterance, that is, the subject that speaks and the subject in speech. According to the linguist Emile Benveniste, "I" is a shifter; it has no specific referent but in the act of speech designates the person who says "I." Lacan was to take this one step further and insisted that the I does not refer to anything stable at all, but rather as a site within speech it could be occupied by a number of different phenomena: the subject, the ego or the unconscious. Lacan de-essentializes the I. The subject emerges at the point at which it is able to symbolize itself as an I in the symbolic order, that is to say, the point at which it can *separate* the "me" as ego from the "I" as subject in relation to others. This distinction corresponds to a further distinction in Lacan's theory between the "ideal ego" and the "ego ideal." The ideal ego originates in the imaginary and is the image one aspires to; the ego ideal on the other hand is a symbolic position. The ideal ego always accompanies the ego as the promise of future unity and cohesiveness to which the ego aspires. The ego ideal is based on the signifier operating as ideal or a point within the symbolic order that guarantees one's position and anticipates secondary (Oedipal) identification. The subject, therefore, is split and de-centered in relation to the ego or individual; it is not self-identical with itself, or as Lacan puts it, *I is an other*.

Lacan's 1966 seminar on Edgar Allan Poe's "The Purloined Letter" clearly illustrates this conception of the subject as *the Subject of the Signifier* or, as that which *one Signifier represents to another Signifier*. The seminar placed at the beginning of the *Écrits* demonstrates Lacan's central thesis: *the insistence of the signifying chain and the determination of the subject by the Signifier*. The term *insistence* refers to the bar separating the Signifier and the signified, and hence Lacan's contention that meaning no longer "consists" in the signifying chain but is excluded and continually "insists" on expression. It also emphasizes that the subject of the unconscious is continually "pressing" or "insisting" on manifesting itself in the symbolic. In relation to Poe's tale, Lacan showed how each character in the story was unknowingly displaced and repositioned depending on their relationship to an incriminating letter. The letter functions as a floating signifier that passes along the signifying chain, with each person unconscious of the full import of what is taking place and how it subjectivizes them. This early "structuralist" Lacan provides us with one definition of the subject, the subject as *precipitate*, as the retroactive effect of one signifier upon another. At this point, the Signifier always interpellates the subject successfully and Lacan concludes with the assertion that "the letter always arrives at its destination." As we will see later, this conclusion opened up Lacan to a brilliant and incisive critique from the philosopher Jacques Derrida.

Lacan subsequently revised his notion of the subject to account for that which falls outside of the signifying chain, or as a *breach* within the signifying chain. In *Seminar XI* (1977[1973]) Lacan substituted the linguistic categories of metaphor and metonymy with the operation of *alienation* and *separation*. Alienation and separation describe the process by which the subject realizes him/herself in the Other. Alienation designates the process through which the subject first identifies with the signifier and is thereafter determined by the signifier. This is essentially the subject of speech and language I outlined earlier. From the mid-1960s onward Lacan no longer spoke of two moments of alienation (the mirror stage and the entry into language), but elaborated a single process that designates the subject's determination by the signifier. From a Lacanian perspective the subject is not alienated from itself but within itself, we cannot escape language and language inscribes us in a certain position within the symbolic. The subject, however, is more than language; it is also what exceeds language.

Separation defines the process through which the child differentiates itself from the (m)Other and is not simply a subject of language. Separation takes place in the domain of desire and requires from the subject a certain "want to be," a "want to be" separate from the signifying chain. It also involves a "want to know" of that which is outside structure, beyond language and the Other. I will return to the issue of the Other in a moment, but first we need to clarify what Lacan means by desire. Lacan is very careful to distinguish between a "need" and "desire." A need such as hunger or thirst can be satisfied; desire on the other hand refers to something beyond basic human needs that cannot be satisfied. Desire is the remainder that arises from the subtraction of *need* from *demand*, it is "the phenomenon of their splitting (*Spaltung*)" (Lacan, 2006[1966], p. 580).

Desire is always the manifestation of something that is lacking in the subject and the Other. As Bruce Fink puts it,

> [in] the child's attempt to grasp what remains essentially indecipherable in the Other's desire – what Lacan calls the X, the variable, or (better) the unknown – the child's own desire is founded; the Other's desire begins to function as the cause of the child's desire.
>
> *(1995, p. 59)*

The infant's earliest experiences are characterized by an absolute dependence upon the (m)Other, as she fulfils the child's needs of feeding, caring and nurturing. In this scenario the infant fantasizes that the (m)Other can fulfill all its needs and desires and, as it is the center of attention, the infant assumes that it equally fulfills the mother's desire. Gradually, the infant realizes that the mother is not as dependent upon it as he/she is upon her, and that a part of the mother's desire is directed elsewhere. Faced with this dilemma Lacan suggests that the child poses a series of questions to itself: What does she want from me? What am I for her? What does she desire?

The infant is forced to recognize that not only is he/she a split and lacking subject but also that the (m)Other is a desiring subject and therefore lacking something. The (m)Other is never perfect, and the infant's demand for love goes *beyond* the objects that satisfy its needs. For Lacan it is this irreducible "beyond" of the demand that constitutes desire.

As with the subject the Other is also lacking, the Other is also "barred." There remains something essentially unfathomable in the desire of the Other for the subject. What Lacan calls separation is this encounter with the lack in the Other and the "want to be" more than merely lack. Separation involves the coincidence, or overlapping, of two lacks, the lack in the subject and the lack in the Other. The interaction between these two lacks will determine the constitution of the subject.

Separation, therefore, takes place at precisely the point that the subject can formulate the question, What am I in the Other's desire?, and can thus differentiate itself from the desire of the Other. While the desire of the Other always exceeds or escapes the subject, there nevertheless remains something that the subject can recover and thus sustain "him or herself in being, as a *being of desire*" (Fink, 1995, p. 61), or a desiring subject. That remainder is the *objet petit a*, the object-cause of desire.

## *The* objet petit a

If Lacan's most celebrated contribution to the field of psychoanalysis was extracting a theory of the subject from Freud, he made no less an important contribution to the psychoanalytic understanding of the object with the notion of the *objet petit a*, or the object-cause of desire. The *objet a* belongs to neither the subject nor Other but falls between subject and Other. This notion was first elaborated in Lacan's 1959 seminar, *The Ethics of Psychoanalysis*, as *das Ding* (the Thing). The Thing is a lost object that must continually be re-found, but paradoxically it is an object that was never there in the first place to be lost. Desire is always the desire for something that is missing and thus involves a constant search for the missing object. The *objet a* is not an object we have lost, as this would imply that we could find it and satisfy our desire. It is rather the constant sense we have that something is lacking or missing from our lives. We are always searching for fulfillment, for knowledge, for possessions, for love, and whenever we achieve these goals there is always something more we desire; we cannot quite pinpoint it but we know that it is there. This is one sense in which we can understand the Lacanian real as the void or abyss at the core of our being that we constantly try to fill out. The *objet a* is both the void, the gap, and whatever object momentarily comes to fill that gap in our symbolic reality. The *objet a* is not the object itself, however, but the function of masking the lack; the object is not part of the signifying chain, it is a hole in the chain. Like so many of Lacan's concepts, the paradox of *objet a* is that it functions retrospectively. The *objet a* is "objectively" speaking nothing. It only exists as something in relation to the desire that brings it about. The *objet a* then is at once the void, the gap, the lack around which the symbolic order is structured and that which comes to mask or cover over that lack. The "Object (a) is the leftover of that process of constituting an object; the scrap that evades the grasp of symbolization" (Fink, 1995, p. 94). The *objet a*, in other words, is the leftover of the real; it is that which escapes symbolization and is beyond representation. I will come back to the real later, but first I will consider two more objects that Lacan introduced into psychoanalytic theory: the gaze and voice as part objects.

## *Gaze and voice as part objects*

The *objet petit a* was not Lacan's only contribution to the psychoanalytic theory of the object. He also introduced two new part objects to complement Freud's feces, breast and penis – the gaze and voice. In *Seminar XI* Lacan drew on Merleau-Ponty's posthumously published *The Visible and the Invisible* to develop the idea of a gaze that preexists the subject. While Merleau-Ponty had posited a Platonic conception of an absolute, all-seeing subject from which this gaze emanates,

Lacan suggests, to the contrary, that there is a "given-to-be-seen." We are not primarily discrete consciousnesses viewing the world but rather we are always already "beings that are looked at." Lacan thus inscribed a separation between the eye and the gaze: while I see from only one point, I am looked at from all sides by a gaze that preexists my subjective view.

Lacan is in effect proposing a reversal of the relationship set up in the mirror stage between the subject and other, since the subject is now constituted as the object of the Other. The gaze therefore positions us as an object and at the same time it is excluded from our field of vision. The gaze is in a sense the underside of consciousness: it is that which is elided in the illusion of consciousness *seeing itself seeing itself.*

While the theory of gaze has been incredibly influential in relation to film and visual studies, the idea of the voice as object has attracted much less attention. For Lacan, the voice is the sense-less remainder of the signifying operation; it is that which is left after the stabilization of signification. The object voice is always the intractable in the voice of the Other that imposes itself on the subject. In this sense the voice operates not as a medium of transparent self-presence but as the point of the eclipse of meaning, the senseless non-subjectivizable remainder (Salecl & Žižek, 1996, p. 102). The object voice, in other words, is that which radically undermines the possibility of self-expression and self-presence, insofar as it introduces a rupture at the core of subjectivity. The voice is exemplary of what Freud called the uncanny, that which is at once familiar and unfamiliar, homely and unhomely; it is something that is always "in-between," or *extimate* to use Lacan's neologism – that is to say, at once interior and exterior, intimate and external (1992[1986], p. 139). The voice appears to belong to oneself, but in order to find one's voice one must first incorporate the voice of the Other, introducing a fundamental asymmetry between one's own voice and the voice of the Other (Dolar, 2006, p. 81). The gaze and voice are thus two paramount embodiments of the *objet petit a.*

## The real of jouissance

The *objet petit a* is the leftover of the real, that is to say, that little bit of the real that the subject has access to. The real is at once one of the most difficult concepts within Lacan to grasp and, at the same time, one of his most significant contributions to psychoanalysis. The real is not a "thing" that can be defined but designates a limit that the subject encounters. Initially the real was opposed to the notion of the imaginary in the sense that it was beyond the realm of appearance and images. In "The Rome Discourse," Lacan elevated the concept to one of his three orders and it was now opposed to both the imaginary and the symbolic; at this time the real roughly corresponded to Freud's notion of psychic reality. Lacan added to Freud's notions of unconscious desire and fantasy, however, a certain morbidity derived from the heterological science of his friend Georges Bataille. The real is that which resists symbolization absolutely and is inaccessible to thought; in this sense the concept increasingly became associated in Lacan's later work with the idea of "impossibility." The real is also closely identified with the death drive and jouissance.

Jouissance is one of those Lacanian neologisms that has created a great deal of misunderstanding. The term is not directly translatable into English, and the Oxford English Dictionary has now recognized it as a specifically psychoanalytic contribution to the English language. Following its popularization by Slavoj Žižek, jouissance is frequently translated as "enjoyment," but this is insufficient to grasp the essential ambiguity of the term, as it combines both pleasure and pain, or more accurately, pleasure *in* pain. Again, Lacan drew here on Bataille's insight that ecstatic experience and horror spring from the same source. Jouissance expresses that paradoxical situation where patients appear to enjoy their own illness or symptom. In 1966 Lacan defined jouissance as "always in the nature of tension, in the nature of a forcing, of a spending, even of an exploit" (cited in Braunstein, 2003, p. 103). In *Seminar XX* he described jouissance as a "substance," the only substance that the analytic experience presupposes and works with (1998[1975], p. 23). The example of jouissance that Lacan usually provides is of religious or mystical ecstatic experience, which, as recent scholarship has revealed, came directly from Simone de Beauvoir's seminal feminist text *The Second Sex* (Collin, 2013[1999], pp. 23–24).

Much of the confusion and controversy around jouissance derives from its relationship to desire and the drive. If desire derives from lack and metonymically moves from one Signifier to another in search of satisfaction, jouissance has been seen as its opposite, as satisfaction and certainty.

Lacan lent credence to this view when in *Seminar VII* he described jouissance as the satisfaction of the drive (1992[1986], p. 209), although Lacan is referring to the death drive and this is not a form of satisfaction that most of us would wish for. The drive, for Lacan, is constant force; it is that force that, upon finding the path to the lost object blocked, presses forward. In *Seminar XI*, however, Lacan reiterates time and again that the whole object of the drive is to stress the impossibility of satisfaction and, in this sense, jouissance is what the drive aims at but never achieves. Néstor Braunstein summarizes the distinction between desire and jouissance well:

> Desire points towards a lost and absent object; it is lack in being, and the craving for fulfillment in the encounter with the lost object. Its concrete expression is the phantasy. Jouissance, on the other hand, does not point to anything, nor does it serve any purpose whatsoever, it is an unpredictable experience, beyond the pleasure principle, different from any (mythical) encounter. The subject finds himself split by the polarity jouissance/desire. This is why desire, phantasy and pleasure are barriers on the way to jouissance.
>
> *(2003, pp. 106–107)*

Jouissance and desire, therefore, are not opposed but intimately related and, as with desire, jouissance is also approached through language and the Other. The Other is believed to experience a level of enjoyment beyond our own experience. The important point here is that jouissance does not exist but rather *insists* as an ideal, as a belief that there must be something more, and it is the strength of this belief that brings it into existence. The real of jouissance, then, is impossible insofar as – whatever we try – full satisfaction can never be achieved.

## The theory of sexuation

Lacan's speculations on jouissance eventually led in his final seminars to some of his most controversial statements on women and feminine sexuality, especially: "the woman does not exist" and "there is no such thing as a sexual relation." Freud's theorization of sexual difference through the Oedipus complex, castration anxiety and penis envy had always presented problems for psychoanalysis in terms of its phallocentrism and the assertion of feminine passivity. Lacan's privileging of the phallus as the one indivisible Signifier that anchors his whole system would seem to exacerbate this situation even further, so it may seem paradoxical that Lacan's work has been so influential for feminists. Crucially, Lacan reformulated the notion of the phallus and castration as a symbolic process that affects both men and women. Lacan's Oedipus complex marks the transition from nature to culture and in this sense involves the constitution of the child's desire but also the recognition of the desire of the other. The child is forced to accept that the mother cannot satisfy its desire any more than it can fulfill the desire of the mother. The mother's desire is elsewhere. The phallus is the signifier of this rupture; it is not a thing-in-itself but a signifier of loss or lack. The phallus represents a moment of division and the recognition of a "lack-in-being" that reenacts the original splitting of the subject; castration involves the symbolic process of the loss of jouissance. It has nothing to do with the fear of losing one's penis but rather giving up part of one's jouissance, and in this sense it applies to both men and women.

Sexual difference rests on the presence or the absence of the phallus, and every subject is faced with two potential positions: that of *having* or *being* the phallus. Each position is theoretically open to both men and women, although men usually pretend to have the phallus while women are seen to struggle to be the phallus. The point is that both masculinity and femininity in this account can be seen as forms of masquerade; men cannot possess the phallus any more than women can be it. Sexual difference is *not* anatomical difference, as in Freud, but it is anatomical difference that comes to represent or figure sexual difference in our culture. Lacan, therefore, suggests that the phallus has both an imaginary function, insofar as it is the object presumed to satisfy the mother's desire, and a symbolic function, insofar as it is the signifier of lack.

Sexual difference, for Lacan, can only be understood in terms of the symbolic through which our subjectivity is structured and, thus, the phallus is the signifier of that which cannot be accounted for by biology. As both men *and* women are subjects of the signifier and alienated through language, there can be no such thing as a sexual relationship because there is no "direct" relationship between men and women. Men and women are divided, split, within themselves and from each other; they do not interact with each other as men and women, as there is always something that intrudes and disrupts that relationship, that is, the signifier. Men and women are not defined in relation to each other, as the opposite but complementary sex, but separately and in relation to a third term. According to Lacan, men are completely determined by the phallic function, they are subject to symbolic castration and wholly alienated within language. Women, on the other hand, are *not* wholly determined by the symbolic and castration. While men's jouissance is limited and bound by the symbolic, that is phallic jouissance, women can also experience another form of jouissance, or something more than the phallic jouissance. Lacan likens this experience to the ecstasy of mystical experience, through which one is at once possessed and annihilated as a subject. Lacan's slogan, therefore, that "the woman does not exist," that she is not One, does not mean that women are any less complete, defined or whole than men but that woman is "subjected" to the signifier differently. Woman does not exist as a whole, unified category; she also has access to a surplus enjoyment that man is denied, although this surplus enjoyment cannot be spoken or symbolized.

## Contributions to the field

The influence of Lacanian psychoanalysis has been extensive and profoundly controversial both within the clinical field and the university. In this section I will focus on Lacan's impact within the fields of film and literary studies, social theory and feminism. In the final section I will address some of the theoretical objections to Lacan.

### Film theory

The initial impact of Lacanian psychoanalysis in the Anglo-American academy in the 1970s came through film and visual studies and what subsequently became known as apparatus or *Screen* theory, after the British film journal. Associated with figures such as Stephen Heath, Jean-Louis Baudry, Christian Metz and Laura Mulvey, the apparatus theorists set out to show how the technical base of film production, projection and consumption is constitutive of meaning in its own right. The significance or meaning of a specific film does not lie in its content but in the way in which the cinematic apparatus constructs our position as film spectators through the camera and the process of projection. Drawing upon Lacan's mirror stage Baudry argued that it is the subject, the film spectator, that makes the necessary links and connections between the series of images displayed before him/her in order for these discrete images to become meaningful as a whole sequence. Therefore, it is the cinematic subject that is the proper object of study for a politically engaged film theory, and Baudry concluded by conflating the Lacanian divided subject with the cinematic subject. Stephen Heath subsequently developed this identification between the cinematic spectator and the emergence of the Lacanian subject in the symbolic through Jacques-Alain Miller's concept of "suture" (see Stam et al., 1992, for an overview of psychoanalytic film theory).

These ideas were further elaborated in the cine-psychoanalysis of Christian Metz, who argued that the primary identification in the cinema is not with something that is *seen* (as in the mirror stage) but with something *seeing*, a pure, all-seeing and invisible subject. What is seen in this situation, the object on the screen, does not know it is being seen and it is this lack of awareness that facilitates the essentially voyeuristic quality of the cinema. Film spectatorship, therefore, does not replicate the specular dynamics of the mirror stage but operates in the symbolic through the creation unconscious voyeurs. For Metz, it is the psychoanalytic concepts of scopophilia and fetishism that are essential for understanding cinematic spectatorship. Laura Mulvey highlighted the essentially male nature of the cinematic spectator in apparatus theory. Drawing upon Lacan's later work, Mulvey argued that cinema produces a male gaze or look and that woman is always the object of this gaze. She suggested that the gaze functioned on three levels. First, there is the voyeuristic gaze of the camera as it is filming. Second, there are the looks intrinsic to the film narrative, and these are usually the looks of male protagonists, as they position women characters within the narrative itself. Finally, there is the gaze of the spectator, and as this gaze is facilitated by the previous two positions it is an inherently male position to adopt. Mulvey's formulation of the male gaze provided the starting point for many debates around the possibility of elaborating feminine, black and gay spectator positions and for a more critical use of psychoanalysis in film theory.

What all of the early theories of the gaze seemed to miss is that the gaze derives from the object and not the subject. Lacan's conception of the gaze has far-reaching implications for film theory, insofar as it is in the split between the eye and the gaze that the drive is manifested in the visual field (1979[1973], p. 73). The gaze is that which escapes the field of vision, but it is something that can be represented in the form of the *objet a*. Lacan's theory of the gaze, therefore, directs us to the function of the *objet a* and fantasy in film. From a Lacanian perspective, fantasy is the mise-en-scène of desire. Mise-en-scène refers to the setting or arrangement of everything within the film frame and provides the link between fantasy, as the staging of desire, and film, as the setting for the desire of the spectator. Film provides a complex set of positions and potential relations through which spectators can play out their desire. The role of narrative is central here, in that it provides recognizable structures and coherence at the level of both fantasy and film. The pleasure we derive from fantasy is not so much a consequence of it achieving its aim, its object, but rather of the way desire is able to play itself out through the narrative structure. The implications of Lacan's later work for film studies has been explored in the many books of Slavoj Žižek as well as the work of Joan Copjec (1993) and Elizabeth Cowie (1997).

## Literary theory

In the 1980s Lacanian psychoanalysis completely rejuvenated the moribund field of psychoanalytic literary criticism that had degenerated into a content-based practice of symbol hunting and psychobiography. Lacan's injunction to follow the path of the Signifier opened up a whole new way of reading unconscious desire in literary texts. As with Freud, Lacan was an avid and close reader of literature; writing influential studies of *Antigone*, *Hamlet* and courtly love poetry, as well as essays on E. A. Poe, André Gide, Marguerite Duras and James Joyce. Literature was also essential for Lacan in the development of such concepts as the "letter" and the "sinthome." Shoshana Felman (1982) has characterized this paradigm shift as a transition from *application* to *implication*; that is to say, literature is no longer seen as a separate discourse outside of psychoanalysis but rather as that through which psychoanalysis can speak its concepts and its truths. The focus of such a criticism will not be on *what* the text means, but *how* it achieves certain effects and how the reader's desire is caught up in a chain of signification.

One of the most fruitful developments in contemporary psychoanalytic criticism has been the use of Lacan's reformulation of "transference" as "the subject supposed to know" in *Seminar XI*. Peter Brooks (1987) argues that transference is essentially textual in nature as all texts have an implied addressee, a reader. The text is inherently dialogic in structure. We intervene in the text through the very act of reading, just as much as the text guides and manipulates our desires as readers. The process of reading is in this sense both transferential and counter-transferential. Transference illuminates the complex encounter between reader and text that takes place in a symbolic space that is at the same time the place of real investments of desire. What motivates us to read and study literature is really a very intense desire, a love of literature that is played out in the dynamics between reader and text.

## Social theory

In 1964 the Marxist philosopher Louis Althusser published a groundbreaking essay entitled "Freud and Lacan" (1984). According to Althusser, Marxism and psychoanalysis converge upon a specific problematic, that is, a particular *structure of misrecognition*. For Marxism, this is the misrecognition that individuals make history; for psychoanalysis, it is the subjects' misrecognition of themselves as centered autonomous egos. Seeing an analogy between Lacan's mirror stage and Marx's account of ideology, Althusser argued that ideology is not a set of ideas or a system of beliefs but a *system of representations*, a system of images, concepts and above all "structures" that are *lived*. In other words, ideology represents a subject's imaginary relation to their real conditions of existence. While Althusser's conception of ideology as a subject's "imaginary" relation to the "real" conditions of existence clearly resonates with Lacanian theory, the analogy proved to be rather tenuous. Marxism's primary interest lies with the representation of *social* reality, while psychoanalysis is concerned with the representation of *psychical* reality, which from a Lacanian perspective undermines the premise upon which Marxist theories of ideology operate, that is to say, that the represented (the object) always exists prior to the representation.

Althusser's Lacanian-inspired account of ideology initially generated an extraordinary outpouring of theoretical construction from Marxist social and cultural theorists before it collapsed under the weight of its own contradictions in the mid-1970s. Two key figures in this respect were the ex-Althusserians Ernesto Laclau and Chantal Mouffe, whose influential work *Hegemony and Socialist Strategy* (1985) inaugurated a current of Lacanian post-Marxism that would transform psychoanalytic social theory throughout the 1980s and 1990s. Drawing on the experience of the new social movements, Laclau and Mouffe argued that politics in the traditional sense of party politics was finished, and that we must rethink the *political* as something that permeates every aspect of society and our lives. Where Laclau and Mouffe differed from other social theorists in the 1990s was their insistence, following Lacan, that both the subject and society are constituted through *lack*. Transposing Lacan's idea that "there is no such thing as a sexual relationship" onto the social, they argued that there "can be no such thing as society."

Sean Homer

From a Lacanian perspective there is no identity prior to its discursive constitution. All identity is equivalent to a differential position in a system of relations – or, to put it another way, all identity is discursive and based on difference. Social identity, just as much as individual identity, cannot be said to be based upon some ultimate self-identity with its object, on the capacity of society to fully constitute itself – to be, if you like, objectively given and knowable. There is always something in excess, something that slips away from the attempt to ideologically fix it. The social, in other words, is an "impossible object." Laclau and Mouffe's work was crucial in the emergence of the most influential Lacanian political and cultural theorist of the past 25 years, the Slovenian philosopher and psychoanalyst Slavoj Žižek. In *The Sublime Object of Ideology* (1989), Žižek argued that a properly psychoanalytic theory of ideology must take into account the constitutive role of fantasy, or what he called the *social-ideological fantasy*. It is not the case that ideology is merely the false or illusory representation of reality but rather it is reality itself that is "ideological." What psychoanalysis teaches us through notions of unconscious desire and fantasy is that the very idea of a "true" representation of reality as self-identical (or nonideological) to that which it represents is inherently impossible; there will always be something that escapes, the *objet a* as remainder of the real. The function of the social-ideological fantasy, therefore, is to mask the trauma that society itself is constituted by this inherent *lack*.

For Žižek, the truly radical aspect of Lacanian theory is not the divided subject but the recognition that the big Other, the symbolic order, is also lacking; it is not whole. The recognition that the Other is lacking is a traumatic moment for the subject and the function of fantasy is to mask this trauma, to make it bearable for the subject in some way. In social terms, Žižek identifies this traumatic moment as the fundamental *antagonism* at the root of all societies. We like to think of our society as naturally and harmoniously evolving over time and through the democratic consensus of the people. For Žižek this is not the case: *all* societies are founded upon a traumatic moment of social conflict, and the social-ideological fantasy masks this constitutive antagonism. As Žižek writes, the "ideological" is precisely "a social reality whose very existence implies the non-knowledge of its participants as to its essence" (1989, p. 21). That "essence" is the moment of barbarity, conflict and antagonism that must be repressed if a society is to claim legitimacy as a "natural," peaceful and democratically evolving state. Žižek has demonstrated this very well in his analysis of the conflicts in the Balkans throughout the 1990s. The function of ideology, writes Žižek, "is not to offer us a point of escape from our reality but to offer us the social reality itself as an escape from some traumatic, real kernel" (1989, p. 45).

## Feminism

The Lacanian account of sexual difference has had a far-reaching, albeit rather ambivalent, impact on Anglo-American feminism. The significance of Lacanian psychoanalysis for feminist politics was first acknowledged in Juliet Mitchell's groundbreaking work *Psychoanalysis and Feminism* (1974) and consolidated shortly after in her coedited (with Jacqueline Rose) book *Feminine Sexuality* (1982). If political theory is concerned to give an account of how social norms are successfully internalized by subjects, what a psychoanalytic understanding of the unconscious forces us to recognize is how this internalization necessarily fails. It is this resistance to any stable identity at the heart of psychic life that creates a particular affinity between psychoanalysis and feminism. The inherent instability of identity undermines traditional conceptions of political identity and solidarity, but it also opens up the possibility for nonnormative theories of subjectivity. The implications for feminist politics of this encounter with Lacanian psychoanalysis would be most fully explored in the pages of the journal *m/f* (Adams & Cowie, 1990).

In its opening editorial *m/f* declared itself to be a journal committed to the "women's move-ment," but at the same time against the essentialism to which many parts of that movement subscribed. The journal set out to systematically interrogate the categories of gender and sexual difference and to show how these identities are not pre-given but produced through complex sets of social and psychic investments. For example, the category of the "feminine" is not something determined by one's anatomy but, as Lacan showed, the result of psychic processes that cannot be accounted for by either biology or social processes. To suggest that women's unequal position within society can be explained simply through sexual difference or gender is to impute a fixed and unchanging essence to the notion of feminine that psychoanalysis reveals as untenable.

The category "woman" cannot be said to exist, as there is no inherent feminine nature or fixed identity to which the term applies. One result of Lacanian feminism, therefore, was to dissolve the boundary between men and women, on which the women's movement was founded. As there is no innate sexual division between men and women based on fixed identities, what is at stake for feminism is the organization of *sexual difference* through social practices and within social rela-tions. The legacy of *m/f* was thus to make "a general theory of women's oppression a thing of the past" (1990, p. 4). For other feminists this has also been the main problem with Lacanianism and the deconstruction of woman as a category. If the notion of the woman no longer exists, then on what grounds can a feminist politics be elaborated? As we will see later, a more critical feminist appropriation of Lacan was developed though the work of Luce Irigaray and Julia Kristeva.

## Main criticisms

Given the claims that Lacan made over the years for the revolutionary impact of his return to Freud and his frequent assertions that he spoke the truth of the Freudian legacy, it is not surpris-ing that his work has attracted an enormous amount of criticism. In this section I will focus on those criticisms that relate to the wider dissemination of Lacan's ideas within the humanities and social sciences rather than on specific clinical controversies surrounding the variable session, the training of analysts and the pass.

### The language of psychoanalysis

I suggested earlier that for Lacan psychoanalysis as a practice, as a theory and as an institution is inex-tricably bound up with questions of language. The Freudian unconscious, however, is that which is at once embedded within language and that which falls outside of it. For Freud, the unconscious is representation in the sense that it contains memory traces of past traumas and experiences; it is the psychical representatives of the drives, and Lacan's critics argue, this is not the same as saying that the unconscious is essentially linguistic in nature. Cornelius Castoriadis, a former member of the École Freudienne and later critic of Lacan, argues that the great paradox of Freudian psychoanalysis is that while "Freud's entire life's work deals with nothing but imagination" (1995, p. 16), the term *imagination* hardly appeared in his work, and he never attempted to systematically theorize the role and function of imagination. For Castoriadis, contra Lacan, the psyche *is* imagination, or what he terms "radical imagination." What distinguishes "man" from animals, he argues, is not logic or reason – or as Lacan would say, his insertion in the symbolic order – but rather his imagination:

> As radical imagination of the singular psyche and as social instituting imaginary, this sort of imagination provides the conditions for reflective thought to exist, and therefore also for a science and even a psychoanalysis to exist.
>
> *(Castoriadis, 1995, p. 15)*

Our subjectivity, in other words, is founded upon the basis of the radical imaginary and the unconscious possibility to create representations rather than the Lacanian determination of the Signifier. The radical imaginary is our human creative potential, it creates ex nihilo, it is self-creating; moreover, it is because radical imagination exists that "reality" exists for us. The unconscious, is a Heraclitean flux of representations, affects and intentions, or desires, and within the unconscious representation, affect and desire emerge in an absolutely spontaneous way. As Anthony Elliott summarizes, "representation, unconscious flux, originary fantasmalization: these are [the] necessary conditions for the possibility of reflectiveness in the individual human subject" – or to put it even more succinctly, "the 'subject' begins life as representation, no more and no less" (1995, p. 40).

## Deconstructing the letter

Early critics of Lacan highlighted his misunderstanding of the Saussurian sign and his unfounded prioritization of the Signifier (Rabaté, 2003, pp. 5–6), but Lacan's theory of language derived from Jakobson rather than Saussure. It was Jacques Derrida (1987[1975]) who launched one of the most incisive critiques of the Lacanian theory of the Signifier in his riposte to Lacan's seminar on "The Purloined Letter." Derrida highlighted two main issues in Lacan's text: the question of truth in psychoanalysis and the function of the Signifier. According to Derrida, Lacan completely ignored the formal, literary structure of Poe's text, reducing it to a poor formalism from which he could extract a semantic content for psychoanalytic interpretation. Lacan's text, thus, demonstrates exactly what it sets out to show is impossible, that there can be a fixed determinable meaning. Lacan insists that the signifier is missing from its place, indeed that it has no fixed place in the symbolic and that the letter has no meaningful content but functions as a symbol of an intersubjective pact. Derrida reveals, however, that the letter not only has its own place but it also follows a specific itinerary. The letter has both an origin and a destination; it has a route that guarantees that it arrives at its proper meaning. For Derrida, this "is the place of castration: woman as the unveiled site of the lack of a penis, as the truth of the phallus, that is of castration" (1987, p. 439). Beneath the notion of an intersubjective symbolic pact, then, we find the idea of "veiling/unveiling," which turns the whole seminar into a Heideggerian discourse on the nature of truth. In short, this is the truth to which Lacan's text aspires, nothing less than the truth of psychoanalysis itself, the truth of castration. Psychoanalysis always finds what it is looking for in literature, which is the validation of its own truths, of its own discourse as truth.

## Challenging the phallus

If the encounter between Lacanian psychoanalysis and feminism has on the one hand been remarkably productive of nonnormative theories of sexuality, it has on the other hand been no less criticized for its phallocentrism. Luce Irigaray trained as a psychoanalyst with Lacan's École Freudienne, but she was expelled with the publication of her doctoral thesis *Speculum of the Other Woman* (1985[1974]). Irigaray is both indebted to Lacanian psychoanalysis and highly critical of it insofar as she has challenged the phallocentrism of the symbolic order through the articulation of a feminine imaginary. Irigaray develops three main lines of critique. First, both psychoanalysis and its attitude toward women are historically determined, as the discipline does not recognize this it is inherently phallocentric. Second, the symbolic order rests on an unacknowledged incorporation of the mother. Finally, psychoanalysis is governed by and perpetuates dominant cultural fantasies, especially with respect to women, and as it does not acknowledge these fantasies we can see repression and defenses at work within the theory itself.

Irigaray argues that the feminine is the unacknowledged unconscious of psychoanalysis and of Western culture in general.

The problem for Irigaray is how to define the feminine without being locked into patriarchal frameworks. The psychoanalytic understanding of sexual difference is based on the *visibility* of difference, and therefore the feminine is always perceived as the absence or negation of the masculine norm. Consequently, women are excluded from representation. The imaginary for Irigaray is *sexed* as she distinguishes between the male imaginary of identity, rationality and phallocentrism and the female imaginary of multiplicity, fluidity and flux. Irigaray is not suggesting that women are irrational but rather that rationality itself has been historically constructed in such a way that the feminine is inevitably repressed. For Irigaray, therefore, the feminine is something that has to be created and given symbolic form and she proposes a strategy for doing this through "speaking (as) woman." We have to imagine the unimaginable and think the beyond of sexual difference.

In the same year that Irigaray published *Speculum*, Julia Kristeva published *Revolution in Poetic Language* (1984[1974]). Kristeva, like Irigaray, was at once influenced by Lacan and tried to move beyond his theory of sexuation. She defines the "signifying process" as a dialectical interaction between the "semiotic" and the "symbolic." The symbolic, for Kristeva, is the formal structure of language, while the semiotic is linked to the pre-Oedipal primary processes. The semiotic is thus linked to the body and the drive that Kristeva locates in the *chora* (usually translated from the Greek as enclosed space or womb). The *chora* is not a fixed place but an endless movement and pulsation beneath the symbolic. The semiotic functions as a disruptive pressure on the symbolic and can be traced through the gaps in language, the tendency to meaninglessness and laughter. Kristeva's views on feminism and women are as controversial as Lacan's. "To believe that one 'is a woman,' Kristeva once remarked, "is almost as absurd and obscurantist as to believe that one 'is a man'" (cited in Moi, 1985, p. 163). For Kristeva, one cannot *be* a woman because "woman" is a social construct. Kristeva defines *woman* as that which is outside of representation, that which cannot be spoken. Unlike Irigaray, though, she stresses the negativity of women's position in relation to the phallocentric order rather than attempting to articulate positive representations of the feminine. What women share with other oppressed groups within society is a position of marginality with respect to the dominant ideology and language. It is in this respect that women and other marginal groups are associated with the semiotic, as that which is outside the dominant discourse.

## Queering the phallus

Judith Butler's (1993) critique of Lacan foregrounds "heteronormative" bias of the phallus. She reads Lacan's "The Mirror Stage" and "The Signification of the Phallus" against Freud's paper "On Narcissism" to highlight the inherent instability and contingency of the psychoanalytic conception of the phallus. She does not reject the notion of the phallus per se but its privileged status within psychoanalytic theory. What we can see in Freud's text is a certain ambivalence at the very heart of his theory, insofar as "the phallus belongs to no body part, but is fundamentally transferable and is at least within this text, the very principle of erotogenic transferability" (1993, p. 62). Paradoxically, the lesson of Freudian psychoanalysis is not that there is a single privileged signifier but rather that anatomy cannot provide the stable referent that anchors the signifying chain. Our bodies cannot be taken for granted because they are always acquired, insofar as our bodies bear on language they can never fully escape from the process through which they are signified. Following Irigaray, Butler argues that there is not one imaginary schema but alternative schemes – female, male, heterosexual, bisexual, homosexual and so forth – and in each of these schemes the phallus will function differently. More specifically, Butler argues for a lesbian phallus that depends on its displacement as a signifier from the penis to other body parts and thus undermines psychoanalysis' phallocentric view of castration anxiety and penis envy.

## Lacan today

Today over 50% of the world's psychoanalysts practice some form of Lacanian analysis, and the Lacanian orientation predominates in many parts of the globe. Lacanian theory also continues to develop within the confines of the New Lacanian School, founded in 2002 and presided over by Jacques-Alain Miller, as well as the multitude of smaller Lacanian organizations. At the same time, the seemingly ceaseless production of books by Slavoj Žižek has kept Lacanian ideas at the forefront of radical social theory. Since the late 1990s, Žižek has shifted the focus of his analysis from the socio-ideological fantasy that sustains capitalist society and the possibility of "traversing the fantasy" to the need for an authentic political "act" to transform the socio-symbolic network itself. This shift registers the impact of Alain Badiou's philosophy, specifically *Being and Event* (2005[1988]) on Žižek's thinking (see *The Ticklish Subject*, 1999, pp. 127–170), and subsequently the "politburo of the two" has advanced an increasingly radical agenda to rehabilitate dialectical materialism and the "idea" of communism. With the belated translation of Badiou's Lacanian-inspired *Theory of the Subject* (2009[1982]) and some of the key texts and commentaries from the *Cahiers pour l'Analyse* (Hallward & Peden, 2012a, 2012b), the high point of Lacano-Althusserianism at the École Normale Supérieure in the late 1960s, there has been a renewed interest in the political implications of the Lacanian divided subject. For Badiou it was never enough to see the subject as merely lack; the subject must also have a positive, transformative dimension. Thus he argues for the necessity of splitting the real into its negative, the subject as lack, and positive aspect, that which can force through change. For the young Normaleans, the Lacanian subject resolved the old Althusserian dilemma of structural transformation by locating the split subject as a "placeholder" within the structure, as that which puts the structure in motion. The ongoing exchanges between Žižek and Badiou over the nature of the event or act, the status of the real, the function of the imaginary and politics as a decision or process have completely overturned debates within Lacanian social and political theory from an emphasis on the impossibility of the social to the possibility of a rupture with the present system.

In *The Parallax View* (2006) Žižek developed a critique of the new brain sciences insofar as they cannot account for the Lacanian divided subject and the psychoanalytic notion of the death drive. In response Adrian Johnston has argued that any genuinely materialist psychoanalysis worthy of its name can only be achieved through a rapprochement with the neurosciences, or, as Johnston provocatively writes, "through Lacanianizing non-Lacanian neuro-psychoanalysis" (2013, p. xii). In their co-authored work *The Emotional Self* (2013), Johnston and Catherine Malabou advance a sustained engagement with the new neurosciences that, far from undermining psychoanalysis, supports many of the more speculative ideas of Freud and Lacan. Johnston and Malabou vigorously reject the commonplace criticism of Lacan that he does not deal with affect. Malabou focuses on "wonder" as the primordial affect, a "pure openness to the extraordinary" (2013, p. 17), and the origins of affect in autoaffection, or self-touching, the self-representation of the subject to itself, prior to any relationship with objects. Drawing upon Derrida as well as Lacan, Malabou develops the concept of hetero-heteroaffection, or, the impossibility of self-touching. Johnston on the other hand focuses upon guilt, and meticulously draws out of Lacan, against the tenor of Lacan's own pronouncements, a theory of "unconscious affects," or (mis)felt feelings. For Johnston in particular, contemporary neuroscience provides psychoanalysis with the resources to confirm its hypotheses around the unconscious and the possibility of unconscious affects, to radically rethink our notions of subjectivity and what it means to be human and, above all, to ground psychoanalysis in a coherent materialist metapsychology of affect.

## References

Adams, P & Cowie, E (eds) 1990, *The woman in question: m/f*, Verso, London.

Althusser, L 1964, 'Freud et Lacan', in *La Nouvelle Critique*, pp. 161–162.

Badiou, A 2005, 1988, *L'Être et l'événement*, Oliver Feltham (trans), *Being and event*, Continuum, London.

Badiou, A 2009, 1982, *Théorie du sujet*, Bruno Bosteels (trans), *Theory of the subject*, Continuum, London.

Braunstein, N 2003, 'Desire and jouissance in the teachings of Lacan', in J-M Rabaté (ed), *The Cambridge companion to Lacan*, Cambridge University Press, Cambridge, pp. 102–115.

Brooks, P 1987, 'The idea of psychoanalytic literary criticism', in S Rimmon-Kenan (ed), *Discourse in psychoanalysis and literature*, Methuen, London, pp. 1–18.

Butler, J 1993, *Bodies that matter: On the discursive limits of 'sex'*, Routledge, London.

Castoriadis, C 1995, 'Logic, imagination, reflection', in A Elliott & S Frosh (eds), *Psychoanalysis in contexts: Paths between theory and modern culture*, Routledge, London, pp. 15–35.

Collin, F 1999, 'Nom du père, On de la mère: De Beauvoir á Lacan', *Lectora*, vol. 4, pp. 23–35; Philip Derbyshire (trans), 2013, 'Name of the father, "one" of the mother: From Beauvoir to Lacan', *Radical Philosophy*, vol. 178, pp. 22–29.

Cowie, E 1997, *Representing the woman: Cinema and psychoanalysis*, Macmillan, Hampshire.

Derrida, J 1975, 'Le Facteur de la Vérité', *Poétique* 21, Alan Bass (trans) 1987, 'The purveyor of truth', in *The postcard from Socrates to Freud and beyond*, University of Chicago Press, Chicago, pp. 96–147.

Dolar, M 2006, *A voice and nothing more*, MIT Press, Cambridge, MA.

Elliott, A 1995, 'The affirmation of primary repression rethought', in A Elliott & S Frosh (eds), *Psychoanalysis in contexts: Paths between theory and modern culture*, Routledge, London, pp. 32–52.

Felman, S 1982, *Literature and psychoanalysis, the question of reading: Otherwise*, Johns Hopkins University Press, Baltimore.

Fink, B 1995, *The Lacanian subject: Between language and jouissance*, Princeton University Press, Princeton, NJ.

Hallward, P & Peden, K 2012a, *Concept and form. Vol. 1: Selections from the Cahiers pour l'Analyse*, Verso, London.

Hallward, P & Peden, K 2012b, *Concept and form. Vol. 2: Interviews and essays on the Cahiers pour l'Analyse*, Verso, London.

Irigaray, L 1974, *Spéculum de l'autre femme*, Gillian C Gill (trans), 1985, *Speculum of the other woman*, Cornell University Press, Ithaca, NY.

Johnston, A & Malabou, C 2013, *Self and emotional life: Philosophy, psychoanalysis and neuroscience*, Columbia University Press, New York.

Kristeva, J 1974, *La Révolution du language poétique*; Margaret Waller (trans), 1984, *Revolution in poetic language*, Columbia University Press, New York.

Lacan, J 1966, *Écrits*, Bruce Fink (trans), 2006, *Écrits*, W.W. Norton, New York.

Lacan, J 1973, *Le Séminaire de Jacques Lacan, Livre XI, Les quatre concepts fondamentaux de la psychanalyse*, Alan Sheridan (trans), 1977, *The four fundamental concepts of psycho-analysis*, Penguin, Harmondsworth.

Lacan, J 1975, *Le Séminaire, Livre XX, Encore, 1972–1973*, Bruce Fink (trans), 1998, *The seminar, book XX, on feminine sexuality, the limits of love and knowledge, 1972–1973*, W.W. Norton, New York.

Lacan, J 1979, 1973, *The Four Fundamental Concepts of Psycho-Analysis*, Jacques-Alain Miller (ed), Alan Sheridan (trans), Penguin, Harmondsworth.

Lacan, J 1986, *Le Séminaire, Livre VII, L'ethique de la psychanalyse, 1959–1960*, Dennis Porter (trans), 1992, *The seminar, book VII, the ethics of psychoanalysis, 1959–1960*, Routledge, London.

Lacan, J 2005, *Mon enseignement*, David Macey (trans), 2008, *My teaching*, Verso, London.

Laclau, E & Mouffe, C 1985, *Hegemony and socialist strategy: Towards a radical democratic politics*, Verso, London.

Moi, T (ed) 1985, *The Kristeva reader*, Columbia University Press, New York.

Mulvey, L 1999, 'Visual Pleasure and Narrative Cinema', in L. Braudy & M. Cohen (eds), *Film theory and criticism: Introductory readings*, Oxford University Press, New York, pp. 833–844.

Rabaté, J-M (ed) 2003, *The Cambridge companion to Lacan*, Cambridge University Press, Cambridge.

Roudinesco, E 1993, *Jacques Lacan: Esquisse d'une vie, histoire d'un système de pensée*, Barbara Bray (trans), 1997, *Jacques Lacan: An outline of a life and a history of a system of thought*, Polity Press, Cambridge.

Roudinesco, E 2003, 'The mirror stage: An obliterated archive', in J-M Rabaté (ed), *The Cambridge companion to Lacan*, Cambridge: Cambridge University Press, pp. 25–34.

Salecl, R & Žižek, S (eds) 1996, *Gaze and voice as love objects*, Durham, NC: Duke University Press.

Stam, R, Burgoyne, R & Flitterman-Lewis, S 1992, *New vocabularies in film semiotics: Structuralism, post-structuralism and beyond*, Routledge, London.

Wallon, H 1931, "Comment se développe chez l'enfant la notion du corps proper," *Journal de psychologie*, vol. 28, pp. 705–748.

Žižek, S 1989, *The sublime object of ideology*, Verso, London.

Žižek, S 1999, *The ticklish subject: The absent centre of political ontology*, Verso, London.

Žižek, S 2006, *The parallax view*, MIT Press, Cambridge, MA.

# 7

# Attachment theory and mentalization

*Peter Fonagy and Chloe Campbell*

Attachment theory was pioneered by the British psychiatrist and psychoanalyst John Bowlby. Its fundamental tenet is that in order for an infant's healthy emotional development to take place, they need to have a secure relationship with at least one primary attachment figure – a consistently present and emotionally available caregiver. Bowlby was medically and psychoanalytically trained, but he was significantly informed and inspired by evolutionary thinking and ethology. It was this integration of an evolutionary and biological approach with a psychoanalytic one that has made Bowlby's work both so powerful, and at times controversial. He described attachment as a universal, evolved process, that infants are innately programmed to form attachments. The attachment created between the infant and carer early in life not only provides the basis for physical protection and care; it also meets the infant's essential emotional needs, allowing him or her to acquire the capacity for mentalizing (the imaginative interpretation of others' and one's own mental state), and for the infant's sense of self-agency. As attachment work has developed, many of its findings have proved congruent with our growing neurobiological understanding of the brain, as well as new thinking on how young children learn, both about the world at large and about their own inner, emotional world. As such, attachment is increasingly understood as providing both the neurological and the psychological framework for the development of personality.

Despite John Bowlby's psychoanalytic background, his biological and apparently mechanistic approach to the ways in which early experience and early relationships shape an individual's emotional life caused opposition and eventual schism from the mainstream psychoanalytic world. Over the last 30 years, attachment theory has developed considerably, and its relationship with psychoanalytic thinking has changed too; it has a growing and increasingly sophisticated theoretical and experimental hinterland and an extensive research base, with systemized forms of measurement. As attachment research has produced a compelling and coherent body of findings, it has been increasingly accepted that attachment patterns in infancy fundamentally affect adult relationships and ways of relating. This understanding has had fruitful bearing on the way we examine enduring difficulties that an individual may manifest in the ways that they relate in others, most notably in the field of personality disorder. What is more, in the last decade or so, the gap between psychoanalysis and attachment thinking has become conspicuously smaller. This rapprochement has been further helped by the growth of the concept of mentalizing, which combines psychoanalytic thinking, attachment theory and recent research on social-cognitive development to shed light on the human impulse and capacity to understand and imagine one's own and other people's thoughts. The creatively interdisciplinary quality that has always characterized attachment theory – its relationship with ethology and evolutionary thinking, cognitive development, and its stormy but undeniable connection with psychoanalysis – has been maintained and developed in recent years through its relationship with the latest neuroscientific work. Across this chapter, we will set out the major principles of attachment theory and the key developments in its intellectual history, and will discuss criticism of attachment theory and its relationship with psychoanalysis, and also the most current innovations in attachment theory and mentalizing.

## History

John Bowlby, who was born in London in 1907, trained as a psychiatrist and a psychoanalyst. In his early twenties, between finishing his undergraduate degree at Cambridge and beginning his medical training, he worked as a teacher; most significant for him were the 6 months he spent at a progressive school for maladjusted children, Priory Gate. He said later of this experience, "when I was there I learned everything that I have known; it was the most valuable 6 months of my life, really" (Kraemer et al., 2007). It was through the children that Bowlby met here that he first started to make his observations about the intense importance of the relationship between child and mother, and the effects that deprivation in maternal care can have on children, both in terms of their immediate distress and their long-term behavior and mental health. It was this fascination with how and why the mother-figure (or primary caregiver as we would now describe it) matters so much that shaped Bowlby's life's work.

On his return to London for his medical training, Bowlby, partly influenced by his experiences at Priory Gate, began his psychoanalytic training. His continuing work with deprived and delinquent children in the 1930s and 1940s led to his being commissioned by the World Health Organization (WHO) to write a report on the effects of institutionalization on young children. *Maternal Care and Mental Health* was published in 1951 and laid out Bowlby's thinking on maternal deprivation, presenting evidence for how "when deprived of maternal care, the child's development is almost always retarded – physically, intellectually and socially – and that symptoms of physical and mental illness may appear" (Bowlby, 1951, p. 15). He cited – in a fascinating precursor to the seminal research on attachment in Romanian orphanages in the 1990s – studies of rates of babbling and crying in babies in orphanages, which demonstrated that institutionalized infants were, by the age of 2 months, measurably less vocal than their counterparts in families.

In 1946, Bowlby became Deputy Director of the Tavistock Clinic in London, and Director of its Children's Department, which he renamed the Department for Children and Parents (Bretherton, 1992). It was his perspective on the significance of the infant's maternal environment that first opened a rift within psychoanalytic thinking. Although Bowlby had trained as psychoanalyst in the tradition of Melanie Klein (his training analyst was Joan Riviere, an influential Kleinian theorist, and his later analytical supervisor was Melanie Klein herself), Bowlby put increasing emphasis on the effect of a child's emotional environment – in contrast to the Kleinian emphasis on the child's internal phantasies as a driver of psychic development, or the Freudian emphasis on the infant's desire for its mother being driven by the sensuous seeking of oral gratification.

The impact of separation from a primary attachment figure became an early focal point for attachment thinking – famously depicted in the film *A Two-Year-Old Goes to Hospital*, an account of the devastating impact of parental separation for a young child. Made by the psychoanalyst and social worker James Robertson, it is a painfully forensic depiction of the toddler's distress and descent into despairing listlessness across an 8-day hospital stay without her mother. The film had so much resonance partly because the effects of separation had hitherto been so little considered in social care and medical practice. The dominance of secondary drive theory – which posited that an infant's desire for proximity with its primary caregiver was driven by their association with providing food and physical care – led to the conclusion that as long as the infant received consistent sustenance and physical protection elsewhere, they would be able to adapt smoothly to changing circumstances. Although contentiously received (some psychoanalysts pointed out, for example, that the child's mother was pregnant, and that the child's desperation may have derived from her feelings about this), the film paved the way for a rethinking of the way hospitalization and institutionalization should be managed for young children. The film, which was very basically and naturalistically shot, showed the visceral reality of attachment needs, as a primitive and defining prerequisite for emotional health in infancy.

Across the 1950s, Bowlby's thinking further evolved away from a psychoanalytic approach through the influence of animal behaviorists, such as Konrad Lorenz and Robert Hinde. Lorenz's work on imprinting in geese and other birds – showing how a young animal, at the right developmental window, is susceptible to learning behavioral traits from its parent – resonated with Bowlby's fascination with teasing out all the wider implications of the infant–caregiver relationship. Particularly relevant was Lorenz's observation that young geese would follow – become attached to – parents, or even objects, even though they did not feed them, if they were exposed to these objects at the right developmental moment (hence the famous black and white film footage of a lanky Lorenz trotting round a garden being followed by a small flock of eager goslings). Similarly, Harry Harlow's experiment with infant rhesus monkeys observed that when distressed the monkeys sought comfort not from their metallic, mechanically feeding "mother" but from the inert but soft, clothed object also placed in their cage. These findings were significant as a riposte to the commonly held view that a young baby's interest in his or her mother was primarily motivated by the need for food ("cupboard love," as the shorthand had it) or the seeking of pleasurable sensation that becomes associated with the mother's presence. Partly bolstered by ethological findings, Bowlby concluded that the infant's drive to be close to its mother was a biological need in itself, not a secondary drive arising from other physical desires. Bowlby took an evolutionary perspective on a child's emotional and cognitive developmental imperatives, as well as its most basic physical needs. Through his ongoing, mutually enriching, intellectual collaboration with the influential Cambridge ethologist Robert Hinde, Bowlby widened the idea of the biological and evolutionary perspective on infancy to encompass the developmental requirement for emotional closeness and psychic support.

Bowlby developed his thinking on attachment substantially across the 1950s, presenting three important papers to the British Psychoanalytic Society that laid the basis for attachment theory (Bretherton, 1992). His first paper was "The Nature of the Child's Tie to His Mother" (Bowlby, 1958), followed by "Separation Anxiety" (Bowlby, 1959) and "Grief and Mourning in Infancy and Early Childhood" (Bowlby, 1960). Published at a period when the two main opposing schools of British psychoanalytic thinking, Melanie Klein's grouping and the more classically Freudian grouping (under the leadership of Freud's daughter Anna Freud), were divided over theoretical differences about the intellectual legacy of Sigmund Freud, Bowlby simultaneously enraged both factions with his rejection of the physical, sensuous nature of the infant's desire for maternal contact. The initial paper was Bowlby's first major presentation of his belief that psychoanalysts underappreciated the significance of the infant–mother tie in early life. Although this initial sally was conducted with a certain well-mannered whiggishness – Bowlby appealed to Freud's movement toward a greater appreciation of the centrality of the emotional nuances of this early relationship toward the end of his life – the results were nevertheless explosive in psychoanalytic circles; for once the Freudians and Kleinians were united in dismay at Bowlby's intellectual heresy.

All the same, Bowlby remained a lifelong member of the British Psychoanalytic Society, and he also maintained that "a great number of the central concepts of my schema are to be found plainly stated in Freud" (Kraemer et al., 2007, p. 305). Looking at Bowlby's work now, we can see that one of his great contributions was his creative integration of the work of the two great thinkers who preceded him, Freud and Charles Darwin (Bowlby's final work was a biography of the latter). The question of Freud's intellectual legacy was, in the 1950s however, a hotly contentious and divisive enough issue within mainstream psychoanalysis; Bowlby's rather maverick appropriation of Freudian thinking was beyond the pale.

Bowlby substantially expanded and enriched his theory in a trilogy of books: *Attachment* (Bowlby, 1969), *Separation* (Bowlby, 1973) and *Loss* (Bowlby, 1980). Across these three texts, Bowlby set out his full elaboration of attachment theory, starting with the evolutionary basis for attachment using ethological as well as human examples. Attachment was described as a form of behavior that the infant adapts according to environmental stimuli. Attachment behaviors are actions that infants use to bring about proximity with the caregiver (these can be crying, smiling, vocalizing, or as the infant becomes mobile, physically approaching and following the caregiver). Taken together, such actions constitute a behavioral system – in other words, an inherently motivated, evolutionarily driven set of behaviors. The innate quality of the need for attachment is indicated by the fact that infants still attach to mothers who maltreat or neglect them, a notion harder to square with secondary drive theory. As a biological driven need, almost all infants form an attachment, but in response to the signals supplied by the attachment figure, the infant develops their own pattern of relating, or attachment style.

The ultimate function of the attachment system is evolutionary, but its repercussions are subtle and wide-ranging. The signals and quality of the exchanges provided by the attachment figure forge internal working models (IWMs) – expectations and perceptions of the self and of others – which persistently shape the tenor of emotional/social interactions:

> In the working model of the world that anyone builds a key feature is his notion of who his attachment figures are, where they may be found, and how they may be expected to respond. Similarly, in the working model of the self that anyone builds a key feature is his notion of how acceptable or unacceptable he is in the eyes of his attachment figures.
>
> *(Bowlby, 1973, p. 203)*

Bowlby more fully elucidated the concept of the IWM across the last two volumes of his trilogy, *Separation* and *Loss*. He described the IWM as the mechanism via which attachment was transmitted across the generations. A caregiver who acquired a stable, healthy IWM through their own experiences in childhood can help the infants for whom they care to build their own IWM that is autonomous, self-protective and able to relate to others. Through the working model, Bowlby conceptualized a more complex and subtle model for the psyche than is sometimes recognized in more simplistic depictions of attachment theory. The mental representations that a person constructs, through their IWMs, particularly in relation to themselves and attachment figures, are central to how they expect others to behave, and how they might be predicted to respond to other people's behavior. In *Loss*, Bowlby described how experiences – often involving other people's emotional states or attachment needs – that are not compatible with the IWM are defended against and disregarded. This led to a new exploration – through the attachment model – of repression and dissociative phenomena, which most typically occur with the deactivation of the attachment system in a disorganized individual dealing with grief.

## Key developments: the Strange Situation and the Adult Attachment Interview

Bowlby's work on attachment was substantially developed, empirically and theoretically, by the work of the Canadian developmental psychologist, Mary Ainsworth (1913–1990). Ainsworth worked for a time with Bowlby at the Tavistock in the early 1950s before performing observational studies of maternal–infant interaction while based in Kampala, Uganda, and Baltimore in the United States. Ainsworth's close observation of maternal patterns of behavior toward and interactions with their children showed significant individual differences. In the Baltimore study in particular, Ainsworth undertook a beautifully observant and meticulous study of the ways in which maternal styles and maternal sensitivity in the early months of life correlated with smoother and more harmonious interactions at around 12 months (Bretherton, 1992).

In the 1970s, Ainsworth and colleagues developed the Strange Situation protocol, which was designed to assess attachment behavior in infants in a standardized way. The Strange Situation takes a vignette from the drama of a toddler's everyday life – exploring new toys, meeting strangers and seeking reassurance from caregivers – and formalizes it into a compellingly revealing account of the infant–caregiver dyad. During this procedure, which takes about 20 minutes from start to finish, a mother and infant are introduced into an unfamiliar playroom. To start with, the mother and child are left alone and the child is free to explore; the mother is asked to watch and quietly engage, but not lead this exploration and play. A stranger (usually a woman) then enters the room, exchanges a few words with the mother before approaching the infant, at which point the mother discreetly exits, leaving the infant with the stranger, who interacts with the child and seeks to encourage play. The parent then returns, and is reunited with and comforts the infant, at which point the stranger slips out. Having reassured the infant, the parent then leaves the room, leaving the infant altogether on its own. At this point the stranger returns and attempts to engage with the child (who by this point is often rather upset and bewildered). Finally the parent returns to the room and comforts the child and the stranger again discreetly leaves.

From their first experiences of the Strange Situation, Ainsworth and her colleagues were particularly struck by the differences in the ways that infants responded to their mothers when they were reunited. Most of the infants were quickly and easily comforted, despite often having been quite distressed moments before, whereas others would express anger or frustration with the mother, or they would allow the mother to comfort them, but would not tolerate a full embrace. Others still would appear disinterested, and even cold-shoulder their mother on their return. As this work went on, it became increasingly apparent that infants were consistently displaying particular behaviors, or styles of behavior, in response to particular parenting styles.

These different styles of response to the Strange Situation were categorized into three patterns: secure, avoidant, and resistant or ambivalent. Further work by Mary Main and colleagues at Berkeley in the 1980s revealed a fourth pattern, that of disorganized attachment.

According to these patterns, a securely attached infant (who normally constitute approximately two-thirds of the nonclinical population) quickly starts to play in the primary caregiver's presence, is tentative around the stranger, and is upset and often tearful at their caregiver's absence. They may accept a degree of comfort from the stranger, but show a clear preference for their caregiver, and are easily comforted by their caregiver on their return. A securely attached child firmly expects their distress to be met with comfort and reassurance.

An avoidant infant appears unconcerned at their carer's disappearance, may not seek contact with the caregiver on their return, and may not seem to prefer the caregiver to the stranger. An avoidant individual has adapted to less responsive caregiving by deactivating their attachment system, learning not to use attachment behaviors to solicit comfort and obtain proximity from their carer, instead seeking to manage alone. A resistant infant tends to keep their focus on their caregiver rather than immersing him or herself in exploration and play when they are first introduced to the playroom; seems highly distressed by the separation; and is not easily comforted on being reunited with the carer. Resistant attachment involves the hyperactivation of attachment behaviors; the infants tend to display high levels of vigilance toward possible attachment threats, and seek reassurance in a particularly urgent manner. A disoriented/disorganized infant is so called because of their unusual attachment behavior, which seems to suggest a breakdown, freezing or disorientation when faced with their own attachment needs. This may manifest itself in apparently chaotic or surprising behaviors such as becoming very still; stereotypical actions such as head banging; or simply appearing frightened of the parent.

Building on this work with infants, further studies were undertaken in the 1980s to see how different attachments styles and behaviors are shown by adults. Attachment styles were found to be relatively enduring across life, with significant implications for thinking about the role of attachment in personality development. Attachment in adults was first rendered measurable when Mary Main, Carol George and Nancy Kaplan produced the Adult Attachment Interview (AAI) in 1984. The AAI is a semistructured interview that asks subjects to describe their childhood experiences that relate to attachment, and to consider how these experiences might affect their relationships and their functioning as adults.

Corresponding with the classifications for infancy, adult attachment styles are categorized as secure/autonomous, avoidant/dismissing, anxious/preoccupied and unresolved/disorganized. An adult who is secure/autonomous during the AAI coherently integrates attachment memories into a meaningful narrative and shows appreciation for the importance of attachment relationships. Avoidant/dismissing AAI narratives will be less coherent: patients will be unable to recall specific memories in support of general arguments and will idealize or devalue their early relationships. Anxious/preoccupied adults will also show a lack of coherence, and will express confusion, anger, or fear in relation to early attachment figures. The narratives of unresolved/disorganized adults, particularly on the subject of bereavements or childhood traumas, will contain lapses in reasoning or expression, such as non sequiturs, and exaggerated, unnecessary detail, or changes in register and uncharacteristic grammatical mistakes. The unresolved state has been described as a temporary breakdown of attention when distracted by traumatic memories, whether during the AAI or through interacting with an infant. Adults showing this pattern are also classified within one of the three primary categories.

The persistent quality of attachment styles produces similarly enduring strategies for dealing with emotions and social contact. For example, the increased sense of agency of the secure child permits him/her to move toward the ownership of inner experience, and toward an understanding of self and others as intentional beings whose behavior is organized by reasonably predictable mental states, thoughts, feelings, beliefs and desires. Longitudinal research indicates that securely attached children are rated as more resilient, self-reliant, socially oriented, and empathic to distress, and tend to have higher self-esteem. Securely attached individuals are able to invest trust in their attachment figures and do not overestimate environmental threat; they can respond proportionately to emotional and social challenges.

Dismissing individuals may have a higher tolerance for experiencing negative emotions, while preoccupied individuals are likely to have a lower threshold for perceiving environmental threat and, therefore, stress. This is likely to contribute to frequent activation of the attachment system, with the concomitant distress and anger such activation can cause likely to manifest as compulsive care-seeking and over-dependency.

Unresolved/disorganized individuals – the adult analogue of disorganized/disoriented infants – frequently have parents who are themselves abusive or unresolved regarding their own losses or abuse experiences.

Evidence linking attachment in infancy with more general personality characteristics is stronger in some studies than in others. Findings from the Minnesota Study cohort indicate a correlation between infantile attachment insecurity and adult measures of psychiatric morbidity, with many potential confounding factors controlled for, linking insecurity and adversity to indications of personality disorder (Carlson et al., 2009). However, in contrast to Bowlby's prediction, the avoidant and resistant classifications tend not to be strongly related to later measures of maladaptation. The disorganized/disoriented infant category appears to be most strongly associated with psychological disturbance (Fearon et al., 2010), although there is also some evidence to suggest a connection between avoidance and internalizing conditions (depression and anxiety) (Groh et al., 2012).

## Criticisms of attachment theory

There has been a history of extensive criticism of attachment theory from within the field of psychoanalysis. The common theme of these critiques has been that by requiring theoretical constructs to be measurable and by focusing on observable behavior rather than on drives and unconscious fantasy, attachment theory drastically reduces the explanatory power of psychoanalytic observations and misses the point of its theory. The definitive review of the first volume of *Attachment*, by George Engel in the *International Journal of Psychoanalysis*, was remorselessly negative:

> Despite Bowlby's inexact treatment of psychoanalytic theory and the logical fallacies that follow, and his misapplication of general systems theory, this is still an important book for psychoanalysts . . . Unfortunately Bowlby fails as an expositor leaving the reader the task of identifying what has germinal value for psychoanalysis.
>
> *(Engel, 1971, p. 193)*

The psychoanalyst Gregory Rochlin was even more despairing:

> The enormous difficulties encountered in attempting to understand the nature of a child's earliest relationships, especially with his mother, are never better illustrated than by Bowlby's efforts . . . His recent turning to studies of primates and control systems in the hope that this will be a more rewarding direction may content him but it will disappoint his reader. Bowlby can convince only if one grants his broad suppositions, is willing to overlook the important distinctions between infants and young primates, and accepts the notion that circuitry between living organisms and robots have little to distinguish them.
>
> *(Rochlin, 1971, p. 506)*

As mentioned earlier, recent trends have reduced the gulf between attachment and psychoanalysis. One of these is that the psychoanalytic world has become increasingly tolerant of heterogeneity. Another factor in this shift has been that the impact of the environment, especially the consequences of trauma, have been increasingly embraced by psychoanalytic thinking. The emergence of a relational and relationship-focused emphasis in modern psychoanalysis in recent decades has particularly resulted in an increasing interest in the formative nature of the child's social environment. This relational orientation has inexorably moved psychoanalysts closer to an attachment model, both theoretically and in their clinical approach.

Concern with child's actual environment was driven by an increasing interest in infant development as a legitimate way of explaining differences in adult behavior. For example, according to object relations theory, as described by the British psychoanalyst Ronald Fairbairn, people are fundamentally driven by relationships and their need for them; the pursuit of relationships is not a secondary by-product of the primary drives for gratification described by Freud. Consequently, an infant's psyche is shaped by its early relationship experiences. There are clear congruencies here, then, with attachment theory. As the object relations model has emerged as the dominant psychoanalytic paradigm, attachment theory's emphasis on the innate need for a relationship has been regarded as increasingly viable. Also important has been the emergence of neuroscientific data from both animal and human work, which has shown the profound impact of early experience on brain development and on social and emotional development. This has served to strengthen the common interests of psychoanalysts and attachment theorists in infant–parent relationships and the role of early experiences in the emergence of emotion regulation.

Nevertheless, psychoanalytic reservations have remained. Attachment theory's continuing neglect of sexuality in general, and infantile sexuality in particular, for example, has been raised (Zamanian, 2011), and there are ongoing concerns about the erosion of the unique complexity and humanism of the psychoanalytic project in the face of the research-driven focus of attachment studies (Hoffman, 2009). Such critiques highlight a real and fundamental disparity in approach between attachment theory and psychoanalysis: the sense that the paradigm-driven schematic constraints of attachment research have resulted in the loss of clinical subtlety and the wealth of psychological complexity allowed for by psychoanalysis. However, it would be an impoverished understanding of attachment theory to portray it as unconcerned with the "dynamic unconscious." Bowlby's own later thinking on unconscious defenses against memories of traumatic separation and loss, for example, and the work of other attachment theorists on the defenses that unconsciously structure the developing personality and capacities for relating, are testament to this. The major difference between Bowlby's thinking and Freud's was in Bowlby's perception of the human emotional need for others as innate, universal and evolutionarily driven. Freud, on the other hand, saw the specificities and complexities behind the impulses involved in relationships, allowing for an exploration of the mind that more readily allows for the difficult and contradictory nature of human subjectivity.

The use of well-established and easily replicable assessment measures such as the Strange Situation protocol and the Adult Attachment Interview has perhaps served to fade out some of the subtleties and nuances of Bowlby's thinking. Inge Bretherton's work on IWMs, for example, has shown attachment theory did seek to engage with internal, symbolic processes: the IWM was described as a representation of the self in metaphorical conversation with the other (Bretherton & Munholland, 1999). The internal, psychic power of the IWM as expressed by Bowlby was also partly disguised by his antipathy toward the psychoanalytic tendency to focus on internal fantasy at the expense of real-life experience.

Bowlby's emphasis on how early environmental experiences mold the IWM does not in fact detract from the richness and imaginative complexity of the IWM that each child devises from their experiences. As the value of attachment thinking has become well established – empirically, clinically and theoretically – the future of attachment thinking and research seems to suggest a further refinement of some of the established thinking, and to seek to locate attachment's role in a wider story about the formation of subjectivity and selfhood, driven by the imperatives of genes and environment – in particular how the social world around us teaches us to mentalize, and the level of epistemic trust we learn to invest in our closest relationships (to which we will return in the next section).

Attachment theory has also received feminist criticism. Attachment is in itself not gender specific, in that the primary attachment figure can be male or female, and it need not be a genetic relation. However, the emphasis on maternal deprivation and the conflation of the mother with the normal primary attachment figure drove a critique of attachment thinking that saw it as a means of defining – and limiting – women according to their reproductive roles. In particular, the emphasis on the possible consequences of being deprived of maternal contact was interpreted as a challenge to the need and desire of women to work out of the home environment. In fact, as early as Bowlby's 1951 WHO report, Bowlby was clear that the primary attachment figure was not necessarily the mother herself: "the infant and young child should experience a warm, intimate, and continuous relationship with this mother (or permanent mother substitute) in which both find satisfaction and enjoyment" (Bowlby, 1951, p. 11).

In the context of Western domestic norms at the time when attachment theory was being developed, it was perhaps inevitable that the biological mother was constantly referred to as the primary attachment figure. The historian Marga Vicedo, in her recent work on the history of attachment theory, has located the power of attachment in the United States in the 1950s within a hardening of attitudes toward gender roles in a context of rising numbers of married women in the workplace, anxiety about increasing levels of divorce and juvenile delinquency, and an intellectual environment where women and female identity were being increasingly contested (Vicedo, 2011). She points out that Bowlby's bestselling book, *Child Care and the Growth of Love* (Bowlby, 1953) (based on his 1951 WHO report), was published in the same year that Alfred Kinsey's groundbreaking book on female sexuality, *Sexual Behaviour in the Human Female* was first published, and Simone de Beauvoir's *The Second Sex* was first translated into English (Vicedo, 2011, pp. 410–411). Vicedo argues that Bowlby's work put exceptionally strong emotional pressure on women as mothers, and reinforced the moral dimension and responsibilities of appropriate maternal love by formulating it as a biological imperative (Vicedo, 2013).

Attachment theory is not a static monolith, captured in the stultifying aspic of post-war cultural preoccupations: aspects of its have been refined and others jettisoned as research has progressed and continues to progress. In the following section we look forward to future directions in attachment thinking.

## New developments: mentalizing, attachment and epistemic trust

A relatively recent concept, mentalizing, has been of some significance in integrating psychoanalytic thinking with attachment theory and research. Mentalizing – defined as the impulse to seek to understand, to imagine other people's thoughts – is one of humanity's most pervasive and powerful characteristics. The first minds that small children are presented with, to wonder about and interpret, are of course those of their most intimate family. Close family – primarily the major attachment figures – provide the earliest formative lessons in other people's thinking, and also, through these people's reactions, for learning about how our thoughts are perceived: who we are imagined to be by others. The mentalizing model is concerned with the caregiver's understanding and reflection on the infant's internal world; through the lessons in reflection and self-reflection that are part and parcel of child–caregiver interaction, mentalizing claims a vital relationship between attachment processes and the growth of the child's capacity to understand interpersonal behavior in terms of mental states (Fonagy et al., 2002).

The theory of mentalizing grew out of developmental research into the growth of understanding of mental states in the self and other. The mentalizing model was first outlined in the context of a large empirical study in which security of infant attachment with each parent proved to be strongly predicted not only by that parents' security of attachment during the pregnancy

(Fonagy et al., 1991), but even more by the parents' capacity to understand their own childhood relationships with their own parents in terms of states of mind. The capacity to mentalize is a key determinant of self-organization and affect regulation, and it emerges in the context of early attachment relationships. Mental disorders in general can be seen as the mind misinterpreting its own experience of itself and therefore of others. The concept of mentalizing postulates that one's understanding of others depends on whether one's own mental states were adequately understood by caring, attentive, nonthreatening adults. Problems in affect regulation, attentional control, and self-control stemming from dysfunctional attachment relationships are mediated through a failure to develop a robust mentalizing capacity (Bateman & Fonagy, 2010).

Mentalizing enables a child to distinguish inner from outer reality, construct representations of his or her own mental states from perceptible cues (arousal, behavior, context) and infer and attribute others' mental states from subtle behavioral and contextual cues. The full development of mentalizing depends on interaction with more mature and sensitive minds. Many studies support the suggestion that secure children are better than insecure children at mentalizing (measured as passing theory of mind tasks earlier; see, e.g., de Rosnay & Harris, 2002). Children with secure attachment relationships assessed by the Separation Anxiety Test do better than children with disorganized attachment on a test of emotion understanding. The first of these findings, reported from the London Parent–Child Project (Fonagy et al., 1997), found that 82% of children who were secure with the mother in the Strange Situation at 5.5 years passed Harris's Belief-Desire-Reasoning Task (which measures an individual's ability to predict someone else's behavior based on an understanding of their beliefs and desires), compared with 50% of those who were avoidant and 33% of the small number who were preoccupied. Findings along these lines are not always consistent, but it generally seems that secure attachment and mentalizing are subject to similar social influences.

The caregiver's capacity for insightfulness and reflective function appears to be associated with both secure attachment and mentalizing. Meins et al. (2001), Oppenheim and Koren-Karie (2002), and Slade (Slade et al., 2005) have sought to link parental mentalizing with the development of affect regulation and secure attachment by analyzing interactional narratives between parents and children. Meins's group assessed parents' quality of narrative about their children in real time (while the parents were playing with their children) whereas Oppenheim's group did this in a more "offline" manner (parents narrating a videotaped interaction). Both groups, however, concluded that maternal mentalizing was a more powerful predictor of attachment security than, say, global sensitivity. Meins and colleagues found that mind-related comments by caregivers at 6 months predicted attachment security at 12 months (Meins et al., 2001), mentalizing capacity at 45 and 48 months (Meins et al., 2002), and performance in a stream-of-consciousness task at 55 months (Meins et al., 2003). Oppenheim et al. found that a secure caregiver–child relationship was predicted by high levels of mentalizing about the child's behavior.

Slade and colleagues (Slade et al., 2005) also observed a strong association between infant attachment and the quality of the parent's mentalizing about the child. Rather than using an episode of observed interaction, Slade and her colleagues used an autobiographical memory-based interview about the child, the Parent Development Interview (PDI). High scorers on the PDI's mentalizing scale are aware of the characteristics of their infant's mental functioning, and they grasp the complex interplay between their own mental states and the child's putative inner experience. They are likely to have secure relationships with infants whom they describe in a mentalizing way. Low mentalizing mothers were more likely to show atypical maternal behavior on the AMBIANCE (Atypical Maternal Behavior Instrument for Assessment and Classification) system, which relates not only to infant attachment disorganization but also to unresolved (disorganized) attachment status in the mother's AAI (Grienenberger et al., 2005).

Taken together, these results suggest that a mentalizing style of parenting might well facilitate the development of mentalizing in the child. Consistent with this is a range of findings covering aspects of parenting that have been shown to predict performance on theory of mind tasks. The process of acquiring mentalizing is so ordinary and normal that it may be more correct to consider secure attachment as removing obstacles to it, rather than actively and directly facilitating its development. Coherent family discourse characteristic of secure attachment helps to generate explanatory schemata by means of which the behavior of others can be understood and predicted. It is fair to say that, under normal circumstances, conversations with frequent accurate elaboration of psychological themes may be the "royal road" to understanding minds. Main's (2000) groundbreaking work has linked attachment to this kind of communication with words. The key to understanding the interaction of attachment with the development of mentalizing may be to look at instances where normally available catalysts for mentalizing are absent.

Maltreatment disorganizes the attachment system. There is also evidence to suggest that, by impeding or distorting open reflective communication between parent and child, maltreatment may disrupt mentalizing. Young maltreated children display certain characteristics indicative of impaired mentalizing: they engage in less symbolic and dyadic play; they sometimes fail to show empathy when witnessing distress in other children; they have poor affect regulation; they make fewer references to their internal states; and they struggle to understand emotional expressions, particularly facial ones. Maltreated children tend to misattribute anger and show elevated event-related potentials to angry faces (for a comprehensive review, see, Cicchetti & Toth, 2005).

Maltreatment may disrupt the development of a coherent understanding of the connection between internal states and actions in attachment relationships (e.g., the child may be told that they "deserve," "want" or even "enjoy" the abuse). This is liable to be more damaging if the maltreatment is perpetrated by a family member. Even when this is not the case, parents' ignorance of maltreatment taking place outside the home may invalidate the child's communications with the parents about his/her feelings. The child finds that reflective discourse does not correspond to these feelings, a consistent misunderstanding that could reduce the child's ability to understand/ mentalize verbal explanations of other people's actions. In such circumstances, the child is likely to struggle to detect mental states behind actions, and will tend to see these actions as inevitable rather than intended. This formulation implies that treatments should aim to engage maltreated children in causally coherent psychological discourse.

Disturbance of attachment relationships, by inhibiting the capacity for mentalizing, disrupts key social-cognitive capacities (the ability to conceive mental states as explanations for behavior in oneself and in others) and thus creates profound vulnerabilities in the context of social relationships. Difficulties in mentalizing appear to be the developmental mechanism for the connection between attachment problems and the enduring difficulties in relating to others that characterize personality disorders. Missing out on early attachment experience (as was the case for the Romanian orphans) creates a long-term vulnerability from which the child may never recover: the capacity for mentalizing is never fully established, leaving the child vulnerable to later trauma and unable to cope fully with attachment relationships (e.g., Rutter & O'Connor, 2004). More importantly, by activating attachment, trauma will often decouple the capacity for mentalizing. This, of course, is further exacerbated when the trauma is attachment trauma. The capacity for mentalizing in the context of attachment is likely to be in certain respects independent of the capacity to mentalize about interpersonal experiences outside the attachment context. For example, in a quasi-longitudinal study based on interviews and chart reviews with young adults, some of whom had suffered trauma, we found that the trauma affected mentalizing in attachment contexts (in this case, adult romantic relationships), but mentalizing was not adversely affected when measured independently of the attachment context (using the Reading the Mind in the Eyes test, which measures how well an adult can judge mood from a photo of their eye area; it is used as a measure of empathy and general capacity to mentalize; Fonagy et al., 2003). It seems that measuring mentalizing in the context of attachment might measure a unique aspect of social behavior.

Insecure and unpredictable attachment relationships between parent and infant may create an adverse social environment that limits the infant's opportunity to acquire "mind reading." But why should evolution allow for such variation if mentalizing is such a valuable adaptive capacity? In social environments where resources are limited, non-mentalizing might be adaptive. The parent's lack of mirroring behavior may serve as a signal for limited resources, warning the child that they will need to use physical force (even interpersonal violence) to survive. Violence is incompatible with mentalizing: if violence rather than collaboration is required to survive, and violence is possible only when we avoid contemplating the mental state of the victim, then the child's lack of mentalizing capacity may increase his/her chances of survival. By contrast, in resource-rich environments, adult carer-teachers are in a better position to facilitate the child's access to subjectivity. If parent–child interaction lacks marking, contingency and other ostensive cues, mentalizing will be less firmly established and more readily abandoned under emotional stress. The child may then manifest early aggression and conduct problems. From the point of view of appropriate intervention, it is probably more helpful to view this kind of aggression as an understandable adaptation rather than demonizing it as an incomprehensible genetic aberration, even if these behaviors are primed in some individuals by a sizeable genetic component acting transactionally.

Linking attachment and mentalizing has been made easier by recent neuroscientific research. Neuroimaging studies, for example, have confirmed the association between attachment and mentalizing: the dopaminergic reward-processing system and the oxytocinergic system have been shown to play a vital role in establishing social bonds and regulating emotional behavior. The role of the dopaminergic reward system in attachment behavior is considered an evolutionary mechanism to motivate reproductive mating, maternal care and offspring survival: it leads individuals to seek close relations with other humans and produces satisfaction when close relations are achieved.

Oxytocin is a neuroactive hormone produced in the hypothalamus and projected to brain areas that are associated with emotions and social behaviors. It plays an important role in the activation of the dopaminergic reward system and in the deactivation of neurobehavioral systems related to social avoidance. Laboratory animals with a genetic mutation rendering them devoid of oxytocin do not develop normally in terms of sociability and caregiving. Oxytocin helps promote social behavior; for example, monkeys without oxytocin do not read social cues as well as those with oxytocin, and they fall to the bottom of the troop status hierarchy. Oxytocin also promotes the "caregiver's bond." Female rats without oxytocin mother poorly, and this has downstream effects on their female offspring, which themselves grow to have limited competence in maternal behavior. Oxytocin is a facilitator of attachment: it enhances sensitivity to social cues, accelerates social connectedness (Bartz & Hollander, 2006), improves social memory and facilitates the encoding and retrieval of happy social memories. By attenuating activity in the extended amygdala, oxytocin also acts to neutralize negative feelings toward others and enhance trust. Oxytocin can inhibit hypothalamic-pituitary-adrenal (HPA) axis activity when the attachment system is activated: secure attachment leads to "adaptive hypoactivity" of the HPA axis, which in turn reduces social anxiety.

The effects of oxytocin on an individual's behavior depend on social circumstances. It seems to facilitate prosocial behavior toward members of the in-group only, and to enhance trust toward reliable and neutral peers but not those who have proven to be unreliable. Oxytocin, therefore, does not always facilitate trust and prosocial behavior: its behavioral effects are mediated by the social context, personality traits and the quality of early attachment (Simeon et al., 2011). Similarly, insecure attachment is bound to the divergent effects of oxytocin. Oxytocin is found in lower concentrations in maltreated children, adults with a history of early separation, and in insecurely attached mothers during the puerperal period (Fonagy et al., 2011).

There are, then, three types of association between aspects of social cognition and attachment:

1   Mediated by dopaminergic structures of the reward system in the presence of oxytocin and vasopressin, the love-related activation of the attachment system can inhibit the neural systems that underpin the generation of negative affect.
2   Threat-related activation of the attachment system (e.g., triggered by perceived threat, loss, or harm) may evoke intense arousal and overwhelming negative affect, bringing about an activation of posterior cortical and subcortical areas and switching off frontal cortical activity including mentalizing.
3   Meanwhile, a secure and predictable attachment relationship may be most effective in *preempting* threat, which possibly reduces the need for frequent activation of the attachment system.

Disturbance of attachment relationships undermines the acquisition of balanced mentalizing abilities, a key social-cognitive capacity, and thus creates profound vulnerabilities in the context of social relationships. Mentalizing clearly has great significance in terms of clinical practice: the development of mentalizing-based therapy, in the first instance for individuals with borderline personality disorder, seeks to improve the capacity to mentalize, creating a more stable sense of self, stabilizing relationships and strengthening affect regulation. As a theoretical formulation rooted in attachment theory and with significant therapeutic applications that are derived from psychoanalytic practice, mentalizing provides a practical mechanism for the psychoanalytic integration with attachment.

In the foregoing paragraphs, we have discussed how insecure and unpredictable attachment relationships may create an adverse social environment for the acquisition of mentalizing. This work is based on the theory of natural pedagogy, which explains how this acquisition or learning process is smoother for secure infants (Csibra & Gergely, 2009, 2011). Pedagogy theory predicts that young children will initially view everything they are taught as generally available cultural knowledge, shared by everyone (Csibra & Gergely, 2006): when they learn a new word for something, they do not need to check that everyone else knows this word. Similarly, young children assume that knowledge of subjective states is shared and that their thoughts or feelings are not separate or unique; only gradually do they learn a sense of the uniqueness of their own perspective.

The establishment of subjectivity is linked to attachment via the experience of consistent ostensive and accurate referential cueing, which in most normative experience would be experienced via what attachment theorists describe as "sensitive parenting." By providing second-order representations on the one hand, and modeling mental reasoning schemes to make sense of action on the other, the relationship with the mind–minded reflective caregiver transforms the child's implicit and automatic mentalizing into an explicit, potentially verbally expressible, and systematized "theory of mind." Aspects of secure attachment such as attunement sensitivity serve to teach us what we cannot learn about the world by simple observation: subjectivity is a clear example of this kind of epistemically opaque phenomenon. Secure attachment and mind–minded reflective mirroring from caregivers build awareness to include internal states, eventually making self-prediction and emotional self-control possible. The benign effects of secure attachment arise at least in part out of superior competence at ostensive cuing in the infant's environment: the caregiver is able to mentalize the infant, and by appropriately responding to and mirroring the infant's state, the infant can learn about their own subjective self.

Secure attachment and skilled mentalizing also assist the infant in another problem that arises in relation to learning: protecting oneself from misinformation from individuals who, whether through hostile intent, competition or indifference do not have a shared investment in the juvenile's learning. It is adaptive to adopt a vigilant stance toward unproven or untrustworthy sources. By the age of 3–4 years, children become aware not only that knowledge is not invariably shared, but also that it is not necessarily communicated with benign intent. In one study, preschool children responded differentially to information supplied by a "good guy" versus a "bad guy." Passing the false-belief test – that is, having a theory of mind – was associated with sensitivity to information coming from positively versus negatively connoted sources (Wilson & Sperber, 2012).

As learning is triggered by ostensive cues that share characteristics with secure parenting, the teaching of secure infants may be smoother than that of insecure ones. By contrast, disorganized attachment interferes with ostensive cues and would be expected to disrupt learning. It is expected that the influence of secure attachment will be particularly crucial in teaching the infant about his/her own subjectivity. Finally, the characteristics of communication associated with sensitive caregiving also reassure the infant about the trustworthiness of the information to be communicated. From an evolutionary standpoint, we may consider such ostensive cues (at least in infancy) to trigger a "basic epistemic trust" in the caregiver as a benevolent, cooperative and reliable source of cultural information (Gergely, 2007). This basic trust enables the infant to rapidly learn what is communicated without the need to test for social trustworthiness. Adults mainly teach infants they look after, for whom they have genetic reasons to care. Infants preferentially select their attachment figures to teach them what in the world is safe and trustworthy, but further to teach them how they can make sense of their own thoughts and feelings, and how knowledge of such internal states can help them navigate the wider social world (Fonagy & Allison, 2014; Fonagy et al., 2014). In terms of thinking about psychopathology, the interaction between attachment, mentalizing and epistemic trust relates to the experience of a breakdown in epistemic trust – the disruption or closing down of the channels learning about the social environment – as a result of social adversity, especially attachment trauma. We suggest that epistemic mistrust may be the general factor that underlies the severity and entrenchment of psychopathology, and that this may be a more productive approach to understanding psychopathology than the discrete diagnostic categories that currently shape approaches to mental illness. The latter fail to capture the variability and symptomatic complexity of individuals' experiences of psychopathology across the life course.

## Conclusion

Secure attachment involves the firm expectation of distress being met with comfort and reassurance. But further, because secure attachment facilitates the emergence of psychic structures linked to emotion, an individual's entire representational system is likely to be more stable and coherent with a history of generally secure attachment experiences. The way we experience thoughts, including attachment-related thoughts and the cognitive structures that underpin these, may be seen as linked to physical aspects of early infantile experience. We now see insecure patterns of attachment as adaptations that maximize the chances of survival of the infant to reproductive maturity despite adverse conditions for child-rearing. In that sense, attachment – according to latest developments in our thinking – might best be understood as a form of adaptive social learning transmitted from primary caregivers about how best to navigate their particular social environment, with all its cultural and material complexities and challenges. This development in our thinking represents a turning toward the role of communication, and the communication of social understanding that is tailored to maximize the individual's functioning in their particular setting, as key to understanding the complexity of human subjectivity and psychopathology. Classical psychoanalytic thinking was concerned with the role of drives – particularly sex and aggression – and the unconscious motivations relating to them that shape the psyche; later 20th-century psychoanalytic thinking has emphasized the role of interpersonal relationships and their intrapsychic counterparts, again often unconsciously. We suggest that the acquisition of mentalizing and the development of epistemic trust in social communication, which in most normative human experience occurs in the context of early relationships with primary caregivers, may constitute a fruitful future focus for thinking about psychopathology and development. Such an approach may speak to some of the psychoanalytic criticism of the failure of attachment thinking to accommodate the full complexity of individual subjectivity. It also speaks to a criticism that has been aimed at both attachment and psychoanalysis: their perceived failure to truly accommodate the complexity of cultural differences.

# References

Bartz, JA & Hollander, E 2006, 'The neuroscience of affiliation: Forging links between basic and clinical research on neuropeptides and social behavior', *Hormones and Behavior*, vol. 50, pp. 518–528.

Bateman, A & Fonagy, P 2010, 'Mentalization based treatment for borderline personality disorder', *World Psychiatry*, vol. 9, pp. 11–15.

Bowlby, J 1951, *Maternal care and mental health: WHO Monograph Series, No. 2*, World Health Organization, Geneva.

Bowlby, J 1953, *Child care and the growth of love*, Penguin, London.

Bowlby, J 1958, 'The nature of the child's tie to his mother', *International Journal of Psychoanalysis*, vol. 39, pp. 350–373.

Bowlby, J 1959, 'Separation anxiety', *International Journal of Psychoanalysis*, vol. 41, pp. 1–25.

Bowlby, J 1960, 'Grief and mourning in infancy and early childhood', *Psychoanalytic Study of the Child*, vol. 15, pp. 3–39.

Bowlby, J 1969, *Attachment and loss, Vol. 1: Attachment*, Hogarth Press and Institute of Psychoanalysis, London.

Bowlby, J 1973, *Attachment and loss, Vol. 2: Separation: Anxiety and anger*, Hogarth Press and Institute of Psychoanalysis, London.

Bowlby, J 1980, *Attachment and loss, Vol. 3: Loss: Sadness and depression*, Hogarth Press and Institute of Psychoanalysis, London.

Bretherton, I 1992, 'The origins of attachment theory: John Bowlby and Mary Ainsworth', *Developmental Psychology*, vol. 28, pp. 759–775.

Bretherton, K & Munholland, KA 1999, 'Internal working models in attachment relationships: A construct revisited', in J Cassidy & PR Shaver (eds), *Handbook of attachment: Theory, research and clinical applications*, Guilford, New York, pp. 89–111.

Carlson, EA, Egeland, B & Sroufe, LA 2009, A prospective investigation of the development of borderline personality symptoms. *Development and Psychopathology*, vol. 21, pp. 1311–1334.

Cicchetti, D & Toth, SL 2005, 'Child maltreatment', *Annual Review of Clinical Psychology*, vol. 1, pp. 409–438.

Csibra, G & Gergely, G 2006, 'Social learning and social cognition: The case for pedagogy', in MH Johnson & Y Munakata (eds), *Processes of change in brain and cognitive development: Attention and Performance XXI*, Oxford University Press, Oxford, pp. 272–294.

Csibra, G & Gergely, G 2009, 'Natural pedagogy', *Trends in Cognitive Sciences*, vol. 13, pp. 148–153.

Csibra, G & Gergely, G 2011, 'Natural pedagogy as evolutionary adaptation', *Philosophical Transactions of the Royal Society of London. Series B, Biological Sciences*, vol. 366, pp. 1149–1157.

de Rosnay, M & Harris, PL 2002, 'Individual differences in children's understanding of emotion: The roles of attachment and language', *Attachment and Human Development*, vol. 4, pp. 39–54.

Engel, GL 1971, 'Attachment behaviour, object relations and the dynamic point of view: A critical review of Bowlby's attachment and loss', *International Journal of Psychoanalysis*, vol. 52, pp. 183–196.

Fearon, P, Bakermans-Kranenburg, MJ, Van IJzendoorn, MH, Lapsley, AM & Roisman, GI 2010, 'The significance of insecure attachment and disorganization in the development of children's externalizing behavior: A meta-analytic study', *Child Development*, vol. 81, pp. 435–456.

Fonagy, P & Allison, E 2014, 'The role of mentalizing and epistemic trust in the therapeutic relationship', *Psychotherapy*, vol. 51, pp. 372–380.

Fonagy, P, Gergely, G, Jurist, E & Target, M 2002, *Affect regulation, mentalization, and the development of the self*, Other Press, New York.

Fonagy, P, Luyten, P & Allison, E 2014, 'Teaching to learn from experience: Epistemic mistrust at the heart of BPD and its psychosocial treatment', manuscript in preparation.

Fonagy, P, Luyten, P & Strathearn, L 2011, 'Borderline personality disorder, mentalization, and the neurobiology of attachment', *Infant Mental Health Journal*, vol. 32, pp. 47–69.

Fonagy, P, Steele, H & Steele, M 1991, 'Maternal representations of attachment during pregnancy predict the organization of infant-mother attachment at one year of age', *Child Development*, vol. 62, pp. 891–905.

Fonagy, P, Steele, H, Steele, M & Holder, J 1997, 'Attachment and theory of mind: Overlapping constructs?' *Association for Child Psychology and Psychiatry Occasional Papers*, vol. 14, pp. 31–40.

Fonagy, P, Stein, H, Allen, J & Fultz, J 2003, 'The relationship of mentalization and childhood and adolescent adversity to adult functioning', Biennial Meeting of the Society for Research in Child Development, Tampa, FL.

Gergely, G 2007, 'Learning "about" versus learning "from" other minds: Natural pedagogy and its implications', in P Carruthers, S Laurence & S Stich (eds), *The innate mind. Vol. 3: Foundations and the future*, Oxford University Press, Oxford, pp. 170–198.

Grienenberger, JF, Kelly, K & Slade, A 2005, 'Maternal reflective functioning, mother–infant affective communication, and infant attachment: Exploring the link between mental states and observed caregiving behavior in the intergenerational transmission of attachment', *Attachment and Human Development*, vol. 7, pp. 299–311.

Groh, AM, Roisman, GI, Van Ijzendoorn, MH, Bakermans-Kranenburg, MJ & Fearon, RP 2012, 'The significance of insecure and disorganized attachment for children's internalizing symptoms: A meta-analytic study', *Child Development*, vol. 83, pp. 591–610.

Hoffman, IZ 2009, 'Doublethinking our way to "scientific" legitimacy: The desiccation of human experience', *Journal of the American Psychoanalytic Association*, vol. 57, pp. 1043–1069.

Kraemer, S, Steele, H & Holmes, S 2007, 'A tribute to the legacy of John Bowlby at the centenary of his birth', *Attachment and Human Development*, vol. 9, pp. 303–306.

Main, M 2000, 'The organized categories of infant, child, and adult attachment: Flexible vs. inflexible attention under attachment-related stress', *Journal of the American Psychoanalytic Association*, vol. 48, pp. 1055–1096; discussion 1175–1187.

Meins, E, Fernyhough, C, Fradley, E & Tuckey, M 2001, 'Rethinking maternal sensitivity: Mothers' comments on infants' mental processes predict security of attachment at 12 months', *Journal of Child Psychology and Psychiatry*, vol. 42, pp. 637–648.

Meins, E, Fernyhough, C, Wainwright, R, Clark-Carter, D, Das Gupta, M, Fradley, E & Tuckey, M 2003, 'Pathways to understanding mind: Construct validity and predictive validity of maternal mind-mindedness', *Child Development Perspectives*, vol. 74, pp. 1194–1211.

Meins, E, Fernyhough, C, Wainwright, R, Das Gupta, M, Fradley, E & Tuckey, M 2002, 'Maternal mind-mindedness and attachment security as predictors of theory of mind understanding', *Child Development*, vol. 73, pp. 1715–1726.

Oppenheim, D & Koren-Karie, N 2002, 'Mothers' insightfulness regarding their children's internal worlds: The capacity underlying secure child-mother relationships', *Infant Mental Health Journal*, vol. 23, pp. 593–605.

Rochlin, G 1971, 'Review of Bowlby, J., *Attachment and loss: Attachment*', *Psychoanalytic Quarterly*, vol. 50, pp. 504–506.

Rutter, M & O'Connor, TG 2004, 'Are there biological programming effects for psychological development? Findings from a study of Romanian adoptees', *Developmental Psychology*, vol. 40, pp. 81–94.

Simeon, D, Bartz, J, Hamilton, H, Crystal, S, Braun, A, Ketay, S & Hollander, E 2011, 'Oxytocin administration attenuates stress reactivity in borderline personality disorder: A pilot study', *Psychoneuroendocrinology*, vol. 36, pp. 1418–1421.

Slade, A, Grienenberger, J, Bernbach, E, Levy, D & Locker, A 2005, 'Maternal reflective functioning, attachment, and the transmission gap: A preliminary study', *Attachment and Human Development*, vol. 7, pp. 283–298.

Vicedo, M 2011, 'The social nature of the mother's tie to her child: John Bowlby's theory of attachment in post-war America', *British Society for the History of Science*, vol. 44, pp. 401–442.

Vicedo, M 2013, *The nature and nurture of love: From imprinting to attachment in Cold War America*, University of Chicago Press, Chicago.

Wilson, DB & Sperber, D 2012, *Meaning and relevance*, Cambridge University Press, Cambridge.

Zamanian, K 2011, 'Attachment theory as defense: What happened to infantile sexuality?', *Psychoanalytic Psychology*, vol. 28, pp. 33–47.

# 8

# Psychoanalysis and the analytic field

*Antonino Ferro and Giuseppe Civitarese*

## The Bionian model of the analytic field (BFT): historical outline

The roots of analytic field theory – or, shall we say, Bionian analytic field theory (BFT) – ultimately lie in gestalt theory, the work of Kurt Lewin and the philosophy of Merleau-Ponty. The underlying idea is that certain phenomena can be studied only in their dynamic totality, which is seen as more than the sum of its components. In addition, it is postulated that investigation of the human mind calls for a psychology of the subject in relation to the object, a psychology inspired by the French philosopher's famous adage "I am a field, an experience" (Merleau-Ponty, 1945, p. 473) – that is, a system of relations. During the 1960s, two important authors reached the same conclusion: Winnicott noted that a child had no existence (unless seen as a part of the mother–child dyad/system); while Bion, profoundly influenced by his first analyst, Rickman, held that the essential point was to consider the analyst–patient couple as if it were a group. From a different perspective, Lacan too stressed the radically intersubjective nature of the ego. The initial attainment of subjecthood arose from the subject's primordial alienation on seeing itself reflected by the object.

Bion's writings on "basic assumptions" –unconscious group fantasies – date back precisely to those years. In them he conceives the idea that individuals are endowed with "valencies." Just as in chemistry atoms bond together to form molecules, so people instinctively forge emotional bonds "for sharing and acting on a basic assumption" (Bion, 1961, p. 153). This constitutes "behaviour in the human being that is more analogous to tropism in plants than to purposive behaviour" (pp. 116–117). The basic assumption, whether it be pairing, fight–flight, or dependence, gives rise to "mental activities that have in common the attribute of powerful emotional drives" (p. 146); it is "the 'cement' that keeps the group assembled" (López-Corvo, 2002, p. 39).

To explain why individuals have such a strong tendency to bond together, Bion postulates the existence of a "proto-mental system." This must obviously be thought of as a totality of which the individuals are merely dynamic elements in relation to all the others. In this totality all the basic assumptions, even if inactive, are considered to be deposited. For Bion too, therefore, the subject is inconceivable except in terms of the intrinsic social dimension. An individual's psyche transcends the physical limits of that individual; it is transindividual. Furthermore, within this system there is no distinction between the bodily and mental realms.

While lying on a continuum that includes classical and Kleinian psychoanalysis, quite a few of Bion's concepts in fact represent a paradigm shift as described by Kuhn (1962). A completely new vocabulary is introduced, including in particular the notions of transformation, the container–contained relationship, reverie, negative capability, the selected fact, waking dream thought, the alpha function, beta and alpha elements and dream thoughts. The concept of projective iden-tification too is used in an idiosyncratic sense, to denote not a pathological phenomenon but a physiological means of communication.

In the context of a psychoanalysis based on an essentially unipersonal psychology, projec-tive identification does not appear as a truly relational concept. If, however, it is accommodated within a two-person psychology rather than a psychology of the subject in isolation, it immedi-ately proves valuable for imparting clinical and technical substance to the concepts of the field and the proto-mental system. Projective identification, in its strongly relational sense as a mode of unconscious communication that also entails actual interpersonal pressure, facilitates understand-ing of how, through what channels, and it what ways this common unconscious area can form, and how the actual processes of interindividual influencing take place.

Nor is that all. Bion overturns the traditional conception of the unconscious and dreams. Dreams are no longer the royal road to the unconscious; instead, dreaming creates the uncon-scious, "dreaming" here being understood as the ability to assign a personal meaning to expe-rience or, if you will, to create symbols; the ability is acquired from the mother at birth. The unconscious becomes a psychoanalytic function of the personality. The identification of the unconscious with sociality, with the symbolic, and with both verbal and preverbal language – with everything that underlies the attainment of subjecthood and the specifically human capacity to think thoughts – is perhaps nowhere clearer than in Bion. There can be no confusion with the unconscious of interest to the neurosciences, whose discoveries of course constitute a limit for psychoanalytic theoretics.

For BFT, patient and analyst are places in an intersubjective field. As noted by Ogden (2008), when a patient comes into analysis, he[1] in effect loses his own mind. A new connection is forged with the reestablished proto-mental area. The patient sets up a communication that can, because it involves him in depth, be channeled so as to repair dysfunctional areas in his internal group structure, and to reinstate the incessant conversation between the various parts of his mind in their constant search for better ways of "thinking" (here unconscious thought, dreaming, think-ing, etc., must be seen as virtually synonymous) of the emotional problem of the moment. For this reason, the use of the classical concepts of transference and countertransference to denote the characteristics of the analytic fields may be misleading, because they presuppose a situation in which analysand and analyst confront each other "face to face" as two positive, pure, complete, and separate subjectivities, each somehow "external" to the other.

The term *field* can already be found in Bion. For instance, in a letter to Rickman dated March 7, 1943, he writes: "The more I look at it the more it seems to me that some very serious work needs to be done along analytical and field theory lines to elucidate" (Conci, 2011, p. 82). What is unequivocally a field theory can then be found in the paper, published in the *Lancet* in the same year and signed by both, entitled "Intra-group Tensions in Therapy: Their Study as the Task of the Group." This was the future first chapter of *Experiences in Groups* (1961), described by Lacan (1947) without hesitation as a "miracle." However, it was Madeleine and Willy Baranger who were the first to use it as the basis of a thoroughly new model in psychoanalysis. In their paper "The Analytic Situation as a Dynamic Field" (1961–1962), which has only recently appeared in English translation (Baranger & Baranger, 2008), they focus on the unconscious couple-related resistances that impede the analytic process – the so-called bastions. Overcoming these resistances is in their view one of the principal aims of analysis. Implicit in this model is the notion that the analyst participates in the relationship with all his subjectivity – that he is inevitably caught up in interactive sequences with the patient, and may grasp their unconscious meaning only afterwards.

Although the Barangers do not quote Bion in their now classical paper, Madeleine Baranger (Churcher, 2008) later acknowledged that she had been influenced by him since the early 1950s:

> It was when we reviewed Bion's studies on small groups that we modified and added precision to our thinking in a direction different from transference–countertransference interaction [. . .]. We then understood that the field is much more than interaction and intersubjective relations [. . .] Translating what is described as the group's "basic assumption" to the individual analytic situation, we spoke of the "basic unconscious phantasy" that emerges in the analytic situation, created by the same field situation [. . .] This phantasy is not the sum or combination of the individual fantasies of the two members of the analytic couple, but an original set of fantasies created by the field situation itself. It emerges in the process of the analytic situation and has no existence outside the field situation, although it is rooted in the unconscious of the members.
>
> *(Baranger, 2005, pp. 62–63)*

Antonino Ferro (1992) has imparted a radical twist to the Barangers' theory of the analytic field by combining it with Bion's psychoanalysis, thus establishing a comprehensive and original model of BFT. Over the years, this model has gradually come to be characterized internationally as the "Italian school."

In particular, in BFT Ferro brings the theoretical contributions of the Barangers and those of Bion together with certain ideas borrowed from narratology and developed in Italy mainly by Umberto Eco. Specifically, Ferro was inspired by Robert Langs's innovative conception of the "interactional spiral" of the patient–analyst dialogue at unconscious level. Ferro has in addition always set great store by Bleger's fundamental study (1967) of the "institutional" nature of the setting and of the various components of the individual's so-called meta-ego (Civitarese, 2008).

## A brief account of the theory and technique of BFT

It must be stated at the outset that it is difficult to illustrate a theoretico-clinical model to which so many authors have contributed, and that the thought of Bion himself cannot readily be isolated from its subsequent developments. There may well be no better occasion than this for applying Freud's logic of Nachträglichkeit. For the sake of simplicity and to facilitate an overall view, the analytic field model of which some focal points are addressed here will be mainly that due to Ferro and his followers.

According to BTF, the mind has the function of constantly alphabetizing crude proto-emotional and proto-perceptual elements (beta elements). The alpha function, which uses an unknown to denote this faculty of whose operation we are ignorant, continuously transforms unthinkable emotions (the result of "friction" with reality) into alpha elements. The alpha elements can join together like interlocking toy bricks to yield dream thoughts that can be memorized or used for dreaming and thinking. So two main entities are available for moving along the continuum that links psychic products from unthought stimuli to abstraction: the alpha function and the apparatuses for thinking thoughts and for dreaming dreams. Each may be a locus of pathology. Some patients have difficulty in forming pictograms, while others have problems on more mature levels.

This capacity to form pictograms (as well as audiograms, tactograms, etc.), and then to dream/think, is not innate. All that is innate is a kind of rudimentary consciousness, an analogue of

Chomsky's generative grammar (Grotstein, 2007) – the capacity to perceive, which, however, must encounter the mind of the other in order to become full consciousness of self.

What happens is that a child communicates with the mother, using projective identification to transmit his unthought ideas to her, for her to receive and transform them and in turn to communicate her understanding through various channels. Upon each successful engagement, a building block of the mind is constructed. An emotional thread is added to other emotional threads to form a container, a structure, a *chora semiotica* (Kristeva, 1998), which confers meaning on the formless, infinite and insensate.

The underlying mechanism of this process is the container–contained relationship, which Bion represents by the symbols for male and female. In order to "contain" an emotion, the container must be neither too small, as it might then shatter; nor too large, because, while it would contain, it would then do so without imparting a form, and although present it would not be seen. Freud fails to give such an account of the qualities this mind must possess in order to promote thought, although he does state in his *Moses and Monotheism* (1939) that individual psychology immediately becomes social psychology.

The model of the mother–child relationship, however, is the key metaphor underlying all Bion's thought and hence also the analytic field model, so that the situation of emotional sharing or unison becomes another name for "truth." Of course, nothing prevents the analytic couple from lapsing into delusion, but as a rule the couple is in turn contained within a number of containers, represented by the ideal and real communities to which its members belong, which act as a limit to the construction of arbitrary truths/contents. As long as this overlap of areas of consensuality persists, the couple is never genuinely alone.

Some other powerful metaphors also inform both theory and clinical work. Thinking is the way the mind digests emotions. In terms of the container–contained relationship, what matters is the mating of minds in the analytic session. Given that any form of verbal and preverbal communication has an unconscious aspect, the dream paradigm, which expresses this concept, can be reformulated in Derridian terms, by the proposition that nothing is outside the text – that is, that everything is seen in its context and nothing escapes the field of the symbolic. Alternatively, everything on the analytic stage can be regarded as belonging to the "fiction" of analysis, just as any object on the boards of an actual theater is "theatrical."

"Digestion," "sex," and "text/dream of the session" are the key drivers of the attribution of meaning in BTF. In accordance with the mother/analyst and child/patient analogy, the analyst places his capacity for reverie at the disposal of a patient whose ability to transform/digest/dream excessively violent emotions has reached its limit. For this reason, the analyst needs a sufficiently well-developed, intact alpha function coupled with a receptive capacity. The way to make oneself receptive is to make good use of one's "negative capability" – that is, to eschew memory and desire and to have "faith" that the ongoing unconscious psychological process may present one with images that will help one to make sense of what is happening.

Eschewing memory and desire is a highly paradoxical precept, which is also inspired by a Cartesian principle of systematic doubt. The patient should be seen on each occasion as if it were the first time and psychoanalysis should be discovered anew with him each time (Ogden, 2008). One should trust one's "hallucinations" and practice active, total denial of material reality. Understanding is inappropriate, says Bion; Donald Meltzer and Thomas Ogden add that a dream need not be understood. They of course mean that one should aim for an understanding that does not constitute an abstract, dry operation performed on the other and on his dream, but instead allow oneself time for the birth of a new symbolic form. This will usefully facilitate the achievement of an integrated, non-split-off somatopsychic understanding. The unconscious most often speaks with a quality of truthfulness that conscious experience usually lacks (Ogden, 2008). As noted by Sandler and Sandler (1976, p. 43), "there is an unconscious 'understanding-work' which goes in a parallel but opposite direction to the dream-work described by Freud."

Once this understanding has been gained, one's work is well underway. However, it can also yield interpretations. These will typically be unsaturated. Rather than closing off the sense, they will seek to broaden and impart new momentum to the process in general, the assignment of meaning, and the narrations of the analytic field. Narration is our way of making sense of reality. Avoidance of over-intrusive interpretations is consistent with another essential principle of BFT, that of sustainability. If we are to be in unison with the patient (and, in virtual terms, with all the countless other "clubs" in which we are enrolled from the moment of birth), it is important for our truths to be sustainable. If the patient lacks the space to contain an interpretation, that interpretation may have negative effects. Sometimes, too, the asymmetric patient–analyst relationship may undergo a reversal, just as, indeed, may be the case with the mother–child relationship. A number of container–contained processes, some of them mutual, are always at work. This means that in BFT the analyst is always involved together with his ineliminable subjectivity. Understanding always in effect lags behind, is nonlinear or recursive; it develops and deepens by constantly turning back on itself and using the unforeseen effects of sense to which it has given rise.

Transference interpretations may also be given in a BFT context, but will then constitute just one of the many possible narrative genres. At any rate, the analyst will not be speaking from an absolute position. What matters is that the patient be capable of accepting an interpretation, and not experience it as a systematic refutation of his perceptions. The primary aim is to work toward a situation of emotional unison using either sensory/symbiotic or other, more abstract channels to expand the capacity to think and transform emotions. Of course, it is always possible to use different models in clinical practice and to return to a one-person vision of the analytic relationship.

In BFT, interpretation tends to be unsaturated, "enzymatic," and open, because it is considered more important to contribute to the narrations of the field than to close off these developments in a definitive meaning. An allusive style may sometimes be most suitable. Hence it is a matter not so much of "giving interpretations" as of laying the foundations for a joint search for meaning. Analysis consists in an exchange of reveries. The impression may be gained that even when not talking about himself the analyst is making arbitrary pronouncements, for instance if he uses certain metaphors or permits himself to be creative, but this is not the case if his inner life too is deemed to be one of the places of the field.

Patients so often do not remember our fanciful interpretations, but instead take pleasure in recalling an enlightening metaphor that has enabled them to live better, to endure their pain, and even to smile at it. This was the case with a female patient who had lost much weight after an operation and had difficulty in getting used to the new situation: hearing the analyst say, "What do you know! Before you were a whale, but now you are a mullet!" in effect represented a "little bit" of alpha function. This was of course a living metaphor, but one presented with feeling, sympathy, involvement, delicacy and humor. It is not a question of saying the first thing that comes into one's mind, even if it is sometimes better to speak first and to think later, but of using one's intuitions in a disciplined manner. Metaphors are reveries that think; successful dreams, simple poems that restore body to the mind and, conversely, reinstall the mind in the body. Reality once more becomes poetically ambiguous. Like dreams, metaphors arise from the work of the unconscious seen as the psychoanalytic function of the personality. The abstractions of thought are essential to us as human beings, but it is the emotions that impart flavor to life and meaning to experience.

There is nothing harder for an analyst than to learn to obtain disciplined insight into the facts of an analysis – facts that cannot be perceived with the senses. From this point of view, metaphors, in the context of the fiction or "as-if" of the setting, are tantamount to symbolizations and certainly not symbolic equations. Why is this? Working-in-a-dream, rather than existing in the concreteness of a hallucinatory world, is in fact working after waking up from the dream. The correct definition of a dream is Dreaming + Waking. It is only then that the dream rewards us with the insight that we inhabit a number of possible worlds, that we possess an internal reality that is thoroughly virtual, albeit in its own way just as real as material reality. Conversely, psychotic dreams or symbolic equations are characters of material reality when seen solely as such, and not deconcretized or transformed into a dream. Bion would here invoke transformations in hallucinosis, and Sandler (2005) a "psychosis of everyday life." Rather than assigning logic precedence over dreams, we assign precedence to the logic of a dream – a dream from which we have awoken, for what else is a reverie or the choice of a "derivative" of waking dream thought? – over that of abstract reason, because we are accustomed to think, as Ogden (2003) so tellingly puts it, that the unconscious speaks with a quality of truthfulness that conscious experience lacks.

Conceptualizing the intermediate space of analysis in this way has consequences. In principle, interpretation is no longer directed to the patient, with a view to modifying something in him, but is instead intended to improve the narrative capacity of the field, the latter being seen as an (un)conscious narration à deux. While an interpretation is seemingly addressed to the patient, seen from this vertex the patient is merely a place in the field. The point is to improve the general level of the text composed and progressively presented by analyst and patient à deux. Hence each intervention seeks to increase the couple's capacity to dream the problem that it has not yet succeeded in dreaming. As a rule, an unsaturated interpretation or an interpretation in the transference expands the field's capacity for dreaming to a much greater extent than a "closed" interpretation! Success here improves the "oxygen supply" of the room, the patient can breathe more easily, and the analyst too emerges changed from the encounter.

The analyst chooses appropriate interventions in accordance with this aim, whether they are intended to reveal the patient's unconscious dynamics to him or merely constitute keys for unlocking material or punctuation marks in the dialogue. As a guide, he keeps track of the figures of the discourse, the characters of the session. These represent the thermometer that measures the emotional temperature of the field, the fluctuations of the index of emotional unison, and the associated tolerance range. They provide information on the state and quality of the oneiric functioning of the field – that is, on the system's capacity to undertake a certain (un)conscious psychological work of transformation of emotions. Analysis is no longer a struggle between good and evil, as in Freud between reason and the demoniac drives seething in the unconscious, but instead between meaning and the absence of meaning, between the capacity and the lack of capacity to make use of the po(i)etico-constructive-aesthetic virtuality of the unconscious.

With the aid of some clinical vignettes, let us now briefly review some of the principal concepts of BFT: casting and transformation in dreaming; narrative derivatives as the patient's unconscious response; and reverie.

## Casting of characters

The concept of casting denotes the choice of a character of the analytic dialogue – or rather, perhaps, the fact that a given character spontaneously engages our attention – as an unconscious vector of emotional "lumps" of the analytic field that are created jointly by analyst and patient. Trying to make the acquaintance of this character, to see what he sees (what is called "vision with" or "internal focalization" in narratology) may be the way to transform or break down such a lump into "thought" emotions (which may also be thought on a "procedural" level) for which responsibility can be assumed, but in particular to apply a method of thinking and engaging in a process aimed at augmenting the general capacity to make sense of things.

## Hate

Eleonora begins her Monday session by saying how much she hates her husband and that she wishes he was dead because he is "lazy, arrogant, and nasty." She then mentions a dream in which she "beat him to death." Seeing that the patient is in tears, the therapist hands her a tissue. The patient then refers to her daughter Daria, who has "put on quite a few pounds and has turned into a monster, fat, and covered in pimples."

Who are the main characters and how are they to be seen? How are they cast?

One character is hate, something extremely violent and uncontainable that looms up inside her. Another is "the husband," who can be imagined as a screen figure for the therapist, who is also hated because she is "lazy," having not worked at the weekend. Then there are the tears, and lastly the tissue, a character that also stands for the capacity to receive and "dry" the patient's suffering. This cleanup operation (for the tears and the hate) is followed by the appearance of Daria, or how the patient sees herself as a fat monster because she is "swollen with hate" and pain. However, another character is the dream whereby the patient demonstrates to us her rage and desire for revenge.

Considered in these terms, the characters are "all" functions of the field, cast in a way that does not correspond to any aspect of external or historical reality. Each character is a vehicle, an excipient that conveys the "active substance" that the patient (or the field) requires to be expressed at the relevant time. Each actor of course carries with himself particular characteristics and a specific halo of associations.

What matters is that the choice of characters – which, we repeat, must be accepted rather than imposed, since it is after all an aesthetic choice – should lead to the weaving of a narration with the potential for favorable development (in the sense of expansion of meaning) of the plot. The field, as a "dreaming ensemble" (Grotstein, 2007) or composition à deux, continuously narrates its own functioning. The greater the increase in the overall narrative capacity of the field, the more readily will each subject participating in it be able to develop his individual capacity to narrate, in the sense of conferring a personal meaning on experience.

The field lives from ongoing casting operations. Access is via the areas of beta elements that surround us all, the possible identities, and the identity-related derivations or multiple potentialities that combine when analyst and patient make contact with each other. Other priority channels are the projective identifications, narrations and stories that begin to come to life, replete as they are with atmospheres, climatic variations, whirlwinds or tsunamis of violent emotions. The field thus constitutes the locus of all possible narrations in all possible times/spaces – past/present/future and the current universe or other possible universes with the "strings" that afford access beyond the barriers of space and time.

In *A Memoir of the Future*, Bion (1991) describes a "field" as the expression of a mind (but, for Bion, mating with the reader's mind is basically always necessary), the mental field being inhabited by "Somites," "Immature," "Full term," "Twenty months," "Moriarty," "Devil," "Priest" and so on, thus immediately suggesting the derivatives of the multiple identities of which we are made and which we attempt to keep closed like a fan, whereas the very formation of the field establishes the preconditions for the unfolding and opening of all the fan's slats, in addition to allowing the addition of further slats and other fans of possibilities.

Bion describes the "changes in pressure" of the analytic field as significant; we would say that they are significant of the as yet unborn thoughts that are apprehended by the concavities or convexities of the psyche of the other or of the place that they inhabit. An example is projective identification, which may be accepted (U) or rejected (∩), and this oscillation will constitute the basic emotional grammar – say, like the triplets of DNA.

$$UU∩$$
$$AUU$$
$$AU∩$$

Lignification of parts of the field is also meaningful: not everything can be turbulence.

The analyst's skill cannot but lie in the transformation of what his senses tell him into food for the mind, bearing in mind that an analytic situation presents an opportunity for a psychoanalytic interpretation. Hence the space of the field is that of the psychoanalytic transformations that come to life within it.

Again, while Bion (1965) described rigid-motion transformations, projective transformations and transformations in hallucinosis, Antonino Ferro, following Francesco Corrao, has added "narrative transformations," and in particular "transformations in dreaming," which open the way to what is specific to analysis – namely, dreams dreamed together in the analyst's office and development of the capacity to dream dreams never before dreamed (Ogden, 2008).

A possible description of the field vertex is given in the following passage from Bion:

> I regard any thing I "know" as transitive theory – a theory "on the way" to knowledge, but not knowledge. It is merely a "resting place," a "pause" where I can be temporarily free to be aware of my condition, however precarious that condition is.
>
> *(Bion, 1991, p. 462)*

In the field, everything is provisional. Indeed, the first description given by Bezoari and Ferro (1989) of the characters that live in it was as "affective holograms" – to indicate both their multiple ownership by analyst and patient and their extreme mutability and oneiric nature.

In the field one works without "memory or desire"; in the field one applies novel, uncommon perspectives.

## Transformation in dreaming

Transformation in dreaming, on the other hand, denotes a valuable technical device – namely, preceding everything that is said in a session by the words "I dreamed that . . . ." We then immediately rediscover the oneiric dimension of the entire session, its character as fiction or virtual reality, and are more readily able to focus on psychic reality. Transformation in dreaming allows reality – including the reality of psychoanalytic theories – to be deconcretized. Of course, over-deliberate application would betray its spirit, which is to reintroduce the work of the unconscious into the session. It would in general be better to immerse oneself in the narrations of the field and then to let oneself be surprised whenever one awakens to this magic perspective.

## Scoliosis

Stefania said:

> You know, my people are a bit cold – caring, but cold. In particular, my father is authoritarian, and never shows any tenderness. When I was 10 years old, I had an operation for scoliosis, which was only diagnosed late on; it was congenital.

If we imagine that Stefania said: "I dreamed that my people had gotten all cold" and so forth, we at once find it easier to ask ourselves what this communication might mean right now. The therapist then has an opportunity of realizing how he is experienced and of modifying his attitude.

## 3-in-One

The session has been somewhat silent. Just before the end, the couch is heard to creak. Anna remarks: "Next time I'll bring some 3-IN-ONE!" This could of course be seen as a reflection on how she has experienced the session – that is, as creaking along rather than flowing.

## A deadly transference

A colleague in supervision reports on a case in which she describes herself as receptive, tolerant, kind and well disposed toward the patient. Then, wishing at a certain point to illustrate a passage in the dialogue and claiming to have interpreted something in accordance with transference theory, she writes in her text not *transferalmente* ["in the transference"] but *trans-feralmente* [*feralmente* means "deadly"]. This slip of the pen betrays in a thousandth of a second the violent, aggressive aspects involved in the relationship, which have hitherto been carefully split off and hidden somewhere in the field. This time, a reflection of how the therapist experienced the session is evident in the supervision by the process of Nachträglichkeit.

## The bathroom

R. has recently moved in with her boyfriend. They immediately start arguing about who should use the bathroom first in the morning. "Is that normal?" she asks me. "Does everyone have these spats?" I tell her that previously they did their best to avoid intimacy, but they had now managed to take a step forward and it was obvious that something like that would happen again. She replies:

> Really?! Well, you know, I'm kind of peculiar: I can't even get used to the cleaning lady. I pay her, but even so I can't stand her touching my things . . . But as for him, he uses my iPad; he wants to play with my games. And I tell him: "What are you up to??? I'm the one that's playing!!" I comment that nothing is more annoying than when someone steals your place [*posto* in Italian] from you. She responds: "It's terrible! It's because he wants to pinch my iPad. Those aren't games that two can play! No way . . . ! I'm terrified about next week: I feel paranoid and nervous because then I'll be changing jobs [also *posto* in Italian]."

What I noticed in the dialogue is that for R. it felt like a forcible entry when I made the rather pedantic, psychologist-like comment that the bathroom is by definition an intimate place and connected this with the need to forge a link, albeit at a safe distance. That was so even if I hadn't really changed places [*posto*] by an explicit transference interpretation. The indirect response came right away in the shape of the reference to the cleaning lady, whom she did not trust even if she paid her specifically to touch her things. It is as if R. felt that I wanted to steal her scene, her toy, the iPad.

## BFT in contemporary psychoanalysis

The influence of Bion has been profound not only in the United Kingdom (Meltzer, Harris Williams), but also in Brazil and Italy, to which he traveled several times to hold seminars, as well as in Los Angeles, where he spent the last 10 years of his life. In South America, prominent Bion scholars are Paulo C. Sandler and Rafael López-Corvo. The contributions of Joan and Neville Symington in Australia and of León Grinberg in Argentina also cannot go unmentioned. It is difficult to draw a detailed map of the various schools that make up the universe of psychoanalysis today, because while there are differences substantial areas of overlap also exist, especially with regard to present-day models inspired by Bion and BFT.

BFT is meeting with increasing recognition and dissemination. In Italy, besides Antonino Ferro (1992, 2010), whose many books have been translated into several languages, there are Claudio Neri et al. (1987) and Giuseppe Civitarese (2008, 2011). In North America, particular mention must be made of Thomas Ogden, who over a period of at least three decades has contributed to the expansion of Bion's heritage with a series of books and papers; these stand out by virtue of their style, originality and sheer number. Some of his concepts are closely related to Ferro's theory of the analytic field. Of central importance are the powerfully relational stamp he impresses on the concepts of projective identification, of the intersubjective analytic third, of analysis as an exchange of reveries, of talking-as-dreaming, of the autistic-contiguous position, of sensory reverie, of interpretive action and of the transference matrix, to mention but a few. It is interesting to note that he draws inspiration from Hegelian dialectics, and in particular from Kojève's lectures on Phenomenology of Spirit,[2] in which the German philosopher establishes a radically social theory of the birth of the subject.

Outside the sphere of analysis, Giuseppe Civitarese, Sara Boffito and Francesco Capello have sought to lay new foundations for psychoanalytic aesthetic criticism based on analytic field theory in the volume *Perdere la testa. Abiezione, conflitto estetico e critica psicoanalitica*. Capello has made a similar attempt in *Città specchio. Soggettività e spazio urbano in Palazzeschi, Govoni e Boine*.

To sum up, a retrospective consideration suggests that the analytic field concept is one of the most radical forms of relational psychoanalysis, the "explosion" of which can be traced back to the mid-1970s in the United States, triggered in particular by Kohut as detonator, but whose foundations had already been laid some 20 years earlier in Europe. Whereas Sullivan in the United States used the concept of the field, he had no influence on these authors because he remained substantially outside the domain of psychoanalysis. Indeed, while sharing a number of assumptions and in particular the field concept, BFT and the Sullivan-inspired North American interpersonalism differ in other important respects.

## BFT and its critics

The principal criticism leveled at analytic field theory is that it neglects the history, trauma, material reality and Oedipus complex. Some hold that it concentrates excessively on the here and now and lives too much in the dimension of dreams, and that the analyst colonizes the patient's mind with ideas that are exclusively his own. The idea is sometimes voiced that the analyst's interventions are arbitrary or that he makes inappropriate use of self-revelation, that he is authoritarian or imposes excessive symmetry on the relationship. Another critique is that BFT takes insufficient account of the unconscious.

These criticisms are cogent and worthy of serious consideration, even if they sometimes appear to presuppose that one should have an answer to every question, and that the analyst may be like an explorer who is in possession of some relatively precise maps and of others in which the details are as yet incomplete. In other cases one is struck, in this and other models, by the tone of superiority in which the critique is expressed – a tone characteristic, according to Bion, of transformations in hallucinosis, a kind of transformation in which fear of the new induces one to cloak oneself not in opinions but in convictions, things being taken at face value. Let us consider these points in succession.

The radical antirealism of the analytic field does indeed fly in the face of our common sense, yet these criticisms continue to confuse reality with the discourse on reality. As biological organisms, we are obviously bound to certain vital parameters, constraints, limitations of reality, of the body and so on. Equally obvious, if we cannot halt the operation of unconscious thought, if at all times we cannot but communicate unconsciously, and if we dream both at night and while awake, then every statement can be seen in terms of its informative and referential quality, or of its real-time unconscious meaning.

While both perspectives are legitimate (as indeed would be any perspective that we agree to use in accordance with certain rules and on whose utility a consensus exists), they are different. Awareness is often lacking of the frame within which a phenomenon or perspective (vertex) is being accommodated. If I am a historian, I am interested in the factual character of an account, even if it is the account of a dream. If I am a classical analyst (in the broad sense), I shall likewise be interested in the facts if I believe that the treatment primarily involves the construction and reconstruction of the past. If, on the other hand, I consider that what matters most is to increase the patient's capacity for independent symbolization, this means not that historical reconstruction is pointless, but that it is relegated to a secondary position, becoming, as Meltzer puts it, a by-product.

This is exactly what happens in child analysis, where play is held to be sufficient to treat the patient. The basic approach of BFT is that we should work with adults in the same way as in an infant therapy setting. An adult's words are his drawings. The facts of reality, when transposed into a drawing, an animated cartoon, or a virtual reality environment, assume meaning within a new frame, even if they inevitably refer to other levels of reality or possible worlds in which we live (the external, internal, past, present and future worlds; worlds inhabited by part-objects, whole objects, etc.). After all, how would it otherwise be possible to communicate with a child in infant psychoanalysis, and thereby to initiate the complex interactions that will enable him to gain access to symbolic thought and permit treatment of his pathology, even without any reference to his personal archaeology? Are we sure that this interaction, made up of rhythms and song and dance, does not remain essential throughout life, besides the more mature capacity to make sense of experience? Is it not the case that – given that loss, separation and pain are omnipresent – what constructs the subject are moments of deep emotional communion?

To augment the capacity for symbolization, great store is set by the experience of emotional sharing, lived consensuality and unison that accrues when the analyst succeeds in seeing what the patient sees, or in transforming the patient's as yet unthinkable anxieties. If the analytic setting has the character of a fiction that is required to enclose material reality in parentheses in order to facilitate access to psychic reality, then everything on this stage is "theater." Anyone who holds that certain communications are confined to the level of reality is failing to observe strictly Freud's principles of the dream paradigm and of communication between the analyst's and the patient's unconscious. Worse, such a person causes the virtual dimension of the analytic field to collapse – that is, he is defending against disturbing contents for which he is not prepared to take responsibility. Reality is then reduced to a nightmare from which waking is impossible.

However, analysis is concerned with psychic and not with material or historical reality; that is the link that must be made to work properly again (which in our case signifies the capacity to name things, which always involves a struggle with ghosts or, if you will, with the absence of the object). If this concerns material reality, it does so only indirectly. Bion writes:

> The past is not important, because you can do nothing about it; the only things about it which you can do anything are the remnants, the vestiges of the past, of past states of mind [. . .] – but it is possible to make use of these vestiges that are discernible in the present if we allow ourselves to discern them.
>
> *(Bion, 1997, p. 44)*

That said, nothing prevents the analyst from aiming for a binocular vision of things that – the differences between them, however, having been clearly established – combines a model of the subject in isolation with one of the subject as a point in the intersubjective analytic field.

BFT is concerned more with containers than with the contained, and with psychic functions more than with mental objects. Yet it would be absurd to draw a sharp line of distinction between these entities. As stated, being interested in *how* rather than *what* entails using mainly open, unsaturated, ambiguous interpretations. The approach is essentially to transmit a method of thinking and of seeking meanings rather than actual results.

Dream theory is thus also modified. Rather than as a text to be deciphered in order to grasp the secrets of the latent thoughts obscured by psychic censorship, a dream is now seen as something to be reworked and transformed on the basis of current emotions by virtue of its rhetoric, which very much resembles poetry. Expression takes precedence over translation.

The analyst listens to everything with an internal setting. He can allow himself more freedom with regard to the classical rules of the setting, but takes more responsibility than that of a mere analyst-as-mirror: listening "without memory or desire," according to Bion, signifies meaningfully relinquishing the barriers to guilt and having to tolerate increased anxiety.

A patient's life history, as narrated by himself or as summarized by the analyst in the medical history, is never pure biography, but always also a narrative derivative of waking dream thought, or the way the analyst dreams or makes sense of his experience with the patient.

Everything depends on the frame, whether our standpoint is inside or outside it. The transference – a concept that we are bound to use, but that strictly speaking is meaningful only within a nonrelational model – is ubiquitous and immediate, albeit variable in intensity. One need only consider the infinite possibilities open to a patient, from his very first session, for organizing a narrative of his life. No other link is available in the selection of what to communicate than the transference. Even when talking about "facts," the patient is conveying a derived or indirect impression of how he perceives himself, the analyst and the emotional quality of their relationship.

BFT is accused of being excessively centered on the dual mother–child relationship and of thus minimizing the role of the third party, the father, in the constitution of the psyche; of taking no account of the Oedipus complex and the drives; and of desexualizing psychoanalysis. In fact, the paternal function is present in field theory from the beginning, from birth itself, in the relationship à deux, as an internal presence (and Oedipal function) in the mind of the mother, who has another object to cathect in addition to the child. It is a "father" or third party who, ideally resting on the concrete reality of a father, is however seen mainly as a function of the caregiver's mind. Again, the analyst is experienced as someone who has a private life of his own, other patients, interests of his own and so on. So the third party/father, as a separating entity, as bearer of the Law, of the sense of a limit and of reality, but also of responsibility and hence as the principle that modulates distance – not too remote and not too close – appears in all the inevitable (and necessary) moments of affective disjunction or nonattunement occasioned by the absence of the other. This is also the case between patient and analyst in an analytic session. This entity is present, lastly, in the structuring function of the setting, which makes for a salutary dialectic of identity and difference, a rhythmic succession of absence and presence, of hate and love.

Self-revelation in no way characterizes the working approach of an analyst who uses this model. In the clinical practice of Antonino Ferro and his followers, there is no trace of the self-revelation that is, instead, the hallmark of North American relational psychoanalysis. Ferro is very concerned to distinguish his model from any notion of corrective emotional experience or interpersonal reciprocity. In general, it is in fact better to avoid this technical device because the patient then feels intruded upon, believing that the analyst is robbing him of the space and time that is rightly his, owing to the asymmetry of the analytic contract.

However, if used with care, it may on occasion represent an extremely significant moment when the patient becomes aware of a particularly attunement with and closeness to the analyst, while noting that the analyst feels free enough to eschew rigid adherence to the rules of the setting.

Two further points must be made. First, self-revelation too involves not only introducing private material of the analyst's, but also bringing to life new characters in the narrations of the session. Second, the idea that the analyst may contribute contents of his own indicates the difficulty of conceiving the analyst's inner life as a point in the field that is dynamically interrelated with all the other points.

Another frequent mistake is to imagine that the analyst constantly loses himself in daydreams that bear no relation to what is actually happening. Nothing could be further from the truth.

On the one hand, the application of this approach, isolating oneself and the material from the context of material reality so as to grasp the essential emotional truth contained within it, is a discipline of the utmost severity. On the other, it is inevitable and indeed also desirable constantly to reimmerse oneself in the commonsense world, in waking sleep (that is, the ingenuous realism whereby we believe we are seeing things as they are), if one is not to betray on the factual level principles of technique supposed to make for greater receptivity.

Again, in some analyses reveries may prove to be completely absent or very rare. Exaggerated emphasis on the concept of reverie leads one to forget that in analysis there is not just one, but instead a number of different therapeutic principles.

A further critique confuses BFT with postmodernism as such, en bloc, as in effect a collective label for things that are in fact quite heterogeneous – or, worse, as a synonym for absolute relativism. In this case, the concept of truth (as is, without quotation marks) is emphatically introduced in the name of a realism that would be tantamount to nothing other than once again eliminating subjectivity. We are unaware of any authoritative scholar who has ever propounded such a notion, which is in fact untenable. It is quite different to maintain, other than in a context of religion or absolute truth, which no one could any longer dream of asserting – even in the pure sciences – that the only remaining foundation lies in consensus within a community, constituting a "minimum realism." What is not easy to grasp is that this consensus is not the fruit of deliberation based on exclusively rational arguments, but also comes into being in hundreds of ways that cannot be reduced to concepts. Moreover, these hundreds of ways somehow include links with reality, although we cannot say how the connection is made. Truth is not said but made; Kuhn's considerations on these matters remain unsurpassed. By introducing a principle of historicity, this author gives a convincing account of the evolution of scientific thought and of the foundations on which we build our human truths.

So it is not true that the analytic field model entails the disappearance of the concept of the subject. This fear too is unfounded. Both the standpoint of the subject and that of dynamic intersubjective interaction are nothing but models and conventions, and not the entity itself. They are constantly evolving perspectives that we carve out of reality in order to acquaint ourselves with something to which we lack direct access. Here again, continuity or discontinuity can be discerned: intersubjectivism, in the particular sense of the term used in BFT, is not an alternative to the concept of the subject, but complements it. In fact, however, the subject is, if only in part, ousted once again, and this time more radically, from the house of the ego; not only is it thrust back toward the unconscious, but the individual unconscious itself is referred to sociality.

As to the critique that BFT renders the analyst–patient relationship too symmetrical, a distinction must be drawn between role and personality. The analyst has a precise role that involves specific responsibilities. At the same time as he performs his role by using his subjectivity, he subordinates that subjectivity to the purposes of the treatment, employing symmetry in order to regain the ideal asymmetry needed to treat the patient. Hence symmetry depends on subjectivity, and asymmetry on the role. The two should not be confused, as seems to be the case when the term *mutuality* is applied ambiguously to denote both unconscious symmetry and a certain conception of the form that ought to be taken, on a basis of parity, by conscious interaction. The only conceivable symmetry, in our view, is that of unconscious communication.

On the level of unconscious communication, however, a dimension of basic symmetry cannot but be postulated. By definition, unconscious communication cannot be observed. We cannot identify the exclusive contribution of the patient or the analyst to one and the same element of the field if considered, precisely, as an unconscious creation à deux. Yet immersion in the symmetrical dimension of the relationship must be placed in the service of the necessary asymmetry of working. The setting defines different times and spaces for patient and analyst. The patient can say anything he likes for as much time as he wishes. The purpose of the meeting is the treatment of his psychological suffering. The analyst, on the other hand, is a professional who is an expert precisely in such matters, having already undergone treatment with his own analysis. For this reason, the direction of "pathological" projective identifications is normally from patient to analyst. Temporary reversals of this flow can, however, be observed, and are referred to as "negative reverie" or "reversal of the flow of projective identifications." That is not a bad thing, but is a fact of life – but the analyst must eventually become aware of the situation so as to put the system of analysis back into working order so that it can properly serve its original purpose.

The distinction between symmetry and asymmetry, although artificial, facilitates the description of two forms of operation of one and the same process. The secondary process constantly seeks to restore asymmetry, but by using unconscious thought and symmetrical communication. This, though, is not something that can be taken for granted, for it entails work. What is, or ought to be, taken for granted are only the external aspects of the relationship, such as responsibility, aims, means or levels of personal suffering.

At the unconscious level, communication is symmetrical. Every element of the field is considered to be co-generated. The characters of the field are functions/holograms of the field that are created by the beams projected by analyst and patient and are no longer recognizable, at least as long as the kind of attributions that would inevitably entail lapsing into a one-person psychology are eschewed. It is a strategic decision. It is of course important for the analyst, and hence also the setting, to be in proper working order – that is, that he be receptive, cathect and be cathected by the patient.

Considered in these terms, his reveries are the way in which dreaming reworks the emotional facts of the field. It is the deepest kind of understanding achievable in analysis. This by no means entails automatically making its contents explicit to the patient. The understanding gained by the analyst through reverie changes his attitude, modulates his capacity for attunement with the patient and modifies the field – something that may already prove decisive. On occasion, all that is needed to turn an impasse or stoppage of time into a living situation of hope restored is an image that makes sense of something that previously seemed quite meaningless.

Finally, with regard to the concept of the unconscious, it is our belief that by radically transforming the exterior of historical and material reality into a dream of the field, we are working with a more rigorous conception of the unconscious than those of other models. In fact, we believe that while perhaps reassuring, it is in part mistaken to consider that we can successfully gain intellectual mastery over a hybrid dialectic of outside and inside that does not make consistent use of a model (rather than using it alternately or, in the limit, simultaneously, these being different things). The unconscious is pervasive and speaks even when it is seemingly silent, not only negatively in micro- and macro-enactments, but also unceasingly with waking dream thought, and above all positively in the form of the poetic activity of the mind (the metaphor is Freud's, from *On Aphasia*), which has the ongoing function of creating meaning. For BFT, the conscious must be made unconscious (rather than the other way round, although that too can be seen in terms of expanding the unconscious), and the efficiency of the personality function that makes for a poetic vision of the ambiguity of things must be enhanced.

## Importance of BFT and its future developments

Bion and BFT accept the challenge of epistemological thought, to the affirmation of which, as it happens, psychoanalysis has made a powerful contribution from Freud on. In this way they demonstrate their extraordinary modernity. It is an open, radically critical kind of thought. It can on no account be identified with a form of nihilistic hermeneutics – that is, with the idea that interpretation has no limits and is devoid of sense. It is not so much a theory as a model, precisely by virtue of its programmatically provisional nature and its resistance to enclosure in a totality or in a system of methods and rules. Its particular fascination lies precisely in the ongoing process of deconstruction and self-deconstruction that is its hallmark, which demands from the analyst not only uncommon discipline of thought but also considerable mental elasticity. BFT does not seek to fix psychoanalysis in definitive forms, or to attain primal truths, but instead feeds on instability and if anything attempts to make reality more (poetically) ambiguous rather than less so. Traditional conceptual structures too are thereby ultimately destabilized, but also enriched and renewed. At the heart of BFT lies the consideration of the irreducible otherness that is the foundation of the subject, as opposed to any concept of experience, presence or identity that is autonomous, primal or self-constituted. As Derrida (1967, p. 56) writes, "alterity [otherness] is even the condition for presence, for presentation, and thus for Vorstellung in general; it precedes all the dissociations that could be produced." Assignment of meaning is not traced back to a consciousness that is master of itself, but emerges from a general textuality made up of references, cross-references, differences, oppositions and relationships. BFT can self-evidently engage profitably in a dialogue with contemporary philosophy.

BFT is just one of the virtually infinite range of models that we could construct to represent for ourselves the relationship between human beings in terms of intermediacy. Other perspectives are always possible. The mistake should not be made of assigning an ontological value to a given model. After all, even the notion of the subject is a construct. Although it works well for a whole set of situations, for all its necessity it is nevertheless a fiction. One need only consider how it has changed since Freud. The point instead is to ask ourselves, which model is most suitable for describing a specific phenomenon because it tells us more, or is more readily understandable, permits the emergence of new aspects, and is, in short, more useful for our purposes. So it was with the introduction of the concept of the field in physics or that of the gestalt in psychology.

The field can also be thought of as a new metaphor that impels us to ask ourselves new questions, to look in new directions and to look at old acquisitions in a new light. Of central importance, for instance, is the concept of "transformation," because it conveys the essence of the psychic processes of representation. It is no coincidence that Bion uses the example of a painter depicting a landscape and wonders how we manage to distinguish one from the other, and what invariants are involved. The emphasis on the aesthetic aspect inherent in representation (in the sense of sensation, as well as the ordinary sense) opens the way to contamination with aesthetic reflection in art. BFT promises a renewal of the psychoanalytic understanding of aesthetic experience, while also in turn causing itself to be interpreted by aesthetics.

Field theory is a newer and more profound theory of unconscious communication between individuals because it involves a more radical notion than other models of the unconscious and of oneiric functioning in a session; because it offers a more accurate description of the working of the analytic relationship; and because it changes our conception of a therapeutic factor and of interpretation.

The blurring of the lines between dreaming and waking life and between the primary and secondary processes is consistent with recent neuroscientific findings.

BFT may also constitute a fruitful approach for group and infant psychoanalysis, because it is to a substantial extent a development of both.

For all these reasons, we believe that the field concept may represent a new and fertile paradigm for psychoanalysis; to paraphrase Bion, it is the probe that gradually expands the area it is investigating.

## Notes

1 Translator's note: For convenience, the masculine form is used for both sexes throughout this translation.
2 Kojève sums up Hegel's conception of the subject as follows: "If they are to be human, they must be at least two in number" (1947, p. 43).

## References

Baranger, M 2005, 'Field theory', in S Lewkowicz & S Flechner (eds), *Truth, reality, and the psychoanalyst*, International Psychoanalytical Association, London, pp. 49–71.

Baranger, W & Baranger, M 2008, 'The analytic situation as a dynamic field', *International Journal of Psychoanalysis*, vol. 89, pp. 795–826.

Bezoari, M & Ferro, A 1989, 'Listening, interpretations and transformative functions in the analytical dialogue', *Rivista di Psicoanalisi*, vol. 35, pp. 1014–1050.

Bion, WR 1961, *Experiences in groups*, Routledge, London.

Bion, WR 1965, *Transformations: Change from learning to growth*, Heinemann, London.

Bion, WR 1991, *A memoir of the future*, Karnac, London.

Bion, WR 1997, *Taming wild thoughts*, Karnac, London.

Bleger, J 1967, 2012, *Symbiosis and ambiguity: A psychoanalytic study*, Routledge, London.

Churcher, J 2008, 'Some notes on the English translation of the analytic situation as a dynamic field', in W Baranger & M Baranger (eds), *International Journal of Psychoanalysis*, vol. 89, pp. 785–793.

Civitarese, G 2008, 2010, *The intimate room: Theory and technique of the analytic field*, Routledge, London.

Civitarese, G 2011, 2012, *The violence of emotions: Bion and post-Bionian psychoanalysis*, Routledge, London.

Conci, M 2011, 'Bion and his first analyst, John Rickman (1891–1951): A revisitation of their relationship in the light of Rickman's personality and scientific production and of Bion's letters to him, 1939–1951', *International Journal of Psychoanalysis*, vol. 20, pp. 68–86.

Derrida, J 1967, *Voice and phenomenon: Introduction to the problem of the sign in Husserl's phenomenology*, Northwestern University Press, Evanston, IL, 2011.

Ferro, A 1992, 1999, *The bi-personal field: Experiences in child analysis*, Routledge, London.

Ferro, A 2010, 2011, *Avoiding emotions, living emotions*, Routledge, London.

Grotstein, JS 2007, *A beam of intense darkness: Wilfred Bion's legacy to psychoanalysis*, Karnac, London.

Kojève, A 1947, 1980, *Introduction to the reading of Hegel: Lectures on the "Phenomenology of Spirit"*, Cornell University Press, Ithaca, NY.

Kristeva, J 1998, 'The subject in process', in F Jameson (ed), *The Tel Quel reader*, Routledge, NY, pp. 133–178.

Kuhn, TS 1962, *The structure of scientific revolutions*, University of Chicago Press, Chicago.

Lacan, J 1947. British psychiatry and the war. *Psychoanalytical Notebooks of the London Circle*, vol. 4, pp. 9–34.

López-Corvo, R 2002, *The dictionary of the work of W. R. Bion*, Karnac, London.

Merleau-Ponty, M 1945, 'The body as expression and speech', in *Phenomenology of perception*, Routledge, London.

Neri, C, Correale, A & Fadda, P (eds) 1987, *Letture bioniane*, Borla, Rome.

Ogden, TH 2003, 'What's true and whose idea was it?' *International Journal of Psychoanalysis*, vol. 84, pp. 593–606.

Ogden, TH 2008, *Rediscovering psychoanalysis: Thinking and dreaming, learning and forgetting*, Routledge, London.

Sandler, J & Sandler, A-M 1976, *Internal objects revisited*, Karnac, London.

Sandler, PC 2005, *The language of Bion*, Karnac, London.

9

# Intersubjectivity

*Jessica Benjamin*

This chapter will discuss how and why the concept of intersubjectivity came to absorb attention from a variety of psychoanalytic schools, however divergent its usage. Intersubjectivity describes the underlying common motive to reorient theory to the reality of contemporary clinical practice leading to convergence around the concept. Despite significant differences between schools, this convergence is evidence of the way that clinical psychoanalysts have moved far beyond the kind of practice that defined psychoanalytic theory in the early decades of its formulation by Freud.

Because the vast dimensions of the change in clinical theory and practice since Freud have remained almost unknown to the average academic or intellectual public, and since the usual form of exposure expected of the educated public consists of the reading of bits of Freud, it would seem an anthology such as this is long overdue. However, for the same reasons, the explication of even one dimension of this change that has occurred within our relatively esoteric culture seems daunting. So I must ask the reader to bear with me as I recapitulate certain key moments in psychoanalytic history that form the background for the shift toward thinking intersubjectively.

## Origins of intersubjectivity in psychoanalysis

Freud (1923) famously wrote about the ego and its objects, that is, the outside world of humans as represented internally. His notion of the person as a tripartite structure involving ego, superego and id always had a different valence in German than in English, of course. Since in German the term *ego* is actually "Ich," which translates as "I," it is a resonant rather than estranging term. Nonetheless, the term *object* to denote other persons is not particularly resonant to describe persons although philosophically customary. More important, the notion that the ego invests (or "cathects") its energy or drive in the object is meant as a description not of actual relationships but of what takes place in the mind, that is, *intrapsychically*. Psychoanalysis was in this sense first developed as an intrapsychic theory and the term *object* designated how the other was represented or manifested inside the mind. Hence, our first point: the term *intersubjective* was adopted, borrowed from philosophy in order to construct the opposite of *intrapsychic*, analogous to Continental philosophers using the idea to oppose the notion of a Cartesian subject–object relation.[1]

To describe the shift toward intersubjectivity I once paraphrased Freud's famous "where id was ego must be," stating: "where objects were, subjects must be" (Benjamin, 1995). But this statement is more rhetorically evocative than it is precise. "Subjects" cannot be inside our mind in the sense Freud meant in speaking of "objects." Others can be represented in our minds, however, perhaps as things located on an axis of uncontrollable–controllable, perhaps as beings with whom we engage in not wholly predictable ways. The idea of more than one subject, of two subjects each with their own mind, holding some view of the other, is essential to the intersubjective position. It insists that the reality of the outside other and the independence of external reality are – if not always experientially accessible to the vagaries of the mind – always a potential, and this notion of the other as "outside" the mind is constitutive of the intersubjective view (Benjamin, 1988, 1994).

But of course inner and outer are codetermining categories, and so we must begin by considering their interrelation. The psychoanalytic precedent for thinking that which is not inside our mind but must somehow get "inside" it was Freud's idea of the outside world or reality and the process of internalization. The relationship to the object is mediated by the function of the object in gratifying instinctual impulses – the mother is not person but provider of satisfaction for oral drives (Freud, 1915). Freud (1911, 1923) variously depicted the ego's relation to the outside world as hostile, resistant or involving the unwilling subjection to the demands of civilization: the renunciation of Oedipal wish fulfillment, the acceptance of "castration" (that one cannot have mother), the repression of sexuality and aggression in order not to lose love or suffer punishment. Thus outside or external referred to the world of others that was either imposing or resisted.

To anticipate the implications of intersubjectivity in regard to Freud's formulation, consider the very different proposition that not castration threats but the simple recognition of the existence of the Other as subject/mind with a will equal to our own sets a limit to our omnipotent wishes or narcissistic aspirations – what we might consider the Hegelian thinking underlying the idea of intersubjectivity (Benjamin, 1988; Ogden, 1994). Further, consider the idea that such recognition comes about through responses from the other that are not primarily imposing but accommodating and thus might be not merely a sad fact but a condition of joy and love. Whether or not one foregrounds and focuses on this fact, as I do, the game changes with the introduction of another subject, an Other who is subject as opposed to a representation subsumed by the notional ego and object in the inner world.

Significantly, the ideas summed up by Freud in his later theories of the ego and the Oedipus complex contributed to the evolution of "ego psychology" (as postwar American psychoanalysis came to be known), concerned with the adaptive or conflictual relationship to "reality." The struggle to accept this reality and the unconscious resistance to it were seen as sufficiently invariant that the analyst's main task was to recognize and interpret their manifestation in the neurotic patient. Organized by an implicit epistemological metaphor of knower and known, clinical theory saw the patient as the analyst's object of knowledge, and the analyst's view of the conflicts being analyzed was, albeit occasionally clouded by countertransference, potentially objective.

Significantly, by the time the second generation of psychoanalysis emerged in British object relations thinking (see Guntrip, 1961), a rather different view of the way the subject accepts reality had developed. Especially beginning with the work of Melanie Klein, a dramatic shift had occurred in which the focus was on the need to maintain love in the face of aggression toward the object, an aggression centered around resentment of dependence on the mother as a source of goodness. Acceptance of reality here implies the fact of dependency and lack of control over the object, and hinges on love balancing hate, a hallmark of what Klein called the depressive position. Klein saw the depressive position as an achievement because the child wants to repair the object it has damaged in fantasy, for example, early Oedipal anxiety relates to the imagined envious attacks on mother and father, in relation to whom the child then needs to restore love and gratitude (Klein, 1945).

While the interest in object relations, with concomitant interest in affects, actions upon or by imagined others, was first elaborated in the work of Klein, her perspective was claimed in the version of analysis carried forward by Bion (1967) and later his followers, Continental analysts like Ferro (2002), as well as the Latin American field theorists such as the Barangers (2009), which emphasized the shared unconscious fantasies that make up the intersubjective field between analyst and patient. Bion's notion of the containing function, the symbolizing reverie whereby the mother/analyst transforms emotional elements that would otherwise be indigestible projections into intelligible thinking, formulated an intersubjectivity of (unconscious) communication via projective identification.

Modifying Klein's contribution to create what was explicitly called object relations theory, Fairbairn, Guntrip and Winnicott stressed the essentially dyadic constitution of a self for whom emotional attachment to the other as a whole rather than as a function is primary. Fairbairn (1952), originator of object relations theory as it came to be called, shifts from Klein's focus on death instinct and aggression; he makes the motivation to maintain attachment to the object a "drive" in itself, and thus reality becomes fully identified with the world of objects who exist outside as well as inside. Winnicott (1958), shortly thereafter, in a similar vein argues for the primacy of the mind developing within the nurturing dyad, expressed in the notion that there can be no baby without the mother. Bowlby (1969), anchored in ethological research, demonstrated the infant's need for a satisfying response to its instinctual urge to attach, to seek proximity in the face of danger/anxiety, and his categories of secure and insecure attachment gradually informed an entirely different view of development than Freud's psychosexual theory. (See Mitchell & Black, 1995, for a summary of these developments.)

On the west side of the Atlantic, Kohut (1977), reacting against the Freudian ego psychology (with its own version of drive-and-defense theory) that dominated North America in the postwar period, developed a psychology of the self: the theory known as self psychology, which argued that healthy development depended on early childhood needs for mirroring and self-cohesion being met by the child's objects, and that these needs for secure attachment persisted in more mature form throughout life. Since the empathic response of the other to these needs is the vital sine qua non of development, the centrality of attachment and need to engage with others as affectively responsive and recognizing persons is highlighted in a way that parallels Winnicott's developmental position on the need for mirroring. Despite continued use of the term *object*, *recognition* as a primary need emerges from these theories in a way it did not previously.

Interestingly, the object relations view of attachment merged with American interpersonal analysis, at the same time that many of its postulates were paralleled by Kohut's (1977) formulation of self psychology. Although there are significant differences to address, for historical purposes it is important that these perspectives joined synergistically in New York where the position now known as relational analysis was officially inaugurated in the late 1980s. Notably, however, relational analysis grew out of the community shaped largely by the American interpersonal school of analysis, which focused on the here and now interaction between analyst and patient (Gill, 1982; Levenson, 1972). Thus it added to these perspectives a focus on the contribution of the analyst's subjectivity to the analysis, the patient's apprehension of that contribution and how the analyst becomes implicated in enactments (Aron, 1996; Hoffman, 1983; Mitchell, 1993). These enactments could be seen not as impurities but as part of a process of revealing dissociated (that is not necessarily fully unconscious but unusable knowledge connected to different parts of self) and unformulated aspects of the patient's mind (Bromberg, 1998, 2006). Relational psychoanalysis

151

placed great emphasis on the issue of mutuality and the contribution of the analyst's subjectivity not merely in the sense of knowing but also of therapeutic action (Aron, 1996; Mitchell, 1993).

It is significant that, despite significant differences, both those who worked in the Klein–Bion tradition and in the relational or self-psychological tradition arrived at the concept of intersubjectivity that refers to some aspect of mutual influence and co-creation between analyst and patient of the contents and process of psychoanalysis. At the same time, a few analysts who grew out of the American ego psychology tradition like Jacobs (2001) and Renik (1993, 1998) began to present strong clinical arguments in favor of the analyst's participation even though they did not embrace the relational turn in metapsychology. Thus by the end of the 1990s there were a number of quite different tendencies in psychoanalysis that brought to the fore either intersubjective theory or a focus on the analyst's subjective contribution.

## The convergence on the concept of intersubjectivity

Addressing the convergence on the idea of intersubjectivity the German analyst Bohleber has recently summed up the shift from an objectivist view thus:

> The subjectivity of the analyst as an instrument of knowledge was integrated into the concept of countertransference, . . . the role of the analyst as a clinical authority and his or her position as an objective observer of analytical events have been transformed [and] analytical knowledge acquisition occurs largely on the basis of the interactional events occurring between analyst and analysand.
>
> *(Bohleber, 2013, pp. 799–780)*

It is significant that regardless of postulates on how the psyche is structured, what conflicts or vulnerabilities constitute the problem psychoanalysis is supposed to cure, these basic assumptions can be shared. So while there are as many recipes as chefs, and we have yet to explicate more fully the term intersubjectivity, it appears true that the evolution of most psychoanalysis worldwide (possibly with an exception of the Lacanians) involved a turn away from the analyst's neutrality or blank screen function adumbrated by Freud and his contemporaries. Thus a break with the idea of analyst as the interpreter and the patient as the one who presents the material to be interpreted, the knower and the known, took shape across many schools. And therefore, in reading the literature from these different schools it is still, to a large extent, possible for the synthetically minded or eclectic student to identify with much of what each says.

If this translatability lies in the fact that there was indeed a shared paradigm shift away from the norms of neutrality and objectivity, then likely it is because there was widespread if unexpressed recognition that these ideals denied the reality of what happens in the room between two people. The presence of two minds – two subjects who in some sense create the known as well as share the process of knowing – both reflects and has shaped changes in the last 25 years of analytic practice. The analyst's knowing proceeded through identification (or receiving and processing the patient's projections as identification) rather than observing and analyzing from outside the patient's verbal productions as if they were a text.

Clearly the universally shared aspect of this shift – the one that makes analysts of different persuasions intelligible to one another even when they disagree – occurred through a critical engagement with both the insights and limits of Freud's view of transference and countertransference, in other words, based on a critique of a shared tradition. And while the demise of the objectivist paradigm of psychoanalysis obviously did not occur in a vacuum but reflected the critiques of positivism and objectivity in modern science and post-modern philosophy, within psychoanalysis itself the practical pressures of working with patients was an equally important motivation for change.

Such clinical pressures – certainly noted but not as readily formulated by Freud given the limits set by the scientific metaphors of his time – led over time to the increased valuation of the analyst's countertransference as a means of knowing the patient's unconscious. However, a close reading suggests that the forces Freud saw but resisted because he could not envision their integration in his method are those we now have the experience and categories to contain: the demand to "play a part" (rejected by Freud in the case of Dora) in the reliving of suffering, the demand for healing and affective connection in the face of psychic catastrophe and trauma (Benjamin, 1998). The degree to which we believe we can overcome these limits, while still adhering to Freud's methods or on the contrary that these methods must be altered, is still a point of great division among analysts. Even in the disagreements provoked by Ferenczi (1933), who today seems amazingly unfettered and contemporary, the issue of mutuality and the nature of the analyst's participation was central. We shall return to the issue of mutuality as one of the chief themes brought into focus by the intersubjective perspective.

Having considered the somewhat unifying focus on intersubjectivity as a way of framing questions about the changing conception of the analyst, let us consider what divisions this synthetic move has given rise to. Some commentators (see Bohleber, 2013; Stern, 2013) have tried to organize these issues by distinguishing two theoretical/practical vectors within the paradigm of intersubjectivity: first, the view that the intersubjective focuses on the relationship between two minds, even perhaps creating a third entity with a life of its own, a field of mutual influence and co-creation within the analytic dyad; and second, the view grounded in developmental psychology that focuses more generally on the capacity and need for recognition between two subjects, equivalent centers of being, each of whom brings to the relationship a different perspective, a unique history and asymmetrical abilities (e.g., mother versus child). The first focus, especially prominent in parts of Europe and Latin America, where it is often referred to as field theory, comes from a psychoanalytic lineage of Klein and Bion, but with a theoretical frame influenced by Lewin's gestalt theory and Merleau-Ponty's phenomenology (see Stern, 2013). This perspective has an epistemological tilt, but follows Bion insofar as its practical and theoretical emphasis is on the creation of a shared fantasy or narrative based on the existence of two unconscious minds participating in the relationship (see Brown, 2011). In North America Ogden, sharing many of the same phenomenological positions, has been a highly influential exponent of this tendency in intersubjective theory, elaborating a notion of the analytic third that bears a similarity to the idea of the field. In Ogden's (1994) conception, the third appears as a dynamic entity co-created by both subjects' minds in shared reverie and unconscious communication. More recently in the American context, Brown (2011) has formalized the Bionian emphasis on unconscious communication and shared reverie in the transference relation.

In the second direction, we can note two main currents. The phenomenological approach to intersubjectivity has also been represented by an influential dynamic systems theory developed in the arena of self psychology by Stolorow, Atwood and Orange (Stolorow & Atwood, 1992; Stolorow et al., 1997), which presented as a critique of Cartesian subject–object thinking. This school of "intersubjectivists" is rather different from the Bionian direction in that it places more emphasis on trauma and history than working through narrative and fantasy.

The relational perspective is closer to the latter intersubjectivist group as it is also oriented to the vector of history and trauma, encompassing a similar broad revision of Freud and making greater claims for the idea of intersubjectivity. However, it places even greater emphasis on developmental theory and infancy (Beebe & Lachmann, 2002; Beebe et al.; Benjamin, 1988). The analytic situation is seen as a mere instance of the human situation, and the dimensions of relationship that form our psyches – attachment or recognition, for instance – are foregrounded rather than the shared content produced by the two unconscious contributions (Stern, 2013).

Another way to sketch this difference is to say that while at the most general level an inter-subjective view implies a concern with the relationship between two persons rather than one person alone, we can already identify a fork in the road regarding the significance attributed to two minds, two persons, two subjects in the room. This fork already became partially discernible with the development of object relations theory: for some (notably Fairbairn, Guntrip, Winnicott, Bowlby and their associates), the importance of the quality of attachment to outside others, the impact of real others on the developing self, issues such as separation and loss, came to have greater weight than Klein's focus on how the ego deals with the inevitable hatred of dependency (fueled by innate aggression), which it solves by means of reparation. To simplify matters a bit, for those who took the Kleinian fork, intersubjectivity has meant primarily a shift in our understanding of what takes place within the analytic dyad, and the existence of the real other, of historical trauma or experience as a source of psychic pain or conflict, is generally less important; the main point of intersubjectivity is that we must use ourselves and our capacity to receive and work through the patient's projections to know them. For those who took the object relations and self psychology direction, which evolved into relational analysis, the evolution of self in relation to real others and historical trauma had as much weight as fantasy, the fate of the need for secure attachment assumed more centrality than aggression in understanding anxiety.

Yet another related matter is the status of intersubjective theory in relation to its object of knowledge/contemplation: Is the intersubjective object of study defined conceptually in terms of something other than superordinate to the individuals who meet? Is there something specific to interaction between persons that is not already contained in the idea of one person? In addressing these questions Bohleber (2013, p. 94) wrote,

> An encounter is always more than the impact it has on those doing the encountering. There-fore, the difficulty facing all intersubjective theory approaches in psychoanalysis lies in describ-ing the intersubjective itself . . . Strictly speaking, when speaking of intersubjectivity, it involves something . . . more than an interactive reciprocal regulation of experience and behaviour.
>
> *(2013, p. xxx)*

The difficulty, Bohleber suggests, is in analyzing these interaction patterns of regulation as we might "events." But in fact, once the study of infancy began, the use of categories that describe interaction patterns rather than individual responses became a hallmark of intersubjective theory, an area of study to which I shall return. I suggest that it is no more inherently difficult to use intersubjective categories to describe events involving the interaction of two or more people than to use intrapsychic categories for events that are purportedly taking place "inside" an indi-vidual mind. Even that bête noire of anti-positivism, the scans of brain alight with colors like pinball machines, can be adapted to show how the scan of one person correlates with the scan of another producing a "replicable" interaction pattern. "*The* intersubjective" is a domain of study, a perspective on the human psyche, a set of categories; it does not refer to or rely on the defini-tion of a singular thing (reification) any more than does "*The* intrapsychic." But just as we might consider intrapsychic theory as properly relating to internalized object relations, structures like superego, ego and id, instincts or anxiety, so might we consider that intersubjective theory should properly focus on processes of mutual identification and projection, mutual affect regulation and attunement, joint dissociation, or mutual recognition of intention, meaning and impact.

In fact, what we mean by intersubjectivity, its domain and concerns qua theory not thing, might best be seen as a question that relates to historical developments in the evolution of theory –

the fork in the road I described earlier. It matters very much whether the point of departure is primarily the analytic dyad or primarily the psychic development of individuals in relationship, or whether the aim is to integrate both those perspectives. And it is equally crucial whether the shift to intersubjective theory retains or turns away from the traditional Freudian idea of triadic development in the Oedipus complex; whether it embraces the contemporary developmental stories emerging from infancy research with its emphasis on procedural levels of interaction or affect regulation rather than narrative. Finally, the range of involvement of the analyst's subjectivity and the weight accorded to enactments varies depending on those theoretical choices. Thus, while these two viewpoints are not mutually exclusive and have been interpenetrating in many thinkers, it is useful to see some divergence in intellectual history as shaping later clinical trends. That said, the constant crossover of concepts, the exchange of ideas that occurs in places like New York, encourages me to seek translation between systems so that we can identify common concerns behind the different languages.

## Intersubjectivity and the idea of recognition

The point of view I shall elaborate here takes the latter broader view of intersubjectivity, clearly more popular in North America, understood both in terms of the philosophically defined problem of recognizing the other as well as the developmentally defined capacity to recognize the other. This perspective, which I elaborated in *The Bonds of Love* more than two decades ago (Benjamin, 1988), is no longer as radical or charged as it was originally, when only a few infancy researchers shared it, before several decades of analysts and infancy researchers expanded it. In this intersubjective perspective the question of the acceptance of reality also emerges, but shifts from something imposed from the outside to an epigenetic process of developing the capacity for mutuality and identification with others. A landmark for intersubjective theory was the influential researcher Daniel Stern's (1985) proposition that at a certain moment the infant has the realization that there are other minds "out there" that feel and think "like me," though with a difference. It follows that minds can know one another, that the independent existence of the other upon whom we depend is not merely a reality to which we are resigned but actually the condition of an enlivening exchange with "more life." In this sense others are not merely love objects but also "like subjects," beings with an equivalent center of subjectivity who share meaning and feeling in ways that are intelligible or communicable but also a center from which things may appear differently (Benjamin, 1988, 1995). Used as a developmental concept, intersubjectivity thus had two interrelated premises: that we need the other, to recognize and be recognized by; and that the psyche grows through the action and impact of one subject on another, subject to subject rather than subject to object.

That the active mental processes that involve the capacity for knowing and being known by the other (also called *mentalization* by Fonagy & Target, 1995) begin in infancy and depend upon the recognizing action of the primary others was, I would argue, most powerfully influenced by the formulations of Winnicott and Kohut, but took on even wider implications with the empirical study of mother–infant interaction. The study of infancy allowed insights into development and affect attunement that support and amplify an intersubjective psychoanalysis in which mutuality or mutual recognition plays a central role.

The developmental view of intersubjectivity that stresses recognition thus came both from those psychoanalytic formulations and from research inspired by and affiliated with the theoretical revisions in late 20th-century psychoanalysis:[2] attachment studies, empirical studies of mother–infant interaction, and later neuropsychological studies. Bowlby's work on internal working models of attachment grew into a major paradigm of understanding the relational style of parent–infant couples, of adult personality based on early childhood.[3] Developmental research exposed how from the beginning of life the self emerges from reciprocal regulation and recognition processes in the primary relationship. On one hand, the paradigm of a passive infant, a "nursling" in the oral phase, was replaced by the view of a little person who could differentiate between self and other, actively explore and try to have an impact on the other, recognize and enjoy rather than shun otherness and novelty. For example, studies of face-to-face play (Beebe & Stern, 1977) between mother and infant at only 3–4 months of age had stunning implications: it was possible to show the early ability to demonstrate and appreciate impact, how actively babies engage with mothers in creating patterns of positive engagement or negatively toned disengagement.

It is noteworthy that what produced this change was not merely the study of infants but of the mother–infant relationship. However, the additional point of recognizing women's, mother's subjectivity – a perspective that could only evolve through the coincidence of feminism with intersubjective theory (see Benjamin, 1988) – amplified the understanding of bidirectional processes, of mutuality. Thus the issue of whether the mother herself enjoyed the engagement, whether she felt in some sense known by her baby as well as vice versa, gradually evolved as a feminist perspective seeped into the world of infancy studies (see Benjamin, 1988), albeit with some limitations imposed by an infantocentric view (e.g., Sander, 2002; Stern, 1998).

The clinical implications of this revision of the basic parental metaphor from Oedipus to mother–infant were considerable. It meant that not only the analyst's knowing but also her or his presence as a receiver of communication constitutes a form of recognition (variously defined in terms of containing, mirroring, understanding, empathy) that feels both safer and more authentic to the patient – contrasting with the metaphor of nonjudgmental safety in the neutrality of the "blank screen" or mirror. The variations in the way that authentic presence is defined and communicated may be seen as dependent not only on theory but how closely the analyst strives for fittedness with a particular patient and not merely on the truth of a one-size-fits-all perspective. Specificity or fittedness was, according to the infancy researcher and analyst Louis Sander (2002), a primary principle of recognition. And as the relational analyst Stephen Mitchell (1997) argued, the tailoring of a specific solution to a specific patient, that which is precisely not-generic, is part of what constitutes the healing process. In other words, the fact that I as analyst am accommodating to you the patient is itself significant, expressing an intent to recognize that can in turn be recognized by the other, even in the presence of misunderstanding or failures in empathy. Subsequent to such research, the clinical implications of these ideas were articulated in a way that had major implications for a shift in practice toward emphasizing affective exchange and interaction, "something more than interpretation" (Beebe & Lachman, 2002; Lyons-Ruth, 1999; Stern et al., 1998).

A crucial clinical perspective evolved from the idea developed by infancy researcher Tronick (1989) of rupture and repair – that is, the inevitability of both micro- and macro-violations of expectancy and disruptions in attunement that must be worked through by the couple to recreate a rhythm of mutual accommodation and affect regulation. It exemplifies the larger concept of recognition and breakdown as a vehicle of relational development. This notion of rupture and repair has merged with the idea of the other, who is able to be more than the projection of one's mind, who can receive as communications such projections along with many other meanings, first formulated by Winnicott (1971). This formulation may be seen in conjunction with the notion that reality must be discovered and created through a *shared* process rather than merely imposed as renunciation of omnipotent wishes for control or gratification. For Winnicott, renunciation was reframed as a positive acceptance of reality, which was facilitated through the intermediate realm of transitional objects, things that were neither definitively real or unreal, neither created nor discovered – whose "thereness" create a potential space beyond subject and object. Winnicott (1971) also wrote compellingly – and for his time heretically – of the need to "destroy the object" so that it could "survive," prove itself to be outside the subject's omnipotent control. That is, he recognized the need of the I for a You who are not "destroyed" by the I's action (mistrust, negativity, withdrawal), such actions as would imply having destroyed You the internal object in my fantasy. Thus, You the inside object have now become You the outside other with whom I communicate, an external reality that I accept or even love, rather than submit to.

Winnicott's (at that time) radical proposal was that of an essential process whereby the developing psyche comes to see the other not merely as an object of its own projections, not merely an object to control or be controlled by, but an outside other who can be loved precisely because she is not identical with that which is created by one's own mind or fantasy. This differentiation, which he thought came about when the other survived ("outside") being attacked or devoured in fantasy ("inside"), he compared to the difference between sucking on a breast that is seen as an extension of self versus actually receiving "not–me" nourishment but an outside source – feeding on the other rather than oneself.

My work (Benjamin, 1988, 1995) aimed to elaborate a theory of intersubjectivity (intersubjective recognition theory) that begins with the issue of recognizing the other, and works with Winnicott's notion of how the other comes to appear to us as a separate but connected being. Separate and connected is a distinction, as Winnicott well knew, crucial to the therapeutic process in order for the patient to be able to make use of or receive something from the other. The distinction also points to the broader dimension of the question: what does it mean to think or analyze with intersubjectivity in mind? To think about the psyche in terms of intersubjectivity means to see the apprehension of the felt experience of the other as a distinct being (neither persecutor nor subjugated) as a central accomplishment of the human subject.

Winnicott's idea of the surviving other as a person of value because they are not simply a mental object also reveals the actual, most primary meaning of recognizing the analyst's subjectivity, the one I have made central to intersubjective recognition theory (Benjamin, 1988, 1995, 2004). It is, incidentally, quite different than one often conventionally assumed by defenders of classical analysis who rejected the relational view of intersubjectivity as being too radical because they reduced its meaning to the idea of "disclosure" – whether the analyst directly expresses thoughts and feelings to the patient based on her or his own subjectivity. While it is true that the issue of disclosure became a valuable fulcrum for showing how the analyst's self-revelation could create space for exploring otherwise closed-off issues (Renik, 1993, 1998), this focus usually avoided the question of satisfying the developmental need for recognition by a vital other.

In particular, the question of what it would mean for the patient to recognize the analyst's subjectivity has been significant in the tension between relational and self psychological views of intersubjectivity, the latter tending to stress the possible interference of the analyst's self-expression with empathic centering on the patient's experience. But the concern with the analyst's intrusion or hijacking of the process arose in relation to many other objections by analysts who think of intersubjectivity while striving to limit the analyst's participation in enactments. The issue at hand is whether the analyst expressing her or his feelings is equated with a kind of absolute symmetry, or whether a form of mutuality is conceptualized that still includes the asymmetry essential to a responsible therapeutic relationship (Aron, 1996).

We will return to the issue of mutuality versus symmetry, but suffice it to say that the question of specific disclosures by the analyst became the focus of discussions of intersubjectivity in the 1990s, mostly prompted by certain analysts from within the American Freudian mainstream who challenged the excessive emphasis on neutrality and nondisclosure of the dominant received wisdom. The narrower controversy around the question of how much and in what way the analyst's subjectivity is "irreducible," as described by Renick (1998, 200-), or how valuable is its

157

expressive use (Bollas (1987, 1989), began to develop into a fuller discussion in the '90s. We can see how the issue of asymmetry takes shape not just as a challenge to neutrality but more broadly in relation to the question of how the analyst participates as a subject.

One reason the relational tendency in psychoanalysis was never fully integrated with Kohut's self psychology movement was that the latter's view of bidirectionality was far more limited; the intersubjective theorists who emerged from self psychology (Stolorow et al., 1997) stressed the need for the analyst to de-center from himself and focus on the patient's subjective experience far more than the patient's need for the analyst to show the impact of his experience on himself or herself. By contrast, the relational analyst (see e.g., Bromberg, 2006, 2011) stresses the patient's need to feel the impact of her or his experience on the analyst's self.

In relation to affect regulation, this implies that the analyst is not adding to the dysregulation the patient is feeling but calming it through her/his understanding. The patient, says Winnicott (1971), comes through the experience of destruction feeling that the analyst who survives destruction is "there to receive the communication" and in this sense a subject outside omnipotent control. In the sense of being *affected* (Bromberg, 2011), but not unhinged (or at least only temporarily so), the analyst survives. In relation to recognition of meaning, it implies the analyst through his/her understanding can, to invoke Holden Caulfield, "catch a body" that is falling into trauma; that he or she can reshape what would otherwise be experienced as disruptive and meaningless "missiles" attacking the sensitive nervous system into "missives" of emotional experience.

This tension between mutuality and asymmetry in the analytic relationship as an aspect of intersubjective theory to my mind has remained a fruitful tension within two schools that are otherwise closely allied and interpenetrating. So far I have been suggesting that we might best identify the sides of the tension in terms of relational and self psychological schools of intersubjectivity.[4] The question of how we limit or expand our uses of self both in terms of emotive expression and content is not only a theoretical but a practical question about the "art" of analysis – relating, for example, to the value we assign directly felt affective exchange versus unknowable unconscious implications. The aim of solving such questions, rather than preserving them for constant interrogation of our practice, seems chimerical. Nonetheless people necessarily lean toward one style of theory and practice over another.

## Hegel, Winnicott and the idea of the third

I suggest these controversies – defined in the past by the shibboleths of correct technique or "what is really psychoanalysis?" – be analyzed intersubjectively and reframed in light of Winnicott's perspective on survival of destruction. The question then becomes, what kind of analytic action makes it possible for the analyst to survive for the patient as a differentiated being rather than succumb to the dynamic of projection and control? How does the analyst show that she or he is receiving the communication, able to bear the weight of the child's/patient's suffering, shame, revelations, use the patient's expression and let the patient use him or her, and, finally, show the emotional impact of this distress without being reactive, that is anxiously withdrawn or aggressive?

This perspective on recognition and survival, the restoration after breakdown or failure might be seen as "intersubjectivity for itself" in the Hegelian sense – that is, not merely an observer's viewpoint of two separate equivalent subjects, but a felt experience of recognizing difference and mutual impact that is (or can potentially be) recognized by the knowing subjects themselves.

Recognition that is recognized is "for itself." Extending this notion to include reciprocal recognition with the patient, the experience is one in which we know ourselves to be trying to recognize each other's communicative intent.

This Hegelian perspective (more accurately, Hegel as filtered through Kojève in Paris in the 1930s), as I shall explicate shortly, was also used in this sense by the psychoanalytic theorist Thomas Ogden (1994) to create a novel paradigm of intersubjectivity mediated by shared unconscious communication. As Ogden put it,

> each individual cannot simply become a self-conscious subject by seeing himself in the other [but] . . . is destined to remain outside of himself (alienated from himself) insofar as the other has not "given him back" to himself by recognizing him.
>
> *(Kojève, 1934–35 in Ogden, 1994, p. 13)*

As I contended in synthesizing Winnicott and Hegel, Ogden likewise stresses that the infant must find himself in the mother as both extension of and other to himself, both through the transitional realm and through the experience of destroying the object.

In a significant contribution Ogden conceived of the analytic third as a dynamic entity co-created by both partners to which both must give over, in effect allowing themselves to be interpenetrated by each other's unconscious fantasies and to some degree "subjugated" by the process of projective identification. As with the idea of enactment (a term he does not use as it implies the analyst "doing" something under the impact of the process), this joint process allows aspects of self, fears and desires, to gradually take shape in a way that can be recognized, so that the third can be refigured as a "recognizing third," a vehicle of understanding and shared knowledge. This transformation depends upon the empathic understanding and interpretation by the analyst and the recognition of the analyst's individuality by the analysand (i.e., using the interpretation). In a sense, both partners are then returned to themselves as separate subjects after enduring and passing through this other-than-self experience within the dynamic third that has overtaken them. In any case, Ogden's views radically transformed the idea of the third from being a representation of theory or knowledge (the "father" with whom the analyst "mother" converses (see Britton, 1988/1997) in the analyst's mind to a co-created process. In that sense it is a true intersubjective third, despite what relational analysts might see as a limited role for the analyst's subjectivity.

In a further development of the Klein–Bion direction, Brown (2011) offers a perspective similar to Ogden's, though less Hegelian. He defines intersubjectivity as "largely an unconscious process of communication and meaning making between the two intrapsychic worlds" (p. 109) that changes both. It culminates in the transformation of the shared emotional field, comprised of our individual unconscious subjectivities into bearable images woven into a narrative. This interweaving occurs through the analyst's ability to mobilize what Bion (1962) called the alpha function, the thinking of emotional meanings that organizes and contains, makes bearable, emotional states so that the patient can identify with this function and gradually increase her own affect tolerance. As we shall see, this view overlaps with important aspects of relational thinking, although his notion is that the intrapsychic worlds of each person are already separate entities that meet, rather than always already mutually constituting as Ogden or the intersubjectivists like Stolorow stress. The key overlapping aspect is that Brown (although this is not explicitly recognized) differs from the contemporary Kleinians in London regarding the effects of trauma, a concept that is controversial for them. The transformational emotional effects of the analyst's witnessing, important for Brown, are constricted by the neo-Kleinians who remain true to a narrow construction of the intrapsychic world and of interpretation and insight as mutative.

From another angle, despite considerable differences, Ogden, the self psychologists and the neo-Kleinians have in common a greater emphasis on the asymmetry of the analytic relationship – asymmetry, that is, regarding the idea that the analyst is primarily a vehicle for recognizing the patient's affects or fantasies. However, their positions diverge along the axis of affect versus fantasy, the history of attachment relations versus here and now exchange of unconscious images, actual trauma versus transference (see Bohleber, 2010). This axis poses different choices than that of symmetry–asymmetry. Thus it is hard to align ourselves along only one axis to determine where we stand in the field. In any case, the question of how the analyst is actually recognized by the patient – including the analyst's failures and difficulties in sidestepping the tendency to reenact original injuries, "repetition" – is more strongly emphasized in the relational school of intersubjectivity, to which I shall now turn.

## Intersubjective recognition theory and the third

Let us now consider how those formulations that emerge from Klein and Bion – and in Ogden's case, mixed with Winnicott and Hegel as well – might translate into or diverge from relational thinking and particularly the idea of the third in intersubjective recognition theory. The experience of thirdness as I conceive it is more like that of Ogden's "recognizing third," in which the difference between self and other is maintained through the sense of an intermediate zone in which contradictions, oppositions, antagonisms or differences have room to be felt, played with or negotiated rather than collapsed. The experience of thirdness is closely related to the dimension of holding tension between opposites or referring to a principle of lawful relating that I would call the third.

In a sense, the ambiguity that applies to the Third – whether it is signifier or signified – can be likened to the Buddhist notions of dharma (as truth, reality, the law, "what is," and the teaching of all the them), or the notion of logos (truth, the law, the nature of things). I grant that at times it also seems compelling to refer, as Ogden does, to that which we co-create, our shared dynamic, as a third – our (inter)personal version of the greater third. Thus we are often faced with slippage as we wonder if the third in any given usage is referring to the dance or the choreography, or even the music to which we dance, while seeing the dancing itself as thirdness. I prefer, therefore, to see Ogden's version of the third, the dynamic interaction that takes on a life of its own, as a very specific instance of something larger. The (capital-T) Third appears to me more as a point in a larger system of dynamic tension or opposition, (originally called "the third term" in Hegelian thinking): perhaps a point of reference, something more like a principle or mathematical function – in this case a function that holds or marks a place in which recognition is restored, in which opposites are held in tension rather than split.

The Third in this larger sense is the principle that represents the world as potentially lawful and meaningful in the face of irreconcilable opposites, polarity and splitting, failures and ruptures in attachment. It holds the place of a possibility that often is contradicted or unrealized, yet can inspire renewed effort to recreate meaning or reconstitute the sense of possible goodness. From this perspective Ogden's usage of the term *subjugating third* to describe a process of joint projective identifications would be paradoxical. A subjugating dynamic, something that takes on a life of its own "outside" the two subjects who create it, which as it were sweeps them up, is not a true third because it always splits the opposites and collapses the in-between space. Even though it is apparently a Third Thing in addition to Us Two, and thus lends itself to be seen as third, it never allows Us Two to be differentiated. Whereas thirdness, in my view, implies a space of differentiation that is not collapsed into the simple opposition of up and down, victim and perpetrator, good and bad, doer and done-to.

My perspective on the concept of the Third is also shaped by the addition of developmental and motivational aspects of intersubjective recognition theory derived from infancy studies. In early development the process of rupture and repair, or of breakdown and restoration of recognition, involves acknowledging the violation of procedural or symbolic patterns that have become part of our expected interaction. In this light recognition points to the idea of the Third as representing a lawful world. This lawfulness is the very basis upon which the other's intentions and one's own actions can be recognized (Benjamin, 2004). With this notion of a lawful world as the basis of the third – what I will call the Moral Third – the contradiction in positing a subjugating third becomes more apparent.

And it is worth emphasizing because a very important correlate to this idea of lawfulness is that ruptures or violations in expectation can and should be acknowledged, so used to enhance resilience and understanding of other minds. In infancy, the acknowledgment of small violations is part of the everyday creation of a lawful world, as when the caregiver acknowledges through gesture and soothing sounds that something is uncomfortable or unexpected (a loud noise, for instance). The use of such "marking" behavior by mothers, elaborated by Gergely and Fonagy, is an example of how soothing entails a proto-symbolic action of both acknowledging the felt distress and mimicking it in a way that shows the caregiver herself is not really frightened or disregulated (Fonagy et al., 2002). Such interactions not only provide affect regulation and protection, but also recognition of the expectation in the baby's mind as well as the pain of violation.

The third is not a simple position of goodness outside such violations – rather the sense of a lawful world begins with the acknowledgment of these violations of expectancy such that we are able to form some sense of what is the rightness or wrongness of things. This lawful quality of experience based on the possibility of repairing ruptures greatly contributes to the safety of attachment and allows for the exercise of agency – in effect, it makes dependency tolerable, not merely a source of pain and anxiety. All of this depends on the background of subject-to-subject co-created patterns: the principle of these patterns being the third, the experience of interacting according to them, thirdness. In this thirdness, the co-created dance is best describable not as an action–reaction or stimulus–response sequence but a form of mutual accommodation or co-action.

The formulation of rupture and repair (Tronick, 1989) has also profoundly changed our view of what is therapeutic or transformational in psychoanalysis. It has allowed us to understand that the inevitable moments of disregulation and dissociation in our processing of what is going on, the possible enactments that result, and the ensuing repair of the therapist's "mistakes" (misattunements, failures in regulation) as a basis for development and change.

Acknowledgment of mistakes becomes the basis for analyzing the dynamic behind them. Insofar as we recognize that the analyst is a subjective participant, and thus she as well as the patient become involved in dissociative processes (Bromberg, 2006), the notion of rupture and repair becomes more essential. However, we should stress that recognizing the analyst's participation goes hand in hand with recognizing how the patient's efforts at repair also help sustain the relationship and (as with infants; see Beebe & Lachmann, 2002) contribute to growth.

Significantly, because intersubjective recognition theory sees the principles of thirdness beginning in earliest infancy relations, we trace those patterns beginning at the procedural or subsymbolic level that may be seen metaphorically as the rhythm between partners. From this I proposed the idea of the *rhythmic third* (formerly "the One in the Third"; Aron, 1996; Benjamin, 2004), the mutual accommodation that brings about the sense of union in thirdness. The principle of accommodation may serve to sum up the earliest procedural version of lawful relating, mutual regulation or recognition, of the attunement that contributes to co-creation of expectable patterns (see Benjamin, 2004; Sander, 2002). In positing a pre-symbolic basis for the third (as opposed to Lacan, see Benjamin, 2004), I am suggesting that the differentiated form of recognizing the other – the other's survival of projective identification or aggression Winnicott described – develops out of fitting in, recognition by an other who is responsive, permeable and recognizing of the self.

On this procedural foundation the more differentiated moral, symbolically mediated third develops based on ability to express our own intentions and to recognize the other as a like subject deserving respect, on whom we must depend without resorting to coercion – with whom we bear the vulnerability of such dependency for realizing our intentions. This *differentiating third* (formerly "Third in the One," Benjamin, 2004) defines a mental position in which the subject can hold in mind different discordant perspectives, recognize the other's separate existence, and thus one in which more than one subjectivity or reality can coexist. Despite the historical ideals of a psychoanalysis based on symbolizing and differentiating, the reality that this aspect of thirdness gets lost or breaks down has preoccupied analysts "drowning in the counter-transference" (Racker, 1968) since Freud struggled to understand what went wrong with Dora (Benjamin, 1998). But it has become increasingly apparent that without attention to affect regulation, to the rhythmic third, exchanges of interpretation and insight in analysis are likely to be a mere simulacrum. They then tend to foster a dissociation whereby the patient keeps their good, insightful part working with the analyst and hides the shame-ridden, less integrated part(s) that feel like a lonely abandoned baby or child.

Thus, in contrast to the version of intersubjectivity that follows the Klein–Bion direction, which stresses the sharing and symbolic processing of unconscious fantasy, the grounding of relational intersubjective theory in infancy studies also brings in what is called implicit relational knowing or the procedural level of action as crucial to the therapeutic process (Lyons-Ruth, 1999; Stern et al., 1998). The co-created thirdness would be constituted not only at the level of fantasy and shared reverie – satisfying and productive as it is – that can be narratively, symbolically given meaning through the function of interpretation or interpretative action. It would also require analyzing the patterns of sub-symbolic, procedural interaction that are seen as transforming the participant's self states and mode of relating.

Thus from the standpoint of relational theories grounded in infancy and concerned with affect regulation, the interactive engagement and attachment patterns themselves shifts something in our minds. Changing these patterns to expand the window of affect tolerance (Schore, 1994; Siegel, 2001), being able to experience more emotion with the other's recognition, as Bromberg (2006, 2011) contends, serves to shift the quality of attachment and frees us from the use of dissociation as a substitute for affect regulation. Thus intersubjective recognition replaces dissociation as it reconfigures the patterns of attachment and the interactive schemas related to agency and impact on the other.

What do I mean by "procedural" and interaction schemas? To name some crucial patterns and schemas: those that together organize the mind to either use social engagement or more dissociative defensive actions (P. Ogden, 2006); the patterns of expectation around rupture and repair, attunement and recognition, which relate to the interactive capacities for self-regulation and mutual regulation (Beebe & Lachmann, 2002; Tronick, 1989); and the linking or dissociation of different self states (Bromberg, 2006, 2011), which relates to capacities for self-reflection and knowing the other. Attention to these changes, in addition to though not excluding elements of narrative and symbolic meaning, extend our notion of how to create affect tolerance (Siegel, 2001) and expand recognition of each other's subjectivity. Since a relational intersubjective view postulates that from the beginning of life we depend on creating patterns of mutual regulation and recognition with the other, including ruptures and breakdowns, experiencing the patterns we have internalized and the possible failures associated with them forms the heart of our work. At times these patterns will be manifest in narrative meanings and symbols, but at other times they must first manifest and shift at the level of the rhythmic third (Benjamin, 2004).

Another sense in which the procedural becomes paramount is the placing of equal or greater significance on the relational fact that we have succeeded as a dyad in *coming through*. The movement from *doer–done to* opposition to feeling conscious of two subjects co-creating, regardless of the content or insight we achieved, is procedurally paramount. This movement is not necessarily facilitated by interpretation or understanding contents in an explicit way, it could be shared laughter or tears, preverbal gestures, that acknowledge our existence as feeling subjects in a world of shared meaning. While Ogden (1994) defines the analyst's laughter as interpretative action, relational analysts consider the possibility that at times it might well be the patient's laughter or other sign of shifting into self-awareness that facilitates the analyst's shift in self state. This ability to have an impact on the analyst enhances the patient's sense of agency.

Going further, Bromberg (1998) adumbrated the idea of standing in the spaces: that formerly unlinked or split apart self states related to the other can now be held in one mind as recognizable parts of self; a person can become aware of more than one feeling, more than one self state or part without one threatening the elimination of the other and thus requiring a defensive dissociation. Dissociation, involving affective shutdown and cutting-off from the other, impoverishes all connectedness and development of the split-off self parts. On this view, enactments occur as both analyst and patient enter into states of joint dissociation, which Bromberg called a "dissociative cocoon"; like Ogden's subjugating dynamic, this shared dissociative state can carry both analyst and patient into enactments that require working through.

However just as dissociation can be seen as a joint process, so the knowledge that in certain ways patients contribute to the recreation of the third and that survival is mutual changes the perspective. Patient and analyst can help *each other* shift from one state of mind: from opposition and projection to shared owning of anger or mistrust. Both need to recover their agency, experience the sense of space for thinking that comes when there is recovery from rupture. Depending on the analyst's ability to acknowledge the patient's contribution and efforts to repair, it can become more apparent how both partners mutually survive destruction, how the patient perseveres despite the analyst's mistakes. This shifts the emphasis toward mutuality, including tolerance of the other's vulnerability as well as appreciation of the other's resilience.

## Mutuality and asymmetry

Our clinical view of enactments and the joint occurrence of dissociation thus depends upon our theorizing of the bidirectionality and co-creation of the interaction as well as the principle of rupture and repair. These postulates are also united by a common focus on regulation of self and other as part of a dynamically interactive system. The question then arises as to the specific nature of mutuality in the analytic dyad.

While some writers, as mentioned earlier, have thought that for relational analysts this mutuality necessarily consists of disclosure that is only one very narrow construction of what it means to use one's own subjectivity or find elements of mutuality in the analytic relationship. However, it is true that an authentic response to the patient may at times be considered the best way to both manifest the impact of the patient's actions and provide a basis for exploring meanings together.

The construction of understanding even in the complex and only partially knowable world of shared unconscious fantasy is never separate from the struggle for recognition and the need to be safely connected. The idea of intersubjectivity suggests that rather than two individual subjects (each with an "intrapsychic" mind) interacting, we recognize the relationship as a matrix in which the reactive points can never be fully determined – no one's transference is really counter to the other, or rather, everyone's is. We are all reactive and, hopefully, other times more reflectively responsive. Not only must the analyst survive the patient, but the patient must survive the analyst. In other words, the analyst aims to facilitate the growth of a relationship, or thirdness, in which both survive, a safe frame or container in which such struggles and resolutions can occur. While the analyst initially may do the heavy lifting, eventually each partner contributes to containing, to building a third. In this way, each analytic dyad strives to create the process of developing secure attachment.

The notion of the analyst's internal process of reflection and use of self analysis followed by interpretation as the solution to coming through enactments or breakdown of thirdness is certainly not *wrong*, but it is limited. It brackets out all the micro-shifts in interaction that help change the self state of both partners, and thus their availability for thinking or sharing affect or getting back into the rhythmic third. Further, it might seriously limit the imagined range of subjective responses that might contribute to recovering the third. For instance, it is often the acknowledgment of the fact of breakdown, injury or mistrust, pain or separation, that helps to restore the third (Benjamin, 2009). Rather than emphasize the aspect whereby the analyst shares her or his personal experience in some *unmediated* way – what is sometimes called "countertransference disclosure" – I like to emphasize the function of acknowledgment in restoring thirdness, which in turn makes possible the that what just occurred.

In this conceptual framework, which includes the analyst's acknowledgment, the process of surviving collisions and moving toward symbolization of enactment, finding meaning together, we recreate the position of the third after having lost it. Rather than thinking of psychoanalysis primarily as the process of creating narrative and symbolic meanings together through the analyst lending the patient her or his thinking function, we might rather think of those intersubjective exchanges in the realm of the third as being created by working through enactments, breakdowns, ruptures, the joint submission to the subjugating dynamic of mutual projective identification. While we might ideally like to be able to surrender when the complementary opposition arises, we almost inevitably resist the dynamic in some way and thus are unable to work our way out without obvious signs of dysregulation, palpable to the other, open to the patient's observation. For this reason *acknowledgment* of our being affected, perturbed, unbalanced is often the sign of our readiness to start processing rather than resisting the experience. The analyst's acknowledgment is therefore often a crucial part of the process of using her or his subjectivity, and it involves a higher level of vulnerability than the idea of the analyst merely thinking, interpreting or containing implied.

But analytic acknowledgment (Benjamin, 2009), eschewed by analysts in the past, is becoming an area of repair that is more plausible as our subjectivity and vulnerability are accepted. And indeed, it may serve to enhance our role as witnesses and carriers of the larger Third. The effect of having the analyst serve as a participating witness to injuries suffered in the past and relived as present enactments – sometimes indeed caused by the analyst's misattunement or dissociation – is an important aspect of the transformation of relational interaction patterns, whether implicit or explicit.

I stress that recognition in the form of acknowledgment is important "for itself" and not merely as a vehicle to some insight as a takeaway for the individual. It means that the patient is not only able to "think" her trauma, a goal expressed from a Bionian viewpoint by Brown (2011) who speaks of "bearing witness as midwife." She is able to have a representation of a caring other, a caring world – a consequence that Gerson (2009) has emphasized in his work on witnessing as an aspect of the third. Changing the Other Within (variously understood in terms of creating new experience, shifting psychic structure, attaining earned secure attachment) is thus as important as narrative formulation in the reorganization of affective experience from chaotic elements to emotions that can be borne through meaning. If the principle of witnessing is integral to the third, as Gerson (2009) maintains, and at the same time as Ullman (2005) portrays integral to the working through of trauma, it may also be more broadly thought of as the very embodiment of recognition in the analytic situation (Stern, 2010). In this paradigm shift it appears that the analyst has to acknowledge moments of failed witnessing and open them for exploration with the patient.

The obstacle to such exploration, which can be addressed once there is a collision of subjectivities, is the "joint dissociative cocoon" (Bromberg, 2006, 2011). The analyst may have avoided the abyss of the patient's fearful memories only to have the patient suddenly emerge with a feeling of being unwitnessed and betrayed. Hence the contemporary appreciation of Ferenczi (1933), who wise beyond his time, asserted that only a full acknowledgment of the recreation in the analytic relationship of childhood injuries can avoid the repetition of mystification and denial that accompanied those injuries. What stands in the way of acknowledgment is usually the analyst's shame or guilt, which pose the obstacle to getting into a more regulated state. Yet these aspects of the analyst's vulnerability can be better held precisely to the extent that this problem is openly acknowledged in the field rather than denied as they were in the period when psychoanalysis was dominated by the belief in objectivity and neutrality.

A summing up of the sensibility of intersubjective recognition theory might read thus: recognition of the pain caused by misunderstanding, by moments of dissociation in which part of the analytic patient feels left alone, by moments of impasse where the projection by each of opposing parts of self into the other creating stuck complementary roles (Davies, 2004), is more crucial in restoring thirdness than was supposed in the days when interpretation and insight were seen as the only medium of analysis. We may consider analytic acknowledgment (Benjamin, 2009) and surrender (Ghent, 1990) to the third – the principle of accepting and owning responsibility for injury – as vital both for creating a new kind of attachment and for restoring affect regulation, for soothing anxiety, fostering the patient's self-cohesion. This in turn makes it possible for the patient (and analyst too) to mentalize more effectively because grasping the other's mind does not mean abnegating one's own feelings and perceptions. In this way acknowledgment can clear the way for deeper understanding for both participants.

Paradoxically, the admission of the analyst's vulnerability functions more as an affirmation of the *asymmetrical responsibility* of the analyst than of mutuality. Thus there is an asymmetry at the level of admitting responsibility even as there is an implicit aspect of symmetry in expecting the patient to survive knowing something about the analyst, recognizing him or her as having a fallible subjectivity, a point stressed by Orange (2011), an analyst of the intersubjective school that developed out of self psychology. The acknowledgment of fallibility, Orange maintains, can be seen as part of a hermeneutics of trust rather than Freudian suspicion. This suggests a position in which analysts recognize their own tendencies toward self-protection, which can create an implicit opposition to the demand for the patient to relinquish that protection. The great challenge for analysts, the problem of our own shame and vulnerability, has become clearer as we relinquish the position of knowing subject – the myth of a healthy person treating a sick one, as Racker (1968), the Argentine analyst who first recognized the power of complementary countertransference, trenchantly put it.

In this way intersubjectivity theory has moved us toward thinking in terms of a two-way process in which there is mutual survival, where each partner survives moments of collision or nonrecognition. For many relational analysts, the intersubjective perspective on mutuality, because it can encompass more experience of vulnerability, has worked in tandem rather than opposing our evolving reflections on trauma and dissociation.[5] Traumatized patients often pull for vulnerability in the analyst. As we tolerate more vulnerability on the analyst's part, we become more conscious of the reciprocal nature of attunement to each partner's self states: the idea that the analyst must show the *impact* of the patient's affect, experience, suffering.

Showing impact is essential to recognizing the other. The idea of therapeutic acknowledgment – based on work with historical trauma that shows how acknowledgment crucially restores a sense of a lawful, caring world – unites elements of mutuality and asymmetry. For even as we realize that the dysregulation and vulnerability may occur in both partners, the requirements of asymmetry must be held in tension with that mutuality – yet another example of the intersubjective effort to hold opposites in a third position. As has already been well established in work with collective trauma outside psychoanalysis, acknowledgment, restoring the role of the witness, is vital in creating a third as well as repair of the injury. The patient can play an active part in repairing and understanding when we welcome, as Ferenczi (1933) said, his criticisms and observations. In this sense the process of creating the third is shared and mutual even though the roles are asymmetrical, creating the third. Thus the binary – asymmetrical or mutual? – will perhaps be deconstructed in the course of an analytic relationship in which the third grows stronger as large and small ruptures are repaired.

Just as in development the intersubjective third develops by acknowledging violations or ruptures, creating a sense of a lawful world, so in clinical work, acknowledgment of violations of expectations for emotional safety, attunement, caring or understanding help to restore a law-ful world of shared meaning in contrast to a world of *doer–done to*. The effect of therapeutic acknowledgment is to validate a person's sense of what has happened and demonstrate that the analyst has also been affected in some way – showing oneself to be responsible for one's own reactions, recognizing the patient's disappointment or fear. In this sense it is another instance of surviving destruction, of showing the sturdiness of the mind that can tolerate the dysregulation of facing its own limits.

One radical implication of intersubjective theory would be that analysts are able to recognize that their own self-regulation and shifting of self state often are dependent upon and facilitated through acknowledging both sides of the interaction. The analyst admits her own part in disrupt-ing the patient's regulation as well as restoring it; she admits the patient's part in disrupting and restoring calm as well. The restoration of the thirdness of mutual regulation and the effort to uphold the third of responsibility would no longer depend on the idealization of the analyst as the well healing the sick. The analyst can ultimately be recognized as an outside other subject who struggles with her/his own limits and tendencies toward dissociation in the face of intense dysregu-lation. The acceptance of our own vulnerability as human subjects who depend on others' recogni-tion is the crux of intersubjectivity to which we repeatedly return – that, as in the Hegelian concept of recognition, we need the other to give us back to ourselves, no matter how much our endeavor is predicated on our giving to them. The suffering that is implied by this predication – that so much of this give back will stumble or fall short – is part of what psychoanalysis asks us to bear.

## Notes

1 While Habermas introduced the term "the intersubjectivity of mutual understanding" into sociology in 1968, this term was actually picked up by Trevarthen (1980), who brought it into infancy studies. He thought the term, although "ungainly," was the best way to describe two subjects in relation to each other.

> In the same period two American psychoanalytic feminists, Dinnerstein (1976) and Chodorow (1977), articulated the problem that the mother was not understood to be a subject in her own right. I undertook the joining of these two perspectives in the 1970s–1980s, culminating in the *Bonds of Love* (1988).

2 This work was done by psychologists and psychiatrists who were trained as analysts but also engaged in infant research.

3 Ainsworth (cited in Benjamin, 1988), for instance, used Bowlby's ideas to formulate the most influential research work on early relational development, the "Strange Situation," in which the ability of mothers and infants to reconnect (mother is soothing, infant can find safety with her) after a brief separation was

observed and categorized in terms of secure and insecure attachment. To this was added a clinically power-ful concept of disorganized attachment, reflecting the fragmentation when the mother is needed for safety yet experienced as frightening and dangerous.

4  For those outside North America, this bifurcated tendency in those who moved away from Freud toward an object relational view has been somewhat confusing, since the term intersubjectivity came to the fore in several different contexts – a confusing case where territorial claims and content differences were hard to sort out. As someone who participated in the early formation of the relational movement but was strongly influenced by self psychology, especially because of its link with infancy research, I have often seen the places where the two schools meet rather than divide. Still, I am more identified with the relational side because of my commitment to the concept of mutual recognition and expression of the analyst's subjectivity.

5  Bohleber (2013) has argued that intersubjective thinking militates against recognizing historical events, trauma outside the here and now of the transference. But this is probably a crucial point of distinction between the relational perspective on intersubjectivity and European field theory, which arguably is less occupied with historical trauma than relational theory whose roots are with Ferenczi, the first real propo-nent of trauma therapy after Freud's famous repudiation.

# References

Aron, L 1996, *A meeting of minds: Mutuality in psychoanalysis*, Analytic Press, Hillsdale, NJ.

Baranger, M & Baranger, W 2009, *The work of confluence*, L Glocer Fiorini (ed), Karnac, London, pp. 63–88.

Beebe, B & Lachmann, F 2002, *Infancy research and adult treatment*, Analytic Press, Hillsdale, NJ.

Beebe, B & Stern, DN 1977, Engagement-disengagement and early object experiences. In N. Freedman (ed), *Communicative structures and psychic structures*, Springer US, New York, pp. 35–55.

Benjamin, J 1988, *The bonds of love: Psychoanalysis, feminism, and the problem of domination*, Pantheon, New York.

Benjamin, J 1994, *The shadow of the other (subject): Intersubjectivity and feminist theory*, Routledge, New York.

Benjamin, J 1995, *Like subjects, love objects: Essays on recognition and sexual difference*, Yale University Press, New Haven.

Benjamin, J 1998, *Shadow of the other: Intersubjectivity and gender in psychoanalysis*, Routledge, New York.

Benjamin, J 2004, 'Beyond doer and done to: An intersubjective view of thirdness', *Psychoanalytic Quarterly*, vol. 63, pp. 5–46.

Benjamin, J 2009, 'A relational psychoanalysis perspective on the necessity of acknowledging failure', *International Journal of Psychoanalysis*, vol. 90, pp. 441–445.

Bion, W 1962, *Learning from experience*, Heinemann, London.

Bohleber, W 2010, *Destructiveness, intersubjectivity and trauma: The identity crisis of modern psychoanalysis*, Karnac, London.

Bohleber, W 2013, 'The concept of intersubjectivity: Taking critical stock', *International Journal of Psycho-analysis*, vol. 94, pp. 799–823.

Bollas, C 1987, 1989, *The shadow of the object*, Free Association Books, Columbia University Press, New York.

Bowlby, J 1969, *Attachment and loss. Vol. 1: Attachment*, Basic Books, New York.

Britton, R 1988, 1997, 'The missing link: Parental sexuality in the Oedipus complex', in R Shaffer (ed), *The contemporary Kleinians of London*, International Universities Press, Madison, CT, pp. 242–258.

Bromberg, P 1998, *Standing in the spaces*, Analytic Press, Mahwah, NJ.

Bromberg, PM 2006, *Awakening the dreamer: Clinical journeys*, Analytic Press, Mahwah, NJ.

Bromberg, PM 2011, *The shadow of the tsunami*, Routledge, New York.

Brown, L 2011, *Intersubjective processes and the unconscious: An integration of Freudian, Kleinian and Bionian perspectives*, Routledge, New York.

Chodorow, N 1977, *The reproduction of mothering*, University of California Press, Berkeley.

Davies, J 2004, 'Whose bad objects are we anyway? Repetition and our elusive love affair with evil', *Psycho-analytic Dialogues*, vol. 14, pp. 711–732.

Dinnerstein, D 1976, *The mermaid and the minotaur*, Harper and Row, New York.

Fairbairn, WRD 1952, *An object-relations theory of the personality*, Basic Books, New York.

Ferenczi, S 1933, The elasticity of the psychoanalytic technique, *Psychoanalytic Review (1913–1957)*, vol. 20, p. 89.

Ferro, A 2009, *In the analyst's consulting room*, Brunner-Routledge, New York.

Fonagy, P, Gergely, G, Jurist, E & Target, M 2002, *Affect regulation, mentalization and the development of the self*, Other Books, New York.

Freud, S 1911, 'Formulations regarding the two principles in mental functioning', in P Rieff (ed), *General psychological theory*, Collier Books, New York, pp. 21–28.

Freud, S 1915, 'Instincts and their vicissitudes', in J Strachey (ed), *Standard edition of the complete psychological works of Sigmund Freud*, vol. 14, Hogarth, London, pp. 111–140.

Freud, S 1923, 'The ego and the id', in J Strachey (ed), *Standard edition of the complete psychological works of Sigmund Freud*, vol. 19, Hogarth, London, pp. 1–66.

Gerson, S 2009, 'When the third is dead: Memory mourning and witnessing in the aftermath of the holocaust', *International Journal of Psychoanalysis*, vol. 90, no. 6, pp. 1341–1357.

Ghent, E 1990, 'Masochism, submission, surrender', *Contemporary Psychoanalysis*, vol. 26, pp. 169–211.

Gill, M 1982, *Analysis of transference*, International Universities Press, New York.

Guntrip, H 1961, *Personality structure and human interaction*, International Universities Press, New York.

Hoffman, IZ 1983, 'The patient as interpreter of the analyst's experience', *Contemporary Psychoanalysis*, vol. 19, pp. 389–422.

Jacobs, T 2001, 'On misleading and misreading patients: Some reflections on communications, miscommunications and countertransference enactments', *International Journal of Psychoanalysis*, vol. 82, pp. 653–669.

Klein, M 1945, 1975, 'The Oedipus complex in the light of early anxieties', in *Love, guilt and reparation*, Hogarth Press, London, pp. 370–419.

Kohut, H 1977, *The restoration of the self*, International Universities Press, New York.

Kojève, A 1934–1935/1980, *Introduction to the reading of Hegel*, Routledge, London.

Levenson, E 1972, *The fallacy of understanding*, Basic Books, New York.

Lyons-Ruth, K 1999, 'The two–person unconscious: Intersubjective dialogue, enactive relational representation, and the emergence of new forms of relational organization', *Psychoanalytic Inquiry*, vol. 19, pp. 576–617.

Mitchell, S 1993, *Hope and dread in psychoanalysis*, Basic Books, New York.

Mitchell, S 1997, *Influence and autonomy in psychoanalysis*, Analytic Press, Hillsdale, NJ.

Mitchell, S & Black, M 1995, *Freud and beyond: A history of modern psychoanalytic thought*, Basic Books, New York.

Ogden, T 1994, *Subjects of analysis*, Aronson, Northvale, NJ.

Ogden, P 2006, *Trauma and the Body: A Sensorimotor Approach to Psychotherapy*, W.W. Norton, New York.

Orange, D 2011, *The suffering stranger*, Routledge, New York.

Racker, H 1968, *Transference and countertransference*, International Universities Press, New York.

Renik, O 1993, 'Analytic interaction: Conceptualizing technique in light of the analyst's irreducible subjectivity', *Psychoanalytic Quarterly*, vol. 62, pp. 553–571.

Renik, O 1998, 'The analyst's subjectivity and the analyst's objectivity', *International Journal of Psychoanalysis*, vol. 79, pp. 487–497.

Sander, L 2002, 'Thinking differently: Principles of process in living systems and the specificity of being known', *Psychoanalytic Dialogues*, vol. 12, no. 1, pp. 11–42.

Schore, AN 1994, *Affect regulation and the origin of the self: The neurobiology of emotional development*, Erlbaum, Mahwah.

Schore, AN 2004, *Affect regulation and the repair of the self*, Norton, New York.

Siegel, D 2001, *The developing mind*, Guilford Press, New York.

Stern, D 1985, *The interpersonal world of the human infant*, Basic Books, New York.

Stern, DB 2010, *Partners in thought*, Routledge, New York.

Stern, DB 2013, *Unformulated experience: From dissociation to imagination in psychoanalysis*, vol. 8, Routledge, New York.

Stern, DN, Sander, LW, Nahum, JP, Harrison, AM, Lyons-Ruth, K, Morgan, AC, Bruschweiler-Stern, N & Tronick, EZ 1998, 'Non-interpretive mechanisms in psychoanalytic therapy: The something more than interpretation', *International Journal of Psychoanalysis*, vol. 79, no. 5, pp. 903–921.

Stolorow, R & Atwood, G 1992, *Contexts of being: The intersubjective foundations of psychological life*, Analytic Press, Hillsdale, NJ.

Stolorow, R, Atwood, G & Orange D 1997, *Worlds of experience*, Basic Books, New York.

Trevarthen, C 1980, 'Communication and cooperation in early infancy: A description of primary intersubjectivity', in M Bullowa (ed), *Before speech: The beginning of interpersonal communication*, Cambridge University Press, New York, pp. 321–347.

Tronick, E 1989, 'Emotions and emotional communication in infants', *American Psychologist*, vol. 44, pp. 112–119.

Ullman, M 2005, 'A cognitive neuroscience perspective on second language acquisition: The declarative/procedural model', in C. Sanz (ed), *Mind and context in adult second language acquisition*, Georgetown University Press, Washington D.C, pp. 141–178.

Ullman, C 2006, 'Bearing witness: Across the barriers in society and in the clinic', *Psychoanalysis Dialogues*, vol. 16, no. 2, pp. 181–198.

Winnicott, DW 1958, *Through paediatrics to psychoanalysis*, Hogarth, London.

Winnicott, DW 1971, 'The use of an object and relating through identifications', in *Playing and Reality*, Tavistock, London.

# 10

# Contemporary European psychoanalysis

*Anthony Elliott*

In her book *Hatred and Forgiveness* (2010, p. 150), Julia Kristeva argues that "a contemporary version of the unconscious appears to be emerging that includes the prepsychical and even Being." For this new outlook, which Kristeva contends is essential to modern European psychoanalysis, theoretical and clinical insights blend to restore a conceptualization of human subjectivity that is always *put into question*.

Kristeva argues that situating psychoanalysis, and specifically the notion of the unconscious, in relation to the very earliest constructions of aliveness in the human subject is essential to investigating the self. The "prepsychical" is a key word. The new European departures of which Kristeva speaks focus on the earliest stages of pre-Oedipal psychic constitution – namely, when the drives are first metabolized into representations and primary processes – and yet these departures also glance backwards to theoretical conjectures sketched in the psychoanalytic tradition.

Considering the more speculative writings of Freud, for example, one finds many related attempts to anchor psychoanalysis in the pre-Oedipal unconscious and its sensorial offshoots. In a jotting from 1938, Freud wrote "Ich bin die Brust" ("I am the Breast"). This sentence – as Cornelius Castoriadis has noted – was no more than speculative conjecture, perhaps a jotting intended to inspire future research. As it happens, Freud was unable to delve further into how the radically unconscious "identifications" or "investments" of the small infant become the very seal of subjectivity. Yet it is this challenge that has been taken up in recent European psychoanalysis and that addresses the repositioning of psychoanalysis as a genealogy of the human subject. The challenge goes right to the heart of the disconnection, mismatch or lack of fit between the internal and external environments of human subjects.

In this chapter, I shall focus on some of the central trajectories, reconciliations and disputes of modern European psychoanalysis. In doing so, I shall pay particular attention to the psychoanalytic approaches developed by Cornelius Castoriadis, Julia Kristeva and Jean Laplanche. While there are other contributions from European psychoanalysts that might have been reviewed, the work of Castoriadis, Kristeva and Laplanche stand out in a most definite way in terms of the comprehensive and radical fashion in which each theorizes the unconscious imagination. Castoriadis conceives of individual imaginaries as ineluctably interwoven with social-historical imaginaries. Kristeva understands human imagination in terms of a permanent state of psychic questioning, of unconscious transformations, an endless dialectic of semiotic and symbolic restructurings. And

Anthony Elliott

Laplanche places the imagination squarely in relation to the demands of interpersonal bonds, the ceaseless work of imaginative, symbolizing activities. The social sciences and humanities now face the challenging work of sifting through the core insights of these three pioneering European psychoanalysts, both for resituating subjectivity in the wake of post-Lacanianism and for reassessing how the repressed unconscious serves to estrange human subjects from what appears most intimate. Through extended analysis and critique of the works of Castoriadis, Kristeva and Laplanche, this chapter is intended as a contribution to that task.

## Castoriadis on imagination: creation "out of nothing"

In his pioneering *The Imaginary Institution of Society* (1987), Cornelius Castoriadis interrogates Freudian psychoanalysis with specific reference to the themes of human creation and imagination. "The imaginary," Castoriadis writes, "is the subject's whole creation of a world for itself" (p. 3). The impact of psychoanalysis – or at least Castoriadis's reinterpretation of Freud – is fundamental in this connection, for Castoriadis's theory of the social imaginary is not only profoundly innovative (stretching the term "imagination" well beyond the narrow meaning accorded to it by the doyen of French psychoanalysis, Jacques Lacan). It also significantly opens a pathway for understanding closures of imagination (e.g., the generalized conformism of institutionalized individualism) in a different light.

Psychoanalysis for Castoriadis centers on imagination from beginning to end. But more than that – in Castoriadis's hands – imagination becomes the basis for a full-blown theory of the social field; yet, this is a kind of imaginary foundation to society that is, paradoxically, non-foundational. For Castoriadis, the imaginary tribulations of the unconscious are utterly fresh, primary fabrications founded purely in themselves, erupting out of nothing and nowhere, and sprung ex nihilo from a disorderly chaos of representational flux (Castoriadis, 1987). While recognizing that the psyche cannot produce everything out of itself, otherwise there would be no reason for the human subject to open itself to other persons and objects, Castoriadis claims it is meaningless to see psychic reality as simply a "receptacle" of the external world, for there can be no social practice without a human subject; with individuals there is psychic organization and emotional experience. Instead, the question of representation, for Castoriadis, centers on the capacity of the psyche itself to *instantiate* representations. Inherent in the Freudian problematic, he writes,

> we can say that the first delegation of the drive in the psyche is the affect, in particular that of displeasure. But we can find nothing in an affect, whether of pleasure or unpleasure, that could account for the form or the content of a representation; at the most the affect could induce the "finality" of the representative process. *It is therefore necessary to postulate (even if this is only implicitly) that the psyche is the capacity to produce an "initial" representation, the capacity of putting into image or making an image.* This may appear self-evident. But this image-making must at the same time relate to a drive, at a time when nothing ensures this relation. This may well be the point of condensation and accumulation for all the mysteries of the "bonding" between the soul and the body.

> *(1987, p. 282, emphasis added)*

Thus, Castoriadis is perhaps the first major modern intellectual to place at the center of his reflections on the social the abstract category of psychical representation itself, both at the levels of the individual ("radical imaginary") and society ("social imaginary"). The imaginary, contends Castoriadis, is not just a question of "the creation of images in society," but rather of the productive energies of self-creation, which, in turn, generates social imaginary significations and the institutions of each particular society. What is radically imaginary about the psychic process of every individual is precisely the representational pleasure of the unconscious monad, initially closed in upon itself and subsequently forced to shift from self-generating solipsistic fantasy to the shared meanings of society (see Elliott, 1999). To the radical imaginary of the psychic monad corresponds the collective order of the "social imaginary," an aesthetics of imagination that holds together the primary institutions of society (language, norms, customs and law) and the form of relation through which individuals and collectivities come to relate to such objects of representational and affective investment (Castoriadis, 1987). Where then does radical imagination originate? What is the condition of possibility for its eruption?

Castoriadis argues that Freud's "primal fantasies" are not genuinely originary fantasies because they involve a relatively developed articulation of "contents" and "relations" between the self and others. Originary fantasy for Castoriadis, by contrast, involves a "lack of distinction between the subject and the non-subject" (1987, p. 286). Originary fantasmatization, or what Castoriadis terms the "radical imaginary," is a primal architecture of representations, drives and passions in and through which the subject creates a world for itself. "The originary psychical subject," says Castoriadis, "is this primordial "fantasy": at once the representation and the investment of a Self that is All" (1987, p. 287). Unconscious representation, according to Castoriadis, is creation ex nihilo. Human imagination is pure creation, the making and remaking of images and forms as self-production. This does not mean, absurdly, that human beings are unconstrained in their representational activity, that is, the making of self and object representations. On the contrary, Castoriadis argues that the self-creating nature of representation "leans on" biological properties of the individual, and is bound up with the symbolically structured character of the social-historical world.

To speak of "originary representation" is certainly at odds with the bulk of modern European thought. From Saussure to Derrida, contemporary theory develops by way of a shift from ideas of "representation" and "mentation" and from the notion that the mind "represents" the world and therefore provides a foundation for knowledge, and toward the study of language and the analysis of discursive practices. This move away from representational theories of the subject might, at first glance, seem to render Castoriadis's stress in imagination and the imaginary outdated or redundant.

Certainly critics have argued that the whole concept of representation, the idea that some transcendental signified automatically assigns a set of stable meanings to the subject, has seriously come to grief since the linguistic turn in modern philosophy. This kind of criticism, however, reflects a fundamental misunderstanding of what Castoriadis means by "originary fantasmatization." The concept of unconscious representation for Castoriadis does not denote an organic bond between image and thing, idea and object; it does not mean the "imitation" or "copying" of a world in the mind of the subject. Rather, Castoriadis suggests that the unconscious comprises a fantasmatic flux, a representational magma of significations, which is strictly unthinkable within the confines of Western rationality and logic. He defines the imaginary as the capacity to posit that which is not. Against the reductive scopic account of the imaginary posited by Lacan, Castoriadis defines the radical/social imaginary not as the creation of images in the mind or in society, but rather in terms of the signifiable.

Castoriadis (1989), following Freud, further contends that originary fantasy and representation underlies the capacity of the subject for critical self-reflection and autonomy. As he says of psychoanalysis itself:

> The possibility of representing *oneself as* representational activity and of putting oneself in question as such is not just a philosophical subtlety; it corresponds to the *minimum* we require

of every patient when we try to lead him/her to discover that X is not Y but that it is very much so for *his/her* own representational activity and that there may be reasons for this.

*(1989, p. 27)*

Representation, unconscious flux, originary fantasmatization: these are, says Castoriadis, necessary conditions for the possibility of reflectiveness in the individual human subject.

In an interview in 1991, Castoriadis reflected on the "incessant flux" of the imagination thus:

> I am not fixated on the "scopic"; one of the gross inadequacies of Lacan's conception of the imagination is his fixation of the scopic. For me, if one is speaking of stages that are worked out, the imagination par excellence is the imagination of the musical composer (which is what I wanted to be). Suddenly, figures surge forth which are not in the least visual. They are essentially auditory and kinetic – for there is also rhythm. There is a marvellous excerpt from a letter of Mozart cited by Brigitte Massin, in which Mozart describes how he composes. Like every self-respecting composer, he composes, obviously, in his head. When deaf, Beethoven heard – imagined – in his head. A true composer writes and hears chords, chordal progressions, as I, in closing my eyes, can review some scene or imagine some scene, bringing into mutual presence characters who have never really been present to each other. Mozart explains that the piece composes itself in his head, and he says the following hallucinatory thing: when the piece is finished, it is all laid out simultaneously before him in its progression. He hears in one moment the beginning, the middle, the end of the first movement of the sonata. As Galileo says of God, the proofs we arduously traverse step by step are laid out before Him instantaneously. That is an imagination. When Mozart says, I have the entire piece laid out in my head, it is not that he sees the score, it is that he hears the totality of the piece. That appears incomprehensible to us because our musical imagination is rather poor: to be able to hear simultaneously the beginning of the symphony in G minor and the minuet. Nor is there anything "visual" in the social imaginary. The social imaginary is not the creation of images in society; it is not the fact that one paints the walls of towns. A fundamental creation of the social imaginary, the gods or rules of behaviour are neither visible nor even audible but signifiable.

*(Castoriadis, 1997b, pp. 182–183)*

Castoriadis's reflections on the imaginary principally concern, one might say, the ways in which a world (at once emotional and social) somehow or other comes to be ordered and organized from groundlessness or chaos; about the creation of imagination from "dull mass"; about creation and invention as a consequence of an "explosion that digs into this mass a hole." The constitution of these imaginary determinations manifests the creativity that appertains to the psyche as such, and that "opens an interior space within it."

Clearly a great deal could be said about the links between imagination and the auditory and kinetic in Castoriadis's reflections, with all this implies of an overvaluation of visual objects in psychoanalysis. Castoriadis is at pains to emphasize that the fetishization of the scopic in Lacanian psychoanalysis has resulted in a harmful neglect of the creativity of the psyche. Freud emphasized, of course, that *visual memory* is fundamental to the unconscious and its expressive processes of condensation, displacement and representation – especially in that aspect of his corpus where he conceived of fantasy in terms of his model of the dream. In some versions of Freud, dreams are the linchpin for an easy fit between representation and imagination. "As an analogue of the mind," writes Harvie Ferguson in *The Lure of Dreams*, "the dream came to represent *both* reflection *and* imagination. Indeed, the plasticity of the dream not only brought to life a picture of the world;

its succession of images also revealed the normally hidden process of representation itself" (1996, p. 7). In Freud's approach, however, the visual domain was not all, for sensory elements also figured in Freud's construction of the dream–work and, by extension, the imagination. The Freudian subject may dream visually, and only be able to report the dream in words, yet the sharpness of the visual perception is an upshot of heterogeneous domains of representation (sensations, affects, verbal and nonverbal representations).

How might the radical imaginary connect with social imagination, and especially possibilities for enhanced freedom? Castoriadis speaks of autonomy rather than freedom, and casts it as an ongoing project. Castoriadis keeps one eye firmly on both ontological and institutional possibilities for personal change and social transformation. "Autonomy," writes Castoriadis "is not closure but, rather opening: ontological opening, the possibility of going beyond the informational, cognitive, and organizational closure characteristic of self-constituting, but *heteronomous* beings" (1997b, pp. 310, 316). The principle that the possibility of challenging established significations and institutions is central to the attainment of autonomy is reflective of a broader movement in history, a movement away from tradition and the sacred and toward the contingency of the social. This amounts to saying that a conception of society has emerged historically that recognizes that there can be no supracollective guarantee of meaning; the end of foundationalism involves an acceptance of the fact that meaning and its actualization always presupposes a social context. As Castoriadis explains:

> if autonomous society is that society which self-institutes itself [*s'auto-institue*] explicitly and lucidly, the one that knows that it itself posits its institutions and significations, this means that it knows as well that they have no source other than its own instituting and significa-tion-giving activity, no extrasocial "guarantee."
>
> *(1997, p. 316)*

The other side of autonomy for Castoriadis is heteronomy, which, with the spread of modernity, has unleashed another social imaginary signification that he calls "the unlimited expansion of 'rational' mastery." Rational "mastery" when expanded indefinitely is, for Castoriadis, "pseudo-rational mastery" and can be detected at work at the individual level in increasing levels of privatization and individualism (that is to say, generalized conformism) and at the societal level in bureaucratic discourse and capitalist ideology. Needless to say, the generalized conformism of institutionalized individualism arises as a version of such pseudo-rational mastery.

## Kristeva on primary identification: the "zero degree" of the psyche

For several decades, Kristeva has focused on recasting the relations between subjectivity and society in a series of works situated at the intersection of psychoanalysis, feminism and modern European thought, including *Tales of Love* (1987), *In the Beginning Was Love* (1988), *Strangers to Ourselves* (1991) and *New Maladies of the Soul* (1993). Her work blends linguistic and psychoanalytical theory to advance a novel account of how preverbal experience – maternal, infantile, poetic – enters into, shapes, distorts and disrupts language through processes of art, literature and psychoanalysis. The result has been a radical opening of the intersections between psychoanalysis and critical social theory, which in turn has provided a transformative political and feminist dimension to Freudian thought and an enhanced psychoanalytical dimension to critical social theory.

Kristeva's various discussions of the constitution of repressed desire demonstrate a persistent concern with human imagination and the creativity of action. In order to adequately grasp

Kristeva's contribution to psychoanalytic theory, it is necessary to situate her work in the context of Lacan's "return to Freud." Having undertaken her psychoanalytic training with Lacan, it is perhaps not surprising that Kristeva's early writings should emphasize the ordering power of the Symbolic, of language as such. In Lacan's rewriting of Freud, the human subject comes to language, and adopts a position of speaker, from a devastating primordial loss. The pain of this loss leads to a repression that at once buries memories of fulfillment experienced through contact with the phallic mother on the one hand, and catapults the subject-to-be into a Symbolic order of individuation, differentiation and cultural signification on the other. This account of how the human subject is radically split off from its own desire by the bar of repression, represented by the signifier of the phallus, was described by Lacan in the following terms:

> All these propositions merely veil over the fact that the phallus can only play its role as veiled, that is, as in itself the sign of the latency with which everything signifiable is struck as soon as it is raised (ausgehoben) to the function of signifier. The phallus is the signifier of this Aushebueng itself which it inaugurates (initiates) by its own disappearance.
>
> *(Lacan quoted in Mitchell & Rose, 1985, p. 82)*

In her early work Kristeva accepts these basic tenets of Lacanian theory, but as noted she contrasts Lacan's account of the Symbolic order with a revaluation of the persistence and force of repressed libidinal desires, somatic dispositions and affects – a kind of unconscious rhythm that Kristeva terms "the semiotic." Prose and poetry are symbolic forms that Kristeva has psychoanalytically deconstructed to try to capture something of "the semiotic" or "maternal body" that remains truly inexpressible. She finds in acts of artistic expression that press language to its limits – that is, in the ruins of the symbolic – a zone, by definition incommunicable, in which desire bursts forth. Is this zone a set of organized subjective meanings, a language, or is it prelinguistic and hence indescribable? It is not so much prelinguistic, according to Kristeva, as an expression of the prolinguistic: affects, bodily dispositions, silences, rhythms.

A powerful indication of how far Kristeva has moved away from Lacan can be gleaned from her more mature work, especially *The Sense and Non-Sense of Revolt* (2000). In a remarkably lucid, eloquent, lethal critique of the linguistification of French psychoanalysis, Kristeva traces and recontextualizes the radical impulse of Freudian thought. Kristeva brands Lacan's "return to Freud" rigorous in developing the insights of Continental philosophy and linguistics, yet narrow (and, in fact, un-Freudian) in dismantling the dualist drive/conscious vision. Lacan himself, she points out, was a pseudo-mathematician of the unconscious, who structuralized psychoanalysis in the wake of the model of language worked out in Freud's *The Interpretation of Dreams*, and who was either unaware or uninterested in how a linguistic interpretation of the unconscious violates Freud's preanalytical studies on the relation between the sexual and the verbal or the master's post-1910 thought on identification, idealization and sublimation. Neo-Lacanian thought also fares badly, and is accused by Kristeva of fatally confusing psychical representations, or formations, with structuring conscious identifications. "If we harden the Lacanian line as I have traced it," writes Kristeva,

> we end up getting rid of what still constituted Freudian dualism at the heart of this second model, a dualism that situates language between the conscious and unconscious while at the same time maintaining the dualist drive/conscious vision. We thus liquidate the instinctual domain as well as the primary processes. This is the tendency of a certain current in French Lacanian and post-Lacanian psychoanalysis that considers the notion of the drive useless.
>
> *(2000, pp. 42–43)*

In her more recent work, Kristeva has become especially interested in Kleinian psychoanalysis, or more specifically Klein's elaboration of Freud's theory of representation or the proto-fantasy. A close reading of Klein, argues Kristeva, demonstrates that the child, from the very beginning of life, is consumed with anxiety. "No matter how far back Klein reaches into childhood," writes Kristeva,

> she always discovers a fantasizing ego. A sundry entity made up of verbal and non-verbal representations, sensations, affects, emotions, movements, actions and even concretizations, the Kleinian phantasy is a wholly impure theoretical construct that defies the purists as much as it fascinates clinicians, particularly those who specialize in children, psychosis, or the psychosomatic disorders.
>
> *(2001, p. 137)*

Moreover, the fantasy-like omnipotent construction of the primary object – the breast – is first and foremost a construction from within, that is, of unstable representational distinctions between *inside* and *outside*, between *inner* and *outer*. "From the outset," writes Kristeva (2001, p. 63) "the primal object of the paranoid-schizoid position emerges, in Klein's view, if and only if it is an *internal object* constructed through a fantasy of omnipotence." As Kristeva notes, rightly in my view, Klein's notion of the internal object is entirely distinct from Lacan's order of the imaginary, for Lacan primarily stressed the visual side of fantasy. Lacan's account of spectral distortion – that narcissism is constituted through the intermediary of the object as a function of the subject's absorption in a reflecting surface – underscores the role of the scopic function in the structuration of the ego and the object. Yet what of transverbal representations, affects, emotions, sensations? Here – and make no mistake about it – Kristeva, a "post-Lacanian," speaks up for Klein's understanding of the internal object, primarily since the Kleinian approach offers a fruitful conceptual map for grasping heterogeneous psychic representations that are altogether missing in Lacan's "return to Freud."

As with her previous work, especially *Tales of Love, Black Sun* and *New Maladies*, Kristeva repositions Klein's clinical and conceptual approach to ask: what is psychic representation? Here Kristeva applauds Klein for uncovering *diverse domains of representation* – not only verbal or symbolic representations, but affects, sensations, gestures and even "concretizations" to which fantasies are sometimes reduced in psychotic suffering. In Klein's theory, says Kristeva, the centrality of wish and fantasy to human subjectivity is borne of sensation and affect. The movement of the Kleinian investigation, routed in clinical experience with children and that contributes significantly to our understanding of both psychosis and autism, is fundamental for grasping the richness and multilayered creativity of the psyche. In exploring the transverbal archaic realm, a realm that belies visual representation, Klein went beyond the "secondary imagination" that runs throughout the whole tradition of Western thought to the primary fantasy or constitutive imagination.

Kristeva makes an interesting case for the contemporary relevance of Klein's hypothesis of a proto-fantasy, or the instituting fantasy. The correctness of Klein's psychoanalytic theory is confirmed, she argues, by more recent studies that portray the psyche, lodged between anxiety and language, in the form of "pre-narrative envelopes" (Daniel Stern), "nameless dreads" (Wilfred Bion) and "life narcissisms" (André Green). Such a focus on the psychic representative prior to representation also connects strongly with Kristeva's own theoretical account of semiotic articulations, defined as a heterogeneous play of unconscious forces – of drives and desires – which exert a pulsional pressure within language itself, and which may be discerned in the rhythm, tone and disruption of speech.

Kristeva is thus out to rescue the notion of drive or affect as potentially radical or subversive. Even so, the tension between psychic repression and unconscious anxiety remains acute. Freud considered that the repression of pleasure, understood in terms of the castration ordeal, generates our distress. This anxiety that can tear us apart, however, is for Kristeva rooted in a much earlier period of psychic development, and so connects directly with the maternal function. Orientating the psychic life of the subject around the pre-Oedipal period and the function of the mother are keys for grasping not only the newborn's psychic pain and its manifold trajectories through-out life, but also the origins of creativity and the capacity for symbolization and thinking. The maternal archaic fantasy, for Kristeva as for Klein, puts flesh on the bones of Freud's theory of the unconscious, as the newborn's drives are directed from the outset toward an object (the mother, or, more accurately, her breast).

This brings us to an important aspect of Kristeva's interpretation of Freud. Kristeva connects the constitution of subjectivity to the imaginary tribulations of the pre-Oedipal phase rather than to the Oedipal symbolic process alone. According to Kristeva, the primary identifications of narcissism already represent an advancement over the affective, representational flux of autoeroti-cism. She describes primary identification as the "zero degree" that shapes psychic space itself, and links this arising of the subject to Freud's notion of a "father in individual prehistory." In this "prehistory," the child forges an initial identification, prior to sexual division, with a maternal-paternal container. As Kristeva explains this *pre-Oedipal* identification:

> Freud has described the One with whom I fulfil the identification (this "most primitive aspect of affective binding to an object") as a Father. Although he did not elaborate what he meant by "primary identification," he made it clear that this father is a "father in individual prehistory" . . . Identification with that "father in prehistory," that Imaginary Father, is called "immediate," "direct," and Freud emphasizes again, "previous to any concentration on any object whatsoever . . . The whole symbolic matrix sheltering emptiness is thus set in place in an elaboration that precedes the Oedipus complex.
>
> *(1987, p. 267)*

And again, on the sexual indistinction of primary identification:

> The archaeology of such an identifying possibility with an other is provided by the huge place taken up within narcissistic structure by the vortex of primary identification with what Freud called a "father of personal prehistory."
> Endowed with the sexual attributes of both parents, and by that very token a totalizing, phallic figure, it provides satisfactions that are already psychic and not simply immediate, existential requests; that archaic vortex of idealization is immediately an other who gives rise to a powerful, already psychic transference of the previous semiotic body in the process of becoming a narcissistic Ego.
>
> *(1987, p. 33)*

Note here that the reference to an *other* ties the emergence of identity to the intersubjective field. Note too that this identification with the imaginary father (which is less a partial object than a pre-object) *constitutes* primary repression; it "bends the drive toward the symbolic of the other" (Kristeva, 1987, p. 31).

Kristeva argues that primary identification arises, not from the child's desire for the pre-Oedipal mother, but from an affective tie with the *mother's desire for the phallus*. Echoing Lacan, she contends that the child comes to realize that the mother herself is lacking, incomplete. In this connection, the child encounters the desire of the other: that the mother's desire is invested elsewhere, in the imaginary phallus. For Kristeva, identification with the imaginary father functions as support for the loss of the maternal object, and provides an imaginary lining to subjectivity that guards against depression and melancholia. Thus,

> "primary identification" with the "father in individual prehistory" would be the means, the link that might enable one to become reconciled with the loss of the Thing. Primary identification initiates a compensation for the Thing and at the same time secures the subject to another dimension, that of imaginary adherence, reminding one of the bond of faith, which is just what disintegrates in the depressed person.
>
> *(1989, pp. 13–14)*

Yet, because the investment in this imaginary father comes from the inside, the emergence of identity is itself a precarious, fragile process.

In her biography *Melanie Klein*, Kristeva also writes about what makes for creative imagination:

> The unconscious or preconscious fantasy is present in all psychic activities and behaviours, so much so that the fantasy is an "active presence of fantasy scenes." Such a fantasy is, strictly speaking, bound up with motivity, taste and food aversions, the sharpness of the perception (particularly the visual perception) of the primal scene, the image of the body, voice-song-and-speech, sporting activities, concert-show-and-film attendance, educational and intellectual activities, neurotic symptoms, and, in the end, the entire organisation of the personality. Not only is the totality of psychic life *impregnated* with fantasies, but in the child whom Klein listened to and analysed, the fantasy – that is, the fantasy that preceded repression – is *united* with psychic life, because this fantasy and this life, "the representative of the earliest impulses of desire and aggressiveness, are expressed in and dealt with by *mental processes far removed from words* and conscious relational thinking."
>
> *(Kristeva, 2001, p. 140, italics mine)*

Kristeva's reflections are in one sense primarily concerned with the presence of fantasy and unconscious work, all to do with the imagination of sensational life. The psychic work of representation is a universal feature "present in all psychic activities and behaviours," by no means restricted to the therapeutic relationship or to particular aspects of mental functioning, such as the standard psychoanalytic menu of daydreaming or erotic imaginings. Rather, it is our ordinary experiences – from sporting activities to the practicalities of learning and education – that are saturated with this originary imagination. All psychic activity, says Kristeva, is "impregnated with fantasies."

What is clear in Kristeva's account of fantasy is that this imaginary domain is inextricably interwoven with the motions of pleasure and unpleasure, the most primitive impulses of desire and aggressiveness that bring a world of subjectivity into being in the first place. Freud astutely captured the theatrical dynamics of sensational life in terms of the logics of dreaming, and it is these affective processes (the dream-work) that for Kristeva dominate the mental apparatus from start to finish. Yet what might Kristeva be gaining by drawing attention to the imaginary resilience – the creative representational refashioning of the senses – of everyday life? And what, we might ask, is gained by thinking of what happens to our wishes (inseparable from figure and fantasy) in categories that emphasize the pro-linguistic: fantasy life is "expressed in and dealt with by *mental processes far removed from words* and conscious relational thinking." Would this not be the other side of language, which is the representational flux of the unconscious ego?

Kristeva conceptualizes what she refers to as the "proto-fantasy" as a kind of oscillation of the imagination, with the human subject internally divided, split between infantile narcissism and the other's lack. Strictly speaking, if representation is an "active presence of fantasy scenes," this is because desire, for Kristeva as for Lacan, is the desire of the Other. To desire the Other is a kind of fashioning, an imagining of what the other dreams, an imitating, an identification with the other's desire. Notwithstanding that it is the inescapability of imaginary misrecognition that leaves the human subject to impute an imaginary fullness to the other's desire that, in fact, pertains only to the representation (that is, the imaginary plenitude that the subject itself desires), the point is there would be no meaning, not to say anything of the possibility for self-knowledge, without these imaginative fashionings.

Kristeva has written in great depth about the length people will go to in creating obstacles to pleasure; in doing so, she has reformulated Freud's account of Oedipal desire as a general theory of the constitution of the subject and its baroque imaginings. I want to emphasize that her reflections on the unconscious or preconscious fantasy – in the earlier quotation – captures something important about the imaginary making and taking of pleasure in daily life. In Kristeva's reckoning, the psychoanalytic theory of fantasy is about the human subject's imaginings that inform, say, perceptions of the body, imaginings about how one sounds and speaks, imaginings about one's sporting prowess, imaginings about pop stars and celebrities, imaginings about educational advancement and intellectual recognition, imaginings about where one is headed or what may be wrong with one's life.

Kristeva's psychoanalytic reflections on the intricate intertwining of psychic representation and revolt alter the stakes of contemporary forms of identity formation. While it is certainly the case that structures of subjectivity appear repressively constituted in Kristeva's writings on "new maladies of the soul," the role that she ascribes to the contribution of individuals and the effort of questioning remains crucial nonetheless. In an interview, Kristeva contrasts revolt to the more general norms of "new maladies of the soul," thus,

> revolt, as I understand it – psychic revolt, analytic revolt, artistic revolt – refers to a state of permanent questioning, of transformation, change, an endless probing of appearances . . . I want to rehabilitate the microscopic sense of the word, its etymological and literary sense in which the root "vel" means unveiling, returning, discovering, starting over. This is the permanent questioning that characterizes psychic life and, at least in the best cases, art.
>
> *(2002, p. 120)*

This notion of "permanent questioning" is particularly significant, I argue, because such a form of revolt appears to be that of tracing alternative possibilities and possible kinds of subjecthood opened in conditions of institutionalized individualism.

More than any other psychoanalyst, perhaps more than Freud's foundational insights, Kristeva captures the complex ways people use their imagination to make life meaningful. For Kristeva, individuals are captured by, in thrall to, their unconscious fantasies – these radically strange, foreign social dreams. Such fantasies, in addition to constituting intercourse between unconscious dreams and practical life, are the very imaginings of imagination. I examine Kristeva's theoretical approach in considerable detail at various points of this book partly because, in my view, she offers us an exemplary social theory of the creativity of imagination. Yet there are now a number of highly original conceptual departures that underscore the creativity of the psyche, and in one sense it is possible that not even Kristeva adequately accounts for what the French psychoanalyst Jean Laplanche – to whom I now turn for a final formulation on the imagination – underscores concerning the importance of creation to social thought.

## Enigmatic messages: Laplanche

Like Kristeva, Laplanche is also concerned with reconceptualizing the conditions of primal identification and repression, with the purpose of mapping the inaccessible, unconscious significations between the individual subject and the intersubjective realm. Laplanche suggests that an
elementary form of subjectivity is constituted when the small infant enters into an identification
with certain "enigmatic signifiers" in the pre-Oedipal phase, a phase that initiates the binding of unconscious drives through primal repression. Though highly technical in formulation,
what Laplanche means by the notion of enigmatic signifier, roughly speaking, is the uncanny
de-centering influence of the Other upon our psychical life. This process of de-centering, says
Laplanche, occurs at the crossroads of language, body and desire – wherever another's "message" (Laplanche's term) implants itself as a perplexing question or foreign body in the human
subject's psyche. Subjectively speaking, the role of enigmatic signifiers is one always at work in
the emotional life of the subject, and yet the sort of specific enigmas or perplexing messages that
tend to dominate a person's experience of self derive, by and large, from childhood. According to Laplanche, enigmatic messages conveyed by parents (at first by the mother) are especially
consequential for the development of subjectivity since such implantations arise prior to the
establishment proper of the signifying character of the symbolic order. As Laplanche puts this:

> The *enigma is* in itself a *seduction* and its mechanisms are unconscious . . . The "attentions of
> a mother" or the "aggression of a father" are seductive only because they are not transpar-
> ent. They are seductive because they are opaque, because they convey something enigmatic.
> *(1987, p. 128, emphasis added)*

If the enigmatic message is integral to the psychic origins of the unconscious, it is equally central to human subjectivity itself, so that Laplanche is able to develop a neo-Lacanian critique of the
trajectory of both psychosexuality and identity. He outlines the foundational force of an opaque,
impossibly paradoxical Otherness – the result of intrusive and exciting adult enigmas – so that the
human subject can never get to the heart of family secrets or sexual researches but must live nevertheless with these enigmas through the continual emotional work of translation, reconstruction
and binding. In any case, this is so since adult messages always already outstrip the small infant's
capacity for emotional processing and affective response. Laplanche calls this the "fundamental
anthropological situation" of humans, the fact that the infant wouldn't survive without the care
and nurturance provided by the adult – a situation that locates the infant as struggling to comprehend the adult's expressions of feeling, gestures of care and conveyances of relatedness. For try as the
infant might to comprehend elements of the adult's communication – attempting a kind of "proto-
understanding" through the primitive translation and binding of adult enigmas – there is always a
leftover or residue, which for Laplanche constitutes the unconscious and primal repressions.

More than merely perplexing, however, enigmatic messages are completely mysterious, for the
enigmatic message is itself, in an uncanny sort of way, always scrambled, overloaded with signification, impenetrable. Laplanche's account of all this might perhaps be likened to the sense of
strangeness an adult might feel when, having entered a room, he or she discovered people talking
a highly specialized language, like the jargon of nuclear physics, nanotechnology or deconstruction. For Laplanche, messages are enigmatic because they are compromised by the repressed
unconscious lodged inside us: a contradictory condensation of unconscious desires invades the
enigmatic signifiers, such that the adult does not know what it wants of the infant in any case.
This is a version of the classic psychoanalytic doctrine that the small infant's unconscious is
formed with reference to the parental unconscious.

From one angle, then, Laplanche is simply making the Freudian point that parents have an unconscious. But, in another sense, he goes further than Freud, underscoring that it is the messages parents do not understand or even know about (due to the dynamic impact of unconscious wishes and the ego's resistance to them) that transfers as a repressed residue within the child's psyche. From this angle, what is on the outside, parental or adult (sexual) messages, constitutes an inaccessible field of significations on the inside, the repressed unconscious. In the words of Laplanche, the implication of this is that there "is no initial or natural opposition between the instinctual and the intersubjective, or between the instinctual and the cultural" (1987, p. 137).

Laplanche's favorite stage of infant development appears to lie with the earliest transactions between mother and child, the pre-Oedipal realm where floating needs and appetites meet with scrambled and mysterious adult messages, which he uses to illustrate the paradox of primal seduction. Returning the Freud's discussion of maternal care and devotion as central to the origins of the infant's psychic life, Laplanche argues that the breast is a carrier of maternal fantasy that transmits opaque sexual significations within the mother–child relation. As Laplanche puts this:

> Can analytic theory afford to go on ignoring the extent women unconsciously and sexually cathect the breast, which appears to be the natural organ for lactation? It is inconceivable that the infant does not notice this sexual cathexis, which might be said to be perverse in the same sense in which that term is defined in the *Three Essays*. It is impossible to imagine that the infant does not suspect that this cathexis is the source of a nagging question: what does the breast want from me, apart from wanting to suckle me, and come to that, why does it want to suckle me?
>
> *(1987, p. 126)*

The child thus receives a sexually distorted message from mother, a message that the child is emotionally unable to comprehend.

Laplanche was one of the first post-Lacanians to write of the strange transformations – the condensations, displacements and reversals – of unconscious repression, which results in the formation of an internal foreign other, of what Freud called a thing-presentation, or, if you will, the depths of imagination itself.[1] He has been one of the few major psychoanalytic thinkers, period, to focus on the irreducible creativity of unconscious work, by which he means specifically the field of symbolizing activity. His psychoanalytic work, to a considerable degree, represents a series of reflections on the ontology of determinism within Freudianism.

For the moment, it is appropriate to detail Laplanche's account of the internal otherness – an unconscious of strange, foreign bodies – at the center of psychic life. As he writes:

> What guarantees the alien-ness of the other? Can one affirm here, with Lacan, the priority of language? If for my part, I speak rather of a "message," this is for at least two well-defined reasons: firstly, the message can just as easily be non-verbal as verbal; and for the baby it is principally non-verbal. Secondly, emphasising "language" effaces the alterity and individuality of the other in favour of transhistorical structures.
>
> *(Laplanche, 1997, p. 660)*

There are a couple of things to note here. Laplanche, like Kristeva, rejects the linguistic imperialism of Lacanian doctrine: "the message can just as easily be non-verbal as verbal." So too, like Kristeva, Laplanche distances himself from a concern with "transhistorical structures" (phylogenesis, language) in favor of the essential uniqueness and individuality of human imagination. In shifting away from Lacan and back to Freud – returning to prelinguistic psychical representatives or fantasmatic constructions made of images and split from words – Laplanche will emphasize that in the act of *psychic translation* the singular individual *creates* in the strongest sense of the term.

It could be said that Laplanche is out to provide a social theory of our *struggle for representation* in the field of symbolizing activity – which, in a sense, has been the subject of all psychoanalytic theories since Freud unearthed the unconscious logics of the dream. For in his preoccupation with the problem of translation – by which is meant the psychic force field of representations, resemblances, contiguities, condensations and reversals – Laplanche's work plays ingeniously on a subtle, but definite, relation between human subjects in the context of symbolic and social formations. For Laplanche, it is essential to grasp that the infant is, from the beginning of life, presented with what he calls "messages" (both verbal and nonverbal) by parents, messages that the infant is ill-equipped to adequately deal with or understand on an emotional plane. It makes perhaps less difference what the soft caresses of a mother actually signify as regards the self-understandings of the adult, though part of Laplanche's interest turns on the way parents always convey far more than they consciously intend. What matters in Laplanche's scheme is that the infant has been addressed or called with a message, a message that is at once exciting and mystifying.

The striking feature of Laplanche's theorization of the message as enigmatic is its sheer open-endedness. His account of the psychosexual development of the individual subject in terms of the ongoing emotional work of translation and retranslation would make no sense were it not for the recognition that, because of the small infant's initially limited ways of trying to emotionally process proffered messages, psychic life is always, necessarily, imaginative, creative, inventive. Unlike the iron determinism of the early Lacan's emphasis on the Symbolic subjection of the subject, it is the mystifying element of the message that for Laplanche sparks imaginative associations in the child. What is inescapable for the infant – and then subsequently for the adult – is that such mystifying messages demand continual psychic work, are in need of continual translation. Indeed, Laplanche himself has acknowledged that he came up with the concept of "message," with all this implies of the need for translation, in order to overcome the rigid determinism of psychoanalysis in France since Lacan.

## Future developments

Some of the most interesting developments in contemporary psychoanalysis persuasively show that the status of the psychic representative prior to representation, and certainly prior to the psyche's Oedipal enmeshment within language and symbolization, may be regarded as having a kind of unconscious (or what Castoriadis has termed the "human Nonconscious") all of its own. The notion of the human nonconscious, or what Kristeva has termed "the prepsychical" and Laplanche "enigmatic implantations," has moved center stage in European psychoanalysis. But it is not just Europe where such clinical and theoretical insights have spread, for North America has also been an important psychoanalytic laboratory for investigations in the genealogy of the Freudian subject – especially the various relational and intersubjective accounts of subject-formation offered in object relations theory and Kleinian psychoanalysis. Rejecting the Lacanian emphasis on the determination of linguistics or discursive codes in the construction of subjectivity, a range of psychoanalysts have argued that the intrasubjective and intersubjective constitution of desire is far more complex, differentiated and nuanced than is dramatized in French (read: Lacanian) psychoanalytic theories. In some approaches, it is the intersubjective constitution and reproduction of psychic life that is especially significant, with theorists referring to "the shadow of the Other" (Jessica Benjamin), "the analytic Third" (Thomas Ogden), the relational force of "thinking in fragments" (Jane Flax), or the transformational "power of feelings" (Nancy Chodorow).

There have been some powerful attempts to trace this interweaving of the prepsychical or proto-affective on the one hand and the unconscious on the other in various psychoanalytic schools. The influence of Bion, for example, looms large in this connection; the writings of Christopher Bollas are illustrative. Bollas emphasizes both the creativity of subjectivity itself and the key place of experience in the formation of psychical constructions and fantasy. He underlines the relational aspect of very early experience in the infant's encounter with the mothering environment.

This represents the core grounding of the self, or what he terms the "idiom," by which he means a psychical grid through which experience is generated and meaning created. According to Bollas we do not move past, or grow out of, this psychological grid. The idiom of psychic organization is not a developmental phase; rather, it is an unconscious space between experience and fantasy. As Bollas puts this:

> The self does not evolve unconsciously; rather, the self *is* unconsciousness, a particular inner presence, reliably vectored by the forms "it" uses to find expression . . . [E]ach of us at birth is equipped with a unique idiom of psychic organization that constitutes the core of our self, and then in the subsequent years of our life we become our parents' child, instructed by the implicate logic of their unconscious relational intelligence in the family's way of being: we become a complex theory for being a self that the toddler does not think about but acquires operationally.
>
> *(Bollas, 1992, p. 51)*

Subjectivity is theorized by Bollas as a kind of dream-work: overdetermined, displaced, condensed, symbolic. Each of us, as human subjects, integrates daily experience into the inner texture of our psychic worlds. We abandon ourselves to the dreaming of life; we immerse ourselves in others and in the object-world; this is a dissolution essential to the inner complexity of psychical life. We dream ourselves into being, says Bollas, "as we dissolve consciousness, disseminate parts of the self in units of experience" and, by turning the self back upon its immersion in experience, "use objects as lexical elements in the elaboration of idiom" (Bollas, 1992, pp. 52–53).

The central subjective tension, according to Bollas, is that of a relationship between unconscious dissemination and reflective subjectivity, of the proto-affective forms that underpin psychic signification (the conversion of beta-element into alpha-element in Bion's terms) and elaborated thinking. In the words of Bollas:

> The concept of self experiencing is ironic, as its referential ambiguity (does it mean the self that experiences or the experiencing of our self?) is strangely true to the complexity of being human. All self experiencing involves this split, which can be described as a division between ourself as simple selves (when we are immersed in desired or evoked experience) and ourself as complex selves (when we think about experience). Naturally such distinctive states may overlie one another, so that I may be reflecting upon an experience in the immediate past while another part of me is already within a disseminating experience.
>
> *(Bollas, 1992, p. 27)*

The central tension or contradiction in self-experiencing is therefore reinscribed in every process of object selection: an unconscious immersion in units of experience that are only partly thinkable (since that immersion is itself a dense condensation of self and object world), and a reflective lifting of such unconscious experience into thinking and articulation.

From this angle, psychoanalysis represents the possibility for confronting fear, nothingness, obliviousness and depression. Psychoanalysis, as indicated by the contributions of Castoriadis, Kristeva and Laplanche in recent European articulations, represents the possibility of continual self-questioning and investigation of the self.

But it is Kristeva who should have the last word here, given that I began the chapter with her recent interventions. The prepsychical or "passionate primary maternal," according to Kristeva, is "the ultimate irrepresentability." Freud for Kristeva opened another spacing of representation, which is the nothing other than the affectivity of representational flux itself. "Didn't Freud write to Fliess," reflects Kristeva, "that he was looking for 'a biological – or rather metapsychological solution,' the synonyms biological and metapsychological contrasting with the 'psychological' solution brought about by 'the theory of wish fulfillment.'" The interface of affectivity and representation, semiotic and symbolic, repressed unconscious and constant self-questioning is – as Kristeva affirms – central to theoretical innovations that are characteristic of psychoanalysis in the 21st century.

## Author's note

This chapter draws extensively from my *Social Theory Since Freud* (Routledge, 2004, London and New York). The chapter is a modified and expanded version of some of the original material.

## Note

1 Having trained with Lacan, Laplanche's early writings indicate a strong conceptual debt to his former analyst. Indeed, the book for which Laplanche is perhaps best known in the Anglo-American world is *The Language of Psychoanalysis* (1967), co-authored with J. B. Pontalis – an encyclopedic coverage of core psychoanalytic concepts through the lens of French Freudianism. Further works of psychoanalytic exposition and critique followed, including the influential tract *Life and Death in Psychoanalysis* (1976), in which Laplanche struggled to remain faithful to the Lacanian modifications to psychoanalysis, principally through expressing his general suspicion of structural theory. It seems likely, however, that Laplanche's lasting contribution to psychoanalysis will be his reflections on otherness in the formation of human subjectivity, as developed in his "general theory of seduction," set out in the five-volume *Problématiques* (1980–1987). A summary of Laplanche's post-Lacanian theory of seduction has appeared in English, in the volumes *New Foundations for Psychoanalysis* (1987) and *Essays on Otherness* (1999).

## References

Bollas, C 1992, *Being a character: Psychoanalysis and self experience*, Hill and Wang, New York.
Castoriadis, C 1987, *The imaginary institution of society*, Polity Press, Cambridge.
Castoriadis, C 1989. 'The state of the subject today', *Thesis Eleven*, vol. 5, pp. 25–43.
Castoriadis, C 1997, *World in fragments: Writings on politics, society, psychoanalysis and the imagination*, Stanford University Press, Stanford.
Elliott, A 1999, *Social theory and psychoanalysis in transition* (2nd ed), Free Association Books, London.
Elliott, A 2004, *Social theory since Freud*, Routledge, New York.
Ferguson, H 1996, *The lure of dreams: Sigmund Freud and the construction of modernity*, Routledge, London.
Kristeva, J 1987, *Tales of love*, Columbia University Press, New York.
Kristeva, J 1988, *In the beginning was love*, Columbia University Press, New York.
Kristeva, J 1989, *Black sun: Depression and melancholia*, Columbia University Press, New York.
Kristeva, J 1991, *Strangers to ourselves,* New York: Columbia University Press.
Kristeva, J 1993, *New maladies of the soul*, Columbia University Press, New York.
Kristeva, J 2000, *Crisis of the European subject*, Other Press, New York.
Kristeva, J 2001, *Melanie Klein*, R Guberman (trans), Columbia University Press, New York.
Kristeva, J 2002, *Revolt, she said*, Semiotext(e), New York.

Kristeva, J 2010, *Hatred and forgiveness*, Columbia University Press, New York.

Laplanche, J 1976, *Life and death in psychoanalysis* (J Mehlman, trans), Johns Hopkins University Press, Baltimore.

Laplanche, J 1987, *New foundations for psychoanalysis*, Blackwell, Oxford.

Laplanche, J 1997, 'Theory of seduction and the problem of the other', *International Journal of Psychoanalysis*, vol. 78, pp. 653–666.

Laplanche, J 1998 [1980–1987], *Problématiques I–V*, Collection Quadrige, Presses Universitaires de France, Paris.

Laplanche, J 1999, *Essays on otherness*, Routledge, London.

Laplanche, J & Pontalis, JB 1968, 'Phantasy and the origins of sexuality', *International Journal of Psychoanalysis*, vol. 49, no. 1, pp. 1–18.

Mitchell, J & Rose, J 1985, *Feminine sexuality and the Ecole Freudienne*, W.W Norton, New York.

# 11

# Twentieth-century American psychoanalysis

*Nancy Chodorow*

American psychoanalysis has recently passed its 100th anniversary. Psychoanalysis was brought to the United States in 1908, when Abraham Brill returned from Europe after studying with Bleuler and meeting Freud, and a year later in 1909, when Freud, Jung and Ferenczi traveled to Clark University in Worcester, Massachusetts, where Freud and Jung delivered lectures (the classic overview of psychoanalysis in the United States is Hale, 1971, 1995). The New York Psychoanalytic Society and the American Psychoanalytic Association were established shortly thereafter, both founded by Brill in 1911.

However, 20th-century American psychoanalysis, as most psychoanalysis outside of its Mitteleuropean countries of origin, can really be said to begin after 1933, when the Berlin Psychoanalytic Institute was Aryanized and refugees from Germany began to arrive in the United States, and after 1938–1940, following the Nazi Anschluss welcomed by Austria in 1938. These émigré (or refugee: immigrants had different self-identities) analysts brought the characteristic identities of their psychoanalytic milieus of origin – Berlin, Vienna, Budapest – and these identities helped to shape a diverse American psychoanalysis.

In spite of this diversity, ego psychology (often referred to as "classical" or "mainstream" American psychoanalysis) has been the hegemonic perspective on psychoanalysis in the United States. Ego psychology has had the most clinical, theoretical, cultural and political influence throughout the psychoanalytic world as a representative *American* tradition, and it is what analysts mean when they refer to "American" psychoanalysis (psychoanalysts and analytic scholars throughout the world use the adjective "American" to refer to the United States and sometimes to Anglophone Canada, though there are thriving psychoanalytic cultures and institutes throughout Latin America).

As ego psychology is the only major psychoanalytic tradition, theory and theory of technique that does not warrant its own chapter in this handbook, the present chapter will mention the variety within American psychoanalysis and conclude by noticing some especial American contributions, but it will focus on American ego psychology, the foundational status of ego psychology in psychoanalysis, and the centrality of the ego in psychic life. It is not possible to do psychoanalytic clinical work or think psychoanalytically without drawing centrally upon ego psychological concepts.

Briefly, alongside ego psychology, a cultural-interpersonal tradition developed, founded in the 1930s by Americans Harry Stack Sullivan and Clara Thompson and Berlin-trained Karen

Horney. This tradition focused on the therapeutic centrality of interaction and the interpersonal in clinical work and development. Over the course of the 1930s, it also came to include a culturalist critique – a view that elements of psychic conflict and neurosis were fostered by particular cultural patterns and pressures. Among these founders, Sullivan was close to the anthropologist Edward Sapir, and Thompson had spent time in Budapest, the home of psychoanalyst-anthropologist Géza Roheim as well as of current and future independent/dissident thinkers Ferenczi, who was Thompson's analyst, and Sándor Radó.

Émigré culturalist Horney, along with Frieda Fromm-Reichman and Erich Fromm, came from Berlin, and this branch of psychoanalysis was related through national and intellectual milieu of origin to the psychoanalytic Marxist Frankfurt Institute.

Descendants of interpersonal-cultural psychoanalysts helped create relational psychoanalysis, which grew to prominence in the United States in the 1980s; relational psychoanalytic feminism; and a vibrant psychoanalytic anthropology in the university that thrived especially from the 1930s through the 1970s. Relational psychoanalysis, in particular, directly inherited the mantle of interpersonal psychoanalysis and continues to coexist with it in overlapping but still differentiated training centers. Some of its founders were trained at the Sullivanian interpersonal William Alanson White Institute, and other relationalists have written extensively about Ferenczi. Other analytic traditions arose in the United States in particular locations – especially Kohutian self psychology in Chicago, which followed upon the earlier Chicago dissidence of Franz Alexander, whose corrective emotional experience became, in Kohut's hands, the analysand's response to a mirroring transference.

It is not surprising that in a large and diverse country, we would find several non-hegemonic psychoanalytic traditions, nor that, in a country where all white inhabitants are some generation of immigrant, these traditions would bear some relation to the countries of origin or training of their proponents – in the case of psychoanalysis, to psychoanalytic center and periphery in Middle Europe. Foundational, hegemonic 20th-century American psychoanalysis, centered in ego psychology, though later fueled by American-born analysts, was first established through an influx of analysts from all three European centers, Vienna, Berlin and Budapest. These analysts shared close, often personal, ties to Freud and to the "late Freud" – those developments beginning with Freud's mid-'teens revision of the psychoanalytic metapsychology, his creation of the structural theory, and his eventual explicit introduction of the psychology of "das Ich": the "I."

By contrast to American ego psychology, developed and elaborated by analysts from all European centers, we can see that alternate traditions in the United States tend to have been fostered more by American-born analysts and by those trained in Budapest or Berlin, away from the Viennese center. Similarly in England, Melanie Klein was formed not in Vienna but in Berlin and Budapest, and we find Michael Balint in 1937a and 1937b contrasting the "Viennese" (Anna Freudian) position on the infant with the (Kleinian) "English" position.

## Ego psychology: historical and intellectual development

American psychoanalysis, whose development coincided with the closing of the European institutes and forced emigration of most members, grew out of an ego psychological foundation initiated by Freud in the 1910s and 1920s. It is useful to consider this prehistory – a prehistory that developed before there was a substantial psychoanalysis in the Americas – because, as we turn to what became, in the latter half of the 20th century in the United States and elsewhere, a widespread object of criticism and dismissal, we can also keep in mind the integral centrality to psychic functioning in general and analytic work in particular of ego activities: ego functions and ego structure. We also remember Hans Loewald's reminder that all object relations theories are equally ego psychologies, as they conceptualize the ego in relation to its internal and external objects, and that in the clinical consulting room, as in development, all clinical encounters involve the intersubjective relating of two egos.

A psychology of the ego is with us from the beginning. In the *Studies on Hysteria*, Freud writes repeatedly of hysteria as consisting in separated or separate "psychical groups" of conflict and repression, and in the case of Miss Lucy R, he specifies "a psychical group divorced from the ego" and "split off [from] ego consciousness." Freud's clinical goal is to return these split-off psychical groups to the ego, to ego consciousness. Still relatively early, we find, in his 1911 "Formulations on the Two Principles of Mental Functioning," Freud telling us about conflicts between the pleasure and reality principles. Our conflicts find their root, he says, when our drives (sexual drives only, at this pre–*Beyond the Pleasure Principle* stage), reaching always toward pleasure, come up against the demands of the reality principle. Already in this 1911 paper we have an ego psychology, as Freud divides the ego into a "pleasure ego" and a "reality ego." The reality ego, he avers, comprises, among other "mental functions" *consciousness*, *attention*, a system of *notation* that includes *memory*, an *impartial passing of judgment* that decides on the truth or falsity of an idea, motoric *action* taken in order to alter reality and *thinking* (Freud italicizes these functions). Only *phantasying* and *daydreaming* remain free from reality testing, but Freud specifies even these as "thought activities." From 1911, then, we see that essential functions of the mental apparatus are "thought activities," including, in addition to cognition and other mental functions, fantasying and daydreaming. As such, we would have to think of them as ego activities.

Ego psychology includes not only the activities, or functions, of the ego but also the ego's subjectivity. We find founding statements in Freud's 1914 "On Narcissism" and in his 1917 "Mourning and Melancholia," essays that initiate both the structural/ego psychological and the object relations traditions. In these essays, Freud tells us that the ego may turn outward toward others or inward toward itself, may attach itself to narcissistically-cathected objects like the self or to anaclitically-cathected objects that perform the function of an other, and may attach to and then internalize objects that are loved or hated. In a fundamental establishing of the ego-structural theory, Freud tells us that the ego forms and develops through internalization, as the "shadow of the object fell upon the ego."

This early theory of internalization and ego formation, expanded throughout the 1920s especially in *The Ego and the Id*, with the elaboration of an account of superego (*das Über-ich*) formation, became the basis both of what came to be known as the structural theory of ego psychology, or ego psychology tout court, and of the object relations and structural theories of Klein and especially of Fairbairn. Fairbairn's diagram of endopsychic structure, with Central Ego, Libidinal Ego, and Anti-Libidinal Ego, each in relation to a particular kind of object, creatively elaborates and specifies what the Freudian structural theory condensed and could as easily have been called an ego psychology as an object relations theory (or an ego-object relations theory).

During this same period, in his 1926 *Inhibitions, Symptoms, and Anxiety*, Freud significantly extended his 1911 description of ego functions and ego psychology, describing the ego as the seat of anxiety – the sensor (and censor) that (unconsciously) decides when a protective or defensive operation is needed.

Ego psychology was consolidated by two establishing texts, Anna Freud's 1936 *The Ego and the Mechanisms of Defense* and Heinz Hartmann's 1939 *Ego Psychology and the Problem of Adaptation*. Anna Freud, in her classic book, describes all the techniques that the ego makes use of to manage conflicts, anxiety, and other internal threats, and her clinical goal is to describe how to help patients to see these, to know and thereby to modulate their own defensive modalities.

She gave us the overarching language of ego defenses and experience-near examples, like "identification with the aggressor" and the "special form of altruism" that defends against anger, in addition to naming for us all the defenses that those who preceded her had in passing described – in addition to repression, turning passive into active, denial, regression, reaction formation, isolation, displacement, undoing, splitting, projection, introjection, turning against the self, reversal, and so forth – defenses that we see in our everyday observation of friends, family and colleagues, as well as, for the analyst and therapist, in our patients and ourselves. As she elaborates, Anna Freud reminds us that defenses, and therefore the ego, are useful and necessary to psychic life. The very existence of the ego, with the ego's observing and assessing capacities and capacity for anxiety, enables the defenses to operate.

A child analyst, Anna Freud suggests that there may be a developmental progression to the defenses, and that different kinds of defenses happen at different stages. Following her work, then, foundational to ego psychology is attention not only to conflict and the character of different conflicts and the defenses that operate to mitigate or resolve these but also attention to the ways that the capacity for defense unfolds over the life cycle and in treatment. For example, you cannot have repression until an ego is differentiated from the drives or what came to be called the id, nor can you identify with the aggressor until ego and superego capacities for identification have begun to develop.

In his 1951 "Ego and Reality" and later, in his 1962 "Internalization, Separation, Mourning, and the Superego," Hans Loewald elaborates upon these developmental observations in a way that applies equally to Kleinian-Fairbairnian theories (Loewald's papers are collected in Loewald, 1980). He claims that ego and external world are subjectively constituted initially by primary differentiation – primary projection and introjection – and that similarly, the object quality of this external world is created as aggressive and libidinal drives come into being. These first proto-ego creations by necessity precede the defensive and aggressive forms of projection and introjection described by Klein and others, as you cannot have projection and introjection before external and internal are constituted, nor sexual or aggressive aims without internal or external drive object.

Heinz Hartmann's *Ego Psychology and the Problem of Adaptation* followed from and extended both Freud and Anna Freud; Hartmann, along with his colleagues Ernst Kris and Rudolph Loewenstein, shortly thereafter brought ego psychology to the United States. Expanding upon Freud, Hartmann asks: What is the ego and who is the person who brings herself to analysis and participates in it? What does the reality principle mean? What is internal reality? Hartmann elaborated the idea of the conflict-free ego sphere and documented, specifically, how conflict and defense may shape the ego capacities themselves. Drawing upon Freud's description of the cognitive, motoric, perceptual, linguistic, fantasy and dreaming functions of the ego, Hartmann showed how these apparently cognitive capacities may become embroiled in unconscious fantasy and conflict, thereby inhibiting and compromising them. According to Hartmann, thinking, remembering, reasoning, speaking, observing the world – those very capacities that enable us to participate in life in general, in work that involves the mind, and in analysis – are ego capacities that can be relatively free from, or relatively entangled in, conflict, since they all have to various degrees fantasy and affect as part of their make-up. Following the Freud of 1911, Hartmann elaborated how the ego functions – including the capacities to dream, symbolize, fantasy, free associate, and access primary process – are part of adaptation, as they respond to and enable response to the reality principle.

Hartmann's ego psychology thus describes how defenses can be pathological or non-pathological. For Freud, fantasy was a defense against reality. By contrast, for Hartmann and the ego psychologists who followed him, perhaps especially Arlow and Loewald, fantasy, symbolism, daydreaming, dreaming, and so forth, are themselves essential ego functions and necessary to health. Here, Hartmann finds common ground also with Kleinian Hannah Segal and with British independents like Milner and Winnicott. Finally, in showing the delicate relations of conflict, conflict-freedom, and ego functions, Hartmann gave us the essential concept of secondary autonomy. Here, he combines an ego psychological metapsychology with a developmental perspective. Hartmann argues that we need to look not only at early conflicts and drive pressures, but also at how these early conflicts and the drive derivatives entangled within them can transform themselves over time. For example, the young child who expresses aggression through an obsession with knives may become a skilled surgeon: the particular form of his early aggression has gained secondary autonomy. Or, as drawn upon by Stephen Mitchell in a 1978 paper that criticizes psychoanalytic pathologizing of homosexuality, a child's by definition intensely and conflictually charged sexuality may find secondary autonomy and drive and identity resolution as gay or straight. Similarly, any gay or straight person's sexuality may also not have found such resolution and be driven by conflict and defense.

## Classical American ego psychology: key contributors and principle contributions

When we look at American psychoanalysis from the point of view of ego psychology, we find two initiating generations born within a short time of one another. Émigré Europeans Hartmann, Kris and Loewenstein, all trained in Vienna, were born between 1895 and 1900, while Americans Jacob Arlow, Charles Brenner and Paul Gray were born between 1912 and 1918.

Loewald, perhaps the most respected classical American psychoanalyst throughout the world, falls exactly in the middle, born in 1906. Loewald was born in Germany and began his professional formation there in philosophy, followed, after his forced emigration in 1933, by medical training in Italy and analytic training in the United States. Self-identified as an ego psychologist, Loewald built upon but went well beyond the Hartmannian contribution. He was critical of Arlow, Brenner and Gray, yet ironically, perhaps the most carefully accurate appreciation and critique, both explicit and implied, of these three also comes from Loewald. My own appreciative but also critical reading indirectly follows Loewald, who has influenced most of my thinking about psychoanalysis. As I suggest below, given the epistemology and history of psychoanalysis, it is impossible not to include some critique in a basic description of American (indeed, of any) psychoanalytic tradition or psychoanalytic locale.

Arlow and Brenner's *Psychoanalytic Concepts and the Structural Theory* (1964), and Brenner's *The Mind in Conflict* (1982), along with other books and articles, established classical American ego psychology. For Arlow and Brenner, as, in a different way for Klein, Freud's topographic theory, describing mental process in terms of primary and secondary process thinking and differentiating unconscious and preconscious in terms of different modes of mentation and their interconnections, became of lesser importance. They were more concerned to conceptualize the different structures of the mind – id, ego and superego – in terms of function, and especially of the conflicts between these. How and whether mental processes were conscious or not conscious, how thought processes, dreams and other language or ideas moved between unconscious and preconscious, expanding primary process fantasy and thinking, and making the unconscious conscious, these were no longer so much primary goals of analysis as was interpreting which drive derivatives had engaged with which ego judgments in forming symptoms and character.

As with structures of the mind, the functions of the different agencies (for Arlow and Brenner, structures with functions) of the mind seemed to matter more than the elaboration and increasing complexity of thought, fantasy and feeling. In a paired set of articles, Arlow (1969a, 1969b) also wrote about fantasy, its centrality as an ego function, and its elaboration in analysis, though it is unclear for the reader how Arlow fit these interests into a functional lens that focused on conflict and compromise formation. At the same time, Brenner through to his last writings would emphasize even more succinctly how psychic conflict was ubiquitous to all mental functioning.

Brenner, whose writings came to be definitional of American ego psychology, saw himself as elaborating upon Freud. For him, childhood progressed through the developmental anxieties (in Brenner's terms "calamities of childhood") enumerated in Freud's *Inhibitions, Symptoms, and Anxiety*: object loss (originally the breast), loss of love (the parent, through separation or rejection), and castration (fears about bodily integrity). All of these engender anxiety – either depressive anxiety about a loss that has already occurred, or anticipatory (castration) anxiety about a loss that is feared. Anxiety leads to unconscious, ideational compromise formations expressed in symptoms and character that include both the initial anxiety and the form of defense against that fear. For Brenner, compromise formations are the basic data of psychoanalysis, and all mental products – thoughts in daily life, fantasies, plans and actions, as well as symptoms and character – are compromise formations borne of conflict. The goal of analysis is, with the patient, to observe defenses expressed in compromise formations like symptoms and character in order to bring to light the underlying conflictual anxieties and fantasies that they contain.

Analysts need to follow the tripartite structural theory, which emphasized the different functions performed, especially by the ego and superego.

Paul Gray, whose work developed separately from Arlow and Brenner, took American structural-functional ego psychology to its farthest rationalist extent (Gray, 2005), and for this reason Gray has among practitioners both devoted advocates and virulent opponents. Gray's goal as a psychoanalyst is to maximize autonomous ego functions and conscious ego solutions for his patients, to make unconscious ego functions conscious and available to observation by the increasingly rational ego, and to minimize defensively induced internal transformations, internalizations and other fantasy processes. He believes that the analyst is shortchanging patients who are capable of developing this degree of conscious rational ego observation if this is not his highest goal.

More than any other analyst, Gray insists upon the analytic goal of everything coming under the sway of the conscious rational ego. Even dreams, Gray argues, should be examined not primarily in order to understand the dream itself, or to valorize and expand upon the remarkable human capacity to connect primary and secondary process, unconscious and preconscious, or fantasy and reality (as would be emphasized, for example, by Loewald), but rather in terms of how the patient's recall of dreams and the way they are talked about in the consulting room serve defensive, resistance functions against immediate feelings in the moment. Similarly, memories of the past, when brought up in analysis, are seen initially as defensive distancing from immediate conflict. For Gray, as for Brenner, autonomous ego functioning, making the ego's conflicts and defenses as conscious as possible, rather than the expansion of dreaming, fantasy, transference and other unconscious processes, is the goal of psychoanalysis. The primary process unconscious in and of itself is not so much of interest. Gray and his followers, whose technique is named "close process," or "the technique of close process attention," have been premier ego psychological leaders (as have been Kleinians throughout the world) in advocating attention to the moment-to-moment ego activity underlying the patient's verbal and nonverbal productions and expression.

When we consider the place of ego psychology in American psychoanalysis, we are considering both the theory of the ego and analytic technique. The classical ego psychologist described, as an expert outside observer, what was going on in the patient, what the patient was expressing in terms of feelings for the analyst, which were, by definition, transference (they came from the past and from within) and resistance against drive derivatives – for Gray, especially drive derivatives of aggression; for Brenner, especially primal anxieties about aggressive and sexual conflicts of early childhood and defenses against these.

## Ego psychology and its critics: toward a psychoanalytic sociology of knowledge

The three American writer-analysts Arlow, Brenner and Gray and their followers have come to epitomize a rationalist, structural-functional, bloodless and affectless ego psychology that is widely excoriated both within American relational psychoanalysis and self psychology and in Kleinian, Latinate, and Latinate Bionian analytic cultures throughout the world. From the point of view of those concerned with preserving the especial role of psychoanalysis as the only theory of mind to valorize and describe unconscious mental life – fantasy, dreaming and primary process – and unconscious communication, and the only therapeutic practice that works to enhance and facilitate these, close process technique can seem overly cognitive, overly reliant on a non-processual structural and functional theory, and overly concerned with enhancing only secondary process functions, and Brenner can seem too much the outside expert on the patient's defenses. These thinkers, and ego psychology more generally, has been extensively criticized for, in the critics' view, losing and invalidating the special nature of mental life that psychoanalysis alone describes theoretically and works through clinical work to enhance. As I discuss later, Loewald, though a self-identified ego psychologist, would share this critique and gives us its most persuasive and careful elaboration. For the non-advocate like myself, it is hard to write about them without a certain critical stance.

Yet, if we keep in mind that no analyst developed a theory or theory of technique without hoping to help patients and help us as humans to understand ourselves and our minds, we can see the significant clinical and theoretical contribution of these exemplars of American ego psychology. Brenner pointed to the process of compromise formation (or compromise creation) as pervasive in psychic life, ensuring that we always have in mind the complexity of mental life and allowing us to consider how and whether particular compromise creations shut down or open up the individual's psychic life. Arlow extended our understanding not so much of the content of fantasy as of how we fantasize, through what capacities and mental agencies. Gray made us aware of the value and goal of insight and self-understanding in analytic work and in everyday life. Moreover, as American psychoanalytic leader Robert Wallerstein pointed out in his presidential address to the International Psychoanalytical Association (1989), all analysts probably have some clinical commonality that overrides theoretical difference. (In Chodorow, 2003, though, I suggest that we can nonetheless divide analytic practitioners according to schools of theory and technique that lead more to "listening for" – along with classical ego psychologists, Kleinian, self-psychological, Lacanian, Italian Bionian, and, in an earlier and more absolutist and embattled period, relational psychoanalysts – and approaches that lead more to "listening to," especially British and American independents, eclectic French analysts like Chasseguet-Smirgel and Faimberg, and many hybrids throughout the world.)

To understand why ego psychology alone among analytic theories and theories of technique has come in for such vociferous and widespread criticism requires both psychodynamic and political explanation, that is, an appeal to a psychoanalytic sociology of emotions. Misreadings are found both inside and outside of psychoanalysis. Hartmann's "problem of adaptation," drawn straight from Freud (1911) and delineating those adaptive ego functions that make living in the world possible, was translated by 1960s radical thinkers like Brown and Marcuse, by the generation of 1968, by many academic critics, and by psychoanalysts throughout the world into an advocacy or acceptance of the sociopolitical and cultural status quo, leading to vituperative criticism. These critics are joined by virulent criticism as well as dismissal of ego psychology among American relationalists and among most psychoanalytic academic humanists (exceptions include feminist object relations literary scholars like Janet Adelman, Madelon Sprengnether, and

191

others), who romanticize and idealize either a linguistically based French psychoanalysis linked to post-structuralism/postmodernism or "the unconscious" as an unmediated cauldron of primal fantasy and affect.

Ironically, ego psychology describes the very dynamic and cognitive processes, those very ego functions, that enable those critics and activists who dismiss it to function and make their critique – to think, write and act efficaciously. Just as you cannot do academic work or critical writing in a consistent enough way without some intact adaptive and integrative ego functions, autonomous ego capacities, an observing ego, and some mastery of drives and conflicts, so also within the field itself. Insight and self-understanding themselves require ego functions, such that you cannot think analytically without many ego psychological assumptions that all analysts share. When we consider the analyst, her patient and fantasy, and we wish to inquire about what agency, what part of the mind, gives shape and content to conscious or unconscious fantasy, we are also in the realm of the ego. Representation and connecting themselves require agency, and the analyst who wishes to help her patient develop this agency needs a conception of this agent, which must be, in the broadest sense, the ego.

It is hard to conceptualize this experiencing agency (which may not be a single agent) other than in terms of ego activities. Accordingly, when we find an analyst who observes and wishes to describe an incapacity to dream or to engage in free-floating association and fantasy in her patient (or herself) but who does not wish to invoke an ego psychology, we often find generalized impersonal, passive descriptives – "the incapacity to dream" – replacing an articulated conception of the seat of dreaming and of unconscious fantasy activity. Except as metaphor, there *are* no thoughts without a thinker. In sum, if we begin from the taken-for-granted and the not-said, as we are asked to do by traditions like phenomenology and ethnomethodology, we find that analysts and academics worldwide have not noticed that they have been speaking and thinking ego psychology all their professional lives.

As one-person psychology and in the realm of the interpretation of defense and resistance against anxiety and conflict, the classical ego psychologists meet the classical and contemporary Kleinians. Just as Gray and his followers seem to focus relentlessly on defenses against drive derivatives of aggression, even to the extent of seeing a patient's looking at a dream as a defense, or feelings about the analyst as a defense, or as Brennerians seem always focused on the "calamities of childhood" and the defenses against these, so also contemporary Kleinians seem focused exclusively on the patient's aggression against the analyst, as they bring everything back to what the patient is doing, through attack, exclusion, or invasion, to the analyst, or to a manic, destructively tinged defense. While classical ego psychological patients live in a world of defense against drive derivatives, anxieties and conflict, Kleinian patients live in a world of projection, introjection and total transference, in which a separate existence is irrelevant and the analyst expects to be, unless defensively excluded by the patient, continually front and center in the patient's analysis. We find among both groups the analyst as expert about the patient's psyche, as Kleinians Betty Joseph, John Steiner, Michael Feldman and others, like Gray, engage in continuous attention to the moment-to-moment activity of the patient's verbal productions, to the resistance and defense expressed in every action, and to what the patient is doing, as much as to the content of what is being said or being expressed about unconscious dream life.

Yet, it is curious: although some British independents are skeptical of the analyst who knows, who cannot wait, and who puts his own mind front and center in the work (see Parsons, 2009), analysts worldwide have had no trouble idealizing and adopting Kleinian theory and technique. They do not bring to their reading and assessment the same critique, concerning too much certainty and too much attention to resistance that has been brought so forcefully and vociferously against classical American ego psychologists. Even the contemporary Kleinian's near-exclusive inward focus on his or her own feelings, countertransference, and self-observation as providing the fullest truth about the patient does not seem to evoke extensive critique. Only ego psychologists are thought to exist in a realm of over-certainty – in the pure, rationalist, defense-obsessed and unrelated way of being that also forms the caricature of them.

By contrast, American psychoanalytic social scientists and historians (of whom there are only a few, given that the basic epistemology of social science and history – that meaning, thought, and action come from without – opposes psychoanalysis) are often more sympathetic to ego psychology. These academics, even if by preference leaning toward one or another psychoanalytic theory, interact with interview and ethnographic subjects and interpret historical actors. They may find it harder to imagine a psychoanalysis that bypasses the ego and that describes and calls only upon an unstructured psyche that fantasizes, dreams and symbolizes.

For them, it is hard to work without assuming ego capacities in their subjects.

## Intersubjective ego psychology: Loewaldian foundations

Even as classical American ego psychology flourished, an alternative ego-psychologically based approach to mind, development, analytic process and change was developing. In "The American Independent Tradition" (Chodorow, 2004), I name this alternative tradition intersubjective ego psychology. The following, edited by the author, describes it:[1]

> Intersubjective ego psychology integrates the two theoretical and clinical developments that have indisputably characterized American psychoanalysis . . . [It holds a] middle terrain between, on one hand, classical structural and contemporary ego psychology and, on the other, classical interpersonal and contemporary relational psychoanalysis, much as the British Independent/Middle Group . . . originally located itself between Klein and Anna Freud. Intersubjective ego psychology involves an apparently contradictory insistence, following the Hartmann-late Freud legacy, on a radical "one-person" intrapsychic perspective centered on fantasy, drive-derivative wishes, resistances, defenses, and compromise formations, and in consonance with the work of Sullivan, Horney, Thompson, Fromm-Reichman, and others, on the "two-person" importance of the analytic, the mother–child, and . . . sometimes, the sociocultural field. Intersubjective ego psychologists use the ego psychological language of interpretation, individuality, autonomy, insight, analytic neutrality, and other similar concepts, and also the language of enactment, transference–countertransference, the contribution of the analyst's mind and subjectivity, and other concepts that arose initially from interpersonal psychoanalysis. Although advocacy of an analytic attitude of uncertainty and curiosity rather than certainty and authority has crossed all psychoanalytic schools in recent years,
>
> > the founding intersubjective ego psychologists, like the founding British Independents, found their way to this attitude sooner.

Loewald is the original theorist of intersubjective ego psychology in mind, development and analytic process. From his 1951 paper, "Ego and Reality," through his classic 1960 "On the Therapeutic action of Psychoanalysis," and on to his last writings, he establishes its terrain.[2] Erik Erikson, whom I discuss later, created an intersubjective ego psychological developmental stage theory and also contributed a cultural-anthropological perspective.

Throughout his writings, Loewald identifies himself as an ego psychologist, as he writes about drives, including the death drive, and makes internalization, structure building and individuation, as well as ego functions like memory and the relation to reality, central. Yet Loewald also differs in fundamental ways from classical ego psychology. First, he stresses the constitutive role of object relations in the psyche and in the psychic changes of analysis, in terms both of an internal world and of *subject–subject relations* – interaction, intersubjectivity – between analyst and patient. Second, although he is not a child analyst, Loewald (as Erikson) advocates, from his earliest paper to his last book, an intersubjective developmental perspective that goes well beyond the classical Freudian and Brennerian drive-sexual developmental model (or the Kleinian recursively expanding projection-introjection model). He pays careful attention to mother–child interaction in the unfolding of the psyche and to the analyst's capacity to range responsively among different developmental levels of psychic functioning in the patient. He is as interested in pre-Oedipal modes of being and the mother–child realm of primary communication as he is in differentiation and the Oedipus complex. Finally, Loewald insists upon the importance of a topographic point of view, focusing on primary-secondary process links and arguing that transference moves between unconscious and preconscious as much as it does from internal to external objects.

From one point of view, beginning with "Ego and Reality," continuing through his emphasis in "Therapeutic Action" on transference as an intrapsychic integration of unconscious and preconscious, and eventuating in his 1979 "The Waning of the Oedipus Complex," Loewald is an ego psychologist in the Hartmannian vein. He is interested in the establishment of ego and reality from the point of view of a single ego, in the differentiation and development of psychic structure out of an ego–id matrix, and in different forms of thinking. He investigates how the individual psyche creates both itself and the world, whatever the givens of innate, cognitive, material or interpersonal reality. In "Ego and Reality," he tells us that his account "does not imply . . . that there is, for the observer, no world, no environment that sends stimuli to the organism. We are concerned here merely with the question how this world becomes psychologically constituted" (Loewald, 1980, p. 11).

Yet even as Loewald's view of the psyche is radically subjectivist, he is equally an ego/object-relations theorist and intersubjectivist. From his claim that the world only exists through its psychological constitution by the individual, he moves, in his 1978 "Primary Process, Secondary Process, and Language," to claim that no subject exists outside of a relational matrix, that "the primary datum for a genetic, psychoanalytic psychology would be object relations. This relatedness is the psychic matrix out of which intrapsychic instincts and ego, and extrapsychic object, differentiate" (1980, p. 216). The object world is thus both created through ego–object differentiation and there as part of primary relatedness to begin with.

In his challenge to classical ego psychological (and other one-person) assumptions, Loewald claims in "Therapeutic Action" that the analyst is a "new object":

> The relationship to the analyst will include resistance, and analytic work includes interpreting transference distortions, but unless it also includes a relation to the analyst as a new object, the analysis won't work. The patient . . . can take the plunge into the regressive crisis of the transference neurosis which brings him face to face again with his childhood anxieties and conflicts, *if* he can hold on to the potentiality of a new object-relationship, represented by the analyst.
>
> *(Loewald, 1980, p. 224, italics in original)*

Yet, even as I claim Loewald as a founding clinical theorist and metapsychologist of intersubjective ego psychology, for founding American relational analyst Stephen Mitchell (2000), Loewald's continuous attention to the mother-child matrix, the analyst as new object, and the complexities of analyst–patient intersubjectivity accord him center stage, along with Bowlby, Fairbairn and Sullivan, as a classical contributor to relational psychoanalysis.

For Loewald, recognition founds development in both childhood and analysis. As he describes in "Therapeutic Action," the analyst, like the parent, is "holding the future," as he describes this in the parent–child case,

> an empathic relationship of understanding the child's particular stage in development, yet ahead in his vision of the child's future and mediating that vision to the child . . . a more articulate and more integrated version of the core of being that the child presents to the parent.
>
> *(Loewald, 1980, p. 229)*

Reciprocally, the child, through affect, body and mind, takes in the mother's vision:

> The child . . . internalizes the parent's image of the child – an image that is mediated to the child in the thousand different ways of being handled, bodily and emotionally. Early identification as part of ego development, built up through introjection of maternal aspects, includes introjection of the mother's image of the child . . . the child as seen, felt, smelled, heard, touched by the mother . . . The child begins to experience himself as a centered unit by being centered upon.
>
> *(Loewald, 1980, pp. 229–230)*

We see in this quote the intrinsic Loewaldian linkage of intrapsychic and intersubjective that marks intersubjective ego psychology. Both child and analysand become "a centered unit by being centered upon." Loewald distances himself from one-person psychologies where the analyst is objective expert (for the American independent Loewald, the critique that matters is of classical ego psychology, but his critique – like that of British independents like Milner and Winnicott in the British context – applies equally to all theories of technique and change in which the analyst is the expert, knowing interpreter and observer of defenses and resistances).

The analyst becomes a "new object," and the collaboration of analyst and patient is "a necessary requirement for a successful analysis, [that] has nothing to do with scientific detachment and the neutrality of a mirror. This identification has to do with the development of a new object-relationship" (Loewald, 1980, p. 227).

Loewald provides the original description of what came to be the fundamental clinical epistemology of intersubjective ego psychology – *two individualities in an inextricably linked interaction that at the same time preserves each.* Here is his formulation, in his 1970 "Psychoanalytic Theory and the Psychoanalytic Process":

> The unit of psychoanalytic investigation is the individual human mind or personality. We single it out – for reasons deeply rooted in that human mind of which we ourselves are specimens – as a subject worthy of study, as a universe in its own right . . . The object of investigation, the analysand, as well as the investigator, the analyst, although each has a considerable degree of internal psychic organization and relative autonomy in respect to the other, can enter a psychoanalytic investigation only by virtue of their being relatively open systems, and open to each other.
>
> *(Loewald, 1980, p. 278)*

As he later puts it, in his 1975 "Psychoanalysis as an Art and the Fantasy Character of the Psychoanalytic Situation": "In the mutual interaction of the good analytic hour, patient and analyst – each in his own way and on his own mental level – become both artist and medium to each other" (Loewald, 1980, p. 369).

More than any writer from any psychoanalytic school, including Freud, Loewald describes the specifics of the psychoanalytic process and of how an interpretation works. He wants to show us precisely, and not generally, not in summary or after the fact, how change happens – what goes on in the minds of patient and analyst; how these two minds come together in the specifics of the clinical interaction; and exactly what happens in a good interpretation and in psychic change.

And although it is certainly the case that Loewald's unique history, character and intelligence are of primary influence here, his self-identified location within ego psychology, where careful elaborations of cognition and affect are central, is also important. As he describes in "Primary Process, Secondary Process, and Language," a good interpretation opens for the patient the possibility of a different integration and organization by naming unconscious, unformulated, primary process and nonlinguistic thoughts, so that the patient recognizes what is named as her own experience. Naming – language itself – includes affective and nonlinguistic tonalities, both in development and in analysis.

Loewald begins at the beginning, walking us through all levels of psychic change. Drawing upon and providing his own translations of Freud, and hovering between topographic and structural metapsychologies, he describes how defensive structures and operations cover over unconscious-preconscious ruptures, where a thing-cathexis has no access to meaning or language but lives in primary or secondary repression and draws available energy to it. A good interpretation, whether from patient or analyst, helps to link this separated off and unavailable confluence of meaning, energy and affect to words. It connects, as Loewald expands upon Freud, a thing-cathexis with a word cathexis, drawing meaning and affect back into lived consciousness. As Loewald claims in "Therapeutic Action":

> if an interpretation of unconscious meaning is timely, the words by which this meaning is expressed are recognizable to the patient as expressions of what he experiences. They organize for him what was previously less organized and thus give him the distance from himself that enables him to understand, to see, to put into words, and to "handle" what was previously not visible, understandable, separable, tangible. A higher stage of organization, of both himself and his environment, is thus reached by way of the organizing understanding which the analyst provides.
>
> (Loewald, 1980, pp. 238–239)

As Loewald describes it, primary process is a particular form of experiencing thing presentations – unconscious proto-thoughts that have never been articulated. Secondary process emerges as thing-presentations gain representation and connection one to the other and a beginning connection to words. It is in this transitional world between primary and secondary process that fantasy, dreaming and genuine self-understanding take place, and at this more organized level, both unconscious and conscious fantasy as well as dreaming require an agency of experiencing that dreams and engages in fantasy (in Bion's language, the move beyond *beta* elements requires *alpha*-function in patient, in analyst and in between them).

Not only an intersubjective ego psychologist, then, Loewald is an ego psychologist whose metapsychology is topographic as well as structural. He does not criticize or abandon the topography of unconscious-preconscious, that move that has made ego psychology anathema in so much of the analytic world. Here is how an interpretation works:

> The interpretation thus creates the possibility for freer interplay between the unconscious and the preconscious systems, whereby the preconscious regains its originality and intensity, lost to the unconscious in the repression, and the unconscious regains access to and

capacity for progression in the direction of higher organization . . . By an interpretation, both the unconscious experience and a higher organizational level of that experience are made available to the patient: unconscious and preconscious are joined together in the act of interpretation.

*(Loewald, 1980, pp. 240, 242)*

What is to be gained in analysis, then, is not, as for many of the interpretive psychoanalyses, including classical ego psychology, predominantly insight through interpretation – though this is of course important – but an experiential shift enabling greater linkage between unconscious, preconscious, and conscious. In "On the Therapeutic Action of Psychoanalysis, Loewald claims:

Transference is the "dynamism" by which the instinctual life of man, the id, becomes ego and by which reality becomes integrated and maturity is achieved. Without such transference – of the intensity of the unconscious, of the infantile ways of experiencing life that have no language and little organization, but the indestructibility and power of the origins of life – to the preconscious and to present-day life and contemporary objects, human life becomes sterile and an empty shell . . . Our present, current experiences have intensity and depth to the extent to which they are in communication [interplay] with the unconscious, infantile experiences representing the indestructible matrix of all subsequent experiences.

*(Loewald, 1980, pp. 250–251)*

## Intersubjective ego psychology: toward an American independent tradition

We can understand intersubjective ego psychology in terms of its sociology of knowledge and its view of mind and change. Along with the founding European-American ego psychologists, Loewald was born and formed in Germanic intellectual culture, in contrast to psychoanalysts formed in those French, Italian and Latin American cultures that have so influenced psychoanalysis in the current period, and perhaps also in contrast to analysts like Klein, Segal, Joseph, Bion and others who created the British Kleinian tradition. Beginning with Freud, this heritage was founded upon respect for the sciences, a view of psychoanalysis as a branch of scientifically based medicine, and a conception of psychology as a science, emphasized further by those middle European analysts who had PhDs in psychology. Further, it included a respect for and interest in the social sciences, along with philosophy and other fields, as Geisteswissenschaften: sciences of the spirit, or human sciences. Following Freud, Hartmann (1950) wrote about psychology and the social sciences, and Loewald, in the 1970s, invited Talcott Parsons to present in a series of seminars on internalization (Loewald's 1973 paper, "On Internalization" was his own contribution).

We find commonality, then, between Loewald's conception of the intersubjective analytic encounter and that of those qualitative, intersubjective and interpretive social sciences grounded in German philosophy and phenomenology, Weber and Simmel. This foundational intersubjectivity met, in the United States, a pragmatic tradition that would lend itself to on-the-ground formulations and conceptualizations of analytic process, Loewald's careful epistemological attention, even in the absence of extensive case material, to exactly how psychic change happens and what is changing is also quintessentially American – on the ground and empirical – qualities that characterize both classical and intersubjective ego psychology. It is perhaps more akin to the interpretive social sciences than to the metaphoric, associative, evocative conceptualizations of psyche and change that we find in the Romance language psychoanalytic cultures, perhaps explaining the especial attraction in these cultures to the English Winnicott and the Francophone post-structuralism/postmodernism favored by many contemporary relational and relational-feminist analysts.

As I noted earlier, the fundamental epistemology of intersubjective ego psychology is an account of the analytic situation as two individualities in an interaction that preserves each, not a more fused interaction that might be said to characterize relational psychoanalysis or analytic field theory, described originally by the Barangers in terms of doubled or mutual projection and later extended especially by Ferro. Intersubjective ego psychologist Poland (2000, p. 29) contrasts a "two-person separate" model of analytic process, neither co-constructed nor fused, with a more relational "two-person unified" theory of analytic technique and change on the one hand and a classical ego-psychological or "one person" model on the other. His conception of intersubjectivity, he notes, is "different from its use [as] unified field" (p. 29). Echoing Loewald, Poland wants to preserve "the patient as a unique other" and a "private universe of inner experience" (1996, pp. 66, 33).

As I read them and hear their work, several contemporary American analysts, as they move into the 21st century, share an intersubjective ego psychological perspective (some of what follows is drawn from Chodorow, n.d.). Their theory of technique, mind, psychic change and analytic process derives from both classical ego psychology and those developments that pay attention to the analytic relationship and transference–countertransference. With some variability among them (I have not, in this chapter, been able to accord sufficient attention to local specificity in American psychoanalysis), these American independents were classically trained and assume an ego psychological metapsychology. They take for granted the ego and its defenses, conflict and compromise formation, and working from the surface. Along with ego psychology and most classical theories, they retain self-understanding, or insight, as a primary analytic goal. In addition to Poland, they include Rosemary Balsam (2008), Dale Boesky (2008), Judith Chused (e.g., 1991, 1992), Glen Gabbard (e.g., 1996, 2007), Theodore Jacobs (e.g., 1991), and James McLaughlin (2005). In recent years, some of those whom I have called American independent have assumed this identity as their own, and, as I have described the American independent tradition in presentations and papers, I have found each time listeners who find the label congenial.

American independents, though ego psychological, are not classical in their attitude toward the patient nor toward the analytic interaction. Like Loewald, they veer away from a portrayal of the analyst as observer, interpreter and expert about the patient's psyche, and the individual analyst's presence matters, as if American independents have absorbed something of the relational-interpersonal traditions. Yet American independents tend not to be relational in their metapsychology, in their attitude toward and use of the countertransference, or in their accounts of clinical work.

Emerging out of a tension I have described (Chodorow, 1999, 2003) between clinical individuality and the generalizations and universalizations that by necessity partially form the basis of all psychoanalytic metapsychologies or theories of mind, as well as of universal prescriptions for analytic activity and technique, American independent metapsychology favors individuality. Its key theoretical feature – and here it is similar to the British independent tradition – is a theory of mind that makes central the particularity and uniqueness of the individual rather than general principles of mental functioning or psychic structure. The therapeutic action of psychoanalysis revolves around helping the patient to elaborate, deepen, unfold and expand his or her individuality, which includes by necessity self-knowledge on the part of the patient, and working to mitigate impediments to this expansion and unfolding. Modell (1993) describes "the private self," I write in *The Power of Feeling* of "the powers of personal meaning and feeling," and McLaughlin says, "I will listen . . . with the intent to understand your meaning and viewpoint, and with the least imposition of my own view or meaning as I can manage" (2005, p. 48). A focus on the relationship and transference–countertransference, then, are not primary technical goals, nor is the analyst's self analysis and self-awareness brought actively and interactively into the consulting room, as we find in the work of many relational analysts.

Following from this, the key feature of American independent conceptualizations of analytic activity and technique is, following Loewald, a portrayal of two *separate* individualities engaged in the work, not co-construction, not a more-than-the-sum-of-the-parts two-person field. Analyst and patient are in a relationship, but this relationship trumps neither unique selfness and otherness nor the asymmetrical focus on the patient. Poland emphasizes "two separate people, two subjects [and] communicative emotional flow between two separate parties" (2000, p. 29), and he advocates "witnessing" as an alternative to interpretation that respects otherness. In a commentary on his identification with British independent Michael Parsons, Poland writes of the patient's "essential otherness and aloneness," of "powerful meanings that arise from the deep," and of the patient as "a distinctly separate person," with "intact otherness" and distinct integrity" (2009, pp. 19, 21, 22, 25). The analyst, by complement, holds a position of "separated otherness," of "firm respect for self and otherness," of an "other" who is "in attendance" or "travels with" the patient (ibid.).

My own writings agree with Poland. In a 2000 presentation subtitled "Why We Still Need One Person Ego-Psychologies," I say:

> By eschewing one-person psychologies as we embrace two-person approaches, we ignore our commitments as clinicians and people to our own individuality, to our "I-ness," and to our hopes that our patients too will integrate an "I" rather than being driven by unavailable, fragmented, split-off overwhelming drives and affects. And we ignore that there is an active person with whom we are interacting, a person who is not entirely a product of their own transference or our own countertransference creation. There are two people there, even as the two of us create a particular reality between us through which we try to understand this patient and our relationship. *It is the perspective of the individual subject that is most at stake.*

Following Loewald, then, the American independent tradition notices the distinct individuality and subjectivity of analyst and patient, even if and as they co-create or co-construct the analytic encounter. This has consequences for technique, because there is a fundamental contradiction, as I remark earlier, between theory-driven listening and a presumption of unique individuality. Not only an exclusive ego psychology, but also an exclusive Kleinian, relational, intersubjective, Kohutian, or Lacanian view cannot meet the individual differences and the moments of particularity of each patient over the course of an analysis. Further, an openness to varieties of intervention fosters *uncertainty* as an attitudinal stance, as well as *curiosity*, on the part of both analyst and patient, about who the particular patient is at the particular moment, and why.

Friedman names "endless curiosity" as one of the "founding attitudes of psychoanalytic treatment" (1997, p. 31), McLaughlin guides the patient toward "how" rather than "what" (2005, p. 203), and I (2003) call curiosity an "undertheorized technical requisite" of analytic work,

> In its emphasis on individuality, the American independent tradition finds common ground with the British independent tradition – Winnicott's true self, Milner's form from formlessness, Bollas's unthought known and personal idiom, Coltart's rough beast waiting to be born. It also shares technical commonality with this tradition, in its emphasis on curiosity and a willingness to wait (see, e.g., Parsons, 2009). For British independents, quick and frequent interpretation (in the British case, concern focuses on Kleinian quickness), and

micro-attention to each utterance of the patient, favors the ego's continual self-scrutiny and awareness and a patient's continual attention to the analyst, rather than allowing for the slow unfolding of individual growth in a facilitating or witnessing environment.

*(p. 479)*

American independents, like British independents and all analysts, feel that the theory and technique they invoke is chosen because it helps patients, but we can see how American independence is also American, how a focus upon personal uniqueness and individuality might have American cultural and intellectual resonance (Chodorow, 2004). And although it is certainly the case that analysts throughout the world treat patients as individuals, British and American independents have *named* individuality in theory and technique, as if there is something American, or Anglo-American, about "independence" or synthetic theoretical thinking (each, of course, influenced by its own psychoanalytic culture of origin). The American and British independent traditions perhaps find commonality in this commitment to individuality, in less concern about the internal cohesion and history of theory, and in empirical and pragmatic groundings to theory, arising both from shared psychoanalytic histories and from common language and related intellectual cultures of origin.

I have named an American independent tradition, but "tradition" itself moves away from uniqueness. Before concluding this section, I point to two 20th-century (and early 21st-century) American independent thinkers whose work is extensive, influential, much cited and thereby independent: Roy Schafer and Thomas Ogden. Both of these thinkers stand on their own, hybrids who draw from and pay tribute to Freud, Loewald and Klein – Schafer listing toward his origins in ego psychology and Ogden with grounding in Winnicott and the British object relations tradition.

Schafer (influential 20th-century works include Schafer, 1976, 1983 and 1992) is one of a generative group of originally research psychologists – in addition to Schafer, Robert Holt, Philip Holtzman and George Klein – who spent time at the Menninger Clinic and at Austin Riggs and who transformed and systematized both the theory and practice of American ego psychology.

Schafer's radical contributions begin with his 1976 *A New Language for Psychoanalysis*, where he argues, drawing upon ordinary language philosophy, for an action language of the psyche that he claims must form the basis for interpretation, in contrast to a widespread view, across most contemporaneous theories, that cast symptom, defense and character in terms of a passive response to drive and defense.

*The Analytic Mind*, which is for some Schafer's best work, describes in great clinical detail, with theory just below the surface, how the analyst should cast ordinary clinical presentations in order continuously to emphasize action and agency – for example, "the analysis of resisting" rather than "*the* resistance" – and how to think clinically about ordinary emotions – for example, disappointment and disappointedness. Beginning with *Retelling a Life*, Schafer turned to the question of narrative in the here and now versus veridical truth in psychoanalysis, and this focus led him subsequently to extensive, original investigation of the various forms of dramatic narrative created by the psyche and in the psychoanalytic encounter. Along the way, Schafer has ranged widely, becoming extremely close for some period to the contemporary Kleinians, but, when asked, never giving up his roots in a personalized version of a Loewaldian ego psychological action language.

Ogden's sui generis contribution (20th-century works include Ogden, 1986, 1989 and 1994) gave to contemporary psychoanalysis several key understandings that, although originally created as extensions to Klein and Winnicott, have entered the psychoanalytic lexicon as universal ways of thinking. Ogden claims that in addition to, and developmentally preceding, the paranoid-schizoid and depressive positions, we refind on the couch what he names the "autistic-contiguous position," that of the infant whose primary sensorium is touch and the skin, or the absence of touch or a skin, which leaves the psychophysical sensorium raw, sometimes sharp, sometimes pins and needles, sometimes bleeding and melding into nothingness.

Ogden's most well-known contribution is what he originally named (and it is hard to remember this, because the term has become so universal and common) the analytic third. Drawing from Winnicott's ideas about transitional phenomena, Ogden suggests that analytic facts that matter are created at a particular moment by both members of the analytic pair and can only be thought of as this new creation. Anything that happens in the consulting room, whether in the mind of the analyst or patient or something named between them, is an analytic third – co-created unconsciously between the two participants. Ogden is almost unique among American analysts in his wide impact throughout the world, as his writings are read extensively and have become taken for granted analytic truths for relational analysts like Stephen Mitchell for many of Ogden's San Francisco colleagues, for British Kleinians and independents, for French and Italian analysts and in Latin America.

## Gender and ethnicity: notes on special emphases and contributions of American psychoanalysis

This chapter on American psychoanalysis in the 20th century has focused on ego psychology and its development, both because of the clinical, theoretical and sociohistorical centrality of ego psychology in American psychoanalysis and in the history of psychoanalysis as a whole and because other chapters focus on other American traditions. I conclude by mentioning two other major foci of attention in 20th-century American psychoanalysis that give it uniqueness within psychoanalysis worldwide.

First, American psychoanalysis followed Freud in emphasizing not only the psychology of the ego but also, more than any other country, in developing branches of psychoanalysis that incorporated the social and cultural. Horney, Sullivan, Thompson and Fromm initiated a thriving cultural school psychoanalysis that influenced and was influenced by generations of psychological and psychoanalytic anthropologists and sociologists. Leading ego psychologists – Hartmann, Loewald, Brenner and more recently Kernberg – have taken social science seriously, devoting plenary and other keynote addresses to this linkage. Psychoanalyst Erik Erikson, especially, brought insight and clinical observation directly to culture in the consulting room.

Here, I describe the contribution of Erikson, who more than any other analyst explored the clinical specificity of culture in the psyche and transformed our understanding of the psyche–culture nexus.

Barely noticed in the current period but a major figure in his own time, Erikson self-identified as an ego psychologist and initiated that branch of intersubjective ego psychology that incorporates the intertwining of ego and society. Beginning in 1951 with *Childhood and Society*, we find a remarkable capacity, unusual for an analyst, for cultural and political curiosity and attention.

Erikson studied Native American tribal groups and wrote about racism, anti-Indian sentiment and actions in the United States, and immigrant identity. He wrote large psychobiographies of Luther and Gandhi, virtually creating the field of psychobiography. Not a medical psychoanalyst in a country that required a medical license for psychoanalytic practice, Erikson found analytic institutional location as one of the lay founders of the San Francisco Psychoanalytic Institute, joined the group of generative ego psychologists at Austin Riggs Hospital in Stockbridge, and had letters and sciences appointments at Berkeley and Harvard.

On the psychocultural ground, what differentiates Erikson from cultural school psychoanalysts and from psychoanalytic anthropologists and sociologists is his fine-tuned attention to subjective as well as objective culture and ethnicity. He sometimes writes about a generalized cultural psyche – "the" American or "the" Russian psyche – but his primary focus is not on objective, or observed psychological culture, but culture in individual clinical minds.

In Erikson's conception of the intersubjective-cultural field, all psychological experience is filtered through the interaction of soma, developmental pattern and society. Erikson more than anyone described in specific clinical detail how history and culture enter into psychic structure, ego formation, identity, character and symptoms, how, as he put it, "history and culture assume decisive concreteness in individual development" and "appear in specific transferences and resistances" (1959, pp. 18, 29).

From its beginnings, psychoanalysis had concerned itself theoretically and clinically with sexuality and gender as central elements in psychic life. Erikson is the analyst who made ethnicity central. Long before American culture and politics became focused on identity, long before a few '60s-influenced and, a generation later, a few '90s post-structural/post-colonialism influenced analysts noticed race and ethnicity, Erikson was obsessed with the particulars of racial-ethnic-cultural identities, spoiled and outcast identities, and identity fragments, all of which must, as Erikson describes this, somehow be cemented into a psychologically working whole (see, e.g., Erikson, 1959, 1964). He tells us about a successful Midwestern businessman who is intrapsychically a Wandering Jew, a blond dancer whose overly rigid posture expresses not only phallicity but also German-Prussian military bearing, and a little boy trying to create an all-American masculine identity in a surround of women relatives (1951, 1959).

Like that of Loewald but with the clinical training and experience of a child analyst, Erikson's intersubjective ego psychology makes foundational the mother–child relational matrix, especially in the constitution of his first developmental stage, basic trust versus mistrust. He expands this into an intersubjective developmental theory that goes throughout the life cycle. For Erikson, an external and internal interpersonal field reappears in the psychosocial crisis of identity, which is more than a sum of identifications but rather a centeredness that at the same time requires confirmation by another, and in the stages of intimacy and generativity. It is only in the final stage of ego integrity that the ego returns to the self, as it needs to function as the recognizing other that once existed in the external world.

A second notable contribution of American psychoanalysis is clinical, developmental and theoretical attention to gender and sexuality. This chapter can touch on this contribution only briefly, but another chapter in this handbook focuses on sex and gender. In the context of this chapter, my point is that this extensive rethinking is uniquely American and thus itself central to an account of American psychoanalysis in the 20th century (and beyond). In no other country do we find, across the analytic spectrum, as extensive clinical and theoretical attention to sexuality and gender, as widespread an influence of a now forty-something-year critique of psychoanalytic theories and clinical treatment of femininity and the homosexualities, the long project within psychoanalysis and in the academy of feminist psychoanalysis and psychoanalytic feminism, and the depathologizing, within the psychoanalytic mainstream, of nonheterosexual object choice. Even in 2013 these developments contrast with many psychoanalytic centers and individual psychoanalysts throughout the world. At meetings, and in conversation with international colleagues from the British, French, Italian and Latin American psychoanalytic communities, Americans find, to their surprise, that there often remains a skepticism about the "analyzability" (or a certainty about non-analyzability) of gays and lesbians, a pathologizing of homosexual object choice, and an ambivalence about training gay analysts. Theoretically, British Kleinians and independents make "the" (presumptively heterosexual) Oedipal couple central to the psyche and the analytic process while often ignoring on-the-ground sexuality and sexual fantasy altogether. Although it is certainly the case that the sexual exploitation of patients, if rare, is found in and found to be troubling in all analytic communities, it nonetheless seems, impressionistically, that American institutes and communities treat such exploitation and its effect more extensively and seriously, through ethics committees, forums and books.

Beginning with the earliest Freudian writings, a focus on gender and sexuality almost defined psychoanalysis, and there was extensive rethinking by Freud and many of his followers during the 1920s–1940s, including Horney's pointing to the defensive and projective construction of masculinity and the sociocultural-psychoanalytic critiques of Horney and Thompson. Yet, when gender and sexuality came again to psychoanalytic attention, in the 1960s and early 1970s, this rethinking, with the exception of Janine Chasseguet-Smirgel and her colleagues, was found almost exclusively in the United States. In the United States, such attention began with the writings of Robert Stoller and Judith Kestenberg in the 1950s and 1960s, and this was followed in the 1970s by a feminist critique from within psychoanalysis and from feminists who themselves became psychoanalysts. Classically trained and medical psychoanalysts Carol Nadelson, Malkah Notman, and Ethel Person initiated this critique. Their rethinking began not only from an analysis of the defenses that led to pathologizing of femininity in patients and in the field itself but also from careful attention to the female bodily-sexual contribution to the psychologies of gender and sexuality. At the same time, beginning in the 1980s, feminists from the academy trained and entered into American mainstream (myself) and relational psychoanalysis – Jessica Benjamin, Muriel Dimen, Jane Flax and Adrienne Harris (Virginia Goldner was already a clinical psychologist), expanding and deepening theorizing, empirical observation and clinical attention to sex-gender concerns (Juliet Mitchell took this route in England). A mid-1970s special issue of the *Journal of the American Psychoanalytic Association* was followed over the next 25 years and beyond by many other special issues and by books and articles by all these early contributors and by Rosemary Balsam, Doris Bernstein, Nancy Kulish, Deanna Holtzman and many others. Founding relational feminists and others created the journal, *Studies on Gender and Sexuality*, devoted to psychoanalytic sex-gender writing.

Complementing the critique of and reformulation of psychoanalytic theoretical and clinical thinking about gender and women as been a powerful challenge to and reformulation of the psychoanalytic theory and treatment of (especially male) homosexuality, beginning with the powerful writings of Richard Isay, Kenneth Lewes and continuing in the current period in the work of Ken Corbett and others. Finally, it is almost exclusively in the United States that analysts have taken on and made problematic not only the classical theory of femininity, but also, beginning with Fogel, Lane and Liebert's *The Psychology of Men* (1986), the classical theory of masculinity and men.

## Conclusion

Twentieth-century American psychoanalysis began just over a century ago. It developed through an initiating group of psychiatrists, expanded during the psychoanalytic diaspora, and branched in several directions. Yet American psychoanalysis has been centered in and defined internally and throughout the psychoanalytic world by ego psychology. Intersubjective ego psychology, a unique American contribution, further describes development, psychological experience throughout the life cycle, and the clinical encounter.

All psychoanalytic theories and theories of therapeutic action were created in order to help patients and to understand the human condition. The theory of the ego and clinical attention to the ego in all its manifestations are essential components of psychoanalytic theory and practice and of all applications of psychoanalytic thought. Intrapsychically and intersubjectively, ego experiences, identifications and activities in all their complexity enable psychoanalyst and patient, psychoanalytic scholar and student, not only to work and to love, but also to live.

## Notes

1  This paragraph edits Chodorow, 2004; quotes should go back to the original.
2  My discussion of Loewald in what follows draws upon, summarizes and paraphrases my earlier writings on Loewald (Chodorow, 2003, 2008, 2009).

## Bibliography

What follows is a guide to reading and contains only some works mentioned. It gives especially short shrift to the extensive contributions of American psychoanalysis in noticing, theorizing and critiquing psychoanalytic understandings of gender and sexuality. Meanwhile, the best overview of the history of psychoanalysis in the United States remains:

Arlow, JA 1969a, 'Fantasy, memory, and reality testing', *Psychoanalytic Quarterly*, vol. 38, pp. 28–51.

Arlow, JA 1969b, 'Unconscious fantasy and disturbances of conscious experience', *Psychoanalytic Quarterly*, vol. 38, pp. 1–27.

Arlow, JA & Brenner, C 1964, *Psychoanalytic concepts and the structural theory*, International Universities Press, Oxford.

Balint, M 1937a, 'Early developmental states of the ego', in *Primary love and psychoanalytic technique*, Karnac Books, London.

Balint, M 1937b, 'Primary object-love', in *Primary love and psychoanalytic technique*, Karnac Books, London.

Balsam, RH 2008, 'The essence of Hans Loewald', *Journal American Psychoanalysis Association*, vol. 56, pp. 1117–1128.

Boesky, D 2008, *Psychoanalytic disagreements in context*, Aronson, New York.

Brenner, C 1982, *The mind in conflict*, International Universities Press, Madison.

Chodorow, NJ 2003, 'From behind the couch: Uncertainty and indeterminacy in psychoanalytic theory and practice', *Common Knowledge*, vol. 9, pp. 463–487.

Chodorow, NJ 2004, 'The American independent tradition: Loewald, Erikson, and the (possible) rise of intersubjective ego psychology', *Psychoanalysis Dialogues*, vol. 14, pp. 207–232.

Chodorow, NJ 2009a, 'A different universe: Reading Loewald through "On the therapeutic action of psychoanalysis"', *Psychoanalysis Quarterly*, vol. 78, pp. 983–1011.

Chodorow, N J 2009b, 'Toward an American independent tradition', unpublished paper.

Chused, J 1991, 'The evocative power of enactments', *Journal of American Psychoanalysis Association*, vol. 39, pp. 615–639.

Chused, J 1992, 'The patient's perception of the analyst: The hidden transference', *Psychoanalysis Quarterly*, vol. 61, pp. 161–184.

Erikson, EH 1951, *Childhood and society*, Norton, New York.

Erikson, EH 1959, 'Ego development and historical change', in *Identity and the life cycle: Selected papers*, International Universities Press, New York.

Erikson, EH 1964, *Identity and uprootedness in our time, Insight and Responsibility*, W.W. Norton, New York, pp. 81–107.

Fogel, G, Lane, F & Liebert, R (eds) 1986, *The psychology of men: Psychoanalytic perspectives*, Basic Books, New York.

Freud, A 1936, *The ego and the mechanisms of defense*, International Universities Press, New York.

Friedman, L 1997, 'Ferrum, Ignis, and Medicina: Return to the crucible', *Journal of American Psychoanalysis Association*, vol. 45, pp. 20–36.

Gabbard, G 1996, *Love and hate in the analytic setting*, Jason Aronson, Northvale, NJ.

Gabbard, G 2007, 'Bound in a nutshell': Thoughts on complexity, reductionism, and 'infinite space', *International Journal of Psychoanalysis*, vol. 88, pp. 559–574.

Gray, P 2005, *The ego and the analysis of defense*, Jason Aronson, Northvale, NJ.

Hale, N 1971, 1995, *Freud and the Americans*. Vol. 1: *The beginnings of psychoanalysis in the United States, 1876–1917*; Vol. 2: *The rise and crisis of psychoanalysis in the United States*, Oxford University Press, London.

Hartmann, H 1939, *Ego psychology and the problem of adaptation*, International Universities Press, New York.

Hartmann, H 1950, 'The application of psychoanalytic concepts to social science', *Psychoanalysis Quarterly*, vol. 19, pp. 385–392.

Jacobs, T 1991, *The use of the self: Countertransference and communication in the analytic situation*, International Universities Press, Madison.

Loewald, HW 1973. On internalization. *International Journal of Psychoanalysis, 54*, 9–17.

Loewald, HW 1980, *Papers on psychoanalysis*, Yale University Press, New Haven.

McLaughlin, JT 2005, *The healers' bent: Solitude and dialogue in the clinical encounter*, Analytic Press, Hillsdale, NJ.

Mitchell, S 1978, 'Psychodynamics, homosexuality, and the question of pathology', *Psychiatry*, vol. 41, pp. 254–263.

Mitchell, S 2000, *Relationality: From attachment to intersubjectivity*, Analytic Press, Hillsdale, NJ.

Modell, AH 1993, *The private self*, Harvard University Press, Cambridge.

Ogden, TH 1986, *Matrix of the mind: Object relations and the psychoanalytic dialogue*, Jason Aronson, Northvale, NJ.

Ogden, TH 1989, *The primitive edge of experience*, Jason Aronson, Northvale, NJ.

Ogden, TH 1994, *Subjects of analysis*, Jason Aronson, Northvale, NJ.

Parsons, M 2009, 'An independent theory of clinical technique', *Psychoanalytic Dialogues*, vol. 19, pp. 221–236.

Poland, WS 1996, *Melting the darkness: The dyad and principles of clinical practice*, Jason Aronson, Northvale, NJ.

Poland, WS 2000, 'The analyst's witnessing and otherness', *Journal American Psychoanalysis Association*, vol. 48, pp. 17–48.

Poland, WS 2009, 'Commentary on paper by Michael Parsons', *Psychoanalysis Dialogues*, vol. 19, pp. 253–258.

Schafer, R 1976, *A new language for psychoanalysis*, Yale University Press, New Haven.

Schafer, R 1983, *The analytic attitude*, Basic Books, New York.

Schafer, R 1992, *Retelling a life: Narration and dialogue in psychoanalysis*, Basic Books, New York.

# 12

# Mexican psychoanalysis in the 20th century

*Rubén Gallo*

## Mexico: a case history

The canonical history of Mexican psychoanalysis – as written in a few articles and a little book – posits that Mexican intellectuals, unlike their Argentinean or Brazilian counterparts, expressed little interest in Freud in the early years of the 20th century. Psychoanalysis did not enter the mainstream until the 1950s, when Santiago Ramírez and Ramón Parres founded the APM (Mexican Psychoanalytic Association), the first Mexican organization to gain the recognition of the International Psychoanalytical Association (IPA).[1]

Interest in a different kind of analysis spiked after Erich Fromm moved to Mexico City in 1950 to teach at UNAM, the National University. His courses and publications brought together a wide spectrum of interests that included psychoanalysis, Marxism, Buddhism and even Talmudic exegesis. Fromm was a charismatic teacher who gained a large following, and eventually his disciples formed a new association, the SPM (Mexican Psychoanalytic Society), that presented itself as an alternative to the orthodox APM. Thus the stage was set for what would become a long-drawn struggle between two analytic tendencies, one Freudian, the other Frommian.

Fromm launched some of the most eccentric projects in the history of psychoanalysis: in 1957 he organized a workshop on "Psychoanalysis and Zen Buddhism" that took place in Cuernavaca and included a public debate with D. T. Suzuki. In the same year Fromm began a "socio–psychoanalytic study" of a small village in the countryside: his goal was to combine the methodologies of psychoanalysis and sociology, using Rorschach tests and interpretative questionnaires, to understand interplay between social conditions and emotional wellbeing in rural Mexico. The study, coauthored by the American sociologist Michael Maccoby, was published as *Social Character in a Mexican Village: A Sociopsychoanalytic Study* (1970) and includes – among other surprising applications of Freudian techniques – a section presenting sociopolitical interpretations of the villagers' dreams.

Led by a similar motivation, Santiago Ramírez (1959, p. 127) used psychoanalytic theories to explain the peculiarities of the Mexican character. In *El mexicano: psicología de sus motivaciones* [*The Mexican: Psychology of his Motivations*] he offered a psychoanalytic critique of the national psyche, emphasizing the detrimental nature of collective neuroses, psychoses and other pathologies. In one of the book's stranger chapters, Ramírez interpreted the childhood enthusiasm for breaking *piñatas* as a "symptom of the aggressive feelings . . . towards the pregnant mother." His was but one of numerous efforts to psychoanalyze Mexican identity.

The psychoanalytic societies led by Fromm and Ramírez were ravaged by internal strife: in the 1960s dissident members resigned from the APM to form new groups. Among these, the most colorful was the AMPP (Mexican Association for Psychoanalytic Psychotherapy), an organization made up almost exclusively of female analysts (in rival groups, the members were known as *las fálicas*, the "phallic girls" (González, 1985, p. 84). Another splinter society, the AMPAG (Mexican Association for Analytic Group Therapy), experimented with group analysis, and made headlines around the world when two of its members – Frida Zmud and Gustavo Quevedo – became the analysts of the controversial Benedictine monastery.

The 1970s brought an influx of Argentinean analysts who arrived in Mexico after fleeing the military dictatorship, including Marie Langer, who was born in Austria, emigrated to Argentina in the 1930s and had become one of the most respected training analysts in Latin America by the time she arrived in Mexico City. Néstor Braunstein, another Argentinean, played a key role in the introduction of Lacanian thought, and remains one of the most prolific authors of psychoanalytic books in Mexico.

Since then the number of psychoanalytic organizations in Mexico has mushroomed: there are now dozens of associations, including Freudian, Frommian and Lacanian groups that identify themselves through ever more complex acronyms: AMPAG, GMEP, APJ, CMPP, CMP, GESE. The dizzying number of splinter societies once led Santiago Ramírez to describe the original APM as "the CTM of psychoanalysis," referring to the powerful Central Worker's Union, an umbrella group for the thousands of unions scattered throughout Mexico.

So goes the canonical history of psychoanalysis in Mexico. But there are several problems with this narrative. First, most articles present partisan accounts, and their authors often seem less interested in striking a balanced viewpoint than in vindicating their own association. The title of one of Santiago Ramírez's books – *Ajuste de cuentas* [*Settling My Scores* (1979)] – illustrates the tone of most of these works. Second, these authors have written institutional histories, focusing on the struggles among various groups and often missing the influence of psychoanalysis on other spheres of Mexican cultural life. But as Thomas F. Glick (1984) has remarked, such an approach is shortsighted and tends to exclude influential discussions of Freud by artists and intellectuals.[2] Third, these histories assume that serious discussions of Freud began only after the founding of the first analytic institutes in the 1950s, while in fact Mexican intellectuals had been reading Freud since the 1920s. As Glick (1994, p. 490) noted, "The early reception of Freud in Mexico has not been studied," even though "his work was amply diffused there in the 1920s and 1930s."

But there is an alternative approach to writing history of psychoanalysis: instead of focusing on psychoanalytic institutes and associations, one can study the influence of Freud on poets, novelists, artists and philosophers. Some of the most audacious interpretations of Freud were devised by figures who were complete outsiders to analytic associations: think of André Breton's *Manifesto of Surrealism*, Salvador Dalí's paranoiac-critical method or the surrealist experiments with free association. Around the world, Freud was read by historians, sociologists, painters, pastors and architects who found ways of extending psychoanalysis into their disciplines.

Two critics have written cultural histories of psychoanalysis focusing on artistic and literary readings of Freud. The first, Elisabeth Roudinesco (1990), published an impressive account of Freud's influence in postwar France, highlighting the psychoanalytic readings undertaken by André Breton, Salvador Dalí, and Georges Bataille among many others. The second, Alexander Etkind (1997), studied how the reception of psychoanalysis in Russia became entangled in revolutionary politics. Leon Trotsky and other Russian intellectuals sought to reconcile Marx and Freud and debated whether psychoanalysis could play a role in Soviet society.

As these studies show, the reception of Freud varied greatly by country and was influenced by the local political and historical context. In France the most influential readers of psychoanalytic theory were avant-garde artists; in Russia they were revolutionary intellectuals. If, as Mariano Ben Plotkin (2001, p. 5) has argued, "an exploration of the way psychoanalysis was disseminated in a particular society and culture tells us something important about both psychoanalysis and that culture" then what does the history of psychoanalysis tell us about Mexico? And what does the Mexican reception of Freud tell us about the history of psychoanalysis?

Freud was read by Mexican poets, novelists, historians, philosophers and artists, as well as by medical doctors and psychiatrists. Salvador Novo was a reader of Freud, and so were Samuel Ramos, Octavio Paz and Frida Kahlo, as well as lesser-known figures like the judge Raúl Carrancá y Trujillo. Some could read German, but most read the Spanish translation of the *Complete Works* issued between 1922 and 1932 by Madrid's Biblioteca Nueva, a publishing house connected to Ortega y Gasset's influential *Revista de Occidente*.

These readings of Freud were framed by the intense debates about national identity that dominated the Mexican cultural scene for the first half of the 20th century, as intellectuals sought to define the new nation that had emerged from a decade of civil war. Government officials hailed the new society as a cultural utopia, while sociologists, historians and philosophers mused on the peculiarities of the Mexican character. Three figures stand out for their innovative applications of Freudian theory to contemporary debates about national identity: Salvador Novo, Samuel Ramos and Octavio Paz.

One of the most eccentric readers Freud ever found was the poet Salvador Novo, who fashioned himself a Mexican Oscar Wilde and led a scandalous public life as a gay man in the 1920s. Novo was one of the first serious readers of Freud in Mexico: he acquired the *Complete Works* published by Biblioteca Nueva, reviewed psychoanalytic publications for literary journals, and wrote an autobiography that doubled as an exercise in self-analysis. Novo was especially interested in the *Three Essays in the Theory of Sexuality*, a book he used to arrive at a new understanding of his sexual identity. At a time when analysts and psychiatrists debated how psychoanalysis interpreted homosexuality, Novo used Freudian theory to affirm his identity as a gay man in an extremely conservative society.

Freud found a very different kind of reader in the philosopher Samuel Ramos. Ramos was the first intellectual to use Freudian theories to understand the national character: his article "Psychoanalysis of the Mexican" (1932) identified a series of collective neuroses afflicting the country, igniting an intense debate about the Mexican psyche that attracted the attention of poets, philosophers and artists, which continued until the 1950s.

Octavio Paz entered the debate about the psychology of Mexicanness, and responded to Ramos's essay in *The Labyrinth of Solitude*, a work that proposes an alternative Freudian interpretation of the national character. Mexicans, Paz argued, suffer from a collective melancholia that has ensnared them in a labyrinth.

Finally, there is the case of Gregorio Lemercier, the Benedictine monk who placed his monastery in psychoanalysis and became famous around the world as a Freudian reformer of Catholicism. Freud was a proud atheist who dismissed religion as an illusion and a private neurosis, and it comes as a surprise that a believer would embrace his theories to enhance monastic life – this was one of the many paradoxes in what became the most eccentric episode in the Mexican reception of psychoanalysis.

Freud's readers in Mexico were a gay dandy, a conservative philosopher, a cosmopolitan poet and a Benedictine monk. This motley crew devised some of the most original, elaborate and influential applications of psychoanalytic theory anywhere in the world.

Novo used Freud to vindicate marginal sexual identities; Ramos, to diagnose the collective neuroses afflicting the country; Paz, the most Freudian of all, launched a psychoanalytic inquiry into the origins of Mexican culture; and Lemercier attempted to reconcile psychoanalysis and monastic life. Had Freud lived to see these experiments, he would have concluded that psychoanalysis had gone completely wild.

A consideration of these four figures will challenge many received ideas about the role of psychoanalysis in 20th-century culture. Many critics have assumed that Freudian theories were put at the service of a conservative, restrictive ideology that sought to normalize sexual identities. Carlos Monsiváis (1995), one of the most respected Mexican intellectuals, has derided psychoanalysis as a fashionable doctrine that led "writers, psychiatrists and psychologists" (1995, pp. 191–192) to analyze Mexican history and cultural life "in light of sublimation, the phallus [. . .] and many other hair-raising stereotypes."[3] In his view, psychoanalysis inherited "the capacities to interpret and cure the soul that were earlier monopolized by the Catholic Church, and ultimately defined a new canon of mental health at the service of the bourgeoisie" (1995, pp. 191–192). The rise of psychoanalysis as a respected discipline, he believes, resulted in an increased marginalization of women, gay men and other minorities.

What a different picture emerges when we revisit Novo's reading of the *Three Essays in the Theory of Sexuality* as a series of modern conceptual tools to affirm his gay identity; when we read Octavio Paz deploying the theories of the Oedipus complex and Geistigkeit to champion the liberating powers of the intellect; or when we discover Frida Kahlo's use of psychoanalytic theories to understand pre-Columbian religions. If I can accomplish one objective in this chapter, it would be to restore Freud to his proper place in Mexican cultural history: as an intellectual model for some of the most original thinkers of the 20th century.

## Freud's correspondence and exchanges with Latin Americans

In 2006 the Freud Museum in London published the complete catalog of the library of Sigmund Freud: *Freud's Library: A Comprehensive Catalogue* (The Freud Museum, London, 2006). It is a monumental work: the result of over a decade of research by Gerhard Fichtner and J. Keith Davies, one of the curators. The book, which includes a CD-ROM, allows the reader not only titles and bibliographic data of all the books that Freud chose for his personal collection, but consular digitized images of autographs, signatures, handwritten notes and other additions listed in each volume. We can see, for example, that one of the few books that Freud annotated was the autobiography of Daniel Paul Schreber, the main source for Freud's essay on paranoia published in 1911.

The compilation of this catalog was a long and complicated project. Freud left Vienna in 1938, a few months after the Anschluss, and moving to London forced him to abandon a part of his library in Austria. After making a selection of about 3,000 volumes that would be sent to England, Freud removed about seven books he sold to a Viennese antiquarian. The lot was bought by Heinrich Hinterberger, a bookseller who eventually sold his entire collection to the medical school at Columbia University in New York. Because of these historical shifts, Freud's library was divided between two continents: most of his books are in London, in the house of Hampstead where he spent the last months of his life and is now the headquarters of the Freud Museum; the other part is at Columbia in New York. Thanks to technology, the reader can now consult the two collections using the CD-ROM that accompanies the catalog. The catalog is also a window into the reading habits of Freud. He owned books in German, English, French, Italian, Spanish and translations of his works in languages that he did not read, such as Hebrew or Japanese. In the Spanish section of his library contains the first translations of his works into Castilian by Luis López Ballesteros and published, starting in 1922 by Biblioteca Nueva in Madrid under the title *Obras completas del Profesor Sigmund Freud* (16 vols). The first volumes bear the following inscriptions: "To Prof. Dr. Sigmund Freud, my greatest admiration and respect, The translator, in April 1922" (Vol. 1); "To the illustrious Professor Freud, respectful homage of admiration, the translator, 6/11/1923" (Vol. 2); "For Dr. Freud, with all admiration and respect, the translator, in June 1923" (Vol. 3). Upon receiving these mailings, Freud wrote a short letter thanking shipping and translation. López Ballesteros included it in the fourth volume of the *Works*: Dr. Luis López Ballesteros and Torres.

As a young student, the desire to read the immortal D. Quixote in Cervantes's original, it took me to learn without teachers, the beautiful Spanish language. Thanks to this youthful fans can now – at an advanced age – I see the success of his Spanish version of my works, the reading always gives me a vivid appreciation for the most correct interpretation of my thought and elegance of style. I admire above all, how you not being a doctor or psychiatrist by profession have been able to achieve so absolute and precise domain of a sick and sometimes intricate dark matter.

Freud.
Vienna, May 7, 1923

In addition to translations, Freud library includes nearly 40 titles in Spanish, most shipments of young Latin Americans, doctors and psychiatrists who were interested in psychoanalysis. These authors include two Chileans (Fernando Allende Navarro and Juan Marin), an Ecuadorian (Humberto Salvador), a Uruguayan (Gerardo Nebel), a Colombian (Edward Weinfeld, author of *Influences of Judaism*, 1935). There are also several Spanish authors (Angel Garma, Santiago Ramón y Cajal, Quintilian Saldaña) and, as expected, more Argentines than any other nationality: there are nine works by Juan Ramón Beltrán, *Addiction* by Gregorio Bermann, and several books of Peter Coscia, Fernando and Jorge Thenon Gorriti.

The vast majority of these books are summaries of Freudian ideas written for a lay audience, and many of them were composed by authors lacking the most basic knowledge of psychoanalysis. In his *Psicoanálisis del sueño profético* (1929), for example, the Spanish César Camargo y Marin presents a "Commentary on the Complete Works of Sigmund Freud in terms . . . the eighth volume of 'Totan and Babu'"! The shallowness of many of these works explains that almost all are now at Columbia's Health Sciences Library: these are books that the teacher decided to leave behind in Vienna. Among the books in Castilian that led Freud to London itself was written by the sole author in this list who had a personal relationship with him: the Peruvian Honorio Delgado, psychiatrist and pioneer of psychoanalysis to his country. Delgado was a great Germanophile who spoke German and visited Freud in Vienna in 1923. His book *Sigmund Freud* (1926) closes with the following recollection of his meeting with the teacher – the only witness to Freud's encounter with a Latin American:

To conclude, we summarize in a few words our personal impression of the teacher. Slender, thin, slightly stooped figure. His traits reveal many past pains and perhaps some sadness. Those eyes have all the accumulated power of thousands of years of dominating will, of immemorial asceticism, which had to be tested countless times, like the mythological hero who only at the expense of bloody deeds reaches the possession of its rightful domain . . . Seeing him, it occurred to my mind, seemed to impress the picture of "Seneca" by Rubens. The personality of the teacher: What simplicity, my goodness! This is what most impressed me, nay, shocked, to find me with the impetus of life, no dizziness, no flicker, without a moment's hesitation, sovereign lucidity. When asked about his health: "It's natural – he replied – so I work." "Oh – I exclaimed – with the war you have lost much and you have to work hard." The dominant note of his person, is, no doubt, serenity. The emotional and spiritual greatness of this man of genius, is comparable to his mental strength." For something Freud himself said: "It is a heavy task for the patient to have the entire human race!"

*(1926, n.p.)*

Beyond this shared meal, Freud and Delgado maintained an intellectual dialogue that lasted several years: he is the only Latin American with whom the professor maintained a regular correspondence. The cross between the two cards are part of the manuscript collection of Sigmund Freud at the Library of Congress in the United States. According to Michael Molnar, director of the Freud Museum, it is quite possible that the only Moche piece in Freud's collection of archaeological artifacts was a gift from Delgado: a clay figurine of a man with wild eyes – possibly a graphical representation of the effects of coca – a topic that interested Freud in his youth.

Finally, I would like to devote a few pages to one of the most eccentric authors in Freud's library. Some time ago I had the opportunity to visit the home of Freud in Hampstead and the Columbia collection to check the contents of his library. There I discovered that there is a single Mexican book in his collection: a work of Mexican criminal law jurisprudence entitled: *General Part*, written by Raul Trujillo Carrancá and published in Mexico City in 1937. The presence of this book among the papers of psychoanalyst seemed implausible: how did this book came to be in the hands of Freud? Unlike other Latin American books, this was not a work of psychiatry, medicine, or psychology but rather an extensive treatise on Mexican law – an issue that could hardly have interested Freud.

## Freud read by judges

*Derecho penal* was among the books Freud chose to leave in Vienna, along with a number of publications in Spanish – mostly elementary introductions to psychoanalysis – that had been sent, often with obsequious dedications, by doctors and psychiatrists from Spain and Latin America, including the Chileans Fernando Allende Navarro and Juan Marín, the Ecuadorian Humberto Salvador, and the Argentineans Juan Ramón Beltrán, Gregorio Bermann, and Fernando Gorriti. Columbia's collection can be thought of as a kind of *salon de refusés*, a collection of the books Freud rejected. The only Latin American author who survived the purge and accompanied Freud to London was Honorio Delgado, a young Peruvian doctor who corresponded regularly with Freud and was mentioned affectionately in "History of the Psychoanalytic Movement."

*Derecho penal* is the odd book out in Freud's collection of Spanish books: all others are introductions to psychoanalysis written by doctors or psychiatrists, and it is easy to see why these authors sent their work to the Viennese analyst. *Derecho penal*, on the other hand, was written by a legal scholar and dealt with a field to which Freud had no apparent connection.

Back in New York, I took the subway uptown to consult the Freud holdings at Columbia's Health Sciences Library. This time I was in luck: an attendant brought me Freud's copy of *Derecho penal*. Judging from its condition, it had never been opened by Freud or by anyone else. Disappointingly, it lacked a dedication or other annotations.

Nevertheless, the book did have some valuable information about the author, Raúl Carrancá y Trujillo (1937), identified on the frontispiece as a "judge, professor of criminal law at the University of Mexico, and recipient of a doctorate from the University of Madrid."

As I was to discover later, Raúl Carrancá y Trujillo was in born in 1897 in the southern state of Campeche to a Spanish father. He received a scholarship to study in Spain, at the Central

University in Madrid, where he completed his undergraduate and graduate studies before return-ing to Mexico City in 1925. He rose quickly through the judicial system and became a university professor, editor of *Criminalia*, a journal of criminology, and eventually a judge. He was an ambi-tious young man, and wrote his first book – an essay on the political evolution of Latin America – in his twenties. By age 35, he had published a novel and four volumes dealing with various aspects of Mexican and Spanish law.

*Derecho penal* includes a chapter that sheds light on how this book might have surfaced in Freud's library. Carrancá (1937, p. 34) presents himself as a disciple of Cesare Lombroso and a firm believer in positivism, and defines criminology as a new science dependent on a series of "auxiliary disciplines." Carrancá believed the modern criminologist needed to employ the methods and investigative techniques developed by a series of related disciplines: anthropology, endocrinology, sociology, statistics, medicine and psychology.

Out of all these auxiliary disciplines Carrancá was most interested in criminal psychology. As he explained in *Derecho penal* (1937, p. 43), he was an avid reader of Freud and considered psychoanalysis an invaluable tool for legal work:[4] like forensic medicine, psychoanalysis could help lawyers and judges reach a well-founded verdict (1937, p. 42). The interpretative techniques discovered by Freud could be used "to analyze the criminal's psychological traits and to pin-point the causes for his transgression" (1937, p. 42). Criminals often suffered from unresolved complexes and other active neuroses, and psychoanalysis could reveal their unconscious motives.

Carrancá presented himself as an authority, telling his readers he had published several articles on criminal psychology, and that one of these had been favorably reviewed by none other than Dr. Freud himself.

The article in question, "A Judicial Experiment With Psychoanalytic Techniques," was pub-lished 3 years earlier, in 1934; it was one of a series of articles Carrancá wrote for *Criminalia* exploring the possible uses of psychoanalytic theories in the practice of criminal law and present-ing one of the most creative – and unusual – readings of Freud anywhere in the world.

## Prison sex

Carrancá's first psychoanalytically inspired article, "Sex and the Penal System" (1933), explored a topic that few had dared to discuss openly in a country that was still largely dominated by Catholic mores: the sexual life of prisoners. In 1924 Mexico had passed a law allowing inmates to receive weekly spousal visits; in theory, this ruling meant that most prisoners could satisfy their sexual needs on a regular basis, but in practice visits were only authorized for male inmates who had demonstrated "good conduct" and were serving long-term sentences. In Carrancá's view, these conditions imposed a terrible hardship on a majority of the prisoners, and his article made a passionate argument for a loosening the restrictions.

To learn more about inmates and their sexual needs, Carrancá interviewed two prisoners: Antonio, a middle-class man who had spent 8 months in jail for robbery, and Juan, a working-class inmate sentenced to 4 years for murder. Carrancá asked the inmates a series of questions about their sexual practices and transcribed their responses. The resulting conversation between the young judge and the prisoners reveals a clash of two very different worlds:

*Carrancá*:  How do those who cannot receive spousal visits satisfy their sexual needs?
*Antonio*:   By means of onanism . . . and by means of the effeminate inmates in cells 56, 58, and 60.
*Carrancá*:  How do these effeminate [inmates] make themselves recognizable to other inmates?
*Antonio*:   By their dress, their make-up, and their use of pet names like "La Eva," "La Miss Mexico," "La Brunette," "La Barbara Lamar," "La Onion Peeler."

*Carrancá:* How could the prison authorities help solve your sexual problems?

*Antonio:* Since I have no money and I can't pay a woman to come see me, I'd ask to be allowed to meet with a woman prisoner of my liking. I've been locked up for eight months, and I'm only twenty-five. Whenever I go see a film, I see couples – men and women touching each other – I see love scenes on screen and my body gets overstimulated; the way the prison is set up, I have no natural means of satisfying my sexual needs" (1937).

Carrancá argued the inmates were subjected to a cruel and unusual form of punishment that amounted to forced abstinence. "Every person with a modicum of culture," he wrote, "knows that sexual satisfaction [. . .] is not an unnecessary luxury but a vital and primal need." Ignoring the prisoners' needs would lead to an unusually high degree of "sexual aberrations" among the prison population: "homosexuality and onanism among men [. . .]; lesbianism among women." If inmates are not allowed to satisfy their sexual needs, their frustration "will unleash the formerly repressed aberrant instincts, which will dominate the individual with such force that nothing will ever succeed in taming them again" (1937, pp. 29–31).

Carrancá closed his article with a passionate plea to judicial authorities for the liberalization of the conditions governing spousal visits. He argued that both men and women should be allowed visits; that these should not be contingent on the inmate's conduct; and that their frequency should be determined in accordance with the inmate's sexual temperament.

We can clearly see echoes of Freud's theories in Carrancá's arguments. Freud argued that sex is a drive, and that a forced repression of sexual impulses paves the way for neuroses. His "Three Essays in the Theory of Sexuality" even considered the case of prison inmates, who were prone to become contingent inverts after prolonged and exclusive relations with persons of their own sex.

Carrancá, however, tinged his argument with a moralism that is absent from Freud's "Three Essays." Freud began his remarks by stating that inversion was no more aberrant than heterosexuality, and that deviations in the sexual aim – including fetishism, scopophilia and sadomasochism – were neither pathological nor examples of degeneration, since these were invariably present, to different degrees, in "normal" sexuality. Carrancá, in contrast, presents homosexuality – as well as onanism – as degenerate practices that should be stamped out from Mexican prisons. There is a striking difference between Freud and Carrancá: Freud wants to understand and analyze all forms of sexuality, without passing moral judgment, while Carrancá – who was a judge, after all – is less interested in delving into psychological motives than in censoring the inmates' sexual practices that fell outside normative heterosexuality.

Despite these differences, Carrancá's article has the virtue of being one of the first attempts to incorporate psychoanalytic theories into legal debates. And notwithstanding his slightly moralistic tone, one has to credit him with breaking one of Mexico's most entrenched cultural taboos by launching a serious, open, and theoretically informed discussion on sexuality.

## Criminals on the couch

A few months after his article on the sexual lives of inmates, Carrancá wrote a second essay inspired by Freud: "A Judicial Experiment with Psychoanalytic Techniques," published in the February 1934 issue of *Criminalia*. Here Carrancá argued that Freud's oeuvre was an invaluable tool for judges and criminologists in elucidating the criminal mind: psychoanalytic theory could be applied to criminal psychology and used to reveal how criminal acts stem from unconscious motivations and desires. Carrancá's article was full of praise for the father of psychoanalysis. "Sigmund Freud," he wrote, that intrepid explorer of the human soul and its dark, subterranean recesses, offers his psychoanalysis to prosecutors as a sort of magic lantern capable of illuminating the way. Freud is an Aladdin with a marvelous lamp, a type of "open Sesame."

*(1934, p. 125)*

Carrancá recommends that judges study psychoanalysis and apply its techniques to criminal cases.

Rather than writing a theoretical comparison between the conceptions of subjectivity presented by psychoanalysis and criminology, Carrancá chose a more pragmatic approach: the young judge decided to play the role of the therapist, turned his office into a consulting room and invited defendants sent to him for judicial examination to talk freely about their lives, dreams, frustrations, desires, sexual fantasies and anything else that might shed light on their unconscious mental processes. To carry out the analysis, Carrancá even considered putting a couch in his office, but in the end opted for a less intimidating option: a chair facing away from him so that his patients could speak without looking at him.

One of his first cases involved a young man identified as "RHV" – like Freud, he referred to patients by their initials to protect their privacy – and accused of shooting his wife in a fit of jealousy. On their first meeting, Carrancá led the defendant into his office, summarized the basics of Freudian methods, and invited him to sit on the analytic chair, facing away from him, and to tell him anything and everything that came to mind.

Dreams, slips and sexual fantasies, he told him, were of particular interest for his work. The judge gave the following account of his first session:

Following Freud's method [. . .] I decided to analyze RHV in a simple and straightforward setting [. . .] I chose to use my own professional office, sheltered from noise and people, especially in the early hours of the morning. I had R brought there, and he remained completely alone with me. In order to gain his confidence, I clearly explained my intentions, my interest in him, the way in which we were to work together. I had taken the precaution of visiting him in prison beforehand, so that he would not fear me. When our [analytic] work started, I had already obtained from him a certain degree of trust, the necessary condition for honesty.

Starting with our first session, I asked R to sit facing away from me, facing a white and empty wall. I told him he could close his eyes if he wished. At first it was a great struggle: he was reluctant to face away from me, fearing I might play some kind of trick on him (or hypnotize him, as he told me later). After explaining in detail my purpose, I told him he was completely free to move about as he wished, and even to turn around and look at me if he so desired (I thus prepared myself for being surprised in the midst of my note taking). This last proposal persuaded him, and a good number of our sessions unfolded in this manner. Sometimes, at the most interesting point in his confessions, he would close his eyes, cover them with his hands, or face away from me. We worked together for several sessions, and I attempted to glimpse into his innermost thoughts, into his subconscious.

*(1937, pp. 127, 128)*

Carrancá published the case study of his first patient in *Criminalia*. After quoting extensively from the defendant's own account of his childhood, family dynamics, work history, marriage, and the fit of jealousy that led him to shoot his wife, the judge offers an analytic interpretation of these events: R had a very "creative imagination," and sometimes confused fantasy and reality; he suspected his wife might be cheating on him, and this fear led him to picture her in bed with another man, a mental image that became as real – and as unbearable – as if it had actually occurred; R was overwhelmed by "violent passions" as he flew into a murderous rage and shot her to death.

During the legal proceedings, the defense argued that R had committed a "crime of passion" – a momentary lapse in judgment that was treated with leniency in Mexican criminal law. The prosecution, in contrast, construed the killing as a premeditated homicide. Carrancá was not persuaded by either argument: based on the unconscious material uncovered during his analytic sessions, he found the defendant guilty of homicide, but ruled that it had not been premeditated, since he had been "provoked by the victim" and by her flirtatious demeanor toward other men. R, the first defendant to be psychoanalyzed by a judge in Mexico, was sentenced on December 27, 1933, to 3 years in prison (1937, p. 127).

Carrancá closed his article by noting that he was the first judge in Mexico – and probably one of the first in the "civilized legal world" – to have delved into the unconscious of a criminal. At the age of 37 Carrancá was already a bold explorer, intent on breaking new ground in the field of criminal law. Some years before Carrancá's experiment, the Mexican philosopher José Vasconcelos called himself "Ulises *criollo*," a Mexican version (*criollo*) of the Homeric hero. Carrancá hoped to become a "Freud *criollo*," an analyst who recreated the experiments of the Viennese doctor on Mexican soil.

One wonders what Freud might have thought of Carrancá's creative but unorthodox use of psychoanalysis. Would he have been pleased to know that his theories were making ripples throughout the world, reaching even Mexican courthouses? Or would he have dismissed these "judicial experiments" as the type of unprofessional abuses that had given analysis a bad name in certain circles? Was this a legitimate branch of psychoanalysis? Would he have seen Carrancá as a faithful disciple or as an imposter?

In 1910 Freud had published a paper criticizing the sloppy methods of certain therapists: "wild psychoanalysis," he quipped, was practiced by doctors who had never undergone proper training, had little or no experience with the technique of free association, and lacked an understanding of unconscious processes. In most cases, these practitioners had reduced Freud's theory of sexuality to a caricature: they understood sexual drives as simply "the need for coitus or analogous acts producing orgasm and emission of the sexual substances" (Freud, 1910, p. 222).

Freud thundered that this vulgar approach to sexuality had nothing to do with psychoanalysis, a complex theory in which "the concept of what is sexual comprises far more; it goes lower and also higher than its popular sense" (Freud, 1910, p. 222). For this reason, he continued, "we prefer to speak of *psychosexuality*, thus laying stress on the point that the mental factor in sexual life should not be overlooked or underestimated" (p. 223). And psychosexuality was a complicated affair, one whose vicissitudes did not always correspond to the patient's sexual practices: "We have long known, too, that mental absence of satisfaction with all its consequences can exist where there is no lack of normal sexual intercourse" (p. 223). Anyone who does not share these views of sexual life, Freud (1912, p. 227) warned, "has no right to adduce psycho-analytic theses dealing with the aetiological importance of sexuality." He concluded by declaring "'wild' analysts of this kind do more harm to the cause of psycho-analysis than to individual patients."

Would Freud have considered Carrancá a wild analyst? The Mexican judge certainly fits the profile sketched in the article: in his writings Carrancá reduced sexuality to its genital component, and his article on prison sex argues that neuroses can be averted or cured by engaging in regular sexual intercourse – the same argument Freud puts in the lips of a wild analyst. Freud recommended that only those familiar with the "technical rules" practice psychoanalysis, and that a treatment was an extremely long process that could not be rushed. Carrancá, in contrast, had little familiarity with the technique of analysis, and his psycho-legal treatments lasted no more than a few days. It seems almost certain that Freud would have considered him a practitioner of wild psychoanalysis – or, in this case, wild psycho-legal analysis.

But contrary to our expectations, Freud had an altogether different response to Carrancá's experiments. Soon after "A Legal Experiment With Psychoanalytic Techniques" appeared in *Criminalia*, Carrancá mailed a copy to Freud. Freud responded with a gracious – albeit brief – letter telling the Mexican judge that he had read his article with great interest, that he approved of the efforts to find new applications for psychoanalysis, and that "it has always been an ideal desire for the psychoanalyst to win two people for our discipline: teachers of youth and judges" (Carrancá, 1934, p. 160). To my knowledge, Freud never made this last assertion anywhere else in his writing.

Far from considering Carrancá a wild analyst who might hurt the cause of psychoanalysis, Freud celebrated his role as a proselytizer, as someone who might win desirable allies for the cause. Carrancá (1934, p. 160), who was understandably proud to have received such a glowing review from the father of psychoanalysis, published a facsimile of the letter in *Criminalia*:

13.2.1934

Hochgeehrter Herr,

Ich habe zum Glück in meiner jungen Jahren Ihre schöne Sprache lesen gelernt und bin so im Stande, mich an der Schätzung und dem Interesse zu freuen, das Sie unserer Psychoanalyse zeigen und an der Anwendungen teilzunehmen die Sie auf ihren Arbeitsgebiet von ihr machen. Leider habe ich es nicht so weit gebracht auch Spanisch zu schreiben und muß sie bitten sich eine deutsche Antwort gefallen zu lassen.

Es war immer ein Idealwunsch des Analytikers, zwei Personen für unserer Deutungsart zu gewinnen, der Jugendlehrer und der Richter.

Ihr herzlich ergebener,
Freud

[2/13/1934

Dear Sir,

I had the good fortune of learning to read your beautiful language in my youth; I was pleased to discover the interest and the appreciation you have shown towards our Psychoanalysis, and to learn of how you have applied it to your discipline.

Unfortunately I cannot go as far as to write you in Spanish, and I must ask you to accept a German response.

It has always been an ideal desire for the psychoanalyst to win two people for our discipline: teachers of youth and judges.

Yours sincerely, Freud]

Freud's letter to Carrancá has never been reprinted, and as of this writing it is not included in the correspondence at the Freud archives in the Library of Congress. It is Freud's only letter to a Mexican correspondent, and one of the very few texts in which he addresses the relation between psychoanalysis and criminology.

## A Stalinist Oedipus

Had the tale of Freud and Carrancá ended here, it would have made an eccentric story about the chance encounter between the father of psychoanalysis and a wildly ambitious Mexican judge; it would have shed some light on the mutual attraction between psychoanalysis and criminology;

and it would have certainly brought to light one of the most surprising episodes in the reception of Freud in Mexico. But there would be one more twist – one worthy of a detective novel – in the story.

In 1938, a year after receiving Carrancá's *Derecho penal*, Freud left Vienna for London, where he died in 1939. Meanwhile, Carrancá continued to climb the echelons of Mexico's judicial system: in the summer of 1940 he was appointed the judge of the district of Coyoacán, the southern neighborhood in Mexico City that was home to Diego Rivera, Frida Kahlo, and many other artists and intellectuals. This was not a particularly troublesome district, and his first cases involved petty crimes and other minor offenses; he led a quiet life in this suburban enclave, with plenty of free time he could devote to reading Freud, until one day he was assigned a high-profile case that would turn out to be the most important of his entire career.

On August 20, 1940, Carrancá was put in charge of a foreign defendant who went by the aliases of Frank Jacson and Jacques Mornard, and was accused of a crime that made headlines around the world: the murder of Leon Trotsky, the Soviet revolutionary who had been exiled in Mexico City since 1937. Jacson had gone to visit Trotsky at his home in Coyoacán with the pretext of showing him an article and struck him on the back of the head with an ice ax while the old man was reading the text. Jacson was immediately apprehended and Trotsky died some hours later at a hospital.

Jacson – his real name turned out to be Ramón Mercader – readily admitted the murder, but the account he gave the police raised suspicions from the beginning. He described himself as a disillusioned Trotskyite, a young revolutionary who had traveled to Mexico to meet the leader of the movement, and had been disappointed to discover that the man he admired had betrayed his ideals. Trotsky, he told the judge, had asked him to murder Stalin, a request that so angered him he decided to kill him.

Carrancá soon found a number of inconsistencies in the murderer's account. He claimed to be a Belgian citizen who only spoke French, yet a visit by a diplomat revealed he knew little about Belgium; he declared he had acted alone, out of disillusionment with Trotsky, but the entire world suspected the assassination had been ordered by Stalin; he assured investigators he did not know any of the Mexican Stalinists who had participated in the first attack against Trotsky's house, yet he rented an office in the same building – Edificio Ermita, near Colonia Condesa – where David Alfaro Siqueiros, the ringleader of an the earlier plot, kept a studio.

Carrancá had a curious case before him: the defendant's guilt had been established – Mercader never denied killing Trotsky – but his motives were unknown. To write his verdict and select the appropriate sentence, the judge had to understand the assassin's motives and their impact on his crime; but since the killer refused to talk, Carrancá had to find a creative way of uncovering his secret.

The "Trotsky case" turned out to be the perfect opportunity for Carrancá to put into practice his psycho-legal theories. Since Mercader refused to talk, and would not reveal his identity or explain his motives for killing Trotsky, the judges decided to probe his unconscious. Freud had once written that nothing was harder to keep than a secret: a person can remain tight-lipped, but in the end he will always give it away through unconscious gestures. Would the same hold true for Mercader?

Carrancá could have analyzed Mercader himself, using – as he had done before – his office as a consulting room for psycho-legal analysis. But in this case the stakes were too high, and he opted to leave the defendant's analysis in the hands of two experts on criminal psychology: Alfonso Quiroz Cuarón, a 30-year-old criminologist with a passion for cracking complicated mysteries; and José Gómez Robleda, a forensic psychiatrist who taught at the National University in Mexico City. Carrancá asked them to apply a battery of psychological exams in order to uncover the unconscious motives behind the assassination. The team visited Mercader in prison and set up a schedule of daily sessions that would include psychoanalysis as well as more traditional psychological tests.

Quiroz Cuarón reported that during the first meeting Mercader was uncooperative and refused to talk. The pair of doctors insisted, telling him the sessions would be beneficial for his mental health. Eventually Mercader agreed, though reluctantly, to work with the two doctors. The team set up an intensive work schedule: for 6 months they met with Mercader 6 hours a day, 6 days a week, spending a total of 942 hours with him. As Trotsky's biographer Isaac Don Levine (1960, p. 150) has written, "No psychological study of comparable magnitude has ever been made of a political assassin."

Following Freud's recommendations on technique, the two doctors asked Mercader to talk freely, and proceeded to analyze his dreams, family relationships, childhood memories, fears, fantasies, slips of the tongue and sexual history. They subjected him to Rorschach tests, word reaction experiments, handwriting analyses and drawing exercises, as well as to a host of other procedures that were beyond the realm of Freud's interests: blood and motor tests, electroencephalograms, and even an examination of body scars. They tested his ability to disassemble and reassemble an assault weapon in the dark; they measured the time he took to put together a jigsaw puzzle; they asked him to draw his family and then interpreted the sketch as an indication of an Oedipal conflict (the parents, they noted, towered over a disproportionately small son); they administered dozens of other tests to gauge his intelligence, quantitative skills and logical capacities. The team was determined to overcome Mercader's secret and to probe into the innermost recesses of his psyche – and of his bodily organs, if it need be.[5]

The doctors also administered a "word response test" – a procedure during which the prisoner was given a word and asked to say the first association that came to mind; the associations were then mined for their unconscious content.

Interestingly, Freud had considered word response tests in his essay on "Psycho-Analysis and the Establishment of Legal Facts," but dismissed them as unreliable, since the associations were made under pressure. Quiroz Cuarón and Gómez Robleda gave Mercader a series of charged words that elicited political associations: he responded to "commerce" with "legal theft"; wealth was "that which will soon belong to the oppressed classes"; religion, "the opium of the people"; and Trotsky, "a self-centered egotist." There is little unconscious content in these associations, expressions of Marxist dogma (Don Levine, 1960).

The two doctors compiled the results of the numerous tests, added their own analyses and interpretations, and submitted their findings to the court. Their 1,332-page brief bore the ominous title "Organic-Functional and Social Study of the Assassin of Leon Trotsky" and was divided into two volumes: the first focusing on Mercader's conscious mind and the second on an "examination of his sub-conscious mental functions" (Colmenares, 1994, p. 287).

The brief opened with a detailed introduction in which Drs. Quiroz Cuarón and Gómez Robleda summarized their findings. Mercader, they wrote, had suffered an "affective trauma" in his early childhood that pushed him into a "neurotic state" and led him to develop "a very active Oedipal complex." Test results suggested that from an early age Mercader felt a violent hatred for his father and for paternal figures in general – a murderous impulse he eventually directed against Leon Trotsky (Quiroz Cuarón, 1957). The real culprit for Trotsky's murder was Oedipus, the report suggested.

When the presiding judge handed down his sentence on April 17, 1943 – Carrancá had been removed from the case some months back – his ruling quoted the doctors' findings and concluded the motive for the crime was "an active Oedipus complex." Mercader was sentenced to 20 years in prison and, despite his lawyer's shrewd legal maneuvers, served his full sentence.

He was released in 1960, whisked to the airport, and put aboard a flight to the Soviet Union, where he was decorated and awarded a military pension. For years he lived a quiet life under yet a new name: Ramón Pavlovich López. In the 1970s he moved to Cuba, the land of his ancestors, where he died of bone cancer in 1978. His ashes were flown to Moscow and buried in the Kuntsevo Cemetery.

Though Carrancá did not stay on as a judge in the case – following a motion by the defense, he was replaced by judge Manuel Rivera Vázquez, who wrote the verdict in 1943 – his theories on criminology and psychoanalysis shaped the trial from beginning to end. His articles for *Criminalia* encouraged the use of psychoanalysis to penetrate the criminal unconscious, and his wish was fulfilled in a high-profile case that was closely followed around the globe. When the judge handed down his sentence, newspapers and illustrated weeklies throughout Mexico reported that an "active Oedipus complex" had pushed Mercader to kill Trotsky. If the use of psychoanalytic techniques in legal proceedings seemed like a utopian dream in 1934, by 1943 it had become accepted practice in Mexico City's criminal courts.

Had Freud lived to see the psychoanalytically inflected trial of Trotsky's assassin, he would have surely objected to the court's focus on the Oedipus complex as a motive for the killing – just as he had done in the Halsmann case. He might have acknowledged, however, that psychoanalytic techniques led to a breakthrough by offering the most complete psychological portrait of Mercader. Julia Kristeva once remarked that the Oedipus complex is not only about parricide – it is also an inquiry into one's origins: Oedipus murdered his father, but he also solved the riddle of the sphinx. Like Oedipus, the analyst wants to know, to make sense of the past and understand the present.

Understood in this way, psychoanalysis emerges as the perfect tool for cracking the mystery of Mercader's true identity. From the moment of his arrest, he lied about his name and origins. One of the objectives of the trial – and of the extensive psychological tests – was to solve the Oedipal riddle of origins. The questions Quiroz Cuarón and Gómez Robleda asked were the same as those posed by Oedipus: who is he and where did he come from? (Though, as Don Levine (1960, p. 150) observes, unlike a real analytic treatment, Mercader's analysis "involved no confidential relationship of doctor and patient [and] it was virtually unlimited in scope.")

Mercader was successful in keeping his secret for many years. He was tried and sentenced as Jacques Mornard, and he continued to live under this assumed name until his release from prison in 1960. Whenever a journalist, a historian or an investigator would ask his real name, he snapped back he had no other name beside Jacques Mornard.

But in the end, a psychoanalyst would unmask him. After the trial, Carrancá moved on to other cases and did not write again about Freud or Mercader. The criminologist Quiroz Cuarón, on the other hand, maintained his interest in both psychoanalysis and the Trotsky case, and spent many years after the trial working diligently to discover the assassin's true identity.

In 1950, 10 years after the murder, he was invited to represent Mexico at the World Congress on Criminology, to be held in Paris that year. He took with him the assassin's fingerprints and photographs and spent some weeks making inquiries at police departments in various European cities. When he got to Madrid he discovered a perfect fingerprint match: the imprints belonged to Jaime Ramón Mercader del Río Hernández, a Catalan radical who had been briefly detained, fingerprinted and charged with subversive activities in the mid-1930s.

Quiroz Cuarón returned to Mexico carrying a set of documents from the Spanish police archives – including Ramón Mercader's photos, fingerprints and handwriting samples – that left no doubt about the true identity of Trotsky's assassin. He published his findings, illustrated with the newly surfaced evidence, in a criminological journal and took credit for being the first to solve the mystery of Jacques Mornard's identity. Mercader, alas, dismissed the findings and insisted, once more, that he was simply Mornard, a Belgian citizen and a disgruntled Trotskyite.

In his articles, Quiroz Cuarón offered a Freudian interpretation of his findings, and invoked the theory of free association to explain the unconscious motives behind Mercader's choice of Mornard as a pseudonym. The name Mornard, he remarked, contains all the letters found in Ramón. Because of psychological determinism, he who devises a false name betrays himself. As Freud had written, nothing in the unconscious is arbitrary. Quiroz Cuarón's article concluded that Mercader's attitude toward his name evoked the primitive beliefs analyzed in *Totem and Taboo*. Like Freud, Quiroz Cuarón compared the behavior of neurotics – in this case a neurotic criminal – to primitive religious practices.

Quiroz Cuarón brought to fruition the ambitious project for integrating psychoanalysis and criminology that Carrancá had proposed in his articles for *Criminalia*, including the use of free association, the focus on pathological complexes and the attention to unconscious motivations. The procedures for psycho-legal analysis that Carrancá had tested on a small scale in the 1930s were now applied, with the blessings of the legal and medical establishment, to one of the most famous criminal cases anywhere in the world. The judicial use of psychoanalysis had become a mainstream practice, fulfilling what had once seemed an idealistic young judge's utopian vision.

## Castrating Caridad

Freud, as we saw earlier, would have objected to the conclusion that "an active Oedipus complex" led Mercader to kill Trotsky – a reservation that many modern readers might be inclined to share. But as outlandish at it might sound today, the diagnosis did point to a crucial factor in the case: Mercader's relationship to his mother.

Caridad del Río was born in Cuba but soon moved to Barcelona, where she married, gave birth to five children, and became a powerful political activist working first for the Spanish Republic and then, after 1939, for the Soviet Union. During the Spanish Civil War she traveled to Mexico, where Diego Rivera painted her portrait. In those years, Caridad became the mistress of one of the most powerful Soviet agents working for the GPU (the espionage agency that would later be known as the KGB): Naum Eitington.

Naum Eitington – who also went by the aliases Leonid Eitington and General Kotov – was one of Stalin's most trusted agents, charged with overseeing the most delicate international operations, like the kidnapping of General Kutepov in 1930 and the assassination of General Miller in Paris in 1937 (Dziak, 1988, pp. 101–102).[6] In 1940 Eitington convinced his mistress, Caridad, to recruit her son for the single most important assignment of his life: the execution of Leon Trotsky. Eitington and Caridad trained the young Ramón, sent him to Mexico, and, on the day of the assassination, waited for him in the getaway car outside Trotsky's house. When Ramón was arrested, the pair returned to Moscow, where Caridad was awarded the Order of Lenin for her services – and for the sacrifice of her son – to the Soviet Union.

Quiroz Cuarón's diagnosis of Mercader was not entirely far-fetched: there was something uncannily Oedipal about a son committing a murder at the behest of his mother and her lover, and a mother willing to sacrifice her son – or at least her son's freedom – for the sake of her lover. Trotsky's assassination also played out as a family romance, as a neurotic triangle featuring a Stalinist agent, his attractive mistress, and her compliant son – a plot that seems taken out of a Greek drama, a Shakespearean play or one of Freud's case studies.

And the plot thickens: as it turns out, there were two degrees of separation between Trotsky's assassin and Freud. While Naum Eitington was fine-tuning the details of the assassination in Mexico, another Eitington – Max Eitington – had become Freud's closest confidant and a pillar of the psychoanalytic movement in Europe. Max, a wealthy, Russian-born analyst, had presided over the International Psychoanalytical Association from 1927 to 1932, emigrated to Palestine in 1934, and maintained a regular correspondence with Freud until his death.

In the 1930s Sándor Radó stunned the psychoanalytic world by claiming that Max and Naum were brothers, and that Max was well informed of his sibling's involvement with Stalin and the GPU. His claim has been debated by historians of Soviet espionage: John Dziak and Stephen Schwartz argued that the Eitington fortune came not from the family fur business, as it was generally believed, but from Stalin's intelligence services, and that Max might have been implicated in some of the operations carried out by Naum. Some historians have suggested that Freud, who received loans from Max during World War I, might have been an indirect recipient of the Soviet money channeled to Naum. It has since been disproved that the Eitingtons were brothers, but some scholars still believe that they were close relatives: Robert Conquest believes they were first cousins, and Alexander Etkind claims that they were brothers-in-law.

Despite having provoked intense – and not always civil – arguments, the exact relation between the Eitingtons has not been definitely established. Rapoport and Alexeev were among the first to argue, in their 1985 book *High Treason*, that the Eitingtons – the authors identify them as Mark and Leonid – were brothers. John Dziak repeated the claim in his 1988 *Chekisty*, but conceded that there is considerable confusion over the identities of the two Eitington brothers. Stephen Schwartz, an article titled "Intellectuals and Assassins – Annals of Stalin's Killerati" and published in the January 24, 1988, issue of the *New York Times Book Review*, repeated the claim that Max and Naum were brothers, and asked to what extent Max might have been implicated in his brother's missions. Historian Theodore Draper responded to Schwartz's article, arguing that Max and Naum were not brothers, and accused Schwartz and Dziak of sloppy historical work. The debate between Schwarz and Draper continued in letters to the *NYRB*, each refusing to cede ground. On July 3, 1988, Robert Conquest published a more level-headed response in the *New York Times Book Review*, reminding all parties in the debate that "Max Eitington's guilt or innocence [is] a question which has been discussed since 1938." The debate was revisited almost a decade later by Alexander Etkind in his *Eros of the Impossible: The History of Psychoanalysis in Russia*, where he argues that Max Eitington could have been an accomplice to Naum's crimes. In my view, the evidence supports the claim that the two Eitingtons were relatives, though not brothers.

Whatever the exact relationship between the them, a prominent historian argued that Max was implicated in at least one of Naum's schemes: the assassination of the Soviet defector General Miller. One of the agents enlisted for this operation was the Russian émigré singer Plevitskaya, an extravagant diva who was a frequent guest at Max Eitington's Berlin home. After the murder, Plevitskaya was convicted in a French court, and her deposition mentioned Max several times, though the analyst was never questioned. Alexander Etkind believes that

> Plevitskaya's testimony and Rado's recollections indicate that Max Eitington could well have been an accomplice in a subtle political game that was being played on a pan-European scale, in which the leader of international psychoanalysis carried out the commands of Stalin's secret service.
>
> *(Gallo, 2010, p. 225)*

Though Etkind concedes "most of the evidence to that effect is circumstantial," he believes that "today there are sufficient data to link Max Eitington in one degree or another with his brother-in-law's schemes" (Etkind, 1997, p. 250).

In my view, the evidence available does not support the claim that Freud actually benefited from Naum Eitington's schemes, and neither does it lend credence to the suggestion that Max might have actively collaborated in Naum's operations. I do believe, however, that the two

Eitingtons were relatives and only one degree separated Max – and Freud – apart from Naum's plots.

The tale of the two Eitingtons – one a Freudian, the other a Stalinist – included a Mexican chapter in which followers of the two relatives crossed paths during the Trotsky case. As president of the IPA, Max Eitington pushed for the worldwide dissemination of Freud's ideas, and it was in part thanks to his efforts that a young judge like Carrancá, living thousands of miles away from Vienna, could study Freud's writings. And it was thanks to the other Eitington that Mercader became a hard-line Stalinist, traveled to Mexico, assumed a false identity and murdered Leon Trotsky. The Trotsky trial pitted a partisan of Max Eitington against an agent of Naum Eitington, a follower of international psychoanalysis against an agent of Soviet espionage. This episode was a historical clash between two institutions, psychoanalysis and Stalinism, each represented by one of the Eitingtons. Naum's agent was subjected to Max's methods, and in the end, Max's follower put Naum's lieutenant behind bars, handing Freud a symbolic victory over Stalin.

One wonders how Max Eitington received the news of Trotsky's assassination in his Palestinian home. Had he been in touch with his relative? Did he know that Naum had masterminded the murder? Did he realize the assassin would be tried by a psychoanalytic judge? Max died in 1943; Naum lived until the 1970s. Did Max see Naum again before his death? Did the two relatives ever discuss Trotsky's death? Was Naum ever analyzed? Historians have debated whether Naum co-opted Max, but they have never considered whether Max might have co-opted Naum, convincing him to undergo an analytic treatment. Readers might be amused by the image of a Soviet agent confessing his secrets to an analyst, but this is exactly what happened in Mexico: when Mercader was ordered to undergo an analysis, psychoanalysis put Stalinism on the couch. In the epic battle between these two Weltanschauungen, psychoanalysis had the upper hand.

Mercader's family romance was more complex than Carrancá or Quiroz Cuarón imagined: it involved a triangle between a Soviet agent, a domineering mother and a complacent son, but it also extended to a powerful father figure: Josef Stalin. Mercader's attack was ultimately directed against the rival of his ideological father.

## Mexicans gone wild

Earlier in this chapter I mentioned Freud's essay on "'Wild' Psychoanalysis" and asked if Carrancá might fit the profile of a "wild" analyst: he did not undergo a training analysis, he reduced sexuality to genital activity, and he did not follow Freud's recommended techniques. But despite these symptoms of analytic wildness, Freud endorsed his practice of psycho-legal analysis and commended him as an ally to the psychoanalytic movement. Carrancá was wild, but not wild enough to qualify as a wild psychoanalyst.

During the Trotsky case, Carrancá came in contact with a type of wildness that would plague Mexico for several decades: wild Marxism. If wild psychoanalysis refers to a superficial and imprecise knowledge of Freudian theories combined with a sloppy clinical practice, wild Marxism entails a vulgar understanding of Marx's writings coupled with dangerous ploys to construct a communist utopia. Stalin – Isaac Deutscher called his doctrines "a grotesque form of Leninism" – was the most striking example of such a wild Marxist, and so were Naum Eitington and Ramón Mercader.

The Trotsky case pitted Carrancá, a wild analyst, against Mercader, a wild Marxist. As we learn from this episode, wild psychoanalysis might raise some eyebrows but is ultimately harmless. In the worst of cases, it could aggravate a neurosis or chip away at the prestige of psychoanalysis. Wild Marxism, on the other hand, left behind a bloody trail of purges, kidnappings, and political assassinations. Both Freudians and Marxists could go wild, but wild analysis, even in its most extreme forms, was merely a form of listening, while wild Marxism was almost always an instrument of murder. Analysis could also be deployed as a weapon – Mercader experienced the battery of psychological tests as a form of torture – but those who found themselves on the couch of a wild analyst, like Mercader, fared much better than those like Trotsky, who found themselves in the bull's-eye of wild Marxism.

What were the repercussions of this epic struggle between the disciples of Freud and Stalin in Mexico? Could we conclude that psychoanalysis triumphed over Stalinism? The efforts of Carrancá and Quiroz Cuarón led to Mercader's sentence and imprisonment, while at the same time raising the prestige of psychoanalysis and exposing the dangers of Stalinism. Freud's doctrines have endured, while Stalin's methods have been repudiated by all but the most recalcitrant of wild Marxists. Some Russian historians have even chosen psychoanalysis as a model to examine the Stalinist past: the recent publication of Alexander Etkind's *Eros of the Impossible*, with its inventive interpretations of Stalinist atrocities, can be read as the most recent in a series of efforts to analyze – in the Freudian sense of the term – the darkest moments of Soviet history. More than seven decades after Carrancá's efforts, analysts are still putting Stalinists on the couch!

## Conclusion

*Derecho penal: parte general*, the single Mexican book in Freud's library, had quite a story to tell: the tale of a Mexican judge who brandished psychoanalysis as a weapon against crime, invented the technique of psycho-legal analysis, and counted Trotsky's assassin as his most famous subject. The plot, as complex as a detective novel, implicated Mercader, Naum Eitington, and even Stalin – an unlikely cast of characters in the history of psychoanalysis.

One of the joys of archival research is to make documents speak, to listen to the story they have to tell. The story told by *Derecho penal*, which sat unopened and unread for almost 70 years at Columbia University's medical library, illustrates the degree of eccentricity that characterized the reception of Freud's ideas in Mexico. In Argentina and Brazil, Freud was read by psychiatrists and doctors, professionals who saw a direct application of psychoanalytic techniques to their professions. In Mexico, however, judges, criminologists and revolutionaries read Freud, and they used his ideas to theorize a radically utopian society – a world in which prophylactic psychoanalysis would eradicate crime, a world in which men would no longer be tortured by neuroses or unconscious traumas. Of all utopias conceived in the 20th century, the one imagined by Trotsky and Carrancá would have been one of the most radical: a society ruled by enlightened, psychoanalytically inclined Marxists protected by Freudian judges. If rumors of this radical utopia had ever reached Freud, he would have certainly concluded, not without some amusement, and perhaps not without some pride, that psychoanalysis had gone completely wild.

## Notes

1 The most comprehensive history of psychoanalytic institutions in Mexico is Fernando M. González, "Notas para una historia del psicoanálisis en México," *Psicoanálisis y realidad*, ed. Armando Suárez, Mexico City: Siglo XXI, 1989, pp. 75–110; Ramón Parres and Santiago Ramírez, two of the APM's original founders, have written a short but informative account of the movement: "Historia del movimiento psicoanalítico en México," *Revista de la Asociación Psicoanalítica Mexicana*, 1968, pp. 19–29; Raúl Páramo Ortega has published two historical overviews that are biased toward his own association: "Mexico," in *Psychoanalysis International: A Guide to Psychoanalysis throughout the World*, ed. Peter Kutter, Stuttgart: Frommann-Holzboog, 1995, pp. II: 149–159; as well as the more extensive *Freud in Mexiko: Ein Essay zur Geschichte der Psychoanalyse in Mexiko*, Munich: Quintessenz, 1992.

2 See also the same author's unpublished manuscript "Huellas de Einstein y Freud en México," n.d.

3 Carlos Monsiváis, "Ortodoxia y heterodoxia en las alcobas (Hacia una crónica de costumbres y creencias sexuales en las alcobas)," *Debate feminista* (April 1995).

4 "Certain crimes," he writes, "can be traced back to the 'complexes' and thus positivist criminal law can turn to psychoanalysis in order to investigate their causes."

5 Quiroz Cuarón and Gómez Robleda incorporated transcripts of the tests in their report to the court. In "Prisoner Against Psychologist," Chapter 8 of *Mind of an Assassin*, Isaac Don Levine draws on these tests to sketch a psychological portrait of Mercader. See Don Levine, 149–194.

6 See also "Naum Eitington" in Vitaly Rapoport and Yuri Alexeev's *High Treason: Essays on the History of the Red Army, 1918–1938*, Duke University Press, Durham, 1985, pp. 391–392.

## References

Carrancá y Trujillo, R 1934, 'Freud to Carrancá y Trujillo', February 13, reproduced in *Criminalia* 8, Academia Mexicana de Ciencias Penales, Mexico City.

Carrancá y Trujillo, R 1937, *Derecho penal: parte general*, Editorial Porrúa, México City.

Colmenares, FH (ed) 1994, *El caso Trotsky*, Consejo Nacional de Posgrado en Derecho, Mexico City, VI, 287ff.

Cuarón, Q 1957. El asesino de León Trotsky y su peligrosidad. *Revista de Criminalística de Cuba. La Habana*, 1956, reeditado en *Etudes Internationales de Psycho-Sociologie Criminelle*, Paris.

Don Levine, I 1960, *Mind of an assassin: The man who killed Trotsky*, New American Library, New York.

Dziak, JJ 1988, *Chekisty: A History of the KGB*, Lexington Books, Lanham, MD.

Etkind, A 1997, *Eros of the impossible: The history of psychoanalysis in Russia*, Westview Press, Boulder.

Freud, S 1910, ' "Wild" psycho-analysis', in J Strachey (ed) *Standard edition of the complete psychological works of Sigmund Freud*, vol. 11, New York: Vintage Books, p. 222.

Freud, S 1912, *Selected papers on hysteria and other psychoneuroses* (AA Brill, trans), New York: Journal of Nervous and Mental Disease, pp. 222–223.

Fromm, E & Maccoby, M 1970, *Social character in a Mexican village: A sociopsychoanalytic study*, Prentice Hall, Englewood Cliffs, NJ.

Gallo, R 2010, *Freud's Mexico: Into the wilds of psychoanalysis,* Massachusetts Institute of Technology, Cambridge.

Glick, T 1994, 'Science and society in twentieth-century Latin America', *The Cambridge History of Latin America. Vol. 6: Part I, 1930 to the Present*, Cambridge University Press, Cambridge, pp. 463–535.

González, L 1985, *Notas para una historia*, Oficina Estatal de Preservacion Historica, Model Offset Printing, Mexico City.

Monsiváis, C 1995, 'Ortodoxia y heterodoxia en las alcobas (Hacia una crónica de costumbres y creencias sexuales en las alcobas)', *Debate feminista*, April issue, pp. 191–192.

Plotkin, MB 2001, *Freud in the Pampas: the emergence and development of a psychoanalytic culture in Argentina*. Stanford University Press, Stanford, CA.

Ramírez, S 1959, *El mexicano: Psicología de sus motivaciones*, Editorial Pax, Mexico City.

Roudinesco, E 1990, *Jacques Lacan & Co.: A history of psychoanalysis in France, 1925–1985*, University of Chicago Press, Chicago.

# 13

# British psychoanalysis in the 20th century

*Caroline Polmear*[1]

In 1906, as English surgeon Wilfred Trotter was talking with Ernest Jones, he mentioned a man in Vienna "who actually listened with attention to every word his patients said to him" (Rayner, 1991). Freud's work was enthusiastically taken up by a group of intellectuals and medics, some of whom went to Vienna for analysis with Freud. In 1913 Jones established the London Psychoanalytical Society, which he disbanded over controversy with the Jungians before founding the British Psychoanalytical Society (BPAS) in 1919 – a firmly Freudian society. Thus the early establishment of psychoanalysis in Britain followed a similar course to that elsewhere following closely the works of Freud. It is as the century progressed, and as Britain became home to the Freuds, Melanie Klein and many other creative analysts, that it began to develop its own particular character.

This chapter is divided into two parts. In the first I trace the development of that particular character looking at clinical theory from Freud's early work to the end of the century. In the second part I explore the penetration of psychoanalytic ideas beyond the consulting room on both British psychoanalysis and wider British society.

Consider the following "construction" that Freud imagines himself "laying before" his patient:

> Up to your nth year you regarded yourself as the sole and unlimited possessor of your mother; then came another baby and brought you grave disillusionment. Your mother left you for some time, and even after her reappearance she was never again devoted to you exclusively. Your feelings towards your mother became ambivalent, your father gained a new importance for you [ . . . and so on].
>
> *(Freud, 1938, p. 380)*

It is a far cry from the communications one might hear an analyst "put to" his patient in a session today or even at the end of the 20th century.

Now consider the following: in this session the analyst has become aware of the patient's irritation with her and detects a sulky atmosphere. The analyst might suggest that the patient is feeling hurt and upset having seen the last patient leave the consulting room and that it has made the patient feel unwanted and angry with her analyst and not feel like talking to her.

Over the course of the century, British analysts have tended to interpret less like Freud in the first example and more like the analyst in the second example. So how has the change come about?

In this section I will attempt to review developments in our clinical practice from 1900 until the end of the century and link these developments with the emergence of various psychoanalytic theories, part theories and concepts that underpin them. It will be a personal view and by no means fully comprehensive; indeed others in the British Psychoanalytical Society will stress different aspects and hold firm to particular ways of working in a session. But I am emboldened to attempt some generalizations about the development of our clinical theory on the strength of the reaction of colleagues overseas who comment that they recognize a British way of working usually associated with the close attention that is paid to the internal world manifest in the consulting room. While the focus of this chapter is on psychoanalysis in Britain, I recognize that there has been a degree of mutual influence with the development of psychoanalysis in other places around the world.

Some terms first need to be defined. When I speak of *British clinical psychoanalysis* I am talking about the work of clinicians of the British Psychoanalytical Society often in this country also referred to as the Institute of Psychoanalysis. The institute is in fact the operational arm of the British Psychoanalytical Society and runs training, publishing activities, outreach and so on. *Clinical theory* referred to here encompasses that which informs clinicians in any psychoanalytical session: when to speak, when to be silent, and when we *do* speak what to speak about and in what manner to speak to our patient about it. It encompasses our theories of psychic development and of what brings about change in analysis. Psychoanalysis covers three different activities: it is a theory of mind, a research method through which we test and change our theories, and a clinical treatment. While treatment is closely related and should be based on the theory of mind *in* psychoanalysis, it also develops through technical and case discussion.

Despite theories being superseded one by another, clinicians do not ever fully give them up; rather they remain in our preconscious mind ready to be called up to consciousness when there is a process at work in the session that seems to call for a particular conceptualization. Joseph Sandler (1983) illuminated the complex and fluid way in which we use psychoanalytic concepts in the consulting room. For example, Freud replaced the topographical model with the structural model of the mind but never reworked *The Interpretation of Dreams* (1900) in the light of his new theory. So it is with clinicians that have followed Freud who use new clinical and technical concepts as they are relevant without being troubling with a complete internally consistent metapsychology. Clinical concepts and phenomena may or may not match exactly theoretical models of psychoanalysis.

## Key developments and theories in British psychoanalysis

In this section I will be charting some of the key developments, clinical concepts, theories and part theories that I believe have affected and influenced the ways British psychoanalysts talk to their patients.

### *Freud's theory of mind: The Interpretation of Dreams (1900)*

With the publication of this great work at the beginning of the century Freud set out his theory of mind: the topographical model. Unconscious wishes largely seen as sexual in nature were described as seeking expression and were opposed by repressive and defensive forces in the mind. The model is one of dynamic conflict between agencies of the mind. The analysis of dreams took center stage in most analyses. Freud famously described it as the "royal road to a knowledge of the unconscious activities of the mind" (1900, p. 608). Dreams are understood as attempts at achieving the fulfillment of unconscious wishes in disguised form. Symptoms were similarly understood as the compromise solutions of these conflicts. In this phase of psychoanalysis the aim of clinical intervention was to relieve the patient's distress by bringing these unconscious wishes and conflicts into consciousness. The work of the analyst resembled that of a detective trying to uncover unconscious wishes through dreams and free associations. It was not felt to be a joint journey of discovery as it is today; rather the work of the physician was to wrestle the facts from the patient and to lay the truth before him or her, as shown in my first quote from Freud.

## The Oedipus complex

A central conflict described by Freud concerned the developmental challenges of the little boy of about 4 or 5 (though Freud saw a similar passage for the little girl in relation to the parent of the opposite sex), who in his love for his mother wishes to own and possess her. In his mind this brings him into conflict with his father, and a fear of the father's retaliation by castration forces him to find a solution to his conflict.

The centrality of the Oedipus complex in Freud's thinking meant that clinical work tended to be dominated by interpretation of conflict at the Oedipal level of functioning. It focused on sexual wishes and it meant that interpretations tended to be in a developed three-person language. As will be noted later, greater understanding of the psychic development of the infant from birth has opened up greater understanding of early developmental disturbances and broadened the scope of work in the consulting room. However, regression in the session tended to be understood as resistance to the difficulties of the Oedipus complex often expressed in a heated transference to the analyst, rather than a valid communication of the central difficulties of patients with early developmental disturbances.

## "The Ego and the Id" (1923)

As a result of his experiences with his patients, Freud found limits to his topographical model: in particular, in relation to what he began to recognize as the unconscious sense of guilt. Ever the true scientist, he put forward a modified model of the mind in the light of new evidence.

This is known as the structural model of the mind. In this model, instinctual wishes derive from the id, which is entirely unconscious and composed of primitive drives. It is dominated by the pleasure principle. During maturation a portion of the id develops and becomes the ego with its task of self-preservation, governed by the reality principle. The superego houses the residue of the child's early conflicts, especially in relation to parents. Large parts of both the ego and the superego are also unconscious. The ego becomes the heart of the character, balancing as best it may the demands of the id, the superego and the outside world.

With this model Freud opened up the world of the ego and began the shift in emphasis from the clinical task of uncovering unconscious wishes and conflicts to that of strengthening the ego. An early contributor to a greater understanding of the ego was Freud's daughter, Anna, whose work *The Ego and the Mechanisms of Defence* was published in English in 1937. She highlighted the work of the ego as defending against both threats from external sources and from internal instinctual ones.

## Curative factors in psychoanalysis and the mutative interpretation

In the late 1920s and throughout the 1930s there was a good deal of interest in curative factors. At this point in the development of psychoanalysis it was no longer sufficient to say that interpretation aimed at making conscious that which was unconscious. James Strachey (1934) published a paper that was to become influential in this debate for years to come. He described the analytic task first in relation to the superego of the patient. He noticed that the patient would imbue the analyst with the severe superego figure he often carried around inside him. As the analyst interprets calmly and nonjudgmentally the patient can take inside him a modified, less severe figure. Deep internal change is brought about by the mutative interpretation, one that arises first from the patient's emotional experience of the analyst as an archaic internal object, and then by contrast as a new object. Strachey believed that this process drove a wedge between the archaic and the new objects and brought about internal change. This important formulation puts transference right at the heart of the session and the analysis.

### Melanie Klein: transference

Freud discovered the clinical phenomenon of transference early on in his work. At first he saw transferences as a hindrance or obstacle to the work of analysis. However, by 1909 he began to recognize that it could be a therapeutic agent, although it was only in the 1930s that the concept began to become the focus of clinical practice.

Melanie Klein's contribution is central in this shift (1952). At the heart of her work is the concept of unconscious phantasy that underlies all thought, rational and irrational. Phantasy (the "ph" is used to denote it is unconscious and unlike conscious fantasy) is a primitive, body-based narrative accompanying the intense loving and hating relationship to the mother. Klein described the developmental achievement of the move from the paranoid-schizoid position with its primitive paranoid anxieties in relation to the mother, to the depressive position in which love and hate can be integrated. Now the phantasied hateful attacks on the object can be borne because through love reparation can be made (see chapter 3 on Klein). For Klein, the patient's unconscious phantasy when in treatment is focused on the person of the analyst. The analytic work is then concerned with the understanding of the unconscious phantasy as expressed in relation to the analyst and this meant a shift from the classical approach to one in which transference interpretation became central in Kleinian analyses (Spillius, 1988).

The controversial discussions in the BPAS in the early 1940s, following Anna Freud's arrival in 1938 (King & Steiner, 1991), were a series of heated scientific papers and debates concerning these issues of theory and technique. The two eminent child analysts, Anna Freud and Melanie Klein, held very different views of both the early development of the child and of psychoanalytic technique and these scientific debates became enmeshed with political and economic divisions in the Society.

From 1921 up to about 1932 Klein's writing often focused on primitive destructiveness, the primitive part object Oedipus complex and the consequent fearful superego. After 1935 she became preoccupied with love, guilt, reparation and mourning as much as with hate and destructiveness. However many of Klein's followers wrote papers throughout the 1950s and 1960s, which tended

> to emphasize the patient's destructiveness in a way that we would now assume might have felt persecuting to the patient. From these papers it seems that unconscious phantasies were

evidently interpreted to the patient immediately and very directly in part-object language (breast, nipple, penis, etc).

*(Spillius, 1988, p. 6)*

There were many in the Society, Kleinians among them, who found this way of talking to the patient quite alien and feared that it forced the patient to submit to the dominance of the analyst's language and understanding.

Perhaps it was the concept of projective identification introduced by Melanie Klein in 1946 that began to bring about a move away from this style of talking to patients. Projective identification is a process by which we get rid of split-off parts of the self and locate them in the object. In unconscious phantasy both the subject and the object are altered by this process. Sometimes the phantasy also involves appropriating parts of the object oneself, so not only projecting an identification but also introjecting one. Although at first this concept was often used rather mechanistically (e.g., "you are putting your messy feelings into me"), with the development of understanding of projective identification as communication and the importance of the containment of projections, clinical use of the concept deepened (discussed later).

We see here how Klein's understanding of primitive psychic processes took the focus in the consulting room away from the triangulation of the classical Oedipus complex and drew attention to much earlier transferences: transferences of split-off parts of the self. This development meant that interpretation of the patient's destructive attacks began to be set alongside the need for the analyst to be able to bear and to understand the use the patient was making of her through projective identification. This is no more crucial than in the analysis of patients with narcissistic and borderline disturbances associated with early developmental failures. In this approach the work was not always about talking to the patient, but rather bearing experiences that the patient found unbearable.

Working with projected parts of the patient first and foremost requires that the analyst *feels and receives* those parts. The work of the analyst no longer resided in the realm of thinking only but now of feeling and thinking together. Alive and emotional contact in the session became the focus of clinical technique, as did understanding the communications in the here and now of the session.

This brought into focus the notion of the countertransference. Paula Heimann (1950, 1960) wrote about the positive value of the countertransference. Her starting point was that the unconscious of the analyst understands the patient's unconscious and that the analytic task was "to sustain the feelings which are stirred up in him, as opposed to discharging them (as does the patient), in order to subordinate them to the analytic task in which he functions as the patient's mirror reflection" (1950, p. 82). She believed that all of the analyst's feelings in the session were to be seen as countertransference that illuminated the patient's transference communication.

## Donald Winnicott: object relations theory

Debate in the Society in these rich middle years of the century was not restricted to classical and Kleinian views only. The work of Ronald Fairburn, Michael Balint and in particular Donald Winnicott – often referred to as object relations theorists – was highly influential. Their work moved psychoanalysis finally away from Freud's emphasis on discharge of drives and pleasure seeking toward seeing people as primarily relationship seeking.

Winnicott was a pediatrician, a child psychiatrist and psychoanalyst who was initially impressed by Klein's ideas. His thinking diverged from hers, however, as his numerous observations of children and their mothers in the consulting room led him to foreground the infant's inextricable relationship with the mother, and noted the important part that both the infant's phantasy and the mother's actual response to the infant played to their development. The quality of the mother's "holding" in the earliest weeks and months is central to the baby's development (Polmear, 2008; Winnicott, 1960a). Winnicott believed that without good enough holding the infant could fail to achieve "being" and instead of becoming able gradually to separate "me" from "not-me" and to dwell in his own body ego, the baby would react to impingements by forming a "false self" (1960b). Thus the mother's attuned and sensitive holding, both physically and emotionally, along with her capacity to hold the child in mind, protects the infant from catastrophic impingement and developmental breakdown.

Winnicott's work contributed to the movement toward seeing the analytic enterprise as a sensitive interrelationship between patient and analyst. It added further weight to the expectation of regression in analysis and that the analyst will need to be able to bear periods of regression without making false or prematurely structuring interpretations. If the analyst can bear the regression in its inchoate form then the patient will have a chance of emerging from the false self and becoming a more spontaneous and authentic person.

## Wilfred Bion: containment

At the same time as the object relations theorists were working and writing, the Kleinian analyst Wilfred Bion – who had worked as an army psychiatrist in the World War II – uncovered the nature of group processes while working with returning traumatized soldiers (Bion, 1961). He became preoccupied with psychotic processes, and his description of maternal and psychoanalytic containment became an important addition to Kleinian theory. Bion's notion of the "containing function" (1962) is similar to Winnicott's notion of maternal and analytic holding, although Bion's theory of container and contained is used more specifically in relation to the containment in the mind of unprocessed affect.

Bion is concerned with the infant's primitive relation to the breast. The hungry baby finds relief from the feeding at the breast, which embodies the container into which the baby projects his anxiety and discomfort. Bion saw this projection as a form of communication rather than simply a ridding of unpleasant affect. The baby receives the milk and love as well as meaning, which change his painful hunger to relaxed satisfaction. He has been contained and will gradually introject this containing function of the mother.

Bion went on to develop his theory of thinking from this starting point. But for our purposes the theory of containment has, I think, become universally accepted by analysts at work with their patients and as such has sealed the shift toward the analyst's function of containment of unbearable affects, working them through in the countertransference (Brenman Pick, 1965) in order to return to the patient a modified experience relieved of the intensely sadistic superego aspects. With this experience the hope is that the patient will also introject the containing function of the analyst and will be able to create more internal space for thinking, both with the analyst and after the analysis has ended.

## Enactment and transference

I began this section with a quote from Freud on constructions in psychoanalysis. Reconstructing the significant events of the patient's past was an important and central aspect of analysis at the beginning of the century. Psychoanalysis is a developmental psychology and the past, or more precisely the unconscious phantasy created in the past, remains at the center of the analytic enterprise. Patients talk about their past experiences in analysis as well as their day-to-day preoccupations. The analyst develops an understanding of the main developmental difficulties faced by the patient as much from the experience that the patient brings into the relationship with the analyst as from what they recall of their past life. The analyst lives through, with the patient, repeated externalizations of internal object relations that owe more to their past than to the present. However, the therapeutic effort is no longer aimed at reconstructing past events. Rather it is aimed at the patient coming to accept and take back their own projected and disowned parts of the self. Construction can be very helpful in this process when it helps the patient to understand how they might have come to this way of psychic functioning. Reconstructing their response to past experiences helps in moderating the shame and the guilt involved in taking back these unwanted parts of the self and thus makes the process more possible.

I have suggested that clinical theory and practice has moved from uncovering past experience and defenses against instinctual wishes, through to a focus on the transference and the here and now of the session, followed by an emphasis on the countertransference and the issue of what is required by the analyst in receiving projected parts of the patient. By this point, making emotional contact with the patient in the session by finding the most pressing affect in the session has become important. Toward the end of the 20th century interest shifted to the issue of enactment. Joseph Sandler and Betty Joseph were influential figures in this development.

## Joseph Sandler

Sandler (1976), writing on countertransference and role-responsiveness, drew attention to the phenomenon of the patient's unconscious attempts to actualize in the behavior of the object his unconscious wished-for phantasy relationship. The pressure, often unconscious, on the analyst may lead to a countertransference enactment; for example, being rather unusually warm, talking more or less than usual, or answering several questions put by the patient. Sandler pointed out that it is when the analyst becomes aware of his role-responsiveness to the patient that he is in a position to begin to understand the patient's dominant transference phantasies and the defenses against them. The analyst is required to adopt a position of "free-floating responsiveness" in order to be able to experience and become fully aware of the complexity and reality of the object relationship being enacted. This work moved the concept of projective identification firmly into the realms of actualization within the analytic encounter.

## Betty Joseph

Betty Joseph, in her famous paper "Transference" (1985), speaks of the "total situation." The total situation broadens the concept of transference by including everything that happens in the session as an aspect of transference. She gives an example in which the patient's immediate anxieties and the nature of her relationship with her internal figures emerge in the whole situation rather than in the immediate associations she brings in the session.

An analyst brought to one of Joseph's seminars work with a patient that she felt very unhappy with. The patient was very hard to help: "schizoid, angry, an unhappy childhood with probably emotionally unavailable parents" (Joseph, 1985, p. 448). The seminar came to the conclusion that what they were all experiencing was in fact the clue they needed to the transference; indeed it was being acted out with the analyst in the session, and again in the seminar. They decided that the patient was letting them experience what it was like to have a mother who could not understand and respond appropriately to her child's feelings but behaved as if she could. In the course of the discussion the members of the seminar sounded as if they understood the material when in fact they struggled to understand. In essence they behaved like the patient's mother. When this could be thought about the patient's experience with her mother was illuminated. Both Sandler and Joseph highlight the importance of communication through projective identification for gaining a deep and complex understanding of the patient's transference.

In this section I have attempted to outline the progression of preoccupations in clinical theory and technique, which seem to me to have moved psychoanalysis from Freud's early work to the end of the 20th century. I do not wish to suggest that all those in the British Psychoanalytical Society work in the same way and with the same emphasis; indeed there are those who very firmly oppose overuse of here and now interpretations. Nevertheless, there is a recognizable general movement through the various phases I have outlined, and I hope to have shown the theoretical concepts that underpin these developments.

## The impact of Freud on 20th-century British psychoanalysis and wider British society[2]

In this section I will explore the relationship between Freud's illumination of the nature of the unconscious mind and the wider society. I will be exploring how far his ideas penetrated the wider culture and in what ways they were taken up. For example, how was psychoanalysis received in this country? How did the psychoanalytic community organize itself? Over the century, what was its relationship with and impact on the medical profession? How did it affect academe and intellectual activity more generally? In exploring these questions I will be looking at some ways in which psychoanalysis has crossed over from "pure" analysis and been applied beyond the consulting room.

Despite Britain being the host country to so many creative intellectual refugees – Marx, Freud, Wittgenstein, Popper, Malinowski, Gombrich, Berlin, Klein to name but a few – the country has always responded ambivalently to their ideas, and in some cases barely engaging with them at all. Perhaps we can say that there is a certain pragmatic, conservative empiricist tradition in this country that makes us wary of intellectual excitement and slow to incorporate new ideas (Anderson, 1968). Yet we have seen how here as elsewhere Freudian ideas have entered the common culture and language. "The Freudian slip," the importance of early childhood experiences, the concepts of repression, resistance, the Oedipus complex and indeed the existence of the unconscious mind itself are all part of everyday accepted language, even "common sense." We can assume then that Freud's influence is far-reaching and has penetrated deep into the culture.

There were pockets of early engagement and interest amongst intellectuals in the interwar years. Famously, members of the Bloomsbury Group were excited by Freud's ideas. Virginia Woolf, writing in her diaries about her meetings with Freud and Klein, shows at first some cynicism and then a growing interest and involvement with the psychoanalytic perspective. Lytton Strachey, a historian and another Bloomsbury intellectual, at first received Freud's ideas with derision, writing a comic parody in an article called "According to Freud." Later, however, he found inspiration in Freud's ideas of unconscious drives to understand the secret passions of the Victorians about whom he wrote. Lytton's brother, James Strachey, trained to be a psychoanalyst. With his wife Alix, James Strachey made a significant contribution by translating, organizing and editing the *Standard Edition* of Freud's work, published under the auspices of Virginia and Leonard Woolf's Hogarth Press. Alix also became an analyst, as did Virginia Woolf's brother and his wife, Adrian and Karin Stephen (Pick, 2003).

The influence of Freud can also be seen in wider culture such as popular literature. D. H. Lawrence grappled with Freud's ideas in his essay, "Psychoanalysis and the Unconscious" (2004), with a mixture of awe and derision. W. H. Auden (1940) was moved to write a poem on the Death of Freud in 1939 with the telling lines:

> if often he was wrong and, at times, absurd to us he is no more a person
> now but a whole climate of opinion
> under whom we conduct our different lives

Even the influential economist Maynard Keynes engaged with psychoanalytic ideas. He thought that discoveries about the unconscious were useful in illuminating the symbolic meaning of money (Pick, 2003).

However, in many quarters Freud's early ideas were derided and summarily dismissed. When David Eder, a psychoanalyst and early follower of Freud, read a paper on psychoanalytic approaches to hysteria and obsessional disorders in 1911 at the British Medical Association's neurological section, it led to the audience (10 in all) departing as soon as he finished speaking. Even the chairman left (Pick, 2003). It is often said that the real resistance in circles such as medical ones was to Freud's ideas on childhood sexuality. Critics in the *Lancet* and the *British Medical Journal* rejected these ideas as unacceptable and unnecessarily and inappropriately erotic.

## The British Psychoanalytical Society

So how was the profession organizing itself in this early period, and what were they contributing to debate?

Ernest Jones, a somewhat controversial figure but a great pioneer, set up the British Psychoanalytical Society (BPAS) with a small group of psychoanalysts in 1919. With the foundation of the BPAS came the establishment of the library and plans to translate the works of Freud and other psychoanalytic writing into English. With the burgeoning of scientific and commercial activity in the BPAS during the 1920s there was a need for a proper administrative structure, and the Institute of Psychoanalysis was set up in 1924, largely through the initiative of John Rickman, to deal with financial and other matters mostly arising from book publication. In 1920 the *International Journal of Psychoanalysis* was established and in 1926 the London Clinic of Psychoanalysis followed.[3]

## Psychoanalysis and the medical profession

Having established the basis of the profession by 1926, an important negotiation was launched by Ernest Jones and his colleagues to try to get psychoanalysis recognized by the medical profession. Following Freud (1926) it was not necessary in this country for an analyst to be a doctor. In 1927 Jones reported that 40 percent of analysts in the British Psychoanalytical Society were nonmedical or lay analysts. The report from this committee broadly recognized the profession of psychoanalyst based on the teachings of Freud and is thought to have been an important milestone in the acceptance of psychoanalysis as an independent profession and not a subgroup of medicine.

With some notable exceptions, such as where psychoanalysts like Bion worked in psychiatric hospitals, psychoanalytic practice has largely been practiced in private consulting rooms outside the National Health Service (NHS). The post–World War II relationship with the NHS, however, has been mixed, with some hospitals adopting psychoanalytic ideas and applying psychotherapeutic models based on those ideas and others rejecting those ideas in favor of organic psychiatry and other forms of psychotherapy such as cognitive behavioral therapy. (I will explore in more detail later some of those applications within the NHS.)

Returning to the early years, while fierce theoretical and technical debate raged within the British Psychoanalytical Society between Melanie Klein and her followers, and Anna Freud and hers about child analysis and child development, there were those who worked to use psycho-analytic understanding more broadly beyond the psychoanalytic community; notably D.W. Winnicott. The reader of his early writing comes across such titles as *A Man Looks at Motherhood* (1949), *Getting to Know Your Baby* (1944), *The Child as a Going Concern* (1949), *Weaning* (1949) and *What About Father?* (1944). These and many other accessible talks and writings are gathered together in his book *The Child, The Family and the Outside World* (Winnicott, 1964). These papers and talks are all written in the language of his intended audience whether they were professionals working with young people or parents of children: they were doctors, nurses, health professionals, health visitors, teachers, social workers, probation officers, parents and foster parents. Winnicott gave talks on BBC radio and wrote copiously in professional newspapers. His tone is that of the kindly pediatrician who has a deep understanding of just how hard it is to be a parent, but how some understanding of child development can help in that difficult task.

Winnicott and fellow psychoanalyst John Bowlby communicated with passion about the deleterious effects of early separation on the development of the child, bringing research work into the public arena to make their case. In a letter to the BMA written on December, 16, 1939, which he wrote with John Bowlby and Emanuel Miller regarding the government's evacuation of small children, he states:

> From among much research done on this subject a recent investigation carried out by one of us at the London Child Guidance Clinic may be quoted. It shows that one important external factor in the causation of persistent delinquency is a small child's prolonged separa-tion from his mother. Over half of a statistically valid series of cases investigated had suffered periods of separation from their mothers and familiar environment lasting six months or more during their first five years of life.
>
> *(Winnicott et al., 1984)*

During World War II (1939–45) Winnicott became a psychiatric consultant to the government's scheme of evacuating children from their homes in areas liable to bombing. Through this work he not only influenced the care of these children but also added to his research knowledge, com-ing to the conclusion that children with good early parenting experience, what Bowlby called "a secure base," were better able to make a constructive use of their new environments.

## Children and psychoanalysis

During the war years Anna Freud and her colleagues set up the Hampstead War Nurseries, providing residential homes for children separated from their parents as a result of the war. The practice was innovative in the emphasis on preserving the child's attachment to their parents by any means possible, and on giving them other stable attachment figures.

Subsequently, in the 1950s at the Hampstead Clinic, later known as the Anna Freud Centre, a small nursery school and several parent–toddler groups were started, which ran with the assistance of a psychoanalytic consultant.

An example of psychoanalytically informed organizational work that had a major influence on child care practice was that of James Robertson, a social worker at the Hampstead War Nurs-eries who later became a psychoanalyst and worked with John Bowlby. Robertson studied the reactions of children admitted to hospital. At the time, in the early 1950s, it was believed that it was unsettling for parents to visit young children in hospital and most hospitals allowed only a few hours of visiting at weekends. Robertson found that children separated for short periods were actively distressed, and as the period of separation grew longer, this gave way to apathy and finally detachment. Finally, mostly to the relief of the hospital staff, the child would make superficial, indiscriminate contact with whatever adult was available. On discharge from hospital a disturbed relationship to the parents persisted for some time.

To try and persuade the hospital authorities to change their practice in relation to children's visiting hours Robertson made a film, *A Two-Year-Old Goes to Hospital* (1951). This showed the processes Robertson was describing, and it still makes harrowing viewing. The film met with outrage and its findings were rejected. Robertson understood this as a fear of a breakdown of the defenses against awareness of the children's emotional pain. In fact it took until 1959 for the Platt Report to recommend an extension of hospital visiting times. However, ultimately this piece of psychoanalytically informed research has had a profound effect on the welfare of children through its influence on hospital policy and on the training of nurses and social workers.

## The tension between psychoanalytic purity and the application of psychoanalysis

From the very beginning there seems to have been tension in the British Psychoanalytic Society between those analysts who focused on deepening their understanding of the workings of the mind and who pursued a career in intensive analytic practice five times a week, and those who, often driven by social conscience, worked to apply psychoanalytic principles to other ventures. This tension continued throughout the 20th century.

Ernest Jones, assisted by Edward Glover, dominated the British Psychoanalytic Society from its inception until after World War II. Jones's mission was to establish psychoanalysis as a respected profession in this country, but in so doing he discouraged analysts – indeed in some cases forbade them – to work at other institutions such as the Tavistock Clinic, founded in 1920, where other forms of psychotherapy were practiced and were available to a wider range of people. Jones himself wrote copiously on art and history, applying psychoanalytic ideas to studying various historical, artistic and literary figures (1910, 1913, 1931). Some of Jones's writing reads a bit like "wild analysis" these days. But the point is that he saw the application of psychoanalytic ideas as valid when it was analytic wisdom that was being offered to other disciplines, but not when it meant, as he viewed it, watering down analytic essentials by adapting psychoanalysis to other professions or ways of working. We see this tension reemerging at various times in the century.

Many psychiatrists and psychoanalysts joined the Medical Corps during World War II – John Rickman, Tom Main and Wilfred Bion, among others. They worked at a small psychiatric army hospital at Northfields in Birmingham treating soldiers with "war neurosis." They became concerned with therapeutic activity not only with individuals but in groups and within the culture of a community. Much was discovered about group processes in these years, and we can trace the development of two different applications of psychoanalytic ideas to groups from those working at Northfields. One branch went on to establish the Tavistock Institute of Human Relations (see Rayner, 1990), while another group contributed to the development of group analytic psychotherapy.

## The Tavistock Institute of Human Relations

The Tavistock Institute of Human Relations (TIHR) was founded in 1948. Knowledge gained in the treatment of soldiers and the study of combat units was applied now to industrial organizations. The economic motivation for this work came from the government's concerns about low levels of productivity in postwar Britain. The projects of the TIHR were concerned with examining unconscious group processes in the workplace, and involved the perspectives of both psychoanalysis and social science, in particular systems theory.

An early action-research project, which continued over 8 years, was of work organization in the newly nationalized coal mining industry (Trist et al., 1963). An important change introduced as a result of this work was "composite working," in which all members of a team working a coal seam were multiskilled so that each could engage in a variety of the tasks that made up the whole operation. This allowed teams to be self-regulating, to feel engaged in a common purpose, and led to a marked improvement in productivity, work satisfaction and labor relations.

As government funding became more difficult to secure, the TIHR shifted its focus from grant-aided research toward consultation directly commissioned by the client organization. For example, the Glacier Metal Company in London requested assistance with negotiating a change from piece-work payment to an hourly rate (Jaques, 1951). The consultant attended the meetings of various groups, workers, management and the two together, over a number of months. His function was not to be part of the process itself but to draw attention to issues in the process of which neither side was fully aware and which were leading to antagonism and stalemate. The outcome of this very successful work was not only that the new wage system was introduced, with satisfaction all round, but also, as a by-product of fully working through the wages problem and all its ramifications, a new shop council was set up that would allow its members fuller involvement in setting policy in future.

Isabel Menzies Lyth, a psychoanalyst working for the TIHR, was commissioned by a London teaching hospital to help devise new methods of carrying out tasks in nursing organization. The resulting report (1959) described nursing practices that were set into the structure of the organization of nursing. The practices Menzies Lyth described included the allocation of work in the form of tasks, for example taking the temperatures of all the patients in the ward, rather than looking after Mrs. Smith and Mrs. Jones, thus preventing individual nurses from becoming close to individual patients. The terrible phrase, "Nurse, get a bedpan for the gall bladder in bed 12," illustrates the kind of depersonalization that had been achieved in the hospital nursing profession.

Menzies Lyth noted the ways the organizational culture encouraged detachment and the denial of feelings, and the attempt to eliminate individual decision making through the use of rules, checks and counter-checks. Menzies Lyth's hypothesis was that these defensive strategies had evolved to protect nurses against the intolerable anxiety that would otherwise be generated as a result of the extreme physical and psychological intimacy inherent in their work. She thought the system was aiding nurses in avoiding awareness of both their patients' intense feelings and their own, to the detriment of their ability to give sensitive nursing care.

Using a psychoanalytic understanding of unconscious processes in the nursing profession continued throughout the century through the work of Julia Fabricius and others. For example, Fabricius has undertaken consultative work both with student nurses (Fabricius, 1991) and with nurse tutors (Fabricius, 1995) and published several papers commenting on the unconscious factors involved in nursing and its organization. She notes that the very junior nurses involved were usually open and sensitive to the emotional issues. They had not yet built up such defenses personally, although these clearly existed in the staff culture of the ward. This pushed the juniors toward either acquiring the institutional defense or feeling near-intolerable anxiety. She postulates that it is thus that institutional defenses are perpetuated and thus also that many of the more sensitive potential professionals are lost from the caring professions through stress and burnout.

## Psychoanalytic group therapy

The use of groups analytically is the second stream to have arisen from the Northfields experiments. Three key names are those of Wilfred Bion, S. H. Foulkes and Tom Main, each of whom contributed a particular perspective to the analytic study of groups. In group analytic psycho-therapy, the principles of individual psychoanalysis are adapted by setting up a neutral, regular, time-boundaried space for a group, which remains largely consistent in its membership. As with individual analytic therapy, unstructured discussion is allowed to arise, rather than a prior agenda being set. The therapist, who may be known as a "conductor" or a "group analyst" has a partici-pant observer role as in individual work, helping the group to find out about what is happening in the room, particularly what may be hidden or unspoken.

Bion (1961) writes about the way the group as a whole functions in relation to itself and to its leader. He describes "basic assumptions," unconscious defenses the group as a whole adopts against anxiety, as opposed to a state of creative group functioning, the "work group."

Foulkes and Anthony (1973) orient themselves more toward the complex matrix of transfer-ences between members and toward the conductor. The group work styles arising from the work of these two thinkers is rather different, although today's analytic groups often incorporate both perspectives.

The third key figure, Tom Main (1989), applied psychoanalytic thinking to therapeutic com-munity treatment, where individuals are helped to learn about themselves and their relationships within a residential community. Main worked at the Cassel Hospital in Richmond, Surrey, an NHS therapeutic milieu for adults, families and adolescents where a key feature of inpatient work is the attention given to the relationship between the staff. Disagreements and differences in perspective between workers are analyzed and worked with for the light they shed on psychic divisions within and between patients.

Other treatment centers run along therapeutic community lines were Peper Harow for very disturbed adolescents; the Cotswold Community for severely disturbed children; and the Henderson Hospital, an NHS provision for disturbed adults. Sadly, by the end of the century all were under severe threat of closure, and only the Cassel Hospital has survived at the time of writing.

## Further developments in psychoanalysis

In 1948 the National Health Service came into being and the Tavistock Clinic developed as a center of excellence within the NHS. Jock Sutherland was chairman from the 1940s until the late 1960s and under his leadership the "Tavi" (as it is often referred to) grew mightily. Many dif-ferent departments with differing underlying approaches flourished. The Child Psychotherapy training (see chapter 3) developed initially under John Bowlby's influence and subsequently developed along Kleinian analytic lines. The Tavistock Clinic became a treatment center for children, adolescents and adults offering individual, couple and group psychotherapy. Its sister organization the Portman Clinic developed as an internationally respected psychoanalytically oriented forensic treatment center. Much research and theory building has arisen from the work of the Portman Clinic, and senior staff undertake consultation work with forensic departments in hospitals, prisons and secure units. Like the Tavistock Clinic, the Portman offers treatment on the NHS, so is free of charge for those needing it.

One of the most obvious areas of tension between the attitude of pure psychoanalysts and those interested in applying psychoanalytic ideas to the wider population was in the area of brief, short and medium-term psychotherapy. There were several eminent psychoanalysts who expounded the virtues of brief work, and perhaps Winnicott and Michael Balint are the most well known. While Winnicott didn't formulate a model of brief psychotherapy, he clearly used it himself. Balint, however, working in the 1950s at the Tavistock Clinic gathered a group of psy-choanalytic colleagues together to study the possibilities of brief therapy based on psychoanalytic understanding. Through their work they recommended that brief work was suitable for those patients who presented with conflicts at the Oedipal level. The more amorphous problems of those with early disturbance were less likely to benefit from brief work. Thus the assessment period was deemed to be crucial and was carefully carried out with the workshop of colleagues providing the clinical discussion for the therapist. It was found that so long as the patients were carefully selected and the length of the treatment was explicitly stated at the beginning of the treatment, then profound and deep work in the transference was possible. It was Balint's pupil David Malan whose work and writing on the subject contributed to an acceptance of a theory and technique of short-term therapy. He also introduced the notion of thorough outcome research to the field of psychoanalysis.

During the middle years of the century the British Psychoanalytical Society was concerned with gaining greater understanding of the mind, and I think in general became inward turning. For this reason perhaps, it is held in high regard within the psychoanalytic community but was again in danger of isolation as it had been in Jones's time. Those who were struggling with bringing together internal and external worlds were sometimes marginalized within the Society. However the pressure to compete in service provision with short term therapeutic models became paramount. Cognitive behavior therapy (CBT) appeared to be able to provide evidence that outcomes of short-term CBT were as good as any long-term psychoanalysis. The "quick fix" appealed to funding bodies whose administrators were interested in the bottom line and not in profound and long-term changes in the internal world.

There were a few brave analysts, however, who worked in the latter part of the century to challenge these claims. Peter Hobson, Anthony Bateman and Peter Fonagy, among others, have made major contributions. The treatment method called mentalization-based treatment (MBT), based on attachment theory derived from the work of John Bowlby, has become accepted as a treatment of choice at many NHS personality disorder units in psychiatric hospitals (Milton et al., 2011).

Humanity's destructiveness has always been a focus of psychoanalytic study. Klein made a strong contribution by placing innate conflict between love and hate at the center of human development. Psychoanalysis is well placed to contribute to the understanding of war, racial hatred and genocide, and perhaps it is surprising that psychoanalysts have not had a stronger voice on these matters outside the consulting room.

Hanna Segal (1987, 1995) elaborated the dangerous psychotic processes that manifest themselves in human groups. In her study of the nuclear threat, she makes a distinction between a state of mind in which one is waging war in order to save or protect something one values as good, and an omnipotently destructive state of mind linked to the sort of obliterating war in which nothing can survive. Segal and others played a part in the nuclear disarmament movement.

## Future developments

### Psychoanalysis in the academy

Unlike in many other countries, psychoanalytic training in Britain has not been linked with universities. Within the Institute the training, while involving theoretical teaching to a high standard, is viewed essentially as clinical training.

*Psychoanalytic studies* as an academic discipline grew up in the 1980s and 1990s but is usually based on Lacanian analysis. In 1991 Michael Rustin (1991) addressed this fact. He thought there was a certain reaction to our clinical and empiricist tradition and that advocates of psychoanalysis in the cultural and academic sphere turned to a mode of thinking as far away from empiricism as possible, that is, to the ideas of Lacan. This meant that what Rustin sees as the distinctive strength of British clinical psychoanalysis, its groundedness in the careful observation of emotional experience within relationships, was relatively neglected by academics. This difference in approach between the teaching of psychoanalysis in the academy and that in the British Psychoanalytical Society has meant that they tended to diverge in the 20th century rather than work creatively and interactively together.

Depending on the background and history of the particular department and the staff within them, different psychoanalytic studies curricula have different emphases. Some give grounding in clinical theory and then foreground a psychoanalytic approach to contemporary cultural phenomena such as literature, film, feminist and political theories. Others have a greater overall emphasis on clinical practice and offer clinically oriented MAs.

This is a rapidly expanding area in the beginning toward the end of the 20th century and emerging further in the first part of the 21st century. It is a close relative of *psychosocial studies* but is distinguished by an emphasis on the interaction between the social and the psychological; indeed psychology itself can be studied as a social construct. The internal and the external worlds and their interaction together are the focus of inquiry. Interdisciplinary investigation lies at the heart of this discipline and psychoanalysis is a key player.

It is interesting to trace some of the contributing factors to the growth of interest in this subject. Sociology departments that flourished in the late 1960s and 1970s became less able to attract students whose interests had shifted away from societal phenomena such as studies of class, status and power and toward interest in the experience and subjective meanings of societal phenomena. Candida Yates (2001) postulates the influence of a therapeutic culture upon the academy; it involved a cultural shift in the way we relate to institutions and relate to authority. In particular, the "new" universities brought in a new kind of student eager to understand his or her own experiences bringing fresh challenges to the psychologists and sociologists working there. At the turn of the century, topics appearing in prospectuses include those as far-ranging as post-structuralism, critical theory, psychoanalysis, systems theory, feminism, humanism, emotion, therapy, memory, risk, sexuality, human rights, suicide, body modification, ethical consumption, identity, race, narrative studies and socio-biography.

## Conclusion

I hope to have shown something of the complex, nonlinear development of psychoanalytic practice and ideas in Britain over the course of the 20th century. It is inevitably a selective account. What I have described as a tension between pure and applied runs through this account as a theme. While the British Psychoanalytical Society sought to refine psychoanalytic theory and technique, many psychoanalytic ideas and applied practices were being developed outside that organization, sometimes by psychoanalysts themselves and sometimes by others.

By the end of the century the British Psychoanalytical Society had begun to respond to criticisms of isolationism and elitism and embarked on a program of joint conferences and applied scientific meetings in which psychoanalysis and other disciplines looked together at issues of joint interest and importance. The 21st century has already seen a growth in this cooperative and creative activity and a far greater degree of openness. However, the 21st century has also seen changes in the economic and political climate. The NHS is responding to budget cuts and to the government's direction to turn hospitals into competing financial concerns – an internal market economy. Psychoanalysts can either respond to this situation with creative proposals backed by research validation or will gradually be replaced altogether within state health service provision.

## Notes

1 I am deeply indebted to Jane Milton and Julia Fabricius for their help in preparing this chapter and in allowing me to use some material from our joint publication, *A Short Introduction to Psychoanalysis* (2011).
2 "The Freudian Century?" was the title of a conference mounted in 2003 by members of the BPAS led by Professor Daniel Pick. The conference brought together psychoanalysts and those from a wide range of disciplines to explore whether or not Freud's views had influenced their discipline in the 20th century.
3 The BPAS and the Institute merged on January 1, 2015.

## References

Anderson, P 1968, 'Components in the national culture' *New Left Review*, vol. 50, July/August, pp. 3–57.
Auden, WH 1940, *Another time*, Random House, New York.
Bion, W 1961, *Experiences in groups*, Tavistock, London.
Bion, W 1962, *Learning from experience*, Heinemann, London (Reprinted Karnac Books 1984, London).
Brenman Pick, I 1965, 'Working through in the counter-transference', *International Journal of Psychoanalysis*, vol. 66, pp. 157–166.
Fabricius, J 1991, 'Learning to work with feelings: Psychodynamic understanding and small group work with junior student nurses', *Nurse Education Today*, vol. 11, pp. 134–142.
Fabricius, J 1995, Psychoanalytic understanding and nursing: a supervisory workshop with nurse tutors, *Psychoanalytic Psychotherapy*, vol. 9, no. 1, pp. 17–29.
Foulkes, S & Anthony, EJ 1973, *Group psychotherapy: The psychoanalytic approach*, Harmondsworth, Penguin.
Freud, A 1937, *The ego and the mechanisms of defence: The international psycho-analytical library*, Hogarth, London.
Freud, S 1900, 'The interpretation of dreams', in J Strachey (ed), *Standard edition of the complete psychological works of Sigmund Freud*, vols. 4–5, Hogarth, London.
Freud, S 1909, 'Notes on a case of obsessional neurosis', in J Strachey (ed), *Standard edition of the complete psychological works of Sigmund Freud*, vol. 10, Hogarth, London.
Freud, S 1926, 'The question of lay analysis', in J Strachey (ed), *Standard edition of the complete psychological works of Sigmund Freud*, vol. 20, Hogarth, London.
Freud, S 1938, 'Constructions in analysis', *International Journal of Psychoanalysis*, vol. 19, pp. 377–387.
Heimann, P 1950, 'On counter-transference', *International Journal of Psychoanalysis*, vol. 31, pp. 81–84.
Heimann, P 1960, 'Counter-transference', *British Journal of Medical Psychology*, vol. 33, pp. 9–15.
Jaques, E 1951, 'Working through industrial conflict: The service department at the Glacier Metal Company', in E Trist & H Murray (eds), *The ailment and other psychoanalytic essays*, Free Associations, London.
Jones E 1910, 'The Oedipus complex as an explanation of Hamlet's mystery: A study in motive', *American Journal of Psychology*, vol. 21, pp. 72–113.
Jones, E 1913, 'The influence of Andrea del Sarto's wife on his art', in E Jones (ed), 1974, *Psycho-myth, psycho-history. Vol. 1: Essays in applied psychoanalysis*, American Edition, Hillstone, New York, pp. 22–38.
Jones, E 1931, 'The problem of Paul Morphy: A contribution to the psychoanalysis of chess', *International Journal of Psychoanalysis*, vol. 12, pp. 1–23.
Joseph, B 1985, 'Transference: The total situation', *International Journal of Psychoanalysis*, vol. 66, pp. 447–454.
King, P & Steiner, R 1991, *The Freud-Klein controversies 1941–45*, Routledge, London.
Klein, M 1946, 'Notes on some schizoid mechanisms', in *Envy and gratitude and other works 1946–1957*, Hogarth Press and the Institute of Psychoanalysis, London (published 1975).
Klein, M 1952, 'The origins of transference', *International Journal of Psychoanalysis*, vol. 33, pp. 433–438.
Lawrence, DH 2004 [1921/1922], 'Psychanalysis and the unconscious', in Bruce Steele (ed), *Psychoanalysis and the unconscious* and *Fantasia of the unconscious*, Cambridge University Press, Cambridge, pp. 1–44.
Main, T 1989, *The ailment and other psychoanalytic essays*, Free Associations, London.
Menzies Lyth, I 1960, 'The functioning of social systems as a defence against anxiety: A report on the study of a nursing service of a general hospital', *Human Relations*, vol. 13, pp. 95–121.
Milton, J, Polmear, C & Fabricius, J 2011, *A Short Introduction to Psychoanalysis* (2nd ed), Sage, London.
Pick, D 2003, Article in *The Guardian*, August 16.
Polmear, C 2008, 'An independent response to *Envy and Gratitude*', in P Roth & A Lemma (eds), *Envy and gratitude revisited*, International Psychoanalytical Association, London, pp. 63–78.
Rayner, E 1990, *The independent mind in British psychoanalysis*, Free Association Books, London.
Rayner, E 1991, *The independent mind in British psychoanalysis*, Jason Aronson, London.

Rustin, M 1991, *The good society and the inner world*, Verso, London.

Sandler, J 1976, 'Counter transference and role-responsiveness', *International Review of Psycho-analysis*, vol. 3, pp. 43–47.

Sandler, J 1983, 'Reflections on some relations between psychoanalytic concepts and psychoanalytic practice', *International Journal of Psychoanalysis*, vol. 64, pp. 35–45.

Segal, H 1987, 'Silence is the real crime', *International Review of Psycho-analysis*, vol. 14, pp. 3–12.

Segal, H 1995, 'From Hiroshima to the Gulf War and after: A psychoanalytic perspective', in A Elliot & S Frosh (eds), *Psychoanalysis in context*, Routledge, London, pp. 191–204.

Spillius, E (ed) 1988, *Melanie Klein today. Vol. 2: Mainly practice*, Routledge, London.

Strachey, J 1934, 'The nature of the therapeutic action of psychoanalysis', *International Journal of Psychoanalysis*, vol. 15, pp. 127–159.

Trist E, Higgin G, Murray H & Pollock, A 1963, 'The assumption of ordinariness as a denial mechanism: Innovation and conflict in a coal mine', in E Trist & H Murray (eds), *The social engagement of social science. Vol. 1: The social-psychological perspective*, Free Association, London.

Winnicott, DW 1960a, 'The theory of the parent-infant relationship', *International Journal of Psychoanalysis*, vol. 41, pp. 585–595.

Winnicott, DW 1960b, 'Ego distortion in terms of the true and the false self', in C Winnicott (ed), 1965, *The maturational process and the facilitating environment*, Hogarth, London, pp. 140–152.

Winnicott, DW 1964, 1987, *The child the family and the outside world*, Penguin Books, US, Addison-Wesley, London.

Winnicott, C, Shepherd, R & Davis, M 1984, *DW Winnicott: Deprivation and delinquency*, Tavistock, London.

Yates, C 2001, 'Teaching psychoanalytic studies: Towards a new culture of learning in higher education', *Psychoanalytic Studies*, vol. 3, pp. 333–347.

## Part II

# Psychoanalysis in the social sciences and humanities

# 14

# History and psychoanalysis

*Michael Roth*

This chapter will explore the connections between psychoanalysis and history beginning with Freud's work, and then consider the impact of psychoanalysis on the approaches to the past taken by historians in more recent years.

## Freud: at the individual level

Psychoanalysis is best read, I have argued, as a theory of history.[1] This means that its central concepts are ones that aim to make sense of the past – or, as I have often put it, to construct a past with which one can live. Psychoanalysis emerged out of hypnosis, which was a technology for changing a patient's past. Hypnotic suggestion, especially as practiced by Charcot, Bernheim and their followers, was a technique to either erase the past or alter it so that it no longer haunted the present. Freud himself was a poor hypnotist, and his limited success with this technique led him to historical consciousness; it led him to try to make meaning out of a painful past rather than to erase that past. Following the case of Emmy v. N (Fanny Moser), I have described this as Freud's "falling into history" (Roth, 2001).

In his early work (writings that precede, roughly, *The Interpretation of Dreams*, 1900) Freud strove to remove the memory's potency, not through forgetting like Pierre Janet but through the discharge of energy that came through a particular form of recollection. Freud came to develop psychoanalysis as a mode of interpretation that would create a past with which one could live. Psychoanalysis emerged out of mourning, out of the work that enables a person to detach him or herself from the past even while retaining some (narrative) connection to it (Roth, 1995). The talking cure demands that one situate oneself (or one's desires) in relation to the past, not that one reconstructs the actual past in the present. Freud developed a hermeneutics of memory rather than a tool for some unmediated expression of the past (whatever that might be) that would pretend to get free of it. That is, Freud developed psychoanalysis as a way of using the past rather than revolting against it.

The significance of this turn to historical consciousness for psychoanalysis is well known, if still controversial. By falling in with the patient's stories, the analyst becomes part of a relationship, a component in a process in which he or she has only limited (albeit important) control. Freud certainly recognized the phenomenon that so impressed Pierre and Jules Janet: patients make an enormous, sometimes bottomless, investment in the relationship with the doctor; they reproduce their illnesses in this relationship. But whereas this phenomenon contributed to therapeutic pessimism about the capacities of the hysteric to lead a normal life, it also became a therapeutic opportunity for the psychoanalyst. That is, the "need for suggestion" and the "perpetual imitation" evinced by patients within the therapeutic process was an exposure of the history of the illness, a revelation of the etiology of its symptoms, if only the analyst were prepared to read it properly. Freud would later understand this exposure through the concept of transference, and the psychoanalytic investigation of the therapeutic relationship itself as a tool for theory and treatment became one of the defining elements of this new approach to the mind and to mental illness.

The concept of the transference also describes the power of the analyst in treatment – the power that the analyst can have to dictate the meaning of the past. This empowerment is a function of the unconsciously repetitive elements of the transference itself. How to use this power without sinking the patients further into the dynamic that was itself at the root of their problems? One can't order the patient to stop being dependent. How to use one's authority to expose one's authority as neurotic? Since Freud's time, psychiatrists and therapists have tried to escape these questions in two very general ways: (1) by denying they really have authority; and (2) by denying that the basis of their authority is neurotic.

Those who favor the first option often underline the *relational* aspects of the psychotherapeutic situation (as if these were not always present in Freud's work), apparently with the happy thought that by telling clients they are in an equal relationship they suddenly acquire equality. The power of suggestion obviously remains strong. The second option assumes that the legitimacy of the therapeutic practice (whether analytic, psychopharmacological, or both) somehow naturalizes and neutralizes the dependence that the client comes to have on the doctor (after all, so this reasoning goes, patients *should* be dependent!). This was the route Janet himself took when he defined the kind of happiness needed by the hysteric and attempted to provide that kind of happiness. Since the dependence is on a reasonable person – a source of reason and progress – it is suddenly no longer supposed to be a symptom. In the tradition in which Janet worked (and that psychoanalysis opposes), analysts can't use their power to create a new history for their patients.

The route taken by Janet has been well traveled by contemporary psychiatry, in which dependence on the authority of the scientific physician is routinely taken for granted. The acceptance of the authority of the doctor goes hand in hand with an indifference to the meaning of the patient's history. Peter Kramer's case of "Lucy" represents a post-Freudian (and post-historical) approach to the self and its pathologies (Kramer, 1994).[2] Lucy is a college student who finds herself taking too many risks in seeking men primed to hurt her. Once in a relationship, Kramer tells us, she invents countless ways to feel rejected. For example, she tests her boyfriend's affections in ways that are bound to show that he is about to leave her. The psychiatrist reveals that Lucy's youth was marked by tragedy and trauma: her mother was murdered by a trusted member of the household, and her subsequent relation to her father was marked by persistent, complex difficulties. But Kramer's treatment protocol ignores this history, and he charts a course of treatment for Lucy that treats her present symptoms at what he calls their "face value." For him this means treating the symptoms not in relation to a history that she might still carry in the present, but as discrete products of an "autonomous syndrome." Kramer is well aware that one could weave together a narrative that would connect Lucy's trauma to what he comes to regard as her "oversensitivity." But he believes that his patient's symptoms, although they may indeed have initially been triggered by early events, now have causes that must be dealt with in the present. "If Lucy can be spared the pain that rejection causes her," he writes, "she will not need to behave in a dependent or self-injurious way." Medication can spare her the pain. In this case "the examination of history, even so evocative a history as Lucy's will be superfluous" (Kramer, 1994, p. 70).

Kramer's discussion of the treatment that renders the examination of history superfluous draws on the psychiatrist Donald Klein's notion of "functional autonomy" (Klein, 1987).[3] Klein introduced this idea to describe how a symptom becomes unmoored from its original cause. A trauma might give rise to what is in that original situation an adaptive response (such as panic or anxiety), but this response persists (now as a symptom) long after that trauma. The original cause (the trauma) is no longer "relevant" to the symptom, which persists as a neurochemical holdover originally called for in specific conditions (like the presence of danger or confrontation with loss). Rather than delving into a person's history to discover the patient's original trauma or subsequent feelings about it, the physician can, through medication, alter the current neuro-chemical context that is provoking the symptom. For example, by chemically raising the thresh-old at which anxiety occurs, the physician can control (or even eliminate) the symptom. This is not, Klein emphasizes, to treat *merely* the symptom. It is to treat the cause that is now producing the symptom *in the present* (Wender & Klein, 1981).[4]

In Kramer's account of Lucy, medication could raise her threshold of responsiveness toward oth-ers (making her "less sensitive"), even as it may have made some of her own feelings more available to her. This leads him to consider that the "set point for sensitivity should be biologically regulated" (Kramer, 1994, p. 96). He does not say by whom, or according to which criteria. How does the doctor (or is it now the insurance company?) determine what is proper or appropriate sensitivity? In making the patient less sensitive, what else is the doctor eliminating from the patient's history, from the patient's life? To his credit, these are not questions Kramer ignores, but they are ones he is willing to bracket in the service of alleviating symptoms causing suffering in the present.

We can see the trajectory from the Janets' hypnotic treatments of pathogenic memories to psychopharmacology today. For them, it was crucial to reduce the potency of the past; if this could be done by providing the patient with an alternate past, so be it. The doctor provided new memories for the patient, a benign past that would not give rise to painful symptoms. In Kramer's treatment of Lucy, medication renders the past, even one with dramatic trauma, superfluous. Lucy's present symptoms are not seen as dependent (any longer) on her history. They have con-temporary neurochemical causes that can be treated with medication. The Janets and Kramer are intent on removing symptoms, on bringing the patient back to normality. The former thought they could do this through hypnotic suggestion that allowed them to give their patients a benign past. Kramer thinks he can bring his patients back into the normal by chemically adjusting things like their "set point for sensitivity." By helping patients into the normal, the doctors want to make it possible for their charges to live more fully in the present – whatever their histories.

In these paradigms of medical intervention, transference, like history, is irrelevant. The author-ity of the doctor is assumed; his or her ability to know the normal and to know what is "super-fluous" is taken for granted. The doctor has both feet planted firmly in the world of science, rationality, normality. How different this medical paradigm is from the transference model of interaction that we can see emerging in Freud's clinical work! The domain demarcated by the transference is tricky ground on which to stand because it is always in danger of shifting under one's feet. As critics of psychotherapy regularly remind us, there is no firm (epistemologically clean) place to stand in this domain. The analysand makes multiple investments in the possibili-ties for insight through the analytic relationship, and doing so is part of the conflicted history that leads the person to desire change; yet doing so is also part of that history that in the present makes any change extremely difficult. The conflicted history of the person *is* the present, and any change that can occur must occur *through* that history. The French hypnosis practitioners and theorists of *amnesics* from whom Freud departed were developing techniques that would remove the troublesome parts of the patient's history, or that would transform the reminiscences causing suffering in the present. They wanted to act on the person's contaminated past *from outside that past*, thereby protecting their intervention (and themselves) from contamination. The same is very much the case of psychopharmacology today. By contrast, for Freud, there was no longer an intervention possible from a point outside it.

Of course, the transference itself can be abused, and there are plenty of examples of the analyst mistreating patients all the while blaming the patients for their desires. The term *countertransference* is used to describe the analyst's projection back onto the patient, and it is a concept that has been used to cover many sins. Freud infamously fell into some of this behavior himself, and my descriptions of how the Freudian model of self-consciousness through understanding the history comes alive in transference might be said to be an aspirational model or an ideal type. Freud himself didn't consistently follow it, as we know from several biographers. Since I cast Kramer's treatment of Lucy in a critical light, perhaps it is best to cite his critical and thoughtful account of Freud's abusive treatment of some patients, and his use of the transference concept to explain away that abuse, especially in the Dora case (Kramer, 2006, pp. 98–100).[5]

Be that as it may, Freud's fall into history has been suggestive, if I can use that word, for theorists of history trying to understand the stories that are left to us from the past. Since the professionalization of history writing in the mid-19th century, there has been an effort to ensure that historians stand outside of – or at a distance from – the events that they are attempting to explain or interpret (Phillips, 2011).[6] The standpoint of objectivity was to ensure that the authority of the historian was derived from established scientific criteria in the present, not from some personal, biased connection to the material from the past being described.

Recent theorists of history have called into question the picture of the neutral, disconnected historian relating past events from the outside. The point of this questioning is not that all interpretations of the past are equally valid, but that it is important to interpret the complex ways historians establish connections between their own present and the past they are bringing to it. Some of these connections can, as Dominick LaCapra has stressed, be usefully described as transferential since they facilitate the unconscious repetition of past patterns in the present. Historians re-present the past, and often in doing so also act out their unconscious or hidden investments in the objects of their research, which are often objects of complex longing and loathing. An acknowledgment of the transferential relations between historians and the pasts we construct enables us to attend to the processes of mediation and unconscious repetition that contribute to any historical representation (LaCapra, 2004; Loewenberg, 1996).[7]

By listening to his patients' stories rather than writing the scripts of their pasts, Freud was beginning to develop psychoanalysis as a form of historical consciousness that focused on the role of desire vis-à-vis the past. How does our relationship to a remembered past, or to the past that we imagine is inaccessible to us, serve particular desires in the present? And how does serving *those* desires make it impossible to serve others? These are questions that would become crucial to the domain of psychoanalysis as a theoretical and clinical enterprise. I have argued that they are also central to the construction of history as a theoretical and practical enterprise. Historical representations attempt to satisfy or stimulate certain desires, and it is usually impossible for them to do so without denying others. The retreat from the transferential, attempts to have uncontroversial museum exhibits, cool detached histories, or neat little positive therapeutic experiences are merely denials of, not solutions to, the problem. One can hope to make the workings of transference in historical representation more apparent, but one cannot avoid this dynamic through some properly hygienic stance toward the past.

How does the remembered or imagined past draw one to it? How does the traumatic past compel our attention, care, or obsession even as it seems to demand acknowledgment that one can never comprehend what happened there? These questions are as important for psychoanalysts as they are for historians. The models of hypnosis and of psychopharmacology point in a different direction. They are alien to modern historical discourse and to psychoanalysis because they are unconcerned with the investment that one has in the past. Contemporary technologies of forgetting have no conceptual space for the desire that one has for the past, a desire that results in an effort to link present and past through narrative. This is Freud's space.

## Freud: at the group level

From the second decade of the 20th century until his death in 1938, Freud increasingly turned his attention to society, its origins, development and crises. He theorized that our societies have created mechanisms – analogous to psychological mechanisms that inhibit our basic desires – to ensure forms of social regulation and repression. At the root of organized human life in common is the prohibition against incest, and Freud speculates that this taboo had its genesis in the guilt stemming from the murder of a powerful patriarch. After the tyrannical father is killed, the sons continue to follow his dictates. Guilt, competition and fear ensure obedience even when the father is not there to enforce his laws. In the psychoanalytic model, violent revolution does not resolve conflict; it just displaces it onto different levels (Freud, 1976a).

The archaic for Freud is not something one outgrows at either the individual or social level but something that remains a vital, and often disruptive, part of existence at any level of development. The emphasis on the archaic as active, on a history that is alive in us, is as important in the psychoanalytic approach to social life as it was in its approach to the individual. Freud's notion of an essential conflict at the core of culture informed all his writing about society, and it was the basis of his general pessimism about the negative effects of powerful, unsatisfied desires. If religion, art and science fail to alleviate the conflicts at the heart of the human condition, then what are the consequences of this failure? If our forms of social life fail to meet our basic psychological needs, then what happens to the unfulfilled desires within society?

Near the very end of his life, Freud returned to the figure of Moses to work through some of these questions. *Moses and Monotheism* was one of Freud's highly speculative works at the intersection of psychoanalysis and history. In it he offered an argument about the origins of religion (in delusion and desire), the identity of Moses (he was really an Egyptian) and the historical destiny of the Jews (how they lived with the trauma of oppression). Some complained that the psychoanalyst was depriving the Jews of images of leadership and consolation when they needed them the most. Although he had started the research years before, Freud released the work in 1938, just when a pogrom of unimaginable horror was getting underway.

Struggling against painful cancer of the jaw, and working within the tightening noose of Nazi oppression, Freud soldiered on to complete his final anti-clerical work. *Moses and Monotheism* remained in the Enlightenment tradition, painting religion as a collective neurosis, a delusion shot through with fantasy, guilt and repression. Freud – in Peter Gay's phrase "the incurable secularist" (Gay, 1988, p. 643) – concluded that Moses was in fact an Egyptian who had been mythologized as a Jew by Hebrew legend. The "man Moses" gave the Jews a stern variation of Egyptian monotheism, and he was probably murdered by his rebellious followers. Freud saw the Jews' embrace of monotheism in a Mosaic (and Egyptian) form as their guilt-filled reaction to the legacy of murder and trauma. The Christian version of communion was a more sentimental repetition of this same process. Moses did bequeath to the Jews a sense of their own chosenness. He, an Egyptian prince, had chosen to lead them, and the one and only God had chosen them as his people. But the burdens of being chosen were great, and the Jews at some point rebelled against them. Following the logic of groups he had previously set forth in *Totem and Taboo*, Freud speculated that guilt following the murder of the leader led to a fervent post-rebellion embrace of the leader's rules, in this case Mosaic monotheism. This was an abstract religion, best symbolized by the prohibition against images of the deity. An "exalted sense of being a chosen people" was linked to tendencies toward intellectual abstraction and a memory of being persecuted by groups that did not appreciate the Mosaic gift of superiority. These traumatic memories reinforced group identity, including an enhanced self-regard. Freud attempted to work through the conflicts between Jewish submission to authority (and suffering) and Jewish self-esteem.

Mark Edmundson has recently argued that the project of *Moses and Monotheism* was less an attack on the Jews than a challenge to what was taking place in Germany: Freud deconstructed the desire for strong leadership and the group erotics of submission – themes all too relevant to Jewish life in the late 1930s (Edmundson, 2007). The Freudian purpose in analyzing desires is to provide new understandings of them that may free us from their unconscious, compulsive dimensions. By rewriting Jewish history, Freud was offering his people the gift of increased freedom through self-awareness.

In *Moses and Monotheism* Freud was returning to group dynamics, a subject that had stimulated his interest for decades. So much of our behavior in groups – be they religious, political or social – is dictated by an urge to escape conflict or uncertainty.

Psychoanalysis teaches that we are ambivalent creatures, that our desires will always be in tension with one another, and that rather than try to resolve those tensions (in faith, in submission to authority) we must learn to manage them. Instead of trying to erase or master conflicts through violence or submission, we must learn to accept that we are imperfect creatures whose needs cannot be fully satisfied. In his study of Moses, Freud was offering a modest yet bold therapeutic intervention for his own time, a deconstruction of patriarchal authority in the ancient past that was again vitally relevant. "To Freud," Edmundson explains, "the present is fundamentally a repetition of what has come before: in fact there is, strictly speaking, no pure present, no 'now' in the thought of Sigmund Freud" (Edmundson, 2007, p. 147). Like Hegel's sense of a present that dialectically contains within it the layers of the past, Freud's present is saturated with repetition. Psychoanalysis provides a "history of the present," a language for understanding our desires as they emerge and for providing us with a past with which we can live.

When Freud undertook the therapeutic intervention of *Moses and Monotheism*, he was near the end of his life, and Europe was on the verge of a cataclysmic war. He offered in this context not advice on how to live but a mode of thinking that might allow us to find, in Edmundson's nice phrase, "words where before there has been only silence and compulsion" (Edmundson, 2007, p. 210). Finding these words meant discovering the desires that make it possible for people or ideas to control us. Finding these words was both a historical and psychoanalytic contribution. They are not "magic words," not keys that master suffering because they get the past exactly right. But they are the vehicles through which we create understanding and shared narratives, constructing a past.

Freud's thinking emerged in the wake of Marx and Darwin, both of whom emphasized struggle as the engine of change. Freud's thought developed in a century in which violent conflicts reached unheard-of dimensions. The conflicts that Freud stressed were within the psyche: people at war with themselves and sometimes with the cultural authorities they had internalized. But he thought that the way we managed (or failed to manage) those conflicts had everything to do with the explosions of violence that marked the modern world. Although much has changed since Freud first formulated his theories, today's concern with the disruptive power of sexuality and aggression has only intensified. Freud did not propose solutions to how one might escape this violence.

Instead, his writings on the connection of culture and conflict identified fundamental problems for the 20th century – problems that show no sign of disappearing in the 21st century.

## Psychoanalysis and the historians

Historians tended to ignore psychoanalysis in the first half of the 20th century, though in his presidential address of 1957 William Langer (whose brother was an analyst) called on his colleagues in the American Historical Association to add it to their toolbox (Langer, 1958).[8] Langer's appeal had little effect on practicing historians, though in the 1950s seminal works in philosophy or critical theory were published that linked the two fields. The first was Frantz Fanon's *Black Skin, White Masks*, first published in French in 1952. Fanon used psychoanalytic categories to diagnosis the persistence of racism, exposing the dynamics of identification that often leads the colonized black subject to imitate the norms of white oppressors. The next two were Herbert Marcuse's *Eros and Civilization* (1955) and his friend Norman O. Brown's *Life Against Death*, first published in 1959. All three books broke away from the American psychoanalytic community's accomodationist view of Freud as a thinker who could help one fit into the mainstream, and imagined him instead as a thinker whose insights into the unconscious could be wed to radical politics. These texts set the stage for a more general effort to link depth psychology with "depth political theory and praxis" in the 1960s. The New Left's and feminism's efforts to link the personal with the political in that turbulent decade would sow the seeds for more extensive use of psychoanalysis among historians in the 1970s.

Fanon showed how alienation and racism were intertwined in the psychopathologies generated by colonialism. Although clearly using psychoanalytic concepts and perspectives, Fanon was also influenced by existentialism and Marxism. Marcuse historicized Freud's theories of the instincts so as to conceptualize a society in which "surplus repression" could be eliminated and Eros could find much fuller expression. *Eros and Civilization* (1955) was one of many attempts to bring Freud and Marx together – to think through how the psychic economy and the forces of capitalism worked together.[9] In the 1950s Brown found much to admire in Marcuse's project, though he himself was more inclined to consider the symbolic dimensions of history without grounding these in the relations of production. Brown's Freud uncovered the contradictions – bodily, psychic and spiritual – that drove us further into senseless labor, dangerous aggression, and painful dissatisfaction. *Life Against Death* (1959) was a call away from the thin gratifications of contemporary social life and toward the ecstatic possibilities that were opened up by acknowledging the force of our desires. Both thinkers argued that only by liberating the erotic from the grips of an economy of repression could we begin to reduce the risks of violent self-destruction.

Fanon was as much revolutionary as psychoanalyst, and he was an active participant in the Algerian struggle for independence. Marcuse was a philosopher and Brown a classicist, but both authors were read by a generation of historians in the United States who came of age in the 1960s. So was the psychoanalyst Erik Erikson, who came to the United States in 1933 and soon was making links between clinical practice and cultural anthropology. His *Childhood and Society* (1951) had forged a bridge between individual psychodynamics and powerful social forces, but it was Erikson's psychoanalytic biographies of Luther and Gandhi really got the attention of historians. In these powerful works written for a general audience, Erikson sought to understand key historical figures using psychoanalytic categories. Luther was seen as having gone through an intense identity crisis, which led to his great acts of defiance and rebellion. *Young Man Luther* was subtitled *A Study in Psychoanalysis and History*, and it was a bestseller in 1958. But many historians were put off by Erikson's anachronistic notion of rebellion (more late 1950s than 16th century), and by the author's speculative reductionism (Luther's rebellion stemmed from a father tyrannical about toilet training, among other things). In 1969 Erikson published *Gandhi's Truth: On the Origins of Militant Non-violence*. Once again the psychoanalyst found a moment in which his subject's identity emerged through crisis, but in this case a crisis of caring for a dying father – not just eliminating him. Erikson's exploration of Gandhi's path to satyagraha was meant as a strong reminder to radicals in America and Europe of how the practice of nonviolence could bring out the latent decency in those perceived as adversaries. The American historian Christopher Lasch began his *New York Times* review of the book as follows:

> *Gandhi's Truth*, even more brilliantly than its predecessor, *Young Man Luther*, shows that psychoanalytic theory, in the hands of an interpreter both resourceful and wise, can immeasurably enrich the study of "great lives" and of much else besides. With these books Erikson has single-handedly rescued psychoanalytic biography from neglect and disrepute.
>
> *(Lasch, 1969)*[10]

But disrepute would hover around psychobiography and other forms of psychohistory throughout the 1970s and 1980s. In France, the *histoire des mentalités* was achieving great success, but this had little to do with psychoanalysis. The attempt to articulate what was thinkable in a given epoch (or at least what was sayable) linked the Annales School's approach to collectivities with the work of Michel Foucault. Both were anti-Freudian (Manuel, 1971). Meanwhile, psychohistory in the United States seemed to many a crude application of Freud (or worse, neo-Freudian ego psychology) to selected batches of evidence from the past. The logic was often faulty, the research thin and the anachronisms heavy. These and other faults were pounced on by critics who saw in psychohistory just the latest attempt to impose contemporary theoretical assumptions onto the distant past.[11] But these deficiencies in psychohistory were also deficiencies in some historical studies more generally. As Thomas Kohut persuasively argued in a sympathetic assessment of the field in 1987, "psychohistory . . . has become a lightning rod, able to absorb some of the historical profession's uncertainty about itself" (Kohut, 1986, p. 337).[12]

Though psychohistory engendered fierce debates, the integration of some psychoanalytic concepts with historical research did gather momentum from the 1960s onward. In a recent brief essay, Peter Burke shows that historians in Europe and the United States – from Norbert Elias to Richard Hofstadter, from George Devereux to Lynn Hunt – were using psychoanalytic concepts in projects that became widely admired contributions to historical understanding. Carl E. Schorske, for example, although never considered a psychohistorian, used psychoanalytic concepts in his study of Vienna (and of Freud himself). Schorske was close to Brown and Marcuse – the three had first met in the Office of Strategic Services (OSS), and it was probably in that context that their mutual explorations of Freud began. Schorske had been a graduate student of William Langer's at Harvard, and Langer's brother Walter was a psychoanalyst who had trained under Anna Freud and accompanied the family into exile. Head of the OSS William Donovan asked Walter Langer to produce a psychological profile of Hitler in 1943.[13] Meanwhile, working in what Schorske recalls as the "morale unit" of the OSS, German émigrés and American intellectuals like himself were using psychoanalytic concepts to try to understand the social-psychological dynamics that made Nazism so attractive to so many Germans. After the war, many found standard historical interpretations inadequate because they neglected either the deep wounds of collective trauma or the vicissitudes of conflicting, hidden instincts.[14] They turned to Freud for new ways to understand the dynamics of desire and the eruption of violence.

Schorske has been intensely interested in Freud's changing relationship with the archaic in particular and with the past in general. In Freud's younger years, Schorske wrote, historical understanding was ascendant in his thinking, but as he developed psychoanalysis as a universal doctrine based on ahistorical notions of the structure of the psyche, Freud left history behind. "Clio was in eclipse in psychoanalysis," Schorske wrote, "but she had not vanished from Freud's mental life" (1981, p. 14). In his last major project Freud would depart from his antihistorical modernist psychologism in order to come to terms with the triumph of National Socialism. With *Moses and Monotheism,* Schorske wrote, "Freud not only resumed thinking with history, but became a historicist himself" (Schorske, 1981, p. 15). He did so under the pressure of events, giving the Jews a heroic, if fraught, role as the protectors of Geistigkeit, a term that combines spirituality and intellectuality:

> Thanks to their intellectual and ethical strength, the Jews as *Kulturvolk* (cultural people) par excellence would always be attacked whenever repressed instinct broke loose in civilized society; thanks to the same masculine virtues, they would have the power to endure in adversity.
>
> *(Schorske, 1999, p. 209)*

This "power to endure," according to Schorske, came at the cost of repressing Sinnlichkeit, the realm of the senses.

The experience of World War II and the confrontation with Nazism's particular mobilization of the archaic on behalf of violence and control was crucial for Schorske and his intellectual cohort in the 1950s. Could they reimagine a connection to the deep past that would be in the service of life, of music, of Eros? In the introduction to his *Vienna* book, and throughout *Thinking With History,* Schorske reminds his readers that this effort at "re-imagination" was undertaken "under the pressure of new, uncongenial turns in the world of politics" (Schorske, 1981, xxiv). The turn to the psychological was part of an effort to understand why the world of politics had turned out so wrong, and why the political dreams of deep-seated change had run aground so badly. Political disappointment in late 19th-century Vienna and in mid-20th-century America was Schorske's context of understanding the modernism's retreat from the historical. In writing about Vienna's past, he was also engaging with the decline of the public sphere in his own present.

Schorske's influential "Politics and Patricide in Freud's *Interpretation of Dreams*" was first published in 1973, and he had already given a version of it at the American Psychoanalytic Society meetings in 1971. The argument is that Freud abandoned politics and developed psychoanalysis as a counter-political mode of thinking because of his frustrations with the public sphere. Schorske develops an interpretation of one of Freud's own dreams to integrate the psychoanalyst into the Viennese political context. In the final sentence of the essay, he concludes: "Freud gave his fellow liberals an a-historical theory of man and society that could make bearable a political world spun out of orbit and beyond control." (Schorske, 1980, p. 203).

With his conclusion, Schorske reinscribed Freud's a historical theory into the warp and woof of temporal connection – historicizing his subject's anti-historicism. Peter Gay is another American intellectual historian who worked to integrate psychoanalysis into broader historical patterns, although he completely rejected Schorske's Vienna-centric approach. Peter Gay had already published an impressive body of work when he began to write more regularly on Freud in the 1980s. At the time he took what we might call a moderate position among those who were looking at history through a psychoanalytic lens, or at psychoanalysis through a historical lens. Among the former were some – mostly writers working within the traditions of critical theory and deconstruction – who saw Freud as a figure who continued the critique of reason and objectivity, the third of the "masters of suspicion" who, like Marx and Nietzsche before him, exposed the lies and self-serving fantasies of bourgeois culture. Among the latter were those – mostly writers of critical biographical studies or skeptical historians of science – who used historical research to debunk Freud's achievements, interpreting them as merely an expression of his own warped experiences, based on a manipulation of evidence and people. In contrast to both of these camps, Gay wanted to bring psychoanalytic concepts into historical work without attempting to put the past on the couch. "A reliance on psychoanalysis, after all, need not entail a naïve reductionist, monocausal theory of history" (Gay, 1985, p. x).[15] He wanted, that is, to pay attention to unconscious factors while using an approach that would be "heavily invested in reality" (1985, p. xi).[16] Borrowing a phrase from Freud's *Totem and Taboo*, Gay wrote: "the 'historical and psychological in one': this states my program with admirable economy" (1985, p. xvi).[17]

The "program" resulted in *Freud for Historians* (1985), which steered a course between those psychohistorians who thought Freud provided all the keys for unlocking the mysteries of the past and critics who rejected any theory of psychological "preconditions" as antihistorical. Gay deplored the reductionist tendencies of the first group and the know-nothing attitudes of the second. For him, psychoanalysis, like historical inquiry generally, depended on a healthy respect for the complexities of human interaction, and people's capacities for concealing their motivations from themselves as well as others. Like the analyst, the historian's task, he argued, is to use evidence to make sense of these hidden elements in human life.

Although Gay could be eloquent in describing the overlapping interests of historians and analysts in deciphering opaque clues from the past, he was more sharply polemical in denouncing those who wanted to confine the relevance of Freud's ideas to a small subsection of Viennese society at the end of the 19th century. He denounced the "myth" that all of the founder's patients were from the same bourgeois, Jewish sector of the capital of the Hapsburg Empire, noting the surprising variety of patient backgrounds in the case studies (Gay, 1985, pp. 80–81). He insisted that Vienna itself, with its rich culture of intellectual and aesthetic innovation, had little to do with the formation of Freud's theories. Freud would have developed the same ideas in any number of cosmopolitan European cities, Gay argued, perhaps thinking (as Freud himself did) that to label psychoanalysis Viennese was to damn it as parochial:

> In truth Freud could have developed his ideas in any city endowed with a first-rate medical school and an educated public large and affluent enough to furnish him with patients . . . the Vienna that Freud gradually constructed for himself was not the Vienna of the court, the café, the salon, or the operetta . . . His psychological theories formed in an intellectual universe large enough to embrace all of Western culture.
>
> *(Gay, 1998, p. 10)*

Confusing the context of discovery with the context of relevance (or verification), Gay seemed to think that Freud's achievement would be diminished if it were seen to have roots that were merely local. Various scientific theories have very particular roots (indeed, one might argue they all do), but this has nothing to do with how widely applicable the theories turn out to be.

The exciting developments in the theory of history in the late 1970s and 1980s, insofar as they paid attention to psychoanalysis, marshaled its insights to point out how jejeune the pursuit of scientific objectivity was for historical practice. Narrativist philosophy of history, deconstruction and postmodernism (especially after the publication of Hayden White's *Metahistory* in 1973) took for granted the constructed, even fictive, nature of historical discourse. Gay's work had no truck with this trend; he was committed to the view that the combination of art and science in the historian's "craft" would produce a relatively stable form of knowledge. His use of psychoanalysis in this regard was thus neither critical nor reductive; that is, he neither used psychoanalysis as a weapon against the historical profession's claims, nor as a hermeneutic key to unlock the secrets of the past. Gay didn't really have much interest in the *theory* of history, but instead continued the *practice* of a historian, increasingly with psychoanalytic tools in his kit. In his preface to *Freud for Historians*, Gay described his interest in the psychological as a complement to his earlier interest in the social. He was still pursuing a broad historical approach to ideas, but now with an enhanced perception of the context in which these ideas took shape. The internal psyche was a complement to the external society.

Schorske and Gay are intellectual historians, and although their work is widely respected within the historical profession, the field in the last decades of the 20th century had moved away from ideas and toward social history. As Lynn Hunt has recently explained, "The rise of social history thus went hand in hand with the rejection of psychological forms of analysis" (Hunt, 2002, p. 345). Social history eschewed the psychological in favor of either the study of economic and demographic trends on the one hand, or in favor of the exploration of cultural expressions on the other. "Psychologizing" was taboo, because it resulted in either pathographies or a tendency to focus on the individual rather than the collective. Those historians who were heavily influenced by post-structuralism or by Michel Foucault also found psychoanalysis anathema. For these writers, language or cultural paradigms formed subjectivity – they were not the expression of subjectivities emerging from psychodynamic conflict (Hunt, 2002, p. 346).

But insofar as social history was concerned with the development of identity, with what was thinkable, with how people imagined authority and social change, it was not surprising that some practitioners turned to psychoanalysis for potentially productive perspectives on traditional historical problems. In the mid-1980s in Britain, an ongoing psychoanalysis and history seminar developed out of the History Workshop Centre for Social History (Alexander & Taylor, 2012).[18] Barbara Taylor and Sally Alexander point out that much of the interest in using psychoanalytic tools came from feminist historians interested in the dynamic creation of gender. Feminist theorists had been largely critical of psychoanalysis, but many also adopted aspects of it in order to understand how the psychodynamic roots of the subordination of women and the creation of patriarchy. Juliet Mitchell's *Psychoanalysis and Feminism* (1974) was a key text in this regard.

Developing a critical, nuanced reading of Freud, and using historical and anthropological research, Mitchell showed how key psychoanalytic ideas could become tools for feminists. Psychoanalysis was not a recommendation for a patriarchal society, she famously concluded; it provided an analysis of one (Mitchell, 1974). For more than three decades feminist historians have taken up these tools in that spirit, whether in Lynn Hunt's analysis of the French Revolution, Lyndal Roper's research into witchcraft, Elizabeth Lunbeck's study of the development of psychiatry in the United States, or Darcy Buerkle's recent work on Charlotte Solomon.[19]

Joan Scott's work has been at the intersection of post-structuralism, social history, and psychoanalysis over the last 20 years or more. She has defended attentiveness to language and structure in opposition to any commonsense realism, and she has insisted on the importance of gender as a vital category of historical understanding (Scott, 1986).[20] Scott has recently turned to psychoanalysis to create another line of productive tension with conventional historical thinking. "Psychoanalysis can force historians to question their certainty about facts, narrative, and cause," she writes. "It introduces disturbing notions about unconscious motivation and the effects of fantasy on the making of history" (Scott, 2012, p. 63). Scott is not thinking of psychohistory in this regard, or of clinical psychoanalysis as it has developed in the United States because she recognizes that both of these have tendencies to reinforce the status quo. Scott is interested in psychoanalysis because it challenges the distinction between fantasy and fact that appears to be at the heart of the historian's enterprise. Psychoanalysis focuses on how we (often unconsciously) construct a past, and in how our investment in the past leads to effects in the present. It begins from those effects, but it does not seek to get to the "really real" behind appearance. Scott quotes Freud's dismissal of the question of whether or not the "primal scene" in the Wolf Man case actually took place as he remembered it: "It is also a matter of indifference in this connection whether we choose to regard it as a primal *scene* or a primal *phantasy*" (Freud, 1976b). Historians are not indifferent about the distinction between what happened and what we remember (or fantasize about), and this is one of the points of "incommensurability" that Scott sees between psychoanalysis and the discipline.

Scott turns to Michel de Certeau's theoretical work and Roper's historical study of witchcraft to tease out the productive power of this incommensurability.[21] The dynamic relation of fantasy and social change, the ways in which history is always mediated by desire, the complex interacting paths through which people pursue (and avoid) satisfaction – all these can all be powerfully framed by the interaction of these traditions of thought.

Unlike the historian who makes an object (an other) of the denizens of the past, the analyst refuses objectification, seeking instead to bring the analysand to recognition of the unconscious agency – the condition and limits – of his or her own subjectivity. It is not, as some have noted, that for Freud, the past always haunts the present, but that the objective times of past and present are confused, often indistinguishable. The point is that time is a complex creation, a constructed dimension of subjectivity, not a chronological given (Scott, 1986, p. 67).

By acknowledging the fruitful incommensurability of psychoanalysis and history we are in a better position – a self-conscious, reflexive position – to make meaning out of change over time.

## Conclusion

In 1905 Freud famously wrote: "He who has eyes to see and ears to hear becomes convinced that mortals can keep no secret. If their lips are silent, they gossip with their fingertips; betrayal forces itself through every pore" (Freud, 1976c, pp. 77–78). The secrets that the patient betrays are signs of our histories, and they may point to ways of making sense of ourselves and of our past to which we have been blind. There need be no end to these stories. Our inquiry into what they might be and mean does not end in some definitive empirical discovery. That's why psychoanalysis and history are so closely linked, both by the stories we tell about the past and by the desire to tell them better (or get them right enough). Some have argued that we have moved into an epoch when "making sense of ourselves and our past" has as little relevance to contemporary reality as privacy on the Internet, psychosomatic erectile dysfunction, or depression as a sensible response to the ways of the world. They have argued, in other words, that history and the narratives through which it was constituted were products of an old bourgeois, or modern, or patriarchal mode of thinking from which we are now liberated. This kind of "liberation" would truly make us post-human, which is the same as being post-historical because it would remove the framework for connecting action to the project of self-understanding.

If we *are* ever liberated from history, if history ever becomes superfluous to how we live in the present and future, Freud will no longer be relevant. This is part of what is at stake in efforts to substitute the reductive forms of neuroscience or affect theory for making sense of the past by working through contested histories. In that case, psychoanalysis (and much else) will certainly disappear. Maybe then the creatures that resemble us will truly be post-human. But if we continue to consider the past important for giving meaning and direction to our lives, then we will continue to turn to psychoanalytic thinking in order to find complex, open-ended ways to tell our histories, to work through who we are, and what we want.

## Notes

1  See Michael S. Roth, *Psycho-Analysis as History: Negation and Freedom in Freud*, Ithaca, NY: Cornell University Press, 1987, 1995; "Why Freud Haunts Us," in *Memory, Trauma and History: Essays on Living With the Past*, New York: Columbia University Press, 2011, pp. 117–124.

2  The case is discussed in the "sensitivity" chapter of Kramer's *Listening to Prozac*, New York: Penguin, 1994, pp. 67–107. Hereafter references to this book will be given in the text.

3  Kramer cites, among other sources, two key articles: Donald F. Klein, "Cybernetics, Activation and Drug Effects," in R. H. Van den Hoofdakker (ed), "Biological Measures: Their Theoretical and Diagnostic Value in Psychiatry," in *Acta Psychiatrica Scandinavica*, vol. 77, suppl. 341 (1988), pp. 126–137; Donald F. Klein, "Anxiety Reconceptualized," in *Anxiety: New Research and Changing Concepts*, ed. D. F. Klein and J. G. Rabkin, New York: Raven, 1981, pp. 235–261.

4  See Paul H. Wender and Donald F. Klein, *Mind, Mood and Medicine: A Guide to the New Biopsychiatry*, New York: Farrar, Strauss & Giroux, 1981, pp. 334–335.

5  Kramer draws especially from the work of Patrick Mahony, *Freud's Dora: A Psychoanalytic, Historical and Textual Study*, New Haven: Yale University Press, 1996.

6  See Mark Salber Phillips, "Rethinking Historical Distance: From Doctrine to Heuristic," *History and Theory*, vol. 50, 2011, pp. 11–23. See also Frank Ankersmit, "The Transfiguration of Distance Into Function," *History and Theory*, vol. 50, 2011, pp. 136–149.

7  See Dominick LaCapra, "History, Psychoanalysis, Critical Theory," in *History in Transit*, Ithaca, NY: Cornell University Press, 2004, pp. 72–105; Saul Friedlander, "History, Memory and the Historian: Facing the Shoah," in Michael Roth and Charles Salas (ed), *Disturbing Remains: Memory, History and Crisis in the Twentieth Century*, Los Angeles: Getty Research Institute, 2001, pp. 277ff; Peter Loewenberg, "Emotional Problems of Graduate Education," in *Decoding the Past: The Psychohistorical Approach*, New Brunswick, NJ: Transaction, 1996, pp. 48–58.

8  See Peter Loewenberg, "The Langer Family and the Dynamics of Shame and Success," in *Decoding the Past: The Psychohistorical Approach*, New York, Knopf, 1983, pp. 81–95.

9  The Frankfurt School of critical theory, out of which Marcuse's work emerged, drew heavily on Marxist and psychoanalytic ways of thinking to understand the persistence of oppression. The works of Max Horkheimer and Theodor Adorno, and of Erich Fromm, are important in this regard.

10  Lasch himself was able to combine psychoanalytic and historical thinking in powerful ways. See his *The Culture of Narcissism: American Life in an Age of Diminishing Expectations*, New York: Norton, 1978; and *Haven in a Heartless World: The Family Besieged*, New York: Norton, 1995.

11  Frank Manuel's essay in *Daedalus* cited earlier contains some of these criticisms, but the most strident critique can be found in David E. Stannard, *Shrinking History: Freud and the Failure of Psychohistory*, New York: Oxford University Press, 1980.

12  Kohut's notes provide a good window onto the field in the mid-1980s. See also Peter Loewenberg, *Decoding the Past: The Psychohistorical Approach*, New York: Knopf, 1983 and Philip Pomper, *The Structure of Mind in History: Five Major Figures in Psychohistory*, New York: Columbia University Press, 1985.

13  The study would be published in 1972 as *The Mind of Adolf Hitler*.

14  In his introduction to *Fin de Siècle Vienna*, Schorske mentions William Langer and Lionel Trilling, as well as Marcuse and Brown, in regard to the growing American interest in Freud (*Fin de Siècle Vienna: Politics and Culture*, New York: Knopf, 1979, p. xxiv). Trilling had been Schorske's undergraduate instructor at Columbia University. In this and subsequent paragraphs I draw upon my conversation with Schorske published as "Energizing the Elemental: Notes on a Conversation with Carl E. Schorske," *American Imago*, vol. 68, no. 4, 2011, pp. 595–604.

15  In this and subsequent paragraphs I draw on my interview with Peter Gay, published as "The Psychoanalytic Corner: Notes on a Conversation with Peter Gay," in Sally Alexander and Barbara Taylor (eds), *History and Psyche: Culture, Psychoanalysis and the Past*, London: Palgrave Macmillan, 2012, pp. 13–26.

16  See also Peter Gay, *Art and Act, on Causes in History: Manet, Gropius, Mondrian*, New York: Imprint, 1977.

17  See also Gay, "Psychoanalysis and the Historian," in *Sigmund Freud: Conflict and Culture*, ed. Michael S. Roth, New York: Knopf, 1998, pp. 117–126.

18  See Sally Alexander and Barbara Taylor, "Introduction," in *History and Psyche*, pp. 2–3.

19  See Lynn Hunt, *The Family Romance of the French Revolution*, Berkeley: University of California Press, 1992; Lyndal Roper, *Oedipus and the Devil: Witchcraft, Sexuality and Religion in Early Modern Europe*, New York: Routledge, 1994; *Witch Craze*, New Haven: Yale University Press, 2004; Elizabeth Lunbeck, *The Psychiatric Persuasion: Knowledge, Gender and Power in Modern America*, Princeton: Princeton University Press, 1995; Darcy Buerkle, *Nothing Happened: Charlotte Salomon and an Archive of Suicide*, Ann Arbor: University of Michigan Press, 2013.

20  See Joan Scott, "Gender: A Useful Category of Historical Analysis," *American Historical Review*, vol. 91, no. 5 (December 1986), pp. 1053–1075; "The Evidence of Experience," *Critical Inquiry*, vol. 17, no. 4, 1991, pp. 773–797.

21  See Michel de Certeau, *The Writing of History* (Tom Conley, trans), New York: Columbia University Press, 1988; Roper, *Oedipus and the Devil*; and Roper, *Witch Craze*.

Michael Roth

## References

Brown, NO 1959, *Life against death: the psychoanalytic meaning of history*, Wesleyan University Press, Middletown, CT.

Edmundson, M 2007, *The death of Sigmund Freud: the legacy of his last days*, Bloomsbury, New York.

Freud, S 1976a, 'Totem and taboo', in J Strachey (ed), *Standard edition of the complete psychological works of Sigmund Freud*, vol. 13, W.W. Norton, New York.

Freud, S 1976b, 'The history of an infantile neurosis', in J Strachey (ed), *Standard edition of the complete psychological works of Sigmund Freud*, vol. 17, W.W. Norton, New York, p. 103.

Freud, S 1976c, 'Fragment of an analysis of a case of hysteria', in J Strachey (ed), *Standard edition of the complete psychological works of Sigmund Freud*, vol. 7, W.W. Norton, New York, pp. 77–78.

Gay, P 1985, *Freud for historians*, Oxford University Press, New York.

Gay, P 1998, *Freud: A life for our time*, Norton, New York.

Hunt, L 2002, 'Psychology, psychoanalysis and historical thought', in L Kramer & S Mazer (eds), *A companion to Western historical thought*, Blackwell, Malden, MA, p. 345.

Klein, M 1987, *The selected Melanie Klein*, Juliet Mitchell (ed.), Free Press, New York.

Kohut, TA 1986, 'Psychohistory as history', *American Historical Review*, vol. 91, no. 2, p. 337.

Kramer, M 1994, 'Sigmund Freud's *The interpretation of dreams*: The initial response (1899–1908)', *Dreaming*, vol. 4, no. 1, p. 47.

Kramer, P 2006, *Freud: Inventor of the modern mind*, Penguin, New York.

LaCapra, D 2004, *History in transit*, Cornell University Press, New York.

Langer, WL 1958, 'The next assignment', *American Historical Review*, vol. 63, no. 2, p. 283.

Lasch, C 1969, 'One man's quest for sainthood and the revolutionary philosophy to which it led', *New York Times*, September 14, available at http://www.nytimes.com/books/99/08/22/specials/erikson-gandhi.html

Loewenberg, P 1996, *Decoding the past*, Transaction Publishers, Piscataway.

Manuel, F 1971, 'The use and abuse of psychology in history', *Daedalus*, vol. 100, no. 1, pp. 187–213.

Marcuse, H 1955, *Eros and civilization: A philosophical inquiry into Freud*, Boston: Beacon Press.

Mitchell, J 1974, *Psychoanalysis and feminism: A radical reassessment of Freudian psychoanalysis*, Allen Lane, London.

Phillips, A 2011, *On balance*, Farrar, Strauss & Giroux, New York.

Roth, MS 1995, 'Freud's use and abuse of the past', in *The ironist's cage: Memory, trauma and the construction of history*, Columbia University Press, New York, pp. 186–200.

Roth, MS 2001, 'Falling into history: Freud's case of "Frau Emmy von N."', *Memory, trauma and history: Essays on living with the past*, Columbia University Press, New York, pp. 104–116.

Schorske, C 1980, *Fin de siècle Vienna: politics and culture*, Knopf, New York.

Schorske, CE 1981, *Fin de siècle Vienna: politics and culture*, Random House, New York.

Schorske, CE 1999, 'To the Egyptian dig: Freud's psycho-archaeology of cultures', in *Thinking with history: Explorations of the passage to modernism*, Princeton University Press, Princeton, NJ, p. 209.

Scott, J 1986, 'Gender: a useful category of historical analysis', *American Historical Review*, vol. 91, no. 5, pp. 1053–1075.

Scott, J 2012, 'The incommensurability of psychoanalysis and history', *History and Theory*, vol. 51, pp. 63–83.

Wender, PH & Klein, DF 1981, *Mind, mood, and medicine: A guide to the new biopsychiatry*, New York: Farrar, Straus & Giroux.

# 15

# Sociology and psychoanalysis

*Michael Rustin*

What is "psychoanalytic sociology"? Does it exist as a recognized field of study, either as a sub-field of sociology or as a subfield of psychoanalysis? Despite the undoubted importance of Freud for some major figures and schools of thought in sociology, the place of psychoanalysis in the sociological field seems nevertheless to be an elusive and tenuous one.[1] From time to time, there have indeed been fruitful interactions between these two powerful paradigms, describing and explaining phenomena that neither could fully grasp alone. But then, each of these "fields" has largely withdrawn to its own primary area of study, avoiding the other as beyond its grasp and concern. In this chapter I will seek to explain how this situation has come about, and ask what might have to happen for this situation to change, and for psychoanalytic sociology to become established on a more resilient basis.

Freud is probably considered by most sociologists to have been essentially a psychologist that is as a scientist or investigator whose primary object of study was the mental life of individuals. Yet in fact, Freud believed that psychoanalysis provided understanding of groups, societies and cultures, as well as of individuals. Among his best known works are *Totem and Taboo* (1913), *Group Psychology and the Analysis of the Ego* (1921), *The Future of an Illusion* (1927) and *Civilization and its Discontents* (1930). Although the second and third of these are related to anthropology and the study of religion more than to sociology as such, all of these works exemplify Freud's belief in the relevance of psychoanalysis to the explanation of societal phenomena.

The origins of sociology as a field precede psychoanalysis. The crucial definitions of the "social" as the object of study that demarcates sociology from its principal rivals among the human sciences[2] were set out by a near-contemporary cohort of writers whose main work preceded Freud's. Even though the lives of all of these writers overlapped substantially with Freud's, and gave them opportunity to take account of the latter's early formative works, there is little indication that any of them did. All of these sociologists were of course in their own ways interested in the relations between changes in social structures and patterns of mental life. For all of them, patterns of motivation of human action – for example "The Metropolis and Mental Life" (Simmel), In the Condition of Anomie (Durkheim), in Gemeinschaft and Gesellschaft Society (Tönnies), or in the "Protestant Ethic and the Spirit of Capitalism" or in Eruptions of Charismatic Authority (Weber) – were central to their understandings of "the transition to modernity," the primary subject matter of this formative phase of sociology. But none of them saw the need to explore the particular dimensions of unconscious or irrational motivation that Freud was putting onto the scientific agenda. Perhaps to do so would have been to blur the boundaries between emergent sociological and psychological frames of investigation that these founding figures were all in the process of marking out. The theoretical tradition of sociology was for many years taught as the exegesis of the great works of these founding fathers (as they used to be called in those unemancipated days). The absence of psychoanalysis and Freud from the definitional framework of sociology removed it from its foundational disciplinary frame.

Even *The Structure of Social Action* (1937), Talcott Parsons's influential reconstruction of that frame as a synthesis of the ideas of several of its founding figures (notably Weber and Durkheim, but excluding Marx), gave no attention to Freud, even though later on Parsons was to acknowledge Freud, with Weber and Durkheim, as his most important role models.[3] The idea that the psychoanalytic field of investigation is in some way alien to sociology, and cannot be readily handled through its methods and sensibilities, has remained a consistent disposition of the sociological field.[4] Even though the tradition initiated by Talcott Parsons departed from this pattern, it is doubtful if has fundamentally changed it.

## Disciplinary questions

Once psychoanalysis had been defined as "outside" sociology (despite the important exception of Parsonian functionalism), persuasive arguments were brought to bear keep it there, or at least to leave it on the margins of intellectual respectability. Insofar as sociology found itself under pressure to conduct itself as a legitimate science, especially during the period of greatest influence of the philosophy of science of Karl Popper and of positivism more generally, association with psychoanalysis, one of Popper's key instances of a "pseudo-science," was for many best avoided. And because some of the most interesting conjunctures between psychoanalysis and sociology came from the neo-Marxists of the Frankfurt School, here was another reason for maintaining a distance between psychoanalysis and sociology's mainstream.

For a period, especially in the two decades after World War II, sociologists responded to the pressure to demonstrate their intellectual respectability by becoming as scientific in their approach as possible. The rigorous demonstration of causal relations between social structures and their effects on behaviors became the empirical staple of the field. Initially, in Britain at any rate, class structures and their consequences for inequalities of all kinds – in education, criminality, life chances – were the main focus of attention. Subsequently the inequalities of gender and race joined those of class as the staples of sociological analysis.[5] Statistical methods became the essential means by which correlations established with relatively small samples were able to lead to generalizations valid over an entire population. (Such methods also became the standard resources of the "applied sociologies" of marketing and psephology, technologies of understanding that have come to have a large role in economically advanced societies.)[6] These approaches led to a prevailing "methodological individualism" (Lukes, 1973) – sociological explanations mostly measured the effects of social structures on the positions or behaviors of aggregated individuals of defined types. But while sociologists might often be methodological individualists – their explanations having to be verifiable in terms of consequences for individual subjects – this did not make them any less concerned to maintain a firm boundary between their field and that of psychology. Psychoanalysis was largely thought of by sociologists, whatever Freud may have written about groups, religion and civilization, as the study of individuals, largely undertaken in clinical settings, so it was common for sociologists to see it as essentially a form of psychology, in which through the definition of their field would take almost no scientific interest.

It did not help the relations between these fields that while psychoanalysis was being disregarded as a *resource* for sociology, it was being found to be of some critical interest as one of its *topics* (to use a distinction usefully made by ethnomethodologists). Psychoanalysis had always found its primarily location in the clinic, or in applied derivatives of clinical settings such as those of social work, education, or organizational consultancy. It was primarily a form of practical knowledge, a human technology as much as a human science. In the post–World War II period it achieved some influence in these spheres, as well as a cultural resonance, measured by its continuing presence in everyday discourse that is probably greater than that of sociology.[7] Psychoanalysts tended for the most part to see themselves as contributing to human enlightenment and betterment, in the spirit of Freud's view of himself as bringing irrational impulses and obstacles to human happiness within the sphere of rational understanding. (Influential sociologists and philosophers provided substantial elaborations of this emancipatory view of psychoanalysis; Habermas, 1971.) But as cultural and social conflict grew in the 1960s, psychoanalysis found itself vulnerable to criticism, as a consequence of its "embeddedness" in established social institutions and practices. For example, some feminists (De Beauvoir, 1952) became critical of the normative positions taken up by psychoanalysts and their institutions on gender roles and on sexuality. One reason for this was because although Freud had written about the normal diversity and complexity of human sexual orientations, psychoanalytic institutes often regarded homosexuality as a pathology, and used sexual orientation as a criterion of admission to psychoanalytic training. For Foucault and his followers, psychoanalysis was one of the most important instances of the absorption of the human sciences into the control system of modern societies, with its intrusive definitions of sexual normality seen as one of its most objectionable features (Foucault, 1998). Consensual, "human relations" approaches to industrial conflicts, which had a significant psychoanalytic component, came under suspicion as a technique of soft managerial control, both theoretically (Rose, 1989) and politically in the harsh climate of industrial relations in the 1970s.[8] And although the radical psychiatry movement had other principal targets than psychoanalysis in its critique of mental health practices, nevertheless the interactionist theories of social labeling on which its analyses drew also placed psychoanalysis under suspicion, as one source of the pathologizing categorizations to which psychiatric patients, like other "deviants," were subjected. And from another side, critical of the romanticism of the 1960s, "the psychoanalytic movement" was assailed by Ernest Gellner (1985) as a leading instance of contemporary irrationalism.[9]

The primary practical involvements of psychoanalysis, in therapeutic and other applied settings, were often intellectually productive. The various sub-paradigms of psychoanalytic knowledge have seen a progressive evolution over a very long period, developing in response to the problems encountered in the consulting room. This reality of a continuing development of concepts, theories and techniques, in the practice of something like a Kuhnian "normal science," is far from the ossified debate about the validity of Freud's fundamental discoveries, which is still presented as if it reflected contemporary psychoanalytic realities. But it is one thing to be generating "practical" and theoretical knowledge in clinical and allied settings, and another to be doing so in the more detached context spirit of academic social science.

At the other end of this spectrum of academic sociological approaches to that of empiricism, referred to earlier, lay the study of sociological theory. This division between empirical sociology and sociological theory was perhaps deliberately modeled on the distinction between theoretical and experimental physics that had been so central to the development of a field that was usually held to be the summit of scientific achievement. In ideologically pluralist Britain, the study of sociological theory consisted of a relatively even-handed exegesis and development of the perspectives of at least three different sociologies – those of Marx, Durkheim and Weber – to be joined as theoretical proliferation began in the 1960s by "symbolic interactionism" as a distinctive

American sociology, by feminist sociology, and by the smaller schools of ethnomethodology, Foucauldian sociology and so forth.

In the United States, theory for a time took the form of the grand synthesis of structural functionalism, an overarching theoretical system that sought to incorporate the main traditions of European sociology in such a way as to largely exclude Marx. This synthesis was in some respects a fruitful one, insofar as it generated hypotheses about the operations of difference instances and regions of the social structure that were amenable to empirical investigation. This synthesis did find a significant place for a version of psychoanalytic ideas, as we shall see, although shorn of their more disruptive and unsettling potentialities.

But while sociology sought intellectual and professional credibility by becoming as scientific as possible, within the then dominant conception of what a science should be, psychoanalysis responded to the challenge of scientific legitimacy in a more uncertain way. Freud had fiercely upheld the aspiration for psychoanalysis to be a new science of the mind, and proceeded to develop its theoretical apparatus in a spirit that was both logical and imaginative. Some of his close associates, such as Abraham and Ferenczi, joined him in a collaborative work of conceptual and theoretical elaboration. They were followed in this formidable work of intellectual production by subsequent generations of psychoanalysts – Anna Freud and Melanie Klein, Heinz Hartman and Heinz Kohut, Wilfred Bion, Donald Winnicott, Herbert Rosenfeld, Ronald Britton, Thomas Ogden – to name only a small number of the most original psychoanalytical theorists. No one could possibly say that psychoanalysis as a field was lacking in conceptual and theoretical elaboration. Indeed some influential voices within psychoanalysis (Tuckett, 2005; Wallerstein, 2005) began to argue in the 1980s that its theoretical proliferation had got quite out of hand. The problem with the field, in their view, was not that there were too few theories, but that there were too many. There were, they argued, no clear demarcations between the fields of application of these theories; they were alleged to use concepts in inconsistent or imprecise ways. The situation was described as corresponding to a "Tower of Babel" (Steiner, 1994).

The weak link in the scientific credibility of psychoanalysis lay not in deficits in its theories but in the unresolved problem of what could be counted as valid psychoanalytic evidence. The challenge laid down polemically by Karl Popper (1963) and by Sidney Hook (1959) and his philosophical associates in the United States, and then developed in a much more rigorous way in two large volumes by Adolf Grunbaum (1984, 1993), was to the validity of what psychoanalysts took to be their primary source of evidence, namely the response by analysands to interpretations offered to them in the consulting room. The idea that these "clinical facts" were hopelessly contaminated by the analyst's "suggestions," by the analysand's emotional dependence on the analyst, and by the unavoidable subjectivity of the whole process of gathering and recording clinical data, was one to which the field of psychoanalysis found no convincing response.

The consequence of what amounted to an academic defeat was that many in the psychoanalytic field abandoned the aspiration for psychoanalysis to be recognized as a legitimate science. It had always been recognized that psychoanalysis belonged to the sphere of the humanities as well as that of the sciences. Its case studies took a narrative, descriptive and developmental form not unlike those of creative literature, although its "stories," unlike fictional narratives, purported to be literally rather than imaginatively true. Since Freud's *Interpretation of Dreams* the understandings of psychoanalysis had depended on the insights conveyed through metaphor and other kinds of poetic association, rather than merely upon the literal description and causal correlation of "facts." Its iconic instances – those descriptions that seemed best to represent its theoretical understandings – were usually of individual cases – for example, Freud's Rat Man and Little Hans and Melanie Klein's Richard. Most of these were individual analysands or patients, treated in the consulting room. But some of them were fictional characters of the imagination, such as King Oedipus or Hamlet, or were interpretations of the imagined history of artists, such as Leonardo da Vinci. The great psychoanalysts showed no embarrassment at all in moving between one kind of "empirical instance" (if one can call them that) and another. No wonder then, that more empirically minded psychologists often said of Freud that while he was undoubtedly an interesting and imaginative thinker, what he had written had little or no scientific basis.

In a situation in which the battle for scientific legitimacy had seemed to be going badly, it was understandable that psychoanalysis would accept the idea of a more hybrid intellectual status, somewhere on the border between the arts and the sciences.[10] Its focus over many decades became largely clinical, offering treatment for various kinds of mental ill-health both to private clients and to those provided by not-for-profit or governmental agencies (e.g., the National Health Service in Britain). Until the recent rise of the movement for evidence-based medicine, the criteria of scientific proof required of professional practitioners were less well defined and rigorous than those that the sciences had learned to prescribe for themselves.

Psychoanalysis developed largely as an independent and largely unlicensed (or self-licensed) profession, and not as an academic or scientific discipline. Its networks of journals, books and conferences were strong and international, but they existed for the most part outside of the broader academic and scientific community.

Thus we can say, apropos of psychoanalytic sociology, that its two prospective partners had travelled in opposite directions in response to the philosophical challenge to prove their scientific credentials. Sociology had by and large accommodated itself to the demands of this epistemological regime – the dominance of quantitative and empiricist sociology in the United States continues to this day. Psychoanalysis, on the other hand, had largely withdrawn itself from the academic fray, and had thus detached itself from the milieus in which interactions with sociologists would be most likely to occur.

## How psychoanalysis found a space for itself within sociology

Despite an environment within sociology that was largely unsympathetic to psychoanalysis, it nevertheless came about that substantial work in psychoanalytic sociology was accomplished. In relation to the greater part of their chosen field of study, sociologists disavowed the unconscious phenomena of mental life, encountered not only in individuals but also in groups and larger social entities, which psychoanalysis claimed as its distinctive field of knowledge. For them, so far as the everyday life of societies functioning in conditions of normality was concerned, such conceptions were at the best highly speculative, offering little solid ground for the scientific investigation to which their field was now committed. Alternatively, such "irrational" dimensions of mental life could best be left to psychiatric clinicians, since in any case it was surely amongst the mentally ill or mad that any disruptive presence of unconscious state of mind would make itself felt.

But for one generation of social scientists, the disturbing presence of the unconscious could scarcely be doubted or disavowed. This was the one most directly affected by Nazism. When an entire society seemed to have become gripped by irrational panics and phobias, and when the public declaration and enactment of sadistic fantasies of persecution and hatred was becoming a fact of everyday life, the idea of the unconscious as a fact of social life imposed itself forcefully onto the attention of some social scientists, initially in Germany. In fact, psychoanalysis has found a place in sociology principally where the presence of unconscious and irrational states of mind and feeling have been so unmistakable, and so disruptive of the normal expectations of behavior, that they have demanded explanation. In mapping the development of psychoanalytic sociology in this chapter, I shall be arguing that it is responses to these social crises of the 20th century that have been central to its development. I shall be describing four major fields of work that in name or substance justify the description of psychoanalytic sociology.

## The Frankfurt School

The first significant group of sociologists to see the relevance of Freud's ideas for the understanding of society were the members of the Frankfurt School, particular Adorno, Fromm, Horkheimer and Marcuse, who brought Freudian and Marxist perspectives together[11] in their profound understanding of Nazism and Fascism. It was clear for this group that Marxist schemes of explanations in terms of economic contradictions and class conflicts were crucial in understanding the crisis of post–World War I Europe, and of the Weimar Republic in Germany in particular. However, they also found the orthodox Marxist models deployed by the political leaders and parties of the left to be inadequate to explain this catastrophic development. Social actors – classes in particular – appeared not to act rationally in pursuit of their economic interests, as orthodox Marxism asserted they would. Instead, political life was becoming dominated by the phenomena of extreme nationalism and xenophobia, anti-Semitism and a cult of leadership that exalted violence over rational deliberation and discourse. It was to understand this profound eruption of irrational passions into political and social life that members of the Frankfurt School turned to psychoanalysis as an intellectual resource.

In brilliant essays, for example Adorno and Horkheimer's *Elements of Anti-Semitism: Limits of Enlightenment* (1944) and Adorno's "Freudian Theory and the Pattern of Fascist Propaganda" (1951) Freud's understanding of the role of irrational transferences in political life was drawn upon to explain the ongoing collapse of civilized values in political and social life. In *Dialectic of Enlightenment* (1944) Adorno and Horkheimer called into question the hitherto optimistic teleology of the West's view of itself. The question they sought to address was "why mankind, instead of entering into a truly human condition, is sinking into a new kind of barbarism." The essential dualism of Freud's view of human nature – based as he saw on dispositions both to love and to hate, on a "life instinct" and a "death instinct" – was incorporated into a social theory that sought to explain the catastrophic failure of human hopes represented by the era of Nazism and Fascism.

In *The Authoritarian Personality* (Adorno et al., 1950) Adorno and his coauthors sought to explain the vulnerability of German society to these irrational appeals by reference to the early socialization of many of its members. A particular division of labor between authoritarian fathers and passive, subordinate mothers reproduced itself, this study argued, in each generation. Exiled to the United States, Adorno, Horkheimer and Marcuse observed affinities between the technologies and processes of propaganda employed by the Nazis, and those of commercial mass culture in the United States. In many ways, theirs was a narrative of disillusionment, written in the context of social and individual tragedies. The potential for an enlightened, humane civilization, anticipated in the writings of both Marx and (in a more skeptical way) by Freud, seemed to the Frankfurt School intellectuals to be in process of being lost. Later, in the 1960s, even such developments as the lessening of sexual repression that had been furthered by psychoanalytic understanding were held by Herbert Marcuse not to be leading to the authentic human fulfilment than might have been anticipated. Instead of self-realization, we had achieved only a condition of "repressive desublimation" and the mass exploitation of sexual fantasy for commercial purposes. Marcuse had earlier analyzed, in his *Soviet Marxism* (1964) and his *Eros and Civilisation* (1955), the links between the regime of repression characteristic of the phase of capital accumulation (whether under capitalism or Soviet Communism) and its apparent weakening as consumer-based capitalism required that libidinal desires be stimulated and converted into action.

The Frankfurt School writers were writing in a particular historical context, and some of their critics subsequently came to see their view of mass culture as unduly negative. It seems in part to reflect the critical response of European intellectuals, steeped in and nostalgic for their own high culture, to the brash populism of the United States, and to demonstrate a blindness to the creative potentials of more democratic culture. Nevertheless, this corpus of writings has a continuing value in demonstrating how psychoanalytic and sociological perspectives can be brought together to explain social phenomena whose irrational elements cannot be ignored. For example, even though Hannah Arendt thought of herself neither as a sociologist nor as sympathetic to psychoanalysis, her *Origins of Totalitarianism* (1951) is a classic example of an analysis implicitly powerful in both of these dimensions. Zigmunt Bauman is a leading sociologist who has integrated these perspectives in a way close to that of the Frankfurt School. His *Modernity and the Holocaust* (1989), which argued that the Nazi death camps were a natural culmination of a perverse process of industrial rationalization, is like a further case study in *Dialectic of Enlightenment*. His account of the hollowing-out of personal identity through the seductions of consumerism develops the Frankfurt School's earlier critique of mass culture. His description (Bauman, 2004) of those reduced to the role of outcasts and wanderers in modern consumer culture describes forms of social persecution whose unconscious mechanisms of projection and scapegoating are similar to those of totalitarian regimes, if less stark.

## Talcott Parsons and psychoanalysis

The other central figure in this period in the incorporation of psychoanalytic ideas within sociology was Talcott Parsons. In his "On Building Social Systems Theory: A Personal History" (1970), Parsons cites Freud as the third of the three theorists who were most important to him. He undertook a personal analysis and a psychoanalytical training (though nonclinical) in the 1940s, and thus became as equipped as a sociologist could be to bring about a synthesis between these fields of ideas. In his own account of his development, the role of psychoanalytic ideas in his construction of a comprehensive model of social systems was primarily to deepen the understanding of attachments to norms and values that he took as foundational for societies.

The problem that Parsons had set out to solve in *The Structure of Social Action* (1937) was what he called the problem of social order. If, as economists and Hobbesian or utilitarian philosophers held, human beings were primarily motivated by the pursuit of rational self-interest, the question was, how could society hold together in face of the conflictful and fissiparous tendencies to which motives of self-interest would surely lead? Parsons's solution, greatly influenced by Durkheim, was to postulate the existence of shared norms and values as the fundamental source of social cohesion. *The Structure of Social Action* is in fact one of the great foundational texts of modern sociology, insofar as it seeks to overthrow the primacy of the rational-individualist ontologies of the sciences of economics and psychology in favor of a theory of normative order as the fundamental social condition.

How then did psychoanalysis, absent from *The Structure of Social Action*, find a significant place in Parsons's subsequent great synthesis? Why were the Durkheimian ideas of shared values, "collective representations," different kinds of common norms, insufficient to explain the viability of persisting social order? Parsons's own account of this development suggests that he became aware of a missing element in his theory. That is, he decided that he needed an explanation of how and why individuals became deeply socialized into systems of meaning and value, and to understand the processes and mechanisms by which they did so. One way in which this psychodynamic element of his theory developed was through his study of the professions, and in particular the medical profession (Parsons, 1954, 1970). Relations between sick patients and their doctors were extremely unequal in regard to their relative power and knowledge. Patients usually had no way of assessing the validity of a doctor's understandings, yet they nevertheless reposed considerable trust in medical judgments. Doctors were given considerable opportunities to exploit this situation to their own advantage, yet most often, in Parsons's view at least, they refrained from doing so. To explain this situation, Parsons referred to the social construction of trust. Professionals, like medical doctors, became socialized into a normative system that required them to act responsibly within the frame of their prescribed roles. Systems of socialization and collective regulation had evolved to enable them to do so. Patients learned that they could rely on medical practitioners to behave responsibly, and that the situation of vulnerability and dependence in which they were placed in their relations with doctors was nevertheless a safe one.

Parsons's understanding of the specific form of authority held by medical doctors takes account of the phenomenon of transference, understood by Freud in the psychoanalytic context. The patient reposes in the doctor the trust whose unconscious source and template is the child's early dependence on its parents' care, and on the projection of powers of agency and judgment onto a responsible other. Obviously such a relationship, with its asymmetry of information and dependence, is vulnerable to exploitation. The normative commitments that Parsons held to be the distinctive attribute of professional organization – a form of collective self-regulation ordered around shared values – was necessary in order for such transferences and dependencies to be rendered safe and positive in their outcomes. Indeed, the normative coordination of the professions becomes a pure type of the most social of all forms of regulation, distinct from those based on instrumental interest or coercive power.

There is a clear parallel between the element of trust, which Parsons identified as central to the doctor–patient relationship, and the phenomenon of irrational transference, which Freud had identified as distinctive of, and essential for, the psychoanalytic encounter. It seems that Parsons's understanding of the role of doctors was influenced in part by his experience of psychoanalytic training. Incidentally, this connection helps to explain the continuing connections between the professional practice of medicine and that of psychoanalysis. In the United States this has taken the extreme form, until recently, that only those qualified as medical doctors would be permitted to train as analysts, but more widely, the ethical regulation of psychoanalytic practice remains close to medical norms, and analysts previously trained in medicine and psychiatry continue to be influential within the psychoanalytic profession. Issues of responsibility and trust that are inescapable in the doctor–patient relationship are even more pressing in the psychoanalytic situation in which an "irrational" transference to the analyst is deliberately cultivated as the source of access to knowledge of unconscious states of mind. Thus the subsuming of the psychoanalytic relationship as a specialized version of one already understood within the practice of medicine provides a source of legitimacy for psychoanalysis.

Parsons went on to undertake a more thoroughgoing integration of Freudian ideas into his theory of the social system. His interest was in how social norms, values and roles became internalized, and the crucial institution in this process of social transmission was the family. Of course, the family is also the primary site of the processes of introjection and identification that take place in infancy. These processes are essential to the formation of personal identity. Parsons and his colleagues looked to Freud's account of early life as a primary resource for understanding socialization. One can say that for Parsons and his colleagues, Freud's work was a kind of sociology of early family life, in its unconscious as well as its conscious dimensions.

These investigations become central to Parsons's and his colleagues' understandings of how in particular norms and expectations governing differences of age and gender become internalized. How does the "standard model" of the American middle-class nuclear family become instilled as unconscious and therefore normally unquestioned expectations in the majority of citizens?

According to this model, which certainly had some correspondence to social reality when Parsons proposed it, instrumental, universalist and affectively neutral traits are located most strongly in men, and expressive, particularistic and affectively charged dispositions are most strongly located in women, Parsons and his colleagues argued that the Oedipal processes described by Freud, in which male children are required to leave the space of maternal intimacy, and in compensation for this affective loss identify themselves with their dispositions and capabilities of their fathers, are necessary to explain the depth of this character formation.[12]

Later stages in the life cycle were made comprehensible in the development of this model of socialization. Parsons saw adolescence as involving a difficult transition from childhood identification with parent figures, to a situation in which young people are obliged to take up roles of relative autonomy, in which they have to compete both for economic opportunities, for example in finding work and establishing careers, and in sexual and marriage markets, in which they eventually form families of their own. He saw the adolescent attachment to peer groups, or in more extreme cases to gangs, and their proneness to the idealization of hero figures (even in the relatively superficial form of leaders in popular culture or sport) as a displacement of transferential bonds formerly located in the secure space of families, now seeking new if temporary forms of attachment and membership within a same-generation group.[13] This functionalist theory of how especially gender roles were unconsciously constructed within the family proved to be highly contentious. However the issue seemed not to be that Parsons's psychoanalytic account was descriptively false, as that it seemed to endorse a normative order that for feminists in particular from the 1960s onward became highly contested.

## Feminist sociology and psychoanalysis[14]

When feminist writers came to challenge the patriarchal order that this model encoded (based on a division of labor that located male activities "in the world," primarily through paid employment, and a female sphere of activity "in the home"), they also found psychoanalytic ideas to be essential to their explanatory task. What for Parsons had seemed to be a natural process through which identities were reproduced across generations was defined by feminists as an unnatural and inequitable one. But critics of this patriarchal order also encountered the fact that this dominant order of values and expectations did seem to be internalized very deeply in its subjects. It became for example a problem for feminists to explain why conscious political struggles to overturn conventional assumptions about gender roles and hierarchies seemed to only to be effective to a point. Even in radical movements, women still seemed to find themselves making the tea and looking after the children.

Many feminists had attacked psychoanalysis for various reasons, including some of the patriarchal assumptions to be found in Freud's writing. But others, such as Juliet Mitchell (1974), Nancy Chodorow (1978, 1989) and Dorothy Dinnerstein (1976) found the psychoanalytic understanding embodied in Parsonian theory, about the deep internalization of gender identities that took place during the parent–child relationships of infancy, to be valuable, once its value orientation was turned on its head. Their argument was that only if the early experiences of infants were made different could women and men escape this unconscious pattern of socialization and its attendant inequalities. For Mitchell a revolutionary overthrow of the bourgeois family was called for.[15] For some radicals, experiments in communal living and child-rearing attempted to implement this vision. For Chodorow and Dinnerstein, it seemed that it might suffice if the division of labor between men and women – mother and father figures within families – was drastically reformed. If infants were to experience fathers as well as mothers as their primary carers, and their mothers as well as fathers as having agency and autonomy in the world beyond the family, then gender identities might take a more varied and diverse form. Some at least of the changes advocated by Chodorow and other feminists have indeed occurred, and the prescriptiveness of gender and sexual identities, in some social milieus at least, has significantly lessened over the last generation or so.[16] Jessica Benjamin (1988) integrated an approach to unequal power and the denial of recognition, derived from Hegel and the Frankfurt School, with a psychoanalytic account of identity formation in early years, to critique the dominant pattern of domination and submission that she held characterized gender relations in contemporary society. Only the reclaiming of subjectivity and agency by women could alter this pattern of domination and subordination of the sexes and its unconscious reproduction.[17]

The challenge that occurred, both in theory and practice, to the standard Freudian account of the formation of identity within the family constellation, was not welcomed by everyone. The attack on the authority of the father, associated in some minds with the feminist movement, has according to some led to a larger crisis of moral authority in society. Christopher Lasch's *The Culture of Narcissism* (1979) had as one of its explanations of a prevailing spirit of hedonism and shallow consumerism the weakening role of paternal authority. (Lasch was regarded with some justice by critics as antifeminist). The negotiation of the Oedipus complex, the necessity to renounce instant gratification, to defer satisfactions, and accept constraints imposed through the superego, was deemed to be essential to the construction of mature, ethical subjects. Thus the Freudian theory of the role of the Oedipus complex in the formation of identity was incorporated into sociological, or quasi-sociological theory, in the service of different conceptions of the possible and the desirable. What was agreed among all these social theorists was that the unconscious dimensions of what happened in infancy, and indeed throughout childhood, had significant effects on the formation of gender identities and of social character more generally.

It might seem from the foregoing that the reasons for the engagement of the Frankfurt School on the one hand, and of Parsons and his associates on the other, were quite different, as was their political orientation. Adorno and Horkheimer were explicitly responding to the implications for rationalist and progressivism ways of thinking of the catastrophic experiences of the mid-20th century with Fascism, Nazism, and the Holocaust in particular. Parsons appeared merely to be providing a deeper sociopsychological foundation than could be found in the mainstream tradition of sociology for his model of a social system based on shared norms and values. Thus the Frankfurt School writers were describing a society in a state of dissolution as a civilized entity. Parsons is setting out the foundations of what he sees as a largely benign democratic and liberal form of capitalism. What could be more different?

However, the fact is that both Adorno and Horkheimer (1944, 1951) and Parsons (1942a, 1942b) wrote crucial essays on the topics both of Fascism and propaganda, at approximately the same time. Parsons notes with a kind of approval that Marxist understandings of Fascism, though different from his own, nevertheless do acknowledge that Fascism must be understood in relation to its larger context of origin. Marxism is thus acknowledged by him as the most serious rival to his own explanation of this crisis.

Parsons's understanding of Fascism focuses on the phenomenon of anomie, on the uprooting of large populations from the previous anchorages in settled expectations and social statuses.

Large numbers of people become amenable to irrationalism sentiments and ideologies because of their acute need for security and meaning. For Adorno, bringing together research undertaken in the 1940s for publication in 1951, Nazi propaganda is described as a diabolical mobilization of emotions and anxieties for perverse ends. Parsons account of propaganda, published in 1944, is more equivocal. He is identified with the democracies in World War II against Nazism and Fascism, and for him propaganda, and its manipulation of the public's emotional styles, is a necessary instrument in the war against dictatorships. In his essay on propaganda, Parsons, like Adorno, notes the importance of the phenomenon of transference as explaining the affective ties between populations and their political leaders.

One might conjecture that not only for the Frankfurt School theorists, but for Parsons and his associates too, Fascism and its exploitation of perverse and destructive emotions represented a significant challenge to the taken for granted status of civilized norms and values. Was one of the reasons why Parsons was led to incorporate psychoanalytic ideas into his theoretical synthesis that it deepened, at the level of affect, his neo-Durkheimian approach to shared norms and values? But was it also because what was happening in Europe was a challenge to his own confidence in the stability of the liberal social order? Was the reason for the strength of Parsons's commitment to the idea of a morally integrated society not, as his radical critics later suggested, that he was essentially a conservative, but that he was aware of how vulnerable societies had proved to be in the Europe of the 1930s and 1940s to the appeal of Fascism? Much of the sociological work influenced by Parsons in the subsequent period, for example in political sociology, set out to clarify the social conditions upon which a democratic and liberal social order depended, against the threats to it from authoritarianisms of both left and right.

Might it not in other words be the case that for functionalist sociology too, the necessary stimulus for giving serious attention to the psychoanalytic study of the unconscious was the unmistakable disruption of the social order by extreme irrationalism?

## Norbert Elias and the civilizing process

The third example of a substantial psychoanalytic sociology to be considered is that of another refugee from Nazism, Norbert Elias (1897–1990). Elias had also worked at the University of Frankfurt, but his formation was different that of the members of the Frankfurt School for Social Research. Whereas Adorno and Horkheimer and the colleagues affected a synthesis between Marxist social science and psychoanalysis in the understanding of Fascism and its origins, Elias's lasting intellectual allegiance was to a form of sociology in which Marxist theories were not central. In his major work of historical sociology, Elias set out nothing less than an account of the development of "civilization," by which he meant a state of society in which instinctual desires of both positive and negative kinds – both those oriented to pleasure and to pain – became over centuries inhibited by social conventions and displaced into constructive forms of social life.

While Adorno and Horkheimer saw society reverting before their eyes to a condition of barbarism, Elias developed (during the 1930s) a historical narrative of long-term social improvement. One might say that whereas the psychoanalytic Marxists of the Frankfurt School faced the horrors of the Nazi period without flinching from their pessimistic and tragic implications, Elias turned away from them, providing what one might see as a compensatory or redemptive narrative of hope. His thesis was that centralization of the means of violence in absolute monarchies, like that of Louis XIV in France, enforced a change in the dominant forms of social character. This argument is consistent with Max Weber's insistence on the significance of the control of violence in the establishment of legitimate governmental authority. Louis XIV required the nobility to leave their warrior fiefdoms and abstain from violence, and instead compete for position and status at the royal court. Elias attributed importance to the development of codes of manners, which he believed to be far from superficial in their effects on behavior. He cited the influence of texts on courtly behavior, by Renaissance writers such as Castiglione on the behavior of the ruling classes, as evidence for this shift in social mores.

Elias's theory of the civilizing process was developed at a time when the Nazis had just risen to power and had driven him from Germany. His study of the growth of civilization was as perhaps a surprising juxtaposition of topic and context. While Elias was studying the development of civility in the early modern period, Adorno and Horkheimer were preoc-cupied with understanding the collapse of civilized life that surrounded them in the 20th century. It seems likely that Elias in his early years in England was continuing, largely in isolation, the project he had formulated during the Weimar years, which like many others he may well have experienced as a period of hope. One might ask how a description of the emergence of manners (which Elias proposed as a key indicator of civilization) could provide any kind of consolation at such a time of universal devastation? Perhaps one can regard Elias's work, undertaken in his rather isolated situation as an academic exile in England, as making an implicit political statement of its own.[18] What after all was being fought for, in the war against Fascism, if not a kind of civility, a society in which violent impulses *could* be restrained by culture and convention, in which people *could* live amongst one another as sociable beings? It is possible that Elias chose to identify himself (as many other exiles from Nazism did) with the milder traditions of his adopted country, and that this provided him with the "secure base," as attachment theorists following Bowlby might put it, in which it made some kind of sense to write a story of historical enlightenment, perhaps for some future audience, even as the civilized world was engaged in its own mass destruction.

No-one however paid much attention to Norbert Elias and his work during those years. Although the two volumes of *The Civilizing Process* (Elias, 1983, 2000) were published in German in Switzerland in 1939, and republished in Germany in 1969, it was not until 1978, when Elias was already 81, that his major work was published in English. His was a career that flourished, as far as his reputation if not his productivity are concerned, only in his old age.

Zigmunt Bauman (1979) in his review of Elias's *The Civilizing Process* when it was first pub-lished in English, noted that Elias had sought to answer in the form of a historical narrative the fundamental questions that Freud had raised in *Civilization and its Discontents* (1930). Indeed, Elias's research during the 1930s can be understood as a historical sociologist's response to the questions raised by Freud's thesis.[19] That is, how can the amoral desires of individuals, seeking only their self-centered gratification, not lead to an impossible state of conflict and disorder? Freud had answered his own question by referring to the repressive functions of the superego, and in a more positive way to the role of the sublimation of desire into the symbolic forms of expression of science and art. Elias sought to show from the historical record how these inhibi-tions and displacements of desire had in fact taken place, making possible a gradual shift (initially among the ruling class, but then diffusing down the social scale) away from the pursuit of bodily and brutish appetites toward morally and aesthetically regulated forms of conduct. He described what in Freud's terms, was a process of sublimation of instinctual drives. Elias argued later (2014) that it would be preferable to replace Freud's concept of the repression of instinctual drives with the more inclusive concept of regulation.

In later work on the sociology of sport, Elias and one of his close associates, Eric Dun-ning (Elias & Dunning, 1986) gave a more specific attention to social processes of sublima-tion. They argued that the primary function of mass spectator sports in modern society is to provide a relatively harmless form of symbolic expression to latently violent emotions. Mass sport, on this account, is seen as a sublimation of emotions that might otherwise seek expression in riot or war.

Elias did not believe that civilization was an irreversible process of improvement. In his later work he explored, with newfound colleagues, the reverse development, the conditions of societal regression or decivilization. One study in which the issues of decivilization were explored in the particularistic way that Elias preferred was *The Established and the Outsiders: A Sociological Inquiry Into Community Problems* (Elias & Scotson, 1965). This was a study of a small community, ficti-tiously called Winston Parva, which was experiencing rather severe group conflicts. This work described the social definition of newcomers to the community as inferior, shiftless and deviant. They were defined as members of the "non-respectable" working class, in contrast to the "respectable" working class status of the established group. The researchers found there was no factual basis for the distinction between these populations. However, as a social definition of the reality it had powerful effects. Subject to this stigmatization, and without the long-established social ties that united the members of the established group, the outsiders remained atomized, and tended to internalize the version of itself held by its established neighbors. Urban legend and gossip gave credence to the stereotypes of inadequacy held of the outsiders by the insider group. We might say, using psychoanalytical concepts developed post-Freud, that powerful unconscious projections were being made by the insider group toward the outsiders, and that these had real effects on the identities of those projected into. One can see how Elias's involvement in the development of group psychoanalysis, with Foulkes, may have contributed to his understanding of these social dynamics.

Elias's explanation, in *The Civilizing Process*, of the transformation of instinctual impulses into more differentiated emotional and mental capacities, lay in a theory of complex social dependencies. His argument was that as the chain of dependencies in society grew, for example through trade, an extended division of labor, and communication, so more complex forms of perception and discrimination grew also. This argument is quite close to that of Durkheim's *Division of Labour in Society*, which argued that individuality depended on the emergence of complex forms of social relation in which individuals became emancipated from subordination to the immediate collectivities to which they belonged.[20] Similarly a court society, in which individuals were confronted with an elaborate social hierarchy in which they were required to compete for status and position, was a more complex system of dependencies than the castle of a local baron or warlord. The regression that Elias and Scotson observed to have taken place in Winston Parva was the consequence of a reduction of complexity of social relationships, to a polarized state in which what mattered most was membership of one of two rival groups. In Durkheimian terms, this was a regression to "mechanical solidarity," in which group membership is based on the idea that members share a uniform identity.[21] The outsider group found itself in a still worse condition, since the disrespect heaped on it inhibited the formation of group ties within its number, and thus further reduced the scope of dependencies. This model is applicable many situations of group conflict, of a sectarian or ethnic nature, especially where these involve violence. Elias's argument, concerning the conditions for both civilization and decivilization was also memorably extended to the analysis of racial divisions in the United States, in articles by Eric Dunning (2004), Elias's close colleague, and Loic Wacquant (2004).

Thus Elias's work offers a further example of how psychoanalytic insights can give an additional dimension to sociological analysis, in capturing the ways in which unconscious desires and fantasies influence social relations. Elias's work is valuable in providing examples of a grounded practice of psychoanalytic sociology, at different levels of the social formation. His concept of "figuration" – the self-organization of patterns of group life and their organization – defines the appropriate object of study in the processual terms that are essential for understanding the interrelations between unconscious and conscious states of mind. Elias's concept of figuration anticipates the later insights of "complexity theory" into patterns of self-organization, which complexity theorists ascribe to physical (for example climatic), biological (evolving embryos, life-forms and ecologies), and social entities and life-forms (Byrne, 1998; Quinodoz, 1997). Figuration is also an apt metaphor for the psychoanalytic understanding of the development of personality organizations, both during infancy and within the transference–countertransference relationships of psychoanalysis.[22] The researchers of the successive generations of the Frankfurt School, Talcott Parsons and his associates, and Norbert Elias, are without doubt acknowledged to be major figures within sociology, or a closely related field of social science, who have all had a productive engagement with psychoanalytic ideas. All this work emerged in an epoch in which the disruptions of civilized life by highly irrational currents of feeling and action could hardly be overlooked.

## The "unconscious defenses against anxiety" thesis

The final field of psychoanalytic sociology to be considered here has a different disciplinary location from the first three. Its primary inspiration was psychoanalytical, not sociological, and was derived from the ideas concerning unconscious mental life that Melanie Klein and her colleagues developed from the mid-1920s onward. While it was firmly located in the tradition of Freud's work, Klein's work gave more emphasis than Freud's had done to destructive states of mind, in contrast to his earlier focus on libidinal desire and its repression and sublimation.

Klein described two kinds of unconscious anxiety that emerge in early development. One of these she called *paranoid-schizoid anxiety* (Klein, 1935). This involves the radical splitting of positive and negative feelings toward the primary figures in an infant's life. She held this paranoid-schizoid configuration to be one that persists as a latent disposition throughout life. The other is *depressive anxiety* (Klein, 1946), which arises when the infant is able to perceive that its feelings of love and hatred are in fact directed toward the same and not different objects, and when it becomes capable of concern for the well-being of whoever has been the object of its own negative feelings. The formation of mind, reflected in the capacity for symbol-formation, is associated in Klein and her successors with the attainment of what she called the "depressive position." This is dominated by depressive anxiety (concerned for others) rather than persecutory anxiety (whose concern is for the self).

It is an issue for the social understanding of psychoanalysis whether this emphasis on states of anxiety and hatred were themselves a response to the extreme violence of the period in which these ideas emerged in their developed form, the 1940s. But most relevant to this discussion is the fact that the idea of unconscious defenses against anxiety became understood, initially by Elliot Jacques (1955) and Isabel Menzies Lyth (1960) as a phenomenon found in social groups and institutions, rather than mainly as the unconscious defense mechanisms of individuals seen in the clinical psychoanalytic situation. Both writers were at the time of undertaking their research working as organizational consultants with the Tavistock Institute of Psychoanalysis. Both were also trained as psychoanalysts.

The field of work initiated by them is located primarily in the field of organizational consultancy, and of psychoanalytic practice as this is applied to groups and institutions. Its closest connection to academic sociology is via the "human relations" tradition in the field of industrial sociology. It has been linked there with socio-technical systems analysis, in the research of social scientists such Eric Trist, A. K. Rice and Eric Miller (Trist & Murray, 1990). However, although it is a potentially highly fertile area of psychoanalytical sociological investigation, the study of unconscious defenses against anxiety still has its main existence outside the academy and the mainstream of sociology.

Isabel Menzies Lyth's seminal 1960 paper "The Functioning of Social Systems as a Defence Against Anxiety: Report on a Study of the Nursing Service of a General Hospital" arose from her employment as a consultant, invited to investigate the apparent dysfunctionality of a hospital's system of nurse training. An unacceptable proportion of nurses either left the service before completion of their training, or soon afterwards. Levels of absence and sickness among them were high. Menzies Lyth observed that the system of care was organized in a depersonalized way, discouraging relationships between nurses and their patients, and organizing nursing care as a series of routinized and often mindless tasks, rather than as the care of individual patients. Errors, or supposed errors, were harshly regarded and punished by superiors.

Menzies Lyth explained this situation by reference to a process of unconscious denial of the anxieties inseparable from intimate contact with and the care of sick people, especially when this was assigned to young women receiving little supervision or support in their work. Instead of being reflected on and processed in the mind, anxieties were split off into an obsessional demand for conformity with rules and routines of many kinds. The satisfactions that can come from the experience of care for patients and from its appreciation by them (which had probably been the motive for many in choosing a career in nursing) were effectively denied by the impersonal system that prevailed. Patients were referred to by illness and their bed number rather than their name. Menzies Lyth proposed that the system would function more effectively in almost every respect if underlying anxieties were acknowledged rather than denied, and if the hospital system became more committed to maintaining human relationships, both between nurses and their patients and within the nursing hierarchy itself.

This study was replicated in a different kind of hospital and in the context of day care for children, by Menzies Lyth herself, and by a few other writers. But although this study is still regarded in its field as a classic, and is frequently cited in the contexts of psychoanalytic consultancy and professional training, it has received relatively little systematic empirical or theoretical development. One can envisage, however, that the idea of unconscious defenses against anxiety, in various institutional contexts, could be the foundation of a productive sub-paradigm of research in the field of psychoanalytic sociology A socio-technical systems model of analysis makes it possible to identify the central task and purposes of different varieties of organization, and to clarify the particular the anxieties, both conscious and unconscious, that are liable to follow from such tasks. The anxieties pervading a prison full of latently violent offenders, of a day nursery whose work is with small children newly separated during long periods of a day from their families, of a psychiatric hospital with severely disturbed patients, or of a care home in which many residents are suffering from dementia, are each likely to give rise to different forms of anxiety among staff, and thus to different patterns of unconscious defense against them. Here is a potentially rich field for theoretical and empirical study of a psychoanalytic sociological kind (Armstrong & Rustin, 2014). Such studies can be expected to lead to generalizable findings about the attributes of such institutional settings and their cultures. They could also identify, through action research, improvements in practice that could enable institutions beset by unconscious defenses against anxieties to function in more reflective ways. One attribute that at least some forms of psychoanalytic sociology might have in common with clinical psychoanalytic practice is the sharing of its understandings with the subjects of its inquiries, in a shared process of "learning from experience" (Bion, 1962).

## Conclusion

In this chapter I have sought to describe and explain the marginal position of psychoanalytic sociology in the field of sociology today. I have suggested that significant exceptions to this pattern have occurred primarily in response to serious disruptions of the rational order of society, for example during the period of Nazism and Fascism. Several other examples of such work could have been given. These include Mitscherlich's study (1975) of the consequences of the "inability to mourn" during the years after World War II in West Germany, in which they argued that the "German economic miracle" was in terms of collective psychology an enactment of manic denial of and reparation for the catastrophic damage brought about by Nazi Germany, both across Europe and to Germany itself. Paul Gilroy (2006) developed a theory of post-colonial

Michael Rustin

melancholia to understand the inability of former colonial nations, like Britain, to mourn and relinquish their lost objects of imperial domination, the failure to mourn leaving their populations doomed merely to reenact their earlier habits of racial denigration and splitting.

Another example, hardly sociological as such, but nevertheless bringing psychoanalytic and social insights together, is the effervescent work of Slavoj Žižek (1990, 1993). In his writing, as in all the other work discussed, it is the evidence of an unconscious excess in the phenomena being considered that establishes the relevance of socio–psychoanalytic explanation.

However for psychoanalytic sociology to become established as a recognized field of sociological study, considerable changes are needed within the fields of psychoanalysis and sociology. There needs to be a larger number of sociologists who have a sufficient training in psychoanalysis (it does not necessarily have to include clinical practice) to achieve a capacity for psychoanalytic thinking comparable to that of psychoanalysts themselves. And, it needs a number of psychoanalysts who are sufficiently versed in the methods of social science research to be able to work with sociologists on these questions. Neither of these conditions is currently satisfied on a scale sufficient to bring about such a development. There is need for sustained work, with theoretical, methodological and empirical dimensions, if psychoanalytic sociology is to become established (or perhaps reestablished) as a field of significance both for psychoanalysis and sociology.

## Notes

1　For example, most contemporary anthologies (Ritzer, 1996; Ritzer & Smart, 2001) and leading textbooks of sociological theory (Giddens, 1989) scarcely acknowledge the existence of psychoanalytic sociology. (Giddens's textbook *Sociology* devotes two pages out of 814 to psychoanalysis. In a hyper-rationalistic spirit, he writes (1992) about "pure relationships" as an ideal in modern "reflexive" societies, as if no unconscious residues or dispositions need now stand in the way of free choices.) The more eclectic approach of social rather than merely sociological theory has provided more scope for the recognition of psychoanalytical perspectives, as in Elliott (1999). Although some sociologists (Craib, 1989; Smelser, 1998) have argued for the relevance of unconscious mental life to sociological understanding, and have gathered together key writings in the field (Prager & Rustin, 1993), this advocacy has had little influence on contemporary sociology.

2　The competing disciplines against which sociology sought to establish its legitimacy were principally psychology, economics, political science and in a different register, Marxism. Sociology was in a more collaborative relationship with anthropology, the differences between them being defined more by reference to their fields of empirical study than by their methods, although there have always been differences there too.

3　Parsons wrote that he became interested in Freud while he was writing *The Structure of Social Action*, but too late to take account of his work in that book.

4　An interesting late example of this is to be found in Bourdieu's late work, *Sketch for a Self Analysis* (2008). In this work, Bourdieu took up what he saw as the unavoidable challenge of placing himself within the frame of explanations in terms of "habitus" and "field" through which he had been able to describe and explain many varieties of life journey in different societies.

　　Issues that might normally be thought of as psychoanalytic – for example, phenomena of unconscious motivation and identification – are hard to escape in such an account of a life, especially where a writer is determined to explain and not merely justify and rationalize the choices he has made. And sure enough, although Bourdieu refers to his long antipathy to the world of psychoanalysis, ideas drawn from its realm – "collective fantasy," "community of the unconsciousnesses," ambivalence, guilt – find an important place in his narrative. And after all, he describes his work as a "self-analysis," implicitly following the example of no less than Freud himself (see Steinmetz, 2013).

5　When sociology moved into an "antipositivist" phase in the 1970s, characterized both by a proliferation of theories and by the adoption of qualitative research methods, a vigorous rearguard action in defense of scientific sociology was fought by some of the sociologists who had been most prominent in the earlier phase – for example, John Goldthorpe (2006), who had been distinguished for his research into class structures and social mobility in Britain.

6 Psychoanalysis did have a significant influence in the practical disciplines of marketing and opinion formation, where systematic attention needed to be given to the desires and fantasies of potential consumers of all kinds of goods and services. (Samuel, 2013). The "truth" of Frankfurt School theories of mass culture and its manipulations of motives were being demonstrated and absorbed into "social technologies," at the same time as its theoretical schemes were being rejected as unempirical and unscientific.

7 Freud, as John Forrester (1997) has pointed out, is a household name, and his major works best sellers. Those of Max Weber and Émile Durkheim are not.

8 Indeed, this approach was rejected by the end of the 1970s by both sides – it was seen as too "consensual" and organizationally committed for the trade union left, but as far too participative and democratic for the right.

9 Later, Gellner (1995) took a much more sympathetic view of Freud's work, arguing that his critique of sexual repression had given a desirable legitimation to liberal consumer society, while leaving morality where in Gellner's view it should be, a matter for individual responsibility and negotiation, free from religious constraint.

10 The most substantial defense of psychoanalysis in these terms is that by Paul Ricoeur (1977, 2012).

11 From an influential empiricist perspective on the social sciences, influenced by Popper, attempts to synthesize Marxist and Freudian perspectives was a double error, since neither of these was held to qualify as a legitimate scientific undertaking.

12 These interlocking arguments are set out in seminal papers reprinted in Parsons' *Essays in Sociological Theory* (1954) and *Social Structure and Personality* (1970), and in more theoretical term in Parsons and Bales (1956).

13 The well-established fact that the absence or disruption of secure environments of parental care for infants carries with it high probabilities of damaged life chances, and even of the reproduction of difficulties in parenting in the next generation, should be seen as a verification of the model of family socialization developed both in the Parsonian and the psychoanalytic traditions. This correlation is by now so obvious that it is barely recognized as a significant discovery of the social sciences.

14 Just as the persistence of gender differences and inequalities calls for the recognition of a level of unconscious determination, so do the equally obdurate inequalities and conflicts of race. The phenomena of unconscious identification, projection and splitting are important elements in the construction and maintenance of patterns of racial oppression, and help to explain their deep resistance to change. An essential starting point is Fanon (1952). See also Kovel (1970), Dalal (2002), Clarke (2003), Gilroy (2006) and Rustin (1991, 2012).

15 Mitchell later herself became a psychoanalyst.

16 However, see Campbell (2013) for a forceful argument that this revolution has now gone into reverse.

17 Wright's *Feminism and Psychoanalysis: A Critical Dictionary* (1992) is a useful multiauthored work of reference to this field.

18 Perry Anderson (1968) described the intellectual exiles who fled to Britain and America from communist and fascist regimes as falling into the polar groupings of "white" and "red" exiles, the former mainly migrating to Britain, the latter to the US. But there is also a substantial intermediate category, which one might approximately define as social democratic, among whose members were Pevsner, Mannheim and Elias.

19 The editors of Norbert Elias's *Collected Works* (Vols. 1–18) have edited and translated hitherto-unpublished writing by Elias on Freud and his relevance, in "Freud's Concept of Society and Beyond It" (Elias, 2014). This valuable article clarifies Elias's engagement with Freud's ideas, and his revision of them of them in the light of a sociological understanding of human development. It shows how perceptive was Bauman's (1979) interpretation of Elias's purpose in writing his historical sociology of civilization.

20 Thus as with Parsons, the heritages of Weber, Durkheim and Freud become incorporated by Elias into a unified theoretical model of social development.

21 A useful modern psychoanalytic description of this process is Matte-Blanco's (1988) model of thinking in binary "classes," seen as a reductive process, rather than through the discrimination of different particulars.

22 This is by no means the only example of Elias's uncanny aptitude, in his relative academic isolation, to anticipate theoretical developments which later became central in the work of a subsequent generation of sociologists. Anthony Giddens's idea of structuration is one such; Bourdieu's concept of habitus, another.

Michael Rustin

# References

Adorno, T 1951, 1993, 'Freudian theory and the pattern of fascist propaganda', reprinted in J Prager & M Rustin (eds), *Psychoanalytic sociology*, vol. 1, Edward Elgar, London, pp. 115–134.

Adorno, TW, Frenkel-Brunswi, E, Levinson, D, & Sandford, N 1950, *The authoritarian personality, studies in prejudice series*, vol. 1, Harper and Row, New York.

Adorno, TW & Horkheimer, M 1944, 'Elements of anti-semitism: Limits of enlightenment', in *Dialectic of enlightenment*, Allen Lane, London.

Anderson, P 1968, 'Components of the national vulture', *New Left Review*, vol. 1, no. 50, pp. 3–57.

Arendt, H 1951, *The origins of totalitarianism*, Schocken Books, New York.

Armstrong, D & Rustin, M (eds) 2014, *Social defences against anxiety: Explorations in a paradigm*, Karnac, London.

Bauman, Z 1979, 'The phenomenon of Norbert Elias', *Sociology*, vol. 13, January 1, pp. 117–125.

Bauman, Z 1989, *Modernity and the Holocaust*, Polity Press, Cambridge.

Bauman, Z 2004, *Wasted lives: Modernity and its outcasts*, Polity Press, Cambridge.

Benjamin, J 1988, *The bonds of love: Psychoanalysis, feminism and the problems of domination*, Pantheon, New York.

Bion, W 1962, *Learning from experience*, Rowman & Littlefield Publishers, Lanham.

Bourdieu, P 2008, *Sketch for a self-analysis*, University of Chicago Press, Chicago.

Byrne, D 1998, *Complexity theory and the social sciences: An introduction*, Routledge, London.

Campbell, J 2013, *Freudian passions: Psychoanalysis, form and literature*, Karnac Books, London.

Chodorow, N 1978, *The reproduction of mothering*, University of California Press, Berkeley.

Chodorow, N 1989, *Feminism and psychoanalytic theory*, Yale University Press, New Haven.

Clarke, S 2003, *Social theory, psychoanalysis, and racism*, Palgrave Macmillan, London.

Dalal, F 2002, *Race, colour and the processes of racialisation: New perspectives from group analysis, psychoanalysis and sociology*, Brunner-Routledge, Hove.

De Beauvoir, S 1952, *The second sex*, Alfred Knopf, New York, pp. 38–52.

Dinnerstein, D 1976, *The mermaid and the minotaur*, Harper and Row, New York.

Dunning, E 2004, 'Aspects of the figurational dynamics of racial stratification: A conceptual discussion and developmental analysis of black-white relations in the United States', in S Loyal & S Quilley (eds), *The sociology of Norbert Elias*, Cambridge University Press, Cambridge.

Elias, N 1983, *The court society*, Blackwell, Oxford (rev ed), University of Dublin Press, Dublin, 2006.

Elias, N 2000, *The civilising process* (rev ed), Blackwell, Oxford.

Elias, N 2014, 'Freud's concept of society and beyond it', in S Mennell, M Joly & K Liston (eds), *Collected works of Norbert Elias. Vol. 18: Supplements and index to the collected works*, University College Dublin Press, Dublin.

Elias, N & Dunning, E 1986, *Quest for excitement: Sport and leisure in the civilising process*, Blackwell, Oxford.

Elias, N & Scotson, J 1965, *The established and the outsiders: A sociological inquiry into community problems*, Frank Cass, London.

Fanon, F 1952, *Black skin white masks*, MacGibbon and Kee, London.

Forrester, J 1997, *Dispatches from the Freud wars*, Harvard University Press, Cambridge.

Foucault, M 1998, *The history of sexuality. Vol. 1: The will to knowledge*, Penguin, London.

Freud, S 1913, 'Totem and taboo', in J Strachey (ed), *Standard edition of the complete psychological works of Sigmund Freud*, vol. 13, Hogarth, London.

Freud, S 1921, 'Group psychology and the analysis of the ego', in J Strachey (ed), *Standard edition of the complete psychological works of Sigmund Freud*, vol. 18, Hogarth, London.

Freud, S 1927, 'The future of an illusion', in J Strachey (ed), *Standard edition of the complete psychological works of Sigmund Freud*, vol. 21, Hogarth, London.

Freud, S 1930, 'Civilization and its discontents', J Strachey (ed), *Standard edition of the complete psychological works of Sigmund Freud*, vol. 21, Hogarth, London.

Gellner, E 1985, *The psychoanalytic movement*, Paladin, London.

Gellner, E 1995, 'Freud's social contract', in *Anthropology and politics: Revolutions in the Sacred Grove*, Blackwell, Oxford, pp. 62–93.

Giddens, A 1989, *Sociology*, Polity, Cambridge.

Gilroy, P 2006, *Postcolonial melancholia*, Columbia University Press, New York.

Grunbaum, A 1984, *The foundations of psychoanalysis*, University of California Press, Berkeley.

Grunbaum, A 1993, *Validation in the clinical theory of psychoanalysis: A study in the philosophy of psychoanalysis*, International Universities Press, Madison.

Habermas, J 1971, 'Self reflection as science: Freud's psychoanalytic critique of meaning', in *Knowledge and human interests* (J Shapiro, trans), Beacon Press, Boston, pp. 214–245.

Hook, S (ed) 1959, *Psychoanalysis, scientific method and philosophy*, New York University Press, New York.

Jaques, E 1955, 'Social systems as a defence against persecutory and depressive anxiety', in M Klein, P Hermann & RE Money-Kyrle (eds), *New directions in psychoanalysis*, Tavistock, London, pp. 478–498.

Klein, M 1935, 'A contribution to the psychogenesis of manic-depressive states', *International Journal of Psychoanalysis*, vol. 16, pp. 145–174.

Klein, M 1946, 'Notes on some schizoid mechanisms', *Journal of Psychotherapy Practice and Research*, vol. 5, no. 2, pp. 160–179.

Kovel, J 1970, *White racism: A psychohistory*, Penguin, London.

Lasch, C 1979, *The culture of narcissism*, Norton, New York.

Lukes, S 1973, *Individualism*, Harper and Row, New York.

Matte-Blanco, I 1988, *Thinking, feeling and being*, Routledge, London.

Menzies Lyth, I 1960, 'The functioning of social systems as a defence against anxiety: Report on the nursing service of a general hospital', *Human Relations*, vol. 13, pp. 95–121, reprinted in I Menzies Lyth, 1988, *Containing anxiety in institutions: Selected essays*, Free Association Books, London.

Mitchell, J 1974, *Psychoanalysis and feminism*, Allen Lane, London.

Mitscherlich, A & M 1975, *The inability to mourn: Principles of collective behaviour*, Grove Press, New York.

Parsons, T 1937, *The structure of social action*, Free Press, Glencoe, IL.

Parsons, T 1942a, 'Some sociological aspects of the fascist movements', reprinted in Parsons, 1954.

Parsons, T 1942b, 'Propaganda and social control', reprinted in Parsons, 1954.

Parsons, T 1954, *Essays in sociological theory*, Free Press, Glencoe, IL.

Parsons, T 1970, *Social structure and personality*, Free Press, Glencoe, IL.

Parsons, T & Bales, RF 1956, *Family socialisation and interaction process*, Routledge and Kegan Paul, London.

Popper, KR 1963, *Conjectures and refutations*, Routledge and Kegan Paul, London, pp. 33–65.

Quinodoz, J-M 1997, 'Transitions in psychic structures in the light of deterministic chaos theory', *International Journal of Psychoanalysis*, vol. 78, no. 4, pp. 699–718.

Ricoeur, P 1977, *Freud and philosophy*, Yale University Press, New Haven.

Ricoeur, P 2012, *On psychoanalysis*, Polity Press, Cambridge.

Ritzer, G (ed) 1996, *Sociological theory* (4th ed), McGraw-Hill, New York.

Ritzer, G & Smart, B 2001, *Handbook of social theory*, Sage, London.

Rose, N 1989, *Governing the soul: The shaping of the private self*, Free Association Books, London.

Rustin, M 1991, *The good society and the inner world*, Verso, London.

Rustin, MJ 2012, 'Race, ethnicity, nationality', in GO Gabbard, BE Litowitz & P Williams (eds), *Textbook of psychoanalysis* (2nd ed), American Psychoanalytic, Washington, DC, pp. 495–506.

Samuel, LR 2013, *Freud on Madison Avenue: Motivation research and subliminal advertising in America*, University of Pennsylvania Press, Philadelphia.

Steiner, R 1994, ' "The tower of Babel", or "After Babel in contemporary psychoanalysis"?', *International Journal of Psychoanalysis*, vol. 75, pp. 883–901.

Steinmetz, G 2013, 'Towards socioanalysis: The traumatic kernel of psychoanalysis and neo-Bourdieuian theory', in PS Gorski (ed), *Bourdieu and historical analysis*, Duke University Press, London, pp. 108–130.

Trist, E & Murray, H 1990, *The social engagement of social science. Vol. 1: The socio-psychological perspective*, Free Association Books, London, pp. 476–493.

Tuckett, D 2005, 'Some developments in psychoanalytic thinking in Great Britain and Continental Europe', in M Cooper, G Gabbard & E Person (eds), *American Psychiatric Publishing textbook of psychoanalysis*. American Psychiatric, Washington DC and London, pp. 407–422.

Wacquant, L 2004, 'Decivilising and demonising: The remaking of the black American ghetto', in S Loyal & S Quilley (eds), *The sociology of Norbert Elias*. Cambridge University Press, Cambridge, pp. 95–121.

Wallerstein, R 2005, 'Will psychoanalytic pluralism be the enduring state of our discipline?' *International Journal of Psychoanalysis*, vol. 86, pp. 623–626.

Žižek, S 1990, 'Beyond discourse analysis', in E Laclau, *New reflections on the revolution of our time*, Verso, London, pp. 249–260.

Žižek, S 1993, *Everything you always wanted to know about Lacan but were afraid to ask*, Verso, London.

# 16

# Philosophy and psychoanalysis

*Adrian Johnston*

Oceans of ink have been, and continue to be, spilled on addressing the intimate yet fraught rapport between psychoanalysis and philosophy. There are many different approaches to exploring the convergences and divergences between these two fields, including (but not limited to) pinpointing the shared fundamental questions asked and answered by both, however similarly or not; charting the historical and intellectual influences of select philosophers from ancient Greece through 19th-century Europe on Sigmund Freud and his analytic progeny; examining the reciprocal influences exerted by Freudian and post-Freudian analysis on philosophical figures and movements in the 20th and early 21st centuries; philosophically interpreting and/or critiquing psychoanalysis (and vice versa); and reading Freud and other analytic thinkers as philosophers. At this point in history, only a single century into the life of the analytic tradition (and this by contrast with over 2,500 years of Western philosophy), the various bodies of literature mapping the complex intersections between psychoanalysis and philosophy would, by themselves, fill a decent-sized library.

In this targeted intervention, I will combine historical and theoretical angles of approach in the course of explaining how Freud and Jacques Lacan in particular uniquely inspire and underpin a specific contemporary philosophical position. To be more precise, I herein unpack how these two towering giants of analysis provide crucial resources buttressing the apparatus of my "transcendental materialism" (an apparatus I will sketch in what follows, in addition to having defined and characterized it in detail on a number of other occasions) (Johnston, 2008, 2013a, 2013b, 2014).[1] This exercise not only will illustrate one set of possible philosophical ramifications flowing from the ideas of Freud and Lacan; it also hopefully will shed new light on multiple facets of Freud's and Lacan's psychoanalytic reflections. That is to say, what follows strives to initiate a truly interdisciplinary endeavor in which philosophy and psychoanalysis mutually enrich each other, rather than a lopsided pursuit in which one discipline dominates the other.

However, before soon starting the mandatory labor of outlining the central contours of transcendental materialism, some additional preliminary framing promises to be both appropriate and helpful.

Roughly contemporaneous with the turn-of-the-century birth of psychoanalysis – this historical fact is common knowledge among professional philosophers, but perhaps less familiar to others – a rift opens up within Western philosophy between European and Anglo-American factions, namely, what has long since come to be labeled the "Continental-Analytic" divide. (This gulf, however, reflects a much older difference between philosophical temperaments separated by the English Channel, tracing back to the 17th and 18th centuries with conflicts between the Continental rationalists such as René Descartes, Nicolas Malebranche, Baruch Spinoza and G. W. Leibniz and British empiricists such as Thomas Hobbes, John Locke, George Berkeley and David Hume.) Anglo-American Analytic philosophy originates, in part, with the rebellions of Gottlob Frege, Bertrand Russell, Ludwig Wittgenstein and company against the inherited weight of the history of philosophy, with its myriad inbuilt assumptions and presuppositions. Rejecting and repudiating late 19th-century British Hegelianism especially (but, along with this peculiar strain of German-inspired idealism, much of the philosophical history relied upon by G.W.F. Hegel and his exegetes), the founders of the Analytic movement, which eventually established its still-reigning hegemony in English-speaking philosophy departments, in essence mimicked the gesture performed by Descartes in the 17th century. They jettisoned the baggage bequeathed by historical philosophies (in Descartes's case, it was the received wisdom of the ancient Greeks and medieval scholastics) so as to wipe the intellectual slate clean and begin philosophizing once again from scratch, seeking to solve perennial philosophical problems with logically and conceptually airtight arguments instead of dubious appeals to venerated past authorities. Debates within a community of scientist-like problem solvers, rather than proliferations of reconstructions of esteemed canonical writers, is held up by partisans of the Analytic orientation as a superior method of philosophizing in general. Whereas disputes about dehistoricized philosophical topics amid a field of contemporaneous authors is the norm for Analytics (what could be described as a "horizontal" model of philosophizing), Continentalists generally remain reliant upon readings of prior authors as the motors propelling forward their discussions (what, by contrast, could be depicted as a "vertical" model).

In certain respects, Freud can be seen as proximate to aspects of Anglo-American philosophy as briefly and crudely portrayed earlier. Like this philosophical orientation's originators, he is suspicious of (and sometimes even outright opposed to) the assumptions and beliefs of many prior Western philosophers (Freud, 1901).[2] He generally takes care to refrain from recourse to the historically laden and overdetermined conceptual vocabulary of these cultural predecessors, often opting instead to forge his own specifically analytic technical terminology (whereas Lacan, in line with the tendencies of other [French] Continentalists, subsequently reintroduces key concept terms from the history of philosophy into the Freudian domain) (Johnston, 2013).[3] In other words, in a fashion resembling both Descartes and the inaugurators of the Analytic tradition, Freud clears the historical-contextual ground so as to lay new foundations unburdened by various and sundry inherited articles of faith.

Even more strikingly, Freud has a distaste for the same sorts of prior philosophies dismissed by the pioneers of the Analytic movement. He favorably invokes Heinrich Heine's derogatory depiction of the figure of the philosopher, an image undeniably referring to Hegel first and foremost (Freud, 1901).[4] Additionally, Freud's overall suspicion of philosophy as a whole is in no small part due to his disdain for the medical legacy of F.W.J. Schelling's *Naturphilosophie* (Freud, 1901)[5] (although his 1919 essay "The Uncanny" appeals to Schelling in relation to the topics of repression and the unconscious) (Freud, 1901).[6] For both Frege et al. and Freud, late 18th- and early 19th-century German idealism (à la Kant, J.G. Fichte, Schelling, and Hegel) – Kant too, especially his "Transcendental Aesthetic" (in the *Critique of Pure Reason*) and ethics of pure practical reason (as per the *Critique of Practical Reason* as well as the "metaphysics of morals" also articulated in other texts), sometimes is a target of criticisms by Freud (Freud, 1901)[7] – epitomizes the speculative excesses and groundlessly wild flights of imaginative fancy to be eschewed by clear-, hard-, and level-headed thinking informed by and modeled on scientific cognition.

And, as just indicated, Freud, again like much of Analytic philosophy past and present, allies his pursuits to the sensibilities of the empirical, experimental natural sciences of modernity (what he labels the "scientific Weltanschauung") (Freud, 1901).[8] Thus, he ignores such Continental contemporaries – 20th-century European (qua non-Anglophone) philosophy in its entirety springs mainly from Kant and Hegel – as Henri Bergson, Edmund Husserl, and Martin Heidegger, despite the numerous (and, by now, well-documented) overlaps between his and their concerns. Similarly, when these Continentalists are mentioned by their Analytic contemporaries, it almost always is as butts of mockery and scorn.

Nevertheless, although my preceding remarks suggest that there is a substantial amount of common ground shared between psychoanalysis and Analytic philosophy, practitioners of the latter have tended to neglect or dismiss the former. However rightly or wrongly – from a Lacanian perspective, this is a grave mistake (Johnston, 2013c)[9] – many philosophers, especially Analytics, see Freud as the advocate of a neo-Romanticism of dark, unruly depths (in line with the tastes of the later Schelling, Arthur Schopenhauer, and Friedrich Nietzsche – admittedly, Freud favorably mentions these thinkers by name as predecessors (Freud, 1901),[10] while, on a Lacanian reading, such mentions are dangerously misleading). He is perceived as the preacher of an irrationalist gospel according to which human beings are the puppets and playthings of seething cauldrons of brute, raw, animalistic instincts surging and billowing just beneath the thin surfaces of heteronomous consciousness. For most Analytic philosophers, committed as they are to precise and sober dissections of ostensibly self-transparent human mindedness, such (neo-)Romantic irrationalism is nothing less than absolutely anathema. What is more, in light of the Western philosophical tradition's deeply entrenched habit of equating the mental with the conscious, the unconscious of Freudian analysis is not something philosophers are inclined by training to embrace (although this is far from the only reason for this disinclination) (Freud, 1901; Johnston, 2010).[11]

Despite some of the overlap between Freud and the Analytics as underlined earlier, Continental philosophers and their offspring in the theoretical humanities have been those most committed to a serious and sustained reckoning with Freudian psychoanalysis.

Although the transcendental and existential phenomenologies of Husserl and Heidegger maintain wary, skeptical distance from Freud, most of the rest of 20th-century philosophy on the Continent engages closely and passionately with analysis both theoretical and practical – not only post-Heideggerian phenomenologies, but nearly the whole range of Continental movements and figures: existentialism, critical theory, structuralism, post-structuralism, semiotics, deconstruction and feminism; Jean-Paul Sartre, Maurice Merleau-Ponty, Paul Ricoeur, Theodor Adorno, Max Horkheimer, Herbert Marcuse, Claude Lévi-Strauss, Louis Althusser, Michel Foucault, Roland Barthes, Gilles Deleuze, Félix Guattari, Julia Kristeva, Luce Irigaray, Jean-François Lyotard, Jacques Derrida and up through Alain Badiou, Judith Butler and Slavoj Žižek (with Lacan's "return to Freud" crucially shaping many of these thinkers' approaches to Freud himself) (Johnston, 2013c).[12] To these non-exhaustive lists of orientations and authors should be added a wealth of studies putting Freud and his legacy into various connections with the 19th-century roots of 20th-century Continental philosophy, namely, German idealism, early existentialism and Marxism. Thoroughly cataloguing the historical and intellectual forces and factors responsible for analysis generally falling on the Continental side of the Continental-Analytic divide would be a book-length endeavor unto itself. For now, suffice it to say that, unlike most Analytics, most Continentalists gravitate toward Freudian analysis precisely because of its challenging implications for traditional and/or conventional nonanalytic (including philosophical) conceptions of subjectivity, consciousness, agency, autonomy, desire, sexuality, embodiment, ethics and politics, among many other topics. At least on the Continent for the last century, the widespread consensus is that philosophy cannot remain the same, cannot continue as before, in the wake of Freud's discovery of the unconscious and those myriad structures and phenomena related to it.

Against this backdrop, transcendental materialism is an outgrowth primarily of Continental lineages, although I seek to put it into dialogue with Anglo-American Analytic philosophy (especially the neo-Hegelianism of Pittsburgh [John McDowell and Robert Brandom] and Chicago [Robert Pippin]; Johnston, 2011a)[13] as well as, more broadly, philosophy of mind and cognitive science). German idealism, Marxism, and Lacanianism (a triad crucial for Žižek and the Ljubljana School of Psychoanalysis) (Johnston & Žižek, 2013)[14] provide its main 19th- and 20th-century European sources of historical and theoretical inspiration. To oversimplify at this initial stage, transcendental materialism aims to be an interdisciplinary extension of dialectical materialism for the 21st century (Johnston, 2013b).[15] But, what, exactly, is this specific variant of materialism? And, how is it related to psychoanalysis à la Freud and Lacan?

I can start answering the first of these two questions by situating transcendental materialism in relation to nine axes, with each axis being a distinction between the complementary poles of two opposed philosophical alternatives. Some of these distinctions have structured the entire sweep of the history of Western philosophy since its beginnings in ancient Greece (arguably Axes One, Two, Four, Six, and Eight), whereas others have come to play central roles only more recently in the modern and/or contemporary eras (arguably Axes Three, Five, Seven, and Nine) – this is not in the least false to say that the axes with prominent roots in ancient Greece do not remain live fault lines of dispute well after antiquity and even up through today. Particularly for my purposes here, the following nine axes of distinctions are helpful and important to consider:

1   idealism versus materialism
2   theism versus atheism
3   humanism/subjectivism versus antihumanism/subjectivism
4   freedom versus determinism
5   ahistorical/decontextualized contemplation versus historical/contextualized practice
6   dualism versus monism
7   transcendentalism versus immanentism
8   metaphysical realism versus nominalism
9   (re)enchantment versus disenchantment.

From a contemporary synchronic standpoint nonetheless informed by the diachrony of intellectual history, the first terms of each axis-distinction, as I have just enumerated them, are inclined to align and link up with each other, as are likewise the second terms amongst themselves too. In other words, these nine axes tend to generate a more basic hypothetical binary opposition between, on the one hand, a type of stance characterized by idealism, theism, humanism/subjectivism, freedom, ahistorical/decontextualized contemplation, dualism, transcendentalism, metaphysical realism, and (re)enchantment, and, on the other hand, a sharply contrasting type of stance characterized by materialism, atheism, antihumanism/subjectivism, determinism, historical/contextualized practice, monism, immanentism, nominalism, and disenchantment. An Althusserian Marxist might be tempted to identify these admittedly artificial, historically/factually inaccurate models of two clashing stances as symptomatic of "class struggle in theory" (Althusser, 2001, pp. 2, 5–6, 8–9).[16] In this context, the Engels-Lenin thesis about the primacy of the idealism-materialism antagonism (i.e., Axis One) in the history of philosophy could be translated as using the labels "idealism" and "materialism" more broadly to refer to the just-mentioned hypothetical split between opposed tendencies traversing the terms of all nine axes of distinction I am employing here (Engels, 1941; Lenin, 1972).[17] Along these lines (following along with Karl

Marx, Friedrich Engels, V.I. Lenin and Louis Althusser), Plato, Descartes and Kant would, each in his own way, partially fall more into the "idealist" camp (i.e., idealism, theism, humanism/subjectivism, freedom, ahistorical/decontextualized contemplation, dualism, transcendentalism, metaphysical realism and (re)enchantment). Meanwhile, Aristotle, Spinoza and Hegel would, each in his own way, partially fall more into the "materialist" camp (i.e., materialism, atheism, antihumanism/subjectivism, determinism, historical/contextualized practice, monism, immanentism, nominalism and disenchantment). Although this either/or meta-axis of tension is an oversimplifying virtual-synchronic construct somewhat disrespectfully sandwiching together and rather brutally disregarding a plethora of actual-diachronic facts about the history of philosophy, it still helpfully captures a pair of fundamental centers of ideational gravity in the form of two never perfectly instantiated, albeit nonetheless palpably influential, ideal attractor points shaping the real movements of the history of philosophy.

Nearly all, if not all, of the great figures of the Western philosophical canon mix and match elements from the idealist and materialist (in the broad Marxist sense of these two labels mentioned a moment ago) poles of the nine axes of distinction I quickly catalogued in the two preceding paragraphs. Furthermore, interpreters of such figures often try to challenge established categorizations of the canonized greats as per these various distinctions (very recent examples include Badiou's Plato and Žižek's Hegel).

Transcendental materialism is no exception to this rule. It too crosses back and forth between the first-term (generally idealist) and second-term (generally materialist) sides of the nine axes of distinction. Furthermore, it resists identification at the levels of certain of these binary axes. The remainder of this chapter will be devoted to two interrelated tasks: first, situating transcendental materialism in relation to each of the nine aforementioned axes of distinction; second (and in conjunction with the first task), specifying how Freudian-Lacanian psychoanalysis directly informs these nine dimensions delineating the core facets of this philosophical position/system.

Beginning naturally enough with Axis One (idealism versus materialism), transcendental materialism, as its very name announces, is materialist rather than idealist. Of course, construals of exactly what "materialism" means vary, particularly depending on how it is understood in light of other philosophical orientations (such as those enumerated here as Axes Two through Nine). For now, prior to nuancing my presentation of materialism in connection with other relevant philosophical commitments, I will define materialism, with provisional bluntness, as rooted in a thesis about the ontological primacy of matter – with the latter being conceived as the objective corollary of the sorts of empirical observation and experimentation practiced by the a posteriori modern sciences of nature (already, this preliminary definition of materialism brings with it naturalism, empiricism and scientism as accompanying philosophical ingredients). With the phrase "the ontological primary of matter," I have in mind the claim that everything that exists is either itself directly material qua physically inhabiting space and time or has things material as at least necessary (if not also sufficient) conditions for its existence (including, maybe, so-called emergent properties). By implication, materialism thus (crudely) characterized entails a denial of the reality of purely immaterial objects and processes as thoroughly disembodied, metaphysical, spiritual and the like.

As regards Freudian and Lacanian analysis, Freud's proximity to materialism perhaps is easier to discern at first glance than Lacan's. Freud begins his career in the late 19th century as an investigator of mental life under the dual dovetailing influences of his medical education in neurology and the physicalism of Gustav Fechner, Hermann von Helmholtz, Carl Claus and Theodor Meynert. From his pre/proto-psychoanalytic writings of the 1890s (such as the posthumously published 1895 "Project for a Scientific Psychology") onward, he frequently appeals to biology especially as a present or future support for his analytic metapsychology, even as the theory and practice of analysis are running far ahead of the state of the life sciences circa the turn of the 20th century. For Freud, not only is there no psyche without a brain (i.e., the latter is, at a minimum, a necessary condition for the former) – the body of which the central nervous system is but a part, through what soma substantially contributes to psyche at the levels of sexuality and the libidinal economy with its drives (Triebe), is absolutely central to mindedness as comprehended by analysis. Moreover, and as I noted earlier, Freud tethers the field he founds to the overarching worldview (Weltanschauung) of the a posteriori experimental natural sciences of modernity. Hence, his materialism is colored by these sciences and a related empiricism. However, by contrast with most other materialisms of these hues, Freud's is not mechanistic, reductive or eliminative, being closer to historical and dialectical materialisms (of which transcendental materialism is a 21st-century extension – with this to be fully explained in what follows in connection with Axes Three through Nine).

Although Freud shows no signs of recognizing his affinities with historical/dialectical materialism, Lacan, particularly during later phases of his teaching, explicitly draws attention to them (Lacan, 1971[2006], 1990; Johnston, 2014).[18] Despite Lacan's repeated self-identifications as both a Freudian analyst and a (dialectical) materialist, many of his interpreters situated largely in the theoretical humanities have failed to register the significance of his materialism. This is partly due to the fact that Lacan, insofar as he is a 20th-century French thinker openly engaged with his European philosophical predecessors and contemporaries, tends to be studied by students and scholars under the spell of those strains of the Continental tradition wary of and/or hostile to the empirical sciences of nature. These strains originate in late 18th-century German Pietism and Romanticism, subsequently taking shape through a line of transmission running through the aging Schelling, Søren Kierkegaard, Schopenhauer, Nietzsche, and on through the 20th century, deeply influencing phenomenology and its offshoots in particular; an alternate tendency to this neo-Romantic one can be traced through Hegel, Marx, Engels, Lenin, the later Georg Lukács, Badiou, Žižek and, as per the exegeses I am proposing here, Freud and Lacan too. Continental types often negatively associate science-informed materialism with the vulgar horrors of reductivism and eliminativism (such associations usually are linked to an oversimplifying view of Analytic philosophy as a homogeneous, monolithic whole – as though, for instance, all Anglo-American philosophers of mind are eliminativists in the mold of Paul and Patricia Churchland). Consequently, Lacan's science-informed (yet neither reductive nor eliminative) materialism – on other occasions, I have argued at length and in detail that his materialism is not, as it too often is taken to be, categorically opposed to the natural sciences (Johnston, 2011a, 2014)[19] – typically is distorted or ignored altogether by his readers. On my interpretation, his complaints and critiques directed at such overlapping targets as biology and naturalism do not express a sweepingly unqualified anti-naturalist dismissal of the life sciences and those materialisms wedded to them so much as a narrower, more precise rejection of the ideologically compromised biologisms and scientisms operative within certain sectors of the post-Freudian psychoanalytic world both clinical and theoretical (the main guilty party being, for Lacan, classical American ego-psychology, with naturalistic rationalizations accompanying its therapeutic norms) (Johnston, 2012b; Lacan, 2006).[20]

The two main dimensions of Lacan's materialism can be aligned with two of his three registers, the Real and the Symbolic (with the Imaginary being the third register) (Johnston, 2013a).[21] At the level of the Real, Lacan, taking his lead from Freud's reflections on human prematurational helplessness (i.e., the biological givens of infantile anatomical and physiological Hilflosigkeit) (Freud, 1901),[22] posits a fragmentary, internally conflicted, and libidinally animated and agitated body-in-pieces (corps morcelé) as the bio-material ground zero of ontogenetic ego- and subject-formation (Johnston, 2012a; Lacan, 1959, 1988).[23] Particularly in his various narrations of the famous "mirror stage," Lacan subtly links Hilflosigkeit to Freud's emphases on originary, id-level conflicts as hard-wired into the fractured foundations of the psyche's libidinal economy (Freud, 1901; Johnston, 2012a; Lacan, 1955[1988], 1956a)[24] (this motif of conflict will be quite important in the discussions of Axes Two and Four later).

In addition to this, as it were, corpo-Real (and in complex dialectical interaction with it), Lacan, at the level of the Symbolic, advances a doctrine concerning the "materiality of the signifier" (Lacan, 1953–54[1988], 1954–55, 1956, 1970, 1988a; Johnston, 2009, 2014).[25] To cut a long story short (albeit one to be taken up again later apropos Axis Eight), Lacan widens the scope of the word "matter" to include the graphic and acoustic substances composing written and spoken language in its material, rather than meaningful, dimensions (i.e., the Real side of the Symbolic itself or, in more traditional Freudian metapsychological parlance, the side of psychical "word-presentations" [Wortvorstellungen] directly functioning as "thing-presentations" [Sachvorstellungen] (Freud, 1901, pp. 202–203; Johnston, 2005, pp. 300–315; Laplanche & Pontalis, 1973, pp. 447–448).[26] Not only is the meaningless materiality of linguistic signifiers audible in drive-saturated poetic and musical employments of language – as first revealed in detail within such foundational analytic texts by the early Freud as *The Interpretation of Dreams* (1900), *The Psychopathology of Everyday Life* (1901), and *Jokes and Their Relation to the Unconscious* (1905), the formations of the unconscious are constructed, at least in large part, out of associations governed by logics of linkage other than those recognized as coherent, grammatical, intelligible, sensible and the like. In other words, Lacan's extrapolation of Saussurian structuralism beyond the confines of linguistics (an extrapolation allowing for Freudian thing-presentations to count as signifiers in a broadened sense) permits him to recast with surprisingly high fidelity Freud's "primary process" model of unconscious mentation as dynamics of interaction between material signifiers qua ideational representations (Vorsellungen) interacting in fashions unconstrained by conscious considerations of meaningfulness (as per the constraints of "secondary process" thinking, with its respect for the conventions of recognized semantics and syntax, classical bivalent logic, and linear chronology) (Freud, 1901; Laplanche & Pontalis, 1973).[27] Subverting standard manners of opposing idealism and materialism, Lacan, with his theory of the material signifier, posits the effective existence of material elements internal (or, more precisely, "extimate" as per a Lacanian neologism signifying intimate externality or inner exclusion) (Lacan, 1959–60[1992], p. 139; 1968–69[2006])[28] to what typically is taken to be the sphere of ideality, namely, that of linguistically mediated psychical subjectivity (i.e., Lacan's *parlêtre* [speaking being]).

Turning now to Axis Two (theism versus atheism), transcendental materialism is a stringent atheism, albeit one seeking to explain those apparently more-than-material entities and events sustaining the enduring temptations of spiritualist idealisms in a non-reductive/eliminative, and yet uncompromisingly materialist, manner. In terms of this dimension of transcendental materialism's debts to psychoanalysis, identifying Freudian analysis as atheistic hardly should be controversial. Freud's 1927 *The Future of an Illusion* is one of the fiercest and most powerful antireligious manifestos of all time.

Other Freudian texts (such as "Obsessive Actions and Religious Practices" [1907], Totem and Taboo [1913], Civilization and Its Discontents [1930], and Moses and Monotheism [1939]) likewise severely undermine the plausibility of religions, casting multiple shadows of massive doubts over anything and everything otherworldly, spiritualistic, theistic, and so on. In addition to specifically analytic reasons for being skeptical apropos all things religious (reasons having to do with clinical and metapsychological understandings of the unconscious, defense mechanisms, affect regulation, libidinal tendencies, familial influences, etc.), Freud sees his self-proclaimed alliance with the worldview of the secular sciences of modernity as augmenting the atheistic thrust of analysis (Freud, 1901).[29] This is a consequence of Freud's adherence to the perspective of an

Enlightenment story according to which the rift between religion and science (in the Baconian-Galilean sense as empirical and experimental) opening up with the birth of the latter in the early 17th century divides two sides along the lines of a zero-sum antagonistic relationship. As per certain 18th-century predecessors (as well as some from the 19th century – Marx, most notably), Freud anticipates that religion will wane in precise proportion to the waxing of science, with technoscientific progress driving along, as one of its by-products, correspondingly progressive sociocultural secularization. Moreover, this anticipation reflects Freud's tacit acceptance of the strong mutual attraction, both historical and philosophical, between materialism (here as scientific naturalism and empiricism) and atheism, a bond tracing back to the godlessness of the atomists and Epicureans of antiquity.

Lacan significantly complicates Freud's avowed atheism without, for all that, abandoning or betraying it. To begin with, he locates the atheistic essence of analysis not in its fidelity to the secular scientific Weltanschauung, but, instead, in its fundamental stress on conflict and inconsistency (Johnston, 2013a, 2014)[30] (as will be seen, conflict and inconsistency also play important roles in tandem with Axis Four below). On Lacan's construal, the scientistic outlook of modernity to which Freud appeals is, in actuality, not fully and thoroughly atheistic insofar as its faithful adherents merely transfer the attributes and powers previously ascribed to the God of monotheisms to their more-than-empirical vision of Nature as a single omnipotent Being, as a grand cosmic One-All in which each and every scrap of being has its precisely determined place in a seamlessly cohesive order ruled by eternal, inviolable laws (Johnston, 2013a, 2014; Lacan, 1959–60; 1969–70[2007], 1972–73[1998]; 1976–77).[31] In Lacanese, this Nature-with-a-capital-N, that of Laplace's Demon and assorted naturalist ideologies, is just another figuration of "the big Other," namely, the fantasy of an ultimate authority guaranteeing that existence has its final rhymes and reasons (Johnston, 2013a, 2014).[32] By contrast, what renders Freudian analysis (in its Lacanian reincarnation) truly and uncompromisingly godless is its advancement of the thesis that, "*Le grand Autre n'existe pas*" ("The big Other does not exist" – and this whether as God, Nature, Society, the Analyst qua "subject supposed to know" ["*sujet supposé savoir*"], and whomever or whatever else erected in this transcendent transferential position) (Johnston, 2013a, 2014; Lacan, 1962–63[2004]; 1964[1977]; 1968–69; 1969–70).[33] Specifically apropos nature (qua the ultimate ontological foundation of factical material substance[s]), Lacan implicitly draws out a logically consequent ramification of Freud's emphases on conflict, particularly as per his post-1920 dual drive model in which the antagonism between Eros and the Todestrieb is primordially incarnated in the id of the embodied psyche (Freud, 1901):[34] As human nature, itself a part of nature *überhaupt*, testifies, nature itself is a discordant disunity, being shot through with collisions, disharmonies, gaps, splits, tensions, and the like (in more Lacanian parlance, nature is an uncoordinated, fragmentary "not all" ["*pas tout*"], a "barred" Real as another nonexistent big Other in addition to the barred Symbolic (Lacan, 1960–61 [2001], 1969, 1973–74, 1975–76 [2005], 1977; Johnston, 2008, 2011a, 2012c, 2013a)[35] – namely, what, following Hegel, I call a "weak nature" (Johnston, 2011a, 2013a, 2013c, 2013d)[36]).

Lacan also is acutely aware of a much more glaringly obvious problem with Freud's inherited Enlightenment assumptions about the relationship between scientific and atheistic worldviews. Almost a century of subsequent history, one overflowing with proliferating new fundamentalisms, has not been kind to the prediction made by Freud in The Future of an Illusion of the withering away of religiosity under the pressures of science-fueled modernization (Freud, 1901).[37] During a 1974 press conference in Rome transcribed and published (in 1975) with the title "The Triumph of Religion," Lacan, without compromising in the slightest his commitment to the atheism proper to Freudian analysis, seeks to explain what went wrong with Freud's 1927 prophecy of the looming defeat of religion. Rather than merely having recourse to the true but (overly) general analytic observation that human psychical subjects can and do sustain split stances in which they simultaneously hold to contradictory positions (such as, for instance, certain mutually exclusive scientific and religious claims), Lacan persuasively argues that the apparent rendering of material/natural being meaningless by the desacralizing effects of relentlessly accumulating technoscientific advances propels many people into the arms of spiritualisms and theisms as providing compensations for lost meanings. That is to say, Lacan's thesis, contra the Enlightenment and Freud, is that religion gets increasingly reinvigorated by the forward march of science insofar as the former absorbs the shocks of the latter; in still other words, religious resacralization is embraced as counteracting the perceived desacralization threateningly promised by the advances of the secular sciences (I subsequently will revisit the issue of de/resacralization in my treatment of Axis Nine).

Lacan accepts Freud's aligning of psychoanalysis with the scientific Weltanschauung specifically to the extent that, in Lacan's eyes, both analysis and the natural sciences, each in their own ways, ultimately reduce the fundaments of existence (whether the objects of science or the subjects of analysis) to the baseless base of a contingent, senseless Real. Hence, he concludes that neither science nor analysis will vanquish religion given the enduring preferences of the vast majority of human beings for meaningful Imaginary-Symbolic realities (however fictive and regressive) over a meaningless Real. The sciences and their technologies, for socioeconomic reasons tightly tied to the ongoing unfurling of global capitalism, will continue to thrive side-by-side with religions (whose own proportionally corresponding thriving is driven by the very acceleration of these same sciences and technologies). For Lacan, analysis, jointly marginalized by both religion and science within the context of late capitalism, can hope, at least for the time being, only to limp along, surviving but not flourishing. He thereby supplements Freud's inventory of "resistances to psychoanalysis" (Freud, 1901; Johnston & Malabou, 2013; Johnston, 2014; Lacan, 2005).[38] For the foreseeable future, both analytic atheism as well as analysis in general must willfully persist in embattled positions vis-à-vis the perverse codependent couple of scientism and spiritualism. However bleak the prospects, this is a struggle worth continuing.

As regards the coordinates of Axis Three (humanism/subjectivism versus antihumanism/sub-jectivism), transcendental materialism aligns itself with the humanist/subjectivist pole. Whereas this is a straightforward and unproblematic move in Freud's wake, it is somewhat contentious in Lacan's. With his avowedly profound indebtedness to the full sweep of Western intellectual/cultural history and focus on uniquely human mindedness and like-mindedness, Freud fleshes out a rich account of human nature and corresponding metapsychological theory of subjectivity (although he does not employ the philosophical term "subject" – Lacan is responsible for explicitly introducing this word into the lexicon of Freudian analysis (Johnston, 2013c)[39] – his mappings of the psyche are open to construal as delineating the contours of what defensibly could be called "subjectivity"). In Freud's conceptual universe, human beings as psychical subjects are distinctively privileged creatures different-in-kind from everything else under the sun.

Lacan complicates matters at the level of Axis Three. On the one hand, in line with his engagements with structuralism and its aftermath, he embraces an antihumanist outlook, one according to which psychoanalysis undermines traditional notions of "man" and "human nature." On the other hand, and by contrast with structuralist-style sensibilities, he does not lump together anti-humanism and anti-subjectivism, instead retaining the centrality of the concept of subjectivity (including the Cogito-like subject of modern philosophy) within a postwar French context in which this concept had been deemed to be passé at best. In short, Lacan is simultaneously an antihumanist and a subjectivist.

Yet, despite his participation in then-fashionable choruses proclaiming the "death of man," Lacan shares with Freud a special concern with the idiosyncrasies, oddities and peculiarities of human animals, with both the first and second natures of these weird, denaturalized organisms. On my reading, Lacan's version of analysis, notwithstanding some of his rhetoric borrowed from a mid-20th-century Parisian Zeitgeist, is not so much antihumanist as an innovative, radical transformation of humanity qua the object-referent of classical humanism.

As is common knowledge, Axis Four (freedom versus determinism) represents one of the perennial "big questions" of the entire history of philosophy up through the present day. Many people both within and beyond psychoanalytic and philosophical circles take Freudian analysis fundamentally to be a discourse of determinism. Is not one of the major consequences of the discovery of the unconscious the conclusion that persons' conscious senses of being free-willed, self-determining, autonomous agents are empty delusions masking heteronomous (over)determination by defensively occluded forces and factors?

In his later reflections on the superego – practical philosophy (ethics, morality, politics, etc.), itself tethered to the freedom-or-determinism problem, is directly impacted by the analytic account of the psychical agency of the Über-Ich – Freud articulates an important insight – "the normal man is not only far more immoral than he believes but also far more moral than he knows" (Freud, 1901, p. 52)[40] (i.e., not all of conscience is conscious, with there being an unconscious underbelly to the superego ["far more moral than he knows"] in addition to the unconscious dimensions of the id-based libidinal economy ["far more immoral than he believes"]). Arguably, for both Freud and Lacan, it similarly could be said, paraphrasing this quotation, that the normal man is not only far more determined than he believes but also far freer than he knows (Johnston, 2008).[41]

An integral aspect of the analytic experience, Freudian and/or Lacanian, is confronting the groundless ground of an unconscious freedom, facing up to the defensively eclipsed presences of underlying contingencies, decisions and responsibilities significantly shaping one's life and its history (as something not governed by the iron necessity of a preordained single destiny). Whether as Freud's "choice of neurosis" (Freud, 1901; Lacan, 1959–60[1992]; 2014)[42] or Lacan's subject (sujet) beyond the ego (moi), analysis not only brings to light the autonomy-inhibiting influences of repressed or disavowed drives, fantasies, and traumas – it also reveals the analysand's far from fated complicity in maintaining his/her psychopathological prison as a (partially) self-constructed enclosure. This is one of the resonances of Lacan's translation and deciphering of Freud's "Wo Es war, soll Ich werden" as "Where it was, there must I come to be" (Hegel, 1977; Lacan, 1977, 2006: 1953–54[1988], 1954–55[1988], 1959–60[1992], 1962, 1967, 1968, 1964[1977]).[43]

As I mentioned earlier in connection with Axis Two, Freud's foregrounding of conflict, especially as taken up by Lacan, is relevant to the freedom–determinism problem. More specifically and on the philosophical terrain of fundamental ontology, the joint Freudian and Lacanian emphases on disunities and disharmonies both somatic and psychical highlight necessary (albeit not sufficient) conditions of possibility for the geneses of subjective agencies not heteronomously encoded and ruled by nature, nurture or any combination thereof. Particularly with Lacan's earlier-noted barring of both the natural Real and sociolinguistic Symbolic (as failing truly to be authoritative big Others, commanding Totalities or Wholes, by virtue of the self-subverting, short-circuiting inconsistencies and contradictions within and between them), spaces are held open for the coming to be of entities and events that are more than just the residual effects of crude causal compulsions. Although, by themselves, the ontological conflicts highlighted by psychoanalysis are not sufficient conditions of possibility for full-fledged autonomous subjectivity – these conflicts disrupt presupposed determinisms, but mere indeterminism by itself is not tantamount to freedom proper qua self-determination – they nonetheless indeed are indispensably necessary for it. Transcendental materialism, in tandem with resources extracted from German idealism, Marxism, and the life sciences of today, incorporates this aspect of Freudian-Lacanian analytic metapsychology into a philosophical system detailing both the necessary (as a meta-transcendentalism of substance) and sufficient (as a transcendentalism of subjectivity) conditions of possibility crucial to such a (theory of the) subject; Johnston, 2005, 2008, 2011b, 2013a, 2013b, 2013c.[44]

From a transcendental materialist position, Axis Five (ahistorical/decontextualized contemplation versus historical/contextualized practice) is to be understood principally in reference to the historical/dialectical materialist movement initiated by Marx (as per, first and foremost, his 11 "Theses on Feuerbach" [1845]) (Johnston, 2013b, 2014).[45] Without here wading into the tangled thickets of numerous controversies concerning Marx's texts and legacies, I will limit myself for now to saying that I interpret Marxism and Freudian-Lacanian analysis as sharing in common, among other things, a commitment to striking a delicate balance between an ahistoricism of the basic "human condition" and a historicism in which this condition is continually inflected and modified by the variable surroundings with which it invariably is entangled (with this interpretation, indebted to Žižek and his brand of Lacano-Marxism, diverging from the more exclusively historicist leanings of mid-20th-century Freudo-Marxism à la the Frankfurt School). In fact, for both Marxism and psychoanalysis, as for Hegel's philosophy preceding them, the ahistorical dimensions of human subjects (as natural and/or transcendental) can and do transition from being implicitly "in themselves" to becoming explicitly "for themselves" (both practically/clinically and theoretically/metapsychologically) only under very precise historical-contextual circumstances (Johnston, 2008).[46]

Marx's first thesis on Feuerbach distinguishes his own materialism from the "contemplative" variety (Marx, 1977).[47] This adjective designates ahistorical and pre/non-dialectical materialisms from antiquity through 18th-century France (with Julien Offray de la Mettrie, Claude Adrien Helvétius, the Baron d'Holbach, Denis Diderot, and the Marquis de Sade) and up to Feuerbach and his fellow Left Hegelians of the 1830s and early 1840s. Marx's critical stance with respect to this older variety of mechanistic materialism entails three interrelated points of concurrence between his novel type of materialism and select aspects of psychoanalysis. First, both historical/dialectical materialism and the materialism of analytic metapsychology (as parsed in and through transcendental materialism – see also the handling of Axis One earlier) are vehemently opposed to reductivist or eliminativist agendas according to which features and facets of human mindedness and like-mindedness evidently exceeding determination by rigid, innate bio-material bases are mere epiphenomena devoid of actual, factual causal efficacy (I will say more about this apropos Axes Six, Seven and Eight later). Second, neither Marx's materialism nor that of Freud and Lacan is contemplative insofar as what the Marx of the "Theses on Feuerbach" means by "contemplation" is a philosophical posture in which the philosopher stealthily assumes the position of a hypothetical eternal gaze externally reflecting upon the equally dehistoricized matters of nature generally and human nature specifically as the fixed, static referents of its vulgarly naturalistic deliberations. On each side of the subject–object distinction, Marxism and analysis jointly break with this sort of oversimplifying contemplation; for both of these traditions, there is neither a neutral, timeless "view from nowhere" from which theories are constructed by an anonymous theorizing subject nor a decontextualized, ahistorical and universal essence of humanity serving as the object for the practical applications of theories. Third (and following closely from the immediately preceding point), historical/dialectical materialism and psychoanalysis, as non-contemplative, must include within themselves explanations on their own terms for their emergences as bodies of theories and practices (i.e., historical/dialectical materialist or psychoanalytic explanations for the genesis and content of historical/dialectical materialism or psychoanalysis). In being self-reflexive in this anti-contemplative way, Marxism, Freudianism and Lacanianism are able to become immanently self-critical, often in highly productive manners (e.g., critically scrutinizing Freud through employing his own analytic insights sometimes sparks unique breakthroughs in which the deadlocks and impasses limiting Freud himself can be specified and surpassed in a non-fungible Freudian fashion) (Johnston, 2014).[48]

As seen with the first five axes listed here, transcendental materialism and its rendition of psychoanalysis are decisively positioned on one end of each of these binary oppositions. However, in relation to Axes Six through Nine, I opt for a refusal of these four either/or dichotomies, staking out a both/and stance as regards Axes Six and Seven and a neither/nor one as regards Axes Eight and Nine. In terms of Axis Six (dualism versus monism), my transcendental materialist take on analytic metapsychology construes the temporally elongated ontogeny of the psychical subject out of somatic substance (with this substance as a barred Real – see Axis Two) as being done the best philosophical justice by something along the lines of an ontology of emergent dual-aspect monism. But, because the emergent constellations and dynamics here (i.e., psyche, subject and the like) are far from inefficacious, insignificant epiphenomena (see also Axis Eight) – this likewise entails that the division itself between psyche/subject and soma/substance also has ontological standing as the negativity of a real rift – my version of this option differs from that of Spinoza as the best-known historical instantiation of dual-aspect monism (and this in that Spinoza's dual aspects, the two "attributes" of "thinking" and "extension," are mere appearances relative to the sole truly existent being qua the infinite One-All of "substance," itself different from either of these aspects/attributes) (Johnston, 2013a, 2013b, 2014).[49] With reference to Spinoza's Continental rationalist predecessor Descartes in addition to Spinoza himself, the Freud- and-Lacan-inspired emergent dual-aspect monism of transcendental materialism attempts to capture and describe the genesis of something more along the lines of Cartesian dualism in and out of something else more along the lines of Spinozist monism (in this vein, transcendental materialism's genetic transcendentalism involves an analysis-informed reactivation of the agenda of post-Fichtean German idealism starting with Tübingen trio of Friedrich Hölderlin, Schelling, and Hegel as a program to synthesize a naturalized Spinozism with the transcendental idealism of Kant and Fichte) (Johnston, 2013b, 2014).[50]

Directly related to the preceding, transcendental materialism, as regards Axis Seven (transcendentalism versus immanentism), does not, as its name might suggest, favor the first over the second pole of this distinction. As an emergent dual-aspect monism in the qualified senses stipulated in the prior paragraph, transcendental materialism charts the bottom-up material genesis of the transcendental, with the latter as a subject thereafter remaining transcendent-while-immanent (à la the dialectical-speculative logic of the Hegelian-Schellingian "identity of identity and difference") (Hegel, 1977a, 2002; Schelling, 1984)[51] vis-à-vis its biological and libidinal grounds. That is to say, a weak nature (in Lacanian locution, a barred corpo-Real) is the material substance providing the first-order set of meta-transcendental conditions of possibility for the transcendent(al) subject as itself a second-order set of more-than-material conditions of possibility for forms of sapient psychical existence (i.e., the conflicted and conflicting split subjects [Lacan's] of concern to analysis) (Johnston, 2013).[52] As both monist and dualist, transcendental materialism similarly is both immanentist and transcendentalist too.

Axis Eight (metaphysical realism versus nominalism) arguably is the most ancient front of dispute in the Western philosophical tradition. This fault line of tension already surfaces between the tradition's two early great grandfathers, namely, Plato and Aristotle. In the shadows of such Greek giants, the entire medieval stretch of European philosophy fairly can be viewed as organized primarily around this specific ontological antagonism. Although the transition to the early modern period in the first half of the 17th century re-centers philosophical debates around the epistemological divide between rationalism and empiricism (a divide severely problematized at the end of the 18th century by Kant's neither rationalist nor empiricist critical transcendental idealism, with Kant bringing the early modern era of philosophy to a close), the philosophers of this period nonetheless continue taking sides in the long-running war between metaphysical realism and nominalism.

Viewed through the philosophical prism of transcendental materialism, psychoanalysis occupies, as with Axis Nine, a neither/nor position in relation to Axis Eight. To be more exact, Lacan in particular establishes links between, on the one hand, the phenomenal and structural abstractions essential to the subject's Imaginary-Symbolic realities and, on the other hand, the Hegelian-Marxian notion of "real abstractions." In both their Hegelian-Marxian and Lacanian versions, these abstractions are bound up with the organization and functioning of imagistic and linguistic contents operating as mediators of intertwined psychical and social life (i.e., Hegelian subjective and objective "spirit" [Geist] respectively). Traditional nominalists dismiss the "spiritual" (quasi)materials of images and words as ontologically inconsequent mere names or signs and nothing more. By contrast, Freudian-Lacanian analysis, as testified to by such core analytic concepts as fantasy and transference, reveals in countless ways just how really consequent (i.e., non-epiphenomenal qua causally efficacious) everything a strict nominalism would deem to be unreal (as purely fictitious, virtual, etc.) is for the concrete cognition and comportment of flesh-and-blood persons. In this vein, it might be remarked that people live and die by illusions, but certainly not by epiphenomena. For psychoanalysis, as (once again) for Hegel before it (with Hegel's ontology sublating [à la his Aufhebung] the opposition between metaphysical realism and nominalism), the idea of the concrete apart from the abstract is itself the height of abstraction. Furthermore, although the analytic belief in the ontological reality of "abstract" ideational representations (whether as Freudian Vorstellungen or Lacanian signifiers) is anti-nominalist, this is not tantamount to an endorsement of metaphysical realism as nominalism's contradictory extreme. Given both its genetic accounts of the emergences of these abstractions out of a non-metaphysical real(ity) as well as its insistence on the irreducible uniquenesses of the idiosyncratic psychical subject's networks of peculiarly particularized ideational representations (Freud's and Lacan's objections to Jung entail, among other things, a repudiation of Jungianism's spiritualistic metaphysical realism of the transhistorical archetypes of a transcultural collective mind), Freudian-Lacanian analysis does not subscribe to classical metaphysical realism (with its ethereally universal and immaterial forms), either (Johnston, 2013a).[53]

Finally, there is Axis Nine ([re]enchantment versus disenchantment). The inauguration of empirical, experimental modern science by Bacon and Galileo (as I remarked previously, this momentous event four centuries ago also is highly relevant to Axis Two) frequently is depicted as bringing about "disenchantment," namely, the erasing from the picture of earthly existence of all things supernatural and the "enchantment" they purportedly sustain. From this angle, the profane scientific liquidation of everything held sacred by various religious dogmas (i.e., gods, souls, afterlives, theodicies, final causes as ultimate ends and so on) brings about a general cultural crisis of purposelessness and valuelessness, allegedly throwing out the baby of "meaning" with the bathwater of superstition. From Kant's time, with the German Pietists and Romantics, to the present, the landscape of European philosophy has remained continually well-populated with advocates pleading for an antiscientific "reenchantment" of the world as a much-needed counter-thrust against a spiritual wasteland of nihilism whose steady expansion is said to be driven by the natural sciences, their technologies, and their pervasive influences on societies (interestingly, F. H. Jacobi, a Pietistic contemporary and critic of Kant, introduces the term "nihilism" into the vocabulary of Continental philosophy) (Jacobi, 1815[2009]).[54]

Not only, as I observed earlier, does Freud ally himself with the Weltanschauung of secular science – Lacan directly asserts that the 17th-century advent of scientific modernity is an absolutely pivotal historical condition of possibility for Freud's later founding of psychoanalysis (Johnston,

1964 [1977], 2005, 2013, 2014; Lacan, 1977).[55] However, both Freud and Lacan, each somewhat differently, would refuse as a false dilemma the loaded alternative between either disenchantment or (re)enchantment – it ought to be noted that those who invoke this very distinction almost always are partisans of (re)enchantment – although, admittedly, the analytic experience integrally involves passing through aspects associated with disenchantment and nihilism broadly conceived, especially for Lacan. Transcendental materialism once more takes its lead from Freudian-Lacanian analysis, refusing this forced choice still brandished by backward-looking, idealistic neo-Romantics and neo-Luddites who are either overtly or (self)deceptively covertly religious when all is said and done (2013a).[56]

In the history of post-Kantian Continental European philosophy, Heidegger is a massively influential recent representative of the neo-Romantic line tracing back to the Protestantism of the dying Holy Roman Empire (Johnston, 2013a).[57] During a July 9, 1964, session of his Zollikon Seminars on Freud (these seminars put forward an extremely contentious and problematic picture of Freud's thinking), Heidegger emphatically utters a statement repeated many times both before and after him – "Science is the new religion" (Heidegger, 2001)[58] (Heidegger's source of inspiration for this sentiment most likely is Nietzsche (Nietzsche, 1974, 1989a).[59] Obviously, coming from Heidegger and countless others, this now commonplace statement is intended as a critical insight.

Instead of externally challenging it as inaccurate – it indeed is – I want to turn the tables here and propose reinterpreting it (or, deliberately misinterpreting and misappropriating it) instead as a noncritical observation. More precisely, science is "religious" not in the standard old sense negatively meant by Heidegger et al., but, rather, only in the sense of not being automatically equivalent to nihilistic disenchantment as the ostensible opposite of supposedly "enchanting" religiosity.

The early 20th-century theologian G.K. Chesterton (one of Žižek's favorite writers) creatively addresses these same issues around the science-religion rapport. In his 1908 Christian apologetic *Orthodoxy*, he maintains,

> The whole secret of mysticism is this: that man can understand everything by the help of what he does not understand. The morbid logician seeks to make everything lucid, and succeeds in making everything mysterious. The mystic allows one thing to be mysterious, and everything else becomes lucid.
>
> *(Chesterton, 1995, p. 33)*[60]

As much of the rest of *Orthodoxy* makes evident, the distinction in this quotation between the "mystic" and the "morbid logician" is a terminological variation on the clash between the (re)enchantment of idealist religion and the disenchantment of materialist science respectively (Chesterton, 1995).[61] The dialectical finesse of Chesterton's move here, as a fully immanent critique of the scientific worldview, must not be missed: he judges science to fail by what he takes to be its own gold standard (i.e., "lucidity" as rigorous, rational transparency) insofar as it allegedly generates more "mystery" than it debunks.

From my transcendental materialist position, I wish to execute a maneuver in response to Chesterton that I will link up with Freud momentarily. Of course, especially if one is invested in at least some (if not all) of the philosophical commitments affirmed at the levels of Axes One through Eight, one could and should externally critique, on both epistemological and ontological grounds, the legitimacy and defensibility of the "one thing" posited by Chesterton's mystic as the alpha-and-omega axiomatic truth of Christian monotheistic spiritualism ("the one created thing which we cannot look at is the one thing in the light of which we look at everything. Like the sun at noonday, mysticism explains everything else by the blaze of its own victorious invisibility") (Chesterton, 1995, p. 33).[62] This perhaps even deserves being met with the comment that anyone who cannot make "everything else . . . lucid" after being permitted to posit something on the order of God suffers from a variety of stupidity so severe that the English language lacks a name for it. But, more interestingly and productively, Chesterton's formulation of his immanent critique of science (as quoted and explained in the earlier paragraph) can itself be immanently critiqued in turn. How so?

If enchantment in the guises of awe-inspiring sublimity and wondrous creations are what is desired, as they are in Chesterton's mysticism, then, according to Chesterton's own immanent critique of science (insofar as it "succeeds in making everything mysterious"), is not science in a way more enchanting than the most mystical of religions – and, hence, a better "religion" (i.e., a "new religion" in a different sense than that intended by Heidegger and company) than all previous, so-called religions (and this again by Chesterton's own lights)? If scientific rationality renders everything incredible through refusing the religious maneuver of enshrining a single mysterious axiom, then does this not bear witness against the charge that such rationality leads straight to outright disenchantment? Furthermore, with Christianity, even the "one thing" allowed "to be mysterious" is not in the least bit unfamiliar (i.e., "mysterious") to humdrum quotidian consciousness: an image of a (mega)subject clearly modeled on the intentional agency of human subjectivity (Chesterton might have benefitted from spending more time with Ludwig Feuerbach). Just how miraculous really are the miracles performed by an anthropomorphic God compared with the most typical occurrences in the physical universe as depicted by the natural sciences? Or, to take the instance of an individual human birth, how mind-bogglingly amazing is the divinely preordained incarnation of one soul in one body by comparison with this same event seen as the outcome of the infinitely improbably chance meeting, not arranged by any top-down guidance whatsoever, of a single sperm and a single egg (with the improbabilities contained in this meeting dizzyingly multiplying: these two people coming together and procreating, these two people themselves being born, the human race having evolved as it did, the earth and the solar system having congealed as they did, and on and on)? For any religion resembling Chesterton's, a living person, for example, represents part of God's plan for creation as a whole, as a manageable total organization ruled by reasonable, sensible final causes in which each and every thing has its proper assigned position and role. By contrast, for the sciences as glossed by transcendental materialism, a living person is a staggeringly unlikely uniqueness that nonetheless "miraculously" has come to be despite the overall statistical odds against this.

Viewed from vantage points furnished by such diverse fields as quantum physics and evolutionary theory, the anthropomorphizing picture-thinking of theologies is far from being imaginative enough to encompass much of creation. The fashions in which this limited, constrained cogitating struggles to get to grips with the this-worldly predictably tosses whatever it is faced with into a one-and-only monochromatic abyss of divinity (as Chesterton says himself, his mystic "can understand everything" by always boringly dissolving all of reality into the dark night of his/her one God without feeling the slightest twinge of awe or marvel in response to what he/she thereby makes vanish). The pre-Cantorian infinite of religions is not infinite enough; the miraculousness of their miracles pales side-by-side with the mere fact of the spatiotemporal existence of any matter at all. Paraphrasing a cliché adage, scientific truths indeed are far stranger than religious fictions. Wonder is as much the effect of science as the cause of philosophy – while being a source of disturbance and trouble for religion.

To refer back to the (re)enchantment versus disenchantment dichotomy (i.e., Axis Nine), science à la transcendental materialism does not inevitably result in nihilistic disenchantment, although the "enchantment" of incarnate existence it can bring about is not the same as that associated with religion hitherto. That is to say, this materialism is neither disenchanting nor (re)enchanting as these alternatives are defined and characterized by those who typically tend to invoke them. Moreover, another reference to the first of Marx's "Theses on Feuerbach" is again appropriate at this juncture (with me having touched upon this thesis in the course of addressing Axis Five). Marx convincingly illuminates how contemplative materialism (i.e., pre/non-dialectical materialisms as mechanistic, reductive or eliminative), through its failure and/or refusal to account for everything that resists being boiled down to the efficient causes of purely natural matter-in-motion (things that appear to be [partially] more-than-material, including activity, agency, consciousness, culture, mind, sociality, etc.), fuels a dissatisfaction propelling people into embracing antimaterialist idealisms. By Marx's own admission, idealisms have the appealing virtue, by sharp contrast with contemplative materialisms, of preserving room in their ontologies for subjectivity, its practices, and the trans-individual historical-linguistic matrices of mediation with which acting subjects are inextricably intertwined. Transcendental materialism, as a contemporary extension of Marxian historical/dialectical materialism, takes this invaluable lesson to heart, avoiding reductivists' and eliminativists' fatal mistake of writing off and leaving behind what inevitably become unexplained leftovers feeding idealist reactions against the understandably perceived poverty of materialist perspectives. Hence, transcendental materialism seeks to advance a non-reductive/eliminative account of more-than-material structures and phenomena formulated nevertheless in the strictest of materialist terms, with no surreptitious spiritualist cheating whatsoever – and this in addition to its portrait of the sciences outstripping religions as measured by the religious yardsticks of sublimity qua incredibleness, mysteriousness, wondrousness, and the like (Johnston, 2013b, 2014).[63]

Finally, to close by returning to Freud, a parallel can be drawn between my neither/nor route through Axis Nine and Freud's very short 1916 essay "On Transience." (Freud, 1901, pp. 303–307).[64] Therein, Freud addresses a piece of quotidian psychopathology, responding to neurotic sadness or withdrawal in the face of objects of beauty or love because of these objects' transience. Certain neurotics' preemptive defensive mourning for or recoil from future losses (via the eventual demise and disappearance of whatever perishable beings or others they are attached to) can come to spoil their current enjoyment of the transient things in question. Freud's description of this neurotic response, in tying it to a stubborn investment in the idea of immortality, hints that it is another illustration of the profound links between neurosis and religion (as per his earlier essay "Obsessive Actions and Religious Practices") (Freud, 1901, pp. 115–127).[65] That said, Freud speaks to this everyday snippet of not-so-secular neurosis by inverting its evaluation of transience as entailing a "loss in . . . worth":

> On the contrary, an increase! Transience value is scarcity value in time. Limitation in the possibility of an enjoyment raises the value of the enjoyment. It was incomprehensible, I declared, that the thought of the transience of beauty should interfere with our joy in it . . . The beauty of the human form and face vanish for ever in the course of our own lives, but their evanescence only lends them a fresh charm. A flower that blossoms only for a single night does not seem to us on that account less lovely.
>
> *(Freud, 1901, pp. 305–306)*[66]

As per my transcendental materialist gloss on the scientific Weltanschauung with which Freud himself aligns psychoanalysis, the reinterpretation of transience offered in this quotation applies equally well to the science-revealed accidents, contingencies, finitudes, fragilities, improbabilities, rarities and vulnerabilities marking life in general and human life in particular. Sources of purportedly disenchanting (and depressing) nihilism are thereby transubstantiated into exhilarating catalysts of awestruck appreciation and amazement. Through its combination of philosophy and psychoanalysis, transcendental materialism not only rebuts the accusation that science devalues life – it counter-offensively accuses science's religious adversaries of not being able to value it nearly enough.

## Notes

1 Adrian Johnston, *Žižek's Ontology: A Transcendental Materialist Theory of Subjectivity*, Evanston, IL: Northwestern University Press, 2008, pp. 269–287; Adrian Johnston, *Prolegomena to Any Future Materialism, Volume One: The Outcome of Contemporary French Philosophy*, Evanston, IL: Northwestern University Press, 2013, pp. xi–xv, 175–209; Adrian Johnston, "Points of Forced Freedom: Eleven (More) Theses on Materialism," *Speculations: A Journal of Speculative Realism*, no. 4, June 2013, pp. 91–99; (Adrian Johnston, *Adventures in Transcendental Materialism: Dialogues with Contemporary Thinkers*, Edinburgh: Edinburgh University Press, 2014.

2 Sigmund Freud, *The Standard Edition of the Complete Psychological Works of Sigmund Freud* (24 vols.) [ed. James Strachey] (hereinafter *SE*), 13: 185; 14: 96–97; 15: 97–98; 17: 261.

3 Adrian Johnston, "Jacques Lacan (1901–1981)," *Stanford Encyclopedia of Philosophy*, 2013, http://plato.stanford.edu/entries/lacan.

4 *SE* 22: 160–161.

5 *SE* 15: 20; *SE* 17: 105–106.

6 *SE* 17: 224–226, 241.

7 *SE* 4: 68; *SE* 18: 28; *SE* 19: 167; *SE* 22: 61–62, 74, 163–164; *SE* 23: 300.

8 *SE* 22: 158–182.

9 Johnston, "Jacques Lacan."

10 *SE* 14: 15–16.

11 *SE* 13: 178–179; *SE* 19: 216–218; *SE* 23: 158–159, 282–283, 286; Adrian Johnston, "Freud and Continental Philosophy," *The History of Continental Philosophy*, eight volumes [ed. Alan D. Schrift], *Volume III: The New Century – Bergsonism, Phenomenology, and Responses to Modern Science* [ed. Keith Ansell-Pearson and Alan D. Schrift], Durham: Acumen, 2010, pp. 319–346.

12 Johnston, "Jacques Lacan."

13 Adrian Johnston, "Second Natures in Dappled Worlds: John McDowell, Nancy Cartwright, and Hegelian-Lacanian Materialism," *Umbr(a): A Journal of the Unconscious – The Worst* [ed. Matthew Rigilano and Kyle Fetter], Buffalo: Center for the Study of Psychoanalysis and Culture, State University of New York at Buffalo, 2011, pp. 71–91; Adrian Johnston, *Prolegomena to Any Future Materialism, Volume Two: A Weak Nature Alone*, Evanston, IL, Northwestern University Press [under review].

14 Adrian Johnston, "Slavoj Žižek," *The Blackwell Companion to Continental Philosophy*, 2nd edition [ed. William Schroeder], Oxford: Blackwell, 2013.

15 Johnston, "Points of Forced Freedom," pp. 91–99.

16 Louis Althusser, "Philosophy as a Revolutionary Weapon (Interview conducted by Maria Antonietta Macciocchi)," *Lenin and Philosophy and other essays* [trans. Ben Brewster], New York: Monthly Review Press, 2001, pp. 2, 5–6, 8–9.

17 Friedrich Engels, *Ludwig Feuerbach and the Outcome of Classical German Philosophy*, New York: International, 1941, pp. 31; V.I. Lenin, *Materialism and Empirio-Criticism*, Beijing: Foreign Languages, 1972, pp. 22–23, 33–34, 95, 106, 128–129, 140–142, 145, 167, 188–189, 191, 232, 321, 344, 407–413, 416–417, 431, 434.

18 Jacques Lacan, *Le Séminaire de Jacques Lacan, Livre XVIII: D'un discours qui ne serait pas du semblant*, 1971 [ed. Jacques-Alain Miller], Paris: Éditions du Seuil, 2006, p. 28); Jacques Lacan, "Responses to Students of Philosophy Concerning the Object of Psychoanalysis" [trans. Jeffrey Mehlman], *Television/A Challenge to the Psychoanalytic Establishment* [ed. Joan Copjec], New York: W.W. Norton, 1990, p. 112; Jacques Lacan, "*L'étourdit*," *Autres écrits* [ed. Jacques-Alain Miller], Paris: Éditions du Seuil, 2001, p. 494; Johnston, *Adventures in Transcendental Materialism*.

19 Adrian Johnston, "The Weakness of Nature: Hegel, Freud, Lacan, and Negativity Materialized," *Hegel and the Infinite: Religion, Politics, and Dialectic* [ed. Slavoj Žižek, Clayton Crockett, and Creston Davis], New York: Columbia University Press, 2011, pp. 159–179; Adrian Johnston, "Reflections of a Rotten Nature: Hegel, Lacan, and Material Negativity," *Filozofski Vestnik*, vol. 33, no. 2, 2012, special issue: "Science and Thought" [ed. Frank Ruda and Jan Voelker], pp. 23–52; Adrian Johnston, "Drive Between Brain

and Subject: An Immanent Critique of Lacanian Neuro-psychoanalysis," *Southern Journal of Philosophy*, vol. 51, September 2013, special issue: "Spindel supplement: Freudian Future(s)," pp. 48–84; Johnston, *Adventures in Transcendental Materialism*.

20 Jacques Lacan, "Science and Truth," *Écrits: The First Complete Edition in English* [trans. Bruce Fink], New York: W.W. Norton, 2006, p. 728; Adrian Johnston, "Turning the Sciences Inside Out: Revisiting Lacan's 'Science and Truth,'" *Concept and Form, Volume Two: Interviews and Essays on the* Cahiers pour l'Analyse [ed. Peter Hallward and Knox Peden], London: Verso, 2012, pp. 105–121).

21 Johnston, "Jacques Lacan."

22 *SE* 1: 318; *SE* 20: 154–155, 167; *SE* 21: 17–19, 30.

23 Jacques Lacan, 1988, "Les complexes familiaux dans la formation de l'individu: Essai d'analyse d'une fonction en psychologie," *Autres écrits*, pp. 33–35, 41–42; Jacques Lacan, "Some Reflections on the Ego," *International Journal of Psychoanalysis*, no. 34, 1953, pp. 13, 15; Jacques Lacan, 1956 [2006], "On My Antecedents," *Écrits*, p. 55; Jacques Lacan, "The Mirror Stage as Formative of the *I* Function as Revealed in Psychoanalytic Experience," *Écrits*, pp. 76, 78; Jacques Lacan, "Aggressiveness in Psychoanalysis," *Écrits*, p. 92; Jacques Lacan, "On a Question Prior to Any Possible Treatment of Psychosis," *Écrits*, p. 461; Jacques Lacan, *Le Séminaire de Jacques Lacan, Livre VI: Le désir et son interprétation, 1958–1959* [unpublished typescript], session of January 7, 1959; Johnston, "Reflections of a Rotten Nature," pp. 23–52.

24 *SE* 18: 52–53, 60–61; *SE* 19: 40–41, 59, 218, 239; *SE* 21: 118–119, 122, 141; Jacques Lacan, *The Seminar of Jacques Lacan, Book II: The Ego in Freud's Theory and in the Technique of Psychoanalysis, 1954–1955* [ed. Jacques-Alain Miller; trans. Sylvana Tomaselli], New York: W.W. Norton, 1988, pp. 322–323, 326; Lacan, "The Mirror Stage as Formative of the *I* Function as Revealed in Psychoanalytic Experience," p. 78; Lacan, "Aggressiveness in Psychoanalysis," pp. 94, 101; Jacques Lacan, "*Le mythe individuel du névrosé, ou Poésie et vérité dans la névrose*," *Le mythe individuel du névrosé* [ed. Jacques-Alain Miller], Paris: Éditions du Seuil, 2007, p. 46.; Johnston, "Reflections of a Rotten Nature," pp. 23–52.

25 Jacques Lacan, "The Function and Field of Speech and Language in Psychoanalysis," *Écrits*, p. 248; Jacques Lacan, "The Direction of the Treatment and the Principles of Its Power," *Écrits*, p. 496; Jacques Lacan, "*Discours de Rome*," *Autres écrits*, pp. 137–138; Jacques Lacan, "Problèmes cruciaux pour la psychanalyse: Compte rendu du Séminaire 1964–1965," *Autres écrits*, p. 199; Jacques Lacan, "Of Structure as an Inmixing of an Otherness Prerequisite to Any Subject Whatever," *The Structuralist Controversy: The Languages of Criticism and the Sciences of Man* [ed. Richard Macksey and Eugenio Donato], Baltimore: Johns Hopkins University Press, 1970, pp. 187; Jacques Lacan, *The Seminar of Jacques Lacan, Book I: Freud's Papers on Technique, 1953–1954* [ed. Jacques-Alain Miller; trans. John Forrester], New York: W.W. Norton, 1988, p. 244; Lacan, *The Seminar, Book II*, p. 82; Jacques Lacan, *The Seminar of Jacques Lacan, Book III: The Psychoses, 1955–1956* [ed. Jacques-Alain Miller; trans. Russell Grigg], New York: W.W. Norton, 1993, pp. 32; Jacques Lacan, *Le Séminaire de Jacques Lacan, Livre IX: L'identification, 1961–1962* [unpublished typescript], session of January 10, 1962; Jacques Lacan, *Le Séminaire de Jacques Lacan, Livre XIV: La logique du fantasme, 1966–1967* [unpublished typescript], sessions of February 1, 1967 and May 10, 1967; Adrian Johnston, *Badiou, Žižek, and Political Transformations: The Cadence of Change*, Evanston, IL: Northwestern University Press, 2009, pp. 122–124; Johnston, *Adventures in Transcendental Materialism*.

26 *SE* 14: 202–203; Jean Laplanche and Jean-Betrand Pontalis, *The Language of Psycho-Analysis* [trans. Donald Nicholson-Smith], New York: W.W. Norton, 1973, pp. 447–448; Adrian Johnston, *Time Driven: Metapsychology and the Splitting of the Drive*, Evanston, IL: Northwestern University Press, 2005, pp. 300–315.

27 *SE* 1: 324–327, 333–340, 357–359, 381; *SE* 5: 599–611; *SE* 14: 186–188, 199, 201–203, 228–229; *SE* 18: 10, 34–35, 62–63; *SE* 19: 45, 138; *SE* 23: 164, 168, 198, 225; Laplanche and Pontalis, *The Language of Psycho-Analysis*, pp. 339–341.

28 Jacques Lacan, *The Seminar of Jacques Lacan, Book VII: The Ethics of Psychoanalysis, 1959–1960* [ed. Jacques-Alain Miller; trans. Dennis Porter], New York: W.W. Norton, 1992, p. 139; Jacques Lacan, *Le Séminaire de Jacques Lacan, Livre XVI: D'un Autre à l'autre, 1968–1969* [ed. Jacques-Alain Miller], Paris: Éditions du Seuil, 2006, pp. 224–225, 249.

29 *SE* 21: 38, 49–50, 54–56; *SE* 22: 34, 160–161, 167–169, 172–174.

30 Johnston, *Prolegomena to Any Future Materialism, Volume One*, pp. 13–38; Johnston, *Adventures in Transcendental Materialism*.

31 Lacan, *The Seminar, Book VII*, pp. 213–214; Jacques Lacan, *The Seminar of Jacques Lacan, Book XVII: The Other Side of Psychoanalysis, 1969–1970* [ed. Jacques-Alain Miller; trans. Russell Grigg], New York: W.W. Norton, 2007, p. 66; Jacques Lacan, *The Seminar of Jacques Lacan, Book XX: Encore, 1972–1973* [ed. Jacques-Alain Miller; trans. Bruce Fink], New York: W.W. Norton, 1998, pp. 68, 70; Jacques Lacan, *Le Séminaire de Jacques Lacan, Livre XXIV: L'insu que sait de l'une- bévue s'aile à mourre, 1976–1977*

[unpublished typescript], session of May 17, 1977; Johnston, *Prolegomena to Any Future Materialism, Volume One*, pp. 13–38; Johnston, *Adventures in Transcendental Materialism*.

32   Johnston, "Jacques Lacan"; Johnston, *Prolegomena to Any Future Materialism, Volume One*, pp. 13–38; Johnston, *Adventures in Transcendental Materialism*.

33   Jacques Lacan, *Le Séminaire de Jacques Lacan, Livre X: L'angoisse, 1962–1963* [ed. Jacques–Alain Miller], Paris: Éditions du Seuil, 2004, pp. 357–358; Jacques Lacan, *The Seminar of Jacques Lacan, Book XI: The Four Fundamental Concepts of Psychoanalysis, 1964* [ed. Jacques–Alain Miller; trans. Alan Sheridan], New York: W.W. Norton, 1977, pp. 230–233; Lacan, *Le Séminaire, Livre XVI*, pp. 280–281; Lacan, *The Seminar, Book XVII*, p. 119; Johnston, "Jacques Lacan"; Johnston, *Prolegomena to Any Future Materialism, Volume One*, pp. 13–38; Johnston, *Adventures in Transcendental Materialism*.

34   *SE* 18: 36–41, 60–61, 258–259; *SE* 19: 40–41; *SE* 21: 118–119, 122; *SE* 22: 210–211; *SE* 23: 148–149, 197–198, 243, 245–247.

35   Lacan, "The Direction of the Treatment," p. 514; Jacques Lacan, *Le Séminaire de Jacques Lacan, Livre VIII: Le transfert, 1960–1961* [ed. Jacques–Alain Miller], Paris: Éditions du Seuil, 2001 [seconde édition corrigée], p. 117; Lacan, *The Seminar, Book XVII*, p. 33; Lacan, *Le Séminaire, Livre XVIII*, pp. 55–75; Jacques Lacan, *Le Séminaire de Jacques Lacan, Livre XIX: . . . ou pire, 1971–1972* [ed Jacques-Alain Miller], Paris: Éditions du Seuil, 2011, pp. 93–110; Jacques Lacan, *Le Séminaire de Jacques Lacan, Livre XXI: Les non-dupes errent, 1973–1974* [unpublished typescript], session of May 21, 1974; Jacques Lacan, *Le Séminaire de Jacques Lacan, Livre XXIII: Le sinthome, 1975–1976* [ed Jacques-Alain Miller], Paris: Éditions du Seuil, 2005, p. 12; Lacan, *Le Séminaire, Livre XXIV*, sessions of April 19, 1977 and May 17, 1977; Johnston, *Žižek's Ontology*, pp. 269–287; Johnston, "The Weakness of Nature," pp. 159–179; Johnston, *Prolegomena to Any Future Materialism, Volume One*, pp. 13–38; Johnston, "Reflections of a Rotten Nature," pp. 23–52; Johnston, "Drive Between Brain and Subject," pp. 48–84.

36   Johnston, "The Weakness of Nature," pp. 159–179; Adrian Johnston, "The Voiding of Weak Nature: The Transcendental Materialist Kernels of Hegel's *Naturphilosophie*," *Graduate Faculty Philosophy Journal*, vol. 33, no. 1, 2012, pp. 103–157; Johnston, "Drive Between Brain and Subject," pp. 48–84; Adrian Johnston, "Misfelt Feelings: Unconscious Affect Between Psychoanalysis, Neuroscience, and Philosophy," in Adrian Johnston and Catherine Malabou, *Self and Emotional Life: Philosophy, Psychoanalysis, and Neuroscience*, New York: Columbia University Press, 2013, pp. 173–178; Johnston, *Prolegomena to Any Future Materialism, Volume One*, pp. 13–38; Johnston, *Prolegomena to Any Future Materialism, Volume Two*.

37   *SE* 21: 38, 49–50, 53–56.

38   *SE* 19: 211–222; Jacques Lacan, *"Le triomphe de la religion,"* *Le triomphe de la religion, précédé de Discours aux catholiques* [ed. Jacques–Alain Miller], Paris: Éditions du Seuil, 2005, pp. 67–102; Johnston, *Prolegomena to Any Future Materialism, Volume One*, pp. xiii–xiv, 32–38, 175–180; Johnston, *Adventures in Transcendental Materialism*.

39   Johnston, "Jacques Lacan."

40   *SE* 19: 52.

41   Johnston, *Žižek's Ontology*, pp. 102.

42   *SE* 1: 231, 270–271, 279; *SE* 3: 220, 255; Lacan, *The Seminar, Book VII*, p. 54; Johnston, *Adventures in Transcendental Materialism*.

43   Jacques Lacan, "The Freudian Thing, or the Meaning of the Return to Freud in Psychoanalysis," *Écrits*, pp. 346–348, 353–354; Jacques Lacan, "The Instance of the Letter in the Unconscious, or Reason Since Freud," *Écrits*, p. 435; Jacques Lacan, "The Subversion of the Subject and the Dialectic of Desire in the Freudian Unconscious," *Écrits*, p. 678.; Jacques Lacan, "Position of the Unconscious," *Écrits*, p. 714; Lacan, "Science and Truth," pp. 733–734; Lacan, *The Seminar, Book I*, p. 232; Lacan, *The Seminar, Book II*, pp. 246–247; Lacan, *The Seminar, Book VII*, p. 7; Lacan, *Le Séminaire, Livre IX*, sessions of January 17, 1962 and March 28, 1962; Lacan, *Le Séminaire, Livre XIV*, session of January 11, 1967; Jacques Lacan, *Le Séminaire de Jacques Lacan, Livre XV: L'acte psychanalytique, 1967–1968* [unpublished typescript], session of January 10, 1968; Lacan, *The Seminar, Book XI*, pp. 44–45.

44   Johnston, *Time Driven*, pp. 340–341; Johnston, *Žižek's Ontology*, pp. 269–287; Johnston, "The Weakness of Nature," pp. 159–179; Johnston, *Prolegomena to Any Future Materialism, Volume One*, pp. 208–209; Johnston, "Points of Forced Freedom," pp. 91–99; Johnston, "Drive Between Brain and Subject," pp. 48–84; Johnston, *Prolegomena to Any Future Materialism, Volume Two*.

45   Johnston, "Points of Forced Freedom," pp. 91–99; Johnston, *Adventures in Transcendental Materialism*; Johnston, *Prolegomena to Any Future Materialism, Volume Two*.

46   Johnston, *Žižek's Ontology*, pp. 265–268.

47 Karl Marx, "Theses on Feuerbach" [trans. S. Ryazanskaya], *Karl Marx: Selected Writings* [ed. David McLellan], Oxford: Oxford University Press, 1977, pp. 156.

48 Johnston, *Adventures in Transcendental Materialism.*

49 Johnston, *Prolegomena to Any Future Materialism, Volume One*, p. 180; Johnston, "Points of Forced Freedom," pp. 91–99; Johnston, *Adventures in Transcendental Materialism.*

50 Johnston, "Points of Forced Freedom," pp. 91–99; Johnston, *Adventures in Transcendental Materialism.*

51 G.W.F. Hegel, "Fragment of a System" [trans. Richard Kroner], *Miscellaneous Writings of G.W.F. Hegel* [ed. Jon Stewart], Evanston, IL: Northwestern University Press, 2002, p. 154; G.W.F. Hegel, *The Difference Between Fichte's and Schelling's System of Philosophy* [trans. H.S. Harris and Walter Cerf], Albany: State University of New York Press, 1977, p. 112; G.W.F. Hegel, *Faith and Knowledge* [trans. Walter Cerf and H.S. Harris], Albany: State University of New York Press, 1977, pp. 59–60, 113; F.W.J. Schelling, *Bruno, or, On the Natural and the Divine Principle of Things* [trans. Michael G. Vater], Albany: State University of New York Press, 1984, pp. 136, 143.

52 Johnston, *Prolegomena to Any Future Materialism, Volume One*, pp. 175–180, 203–209; Johnston, *Prolegomena to Any Future Materialism, Volume Two.*

53 Adrian Johnston, "Lacking Causes: Privative Causality from Locke and Kant to Lacan and Deacon," *Speculations: A Journal of Speculative Realism*, 2013 [forthcoming]; Johnston, *Adventures in Transcendental Materialism*; Johnston, *Prolegomena to Any Future Materialism, Volume Two.*

54 Friedrich Heinrich Jacobi, "David Hume on Faith, or Idealism and Realism, a Dialogue: Preface and Also Introduction to the Author's Collected Philosophical Works" (1815), *The Main Philosophical Writings and the Novel Allwill* [trans. George di Giovanni], Montreal and Kingston: McGill-Queen's University Press, 2009, p. 583.

55 Lacan, "Position of the Unconscious," p. 712; Lacan, *The Seminar, Book XI*, pp. 47, 231; Johnston, *Time Driven*, pp. 61–71; Johnston, *Prolegomena to Any Future Materialism, Volume One*, pp. 39–58; Johnston, *Adventures in Transcendental Materialism.*

56 Johnston, "Points of Forced Freedom," pp. 91–99.

57 Ibid.

58 Martin Heidegger, *Zollikon Seminars: Protocols-Conversations-Letters* [ed. Medard Boss; trans. Franz Mayr and Richard Askay], Evanston, IL: Northwestern University Press, 2001, p. 18.

59 Friedrich Nietzsche, *The Gay Science* [trans. Walter Kaufmann], New York: Vintage Books, 1974, §300 [pp. 240–241]; Friedrich Nietzsche, *Beyond Good and Evil* [trans. Walter Kaufmann], New York: Vintage Books, 1989, §14 [pp. 21–22], §206 [pp. 125–126]; Friedrich Nietzsche, *The Genealogy of Morals, On the Genealogy of Morals and Ecce Homo* [trans. Walter Kaufmann], New York: Vintage Books, 1989, §23 [pp. 145–148], §24 [pp. 151–153], §25 [pp. 153–155].

60 G.K. Chesterton, *Orthodoxy*, San Francisco: Ignatius Press, 1995, p. 33.

61 Ibid., pp. 32–33, 55–56, 65–66.

62 Ibid., p. 33.

63 Johnston, "Points of Forced Freedom," pp. 91–99; Johnston, *Adventures in Transcendental Materialism.*

64 *SE* 14: 303–307.

65 *SE* 9: 115–127.

66 *SE* 14: 305–206.

# References

Althusser, L 2001, 'Philosophy as a revolutionary weapon (interview conducted by MA Macciocchi)', in L Althusser (ed), *Lenin and philosophy and other essays* (B Brewster, trans), Monthly Review Press, New York, pp. 2, 5–6, 8–9.

Chesterton, GK 1995, *Orthodoxy*, Ignatius Press, San Francisco.

Engels, F 1941, *Ludwig Feuerbach and the outcome of classical German philosophy*, International, New York, p. 31.

Freud, S 1901, *Standard edition of the complete psychological works of Sigmund Freud* (J Strachey, ed), Hogarth, London, *SE* 1, pp. 231, 270–271, 279, 318, 324–327, 333–340, 357–359, 381; *SE* 3, pp. 220, 255; *SE* 4, pp. 68; *SE* 5, pp, 599–611; *SE* 9, pp. 115–127; *SE* 13, pp. 178–179, 185; *SE* 14, pp. 15–16, 96–97, 186–188, 199, 201–203, 228–229, 303–307; *SE* 15, pp. 20, 97–98; *SE* 17, pp. 105–106, 224–226, 241, 261; *SE* 18, pp. 10, 28, 34–35, 36–41, 52–53, 60–61, 62–63, 258–259; *SE* 19, pp. 40–41, 45, 52, 59, 138, 167, 211–222, 216–218, 239; *SE* 20, pp. 154–155, 167; *SE* 21, pp. 17–19, 30, 38, 49–50, 54–56, 118–119,

122, 141; *SE* 22, pp. 34, 61–62, 74, 158–182, 160–161, 163–164, 167–169, 172–174, 210–211, *SE* 23, pp. 148–149, 158–159, 164, 168, 197–198, 225, 243, 245–247, 282–283, 286, 300.

Hegel, GWF 1977a, *The difference between Fichte's and Schelling's system of philosophy* (HS Harris & W Cerf, trans), State University of New York Press, Albany, p. 112.

Hegel, GWF 1977b, *Faith and knowledge* (W Cerf & HS Harris, trans), State University of New York Press, Albany, pp. 59–60, 113.

Hegel, GWF 2002, 'Fragment of a system' (R Kroner, trans), in J Stewart (ed), *Miscellaneous writings of GWF Hegel*, Northwestern University Press, Evanston, IL, p. 154.

Heidegger, M 2001, *Zollikon seminars: Protocols-conversations-letters* (M Boss, ed), F Mayr & R Askay, trans), Northwestern University Press, Evanston, IL, p. 18.

Jacobi, FH 1815, 'David Hume on faith, or idealism and realism, a dialogue: Preface and also introduction to the author's collected philosophical works', in *The main philosophical writings and the novel Allwill*, 2009 (G di Giovanni, trans), McGill-Queen's University Press, Montreal and Kingston, p. 583.

Johnston, A 2005, *Time driven: Metapsychology and the splitting of the drive*, Northwestern University Press, Evanston.

Johnston, A 2008, *Žižek's ontology: A transcendental materialist theory of subjectivity*, Northwestern University Press, Evanston, IL, pp. 269–287.

Johnston, A 2009, *Badiou, Žižek, and political transformations: The cadence of change*, Northwestern University Press, Evanston, IL, pp. 122–124.

Johnston, A 2010, 'Freud and continental philosophy', in A Schrift (ed), *The history of continental philosophy*, in K Ansell-Pearson & A Schrift (eds), *The new century – Bergsonism, phenomenology, and responses to modern science*, vol. 3, Durham, Acumen, pp. 319–346.

Johnston, A 2011a, 'Second natures in dappled worlds: John McDowell, Nancy Cartwright, and Hegelian-Lacanian materialism', in M Rigilano & K Fetter (eds), *Umbr(a): A journal of the unconscious – The worst*, Center for the Study of Psychoanalysis and Culture, State University of New York, Buffalo, pp. 71–91.

Johnston, A 2011b, 'The weakness of nature: Hegel, Freud, Lacan, and negativity materialized', in S Žižek, C Crockett & C Davis (eds), *Hegel and the infinite: Religion, politics, and dialectic*, Columbia University Press, New York, pp. 159–179.

Johnston, A 2012a, 'Reflections of a rotten nature: Hegel, Lacan, and material negativity', *Filozofski Vestnik*, in F Ruda & J Voelker (eds), special issue: *Science and Thought*, vol. 33, no. 2, pp. 23–52.

Johnston, A 2012b, 'Turning the sciences inside out: Revisiting Lacan's "Science and truth,"' *Concept and form*, in P Hallward & K Peden (eds), *Interviews and essays on the Cahiers pour l'Analyse*, vol. 2, Verso, London, pp. 105–121.

Johnston, A 2012c, "The voiding of weak nature: The transcendental materialist kernels of Hegel's *Naturphilosophie*," *Graduate Faculty Philosophy Journal*, vol. 33, no. 1, pp. 103–157.

Johnston, A 2013a, *Prolegomena to any future materialism, the outcome of contemporary French philosophy*, Northwestern University Press, Evanston, IL, vol. 1, pp. xi–xv, 175–209.

Johnston, A 2013b, 'Points of forced freedom: Eleven (more) theses on materialism', *Speculations: A Journal of Speculative Realism*, no. 4, pp. 91–99.

Johnston, A 2013c, 'Jacques Lacan (1901–1981)', in *Stanford encyclopedia of philosophy*, available at http://plato.stanford.edu/entries/lacan

Johnston, A 2013d, 'Drive between brain and subject: An immanent critique of Lacanian neuro-psychoanalysis', *Southern Journal of Philosophy*, special issue, *Spindel supplement, Freudian Future(s)*, vol. 51, pp. 48–84.

Johnston, A 2013e, 'Misfelt feelings: Unconscious affect between psychoanalysis, neuroscience, and philosophy', in A Johnston & C Malabou (eds), *Self and emotional life: Philosophy, psychoanalysis, and neuroscience*, Columbia University Press, New York, pp. 173–178.

Johnston, A 2013f, 'Lacking causes: Privative causality from Locke and Kant to Lacan and Deacon', *Speculations: A Journal of Speculative Realism*, vol. 6, pp. 19–60.

Johnston, A 2014, *Adventures in transcendental materialism: Dialogues with contemporary thinkers*, Edinburgh University Press, Edinburgh.

Johnston, A & Malabou, C 2013, *Self and emotional life: Philosophy, psychoanalysis, and neuroscience*, Columbia University Press, New York.

Johnston, A & Žižek, S 2013, *The Blackwell companion to continental philosophy* (2nd ed) (W Schroeder, ed), Blackwell, Oxford.

Lacan, J 1954–1955, 1988, *The seminar of Jacques Lacan, book II: The ego in Freud's theory and in the technique of psychoanalysis* (S Tomaselli, ed, J-A Miller, trans), W.W. Norton, New York, pp. 322–323, 326.

Lacan, J 1954–1955, *The seminar of Jacques Lacan, book II*, p. 82.

Lacan, J 1956, 2006, 'On my antecedents', *Écrits*, p. 55.

Lacan, J 1956a, 2006, 'Aggressiveness in psychoanalysis', *Écrits*, pp. 92, 94, 101.

Lacan, J 1956b, 2006, 'On a question prior to any possible treatment of psychosis', *Écrits*, p. 461.

Lacan, J 1959, *The seminar of Jacques Lacan: The ethics of psychoanalysis*, W.W Norton, London.

Lacan, J 1969, 2006, *The seminar XVII, the other side of psychoanalysis*, (J-A Miller, ed, R Grigg, trans), W.W. Norton, New York.

Lacan, J 1970, 'Of structure as an inmixing of an otherness prerequisite to any subject whatever', in R Macksey & E Donato (eds), *The structuralist controversy: The languages of criticism and the sciences of man*, Johns Hopkins University Press, Baltimore, p. 187.

Lacan, J 1971, *D'un discours qui ne serait pas du semblant, Le Séminaire*, Livre XVIII (J-A Miller, ed), Éditions du Seuil, Paris, 2006, p. 28.

Lacan, J 1973–74, 1998, *The seminar XX, encore: On feminine sexuality, the limits of love and knowledge* (J-A Miller, ed, B Fink, trans), W.W. Norton, New York.

Lacan, J 1975, 1982, 'The seminar XXII of 21 January 1975—RSI', J. Rose (trans), in J Mitchell and J Rose (eds), *Feminine sexuality*, W.W. Norton, New York.

Lacan, J 1977, 'A Lacanian psychosis: Interview by Jacques Lacan, 13 Feb. 1976', in S Schneiderman (ed), *Returning to Freud: Clinical psychoanalysis in the school of Lacan*, Yale University.

Lacan, J 1988a, *The seminar of Jacques Lacan, book I: Freud's papers on technique, 1953–1954* (J-A Miller, ed, John Forrester, trans), W.W. Norton, New York, p. 244.

Lacan, J 1988b, 'Les complexes familiaux dans la formation de l'individu: Essai d'analyse d'une fonction en psychologie', in *Autres écrits*, pp. 33–35, 41–42.

Lacan, J 1990, 'Responses to students of philosophy concerning the object of psychoanalysis', J Mehlman (trans), in J Copjec (ed), *Television/a challenge to the psychoanalytic establishment*, W.W. Norton, New York, p. 112.

Lacan, J 1998, *The seminar XX, encore: On feminine sexuality, the limits of love and knowledge* (J-A Miller, ed, B Fink, trans), W.W. Norton, New York.

Lacan, J 2001, 'Merleau-ponty: In memoriam, 2001', W ver Eecke and D de Schutter (trans), in K Hoeller (ed), *Merleau-ponty and psychology*, Humanities Press, Autres Écrits, Seuil, Paris.

Lacan, J 2004, *The seminar, book X: Anxiety, 1962–1963* (J-Alain Miller, ed, AR Price, trans), Polity Press, New York.

Lacan, J 2006, 'Science and truth', in B Fink (trans), *Écrits: The first complete edition in English*, W.W. Norton, New York, p. 728.

Lacan, J 2007, 'Le mythe individuel du névrosé, ou Poésie et vérité dans la névrose', in J-A Miller (ed), *Le mythe individuel du névrosé*, Éditions du Seuil, Paris, p. 46.

Lacan, J 2007, *The seminar XVII, the other side of psychoanalysis* (J-A Miller, ed, R Grigg, trans), W.W. Norton, New York.

Laplanche, J & Pontalis, J 1973, *The language of psychoanalysis*, The Hogarth Press and the Institute of Psycho-Analysis, London.

Lenin, VI 1972, *Materialism and empirio-criticism*, Beijing: foreign languages, pp. 22–23, 33–34, 95, 106, 128–129, 140–142, 145, 167, 188–189, 191, 232, 321, 344, 407–413, 416–417, 431, 434.

Marx, K 1977, 'Theses on Feuerbach' (S Ryazanskaya, trans), in D McLellan (ed), *Karl Marx: Selected writings*, Oxford University Press, Oxford, p. 156.

Nietzsche, F 1974, *The gay science* (W Kaufmann, trans), Vintage Books, New York, vol. 300, pp. 240–241.

Nietzsche, F 1989a, *Beyond good and evil* (W Kaufmann, trans), Vintage Books, New York, vol. 14, pp. 21–22, vol. 206, pp. 125–126.

Nietzsche, F 1989b, *The genealogy of morals, on the genealogy of morals and Ecce Homo* (W Kaufmann, trans), Vintage Books, New York, vol. 23, pp. 145–148, vol. 24, pp. 151–153, vol. 25, pp. 153–155.

Schelling, FWJ 1984, *Bruno, or, on the natural and the divine principle of things* (MG Vater, trans), State University of New York Press, Albany, pp. 136, 143.

# 17

# Literature and psychoanalysis

*Madelon Sprengnether*

What do psychoanalytic discourse and literary discourse have in common, and how do they diverge? There is no simple set of answers to these questions, as neither psychoanalysis nor literature can be apprehended as a single, definable entity. We speak of psychoanalysis and of literature as if they were nouns or objects, when they function more properly as verbs or forms of motion.

That Freud took inspiration from literature, most notably in his theorization of the Oedipus complex, and credited poets and fiction writers with intuitive knowledge about dreams and the working of the unconscious is widely recognized. Teasing out the meanings in Freud's acknowledgment of his indebtedness to literary artists is a more troubled and troubling endeavor.

Adding to the complexity of this question, psychoanalysis as Freud conceived it does not come down to us as a fixed and internally consistent body of theory. Freud's texts interact with one another in myriad ways, repeating, revising and commenting on one another as if to represent an ongoing internal conversation, rather than a logically ordered set of ideas.

Freud's speculative bent not only gave him the freedom to posit the Oedipus complex as a universal psychic structure, but also to imagine Leonardo da Vinci's early life (1910), to propose a myth of the primal horde to explain the development of human morality and civilization (1913), and to invent an entirely new history for Moses as a non-Jew (1939). It also allowed him (when necessary or convenient) to change his mind. A case in point is Freud's shift from the so-called topographical model of psychic functioning based on the relationship of conscious to unconscious mental processes to the structural model of mind that posits interactions among the ego, superego and id.

The mobility and flexibility of Freud's thinking proved an asset to him in the accretive, revisionary and evolutionary nature of his theorizing. It also opened the door to further revisions and alterations of his ideas, authorizing his followers to exercise their own innovative and creative powers. Hence, it makes more sense to refer to psychoanalysis in the plural than in the singular form. When we talk about this highly complex and mobile body of theories and practices, we are engaging not with psychoanaly*sis* but rather with psychoanaly*ses*.

The same may be said of literature, which consists of many genres (poetry, fiction, drama, creative nonfiction), which have diverse points of origin, evolutionary histories and cultural manifestations. The history of literary criticism is equally complex, spanning many centuries, cultural traditions and national boundaries.

How, then, is it possible to address the question of the relationship between two such power-fully influential, yet also challengingly mobile, modes of discourse and representation? For the purpose of this chapter, I want to begin with the assumption that literature and psychoanalysis are plural entities in themselves, subject to mutation and change, yet mutually and fruitfully inter-involved over the course of the 20th century – and beyond. Each, you might say, is a moving target, yet their individual trajectories may be examined at significant moments of intersection.

This chapter also assumes that both psychoanalysis and literature – as diverse and distinctive as they are in their histories and concerns – participate in the broad sociocultural movements of their time. Neither exists in a vacuum, but rather as one strand among many of the material, intellectual, social, aesthetic and political forces that shape our time.[1]

Yet there is also a significant difference between these two powerful modes of discourse: psychoanalysis originated fairly recently, with the theoretical endeavors of Sigmund Freud, who took pains to establish himself as sole founder of a new discipline. From this point of view, one might say that Freud, like other great thinkers before him, contested major tenets of the belief system he inherited – as a physician, neurological researcher, and bourgeois citizen of fin-de-siècle Vienna – and effectively transformed them. Over 150 years after his birth one may also say that his ideas (admittedly in diluted form) have permeated Western culture. Who, for instance, is unfamiliar with the terms Oedipus complex, penis envy, castration anxiety, infantile sexuality, the unconscious, or the id?

And who, after Freud, would deny the wish-fulfilling properties of dreams or the hidden significance of everyday slips of the tongue? Not only have Freudian neologisms entered our common vocabulary, but Freud's focus on the irrational properties of the human mind has also contributed to modernism's subversion of the Enlightenment ideal of reason as a guide to politics and human behavior.

Beginning with these assumptions – that neither literature nor psychoanalysis is unitary, that both discourses are embedded in the specifics of their time and place, and that they are complexly inter-involved over the course of the 20th century – I nevertheless want to highlight some very general points of convergence between them.

Both forms of discourse assume that meaning is (in Freud's terms) latent rather than manifest. Hence all forms of discourse, whether literary or individual, call for (and benefit from) interpre-tation. In addition, they both make use of and seek to elucidate strategies of displacement and concealment – most commonly symbol and metaphor. As such, they are equally overdetermined, hence irreducible to a single set of meanings.

These areas of resonance are significant, I believe, in terms of the broad shift from modernism to postmodernism over the course of the 20th century. The relationship between psychoanalytic and literary (cum philosophic) discourse both reflects and contributes to this trend.

Finally, I want to suggest that the current tendency (among psychoanalytic as well as literary scholars and theorists) to read Freud's texts through a mobile set of interpretive strategies returns Freud to his own literary and autobiographical bases.[2] In this respect, his ideas remain interesting and useful insofar as they continue to open themselves to new insights and meanings – just as literary texts sustain their readership through ever-evolving processes of interpretation.

## Broad developments and significant interactions

Much of the early history of psychoanalysis and literary interpretation, in the United States at least, reflects the emphasis on orthodoxy that Freud himself fostered among his followers and that flourished in postwar American culture through a generation of analysts who fled Nazi Germany. Many of these practitioners, trained by Freud or members of his inner circle, helped to found institutes that emphasized adherence to such key Freudian concepts as the Oedipus and castration complexes, with their concomitant formulations of masculinity and femininity. Such ideas not only resonated with the ideal of the nuclear family that evolved in the aftermath of World War II, but also helped to sustain it.

Many literary critics, discontent with the strictures of the 40-year domination of the New Criticism, which banished all forms of "extraliterary" consideration (such as cultural, biographical, historical or psychological issues) from the realm of textual interpretation, rebelled, in part, by embracing Freud's focus on the role of sexuality in human behavior, as well as his theory of coded meaning. Such critics happily discovered phallic symbols, as did Freud, in images of upright or elongated objects and female symbols in any kind of enclosed or inner space. For some writers as well as critics, such symbol hunting seemed not only obvious but also reductive. Yet it was hard to ignore this new approach to literature and literary criticism.

A writer like Vladimir Nabokov would publicly reject Freudian ideas while clearly flaunting them in his comic/satiric and profoundly transgressive novel *Lolita*. A much younger (though now aging) writer such as Philip Roth would not only embrace Freud but also turn him on his head in his equally comic/satiric and profoundly transgressive novel *Portnoy's Complaint*. Once writers themselves began to engage with Freud's ideas through adoption or contestation, the game changed. Freud was now a part of the culture at large – and, as such, subject to deformation, alteration and creative invention.

Social movements also had an impact. The 1950s American ideal of the father-dominant, mother-submissive family in which dads worked to support families domestically managed by women raising children at home gave way to the social upheavals and challenges of the second wave of feminism initiated by Betty Friedan's *The Feminine Mystique* (1963), published in the midst of the Civil Rights movement of the 1960s.

Combined with the anti-Vietnam War movement of the late 1960s and early 1970s, the feminist movement challenged Freud's ideas about female sexuality and feminine development, hence also helping to undermine Freud's focus on the foundational status of the Oedipus complex.

In the meantime, post-Freudian theorists (including his own daughter Anna Freud) had noticed something missing from the magisterial Oedipal construct: the newly significant pre-Oedipal period, which Freud acknowledged but chose not to theorize (Sprengnether, 1990), and which vitally involved those of his followers (many of them women) who undertook child analysis and/or observed mother–infant interactions. The school of object relations (Bowlby, 1969; Fairbairn, 1952; Guntrip, 1968; Klein, 1975; Mahler, 1968; Winnicott, 1971), which emphasized the role of the mother in early infant development, introduced many new paths in psychoanalytic theory and practice, which resonated with the feminist focus on women writers (past and present) and on themes that concern women in their roles as mothers and daughters. Feminist literary critics now turned their attention from a critique of stereotypical forms of "masculine" behavior in male-authored texts, to women writers' explorations of female issues and concerns, including the various possibilities of feminine subjectivity and desire (Abel, 1989; Gardiner, 1985; Gilbert & Gubar, 1979; Hirsch, 1989; Lilienfeld, 1980; Showalter, 1977; Suleiman, 1985).

The broad shift in psychoanalytic theory from Oedipal to pre-Oedipal matters of investigation corresponded with the social movement of second wave feminism in a way that supported not only the claims of women writers to equal time in the publishing world, but also to literary critics' focus on the ways that women authors have represented their experience(s) across the centuries. Some elements of idealization of women as mothers, present in Freud's own texts, persisted in this period, with the result that women's capacities for relatedness, empathy and ethical concern for the welfare of others were celebrated over men's focus on abstract reasoning and principles of justice and morality (Chodorow, 1978; Gilligan, 1982; Ruddick, 1989). The attempt to articulate a new and positive form of feminine identity – based in part on assumptions about mothers' capacities for and commitment to caregiving – has come under attack from many quarters and remains (to this day) a matter of debate.

Part of the difficulty, both in theory and in literary production, may lie in the problem of infinite regress when it comes to matters of origin. Freud rather neatly sidestepped this issue by beginning his theoretical labor not with the moment or fact of birth, as his friend and contemporary Otto Rank did in his articulation of "birth trauma" (Rank, 1952), but with the advent of the Oedipus complex, a much later development focused on the male child's rivalry with his father for the love and possession of his mother. To the extent that Freud thought about the pre-Oedipal period, he consigned it to shadows, like the Minoan-Mycenaean period of human prehistory (Freud, 1931). What we cannot remember, we may not theorize, he appears to have maintained – failing to imagine the practices of his own daughter Anna Freud in observing the behavior of very young children, much less the theoretical activities of Melanie Klein, who also pioneered the field of child analysis (A. Freud, 1922–1935; Klein, 1975).

Freud's avoidance of theoretical investigation of the pre-Oedipal period allowed him to preserve his personal idealization of maternal care – in his famous statement about the relationship of a mother to her male child as "altogether the most perfect, the most free from ambivalence of all human relationships" (Freud, 1933, p. 133), yet he also had a point about our collective lack of memory of the earliest stages of life. Mothers may remember, but babies do not. An entire body of speculative theory has arisen around this problematic awareness. How can we describe our own origins if we simply cannot recall them, much less articulate them?

Pre-Oedipal theory, post-Freud, has taken several different paths. The British and American branches of the object relations school have focused on the figure of the mother and the significance of how she relates (in healthy or troubled ways) to her newborn and developing infant. Even at best, these schools, however sensitive to individual styles of parenting, tend to lay the burden of normal or optimal child development on the mother. The more recent school of attachment theory – based on close mother–infant observations and hence more "evidentiary" in its processes and formulations – is even more focused on the mother's responsibility for her child's early ego development and capacity for relationship (Bowlby, 1969; Fonagy, 2001; Schore, 1994; Stern, 1985). Neither of these schools takes into consideration the mother's own history of mothering, much less the notion that no one is ideally mothered into the world.

Freud's own mother, as we know from various biographical sources, was unable to offer her undivided attention to her firstborn son, given that she was pregnant with his younger brother Julius, not long after his own birth and suffered the loss of this child within a year. Her successive pregnancies with Freud's six surviving siblings indicate that she had many children's needs to attend to. Although one may credit Freud's conviction that his mother was particularly devoted to him and believed in the special nature of his destiny, one can also understand how Freud as a child may have experienced her distraction with the cares of her household, including those of his younger sisters and surviving brother Alexander (Sprengnether, 1995). That he was entrusted to the care of a nanny in his earliest years suggests as much. Freud, at least, did not experience the kind of undivided attention from his mother that both object relations theory and attachment theory seem to prescribe for optimal infant development.

A counter-idealizing yet ultimately unrevolutionary trend emerged in France through the influential writings of Jacques Lacan. Lacan – who regarded himself as Freud's true heir, rescuing his radical insight into the irrationality of the unconscious from what he viewed as the reductive emphasis of American ego psychology – made use of French Structuralism and Saussurian linguistics to perform a transformation of Freud's ideas into his own idiom (Lévi-Strauss, 1969; Saussure, 1977).

For Lacan, who was also sensitive to the Dada and Surrealist movements in art, the realm of the pre-Oedipal represented a field of speculation as well as potential subversion of the Oedipal drama, which both instigates and sustains patriarchy. Given that the pre-Oedipal period precedes the onset of memory, along with verbal control, it represents a time when the ego is both fluid and disorganized. In this state of disorientation, it does not differentiate itself from the maternal matrix, nor does it conceive of individual identity as it may function in the social order.[3]

In Lacan's myth of origins, the authority and presence of the father (his "non" prohibiting incest, along with the power of his "nom," his name and what it signifies in terms of his role in maintaining the structure of the family and society) incur a rupture in the (quasi-blissful) mother–infant relationship. The father, in this narrative, represents the necessary third term that not only signals the infant's access to language and signification, but also its introduction into the social order.

Lacan's reformulation of Freud's Oedipus and castration complexes, de-emphasizes the role of drive or desire (i.e., the wish to murder one's father in order to have sex with one's mother) in favor of a more abstract conceptualization of how and why infants separate from their mothers. Each narrative has its tragic aspect, as neither permits the infant (presumably male) to achieve satisfaction in terms of having the mother all to itself.

Renunciation (as in Freud's key concept of sublimation as the effort to redirect prohibited wishes and desires into socially acceptable activities) marks both stories. Yet there is a significant difference, which stimulated Lacan's feminist follower-critics to introduce new psychoanalytic and writerly options.

There is no question that Lacan himself valorized the position prior to paternal intervention as represented by the father's "non," while also insisting on its necessity to participation in society and culture. His writings, as a result, have the paradoxical effect of both undermining and affirming the patriarchal status quo. The pre-Oedipal period (renamed the Imaginary in his unique terminology) represents the actual or primary state of confusion, disorientation and fragmentation of the ego, over which a socially acceptable form of integration (imposed by the father's function) is overlaid.

Civilization, thus linguistically and psychically organized, is something of a sham. Exposing the nature of this sham allows Lacan to dance on the border, as it were, between the pre-Oedipal and Oedipal periods, seeming to endorse the revolutionary prospect of ego dissolution, while also affirming the necessity of the father's role and function in maintaining the patriarchal organization of human society.

It is perhaps no wonder that the writings of Lacan's feminist followers (most notably Hélène Cixous and Clément (1986), Luce Irigaray (1985) and Julia Kristeva (1986)), seem both liberated and constrained by his theoretical formulations. Each has sought – through theoretical formulations and writerly practices – to investigate the potential for creative disruption embedded in the pre-Oedipal period. For these women, the lack of firm ego boundaries that characterizes the infant's relationship to its mother permits a freedom of internal organization, which may find adult expression in certain forms of writerly representation, loosely described as *l'écriture féminine*. Such so-called feminine writing – in contrast to rationally ordered or logically sequential forms of expression – allows for the eruption of unconscious images, fantasies and desires.

In some instances, these women associate the capacity for producing this kind of writing with the biological condition of being female and celebrate women's special proclivity for and access to *l'écriture féminine*. At other times, they maintain that such kinds of writing are not only open to men but have also been successfully practiced by them – as works by Marcel Proust, James Joyce, Jean Genet and others demonstrate.

French feminism, as represented by these women's collective writings, had a significant impact on advancing awareness of and appreciation for avant-garde forms of literature, as experimental kinds of writing seemed more closely to approximate pre-Oedipal experience(s) than did male-centered, Oedipally organized texts. In this sense, French feminist theory and writing endorsed the literature of modernism over that of 19th-century realism. At the same time, French feminists' adherence to Lacan's model of the acquisition of language and access to the Symbolic order (Lacan's substitution for Freud's term *civilization*) prevented them from finding an alternative to patriarchy. To some degree also, their idealization of the mother–infant bond and the pre-Oedipal period as one of freedom from patriarchal constraint led to criticisms of their work for reinstating stereotypes of women as creatures ruled by nature and emotion, as opposed to culture and reason.

The conflicts within feminist literary criticism – as a result of conflicting theoretical currents – seem not to have come to resolution so much as they have shifted ground. Social concerns, instead, have taken center stage in recent decades – focusing on such issues as race, class, and gender identity, including issues of sexual orientation and transsexuality. In this arena, the work of Lacan has been less significant than that of his French philosophical contemporary, Michel Foucault.

Foucault's work critiques psychoanalysis as a discipline enmeshed in the culture of its time (especially in terms of its understanding of the diverse forms of human sexual expression), hence one that is subordinate to historical/materialist analysis (Foucault, 1978). Foucault, in this sense, takes aim at Freud's somewhat easy assent to the assumptions about masculinity and femininity embedded in the social order of his day.

Foucault's work inspired and intersects with trends in contemporary LGBT (lesbian/gay/bisexual/transgender) studies, which flourish in the United States and elsewhere. If gender identity – as Judith Butler claimed in *Gender Trouble* (1990) is not a matter of anatomical or biological destiny but rather one of social construction, then we may all be freed from gender stereotypes based on how we look or are perceived by others.

Butler's early work owes much to Foucault's efforts to expose and to deconstruct the cultural assumptions about sexual behavior that Freud inherited and partially transformed but also transmitted in his formulation of the Oedipus complex. Despite Freud's affirmation of the bisexual disposition of both sexes, his Oedipus construct assumes that boys are normally heterosexual, as are girls – regardless of the fact that this construct does not explain female development as comfortably as it does the evolution of heterosexuality in boys and men. In her emphasis on the social construction of masculinity and femininity, Butler strove to liberate both men and women from the constraints of heteronormativity.

## Toward postmodernism

Movements in psychoanalytic theory and in literature and literary studies, as I have suggested earlier, do not move together in lockstep but rather speak to one another across disciplinary developments, as across national, historical and cultural boundaries. As a result, I have chosen to focus on moments where these two powerful modes of representation have impacted and challenged each other, with the effect of stimulating new forms of psychoanalytic and literary discourse.

The opening of psychoanalytic investigation and theory to the pre-Oedipal period neglected by Freud proved both productive and problematic in terms of literary/cultural study. On the one hand, it alerted women writers, readers and critics to a field that had been obscured and prompted vital responses – not only in terms of the publishing world (which began to recognize the quality of women's writing as well as the possibility of reaching new markets), but also in terms of the exploration of new subjects (e.g., women as daughters and as mothers, in addition to their forms of sexuality and expressions of subjectivity). On the other hand, it revived discussion about women's roles as mothers and caregivers, which has led (in some instances) to an intensification of pressure on mothers to provide "ideal" care to their newborns and preschool-age children. The contemporary (admittedly middle-class) liberated woman seems to be able to have it all, but cannot embrace this role without internal conflict, and in some instances, intense anxiety and/ or guilt.

While the debate about women in the workplace continues as a matter of social concern, the writerly and literary critical exploration of women in their roles as mothers and daughters seems to have subsided – due perhaps to the theoretical impasse reached in the conflict between the object relations view of women and that of French feminism, neither of which found a way of undermining or overturning the Oedipus complex as the engine of civilization and (patriarchal) culture. Instead, historical pressures and considerations, combined with the Foucauldian social constructivist turn toward cultural-political analysis, introduced new subjects of interest. I would describe the nature of this turn – in its broadest sense – as postmodern.

From a psychoanalytic perspective, this shift may be attributed to two important developments: the recognition of the subjective involvement of the analyst in the process of treatment (under the general rubric of countertransference and intersubjective theories), and the emergence of trauma theory. These two strands of psychoanalytic thought, developing along somewhat parallel lines, have not only affected each other but also have connected with a significant trend in literary/cultural studies toward the investigation of the history of the 20th century as traumatic – hence disruptive of previously understood notions of stability in human nature and behavior.

There is an additional point of intersection here between Freud's (and his successor Lacan's) emphasis on the driving and determining forces of human behavior as beyond our rational control (represented in dream formation, the unconscious, eros, the death instinct and the id), but postmodern psychoanalytic literary and theoretical practices take these assumptions further.

Early in his practice as an analyst, Freud observed the phenomenon of transference: the patient's tendency to replay and relive emotional dramas from the past, as evident in his or her feelings of love/hate toward the therapist (Freud, 1905, 1912a, 1915). Much later, he recognized the ways that the (insufficiently self-aware) analyst might do the same in reverse, reacting to his or her patient on the basis of personal issues and conflicts (Freud, 1912b, 1937). While Freud readily acknowledged that the process of self-analysis continues throughout life and may never be complete, he did not actively theorize the concept of countertransference as it is understood today.

Over the course of the latter half of the 20th century, the representation of the analyst as securely in possession of the kind of knowledge that enables him to apprehend and articulate the unconscious conflicts of his patient has diminished to the point of near vanishing. In place of the image of an all-knowing and largely silent analyst, whose mind serves as a blank screen for projection of the emotions of his patient, a radically different conception and set of practices has emerged. Instead of being a one-way street of disclosure, the psychoanalytic process is now generally understood as a two-person form of engagement, in which both partners are subjectively involved. The difference between analyst and patient is less one of emotional distance or disinterested observation on the analyst's part than one of specific training, including years of personal analysis, leading to the capacity for insight.[4]

Although this crucial development in psychoanalytic theory might seem, to many of us today, a matter of common sense, it has had significant consequences. Freud's conception of the superior, self-contained, and scrupulously objective analyst – as best represented perhaps by himself – can no longer be sustained. Even Lacan, one of Freud's most staunch defenders, challenged the role of the analyst as the one ideally "supposed to know." In his emphasis on the turbulent and disruptive tensions of the pre-Oedipal (Imaginary) period, Lacan sided with artists and revolutionaries, hence contributing to the undermining of all forms of authority, including his own as well as that of Freud.

Countertransference theory does not seek to undermine key psychoanalytic formulations, such as the Oedipus and castration complexes, but rather to focus on the mobile and contingent process of interaction established in the consulting room (Gabbard, 1995; Jacobs, 1999). It introduces its own kind of "relativity theory" into psychoanalysis as a collection of ideas and practices. At the same time, it cannot exclude from consideration the kinds of social, political, material and cultural concerns highlighted by Foucault. In this respect, the evolution of psychoanalysis over the course of the 20th century corresponds with dominant movements in literature and literary criticism. Each has moved away from the kinds of grand narrative that characterized the 19th century – along with their emphases on human order, reason and (the potential for) progress.

Intersubjective theory takes the ideas embedded in countertransference theory to new levels of speculation and uncertainty (Mitchell, 1993). If, as seems the case, the analyst is involved in a profoundly emotional and culturally inflected subjective encounter, what kind of communication occurs – and how might one describe it?

Following Lacan and other theorists' leads into the realm of the nonverbal as represented by the pre-Oedipal period, some analysts, for example Wilfred Bion (1962) and Thomas Odgen (1994, 1997), have posited a form of nonverbal interaction between analyst and patient that "happens" on the level of the unconscious in each partner. This unconscious and inarticulate type of communication may then find its way into words – via the special sensitivity of the analyst – and thence into conscious processing.

Melanie Klein's notion of projective identification (Klein, 1975), which theorized some of the ways in which patients might induce their analysts to feel what they were feeling, spoke to this kind of unconscious communication, although her near-contemporary Wilfred Bion immersed himself more intimately in this realm of speculation. The contemporary American psychoanalyst Thomas Ogden has made this idea more accessible in his articulation of the "intersubjective analytic third," by which he attempts to delineate the space in which the unconscious of both the analyst and the patient may communicate. For Ogden, access to this realm of communication involves the analyst's activity of reverie – which Ogden does not view as an expression of the analyst's distraction, boredom or lack of connection with his patient, but rather as a sign of his deep, unconscious communication.

The turn, in psychoanalytic theory and practice to an emphasis on the nonverbal realm of the pre-Oedipal period not only parallels but also supports the turn toward recognition of the analyst's subjectivity in the process of treatment and the unconscious (unverbalized) elements of his or her response to patients and the interaction between them.

Rather than pursuing Freud's emphasis on the significance of renunciation and sublimation in the evolution of human culture and civilization, his followers (intentionally and to some degree inadvertently) stress the unpredictable, unruly, inarticulate and sometimes destructive urges that reside in and emanate from the realm of the unconscious. The development of trauma theory in the latter half of the 20th century not only coincides with this overall trend but also furthers it in significant respects.

In the aftermath of World War I, Freud commented on the effects of trauma as a physical and/or psychic shock to the system so profound as to unhinge a previously "healthy" personality, but he did not pursue this subject at length – other than to posit the existence of an ominous "death instinct" in human nature that accompanies the desire to live and sustain life, and to observe the tendency to repeat past experiences of pain and suffering rather than act to resolve them (Freud, 1920).

While clearly indebted to Freud's formulations, trauma theory was slow to develop, achieving significant momentum in the post–Vietnam War era in the United States as a result of two forms of activism: Vietnam War veterans who spoke out about their enduring psychic and physiologic wounds, and women who called attention to the long-term bodily and emotional effects of rape, battery, incest and other forms of sexual abuse (van der Kolk et al., 1996). Once again social experience intersected with and helped to stimulate new areas of research and development in literary and psychoanalytic production. Not only is this field in a state of fluid and rapid development, but there is also an interesting new partner in the game – neuroscience, with its technology of real-time brain imaging (functional magnetic resonance imaging, or fMRI) and related research into the functions and dysfunctions of memory.

A consensus has emerged among psychoanalysts and neuroscientists regarding a specific aspect of trauma: its inaccessibility to verbal processing and (hence) narrative construction. For members of the psychoanalytic community, this means that trauma victims have no effective form of speech or language through which to integrate their disruptive experience(s) into the ongoing narrative of their lives (van der Kolk et al., 1991). The field of Holocaust studies, especially as it relates to the testimonies of its survivors, has a particular interest in this concept, as it correlates with an understanding of the Holocaust as essentially unspeakable, hence outside the realm of ordinary narrative representation. For many in this field (as for others who research the effects of other historical traumas), there is no way to give expression to the full horror of such events (Lanzmann, 1991).

Neuroscientists approach this issue from a different yet corroborating perspective. In their view, the sudden (or repeated) shock of trauma releases the stress hormone cortisol in such a way as to interfere with the normal, memory-forming function of the hippocampus (Schacter, 1996). Not being able to compose a proper memory of the event, the trauma victim relives it as if it were still happening – in the form of flashbacks, fight or flight responses, and recurring nightmares (Schacter, 1996). In this view, the past is never past, but rather a daily, unbidden and violent presence.

Although Freud did observe some of these phenomena, he did not investigate them in depth, due in part to his commitment to the process of bringing previously unconscious and nonverbalized aspects of human experience into the light of psychoanalytic treatment and dialogue. Trauma theory poses a challenge to this perspective. The increasing emphasis within psychoanalysis as a developing body of theory and practice on the pre-Oedipal period (inaccessible to individual consciousness and articulation) leads, however, to precisely this kind of impasse.

What we cannot remember, we cannot put into words, which in turn we cannot make meaningful sense of. In a curious way, the trajectories of psychoanalytic theory and practice, of literature and literary analysis – and more recently the neuroscience of trauma – articulate similar problems over the course of the 20th century. If key aspects of human experience are truly beyond words, how are we to speak or write?

I do not want to suggest that psychoanalysts – and here I mean to include psychologists and clinical social workers – despair of treating their patients because they are no longer certain of what they know, or how to deal with the murky realms of nonverbal experience and communication. On the contrary, psychoanalysis as a set of theories and treatment modalities appears to be thriving, as it attempts to come to grips with some of the more extreme forms of human suffering that characterize our time. That definitive answers are not forthcoming does not invalidate the energy engaged, but rather speaks to the density and complexity of the problems at issue.

Nor do I wish to indicate that the modernist experiment in literature and literary study has reached a dead end with the advent of postmodern theories and practices. While it is clear that many writers (poets, fiction writers and memoirists) have adopted a set of postmodern ideas and forms of writing that strive to embody the problem(s) inherent in the process of representation, it would be difficult to find any who argue against writing, authorship or publication per se. Even those who assent to Roland Barthes's (1968) notion of textual production as an effect of social and material culture (the so-called death of the author) claim individual responsibility and ownership when it comes to matters of royalty or copyright.

To state this case as simply as possible: we keep trying to give expression to what seems to be – by its very nature – elusive and ultimately (perhaps) inexpressible.

## Postmodernism

Psychoanalysis, like literature and other forms of meaning-making, strives to illuminate the most urgent questions of our time. In the current shift – still underway – between modernist and post-modern worldviews, it reflects our deep concern, as well as our anxiety and uncertainty, about the future. Psychoanalysis as a discipline is not unitary (as Freud had hoped), but rather highly heterogeneous – containing within its broad embrace many conflicting theories and treatment modalities.

The same might be said of the world of literary production and reception – where there is no longer an agreed-upon canon of great authors, much less a hierarchy of literary value, but rather a plethora of genres, styles, voices and critical views, all competing for attention in a rapidly changing media environment and equally evolving set of social networks connecting writers, audiences and critics. Most people most of the time, I believe, would find such developments more hopeful and salutary than otherwise.

Modernism contained within itself the seeds of postmodernism, the consequences of which we have yet to comprehend, much less to theorize, in terms of the world we live in today – as dominated as it is by international conflict, local genocidal actions and violations of human rights, extremist movements and ideologies, financial markets and practices that only the most elite among us can manipulate or understand, as well as nuclear and environmental threats to global survival.

The current focus on trauma theory may represent a very real engagement not only with the extremely painful history of the 20th century but also with our own (terrified if not terrorized) concern about what may lie ahead. Many contemporary writers seek to engage these kinds of issues on the level of subject matter as well as narrative form (e.g., Don DeLillo, Louise Erdrich, Colum McCann, Toni Morrison, Zadie Smith and David Foster Wallace, to name only a handful of fiction writers). At the same time, popular literature hardly seems to change, relying as it does on clearly defined characters and conventional structures of conflict and resolution.

The upside to this confusion of tongues in the state of contemporary culture is the freedom (in plural political societies) to choose the narrative or treatment modality that is not only most resonant with one's history, cultural background and system of belief, but also most individually useful and productive. The downside is that there is no universal psychic paradigm to which anyone/everyone can turn for insight and understanding.

Freud himself – though a participant in this series of developments – hardly imagined such a cacophonous state of affairs. Rather, he pictured a seamless line of descendants who would promulgate his ideas for the benefit of future generations. Early in his career, he conceived of an ideal successor, a "crown prince," who would ensure the continuity as well as the purity of the ideas he articulated. One after another, however, these younger (primarily male) followers fell away. Even his own daughter Anna Freud, who professed her loyalty in personal and ideological ways, helped to inaugurate the field of child analysis and pre-Oedipal studies, which have called many of his most cherished concepts into question.

Freud, in spite of his particular genius, seems not so much to have provided a means of relieving the neurotic dilemmas he observed in himself and his late Victorian and early 20th-century compatriots, as to have opened a Pandora's box of problems and issues for our own and future generations to address.

## Conclusion

If, in our current state of global (multi-sexual, multicultural, multi-historical, multinational, multi-financial) awareness, we no longer feel comfortable with the idea of mastery – in terms of philosophy, religion, social theory, literature or psychoanalysis – how might we move forward? I'd like to propose a rather humble thesis, beginning with the assumption that each of us, born into our own family system, time and place, attempts to find personal meaning in our lives – even when these attempts appear to be thwarted by conditions (most often material/historical) beyond our control.

Freud was a major thinker in striving to make sense of the world he inherited and vigorously participated in, but which also transcended his ability to theorize in a universal way for all time. In this sense, he reflects many assumptions that most of us no longer take for granted – that he was designated for a special destiny as a result of being his mother's favorite, firstborn son, and that he was the inheritor of a tradition of master theorist/philosophers, who could guide and lead mankind into a less suffering, if not also more enlightened future. At the same time, we continue to read him and to be inspired by his work. Why?

The reason, I believe, is that Freud wrote like a writer – that is to say, in a manner that allows readers to engage with his ideas in multi-textual ways.[5] Because of his somewhat meandering, hypothetical, anecdotal, metaphoric and often self-questioning style, he offers opportunities for us as readers to engage in a silent (perhaps subconscious or even unconscious) conversation with him, allowing us to ponder our own thoughts, feelings and experiences in relation to his.

Freud, on the page, is the least coercive of theorists, allowing for doubt, conjecture and even creative disagreement with him – which, in turn, invites new ideas and formulations. While Freud himself may have deplored the defection of individual disciples, the enduring legacy of his writing (not unlike that of literary authors over time) has been to enable creative response and adaptation.

Like children who become the unwitting legacies of their parents' psychic histories, psychoanalytic as well as literary writers inherit the tangle of history, theory and (partially processed) experience that precedes them. In the best of circumstances, they do not blindly adhere to or repeat these histories. Rather they transform them in the light of their own life trajectories and sources of inspiration.

Ironically, for Freud, the aspects of his writing that exercise the most appeal for contemporary writers and theorists draw from ideas he hinted at instead of fully developing. It's as if late 20th- and 21st-century readers explore the regions that Freud himself could glimpse, but not directly address. These include the pre-Oedipal period (which Freud considered too shadowy to investigate), the phenomenon of mourning (which he regarded as too ordinary to theorize) and trauma – a subject that prompted him to hypothesize repetition compulsion and the death instinct (Freud, 1917, 1920). While opening these areas of interest, Freud himself did not pursue their implications, leaving them for others to mine more deeply. It is for this reason, I believe, that contemporary psychoanalytic theorists routinely pay tribute to him, citing those (mostly fragmentary) statements in his texts that authorize their own views and speculations. Not only do they seek in this way to honor Freud's achievement, but also to establish a line of continuity between his work and theirs. At the same time, contemporary psychoanalytic theories and theorists diverge widely from their source – so much so that Freud himself would regard many (if not most) as defectors and/or apostates.

The current emphasis on the two- (or three-)person nature of psychoanalytic treatment, along with the fascination with preverbal or nonverbal aspects of early life, and their adult corollaries in the unrepresented nature of traumatic experience(s), has moved psychoanalysis in the direction of avant-garde literature, which seeks also to explore such elusive states of mind and being. Both disciplines/discourses seem to be asking the same kinds of questions. What forces beyond our conscious awareness drive or control our actions? Who or what is speaking through us as we struggle to shape our own poetic or narrative structures of meaning? Are some aspects of human experience genuinely inaccessible to representation? If so, what can we hope to comprehend, much less articulate? Finally, what kinds of social/political relations can be formed in the light of these issues and awarenesses?

Although I do not have answers to these questions, I want to suggest that Freud not only contributed to the dominant historical movement of his time toward the shaping of modernity, but also helped – through the polysemous and unstable nature of his own writing practices – to enable postmodernism, which calls into question every aspect of authority (who "authors" our beginnings and what can be said about them), including the authority of Freud himself.

That Freud wrote like a writer – that is to say, recognizing that all forms of writing are tentative forays into the unknown – not only establishes his body of work among the classics of 20th-century literature but also affirms his role in the development of contemporary postmodern reality.

## Notes

1 Freud's insistence on the universality of his theories had a dampening effect on studies of his work in sociopolitical terms. Among those who have sought to locate Freud's achievement in terms of the science and culture of his times, Peter Gay (1988), Peter Homans (1989), Carl Schorske (1981), Frank Sulloway (1979) and Eli Zaretsky (2004) are especially cogent.

2 I have argued elsewhere that Freud's theoretical endeavor, especially in its earliest stages, constitutes a unique form of autobiography, as his major insights, e.g., dream interpretation, the Oedipus and castration complexes, derive from his self-analysis (Sprengnether, 1995). The resonance of Freud's ideas with other social developments of his time have not only ensured his place in the history of modernism, but have also provided the inspiration for contemporary theories and practices, many of which alter his conceptions to the point that he would hardly recognize them. What Freud invented, in my view, is not an objective science of mind but rather a new form of subjective self-inquiry. The power of his discovery is in no way diminished by its lack of "scientific" status. To make such a claim would be like saying that James Joyce's *Ulysses* or Marcel Proust's *In Search of Lost Time* have nothing to teach us about the workings of the human mind.

3 Lacan famously posited a "mirror stage" of development (1977), at which point the infant catches sight of itself in a mirror, which reflects back an image of physical and psychic cohesion. This image provides an illusion of internal coherence, which in turn fosters the infant's developing ego. Such an ego, based on the alluring, yet inaccessible image in the mirror, is as frustrating as it is unreal. In Lacan's mode of thinking, we never coincide with the image of ourselves that we perceive as integrated and whole, at the same time that we rely on just such an image to function within the social order. The "mirror stage" in this way constitutes a "heads you lose, tails you lose" deal, which the drama of human development requires. To accept this bargain involves living with a necessary split – the simultaneous embrace and alienation from a selfhood that is a fictional construct at best. To reject it is not only to refuse participation in the human social exchange that Lacan terms the Symbolic Order, but it is also to consign oneself to the realm of failed interaction and communication that constitutes psychosis.

4 There is an interesting parallel between the development of countertransference theory in psychoanalysis and reader-response criticism in literary studies, which deposed the literary text as the primary source of meaning in order to relocate it in the minds of individual readers (Bleich, 1975; Fish, 1967; Holland, 1968). Whereas the New Criticism had assumed the text itself as the arbiter of its meaning(s), which the assiduous reader could decode or discover through close textual analysis, subsequent modes of interpretation (feminist, Marxist, queer, postcolonial) have assumed the primacy of the reader, including his or her cultural background and individual life history.

5 Steven Marcus, in his seminal essay "Freud and Dora: Story, History, Case History" (1974), considers the radical hypothesis that Freud, in his Dora case history, was writing a unique kind of modernist fiction. Not many critics have followed his lead in regarding Freud primarily as a writer of fiction – or perhaps, even more appropriately, as a writer of memoir. Implicitly, however, philosopher/psychoanalytic/critics such as Jacques Derrida (1978) read Freud's texts not for their overt content but for their subtextual resonances and even subversive implications. A deconstructionist (or postmodern) reading of Freud will, by its very nature, read on the margins of Freud's texts, seeking for the moments of rupture, disruption, contradiction, and/or reversal of conscious meaning. We read Freud today as he taught us to read dreams, that is to say, with an eye to disguise, displacement, and cryptic expression. In this sense, Freud's texts are literary – open to endless conjecture and interpretation.

## References

Abel, E 1989, *Virginia Woolf and the fictions of psychoanalysis*, University of Chicago Press, Chicago.

Barthes, R 1968, 1977, 'The death of the author' (S Heath, trans and ed), in *Image, music, text*, Noonday Press, London.

Bion, W 1962, *Learning from experience*, Basic Books, New York.

Bleich, D 1975, 'The subjective character of critical interpretation', *College English*, vol. 36, pp. 739–755.

Bowlby, J 1969, *Attachment and loss*, Basic Books, New York.

Butler, J 1990, *Gender trouble*, Routledge, London.

Chodorow, N 1978, *The reproduction of mothering*, University of California Press, Berkeley.

Cixous, H & Clément, C 1986, *The newly born woman* (B Wing, trans), University of Minnesota Press, Minneapolis.

Derrida, J 1978, 'Coming into one's own' (J Hulbert, trans), in G Hartman (ed), *Psychoanalysis and the question of the text*, Johns Hopkins University Press, Baltimore.

Fairbairn, W 1952, *An object relations theory of the personality*, Basic Books, New York.

Fish, F 1967, *Clinical psychopathology: Signs and symptoms in psychiatry*, Wright Publishers, Bristol.

Fonagy, P 2001, *Attachment theory and psychoanalysis*, Other Press, New York.

Foucault, M 1978, *The history of sexuality*, vol. 1 (R Hurley, trans), Pantheon, New York.

Freud, S 1905, 'Fragment of an analysis of a case of hysteria', in J Strachey (ed), *Standard edition of the complete psychological works of Sigmund Freud*, vol. 7, Hogarth, London, pp. 1–122.

Freud, S 1910, 'Leonardo da Vinci and a memory of his childhood', in J Strachey (ed), *Standard edition of the complete psychological works of Sigmund Freud*, vol. 11, Hogarth, London, pp. 59–137.

Freud, S 1912a, 'The dynamics of transference', in J Strachey (ed), *Standard edition of the complete psychological works of Sigmund Freud*, vol. 12, Hogarth, London, pp. 97–108.

Freud, S 1912b, 'Recommendations to physicians practising psycho-analysis', in J Strachey (ed), *Standard edition of the complete psychological works of Sigmund Freud*, vol. 12, Hogarth, London, pp. 111–120.

Freud, S 1913, 'Totem and taboo', in J Strachey (ed), *Standard edition of the complete psychological works of Sigmund Freud*, vol. 1, Hogarth, London, pp. 1–161.

Freud, S 1915, 'Observations on transference love', in J Strachey (ed), *Standard edition of the complete psychological works of Sigmund Freud*, vol. 12, Hogarth, London, pp. 157–171.

Freud, S 1917, 'Mourning and melancholia', in J Strachey (ed), *Standard edition of the complete psychological works of Sigmund Freud*, vol. 14, Hogarth, London, pp. 237–258.

Freud, S 1920, 'Beyond the pleasure principle', in J Strachey (ed), *Standard edition of the complete psychological works of Sigmund Freud*, vol. 18, Hogarth, London, pp. 1–64.

Freud, A 1922–1935, *Introduction to psychoanalysis: Lectures for child analysts and teachers, the writings of Anna Freud*, vol. 1, Indiana University of Pennsylvania, New York.

Freud, S 1931, 'Female sexuality', in J Strachey (ed), *Standard edition of the complete psychological works of Sigmund Freud*, vol. 21, Hogarth, London, pp. 221–243.

Freud, S 1933, 'Femininity', in J Strachey (ed), *Standard edition of the complete psychological works of Sigmund Freud*, vol. 22, Hogarth, London, pp. 112–135.

Freud, S 1937, 'Analysis terminable and interminable', in J Strachey (ed), *Standard edition of the complete psychological works of Sigmund Freud*, vol. 23, Hogarth, London, pp. 209–253.

Freud, S 1939, 'Moses and monotheism', in J Strachey (ed), *Standard edition of the complete psychological works of Sigmund Freud*, vol. 23, Hogarth, London, pp. 1–137.

Friedan, B 1963, *The feminine mystique*, Norton, New York.

Gabbard, G 1995, 'Countertransference: The emerging common ground', *International Journal of Psychoanalysis*, vol. 76, pp. 475–485.

Gardiner, J 1985, 'Mind mother: Psychoanalysis and feminism', in G Greene & C Kahn (eds), *Making a difference: Feminist literary criticism*, Methuen, London.

Gay, P 1988, *Freud: A life for our time*, Norton, New York.

Gilbert, S & Gubar, S 1979, *The madwoman in the attic: The woman writer and the nineteenth-century imagination*, Yale University Press, New Haven.

Gilligan, C 1982, *In a different voice*, Harvard University Press, Cambridge.

Guntrip, H 1968, *Schizoid phenomena, object relations and the self*, Hogarth Press, London.

Hirsch, M 1989, *The mother/daughter plot: Narrative, psychoanalysis, feminism*, Indiana University Press, Bloomington.

Holland, N 1968, 'The mind and the book: Past, present, and future psychoanalytic literary criticism', in D Scharff (ed), *The psychoanalytic century: Freud's legacy for the future*, Other Press, New York, pp. 181–194.

Homans, P 1989, *The ability to mourn: Disillusionment and the social origins of psychoanalysis*, University of Chicago Press, Chicago.

Irigaray, L 1985, *Speculum of the other woman* (G Gill, trans), Cornell University Press, Ithaca, NY.

Jacobs, T 1999, 'Countertransference past and present: A review of the concept', *International Journal of Psychoanalysis*, vol. 80, pp. 575–594.

Klein, M 1975, *Love, guilt, and reparation & other works 1921–1945*, Delacorte, New York.

Kristeva, J 1986, *The Kristeva reader* (T Moi, ed), Columbia University Press, New York.

Lanzmann, C 1991, 'The obscenity of understanding: An evening with Claude Lanzmann', in C Caruth (ed), *American Imago*, vol. 48, pp. 473–495.

Levi-Strauss, C 1969, *The elementary structures of kinship*, Beacon Press, Boston.

Lilienfeld, J 1980, 'Reentering paradise: Cather, Colette, Woolf, and their mothers', in E Broner & C Davidson (eds), *The lost tradition: Mothers and daughters in literature*, Frederick Ungar, New York.

Mahler, M 1968, *On human symbiosis and the vicissitude of individuation*, International Universities Press, New York.

Marcus, S 1974, *Representations: Essays on literature and society*, Columbia University Press, New York.

Mitchell, S 1993, *Hope and dread in psychoanalysis*, Basis Books, New York.

Ogden, T 1994, *Subjects of analysis*, Karnac Books, London.

Ogden, T 1997, *Reverie and interpretation*, Karnac Books, London.

Rank, O 1952, *The trauma of birth*, Robert Brunner, New York.

Ruddick, S 1989, *Maternal thinking*, Beacon Press, Boston.

Saussure, F 1977, *Course in general linguistics* (C Bally & A Sechehaye, eds, W Baskin, trans), Fontana/Collins, Glasgow.

Schacter, D 1996, *Searching for memory*, Basic Books, New York.

Schore, A 1994, *Affect regulation and the origin of the self*, Erlbaum, Hillsdale, NJ.

Showalter, E 1977, *A literature of their own: British women novelists from Bronte to Lessing*, Princeton University Press, Princeton, NJ.

Sprengnether, M 1990, *The spectral mother: Freud, feminism and psychoanalysis*, Cornell University Press, Ithaca, NY.

Sprengnether, M 1995, 'Reading Freud's life', *American Imago*, vol. 52, pp. 9–51.

Stern, D 1985, *The interpersonal world of the infant*, Basic Books, New York.

Suleiman, S 1985, 'Writing and motherhood', in SN Garner, C Kahane & F Sulloway (eds), 1979, *Freud: Biologist of the mind*, Basic Books, New York.

Sulloway, F 1979, *Freud, biologist of the mind: Beyond the psychoanalytic legend*, Basic Books, New York.

van der Kolk, B, Weisaeth, L & van der Hart O 1991, 'The intrusive past: The flexibility of memory and the engraving of trauma', *American Imago*, vol. 48, pp. 425–453.

van der Kolk, B, Weisaeth, L & van der Hart, O 1996, 'History of trauma in psychiatry', in B van der Kolk, A McFarlane & L Weisaeth (eds), *Traumatic stress: The effects of overwhelming experience on mind, body, and society*, Guilford Press, pp. 47–74.

Winnicott, D 1971, *Playing and reality*, Tavistock, London.

Zaretsky, E 2004, *Secrets of the soul: A social and cultural history of psychoanalysis*, Knopf, New York.

# 18

# Psychoanalysis and architecture

*Elizabeth Danze and Stephen Sonnenberg*

The past several decades have seen a dramatic increase in interest in examining the theoretical and cultural connections between psychoanalysis and architecture. Considering the two fields in relation to one another creates a richer understanding of each discipline, how one informs the other, how each reflects an underlying set of assumptions about its purpose, and how both may continue to inform contemporary discourse.

Aspects of the disciplines of architecture and psychoanalysis expand our knowledge and instruct our thinking on points of common interest. While architecture operates in the realm of the physical, external world, our experience of it extends into the internal world of emotion, perception, feeling and awareness. All of these overlap the concerns of psychoanalysis. More than simply constructing a building, architecture seeks to illuminate, enhance and inspire. Architecture can promote well-being and peace of mind, encourage introspection as well as expression, and expand understanding of ourselves as both individuals and as a community of human beings.

Contributions made by architects, psychoanalysts, theoreticians and historians describing both fields reveal the connection between buildings and the world of the psyche. The scale of the examination ranges from the urban and environmental context to a room, to the site of the body, and the way we psychoanalytically engage the physical world. This chapter will provide an account of various intersections of psychoanalysis and architecture and create an overview of the broader historical and cultural perspectives brought to bear on both. It includes references to two recently published books on this subject: *Space and Psyche* and *Psychoanalysis and Architecture*, as well as an interactive three-and four-dimensional clinical, research, learning and teaching model of Erik Erikson's Diagram of Psychosocial Development and its use; the Veterans Community Park and Pavilion Project; and three architectural design studios at the University of Texas School at Austin School of Architecture, where an architect and psychiatrist led students in exploring how psychoanalysis informs our thinking of architecture and design.

## Themes and theories

Scholarship explicitly focused on the relationship between architecture and psychoanalysis has historically been sporadic, not gaining considerable footing until the 1980s and 1990s. Until then, architectural themes could occasionally be found in psychoanalytic work, but these tended to manifest as architectural archetypes that served as a metaphor for psychological pathology rather than a true examination of the impact of architecture upon the psyche. A 1964 paper by Gordon Globus and Jeff Gilbert published in the *Psychoanalytic Review* entitled "A Metapsychological Approach to the Architecture of Frank Lloyd Wright," was one of the first essays that examined the intersection of the two disciplines by analyzing the psychological development of Frank Lloyd Wright as it manifested in his architectural works. In this essay the authors emphasize the ego-related aspects of Wright's work through a discussion of several of his most important projects. They demonstrate how the extraordinary changes seen in the development of Wright's architecture parallel the vicissitudes of libido, ego organization and object relations.

Further explorations of architecture and psychoanalysis in the 1970s and 1980s by prominent architectural theorists such as Rem Koolhaas, Mario Gandelsonas, Peggy Deamer and Beatriz Colomina advanced an understanding of this interdisciplinary relationship. For example, in "Le Corbusier and Photography" (1987) Colomina discusses Le Corbusier's nonacademic working methods, including the various ways the architect used photography as a tool for representation. She expands upon this theme in her 1994 book *Privacy and Publicity*. Here the photographic process, from its beginnings as an invisible negative enclosed within the camera to its eventual development into a visible print, is likened to the processes of the conscious and unconscious mind. Colomina claims that "the simultaneous arrival of psychoanalysis and photography marks the emergence of a different sense of space, indeed of a different architecture" (Colomina, 1994, p. 82). From here, Colomina explores the use of photography in architectural representation and the discrepancies between reality and representation that arise from it.

Although not explicitly focused on architecture, many of Sigmund Freud's writings discuss architectural and spatial themes – from the scale of the city to the scale of the psychoanalytic space. In *The Interpretation of Dreams*, one of his earliest and most notable works, he discusses the origins and nature of dreams, as well as his method of dream interpretation. Freud details several of his patients' dreams of their childhoods, one of the most potent sources of dreams, as well as his own dreams, many of which are focused around the psychological aspects of spatial experiences of a country, city, house, shop, attic and so forth. In a later essay, published in 1912 as part of *Papers on Technique: Recommendations for Physicians on the Psycho-Analytic Method of Treatment*, he also outlines many practical aspects for establishing an appropriate analytic setting.

Freud frequently referenced classical architecture, as in *Civilization and its Discontents*, where he uses Rome – the Eternal City – as an analogy of the mind. Just as Rome is composed of the many iterations of the city that have arisen throughout history, so too is the mind composed of all its previous stages of development. Again, drawing from classical architecture, Freud provides a narrative in "A Disturbance of Memory on the Acropolis" (1936) of his own psychological experiences of the Acropolis during a trip in 1904, much earlier in his life. Freud recounts his feelings of disbelief and unreality, which he termed "derealization," upon seeing the Acropolis, rather than his anticipated reaction of admiration. While he *knew* of the historical reality of the Acropolis, his unconscious mind had somehow retained incredulity about the actual existence of this iconic site. Freud attributes this reaction to the unexpected and paradoxical nature of wish fulfillment: that the satisfaction of a certain desire is prevented because of a deep-seated feeling of being undeserving of happiness. Freud believed that his own experiences of derealization and falsification of memory occurred not because he actually doubted the existence of the Acropolis but rather because he doubted that he would ever have the opportunity to travel and experience it personally due to his own childhood experiences with poverty. Fulfilling his desire for success resulted in feelings of guilt at having surpassed his father's accomplishments. How did the architecture of the Acropolis evoke this response in Freud? Some have speculated that he unconsciously identified with the figural

*Figure 18.1* The Acropolis
Source: © Elizabeth Schaub

frieze carvings and the implications of that; others speculate that monuments illicit powerful reactions in us all (Figure 18.1).

In 1919, Freud published "The Uncanny," a paper that has provided some of the most fertile ground for subsequent scholarship on the intersection of psychoanalysis and architecture. Freud begins by acknowledging the need for an intellectual foray into the realm of aesthetics, while simultaneously admitting to his general disregard for the subject in his other writings. Aesthetics, in this sense, is not a theory of beauty but a theory of "the qualities of feeling" (Freud, 1919, p. 218). Specifically, he addresses the uncanny: that which arouses feelings of dread and horror. The German word for uncanny, *unheimlich*, translates to "unfamiliar," but its root and antonym, *heimlich*, literally translates to "homely," as in "belonging to the home" or "familiar." This word contains at its core architectural connotations influenced by psychological experience. Freud provides an etymological analysis of equivalent words from several European languages that also express a negative emotional response of fear of, or disorientation to, that which is foreign or unfamiliar. Freud supports his theories of the uncanny through case analyses and personal accounts, some of which involve distinctly strong architectural motifs and experiences, such as the haunted house and getting lost in rambling Italian hill towns.

Architect Anthony Vidler's 1992 book *The Architectural Uncanny: Essays in the Modern Unhomely*, was a milestone in nuanced cross-disciplinary research on these fields, and dovetails with Freud's "The Uncanny." It also reflects the pervasive influence of psychoanalytic thinking on architectural theorizing. In this book, Vidler traces the development of the *unheimlich*, or uncanny, from its roots in the late 18th century through its manifestation in late 20th-century culture. This broad feeling of insecurity and estrangement developed from the great social revolutions that resulted in the establishment of the middle class and spurred the increasing urbanization from which great cities of unprecedented and inhuman scale were born. The 19th century brought a centralization of political and cultural power that replaced local customs and severed community bonds. Vidler notes that Freud's writings on the uncanny were published in the immediate aftermath of World War I, a time when "the apparently secure house of western civilization was in barbaric regression; when the territorial security that had fostered a notion of unified culture was broken, bringing a powerful disillusionment" (Vidler, 1992, p. 7). This experience of the uncanny was no longer confined to the individual but experienced throughout the collective cultural psyche.

Vidler divides this work into two parts. The first concerns itself with the literary, aesthetic, and philosophical underpinnings of the uncanny, and the second with the examination of several contemporary architectural and urban projects. "Here the question of the homely becomes particularized, embodied in architectural forms that seek to express the precarious relationship between psychological and physical home" (Vidler, 1992, p. xi).

In his 2000 book, *Warped Space*, Vidler builds upon the themes explored in his previous work, portraying the modern individual as caught in spatial systems beyond their control, attempting to make sense of a situation through the means of architectural and artistic representation. He focuses on the psychopathology of modern space itself. Fascinated by the relationship between psychic identity and spatial construction, he conjoins the idea of phobic space and its design corollary, warped space. Phobic space for Vidler is a product of the imaginary displacement or the projection of fear, anxiety, estrangement and their psychological counterparts – anxiety, neuroses and phobias – onto the modern city and architecture.

The first half of the volume offers a genealogy of phobic space that begins with the maladies of agoraphobia and claustrophobia as diagnosed by late 19th-century psychologists. It then focuses on the sense of estrangement produced in modern citizens and reproduced in modernist architecture, art and film to reflect the nervous life of the big city. The second half explores the contemporary zeitgeist through the work of five artists and five architects, extending the idea of warped space to today's technologically sophisticated digital and virtual culture.

Steve Pile, whose research focuses primarily on the relationships between space, identity and the urban environment, has made multiple contributions to the discourse on the psyche and the urban. In his 2010 essay "Sleepwalking in the Modern City: Walter Benjamin and Sigmund Freud in the World of Dreams," Pile addresses themes of the city and the alienation of modernity, and its accompanying fear and desire. He suggests cities and dreams are both built on wish fulfillments and anxieties. In other words, cities are desire and fear made concrete, but perhaps in deceitful, disguised and displaced ways.

In Pile's analysis of Benjamin's *One-Way Street*, he describes the alienation experienced by people in the modern city. Benjamin asserts that it is the revolutionary task of the social critic to shock the dreamers awake. Benjamin seeks the solution to the problem of alienation through the dream itself. In a very real way, just as the dream is most vivid at the point of waking, dreams anticipate and can perhaps promote an awakening. Benjamin focuses on areas of the city that are being altered – as if waking from a dream – and urban artifacts that contain cultural memory. While Freud did not specifically address urban life, he described a walk through the city in his essay on the uncanny, and Pile embraces Freud, using his theories on dream work to illuminate Benjamin's writings: dreams simultaneously mask and reveal unconscious desires.

In the chapter Pile contributed to *Freud 2000* (Anthony Elliott, ed., 1999), "Freud, Dreams, and Imaginative Geographies," he argues that the primary mechanisms of Freud's dream work – *condensation* and *displacement* – are inherently spatial and that correlations can be drawn between it and human geography. Dreams are constructed out of spatial analogies and relationships, and the spatial consciousness of the dreamer is the blending of the social, personal and imagined topography of the body that understands the geography of the dream. The dream fervently traces paths, makes connections, juxtaposes elements and composes symbols within its space.

As psychoanalyst Christopher Bollas writes in "Architecture and the Unconscious" (2000), the way we plan and live in our built environments reflects unconscious forms of thinking realized through architecture. Cities become holding environments that offer inhabitants differing forms of psychic engagement with the object world. Their planning and the types of objects they offer combine to create degrees of "imageability," an attribute of any city that could become part of a psychoanalysis of the built world, or what Gaston Bachelard termed a "topo-analysis." Bachelard, a philosopher and scientist, in his 1958 book, *Poetics of Space*, addresses architecture, poetry, psychoanalysis, and the imagination. His book encourages architects to design based on the experiences a building will engender and encourages an architecture of the imagination.

In "The City Within (2012)," Esther da Costa Meyer's contribution to *Space & Psyche*, the author integrates psychoanalytic thinking with social history, examining these through the lens of architecture. Focusing on the people of Paris during the mid-19th-century's Second Empire, when Napoleon III and his prefect Baron Haussmann destroyed much of the urban landscape in a dramatic urban renewal effort, da Costa Meyer describes the simultaneous erosion of the collective psyche of the affected Parisians. As sites of past insurrections were demolished, Parisians felt disoriented, as spaces associated with their lives disappeared. In the second part of her essay, da Costa Meyer describes how it was discovered through Haussmann's excavations that Paris had also been inhabited by nonhuman species. This occurred in the era of Darwin's theory of evolution, which questioned Western Europe's sense of geographic and historical place in the history of the world and the animal kingdom. Da Costa Meyer explains how the discovery threatened the emotional well-being of the populace, how the past lives on in our psyches, and how the fragility of the psyche is revealed in moments of turmoil in the physical environment.

Architectural historian Joseph Rykwert makes observations on the modern city and its architecture in "Space and Mind (2012)," his contribution to *Space & Psyche*. He articulates a psychoanalytic understanding of the relationship between the psyche and the body, and examines the structure and infrastructure of the city as a manifestation of the same relationship. He describes the progression of the infant's first spatial experiences, which he characterizes as embracing, protective, and womb-like, to the upright posture of the child and its awareness of its separateness in an unprotecting world. This leads the child, Rykwert posits, to an awareness of the need to manipulate the environment for the sake of protection; Rykwert links this to the primary role of architecture: the mediation between the person and the world through the building of shelter. More generally, Rykwert suggests that the modern city, reflected in the skyscraper, has obliterated the conscience and that the city is in need of psychoanalytic help. He describes the progression of the skyscraper as moving from prelude to entrance into heaven – as seen in the era of Protestant religious influence – to demonstrations of the triumph of the superego with the construction of skyscrapers like the Empire State and Chrysler Buildings. Ultimately, Rykwert suggests, this era has been supplanted by an urban architecture that is an extension of the id.

In his essay *Against Redemption: The Arts of Counter-Memory in Germany Today* (2000), James Young examines the transformation of the monument over the course of the 20th century, from the representational figurative icons of the late 19th century to the minimalist conceptual pieces that serve as an intersection between public art and political memory and reflect the ambivalence and uncertainty of late 20th-century postmodernism. Young cites Andreas Huyssen, who suggests that there seems to be an inverse proportion between the memorialization of the past and its contemplation and study. It is almost as if by assigning monumental form to memory we have divested ourselves of the obligation to remember. Young specifically studies the "counter-monuments in Germany," memorial spaces designed to challenge the very premise of the monument. In this essay he looks in depth at the creation of Daniel Libeskind's Jewish Museum in Berlin, and the manner in which it embodies the sense of the "unheimlich."

Faye Carey studies Freud's "A Disturbance of Memory on the Acropolis," using it as a way to study the creation of memory and identity. Carey argues that Freud's description is not so much a disturbance of memory but rather the manner in which the timelessness of the unconscious treats historical events as psychically, resiliently concurrent with those of the present. Psychoanalyst Stephen Sonnenberg also examines this same writing of Freud, arguing that the physical characteristics of the Acropolis contributed to Freud's experience of false memory and foreshadowing the idea which emerged in 2012 of the reciprocal attraction of the unconscious and the visual. In his contribution to *Space & Psyche*, Sonnenberg further illustrates this type of attraction with his interest in the visual aspects of architectural sites in Berlin. Employing the method of self-analytic reflection, he concludes that there exists an oscillation in the architecture of Berlin – and also among its citizens – regarding acceptance and denial of efforts at redemption for the Holocaust. Furthermore, Sonnenberg suggests that a similar ambivalence regarding efforts at redemption from traumatic experiences is seen in the clinical setting.

In "Architecture Figure Death" (2008), Lorens Holm uses Le Corbusier's 1911 visit to the Parthenon as a point of departure to investigate the phenomena that the Parthenon often incites: the unraveling of distinctions between viewer and viewed, subject and object, object and space. This paper draws on psychoanalytic accounts of subjectivity, particularly Lacan's and Freud's accounts of the drives, to understand the function of the Parthenon in Le Corbusier's life and death. This paper covers similar ground to the discussion of the Parthenon in Vidler's "Framing Infinity" and Holm's "Vignettes of Death." In *Adrian Stokes: An Architectonic Eye*, Stephen Kite explores the writings of British art critic and cultural theorist Adrian Stokes. "Stokes's writings sustain and extend the evocative English aesthetic tradition of Walter Pater and John Ruskin, illumined by a personal sensibility to the consolations of art and architecture, and the insights given by psychoanalysis" (Kite, 2009, p. 1). Though Stokes was primarily a writer, painter and poet, Kite suggests his work was clearly influenced by the urban environments he occupied. "Stokes viewed art as a process of reparation of that which is broken and scattered within the psyche, and without in the harshness of our urban culture" (Kite, 2009, p. 1). In this sense, Kite states that Stokes's own creative work served as a mediator between the inner world of the psyche and the outer world of architecture and the greater environment.

Kite develops this idea throughout the book, arguing for the architectonic basis of Stokes's theory of art. "We are sensitized to the plane of a canvas or the textures of a relief, by the fundamental lifelong experiences of cobbled streets, junctures of paving and wall, and haptic encounters with smooth and rough surfaces" (Kite, 2009, p. 2). His book "attempts to isolate the salient features of Stokes's architectonically founded aesthetic and aims to show the crucial experiences whereby his architectonic sensibility was formed and shaped, and to interpret how and in what context these notions were articulated theoretically" (Kite, 2009, p. 2). Kite tells us, too, that Stokes's work was informed by his personal experiences as a patient of psychoanalyst Melanie Klein. Stokes declared that architecture is the mother of the arts, and Kite argues that this was not intended as some "vague cliché, but in the deepest experiential and psycho-physiological ramifications of that definition" (Kite, 2009, p. 2).

Peggy Deamer's contribution to *Psychoanalysis and Architecture*, "Adrian Stokes: The Architecture of Phantasy and the Phantasy of Architecture," also explores the influence of Kleinian and Freudian psychoanalysis upon Stokes's work.

> For those investigating the relationship between architecture and psychoanalysis, Stokes is interesting not just as a "translator" of Kleinian principles in architectural terms, but the manner in which he mines her concepts of phantasy and symbolization to establish a framework to evaluate, indeed proselytize, the virtues of architectural form.
>
> *(Deamer, 2005, p. 126)*

According to Deamer, this is important because most of the aesthetic engagement in psychoanalysis has remained on the level of content rather than form. Deamer outlines Klein's reworking of Freud's three phases of the id, and argues that among the four methods of defense found within Klein's theories, phantasy is the primary mechanism. For Klein, "Phantasy is not an escape from reality, but, rather, the particular way a child 'sees' and interprets reality and copes with being in the world" (Deamer, 2005, p. 128).

> In analyzing how the ego functions perceptually to direct the figures populating the id/superego inner world and their application onto and absorption of the external world, Klein, unlike Freud, depicts an ego that is almost entirely described by its image management.
>
> *(Deamer, 2005, p. 129)*

Deamer goes on to reference Stokes's own writings that illuminate his position on the nature of art and architecture. For Stokes, art is not a denial of reality, as was argued by Freud, but a more complex manifestation of an individual's reality as it is formed by the relationship of his inner and outer worlds. "Paintings should never be about their composition or their perspectival depiction of deep space; rather they should register their layering" (Deamer, 2005, pp. 132–133). As such, Stokes considered architecture to be "the most robust of arts because it promotes the most complex and compelling of phantasies" (Deamer, 2005, p. 133).

Psychoanalyst Adele Tutter explores the work of architect Philip Johnson in "Design as Dream and Self-Representation" (2011). She compares his masterpiece – the Glass House – to a dream and conceptualizes it as containing encrypted and embedded representations of the self. Tutter uses Freud's *The Interpretation of Dreams* as the theoretical and methodological model for this approach to explicating the relationship between architecture and psychoanalysis. Drawing on Johnson's words and forms set in biographical, historical and cultural context, Tutter traces interpretive paths from manifest design elements of the Glass House to overdetermined latent meanings, yielding new and surprising insights into the Glass House, its elusive architect, and the process of its design. A mirror that reflects an image, a lens that focuses it, and a prism that reveals its components, the Glass House, she asserts, turns a lucid eye onto its maker.

In "A Violent Atomization" (2012), Tutter's contribution to *Space & Psyche*, she further examines Johnson and the Glass House from the perspective of how his design efforts were designed to repair unmet needs from his early childhood, and how these efforts changed throughout his lifetime. Moving from Johnson's early attachment to the architecture of Mies van der Rohe to his later shift to the work of Theodate Pope Riddle (an architect and also Johnson's mother's cousin), Tutter invokes the language of clinical psychoanalysis to make the case that Johnson suffered from the threat of emotional fragmentation. Tutter further demonstrates how particular aspects of the Glass House were also influenced by Johnson's other desires and explores this through contributions made in Bachelard's *The Poetics of Space*.

Sylvia Lavin explores the architecture of Richard Neutra, linking his work to themes ranging from birth trauma to domesticity and the house. In *Form Follows Libido* (2005), Lavin notes Neutra's interest in a sensory and psychological approach to the design of the environment. This approach, explored by Neutra in his 1954 book, *Survival through Design*, includes themes of birth and rebirth, and his expression of his own erotic obsessions. Lavin argues that Neutra's approach to design is largely based on his own interpretation of psychoanalytic principles. Neutra, born in 1892, frequented Freud's apartment in Vienna and was friends with his son Ernst. He also read and wrote extensively on psychoanalytic theory, arguing that a house and the broader environment could – and should – have an influence on inhabitants and their psychological well-being.

In "Open the Box: Richard Neutra and the Psychology of the Domestic Environment" (1999), Lavin uses the houses of Richard Neutra to examine the Americanization of psychoanalysis and architecture. According to Lavin, the transformation of the American house in response to changing gender roles has been widely studied; however, little attention has been paid to the eroticization of domesticity during the postwar period and the new architectural effects it engendered. She argues that the impact of psychoanalysis on American everyday life can be measured by its negotiations with the intimate spaces of domesticity, as psychic and spatial conditions merged in the single-family house to produce a new sense of psychophysical environment. Just as the space of psychoanalysis staged the public confrontation with a new phase of modernity, the postwar single-family house staged a private confrontation with one of classical modernity's concluding chapters.

In "Space House: The Psyche of Building," Beatriz Colomina explores Frederick Kiesler's "Space House," a full-size model of a family house, located on the first floor of the Modernage Furniture Company and designed to arouse interest in the 33 furnished rooms on the upper floors. Reporters at the time discussed the house in psychosexual terms, describing its "come hither" appeal. Colomina goes on to provide an in-depth analysis of the sensual characteristics of the Space House, as well as Kiesler's contribution to the field of architecture. She continues a psychoanalytical thread by arguing that, for Kiesler, architecture is always erotic, and psyche and architecture are inseparable (Colomina, 2000, p. 66).

Colomina's contribution to *Sexuality and Space*, "The Split Wall: Domestic Voyeurism" (1992), explores the psychological aspects of Adolf Loos's interiors as manifested in the Raumplan, a design strategy that relies on a series of discrete rooms in which the architectural section is emphasized. Colomina explains how Loos's interiors are notable in that windows are used to provide light, rather than a view to the exterior, and seating is frequently arranged with the occupant's back to the window, providing an inwardly focused experience.

In "Untitled: Housing Gender" (1992), Mark Wigley traces the relationships between the role of gender in the discourse of space and the role of space in the discourse of gender. He specifically focuses on the interrelationships between how gender is housed and the role of gender in housing. Wigley analyzes the gender-space division found within architectural texts by Leon Battista Alberti and Xenophon, wherein the domain of women is relegated to the interior and that of men to the exterior. The house thus serves as a mechanism for the domestication and control of women and their sexuality.

In "A Fitting Fetish: The Interiors of the Maison de Verre," Sarah Wigglesworth examines the modernist architectural agenda in relation to the Maison de Verre, suggesting a connection between the building, specifically its interior treatments, and the female body. She argues that the interiors have taken on the characteristics of fetish objects, "seducing architects with their forms and surfaces" (Wigglesworth, 1992, p. 92). However, this fetish conceals a deeper fear of social unrest and of women's behavior in the period of female emancipation. She draws upon feminist, psychoanalytic, visual, modernist and film theories to gain a deeper understanding of architecture and its hidden agenda of control in relation to the female body, a site of both desire and fear. She argues that from this analysis a crucial issue for architects is uncovered: that of the futility of desiring control over those who occupy their buildings.

Gérard Wajcman discusses the nature of the intimate in his essay "Intimate Extorted, Intimate Exposed" (2008). The space of the intimate can be interior and subjective, or it can take the form of a physical site: it is that part of space where the subject can feel shielded from the gaze of the other. This definition of the intimate – a site free from every gaze – implies a relation to power, or rather a separation from it. This constitutes the real condition of the intimate, which we can associate with the right to secrecy. Thus intimate, secrecy and freedom are inherently linked. Wajcman, blending psychoanalytic perspectives with an understanding of design, asserts that we live in a time in which the intimate is threatened: each person wants to know what is happening in the life of the other and, as a result, an obscene taste for exhibition develops. Each one wants to see and each one wants to be seen, all at once, and this is reflected in how architects think about design.

Lorens Holm has said the aim of his paper *Reading Through the Mirror: Brunelleschi, Lacan, Le Corbusier: The Invention of Perspective and the Post-Freudian Eye/I* (1992) is "to construct an account of architectural space that is an elaboration of the psychoanalytic account of the subject" (Holm, 2009, p. 2). His premise is that Freud and Jacques Lacan revolutionized the conception of the space of an intimate self, and it would seem legitimate, therefore, to ask what this revolution might offer a critique of architectural space. Holm treats the fundamental psychological concept of an intimate self as a topological problem, and ponders the comparisons between structures of subjectivity and the structure of architectural space and its representation.

John Hendrix's book *Architecture and Psychoanalysis* (2006) establishes and analyzes a relationship between architecture and psychoanalysis through the work of Peter Eisenman and Lacan. It examines the parallels and similarities between Eisenman's compositional strategies and Lacanian linguistics and psychoanalysis. The purpose of the study is to demonstrate the importance of psychoanalysis as it can be applied to design strategies and theoretical premises in architecture, and to the reading of architecture, its analysis and criticism. Architectural precedents are analyzed in figures such as Leon Battista Alberti, Giulio Romano, Andrea Palladio and Francesco Borromini from the Renaissance; and Le Corbusier, Giusseppe Terragni, Ludwig Mies van der Rohe and Philip Johnson in the 20th century. Hendrix has focused on the psychoanalytic theories behind the ways in which dreams are constructed. In his contribution to *Space & Psyche*, "Architecture and Dream Construction" (2012), he argues that an architect's design process may be understood through a combination of Freudian and Lacanian dream theories. Hendrix highlights seven architectural projects, dating from 1527 to 1988, outlining how the theories of Freud and Lacan – the latter more linguistic – provide insight into this selection of buildings and offers a range of new and rich terminology as a way of understanding them.

Jane Rendell delves into the analytic setting itself in "The Architecture of Psychoanalysis" (2012) as she explores architectural structures in psychoanalytic theory and practice. She focuses on ways that architectural space registers in psychoanalysis, including a topographic understanding of psychic processes and their representations in drawings, the spatial structuring of psychic life through the screens and folds of memory, and the architectural setting in which psychoanalysis takes place. Rendell's discussion is intended to offer new approaches for understanding the connection between subjects, objects and spaces in architectural research and practice. Elizabeth Danze, in her 2005 essay in *Psychoanalysis and Architecture* writes about the analyst's consulting room, and how it frames, contains and impacts the relationship of the analyst and the analysand.

In "Berggasse 19: Freud's Ear," a chapter from *The Sense of an Interior* (2004), Diana Fuss and Joel Sanders examine the significance of the site that housed Freud's psychoanalytic practice. The authors explore how the spatial configuration of Freud's office, and the arrangement of furniture and objects within it, might frame an understanding of psychoanalytic theory and practice. Using black-and-white photographs of Freud's original analytic space as well as architectural drawings, Fuss and Sanders consider the threshold between the two-dimensional space of the photographs and the three-dimensional space of architecture, and how an architectural study of Berggasse 19 might inform an understanding of the play of vision, power and transference that structures the analytic scene.

Susan Bernstein begins "Housing Freud," a chapter within her larger work entitled *Housing Problems: Writing and Architecture in Goethe, Walpole, Freud, and Heidegger*, by studying the text *Tribute to Freud* by poet H.D. (Hilda Doolittle). H.D. discusses the physical setting of Freud's apartment as part of an understanding of her analytic experience as his patient. Through H.D.'s descriptions Bernstein examines the setting of analysis, primarily in relation to the analytic couch, its psychological impact, and the reasoning for the interior arrangement. From there Bernstein contrasts the methods of display used in the London Museum and Berggasse 19, asserting that the former attempts to replicate and preserve the original rooms, while the latter contains a collection of objects. The author examines these differences in approach in relation to Freud's theories.

## The intersection of architecture and psychoanalysis in the educational setting of an architectural design studio

The preceding summarizes the ways architects view psychoanalysis and the ways psychoanalysts view architecture. In our research and teaching we have attempted to synthesize psychoanalysis and architecture and explore the potential of one's impact on the other. This work has taken the form of writing, teaching seminars, creating symposia, editing books, and creating three architectural design studios and an independent study with one undergraduate student.

The authors' collaboration began in 2003 with the editing by Danze, along with James Anderson and Jerome Winer, of the book *Psychoanalysis and Architecture: The Annual of Psychoanalysis*, in which Sonnenberg had written a chapter, "What Can Psychoanalysis Learn From an Enhanced Awareness of Architecture and Design?"

This book and the discovery of common interests initiated the creation of an international conference on the relationship of these two disciplines. The conference, Space & Mind, was held in 2007 at the University of Texas at Austin. Internationally established and respected speakers from both the fields of architecture and psychoanalysis participated.

In 2006 the authors participated in a study group where they read Erik Erikson's seminal paper, "The Problem of Ego Identity" in the *Journal of the American Psychoanalytic Association*, in which Erikson describes human psychological development occurring in stages represented in a two dimensional organization chart (Figure 18.2). They thought that Erikson's two-dimensional grid could be better redesigned in three dimensions. Working with two graduate students, the authors spent 4 years creating this three-dimensional model, which they presented at the American Psychoanalytic Association's poster session in January 2010; this model continues to be a topic of their ongoing research.

Additionally, the study group spent 2009 examining the relationship of psychoanalysis and architecture in a sequence titled "Mind and Architecture." Readings included sections of Juhani

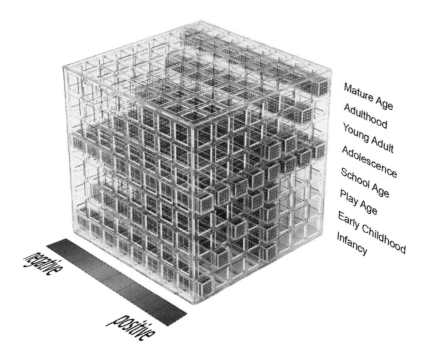

*Figure 18.2* The Erikson model of psychosocial development
Source: © Elizabeth Danze

Pallasmaa's *The Thinking Hand* (2009), Peter Zumthor's *Thinking Architecture* (1997), and Gaston Bachelard's *The Poetics of Space* (1958). These challenging readings and discussions deepened their mutual understanding of the intersections of architecture and psychoanalysis, and contributed to the development of a shared vocabulary.

Work from the Space & Mind conference was compiled and refined and subsequently published in 2012 (CENTER 17: *Space & Psyche*, Danze, E., Sonnenberg, S., eds.), reflecting by then a near decade of collaboration. That volume included original essays by each of the authors, one explaining in detail the development of the Erikson model (Danze, E., CENTER, 17: *Space & Psyche*, 2012a), and the other elaborating on how architecture augments the more traditional psychoanalytic lens in understanding societal reactions to trauma (Sonnenberg, S., CENTER 17: *Space & Psyche*, 2012).

We offer this brief history to introduce the complexity of building the interdisciplinary relationship of architecture and psychoanalysis that exists at the University of Texas at Austin School of Architecture, The resulting integration also reflects a synthesis of the ideas conveyed in the earlier section of this chapter describing its influence on the next generation of practitioners and scholars. We will examine the influence of these studios we co-taught, as well as the honors senior thesis research project we co-supervised, focusing in four cases on particularly high-achieving students.

Throughout our collaborations, a number of interesting case studies emerged that we believe best highlight the potential of these interdisciplinary exchanges. One of the most compelling settings is the advanced architectural design studio. This studio is upper level, combining undergraduate- and graduate-level studio courses and includes approximately

16 students focused on intensive design study on specialized topics. We have collaborated in three such studios, merging the subjects of architecture and psychoanalysis and applying them to specific design problems that engage pressing social issues and human experience in a variety of ways.

## Building as hope: architecture and the ideal self/the Manchester Bidwell Center for Arts and Technology project

Co-taught in 2011 by Danze and Sonnenberg, this graduate design studio utilized psychoanalytic developmental sensibilities in examining and connecting the realms of architecture, the outer, material world of tangible places; and psychology, the inner world of the human mind.

The primary project was the design of a multidisciplinary arts and learning center that fosters a sense of belonging, interconnectedness, and hope within the urban community. The studio directly involved Bill Strickland, president and CEO of Manchester Bidwell and the National Center for Arts and Technology and members of his staff as clients and colleagues. While in college in 1968, Strickland founded the Manchester Craftsmen's Guild to bring arts education and mentoring to inner-city youth in his neighborhood. Today this organization serves public school students as well as adults in transition by offering courses in ceramics, design, digital and photography studios and more recently the culinary arts and sciences. Strickland, a MacArthur Fellowship recipient, had most recently been appointed by President Obama to his White House Council for Community Solutions.

Strickland's philosophy is simple: the environment shapes people's lives. By constructing an empowering atmosphere of art, light and music and guided by staff that strive to realize the genius in everyone, the program enables its students to become productive contributors to society. Students explored the program, investigated and discussed the client-architect relationship, identified potential sites for locating a facility and designed a prototype infused with personal and community motivation.

The studio posed and explored questions from an analytical and psychoanalytic point of view, defining the relationship between the institution and the individual, between artist and the medium, between the city and the building. The psychoanalyst/architect team helped students understand psychoanalytic principles by assisting with self-observation and discussing readings on the relationship between architecture and psychoanalysis. A goal of the studio was to help students recognize how growth is plastic, and how the design process promotes growth in the designer, even as it creates an environment that encourages growth in the users of a new space or building. Like many architectural design projects the challenge to the designer is to understand what the users of the building require and to empathize with the user. The studio work engaged inquiry of two concerns: the identity and use of an educational institution as embodied in its physical environment based on psychoanalytic principles, and psychoanalytic developmental sensibilities – including self-observation – in both the user and designer.

Architecture was considered the container of, and medium for, personal empowerment, freedom and growth. The goal was to create an environment where the architecture participates in and promotes this process. Similarly, introspection and reflection were both subject of, and method for, design. Students studied projects that operated as primary participant in providing well-being, awareness and growth of the individual.

The initial phase of the project involved looking simultaneously at both the large and small scales. Specifically, this involved analysis, evaluation and response to an existing building, as well as the design of a series of short, interconnected exercises examining specific elements of the building as a way to initiate the building design. The first of these involved the design of a pottery studio, and the second a gallery for the display of artwork. Students examined the intentions for making building form through a series of analyses, typological precedents, programmatic organizations and formal composition of individual and multi-unit spaces. Issues of publicity and privacy, boundary, threshold, bodily sensation and spatial phenomena were examined as well as the marriage of the experiential and physical to the psychological.

Another dimension to Strickland intrigued us: he was a patron of psychoanalysis and a trustee of the psychoanalytic training center in Pittsburgh – a man very knowledgeable about psychoanalysis who believed that the innovative program he had developed rested on a psychoanalytic foundation.

From our perspective this was an exciting first effort and blending of clinical psychoanalytic idea and theory with architectural theory and practice in a design studio. In that spirit, we used the Erikson Model as a way to teach architecture students about human development, and also offered it as a way a student could measure her or his psychological development as a result of this studio experience. We invited students to use the model at the start and end of the semester to record and concretize their own emotional growth.

The reading list and didactic portion of the studio was heavily psychoanalytic, and also reflected the ideas the authors were developing about the relationship of architecture and psychoanalysis. The readings included works by Strickland, Erikson and Freud, as well as Danze's and Sonnenberg's own writings, among several others.

Strickland had been influenced in powerful ways by Frank Lloyd Wright's Fallingwater, which he had seen as he was developing his program, and built his facility in the Wright tradition. Strickland felt that an environment that included plant life, light and water was essential in providing a safe and growth-producing environment, and that if troubled youths were welcomed into a beautiful facility they would respond by producing beautiful ceramics and cooperative, empathic behavior. The history of his facility bears witness to how right he is: no episodes of violence or criminal behavior have occurred in the years of his project's existence.

## Housing Homeless Families Studio

This studio, held in the spring of 2013, was co-taught with Sarah Dooling, a professor with a background in wildlife management, social work, urban planning and interdisciplinary research. We believed from the start that the population we aimed to serve had multiple psychological vulnerabilities, and that an interdisciplinary team capable of breaking new ground was necessary. We also believed that because our students would be asked to empathize with and understand the homeless, their task would be both emotionally demanding and potentially productive of psychological growth.

Through a series of short projects, lectures, readings and field trips, this studio's work concerned itself with the purposeful inquiry of research and design in several forms, contexts and scales related to and surrounding issues of homelessness. Students designed housing options and social services centers for homeless families. They collaborated with local institutions in identifying the social and cultural challenges of homelessness facing the city of Austin. Through the process of design, students compared two approaches to locating, distributing and configuring housing and services – high density, concentrated and low density, intermixed. The designs focused on the physical and cultural contexts of selected sites, and design strategies developed with an understanding of the psychological experiences of homelessness for parents and children. This resulted in designs for spaces that support mental health, well-being and addressed the regulatory constraints and opportunities for constructing housing within local cultural, political and economic contexts.

The course also examined how the fields of psychoanalysis and psychology – which are steeped in theory – inform our thinking about architecture and design. Assignments included reading essays from *Space & Psyche* and authors such as Leatherbarrow and Pallasmaa, and looked to films such as *Into Great Silence* and *Wings of Desire* as part of the seminar component of the class.

The first short project used memory as a means of using personal experience as a guiding constraint. The primary project investigated the contemporary "asylum/refuge/sanctuary" as defined by the student. Students also defined relationships between the institution and the individual and applied methods, theories and research explored earlier in the semester to the scale of a small building. The final project included the design of all support functions on a specific site.

Water was introduced as a medium and students examined issues of publicity and privacy, boundary, threshold and bodily sensation and spatial phenomena. Students also explored access and confinement – the explicit or implicit ability to cross a physical or notional boundary – and separation. These examinations aimed to gauge degrees of intimacy – a property or value used to calibrate spatial zones and their thresholds.

Each student made connections between their personal concern and materiality and construction. Analysis, evaluation and means of reporting and revealing information included extensive descriptive studies expressed in drawing, photographs, models and other virtual and physical media. Students examined design values within issues concerning psychology, sociology, materiality, technology and construction and the way they shape and make architectural form.

We again used the Erikson model with our students, encouraging them to use it to enhance their understandings of human development, reflect on the studio's impact on their own development, and serve as a stimulus for individual maturational experiences.

The studio also included an elaborate didactic component. Students had access to a database created by Professor Dooling as part of her research. Additionally, reading included Nooe and Patterson's "The Ecology of Homelessness" from the *Journal of Human Behavior in the Social Environment*; Bassuk, Volk, and Olivet's "A Framework for Developing Supports and Services for Families Experiencing Homelessness" from *The Open Health Services and Policy Journal*; and Danze, Ruckman, Winn, and Sonnenberg's "An Interactive Three- and Four-Dimensional Clinical, Research, Learning, and Teaching Model of Erik Erikson's Diagram of Psychosocial Development'" from the *Journal of the American Psychoanalytic Association*. Students also read Danze's "Modeling Erik Erikson's Diagram of Psychosocial Development" from *Space & Psyche*; Bassuk, Buckner, Perloff, and Bassuk's "Prevalence of Mental Health and Substance Use Disorders Among Homeless and Low-Income Housed Mothers" from the *American Journal of Psychiatry*; and Coldwell and Bender's "The Effectiveness of Assertive Community Treatment for Homeless Populations With Severe Mental Illness: A Meta-Analysis" from the *American Journal of Psychiatry*.

Other readings included additional papers from the *American Journal of Psychiatry*, *Space & Psyche*, Peter Zumthor's *Thinking Architecture* and *Atmospheres*, Pallasmaa's *The Thinking Hand* and Peter Eisenman's *Ten Canonical Buildings 1950–2001*. The studio took field trips to shelters, which illumined the issues of financial setbacks, substance abuse, post-traumatic stress disorders and health care, all of which reliably surround homelessness.

We were impressed with students' emerging nuanced interdisciplinary understanding of a subject that bridged psychoanalytic psychology and architecture. Students presented their designs to policy makers at Austin City Hall, who expressed interest in future planning activities focusing on student designs for housing. One student applied the unique experience of the studio to apply for and receive a prestigious British Marshall Scholarship to pursue graduate studies in the United Kingdom.

Elizabeth Danze and Stephen Sonnenberg

## *Veterans Community Park and Pavilion Studio*

The Veterans Community Park and Pavilion Project Studio was based on research that grew out of the Spring 2010 University of Texas Humanities Institute Faculty Fellows Seminar, which studied intellectual life at moments of crisis. A major focus of the seminar was an examination of the experience of veterans returning from the conflicts in Iraq and Afghanistan. At the time, the behavioral health care epidemic of veterans was already very clear: US military veterans were committing suicide at the rate of 22 a day.

The work of this studio, co-taught by us and Professor John Blood, was a direct response to a critical disconnection between the veteran and civilian communities. The project specifically addressed severe psychological reactions to war among veterans, such as post-traumatic stress, depression, suicide and violent behavior. It also addressed the need to heal the collateral experience of trauma and related psychological problems that arise in the families of veterans and the broader community. Because it had been established that traditional medical interventions for post-combat veterans are not effective in healing their wounds of war, nor the collateral wounds of families and community, students explored the role of architecture in creating a place of healing, engagement and connection. As part of the studio they developed a prototype building that merged architecture and psychoanalysis to improve the experience of these veterans.

Historically, several societies successfully reintegrated combat veterans and healed the collateral psychological wounds of the community. The ancient city of Athens was at war for more than 100 years, and provided a model of a community healing the wounds of war. The Theater of Dionysus is one example of a sanctioned environment where the trauma of war was communally assuaged for combatants, veterans and citizens. Here, veterans and active duty soldiers acted in dramas set in wartime settings, written by playwrights such as Aeschylus and Sophocles (themselves veterans of military campaigns) and were witnessed by other veterans and members of the citizenry. This project was founded on the belief that such a sanctioned public forum that integrates architecture, psychoanalysis, theater and the arts provides a venue for healing. We sought to create such a built environment, and to research and develop such a model, in order to establish a contemporary paradigm to promote the healing that is badly needed in our society.

The project was an interdisciplinary collaboration, sponsored by four entities of UT Austin: the School of Architecture, the Humanities Institute, the Division of Diversity and Community Engagement and the Rapoport Center for Human Rights and Justice. The project's Task Force included leading faculty from across campus disciplines, veterans of war, and other representatives of the community. The specific building proposal was a park and pavilion where soldiers, veterans, their families and civilian community members would interact to detoxify the trauma of war (Figure 18.3).

By merging architecture, psychology and the arts, students developed a prototype that draws on historic examples and the origins of theater to address severe post-conflict psychological problems of both veterans and the broader community, which must accommodate its traumatized veterans. Citing innovative programs such as the Telling Project provided a setting for cathartic and ritualized communal conversation where veterans speak directly to their own communities concerning their experiences, humanizing and making immediate what are otherwise abstract and polarizing ideas and issues.

The design proposal is a place where soldiers, veterans and members of the community come together for a wide range of both planned and spontaneous activities. It is not a memorial, but rather a setting that supports an active process of collective healing. Guidelines and objectives for the prototype were developed with input from veterans and military leaders,

*Figure 18.3* Design proposal by Jessica Glennie

psychologists and psychiatrists, filmmakers, authors, artists, architects and students. The studio produced prototypical designs for the park and pavilion and one student used her work to attain a Rhodes Scholarship.

## *Utilizing Erik Erikson's model of psychosocial development and conducting focus groups to assess student veterans*

The fourth teaching experience involved supervising a student's thesis that used the Erikson model to research adjustment to campus life by the university's war veterans. Erikson's work and our model were designed to encourage reflection on one's past and present, to produce a better understanding of identity in the present and as it evolved over time. It was an aid and stimulus to self-exploration and self-understanding. The thesis described the limitations of looking at the model in a straight-lined fashion, which assumes that development proceeded linearly, and that each phase inevitably followed the one prescribed before it. In fact, the thesis used the model to demonstrate that development does not proceed in a linear and sequential fashion for veterans on campus. An experience in a given phase might change the way an individual saw her or his previous and subsequent development, and there was fluidity in the way phases of development interacted and influenced each other. As such the model acts as a catalyst and useful tool for many perspectives of self reflection. The student who worked on this project made important seminal observations, leading to these conclusions about nonlinear development.

## Conclusion: architecture, mind, body

Distinguished architect and writer Juhani Pallasmaa has examined the stairway as metaphor in "Stairways of the Mind" (2000). He laments the transformation of buildings into machines for living, surely in reference to Le Corbusier's ideas from his pivotal text, *Toward a New Architecture*. Pallasmaa asserts that we have forgotten that the task of the house is not only to provide physical comfort and bodily shelter, but also to create spatial and material metaphors for our fundamental existential encounters. Describing the house as a metaphor for the body, and the body a metaphor for the house, Pallasmaa calls the staircase the symbolic spine of the house, its most important organ. Lamenting the loss of the attic and cellar in the modern home, Pallasmaa infers a loss of memory, in reference to Bachelard's metaphorical connections of the attic to storage of positive memories and the cellar to unpleasant memories. Pallasmaa refers to the staircase as also being the symbolic heart of the house, as it is reserved for vertical circulation, just as the heart pumps blood up and down the body. He connects his ideas to Freud's belief that the regular rhythm of stairs also addresses our dream imagery through its essence as a sexual metaphor. In considering other metaphors of the staircase, Pallasmaa draws attention to the representation of stairs as symbols of cosmological ideas and spiritual aspirations, power and authority, prestige and status, hierarchy and classification. He notes as well the understanding of stairs as a vertical labyrinth, the role of stairs in cinematic dramaturgy, and their use as an instrument of hierarchical classification. Pallasmaa notes that the buildings and townscapes of our time lack a spiritual and emotional content, and that the great challenge for architects is the re-sensualization, remythologization, and re-poetization of the human dwelling.

Pallasmaa begins his *Space & Psyche* essay, "In Praise of Vagueness," with a confession that he was educated during an era in which architectural education emphasized positivism. This was a time when the student was taught to bring focus to his or her design work, to pursue design with precision and certainty, and without ambiguity. Pallasmaa writes that today the computer and computer-aided design inhibit the architect's capacity to imagine deeply and phenomenologically, a point of view clearly compatible with what he describes as the evolution of his own design method: to work *without* focus and precision, embracing uncertainty and vagueness as part of his design process. This reminds us of the psychoanalyst's embrace of freely hovering attention as she listens to the analysand. It is also akin to our embrace of vagueness, ambiguity and openness to the ideas generated in the design work of our students. We see ourselves as teachers who borrow from the psychoanalytic method of clinical supervision.

Psychoanalysis and architecture provide a natural, organic convergence of thought about how we relate to our surroundings, our spatial perceptions, the role of thoughts and memories in our interactions with the world, and how we conduct academic discourse with a wide range of students. We hope this chapter will encourage architects to provide a physical setting for the psychological world where teachers, students and clients vividly experience emotions, memories and desires. Through engagement with psychoanalytic ideas and interdisciplinary collaboration between architects and psychoanalysts, architects can reveal and manifest vast possibilities for the physical realm. This interaction between space and psyche has a long and rich history. Continuing and enhancing this discourse will profoundly inform architectural and psychoanalytical thought as we move forward with deeper and more creative insights, teaching experiences, research and designs.

## Authors' Note

The authors wish to acknowledge the assistance of Amy Freedberg and Ana Calhoun in reviewing the literature on psychoanalysis and architecture for this chapter, and the research conducted by Bethany Hamilton, whose work as a University of Texas at Austin undergraduate is described in the section "Utilizing Erik Erikson's model of psychosocial development and conducting focus groups to assess Student Veterans." The British Marshall Scholarship recipient written about is John Russell Beaumont, and the Rhodes Scholarship recipient is Jessica Glennie.

# Bibliography

Bachelard, G 1958, *Poetics of space*, Press Universitaires de France, Paris, 1994, Beacon Press, Boston.

Bernstein, S 2008, *Housing problems: Writing and architecture in Goethe, Walpole, Freud, and Heidegger*, Stanford University Press, Stanford.

Bollas, C 2000, 'Architecture and the unconscious', *International Forum of Psychoanalysis*, vol. 9, pp. 28–42.

Colomina, B 1987, 'Le Corbusier and photography', *Assemblage*, vol. 4, pp. 6–23.

Colomina, B 1992, 'The split wall: Domestic voyeurism', in B Colomina (ed), *Sexuality & space*, Princeton Architectural Press, Princeton, NJ.

Colomina, B 2000, 'Space house: The psyche of building', in I Borden & J Rendell (eds), *InterSections: Architectural histories and critical theories*, Routledge, New York.

da Costa Meyer, E 2012, 'The city within', in E Danze & S Sonnenberg (eds), *Space & psyche*, Austin, TX: Center for American Architecture and Design.

Danze, EA, Ruckman, R, Winn, P, Sonnenberg, SM 2010, 'An interactive three- and four-dimensional clinical, research, learning, and teaching model of Erik Erikson's diagram of psychosocial development', *Journal of the American Psychoanalytic Association*, vol. 58, pp. 1–11.

Danze, EA & Sonnenberg, SM 2012a, 'Commentary on Adele Tutter's "design as dream and self-representation: Philip Johnson and the glass house of Atreus"', *Journal of the American Psychoanalytic Association*, vol. 60, pp. 533–549.

Danze, EA & Sonnenberg, SM 2012b, 'Modeling Erik Erikson's diagram psychosocial development', in E Danze & S Sonnenberg (eds), *Space & psyche*, Center for American Architecture and Design, Austin, TX.

Deamer, P 2005, 'Adrian Stokes: The architecture of phantasy and the phantasy of architecture', in JA Winer, JW Anderson & EA Danze (eds), *Psychoanalysis and architecture*, Mental Health Resources, Catskill, NY.

Erikson, E 1956, 'The problem of ego identity', *Journal of the American Psychoanalytic Association*, vol. 4, pp. 56–121.

Freud, S 1919, 'The uncanny', in J Strachey (ed), *Standard edition of the complete psychological works of Sigmund Freud*, vol. 17, Hogarth, London.

Freud, S 1930, 'Civilization and its discontents', in J Strachey (ed) *Standard edition of the complete psychological works of Sigmund Freud*, vol. 21, Hogarth, London.

Freud, S 1936, 'A disturbance of memory on the Acropolis', in J Strachey (ed), *Standard edition of the complete psychological works of Sigmund Freud*, vol. 22, Hogarth, London, pp. 237–248.

Fuss, D & Sanders, J 2004, *The sense of an interior: Four rooms and the writers that shaped them*, Routledge, New York.

Globus, G & Gilbert, G 1964, 'A metapsychological approach to the architecture of Frank Lloyd Wright', *Psychoanalytic Review*, vol. 51, pp. 285–297.

Hendrix, J 2006, *Architecture and psychoanalysis: Peter Eisenman and Jacques Lacan*, Peter Lang, New York.

Hendrix, J 2012, 'Architecture and dream construction', in E Danze and & S Sonnenberg (eds), *Space & psyche*, Center for American Architecture and Design, Austin, TX.

Holm, L 1992, 'Reading through the mirror: Brunelleschi, Lacan, Le Corbusier: the invention of perspective and the post-Freudian eye/I', *Assemblage*, vol. 18, pp. 20–39.

Holm, L 2000, 'What Lacan said re: architecture', *Critical Quarterly*, vol. 42, pp. 29–64.

Holm, L 2008, 'Architecture figure death', *Haecceity papers: Psychoanalysis and architecture*, vol. 4.

Holm, L 2009, *Brunelleschi, Lacan, Le Corbusier: Architecture, space and the construction of subjectivity*, Routledge, London.

Kite, S 2009, *Adrian Stokes: An architectonic eye*, Legenda, London.

Lavin, S 1999, 'Open the box: Richard Neutra and the psychology of the domestic environment', *Assemblage*, vol. 40, pp. 6–25.

Lavin, S 2005, *Form follows libido*, MIT University Press, Cambridge, MA.

Neutra, R 1954, *Survival through design*, Oxford University Press, New York.

Pallasmaa, J 2000, 'Stairways of the mind', *International Forum of Psychoanalysis*, vol. 9, pp. 7–18.

Pallasmaa, J 2012, 'In praise of vagueness', in E Danze & S Sonnenberg (eds), *Space & psyche*, Center for American Architecture and Design, Austin, TX.

Pile, S 1999, 'Freud, dreams, and imaginative geographies', in A Elliot (ed), *Freud 2000*, Routledge, New York.

Pile, S 2010, 'Sleepwalking in the modern city: Walter Benjamin, Sigmund Freud, and the world of dreams', in N Whybrow (ed), *Performance and the contemporary city*, Palgrave Macmillan, New York.

Rendell, J 2012, 'The architecture of psychoanalysis: constructions and associations', in O Knellessen, I Haertel & H Mooshammer (eds), *Bauarten von Sexualität, Körper, Phantasmen: Architektur und Psychoanalyse*

[*Ways of building sexuality, bodies, phantasms: Architecture and psychoanalysis*], Bartlett School of Architecture, London.

Rykwert, J 2012, 'Space and mind', in E Danze & S Sonnenberg (eds), *Space & psyche*, Center for American Architecture and Design, Austin, TX.

Sonnenberg, SM 2005, 'What can psychoanalysis learn from an enhanced awareness of architecture and design?', *Annual of Psychoanalysis*, vol. 33, pp. 39–56.

Sonnenberg, SM 2006, 'What can psychoanalysis learn from an enhanced awareness of architecture and design?', in J Anderson, E Danze & J Winer (eds), *Psychoanalysis and architecture: The annual of psychoanalysis*, Mental Health Resources, Chicago.

Sonnenberg, S 2012, 'A psychoanalytic reflection on Berlin, the Holocaust, and interdisciplinary research', in E Danze & S Sonnenberg (eds), *Space & psyche*, Center for American Architecture and Design, Austin, TX.

Tutter, A 2011, 'Design as dream and self-representation', *Journal of the American Psychoanalytic Association*, vol. 59, pp. 509–548.

Tutter, A 2012, 'A violent atomization', in E Danze & S Sonnenberg (eds), *Space & psyche*, Center for American Architecture and Design, Austin, TX.

Vidler, A 1992, *The architectural uncanny: Essays in the modern unhomely*, MIT University Press, Cambridge, MA.

Vidler, A 2000, *Warped space: Art, architecture, and anxiety in modern culture*, MIT University Press, Cambridge, MA.

Wajcman, G 2008, 'Intimate extorted, intimate exposed', *Journal of the Jan van Eyck Circle for Lacanian Ideology Critique*, vol. 1, pp. 58–77.

Wigglesworth, S 1992, 'A fitting fetish: The interiors of the Maison de Verre', in B Colomina (ed), *Sexuality & space*, Princeton Architectural Press, Princeton, NJ.

Wigley, M 1992, 'Untitled: Housing gender', in B Colomina (ed), *Sexuality & space*, Princeton Architectural Press, Princeton, NJ.

Winer, JA, Anderson, JW & Danze, EA (eds) 2005, *Psychoanalysis and architecture*, Mental Health Resources, Catskill, NY.

Young, J 2000, 'Against redemption: The arts of counter-memory in Germany today', in P Homans (ed), *Symbolic loss*, University Press of Virginia, Charlottesville.

# 19

# Cinema (film) and psychoanalysis

*Andrea Sabbadini*

---

*Qu'est-ce que le cinéma?* This deceptively simple title of a seminal book of essays by the French film critic André Bazin (1967) has become over the years the unanswerable question that has occupied the minds of film scholars, including those with a psychoanalytic orientation.

Originally intended by Freud as a form of therapy for the neuroses, psychoanalysis soon became a more ambitious project: a general psychology for the investigation of mental functioning. This opened up a number of areas for the application of psychoanalytic theories outside its original scope: the extraclinical utilization of psychoanalytic knowledge or indeed aspects of the psychoanalytic approach in relation to cultural products and events, or to "explanatory, methodological, or technological problems arising in disciplines or human endeavours other than psycho-analysis" (Edelson, 1988, p. 157). These areas include not only anthropology, education and history, but also the arts and, among them, cinema: a form of representation that seems to entertain an important relationship with our mental activities and emotional experiences.

> [Cinema] is a type of mime of both mind and world . . . Breaking from the confines of photography and theatre, it is unique in its representation of an abundant world in motion. There is a persistent sense that cinema imitates the movement of the mind, that there is *a correspondence (however elusive)* to be discovered between psyche and cinema.
>
> *(Lebeau, 2001, p. 3, italics added)*

The oft-mentioned historical coincidence of birthdays of cinema and psychoanalysis is not coincidental. (The inventors of the new medium of cinema, the brothers Auguste and Louis-Jean Lumière, showed their first short movies in Paris in 1895, the year when the first psychoanalytic book, Breuer and Freud's (1893–1895) *Studies on Hysteria*, was published in Vienna.) Both disciplines, however different, can be construed as having developed from the same ambivalent attitude to the positivistic culture prevalent at the end of the 19th century. Psychoanalytic ideas, such as unconscious motivation, transference, ego defenses, the dream as wish fulfillment, infantile sexuality and the Oedipus complex, have infiltrated many aspects of Western culture. It should not surprise us, then, that they have also been accepted, however unintentionally, by film – the most popular form of mass entertainment throughout the 20th century and beyond.

Some screenwriters and filmmakers adopt psychoanalytic ideas about human experiences. As Claude Chabrol stated in an interview explaining why he collaborated with a psychoanalyst in the writing of his film *La Cérémonie* (1995), "it's very hard, when you deal with characters, not to use the Freudian grid, because the Freudian grid is composed of signs that also apply to the cinema" (Feinstein, 1996, quoted in Gabbard, 2001, p. 1). Other filmmakers may not be as explicit in acknowledging their debt to psychoanalysis, and yet in their work we can identify its influence on such aspects as characterization, choice of narrative themes, emphasis on psychological motivation or oneiric atmosphere.

At the same time, films have often been understood with reference to psychoanalytic concepts. This has been possible because an important aspect of the "correspondence, however elusive," between psychoanalysis and cinema concerns the analogies between filmic language and the analytic idiom used to describe unconscious processes. Not only are words such as *projection* current in the filmic and analytic languages but there are also certain psychoanalytic concepts (e.g., *screen memories* and *primal scenes*) that may be considered as definitions of film. Furthermore, the process of *free associations* (mostly visual in film and verbal in psychoanalysis) has in both idioms the similar purpose of encouraging the exploration of deep emotional meanings and of the often uncertain boundaries between reality and fantasy. In Glen Gabbard's words, "to a large extent, film speaks the language of the unconscious" (Gabbard, 1997, p. 429).

## A psychoanalytic film genre?

Although a "psychoanalytic film genre" as such does not exist, certain films are undoubtedly more suitable than others for a psychoanalytic reading and are in turn more likely to provide analysts with observations and insights potentially useful in their clinical work. These films fall into three broad and to some extent overlapping categories.

### Films with psychologically credible characters

In the first group we find those works in which screenwriters and filmmakers collaborate in portraying their characters in an explicitly psychological way. The emphasis here is not so much on fast-moving action, dramatic plots or the display of striking special effects, but on a detailed, in-depth study of the inner world and personality of the main characters. In these movies generalizations (of the "goodies vs. baddies" kind) are avoided, and people are represented in their ambivalent or conflictual aspects. Their past is taken into account (either by presenting characters as they grow and evolve over time or by using the filmic technique of editing flashback scenes into the main narrative), and their unconscious motivations are hinted at or even openly explored. Spectators can sympathize with the psychologically justified, if often just subtle, transformations that occur to these characters as a result of the vicissitudes they go through in the course of the movie.

These films' characters, in other words, emerge from the flat silver screen as truly three-dimensional, allowing the viewers to recognize them as real people and therefore to identify with them in all their often disturbing contradictions, rather than idealizing or denigrating them as tends to happen in regard to character representations in less psychologically sophisticated movies.

Comfortably fitting into this group are, to give just one example from the many available to film history, many works from the French *Nouvelle Vague* (New Wave) of the late 1950s throughout the 1960s, by such *auteurs* as François Truffaut, Louis Malle, Jacques Rivette and Eric Rohmer. The statement by Rohmer that his movies deal less with what people do than with what is going on in their minds while they are doing it may equally apply to our therapeutic approach to patients.

## Films on themes directly concerning psychoanalysts

The second category of films popular among psychoanalytic critics includes those many works that deal with themes also familiar to analytic inquiries, thus covering disparate aspects of the human condition: crises in subjectivity related to developmental stages or to acute existential and moral dilemmas (by such directors, to name just a few from different cinematic traditions, as Ingmar Bergman, Akira Kurosawa, Krzysztof Kieslowski); loss and mourning; conflictual or abusive family constellations (Jasujiro Ozu, Luchino Visconti, Satyajit Ray), sometimes with an emphasis on incestuous themes; different forms of mental pathology, such as depressive and suicidal, neurotic or narcissistic disturbances (Woody Allen); sexual perversions and gender confusion (Pedro Almodóvar); drug addiction and alcoholism; dissociative, paranoid, and psychotic states; and so on. It must be noted here that unfortunately many movies on psychosis, including some of the best (such as Roman Polanski's *Repulsion* [1965] and David Cronenberg's *Spider* [2002]), tend to associate madness with murderousness, or even to fall in the horror genre, thus reflecting rather than challenging common stereotypes about mental illness.

Specific psychoanalytic interpretations could throw some new light on certain psychological phenomena represented in films: for instance, Alfred Hitchcock's *Rebecca* (1940) could be watched from the perspective of the "replacement child" syndrome; Peter Weir's *The Truman Show* (1998) is enriched by understanding it in the light of the Winnicottian concept of the "false self"; and Alejandro González Iñárritu's *Amores Perros* (2000) is an interesting instance of the enactment of "rescue fantasies."

A cinematic theme particularly important to psychoanalytic investigation is that of scopophilia: when watching films whose characters indulge in voyeuristic activities (prominent among them, Alfred Hitchcock's *Rear Window* [1954], Michael Powell's *Peeping Tom* [1960], Michelangelo Antonioni's *Blow-Up* [1966], or Krzysztof Kieslowski's *A Short Film About Love* [1988]), viewers are no longer just indulging in watching a movie, with all the wishes, anticipation, pleasure or disappointments intrinsic to such an activity. What they are watching now are other voyeurs like themselves. In other words, their identifications and visual excitement have as their objects not only the film itself but also the subjects and objects of the voyeuristic activities projected on the screen.

## Films (mis)representing the psychoanalytic profession

In the third and last group I have included those films that attempt to represent the psychoanalytic profession itself: those movies, that is, that include a psychoanalyst as a main character (e.g., Nanni Moretti's *The Son's Room* [*La Stanza del Figlio*] [2001]), Freud himself (John Huston's *Freud: The Secret Passion* [1962]), psychoanalytic patients (Hugh Brody's *Nineteen Nineteen* [1985]), or both analyst and analysand (Georg Wilhelm Pabst's *Secrets of a Soul* [*Geheimnisse einer Seele*] [1926]). Not surprisingly, prominent patients involved in scandalous relationships have attracted special attention from filmmakers – at least three of them in Sabina Spielrein's case (Elisabeth Màrton in 2002, Roberto Faenza in 2003, and David Cronenberg in 2011).

The earliest example of something approaching the presence of psychoanalysis in a film can be found in *The Mystery of the Rocks of Kador* [*Le Mystère des Roches de Kador*] (Léonce Perret, 1912), in which "a celebrated foreign alienist physician" saves the heroine Suzanne from madness by utilizing the "luminous vibrations of cinematographic images" to induce in her an hypnotic state leading to psychotherapeutic suggestion (see Bergstrom, 1999, pp. 15–20).

However, the first major and arguably still most successful filmic representation of psychoanalysis is the feature *Secrets of a Soul* (1926). Aesthetically located somewhere between the claustrophobic expressionistic world of "*Kammerspiel*" and the emergence of the "*Neue Sachlichkeit*," the film was directed by Georg Wilhelm Pabst, with leading German psychoanalysts Karl Abraham and Hanns Sachs as consultants. Aptly described as "a silent film about the talking cure" (Ries, 1995), *Secrets of a Soul* was an experimental project intended to introduce the general audience to a psychoanalytical understanding of mental phenomena in a thought-provoking and visually engaging form within the structure, not unknown to Freud's own case histories, of a detective story. It is a detailed and respectful account of the fictional case of a neurotic chemist (played by Werner Krauss), a man who develops a phobia of knives and becomes pathologically jealous and sexually impotent when he hears that a young cousin of his wife's is coming to visit them. His not-too-accidental encounter with a psychoanalyst eventually brings about his remarkable recovery.

Having been invited by Abraham to cooperate on this film, Freud replied to him in no uncertain terms: "I do not believe that satisfactory plastic representation of our abstractions is at all possible" (Freud, 1925a). Only a few months earlier, Freud had also declined Samuel Goldwyn's substantial offer of $100,000 for a script on famous love stories.

Psychoanalysis reached Hollywood in the 1940s with Hitchcock's *Spellbound* (1945). It tells the story of a beautiful psychoanalyst (Ingrid Bergman) who falls in love with her handsome patient (Gregory Peck) as she tries to rescue him from being unjustly accused of murder by helping him to uncover, through a most unethical mixture of therapeutic interventions and erotic passion, a traumatogenic childhood memory. The original twist in *Spellbound* is that, through the psychopathological devices of amnesia and guilt complex, the protagonist's main accuser is not some police detective, court judge, or other such authority figure, but a part of himself – his own harsh superego, which has never forgiven him for the accidental death, many years earlier, of his brother. It is only fair to mention that, although this film played a part in popularizing psychoanalysis in the United States in those years, Hitchcock himself had confessed that his movie was "just another manhunt story wrapped up in pseudo-psychoanalysis" (Truffaut, 1984, p. 165).

Freud was reserved about his personal life, skeptical about biographies of any kind and, as we know, unsympathetic to the medium of cinema. However, he reluctantly agreed to be filmed in 1928 by one of his American patients, Philip R. Lehman, for a documentary that was also to include shots of many other prominent psychoanalysts; its final 50-minute version, entitled *Sigmund Freud: His Family and Colleagues, 1928–1947*, was edited, restored, and completed by Lehman's daughter, Lynne Lehman Weiner, and released in 1985 (Marinelli, 2004).

The founder of psychoanalysis would have thought of a feature film about himself – such as John Huston's *Freud* (1962) (the lurid subtitle *The Secret Passion* was added later for commercial reasons) – as anathema. However, this movie turned out to be no conventional Hollywood biopic, being concerned not so much with Freud the man but with a subject matter that we know to be fundamentally resistant to representation: the unconscious itself. Making this movie caused drama among Universal Pictures, John Huston, his first screenwriter (no less than Jean-Paul Sartre, 1985), and the film's star, a sensitive if also disturbed Montgomery Clift.

This film demands its audience to get emotionally as well as intellectually involved, in ways that feel almost physically painful. "Both sights and sounds in this film," wrote Brill (1997), "require constant interpretation; both function more as clues that must be construed than as signposts. Both, as Freud says of dreams, 'speak in riddles'" (p. 183).

Huston's film concentrates on the early years of psychoanalysis, from 1885 to Freud's father's death in 1896, and the publication at the turn of the century of *The Interpretation of Dreams* (Freud, 1900). Crucial to those years are the discovery and then the abandonment (ca. 1897) of the so-called seduction theory of psychoneurosis, which provides the theoretical underpinnings to the movie's narrative. Freud's patient in the film, Cecily (Susannah York), a composite of the cases of Anna O, Dora and others, is affected by severe hysterical symptoms, eventually understood by Freud in relation to her childhood Oedipal phantasies. In Huston's film, Freud and Cecily embark upon a journey toward self-knowledge. The motifs of eyes, mirrors, keys (also present in the Pabst's and Hitchcock's movies referred to earlier) and the insistence on the imagery of light and darkness emphasize the arduous character of such a quest.

A more recent film on psychoanalysis is Hugh Brody's *Nineteen Nineteen* (1985). It is the story about two former patients of Freud's (played by Paul Scofield and Maria Schell) who meet up in Vienna in the 1970s to reminisce about their lives and their tumultuous analytic experiences (their biographies are based on two of Freud's celebrated case studies). The narrative unfolds within a structure of four interrelated levels of discourse. At the first level we witness the interactions and dialogues between the two characters concerning themselves as they are in the present, in their late sixties, and their relationship. At the second level we are spectators to their recounting of events, impressions and fantasies about their personal and collective history. Then, in flashback we are offered, at the third level of discourse, the reliving of the past, either in color during their troubled adolescence on and off the couch or in archival black-and-white newsreels, family movies, and still photographs. Finally, again in flashback, we have the "material" they present to Freud himself in his Berggasse consulting room. We the viewers (and they, the patients) never actually see Freud but only hear his reassuring off-screen voice from behind the couch.

It must be noticed here that one of the problems concerning many of the representations of our psychoanalytic profession in film is a certain confusion, especially in the minds of Hollywood filmmakers and their audiences, between psychoanalysis and psychiatry.[1] Such a confusion is, at least in part, justified by the fact that until not long ago all American psychoanalysts also were psychiatrists. It is a small but significant detail that psychiatrists display portraits of Freud on their walls in such important films on mental institutions as Anatole Litvak's *The Snake Pit* (1948), Nunnally Johnson's *The Three Faces of Eve* (1957) and Samuel Fuller's *Shock Corridor* (1963), a subclass of both our second and third categories that also includes Miloš Forman's popular *One Flew Over the Cuckoo's Nest* (1975).

In the majority of the films belonging to this third category, psychoanalysis has been presented in the dramatically effective, but inaccurate, version of the therapist being engaged in the cathartic recovery of repressed memories of traumas for the explanation of current events, with much use of flashbacks as the filmic device equivalent to memory. This approach has been exploited, among others, in some of Alfred Hitchcock's movies, such as the already mentioned *Spellbound* (1945) and *Marnie* (1964). *Spellbound* is also an example of the way in which psychoanalysis can be misrepresented in cinema by showing analysts acting out their (countertransference) love for their analysands by getting involved in romantic or sexual activities with them. An exception to this can be found in the remarkable television series *In Treatment* (2010), in which the character of the psychotherapist (played by Gabriel Byrne) is shown as emotionally vulnerable to the seductive temptations of one of his patients, but professional enough to resist enacting his erotic feelings for her.[2]

Another distorted picture of our profession on the screen concerns the suggestion, to comical effect, that analysts are more insane than their patients (*Deconstructing Harry*, Woody Allen, 1997; *Analyze This*, Harold Ramis, 1999). Other times analysts are portrayed as naïve, unprofessional, greedy, abusive or even involved in criminal activities.

## Films and dreams

A special place in the dialogue between psychoanalysis and cinema concerns dreams. As their interpretation constitutes, according to Freud, the "royal road" to the unconscious, perhaps also the exploration of films may lead us in the same direction. The association between movies and dreams is powerfully established in our culture. I still remember that, as children growing up in the 1950s, when reporting to our friends our dreams we always mentioned whether they were in color or black and white. I suppose that children of the previous generation may have commented on their dreams as being silent or talkies. And contemporary ones may question whether they see their dreams in 3-D. Hollywood, of course, has always been described as a "dream factory."

Movies and dreams seem to share a morphological equivalence insofar as both can be considered to express our latent unconscious wishes through their manifest contents, and both use, for the purpose of circumventing repression, similar mechanisms. These include (in films, especially at the editing stage) condensation, displacement, symbolic representation and distortions of time and space (Freud, 1900).

Eberwein (1984) suggested a similarity between the *film screen* and the *dream screen* as places of both fusion and separation. The concept of dream screen was originally developed by Bertram D. Lewin:

> I conceived the idea that dreams contained a special structure which I named the *dream screen* . . . I thought of the dream as a picture or a projected set of images, and for the reception of these images I predicated a screen, much like the one we see in the artificial night of a dark motion-picture house before the drama has radiated forth from the window of the projection box.
>
> *(Lewin, 1953, p. 174)*

More recently, Laura Marcus observed that

> cultural commentators have explored the primacy of "wish-fulfillment" in the narrative structures of films, and as equivalent to its function in dreams and daydreams . . . For filmmakers themselves, dreams and dream-states seemed from the outset to be an essential part of film's ontology: while "dream sequences" within films may seem to be bounded, they are never fully sealed off from the film-space which contains them.
>
> *(Marcus, 2001, p. 52)*

The severely neurotic psychopathology of the protagonist of Pabst's already mentioned *Secrets of a Soul*, whose clinical case is based on one of Karl Abraham's own patients, is resolved by a psychoanalyst through the interpretation of a 10-minute-long dream, one of the longest dream sequences in the history of cinema. Its many manifest elements, representing in a condensed and floridly symbolic form the various components of the protagonist's inner world, are explored one by one by his psychoanalyst, leading back to his patient's latent, repressed infantile wishes until his symptoms disappear.

Hitchcock's *Spellbound* is memorable in particular for Salvador Dalí's surrealistic design for the oneiric sequence, represented with an architectural sharpness that contrasts with the more traditional blurred images of filmed dreams. (Dalí had already collaborated in the making of a psychoanalytically significant film, Luis Buñuel's early masterpiece *Un Chien Andalou* [1928].) It is worth mentioning here that although Freud, a son of the Enlightenment, had no patience for any sort of surrealistic irrationalism, "any critical account of the art of Salvador Dalí or of Surrealism in general must take as its point of departure Sigmund Freud whose influence . . . was absolutely fundamental" (Wilson, 1980, p. 9).

In *Spellbound* the interpretation of the patient's dream becomes a way of unlocking a mystery that will pave the royal road to the final dramatic unfolding of the narrative. The function of dreams, at least in classical psychoanalysis, is to express in a distorted form not a repressed memory but an unconscious wish. In *Spellbound* we have instead a decoding of the manifest dream content based on the speculations made by two doctors rather than on the patient's own free associations.

I shall also mention here the famous dream in the opening scene of Ingmar Bergman's *Wild Strawberries* (*Smultronstället*, 1957). It is a compassionate portrait of an elderly man, Professor Isak Borg, coming to terms with the sorrows of an emotionally cold life. The night before embarking on a car journey to his old university where he is to receive an honorary degree, Borg has a disturbing dream. Its representation – which includes a clock without hands, the appearance of the character's double, and his own corpse coming back to life – is one of the most effective filmic illustration of the psychological phenomenon described by Freud (1919) as the "uncanny."

This dream, offering Borg a first opportunity to reflect upon his existence and the choices that led to a life devoid of depth and meaning, helps him move from fear to acceptance of his mortality and thus toward a sort of late redemption.

It may be useful to refer to Francis Baudry's discussion of the psychoanalytic interpretation of literary texts, because what he wrote clearly also applies to the film texts analyzed by psychoanalysts. Baudry outlined four different approaches:

> In the first approach, the analytic writer treats a novel, play, or poem as a case history, ignoring the as-if nature of the literary text and performing a type of character analysis. The second approach relates the text to the mental life (both normal and abnormal) of the author. The text is viewed as a modified form of free association. The third approach considers the text in its own right and carries out a thematic analysis identifying traces or derivatives of mental contents. The fourth approach concerns itself with the reaction of the reader and the production of poetic and aesthetic effect.
>
> *(1984, p. 552)*

We can observe here some similarities with Gabbard's (1997) own helpful classification of psychoanalytic film studies under seven categories: (1) the explication of underlying cultural mythology; (2) the film as reflective of the filmmaker's unconscious; (3) the film as reflective of a specific developmental moment or crisis; (4) the application of Freud's dream work to film; (5) the analysis of spectatorship; (6) the appropriation of psychoanalytic constructs by the filmmaker; and, last but not least, (7) the analysis of a character in the narrative. Examples of psychoanalytic studies about films under these categories are given by Gabbard (2001) in his volume of collected essays selected from the film section of the *International Journal of Psychoanalysis*, which he started in 1997 and edited for a few years.

## Early days

There is a rare and remarkable reference to cinema in a letter Freud wrote from Rome to his family on September 22, 1907. Its relevant section is worth quoting:

> On the Piazza Colonna behind which I am staying, as you know, several thousand people congregate every night . . . on the roof of a house at the other end of the piazza there is a screen on which a *società Italiana* projects lantern slides (*fotoreclami*). They are actually advertisements, but to beguile the public these are interspersed with pictures of landscapes, Negroes of the Congo, glacier ascents, and so on. But since these wouldn't be enough,

the boredom is interrupted by short cinematographic performances for the sake of which the old children (your father included) suffer quietly the advertisements and monotonous photographs. They are stingy with these tidbits, however, so I have had to look at the same thing over and over again. When I turn to go I detect a certain tension in the crowd, which makes me look again, and sure enough a new performance has begun, and so I stay on. Until 9 P.M. I usually remain spellbound; then I begin to feel too lonely in the crowd, so I return to my room to write to you all after having ordered a bottle of fresh water. The others who promenade in couples or *undici, dodici* stay on as long as the music and lantern slides last.

*(Freud, 1907, pp. 261–262)*

What Freud says in this letter promises a future fascination for the new art form; however, not only did he not believe, as we have already pointed out, that psychoanalytic ideas could be represented by cinema, but for the rest of his life he displayed as little interest in films as he had in some other artistic disciplines such as music. "Filmmaking can be avoided as little as – so it seems – bobbed hair," Freud wrote in a letter to Sándor Ferenczi on August 14, 1925, "but I myself won't get mine cut, and don't intend to be brought into personal connection with any film" (Freud, 1925b, p. 222).

Many of Freud's followers, however, had a different opinion. At first analysts who found movies worthy of their intellectual enquiries limited themselves to an *application* to film criticism of the concepts they were familiar with from their clinical work. The first attempt to interpret a film from a psychoanalytic perspective was made as early as 1914 by Otto Rank. In the opening chapter of his psychoanalytic study on the phenomenon of "the double" Rank commented on the German film *The Student of Prague* (*Der Student von Prag*, 1913) directed by Stellan Rye and written by Hanns Heinz Ewers (a follower of E.T.A. Hoffmann, "the unrivalled master of the uncanny in literature" [Freud, 1919, p. 233]). Freud himself mentioned this film when he quoted Rank in a footnote to his text on "The Uncanny" (Freud, 1919, p. 236, n. 1). In that same essay Rank stated, in stark contrast with the position adopted by Freud, that

the uniqueness of cinematography in visibly portraying psychological events calls our attention, with exaggerated clarity, to the fact that the interesting and meaningful problems of man's relation to himself – and the fateful disturbance of this relation – finds here an imaginative representation.

*(Rank, 1914, p. 7)*

The publication of Hugo Münsterberg's (1916) *The Film: A Psychological Study*, the first book on the parallels between the structure of the (conscious) mind and the filmic experience, occurred 2 years later, in 1916. It would take several more years for Hanns Sachs, the Berlin analyst who in 1926 was to contribute, as we have seen, to the screenplay of a major movie on psychoanalysis, to write an article on cinema (Sachs, 1929). In it, among other observations on the formal aspects of the cinematic medium, Sachs identified interesting parallels between silent movies and Freud's theory of parapraxis.

It would not be until the early 1960s, however, that psychoanalysis started to enrich film theory by providing original and often controversial interpretations of individual movies. Depending on the particular author's theoretical orientation, these could include references to castration anxiety (classical Freudian), the symbolic order (Lacanian), self-objects (Kohutian), the paranoid-schizoid and the depressive position (Kleinian), archetypes and the collective unconscious (Jungian), and so on. These scholars focused their attention, sometimes with the help of a detailed textual analysis of film sequences, on narratives and characters, or even on the personality or psychopathology of the filmmakers themselves, as revealed by their work.

Gradually, however, their interest in cinema expanded to include an appreciation of its language, its formal structure, and its psychological, social and more generally cultural functions, whereas the sterile psychohistorical activity of analyzing filmmakers on the basis of their artistic productions was to a large extent given up.

## Lacanian contributions

Jacques Lacan's emphasis on language and its isomorphic relationship to the unconscious produced among some of his followers a number of original contributions to psychoanalytic film studies that, especially in the 1970s and 1980s, dominated the academic field on the pages of the prestigious journals *Cahiers du Cinéma* in France, *Screen* in Britain, and *Camera Obscura* in the United States, and through the seminal essays of such authors as Jean-Louis Baudry (1974) and Christian Metz (1974).

Lacanian film scholars tried to understand spectator identification through the lens of Lacan's theory of the "mirror stage" – that developmental process (an aspect of what he called the imaginary order) occurring in children between 6 and 18 months of age when they misrecognize themselves in the mirror as though their fragmentary body was a whole, and thus build their ego on the basis of such an illusion. These film theorists took as their assumption the analogy between these deluded children and film viewers, for the latter would be using the silver screen as though it were a mirror. The spectator would thus acquire a false sense of power, or indeed of omnipotence, through a primary identification with the movie camera, while in fact being merely a passive viewer of what unfolds in front of him. For Metz this would account for the popularity of cinema insofar as it constitutes an imperfect reflection of the realities it represents while placing the viewers into a regressive dream state. A reason why, according to some Lacanian theorists, this unconscious scenario occurs is that the spectator can remain unseen, a fact facilitated by the absence (typical of mainstream cinema) of self-reflective references to the filming process itself and to the apparatus (the all-seeing, potent, phallic camera) involved in it. In fact, the omnipotent phantasy collapses as soon as a spectator realizes that what is projected on the screen is just a constructed product. In this sense classical cinema was considered as an instance of commodity fetishism, hiding the labor that went into its production – a view providing a political dimension to such film studies.

Although cinema (and, as we have noted, psychoanalysis) was born at the end of the 19th century when the Lumière brothers showed their first films in public, the *idea* of cinema goes back more than two millennia, when Plato (360 B.C.) used the "Allegory of the Cave" to describe how chained prisoners, unable to move or turn their heads back, would mistakenly believe that the wooden and stone statues carried in front of a fire behind them, and whose shadows were thus projected on the cave wall facing them, were real people and not simulacra. "And so in every way," Plato concluded in the *Republic*, "they would believe that the shadows of the objects we mentioned were the whole truth." Jean-Louis Baudry, another prominent Lacanian film scholar, also referred to Plato's myth in developing his own views about what he calls the cinema "apparatus." Following the publication of his article, entitled "Ideological Effects of the Basic Cinematographic Apparatus" (Baudry, 1974), then developed into a book (Baudry, 1975), his apparatus theory became influential within academic film studies throughout the 1970s. This approach emphasized the ideological nature of the mechanics of film representation. In particular, the camera and the editing suite were considered by Baudry and his followers to be key tools in providing ideological points of view to the spectators' gaze, thus making cinema itself instrumental for the transmission of dominant cultural values.

Among the many important issues raised by Metz (1974) in his oft-quoted essay "The Imaginary Signifier," I focus here on just one that seems to me particularly suggestive. Referring to the fact that, given the nature of the film medium itself, what we watch in a cinema is even further removed from the object being represented than, say, what we would witness on a theater stage, Metz conceded that what unfolds on the screen "is real (the cinema is not a phantasy), but the perceived is not really the object, it is its shade, its phantom, its double, its *replica* in a new kind of mirror" (Metz, 1974, p. 45). What is peculiar about cinema, he says, is not only that it allows us to perceive our object from a distance (through the senses of sight and hearing) but also that "what remains in that distance is now no longer the object itself, it is a delegate" (p. 61). This "delegate" is a prime instance of the Lacanian *manque* ("lack"): like any other form of desire, its essence depends on being fulfilled, while its existence comes to an end the moment it is. Film is suspended, for Metz, in the imaginary space of this paradox. Indeed, a frequent critique of Lacanian theories of cinema is that they tend to describe the desire in film audiences in negative terms, as originating from an absence of the objects signified on the screen.

Lacanian analyst Jacques-Alain Miller (1966) proposed the term "suture" to describe the imaginary process whereby the subject is "stitched into" the signifying chain. This concept "found immediate favour amongst film theorists in order to describe the mechanism by which the spectator is positioned as a cinematic subject, [and] takes her or his place in the cinematic discourse" (Cowie, 1997, p. 115). Other authors with a Lacanian orientation, such as Stephen Heath (1981), Ann Kaplan (1990), Slavoj Žižek (1992) and Joan Copjec (1994), have studied specific formal aspects of filmmaking (screenplay, direction, mise-en-scène, camera work) or of film watching, sometimes in the context of their analogy with conscious, preconscious and unconscious mental processes or in relation to the categories of the real, imaginary and symbolic orders. Film editing, in particular, lends itself to be discussed in terms of similar defensive mechanisms as those operating, for instance, in dream work and in symptom formation.

## Studies on "spectatorship"

Under the influence of Lacanian-colored semiotics and feminist theories, a fertile ground of research has also been that of the relationship, under the generic label of "spectatorship," of cinema with its audience. The term "spectatorship" refers to the complex of psychological, socioeconomic and more generally cultural phenomena that affect filmmakers in their construction, and audiences in their reception, of cinematic products as well as the mythologies associated with them.

These studies have covered such varied areas as those concerning regressive elements of film (for some, the dark room of the theater is the symbolic equivalent of the intrauterine experience), voyeuristic aspects (the viewer's curiosity for the primal scene to be enacted on the screen), or fetishistic components (the mass phenomenon of worshipping celluloid stars).

Psychoanalytically influenced film scholars with a feminist orientation, prominent among them Laura Mulvey (1975, 1989), Teresa de Lauretis (1984) and Mary Ann Doane (1987), have provided original perspectives on issues of sexuality in films, such as gender stereotyping and the role of women as fetishes or as the objects of male voyeuristic gaze. Relevant in this context is Joan Riviere's (1929) concept of "womanliness as masquerade," whereby a woman's public success could signify "an exhibition of herself in possession of the father's penis, having castrated him" (p. 305). Riviere explains: "She identifies herself with the father; and then she uses the masculinity she thus obtains by putting it at the service of the mother. She becomes the father, and takes his place; so she can 'restore' him to the mother" (p. 310).

The importance of this for cinema rests on the fact that such a masquerade of female identity and sexuality, it is argued, is also mirrored in the (male) representations of women characters on the screen.

## Reflections on the point of view

As already noted, a topic of major interest to psychoanalysts concerns the tension spectators experience between on the one hand identifying with the perspective of the filmmakers and their camera and on the other immersing themselves in the film's narrative, feeling contained by it, and letting themselves be drawn into identifications with, and relationships to, the different characters on the screen.

Where would the spectator's point of view then be placed? Metz (1974) believed that a viewer could only identify with the camera that has preceded him in the act of looking. Of course, we know that what we are watching is "just" a film, performed by actors, shot by a camera and projected on a screen, in the same way as we know, upon waking up, that what we have lived through in our sleep was "just" a dream. In addition, we understand that the perception of seamless frame-to-frame movement and of three-dimensional images on a two-dimensional surface, and the sensation of regressing in time in the flashback scenes, to mention just a few of the artifices of the cinema medium, are but an illusion. In reality, however, our experience as spectators is mostly a different one.

I would like to draw a parallel here with one aspect of the psychodynamics of the developing child. At first, a baby's primary form of relationship is his identification with the mother: this we can compare with the spectator's identification with the point of view of the camera, which has given birth to the film in the first place. However, as the child grows older, and assuming the primary identification was with a good-enough mother, he or she then gradually (although never entirely) begins to separate from her. This will allow the individual to learn to engage in the lifelong process of getting involved in mature object relationships.

Analogously, we could suggest that movie spectators, while always potentially aware of the existence of a camera somewhere in the background of their viewing experience, grow out of it once they feel settled in their armchairs (sometimes with the help of a drink and a tub of popcorn) and the light in the cinema goes down. They can then immerse themselves in the film's narrative, feel held and contained by it, and let themselves be drawn into a complex play of identifications with, and relationships to, the different characters on the screen. In order to do this, however, our viewers must momentarily forget that they are watching "just" a movie shot by a camera and disengage from their original identification with the camera's point of view.

Occasionally spectators may be made conscious again of the existence of the camera. This happens when they get drawn, as it were, "behind" the film by a moviemaker's self-reflective gesture, by the specific subject of the film (for instance, scopophilia or filmmaking itself), or by the introduction of explicitly subjective shots. The authorial voice sometimes makes itself more audible through a deliberately emphatic use of certain filming techniques – say, an insistent use of a fixed or of a handheld camera, circular movements around a room, close-ups on the eyes of a troubled character – and the audience could therefore be made more aware that there are moviemakers and their creative minds (as well as their tools) behind the film. In a similar way, regressive moves toward primary identifications are always possible in well-adjusted, autonomous adults, but these should be considered as exceptions. The norm for the grown-up is to use the original identification with the good-enough parent as a step toward forming relationships with others, much as the function of the camera is to offer the spectator an opportunity to move away from awareness of the apparatus that had produced the film and relate instead to what is projected on the screen.

It is also worth pointing out that when sitting in a cinema, we do not find ourselves in the presence of a camera but of another machine that represents it: the projector. Although it could be argued that a film's very existence depends on the intercourse between the parental couple of camera and projector (without the former it could not be made; without the latter it could not be seen), in our viewing experience we mostly relate to this offspring by ignoring its parents.

## A Winnicottian approach

Film studies inspired by Donald W. Winnicott's theories are scant, perhaps at least in part because of his own somewhat unenthusiastic attitude to cinema. Yet his developmental model of mental processes proves useful for an understanding of the structural and functional characteristics of cinema as well as to provide original interpretations of individual movies. Particularly relevant here are his concepts of "mirroring" and of "transitional space."

The process of mirroring (Winnicott's own adaptation of the Lacanian mirror stage) refers to the intimate exchanges of gazes between mother and baby, facilitating in the latter the gradual establishment of a sense of personal identity. Winnicott (1967) once quoted a patient saying that the painter Francis Bacon liked "to have glass over his pictures because then when people look at the picture what they see is not just a picture; they might in fact see themselves" (p. 117). This detail seems to confirm the meaning of the screen on which the film gets projected as a distorting mirror surface reflecting what we unconsciously wish to see in it.

As to the transitional space, Winnicott conceptualized it as a sort of playground, "a resting-place for the individual engaged in the perpetual human task of keeping inner and outer reality separate yet inter-related" (Winnicott, 1953, p. 230). Cinema could be seen as an eloquent instance of a playful activity (but, like a child's play, also an entirely serious one) that takes place in what, to use another spatial metaphor, we could call a "bridge space." As an extension of the transitional space, the bridge space is also an intangible yet at the same time real territory located on the boundaries between the internal and the external worlds and linking them together. Film opens up such a creatively ambiguous space in the cracks between reality and fantasy, documentary and fictional narrative, historical events and subjective experiences. The bridge space is what connects external reality to its filmed representation and the filmmakers' imagination to the viewers' experience.

## Toward interdisciplinary dialogues

As we have seen, psychoanalytically informed film scholars have been engaged from a variety of theoretical perspectives in important research on the connections between cinema and psycho-analysis. As a result, the discourse on their complex relationship has become progressively broader and deeper, no longer involving exclusively the application of concepts borrowed from analytic theory to film interpretation.

What is particularly encouraging is the emerging extension of our field of inquiry toward a more sophisticated process characterized by new interdisciplinary dialogues between the practitioners of cinema and those of psychoanalysis. In other words, psychoanalysts are now showing an interest in what films can offer them, in appreciating them also as valuable contributions to their theoretical knowledge about the human mind and to their clinical work with patients.

In particular, psychoanalysts and other analytically oriented therapists believe that they have much to learn from films, especially from those that focus on characters portrayed in all the complexity of their personalities and emphasize subtleties of psychological and interpersonal experience. What the viewing of such movies can do for analysts is to enrich their knowledge of the human condition, both in its normal and psychopathological manifestations, reminding them of how unclear the boundaries can be between the two.

In some cases, film scholars, filmmakers and mental health practitioners cooperate to achieve a deeper understanding of many aspects, both normal and abnormal, of our internal world, subjectivity, sexual identity, social roles and interpersonal relationships for an enrichment of both disciplines. Numerous specialized publications, dedicated Web sites, the regular inclusion of film essays in the main psychoanalytic journals, as well as increasingly frequent professional events at which psychoanalysts debate their approach to cinema with filmmakers and the latter discuss their movies with analysts, attest to the importance of such cross-fertilizing interchanges. Furthermore, the program of most psychoanalytic conferences since the 1990s now includes the screening of films followed by panel discussions with psychoanalysts and filmmakers. International events such as the European Psychoanalytic Film Festival taking place biennially in London constitute meeting points for the practitioners and students of the two disciplines and provide invaluable opportunities for such exchanges.

I now present a couple of personal examples of this fruitful dialogue between cinema and psychoanalysis. The first illustrates how filmmakers, while being sometimes suspicious that psychoanalytic interpretations could impose unintended meanings on their work, can at other times be open to the idea that some of their artistic choices may be motivated by factors outside their consciousness. *Histoire d'Eaux* (2002) is a short film about the passing of time as a subjective experience, showing that different temporal modalities can easily coexist. In the course of the roundtable conversation with its director, Bernardo Bertolucci, I commented that the lyrics of "Un Anno d'Amore" – Mina's love song playing diegetically from a radio in the background – were consistent with the main message of the film. Although this was quite obviously the case (the song suggested that a boyfriend would understand in a single instant the meaning of a whole year of his girlfriend's love for him), Bertolucci at first objected, claiming that he had chosen that music simply as a friendly gesture toward Pedro Almodóvar, who had used that same song in one of his movies.

On second thought, however, Bertolucci admitted that it could not have been a coincidence that, of all the songs available to him, he should have ended up picking one that was so relevant to the content of his film. Unconscious reasons for his choice, and for then justifying it to himself and to our audience with a rationalization, must have been at work there, and he was pleased that our discussion had allowed him to learn something about his movie, and potentially about himself too, of which he had been hitherto unaware. Bertolucci's openness to psychoanalysis is also evident in the following quotation: "Since I started to know analysis I found that I had, in my camera, an additional lens which was . . ., it's not Kodak, it's not Zeiss, it's Freud, it's a lens which really takes you very close to dreams" (Bertolucci & Sabbadini, 2007, p. 384).

My second example illustrates how a film could help us become more conscious of certain aspects of our psychoanalytic work. Michael Radford's *Il Postino* (1994) is the fictional narrative about a simple postman who, charged with the daily delivery of mail to the exiled Pablo Neruda, develops a personal relationship with the famous poet while learning from him about verse, metaphors and rhymes. After watching that film, I realized that there were interesting similarities between their friendship and the analytic relationship itself, that the daily encounters between the village postman and Neruda were comparable with therapeutic sessions and, more specifically, that the feelings that *il postino* was developing for the poet had strong transferential connotations.

Reflecting on that film, I thus became more vividly aware of the extent to which language – and a sensitivity to the sound and shades of emotional meanings of words – is crucial to both the poetic and the analytic experience. Furthermore, as Neruda, having then departed from the island, soon forgot about his friend thus leaving him in a state of bewildered despair, I was reminded of the significance of the phase of termination within the analytic relationship and of allowing for a proper working through of the mourning process in order to minimize the sense of abandonment, betrayal and loss in our patients, if not also in ourselves.

## Conclusion

As we have seen, the relationship between psychoanalysis and cinema is a complex one. Most studies in this area, whether from psychoanalysts or film scholars, originally focused on the application of certain basic analytic concepts, borrowed from Freudian or other metapsychologies, to the interpretation of the contents of individual movies and to the exploration of such themes as their narrative, characterizations and oneiric quality.

Of course, a psychoanalytic film genre as such does not exist. However, there are certain movies that lend themselves better to a psychoanalytic reading: those portraying characters in a psychologically convincing, three-dimensional way; those dealing with themes of direct interest to analysts; and those representing the analytic profession itself.

In the course of the past half century this field has gradually expanded to embrace also a variety of other contributions, most notably those influenced by Lacan's theories. These include studies on the form of cinema (its structure, apparatuses, function, language and so on) and of its reception and impact on its viewers ("spectatorship," point of view). At the same time an ongoing dialogue has been evolving between filmmakers and psychoanalysts, thus recognizing the importance of cinema (both as an art form and a popular medium) for providing psychoanalysis with original insights into human nature – how and why people behave, think, feel and relate to one another – all invaluable material to theoreticians as well as practitioners of the analytic discipline.

In the past few decades lines of communication among filmmakers and psychoanalysts (not to also mention numerous analytically informed film scholars) have been opened on the pages of books and journals, on Internet sites, in academic film studies courses and at conferences and festivals the world over. The large body of work in this area, promising further fruitful developments in the years to come, is a testament to the dedication of those scholars who, through their knowledge about and love for cinema and psychoanalysis, and for their relationship, have believed in the value of interdisciplinary dialogues and cross-fertilization between them.

## Notes

1  See, for instance, the title of the important book on American cinema *Psychiatry and the Cinema* (Gabbard & Gabbard, 1999). In their "Preface to the Second Edition," the authors wrote:

> Since the appearance of our first edition in 1987, psychiatry has continued to distance itself from psychoanalysis and psychotherapy. Nevertheless, in the cinematic world, the emphasis remains on the talking cure. . . . Hence, we continue to use the term *psychiatry* in the broadest possible sense to encompass all mental health professionals, especially those who practice psychotherapy.
>
> *(1999, pp. xix–xx)*

2  Another analyst recently made popular by television is Dr. Jennifer Melfi (played by Lorraine Bracco), the attractive therapist of mobster Tony Soprano in the groundbreaking and hugely successful drama series *The Sopranos* (David Chase, 1999–2007).

## References

Baudry, J-L 1974, 'Ideological effects of the basic cinematographic apparatus', *Film Quarterly*, vol. 28, pp. 39–47.
Baudry, J-L 1975, 'The apparatus: Metapsychological approaches to the impression of reality in cinema', in P Rosen (ed), *Narrative, apparatus, ideology: A film theory reader*, Columbia University Press, New York, pp. 299–318.

Baudry, F 1984, 'An essay on method in applied psychoanalysis', *Psychoanalysis Quarterly*, vol. 53, pp. 551–581.

Bazin, A 1967, *What is cinema?*, University of California Press, Berkeley.

Bergstrom, J (ed) 1999, *Endless night: Cinema and psychoanalysis, parallel histories*, University of California Press, Los Angeles.

Bertolucci, B & Sabbadini, A 2007, 'Psychoanalysis: The 11th muse (a conversation)', *Psychoanalysis Inquiry*, vol. 27, pp. 381–394.

Breuer, J & Freud, S 1893–1895, 'Studies on hysteria', in J Strachey (ed), *Standard edition of the complete psychological works of Sigmund Freud*, vol. 2, Hogarth, London.

Brill, L 1997, *John Huston's filmmaking*, Cambridge University Press, Cambridge, MA.

Copjec, J 1994, *Read my desire: Lacan against the historicists*, MIT Press, Cambridge, MA.

Cowie, E 1997, *Representing the woman: Cinema and psychoanalysis*, Macmillan, London.

de Lauretis, T 1984, *Alice doesn't: Feminism, semiotics, cinema*, Macmillan, London.

Doane, MA 1987, *The desire to desire: The woman's film of the 1940s*, Macmillan, London.

Eberwein, R 1984, *Film and the dream screen*, Princeton University Press, Princeton, NJ.

Edelson, M 1988, *Psychoanalysis: A theory in crisis*, University of Chicago Press, Chicago.

Feinstein, H 1996, 'Killer instincts: director Claude Chabrol finds madness in his method', *Village Voice*, vol. 24, p. 86.

Freud, S 1900, 'The interpretation of dreams', in J Strachey (ed), *Standard edition of the complete psychological works of Sigmund Freud*, vols. 4–5, Hogarth, London.

Freud, S 1907, 1961, 'Letter of 22 September', in EL Freud (ed), *Letters of Sigmund Freud 1873–1939*, Hogarth, London.

Freud, S 1919, 'The uncanny', in J Strachey (ed), *Standard edition of the complete psychological works of Sigmund Freud*, vol. 17, Hogarth, London.

Freud, S 1925a, 1965, 'Letter of 9 June', in H Abraham & EL Freud (eds), *A psycho-analytical dialogue: The letters of Sigmund Freud and Karl Abraham 1907–1926*, Hogarth, London, pp. 193–194.

Freud, S 1925b, 'Letter of 14 August', in E Falzeder & E Brabant (eds), *The correspondence of Sigmund Freud and Sándor Ferenczi. Vol. 3: 1920–1933*, Belknap Press, Cambridge, MA.

Gabbard, GO 1997, 'Guest editorial: The psychoanalyst at the movies', *International Journal of Psychoanalysis*, vol. 78, pp. 429–434.

Gabbard, GO & Gabbard, K 1999, *Psychiatry and the cinema* (2nd ed), American Psychiatric Press, Washington, DC.

Gabbard, GO (ed), 2001, *Psychoanalysis and film*, Karnac, New York.

Heath, S 1981, 1990, *Questions of cinema*, London, Macmillan, reprinted in EA Kaplan (ed), *Psychoanalysis and cinema*, Routledge, London.

Lebeau, V 2001, *Psychoanalysis and cinema: The play of shadows*, Wallflower, London.

Lewin, BD 1953, 'Reconsideration of the dream screen', *Psychoanalysis Quarterly*, vol. 22, pp. 174–199.

Marcus, L 2001, 'Dreaming and cinematographic consciousness', *Psychoanalysis and History*, vol. 3, pp. 51–68.

Marinelli, L 2004, 'Smoking, laughing, and the compulsion to film: on the beginnings of psychoanalytic documentaries', *American Imago*, vol. 61, pp. 35–58.

Metz, C 1974, *The imaginary signifier: Psychoanalysis and the cinema* (A Williams, B Brewster et al., eds, C Britton, trans), Indiana University Press, Bloomington.

Miller, J-A 1977–1978, 1966, 'Suture (elements of the logic of the signifier)', *Screen*, vol. 18.

Mulvey, L 1975, 'Visual pleasure and narrative cinema', *Screen*, vol. 16, pp. 6–18.

Mulvey, L 1989, *Visual and other pleasures*, Macmillan, London.

Münsterberg, H 1970, *The film: A psychological study* (1916), Dover, New York.

Rank, O 1971, *The double: A psychoanalytic study* (1914), University of North Carolina Press, Chapel Hill.

Ries, P 1995, 'Popularise and/or be damned: psychoanalysis and film at the crossroads in 1925', *International Journal of Psychoanalysis*, vol. 76, pp. 759–791.

Riviere, J 1929, 'Womanliness as masquerade', *International Journal of Psychoanalysis*, vol. 10, pp. 303–313.

Sachs, H 1929, 'Zur psychologie des films', *Die psychoanalytische Bewegung*, vol. 1, pp. 122–126.

Sartre, J-P 1985, *The Freud scenario* (J-B Pontalis, ed), Verso, London.

Truffaut, F 1984, *Hitchcock*, Simon and Schuster, New York.

Wilson, S 1980, *Salvador Dalí*, Tate Gallery, London.

Winnicott, DW 1953, 1971, 'Transitional objects and transitional phenomena', in *Playing and reality*, Tavistock, London, pp. 1–18.

Winnicott, DW 1967, 1971, 'Mirror role of mother and family in child development', in *Playing and reality*, Tavistock, London, pp. 130–138.

Žižek, S 1992, 'Enjoy your symptom! Jacques Lacan', in *Hollywood and out*, Routledge, London.

# 20

# Psychoanalysis and the visual arts

*Ellen Handler Spitz*

## From art history to psychoanalysis

As an undergraduate student at Columbia University's Barnard College in New York City, pursuing a degree in fine arts (now termed art history), I studied with the eminent Rembrandt scholar Julius Held (1991), and was assigned to write my first essay on a work of visual art in one of the city museums.[1] I chose a haunting canvas on a wall of the Frick Collection on Fifth Avenue and 70th Street: Rembrandt's mysterious equestrian, the *Polish Rider* (see Figure 20.1).

I recall looking steadily and adoringly at the dashing young man depicted in this painting and trying to commune with him. So many questions: Where was he going? Why was he alone? What sort of mood was he in? I admired his smart red breeches, the arrogant way his right elbow juts out toward us, and the taut carriage of the reins in his left hand. The latter made a special impression because I myself was an ardent, ribbon-winning equestrienne. The young swain gazes out of a rockbound landscape as his open-mouthed gray mount, in profile, traverses the desolate terrain with his rider jauntily astride. An eerie solitude envelops them. The gallant fellow focuses not on where he is headed but peers out in our direction from beneath a brimmed hat as if he actually sees us, as if he knows we are there; yet, he also seems fixated on spaces far beyond us in the distance.

Nobody really knows the subject of this mysterious image nor the name of its protagonist, if indeed it is meant to be a portrait, which I doubt. Scholars have even disagreed as to its authorship and have long disputed whether the canvas was painted by the master himself, or by a student or by a gifted follower of Rembrandt.

What mattered to me, however, was none of that but rather something quite different: I wanted to know why this painting drew me toward it. Why it seemed so necessary for me to write about *it* and none other. How did the image etch itself into my psyche? Why did I feel the way I did when I looked at it and also when I conjured it up in its absence? These were the issues I cared for. The painting seemed to follow me, just as its rider follows along inside the picture space, going we know not where, and with a mood neither joyful nor mournful but quietly alert, self-possessed, and potentially responsive. I fell in love, sans doute, and wanted to know why.

*Figure 20.1    Polish Rider* by Rembrandt van Rijn, oil on panel, 1655
Source: The Frick Collection, New York

These were the aperçus that concerned and thrilled me – matters of aesthetic response, emotional as well as perceptual. Unabashedly, these remain my principal aesthetic concerns. They fuel my abiding love for the visual art of painting, and they form an abiding leitmotiv throughout my long career as writer, critic and professor. Because of this peculiar idiosyncrasy, however, I have been forced to travel in solitude – much like the Polish rider himself – going beyond the pale and into open country, beyond the bounds of a discipline that has often regarded affection, attraction and appreciation as eccentric to its mission.

In the course of my wanderings, principally in graduate school, I came, quite fortuitously, upon psychoanalysis, and turned to it with high hopes. It appealed to me because of its engagement with emotion and fantasy and because it seemed, if not to provide answers (which it rarely did), then, at least, to refrain from slighting my deepest questions. In the following pages, I shall try to give an overview of some of the ways in which psychoanalysis has informed my work as a writer in the arts and demonstrate that it offers a plenitude of interpretive modalities to all who share my passionate concern for the psychological and aesthetic as well as the historical attributes of the visual arts.

## Framing themes[2]

Almost from its origins, psychoanalysis has been applied outside the clinical sphere to works of art and used as a mode of understanding in the aesthetic realm. Consider its contribution to three major areas of concern to those involved with the visual arts. First, how can we connect the nature of creative work with the life histories of artists: how does art grow out of an artist's life? Second, what about the interpretation of works of art independent of their creators: how does psychoanalysis help us to understand art's emotionally puzzling elements? Third, what is the nature of our most personal and meaningful encounters with works of art? Why do we care about art, and how do works of art impact us? Why do we strongly prefer some works to others? Beyond these principal topics, we might add others, such as questions about the unconscious elements of period styles and iconographic choices. For this latter topic, a landmark contribution was made in 1984, when art historian Leo Steinberg published his astonishing study, *The Sexuality of Christ in Renaissance Art and in Modern Oblivion*, which argues that, due to understandable inhibitions concerning the portrayal of Christ's genitalia, artists were forced for centuries to produce strained, concealed, ingeniously disguised representations.[3]

Unlike a clinical psychoanalyst, a writer who applies psychoanalytic ideas to visual art rarely has any therapeutic goal in mind. When she interprets the art of the distant past, in particular, there is no interpersonal context for evolving transferences. Thus, in the absence of live interpersonal exchange, interpretation in the realm of the arts lacks the intersubjective validation fundamental to clinical practice. Yet, even when the object of inquiry is not a live human being, there continues to be a rich dialogue, for works of art *do* answer back when they are attended to, and the finest of them are endowed with transhistorical powers to co-create and transform – even if transiently – their viewers and audiences; therefore, they are best seen as relational rather than fixed. I witness this phenomenon daily in my professorial life, when I observe the power that works of art exert over my students year by year.[4] Nonetheless, the psychoanalytic interpreter of art differs fundamentally from the practicing analyst in her motives, methods, and goals.

Over the years, boundary issues have often interfered with a positive reception on the part of scholars in other disciplines toward psychoanalysts who have wandered into the aesthetic domain and toward non-analysts who have attempted to import psychoanalysis into the realms of art history and criticism. These boundary issues are often due to territorialism in its most primitive forms, that is, protective defenses against the invasion of what is perceived as one's own rightful space, and to failures on the part of some psychoanalytically informed authors to specify limits to their projects (typically, like many others, they tend to claim overmuch). Outsiders to psychoanalysis, therefore, occasionally consider analytic forays into their territory as presumptuous. By the same token, some practicing psychoanalysts reject nonclinical academic authors as hyperintellectual and protest they draw on psychoanalytic theory mechanically. The lurking dangers from such practices are superficiality and premature closure.

When, however, psychoanalytic theory as an approach to art is well grounded and combined sensitively with other approaches, when it is conjoined with qualitatively rich and direct experiences with art works themselves and with knowledge of history and criticism, the interdisciplinary marriage can bear nourishing and delicious fruit. In such cases, the unique contribution of psychoanalysis to the realm of the aesthetic is made manifest. One example of such excellence is by the British art historian Margaret Iverson. Her book, *Beyond Pleasure* (2007) offers a brilliant, carefully researched discourse on the then 21-year-old Maya Lin's minimalist, conceptualist, incredibly moving Vietnam War memorial design in Washington, DC.[5] Iverson makes use of the psychoanalytic notion of the "fetish" to reveal ways in which a public monument can serve both to disavow traumatic knowledge and at the same time to induce memories of trauma by standing simultaneously for and against loss.

Drawing on the psychoanalytic work of Julia Kristeva, Iverson invokes the image of a scar that heals yet maintains afterwards the path of the original gash. She quotes psychoanalyst Octave Mannoni's (1969) formulation of fetishism: "I know, but all the same" to develop her depiction of Maya Lin's work in the context of the political and ideological battles that stormed around it, mirroring the already deep rifts that had ruptured American society in the wake of that wasteful war. Citing Freud's fantasy about an imaginary Londoner who pauses in sorrow before a monument to a former queen (Elinor of Castile) rather than attend to his present lover,[6] she asks whether the purpose (or fate) of such a monument is paradoxically to foster what she calls "the necessary art of forgetting." Telling her reader the precise moment at which tears filled her own eyes when she walked along the wall for the first time, she reveals how Maya Lin's monument negotiates passages between private grief (the highly polished black granite reflecting each mourner's face as he or she passes by) and public mourning. With the help of psychoanalysis, she demonstrates how Lin's stark design acts like a lightning rod for emotions that continued for years to swirl around the Vietnam War: anger and outrage. Such feelings and attitudes, she persuasively argues, are, by virtue of the monument's design, "displaced on to issues of aesthetics – modernism as against tradition, abstraction as against figurative art" (Iverson, 2007, p. 96). Iverson's interpretive work stands as an exemplary model of the application of psychoanalysis to visual art – thoughtful, heartfelt, original and inspiring.

By contrast, we might consider Freud's own controversial discussion of *The Moses of Michelangelo*, that monumental statue located in the church of San Pietro in Vincoli, Rome – one which proved of particular fascination to the founder of psychoanalysis. In *Mirrors of Memory*, Mary Bergstein (2010) traces far-reaching but little explored effects of European fin-de-siècle visual culture on Freud's mind. She discloses that the art and practice of photography were naively assumed transparent and objective ways of documenting and gaining access to a prior reality in many fields at the time (archaeology, ethnology, psychiatric diagnoses, art connoisseurship, criminology): photography as a privileged purveyor of truth. As such, Bergstein argues, photography served to shape Freud's thinking about the statue. Apparently, he pored for hours over photographs of the *Moses* while he was in Vienna, where he wrote his treatise. Freud's immersion in a culture saturated by widespread belief in photography-as-truth persuaded him, according to Bergstein, to see the statue as a portrait of the actual man Moses who was reacting at a discernible moment in real time – as if the statue were a person frozen mid-act and could spring to life. Photography, after all, is a visual medium that seems to promise veracious documentation of moments in time. In fact, however, it is not at all clear that Michelangelo intended to represent any particular instant in the story of the reception of the Ten Commandments, which, as is normally the case in the Hebrew Bible, is an event recounted in broad paratactic strokes, thus leaving much room for speculation and Midrashic commentary.

Italian Renaissance sculpture and portraiture, moreover, aspire to a state of timelessness: *sub specie aeternitatis*. The camera, by contrast, captures, apparently, an instant. Bergstein argues that Freud, years after his visit to Rome, composed his highly debatable interpretation of the famous statue by studying photographs of details that he apparently misunderstood, taking them not as "representations of a representation," but rather as literal pictures of Moses himself; thusly, Freud explained the statue's gestures – hand and beard.

Of course, one might protest that Freud's question about why Moses strokes his beard mirrors my own youthful questions (*vide supra*) concerning Rembrandt's *Polish Rider*. And yet, there is a huge difference. There, I limited my perspective to my own personal quest; I made no claims beyond private aesthetic response. In Freud's case, he claims more arrogantly to have found the key to understanding the statue. This difference underlines one of the most serious reasons for the failure of psychoanalysis to have made greater inroads into interdisciplinary work in the humanities. Freud's insights into Michelangelo's *Moses* are worthwhile. They constitute strong, persuasive critical readings, even if based principally on photographs, and after reading his essay one's experience in Rome may be enhanced and nuanced. But they are critical responses, nothing more. They do not provide an art-historically informed key to understanding the statue, and, if they are taken to be such, they cannot but prove misleading and false. The same is true for Freud's controversial, much maligned essay on Leonardo da Vinci (see Spitz, 1985). At core, we have here perhaps the moot question of the identity of psychoanalysis itself. Is it an interpretive modality and thus an art? Or does it take itself to be a hard science?

## A three-part paradigm

Following the paradigm I mapped out in *Art and Psyche* (1985), let's divide our inquiry into three areas: artistic creativity, the interpretation of works and the nature of audience response. Each of these topics correlates historically with a chapter in the development of psychoanalytic theory and also with a chapter in the history of criticism. Freud (1955) said the best way to understand psychoanalysis is to study its origins and history. Following his counsel, we may take the evolution of psychoanalysis in its relation to the arts as falling into a three-stage sequence beginning with the *Studies on Hysteria* and *The Interpretation of Dreams* (1900–01), in which Freud (Breuer & Freud, 1891) reports his discovery of the dynamic unconscious, develops his notions of mental conflict (repression, repetition and transference) and offers a topographic model of the mind. In this first stage, Freud views artistic form as a pleasurable disguise, however elaborate, for content originally derived from forbidden wishes, both erotic and aggressive. With the development of ego psychology (stage two) by Anna Freud (1936), Heinz Hartmann, Ernst Kris (1952) and others, the viewpoint toward art shifts. Now, rather than taking the buried and disguised wishful content of art as our focus, it is the elaboration of artistic form that comes into the light. Our next question has to do with how form arises. According to some, form is best thought of as representing the relatively autonomous functioning of the ego; in other words, aspects of artistic form arise more or less independently of wishes, drive and instinct. Finally, with the advent of object relations theory (stage three), as exemplified by the writings of Margaret S. Mahler in the US and British-based authors like Melanie Klein, D. W. Winnicott, Hanna Segal, Marion Milner, and others, aesthetic experience is traced back to a young child's first relationship, to "symbiosis" and separation-individuation, to play and to transitional objects and phenomena – things and sounds that evoke the qualities of early formative bonding relationships. In this model, works of art are seen as representing an "intermediate area of experience" (Winnicott, 1987) between the self and the outside world. Artistic form and content fuse; any attempt to separate them is seen as depriving the work of its status as art.

Can these three approaches be integrated, or are they incompatible? Some unification is clearly feasible. In the case of the artist's relation to his work, a classical Freudian approach makes sense because it traces – by studying the artist's life – the putative intrapsychic conflicts that may have motivated or infiltrated his or her works of art. Here too, however, ego functions have their place (as they relate to media, method and style) and object relations theory, as well. In the case of the interpretation of works, ego psychology and object relations theory are primary because they are concerned with unconscious fantasies that involve both id and ego; this matters because when we interpret psychoanalytically we search both surface and depth and seek all the wily ways in which these categories resist and defy their reification. Object relations theory, because of its developmental perspective, has much to say regarding aesthetic response. Thus, the three approaches can serve as mutually interdependent interpretive modes.

Artists, as we know, step back from works in progress to appraise them critically and revise them. Likewise for critics – their perceptual acuity, inventiveness, knowledge and unconscious fantasies determine the quality of their aesthetic judgments. Audience members resonate unconsciously with many aspects of the art they behold. Hence, although to separate these categories serves the needs of academic discourse, what actually happens during creation, criticism and aesthetic experience involves all three. The differences consist in emphasis, and each mode is ever implicit in the others.

A parallel interdependence may be observed among the various aspects of psychoanalytic theory. Early drive theory involves recognition – as yet unformulated – of an agency in conflict with the drives, later to be developed into ego psychology. In ego psychology, there is an implicit awareness of the drives and their derivatives, the wishes out of which unconscious fantasies are made and against which specific defenses are mobilized. Moreover, the analysis of a drive includes a concern with its object as well as its aim, impetus and source. Thus, object relations theory is inextricably tied to the earlier paradigms from which it springs. We may, therefore, regard these modes as parts of a whole with varying stresses. Similarly, art criticism shifts among expressive, objective and phenomenological modes, all of which exist on a continuum. Romantic, formalist, sociological, ideologically driven, response-based and contextual criticisms are likewise mutually interdependent. Furthermore, the absorption of psychoanalysis into 20th- and 21st-century intellectual and cultural life means that it plays (although often covertly) – in concert with them – a significant role.

## Freud's contributions

Freud's interest in art is perhaps best documented by his antiquities collection ("I have sacrificed a great deal for my collection of Greek, Roman and Egyptian antiquities," he wrote in a letter to Stephan Zweig on September 7, 1931, "and actually have read more archaeology than psychology"),[7] as well as by his books and papers devoted to art and the many references scattered throughout his works. Although Freud's theoretical perspectives famously evolved, his artistic taste remained stable, and he never systematized his cultural theories. His major concern, with few exceptions, is with the relation between an artist's inner life and his artistic products. Freud sees the cultural object as expressive of and as the result of internal themes and conflicts.

> Art [he states] brings about a reconciliation between two principles [pleasure and reality]. An artist is originally a man who turns away from reality because he cannot come to terms with the renunciation of instinctual satisfaction which [reality] at first demands, and who allows his erotic and ambitious wishes full play in the life of phantasy. He finds the way back to reality, however, from this world of phantasy by making use of special gifts to mould his phantasies into truths of a new kind which are valued by men as precious reflections of reality.
>
> *(Freud, 1958, p. 224)*

Through art, in other words, one actually *becomes* the king, hero or chosen beloved of one's dreams but without expending all the energy needed in the real world and without the luck necessary to succeed. The artist's success depends on the fact that others share his dissatisfaction: no one wants to replace the pleasure principle with the reality principle! Art gives ersatz gratification; it gives temporary but highly satisfactory wish fulfillment, and it is sanctioned, moreover, by the surrounding culture. This formulation stands up quite well when we apply it to 21st-century popular art, including commercial art, advertising art, movies and television shows. It even works for video games, if we take them too as a species of popular art. Freud's formulation works less well for the fine, often ironic art of our day that focuses on ideological and political themes and that mocks aesthetic gratification as an artistic goal.[8]

Freud also emphasizes communication. Interestingly, he concurs in this with his older contemporary, Leo Tolstoy (1899). The value of aesthetic experience for both thinkers comes from identification. For Freud, however, the specific latent content of an artist's work is not necessarily mirrored by or even revealed to the viewer. As he sees it, the object of identification that matters is far subtler. It is nothing less than the quintessential process of circumventing renunciation. What delights an audience and what constitutes the essence of aesthetic experience is, for Freud, the successful outwitting of the internal censor by making possible the *gratification of wishes in fantasy*: this is what gives us our deepest pleasures in art. So, while instinct and wishes lie at the core of art, it is their *elaboration into form* by the artist's skill that brings about a convergence of reality and pleasure and provides grounds for identification and communication. This is quite different from Tolstoy, whose concerns are far more concrete, didactic and ethically focused.

Speculatively but persuasively, Freud (1908) traces a path from children's imaginative play through daydreaming and fantasy to the work of artists. In various writings, he underscores the continuity of art with other modes of mental function, such as jokes and dreams. Artists exist on a continuum with others who are not artists: Freud writes: "Might we not say that every child at play behaves like a creative writer [or artist], in that he creates a world of his own, or, rather, re-arranges the things of his world in a new way which pleases him?" (Freud, 1908, p. 143). This Freudian image of the child/artist rearranging objects in unique configurations paves the way for Winnicott and others, who have elaborated the derivation of artistic activity from childhood play. Freud's image also prefigures theories about the experiences of audiences for works of art. This is because, similarly, when art seems new and compelling, it challenges us to reorient ourselves. It charges us to reconceive phenomena in novel orderings that disrupt our previous assumptions and tastes. It confronts us with truths heretofore unacknowledged and with fresh possibilities for the fusion of our inner and outer realities. It puts us, in other words, into the place of a child who is experimenting. It forces us to create our own world – or at least some aspects of it – anew.

Recently, apropos, I had an experience of this sort when I attended the Metropolitan Opera's production of Verdi's *Rigoletto*, set stunningly in 1960s Las Vegas, the stage electrified with rainbow-colored flashing neon lights and crowded with supernumeraries, bar girls and shills, gleaming in shimmers and spangles with plumes and mesh-stockings; in Act III, Gilda's moribund body is dumped by Sparafucile into the open trunk of an onstage coupe. Thus, the well-loved 1851 work, in this unexpected form, burst into new life for me as it did for the entire opera house. Enthralled, we gave it ovation after standing ovation.

It is important, therefore, to resist those who would attack Freud for taking art merely as a way of circumventing prohibition by permitting instinctual gratification indirectly, for Freud was profoundly respectful of art's potential to bring us in touch with inner truths. He was not, furthermore, oblivious to his own cursory treatment of artistic form. In the opening paragraph of *The Moses of Michelangelo*, he writes:

> I am no connoisseur in art, but simply a layman . . . the subject matter of works of art has a stronger attraction for me than their formal and technical qualities, though to the artist their value lies first and foremost in these latter. I am unable rightly to appreciate many of the methods used and the effects obtained in art.

> *(1914, p. 214)*

Nonetheless, Freud speculates on the nature of artistic form by asking us to consider why it is that, when ordinary persons tell us their daydreams, we feel bored, but when the daydreams of gifted artists are transformed into sculpture or painting, we awaken from our lethargy and experience intense delight. He analogizes the pleasure of artistic form to sexual foreplay in that it gives pleasure of its own while simultaneously readying us for the even greater pleasure we get from the full liberation of sexual tension. He proposes that the artist's work provides a kind of model, "enabling us thenceforward to enjoy our own dreams without self reproach or shame" (Freud, 1908, p. 153). Form and content work hand in hand, and art, at its strongest, liberates audiences by empowering us to dare to enter into more intimate contact with our own internal worlds, unlocking boundaries that formerly seemed fixed. This idea, which attempts to explain how it is that art can have such dramatic effects on us, constitutes Freud's most telling contribution to the philosophy of art. It is, furthermore, a contribution highly pertinent to much art of our time that – whether it eschews ideology or not – takes risks, shocks into awareness, and opens (technically and conceptually) onto new horizons – hallmarks of this century.

Today's art brings sensations of human selves that fluctuate and metamorphose not only geographically (through exile and emigration) but also physically (one thinks of art-related surgeries – as in the disturbing work of the French performance artist Orlan, for example, who in the 1990s underwent a series of plastic surgeries in order to transform herself into an ideal of perfect beauty, thus critiquing the enslavement of women to ideals of external loveliness; prostheses; hormonally, surgically induced gender changes; and cyborgs. Freud's actual taste in art, while highly cultivated, was retrograde. He clung to the plastic arts of antiquity and preferred them to the exuberant avant-garde art of his own era – fin-de-siècle Vienna (for example, Klimt's endlessly recycled portrait of Adèle Bloch-Bauer) – that swished about him with dazzling brilliance but failed to gain his attention.

## The contributions of ego psychology

During and since Freud's lifetime, other psychoanalytic authors have made significant contributions to our understanding of art. Notable among them is Ernst Kris, who was a curator in Vienna at the Kunsthistorisches Museum before becoming a psychoanalyst.[9] Kris (1952) emigrated and settled in New York to escape the Nazi terrors of World War II. His essay "Aesthetic Ambiguity" tackles the complex relationships that exist between artistic production and aesthetic response. He asks how these two experiences are linked. Picture once more the artist who, during the processes of creation, simultaneously acts as his own work's first critic.

Imagine a painter who, motionless, brush in hand, contemplates his canvas for long moments in silence. Physically inert, he is hard at work on the painting (see Figure 20.2).

He is also communicating with it as its first beholder. Here we have a condensed image of a problem Kris (1952, p. 254) addresses. "Aesthetic creation," he states, "is aimed at an audience," and he actually defines as aesthetic *only* those self-expressions that do communicate. Here again, as with Freud, Kris does not mean – reductionistically – that a work's content, separated from its form, communicates. On the contrary, he understands "communication" to mean far more than what he takes to be the "prior intent" of the artist. Rather, communication consists in "the re-creation by the audience" of the artist's work. Expressing it this way, Kris comes close to the ideas of two American philosophers who were contemporaries of his, John Dewey (1934) and Susanne Langer (1953), who likewise claim that works of art are best taken as mutual co-creations. Authentic responses to works of art according to these thinkers entail contributions of the observing self. Aesthetic experience is a collaborative, interactive adventure. For Kris, artists cannot be seen as active while audiences remain passive, but both parties must be seen as

*Figure 20.2    Artist in His Studio* by Rembrandt van Rijn, oil on panel, 1669
Source: © Museum of Fine Arts, Boston

active. In the example just given, the painter who remains motionless before his canvas should be understood as fully engaged and active, just as when he is when is daubing the canvas with a brush or mixing colors.

This idea matches a quintessential psychoanalytic tenet, namely, that the process of psycho-analytic treatment, the work of therapy, involves *partnership*. Two individuals engage, but they need not, and indeed they *cannot*, be engaged in precisely the same task, and silence is part of the work. Kris postulates a similarity between the processes of artist and audience: not an identity. Turning away from the artist's "prior intent" or inner conflicts, and away from any preexistent condition that must be unearthed, Kris implies that, for communication to occur, whatever was emotionally charged for a particular artist at the time of his work's creation need not be the same for his audience. Information about an artist's life and purposes may be, simply, irrelevant for our appreciation of a particular work. Emphasis shifts, on this model, from the hidden to the manifest. As Oscar Wilde (1891, p. ii) coyly writes, contemporaneous with Freud's early work on hysteria, "All art is at once surface and symbol. Those who go beneath the surface do so at their peril." What matters is what we can actually perceive *in the work itself* what it presents to us and how it resonates with whatever we bring to it in the moments of our interaction with it. An example that springs readily to mind is the oeuvre of Belgian surrealist René Magritte (1898–1967), whose images often seem highly charged and whose symbols are rich with meaning. When we come upon them, we may be moved to respond to them emotionally; yet, the actual occurrences in Magritte's own life, which caused him to create them, have no necessary connection with the particulars of our own lives (Spitz, 1994).[10]

Central to Kris's (1952) approach is the role played by ambiguity. He introduces his notion of the "potential of a symbol," which is "the obverse side of its over-determination" (1952, p. 255). In other words, symbols in works of art arise from a condensation of many psychic (and external) factors, some of which are unconscious, that is to say, either repressed or otherwise unknown to the artist. According to Kris, a potent symbol is potent not merely because of its genesis but because it wields the power to initiate a parallel process in its audience and to inspire a multiplicity of associations. Importantly, these two phenomena – the repressed matter within the artist and the repressed matter within any individual audience member – need not correspond. They are obviously never identical. What is crucial for Kris is that symbols with genuine aesthetic merit stimulate "primary process" thinking in the members of their audience. In other words, a valuable work of art puts viewers in contact with their own unconscious. This idea comes close to that of Freud's when he says that the work of art enables us to enjoy our own daydreams without self-reproach. For both Kris and Freud, art offers its audiences a safe domain in which boundaries may be crossed with minimal risk. Kris stresses that to function aesthetically the symbol must involve us in a shift from secondary (rational) to primary (intuitive) process.

Yet, this condition is necessary but not sufficient. We can easily imagine nonartistic situations (think of heated political arguments) that generate precipitous shifts from logic to irrationality, from serenity to intense feeling, with no accompanying aesthetic pleasure. As a corrective, Kris invokes the notion of psychic distance, familiar to philosophers as "aesthetic" distance or "disinterest" (Kant, 1790). Distance matters because, when form and latent content move too close, we find that we do not have art but something raw and crude: like pornography, propaganda or magic. To elaborate this point, the failure of aesthetic distance may turn works into fetishes that actually stimulate erotic or political acts rather than inspire contemplation.

Going beyond both Kant and Kris, the experience of aesthetic distance is historically and culturally (as well as personally) relative, however. One looks contemplatively today at nudes by Titian, Velasquez or Ingres, for example, just as one looks at Goya's *Executions of May Third* or at Picasso's *Guernica*, despite their manifestly erotic or violent subject matter. Their historical distance from us and their carefully crafted aesthetics and ambiguities invite a many-layered response rather than primitive acting out. When, on the other hand, form and latent content grow too remote, we tend to feel bored. Such work seems dry and dull and rarely attracts us; we are unable to participate and may simply withdraw. The most effective images avoid these twin pitfalls. They are able to effect changes in us both in terms of psychic level and distance. Redolent of ambiguity, they can be interpreted from within the context they themselves create. Therefore, the highest value or best chances for the survival of works of art belong to those works that, according to Kris, possess "as high a degree of interpretability [ambiguity] as is compatible with containing within themselves their own sources of integration (Freud, 1957, p. 264). I return your attention, if I may, to Rembrandt's *Polish Rider*, a work of art that admirably fulfills these criteria for longevity.

How can one highly condensed symbol take on new meaning depending on shifts in the context into which it is placed? One might think of art intended originally to be religious, such as a devotional image (an "*Ecce homo*," perhaps – an image of Christ crowned with thorns and displaying his wounds, intended to stimulate religious fervor and, pari passu, an image often highly effective in goading its viewers to perform acts of anti-Semitic violence). When removed from its church wall niche and placed in an art museum hundreds of miles away, such an image often sheds its spiritual aura, shifts from sacred to secular, but may achieve, by way of compensation, enhanced aesthetic, historical and documentary value. Still, as psychoanalysis would have us understand, vestiges of the repressed spiritual meaning continue to inhere, inducing an element of the uncanny.

Kris's original concept, "regression in the service of the ego," has fallen into disuse among contemporary psychoanalytic thinkers but it retains its heuristic value for students of art. It is a particularly useful notion with regard to the problematic link we have been considering between artistic activity and aesthetic and emotional response. Kris's idea involves the intermittent relaxation of the ego functions (such as thought, planning, control, and critical judgment) so as to permit access to the unconscious. He sees the artist not as prisoner of regressive forces within himself but as endowed with a strong observing ego and thus able, to some degree, to regulate the interplay and shifts among the psychic levels. Aesthetic creation, according to Kris, is largely purposive and controlled.

A small child's experiences with painting are relevant here. Kris suggests how at first a child may be thrilled by bright colors and by the viscous texture of the tempera medium and be motivated instinctually to smear and mess with it. Gradually, however, she becomes fascinated by what is actually happening on the paper itself. She looks at the marks she has made and focuses her attention on her growing ability to manipulate the brush. At this point in the process, instinctual energies are left behind, and the ego begins to function semi-autonomously. When this happens, the child has started to behave like a budding artist. She begins to plan what to do next. In clinical and developmental terms, Kris (1955, p. 37) writes, "as maturation proceeds, as the inner world grows, as new pleasures in fantasy and mastery become accessible, the structure of the activity itself influences the process of neutralization." This formulation is relevant to examples drawn from modern art: think of Josef Albers's exploration of color relationships, Piet Mondrian's concern with graphic structure and design, Jackson Pollock's performances of the elastic relations between freedom and order through the medium of calligraphic line. These activities require skill, technique and problem-solving – in short, functions of the ego.

An earlier contemporary of Freud who contributed to the dialogue on the relation between art and ego was Otto Rank (1932). Rank conceives of form as representing an "ego ideal." Artistic form embodies the human desire to transcend our given biological and social determinants, he explains. It reveals – in architecture especially – the attempt of human beings to gain control over aspects of the external environment (Spitz, 2012). At the same time, Rank analyzes recurring elements in aesthetic form by tracing them to biological sources. He derives the spiral, for example, which is a ubiquitous design, from the human intestines. Another highly perceptive psychoanalytic writer, Phyllis Greenacre (1971), writing about the childhood of artists, underscores Rank's interest in biological *Anlagen* by deriving the predisposition toward adult experiences in the arts from a heightened and broad-based sensuality in early childhood.

It is important before leaving the field of ego psychology to point out that a psychoanalytic approach, which depends *purely* upon the so-called autonomous functions of the ego, would suffer twin shortcomings. One is that it would remove itself from the wellsprings of psychoanalytic thought, which lie in notions of unconscious conflict and of fantasy derived from instinctual pleasures that struggle repetitively, ingeniously and valiantly against both internal and external resistances. The other is that exclusive preoccupation with form is too limiting.

Formal problems are often diverting, it is true, and their solutions fascinating, but not all form carries meaning. For a work of art to be truly great, there must be *content* in Freud's sense, that is to say, not merely perception but a reaching down into the depths of experience. Aristotle underscored this when he spoke of a catharsis of pity and fear, and perhaps the greatest artists of every age have known it. Although we can (and do) spend many profitable hours dwelling on form and technique in Rembrandt, Goya or Van Gogh, their works have survived because their content is nontrivial. They paint the deepest fears and wishes of mankind.

## The contributions of object relations theory

Prototypically developmental, the approach of object relations theory is well characterized by D. W. Winnicott's (1953) seminal paper on the transitional object. Winnicott takes a baby's special blanket or soft toy animal as precursor of eventual adult investment in cultural objects of many kinds, including works of art. Winnicott regards this baby blanket as transitional in several senses: it is a step along the way to full symbolization; it is transitional in that any questions as to whether its soothing properties are inherent or created by the baby herself remain labile; and it represents a developmental marker between total dependence and relative independence, an independence that accrues from the internalization of an ego-supportive environment. Thus, a child's attachment to a transitional object betokens the fact that he or she is well on the way toward internalization. Winnicott sees such attachments as normal and healthy and claims that their highly personal significance is a function of whatever reciprocal cues are developing in the parent-child relationship. From such attachments, Winnicott derives not only an individual's capacity to invest in cultural objects and experiences of all kinds but also to forge creative links between inner and outer worlds. Like Freud, he cites – with great respect – children's imaginative play and claims that it forms a bridge between infantile illusion or fantasy and aesthetic experiences in adulthood, a line of thought pursued also by Greenacre (1971) in her work on the childhood of the artist.

Winnicott stresses that the question we must never ask a child about her teddy bear or blanket is: did you *make* this object or did you *find* it? This is because, like an artist's, a child's experience includes both of these modes. Instead of intruding with our rationalism, we should be knowingly complicit in the transformation of a ragged blanket or scruffy toy into a supremely valued object. Taking this, then, as paradigmatic of our relationships to works of art, we can see how a radical separation of form from content would destroy a work *as art* and annul an experience *as aesthetic*. This is so because such a separation would entail moving outside the experience in such a way as to reduce the experience to something less or other than what it is. An analogy to the psychoanalytic situation seems apt. The psychoanalyst operates within boundaries given by a developing dialogue that takes place between two individuals. Ideally he does not interrupt this privileged space-time to introduce material from outside or to judge the emerging material on grounds imported from elsewhere. The treatment, therefore, seen in this Winnicottian light, resembles a field of play; like a work of art, it comes gradually into being over time during an enactment.

A distinctive feature of Winnicott's theory is that, whereas Freud concerns himself almost exclusively with intrapsychic processes, Winnicott posits a third area of experience, an "intermediate space," he calls it, in which inner and outer, fantasy and reality, are mingled. He is thus alive to the "thing-ness" of the art object. Transitional phenomena differ from dreams and daydreams in that they are not purely mental constructs. Transitional objects have palpable representation and existence in the external world. They cannot, therefore – as is true likewise of the materials, instruments, and tools used by artists – be entirely controlled; as mothers know to their chagrin, blankets and toys are frequently lost. With respect to a working artist, Winnicott implicitly reminds us that, whatever conflicts and secret desires she may have, an artist must cope in her studio with the recalcitrance of paint or stone, with the vagaries of her computer or with the technicalities of her not always cooperative photographic equipment.

As has been noted, there is a clear interdependence among the various modes of aesthetic experience. Philosophers interested in understanding and describing this have sometimes spoken of experiencing an artwork from within and from without. Most of us do, in fact, when visiting an art gallery, alternate between full absorption in the art and a return to a clear consciousness of self. The "aesthetic distance" between any composition and ourselves varies as we experience it. What does psychoanalysis have to offer by way of explanation of the most privileged of such moments when we find ourselves fully transported "within" a work of art, fused with it, and the illusion becomes real? When we dwell momentarily within its aura of magic and power?

Such moments are characterized by a deep rapport of subject and object – a state in which, as psychoanalyst Christopher Bollas (1993, p. 40) notes, "*the subject feels captured in a reverential moment with an aesthetic object*" – held by a "spell which holds self and other in symmetry and solitude [in which] time crystallizes into space [and we experience] the uncanny pleasure of being *held* by a poem, a composition, a painting [emphasis mine]" (Winnicott, 1953). This description returns us to Winnicott, who has described what he calls a "holding environment," which parents create again and again for their children. A work of art, similarly, may elicit states of absorption and embrace for its listeners, beholders or readers. And/or it may push us away.

Then, it may open its arms again for another embrace. What psychoanalysis offers, through the work also of Margaret S. Mahler (1968) on "separation–individuation," is a developmental model that can help explain the power of such experiences and how they exert their long-lasting influence on us.

## Concluding thoughts

Published work on psychoanalysis and art has long relied on Freudian texts, and among Freud's many papers there are several that deserve special mention. *Family Romances* of 1909 offers richly nuanced suggestions about artists' desires for idealization and their counterintuitive needs for devaluation. This essay enriches our notions about symbolism by showing how the present and past mutually revise one another in terms of the imagery we simultaneously remember and invent. *Leonardo da Vinci and a Memory of His Childhood* of 1910 is arguably Freud's most famous paper on art, and, despite its errors and inaccuracies, it continues to enthrall readers and to spawn a vast literature of responses, with more no doubt to come.[11] "'Wild' Psycho-Analysis" of 1910 cautions authors lest they jump too quickly to (erroneous) conclusions, while *Formulations on the Two Principles of Mental Functioning* divides the field into primary and secondary functioning, pleasure and reality, innovation and repetition, all of which have important roles to play in any serious consideration of the formal elements in visual art. *Mourning and Melancholia* of 1917 and *The Uncanny* of 1919 are brilliant essays especially helpful for interpreting the work of artists who dwell in trauma, tragedy and mystery. *The Note Upon "The Mystic Writing Pad"* offers metaphors for creative mental processes and for the structure of various works, such as do *Fetishism* of 1927 and *The Splitting of the Ego in the Process of Defense* of 1940. In short, it is not simply the papers Freud wrote directly about art that can prove useful but the larger corpus of his work where, sometimes in unexpected nooks, he offers stunning insights as he struggles to define concepts that may help us grapple with the emergent art forms of our 21st century as well as the art of the past.

The finest interdisciplinary dialogues between psychoanalysis and art – because there is no clinical agenda – assiduously avoid the diagnosis of artists. Such dialogues grasp the force of the wry comment, attributed to Isaac Bashevis Singer, that "in art, truth that is boring is not true." They seek, in parallel with their subject, to draw closer to the fount from which imagination springs. They search for intuitive feelings of rightness and never pretend to final solutions.

They trade in high degrees of both candor and suspicion (Gay, 1976). They know that memory and desire are connected and forbear to privilege reason over unreason or vice versa. They emphasize the reality of meanings and espouse the truth that meanings, like events, reverberate throughout history – both personal history and history on a more global scale. They model the importance of studying these meanings as they circulate, collide with and supersede one another. They enable us to see how it is that we ourselves, in studying these meanings – through art and through psychoanalysis – take part in altering them. When psychoanalytic interpretations adhere to works of art and become internalized, as it were, the works themselves seem to morph, and our aesthetic experience with them modulates as well. The finest endeavors of this kind, when all is said and done, not only illuminate and the change the objects of their study but teach us to grow, inspire us and, like art itself, turn us as individuals back to our own lives reanimated, expectant and renewed.

I wish to close by saying that psychoanalysts who have ventured into other disciplines have, unfortunately, proven themselves guilty, in many cases, of cavalier treatment of those disciplines, just as authors outside the psychoanalytic orbit have, correspondingly, used psychoanalytic ideas and methods without understanding them well enough. I use the expression "well enough" to conjure precisely the referent that this phrase is meant to evoke for a psychoanalytically informed reader. I refer, of course, to Winnicott's notion of the "good-enough mother." Winnicott, in fact, was notoriously suggestive rather than crystalline in his formulations, and he never did specify precisely what he meant by the "good-enough mother." However, just as Justice Potter Stewart once said of pornography that, although he could not define it, he certainly knew it when he saw it; likewise, in this context, understanding another's field "well enough" may not lend itself readily to clear definition, but it is surely palpable in the pages of interdisciplinary writing. And when this "good-enough" engagement is lacking, the published results are catastrophic for psychoanalysis. In such unfortunate cases, potentially interested independent writers, academics and practitioners in other fields feel understandably alienated and fail to benefit from wondrous potential insights. Meanwhile, psychoanalysts remain in the dark as to the complex (and, in the present instance of the visual arts, predominantly nonverbal) factors that impinge on their own field.

It remains to return to our redoubtable *Polish Rider*, who, within his elegant frame at the Frick, continues to trot along toward some unknown destination. My foregoing discussion seems not to have perturbed him! As stated at the outset, while I cannot claim that psychoanalysis holds full power to illuminate the sway this picture exercised over me as an undergraduate, I nevertheless feel great pleasure and satisfaction in the many rich ways it has given me to approach that question. Above all, psychoanalysis honors questions such as mine, and it does so by teaching us to question ourselves, to search for truth about our hidden desires, to confront our unwelcome conflicts of wish, fear, and aggression, to attend to our cacophonous and contradictory developmental passages through life[12] and our relational[13] polyphonies (to turn momentarily here from visual art to music). Psychoanalysis spurs us on to keep such inquiries alive. The *Polish Rider* seems an apt metaphor for that quest, a great and necessary one, quintessentially and indispensably human.

## Notes

1 See Ellen Handler Spitz, "Warrant to Trespass/Permission to Peer," *Art Bulletin*, vol. 77, no. 4, 1995.
2 In the pages that follow, I draw from discussions to be found in my book, *Art and Psyche*, New Haven: Yale University Press, 1985; I also draw on my prior discussion of these issues in *The Textbook of Psychoanalysis*, 2nd edition [ed. Glen O. Gabbard, B. E. Litowitz, and P. Williams] Washington and London: American Psychiatric Publishing, 2012, pp. 523–535.
3 Leo Steinberg, it is interesting to note, was undergoing psychoanalysis during this period. See also, Ellen Handler Spitz, http://www.artcritical.com/2011/09/24/leo-steinberg/
4 Recently, apropos, a student of mine whose father had been violent and abusive for many years wrote an astonishing essay on Hans Christian Andersen's "The Little Match Girl," in which she focused on the fact that, starving and freezing in the cold of winter, that little girl *could not go home.* Beyond all else, my student wrote, the inability of this child to go home constituted the most abject horror of the tale: Hans Christian Andersen had crystallized the centrifugal theme of her own childhood. Never, she exclaimed, would she let a child of hers feel this way.
5 Maya Lin's 1982 Vietnam Veterans Memorial, Washington, D.C., receives approximately 2.4 million visitors per year. http://www.searchinq.com/webresults?q=Veterans%20Statistics&an=1
6 See the first of Freud's "Clark Lectures" of 1910 on the origin and development of psychoanalysis.
7 See Freud's letter to Stephan Zweig on September 7, 1931.
8 See, for example, Fred Wilson: *Guarded View*, 1991, the Whitney Museum of American Art, a work that addresses the role of race in American art museum settings.
9 See E. H. Spitz, "Kris-Crossing," in *The Brooklyn Rail: Critical Perspectives on Arts, Politics, and Culture*, June 2014. http://www.brooklynrail.org/2014/06/criticspage/kris-crossing
10 See also E. H. Spitz, *Magritte's Labyrinth*, Argo Navis: William Morris Enterprises, 2015, (eBook).
11 One fascinating, easily overlooked essay on this paper of Freud's is by Alan Bass, "On the History of a Mistranslation and the Psychoanalytic Movement," in *Difference in Translation* [ed. Joseph F. Graham], Ithaca and London, Cornell University Press, 1985, pp. 102–141.
12 For work on stages of human development throughout the life cycle, see the writings of Erik H. Erikson (1902–1994).
13 For perspectives on relational psychoanalysis, see Stephen A. Mitchell, *Relationality: From Attachment to Intersubjectivity*, New York: Routledge, 2003.

## References

Bergstein, M 2010, *Mirrors of memory*, Cornell University Press, Ithaca, NY.
Bollas, C 1993, *The aesthetic moment and the search for transformation. Transitional objects and potential spaces: Literary uses of DW Winnicott*, pp. 40–49.
Breuer, J & Freud, S 1891, *Studies on hysteria*, Basic Books, London.
Dewey, J 1934, *Art as experience*, Paragon Books, New York.
Freud, A 1936, *The ego and the id*, International Universities Press, New York.
Freud, S 1908, 'Creative writers and daydreaming', in J Strachey (ed), *Standard edition of the complete psychological works of Sigmund Freud*, vol. 9, Hogarth, London, pp. 142–153.
Freud, S 1914, *The Moses of Michelangelo*, Hogarth Press, London.
Freud, S 1955, 'Two encyclopedia articles: (A) psychoanalysis', in J Strachey (ed), *Standard edition of the complete psychological works of Sigmund Freud*, vol. 18, Hogarth, London, pp. 235–254.
Freud, S 1957, 'Clark lectures' and 'Five lectures on psychoanalysis', in J Strachey (ed), *Standard edition of the complete psychological works of Sigmund Freud*, vol. 11, Hogarth, London, pp. 9–55.
Freud, S 1958, 'Formulations on two principles of mental functioning', in J Strachey (ed), *Standard edition of the complete psychological works of Sigmund Freud*, vol. 12, Hogarth, London.
Gay, P 1976, *Art and act: On causes in history: Monet, Gropius, Mondrian*, Harper and Row, New York.
Greenacre, P 1971, *Emotional growth: Psychoanalytic studies of the gifted and a great variety of other individuals*, vol. 2, International Universities Press, New York, pp. 479–504.
Held, J 1991, *Rembrandt studies*, Princeton University Press, Princeton, NJ.
Iverson, M 2007, *Beyond pleasure: Freud, Lacan, Barthes*, Pennsylvania State University Press, University Park.
Kant, I 1790, *The critique of judgment*, Macmillan, London.
Kris, E 1952, *Psychoanalytic explorations in art*, International Universities Press, New York.
Kris, E 1955, 'Neutralization and sublimation', *Psychoanalytic Study of the Child*, vol. 10, pp. 30–46.

Langer, S 1953, *Feeling and form*, Charles Scribner's Sons, New York.

Mahler, M 1968, *On human symbiosis and the vicissitudes of individuation*, International Universities Press, New York.

Mannoni, O 1969, *Clefs pour i'imaginaire*, Seuil, Paris.

Rank, O 1932, *Art and artist*, Knopf, New York.

Spitz, EH 1985, *Art and psyche*, Yale University Press, New Haven.

Spitz, EH 1994, *Museums of the mind: Magritte's Labyrinth and other essays*, Yale University Press, New Haven.

Spitz, EH 2012, 'Primary architecture and towers of books: Reflections on space and self in childhood', in E Danze & S Sonnenberg (eds), *Center 17: Space & psyche*, Center for American Architecture and Design, Austin, TX, pp. 168–181.

Tolstoy, L 1899, *What is art?* (A Maude, trans), Crowell, Springfield.

Wilde, O 1891, 'Foreword', in *The picture of Dorian Gray*, Bernhard Tauchnitz, Leipzig, pp. i–iv.

Winnicott, D 1953, 'Transitional objects and transitional phenomena', *International Journal of Psychoanalysis*, vol. 34, pp. 89–97.

Winnicott, D 1987, *Through paediatrics to psycho-analysis*, Hogarth Press, London (originally published 1958).

# 21

# Law and psychoanalysis

## *David Caudill*

Over 25 years ago, when I was a practicing attorney in a large law firm in Austin, Texas, I gave a paper on "Freud and Law" at a political science conference in Houston. My law firm regularly published a newsletter to highlight its members' accomplishments, and solicited from its lawyers any newsworthy items. After I submitted the news of my paper, it was announced in the next newsletter that I had given a presentation on "Fraud and Law" – the editor having corrected a seeming typographical error on my part, since it was unlikely that Freud had anything to do with the practice of law.

Among those more familiar with the Freudian tradition, the identification of a field of law and psychoanalysis, or "psychoanalytic jurisprudence," probably raises the image of a psychoanalyst testifying in a criminal trial as an expert witness on insanity. For several reasons, that image has passed into history, as recently explained by a US federal judge:

> In the case of certain kinds of purportedly scientific evidence, courts have sometimes proved quite credulous. A well-known case involves psychoanalytic evidence. In the middle of the twentieth century, American courts were persuaded that psychiatric evidence – which at that time leaned heavily on psychoanalytic theory – had reached a level of scientific certainty sufficient to warrant its admissibility and use in a wide range of cases. This mirrored a growing acceptance of psychoanalysis and psychiatry in the academy, and in "enlightened" society as a whole.
>
> *(Rakoff, 2008, pp. 1386–95)*

That assessment – psychoanalytic evidence, "purportedly scientific," was previously admitted into court by "credulous" judges – reflects contemporary attitudes toward psychoanalysis in US legal contexts. Just as the Freudian tradition has not fared well in the academy or in "enlightened" society as a whole, psychoanalytic evidence does not generally meet the standards for admissibility of scientific expertise. A biological model of the mind has replaced notions of unconscious motives or repressed memories of abuse, both in the academy and in among qualified medical experts. The long-running debate over the scientific status or "validity" of psychoanalysis was, in simplistic terms, won by Freud's critics.

However, a more measured assessment, by a leading evidence scholar, makes some valuable distinctions. Suppose, Professor Imwinkelried writes, that in a psychiatric malpractice case, the plaintiff alleged that the defendant psychiatrist was negligent in using psychoanalytic techniques to diagnose and treat the plaintiff. The defense calls Freud as a witness. Freud proposes testifying that his theories can be used effectively in treating disordered patients. Would that testimony necessarily lack "appropriate validation"?

*(Imwinkelried, 2003, p. 50)*

The issue in that hypothetical is not the controversial question of whether the plaintiff's symptoms were caused by childhood trauma, but whether psychoanalysis is sometimes effective in treating disorders; and

We now have the benefit of the extensive, collective experience of many therapists who have relied on psychoanalytic techniques and witnessed an improvement in the mental health of numerous patients. That experience should be adequate validation in the malpractice case.

*(Imwinkelried, 2003, pp. 50–51)*

Suppose, however, that in a rape case, the prosecutor calls the same psychiatrist to testify that the alleged victim's dreams indicate that she was raped (Imwinkelried, 2003, p. 50).

Now Freud is being invited to draw a different inference . . . Even if the witness's other theories have been verified and other applications of dream theory have been validated, the judge would be entitled to bar this testimony absent a stronger foundation.

*(Imwinkelried, 2003, p. 51)*

The fact that Freud's testimony would be admissible in the malpractice example, because it "comported with a broad rationalist understanding" of validation, "would not mandate or justify [admitting] Freud's testimony about unsubstantiated theories that are nothing more than plausible hypotheses worthy of systematic scientific investigation" (Imwinkelried, 2003, p. 51).

In any event, while the utility of psychoanalytic expertise in the courtroom is quite limited, the scholarly tradition in law and psychoanalysis continues, primarily conceiving of psychoanalysis as a social theory, dealing with a "collective" unconscious (groups as the subject of psychoanalysis) rather than a clinical practice. Nevertheless, one should not conclude that psychoanalytic insights are limited to mere social *theory*, because many of the legal studies employing psychoanalytic theory are practical and address current issues in law. Moreover, psychoanalytic clinical conceptions and categories are drawn upon in social theory, typically by analogy.

In this chapter, I first focus on psychoanalytic jurisprudence as a philosophy of law, including the notion that Freud's corpus constitutes a theory of law. I also survey the uses of psychoanalytic insights in critical legal theory, interdisciplinary studies in law such as law-and-economics and political theory, and traditional Freudian legal thought. Then I explore practical studies in law and psychoanalysis that address contemporary legal doctrines and controversies. I briefly describe the appropriation of psychoanalysis by law and literature scholars. The following section discusses criticism of the law and psychoanalysis project. I conclude with some remarks about the future of psychoanalysis in law.

## Psychoanalytic jurisprudence: the philosophy of law

The term "jurisprudence" has multiple meanings. It can refer to a series of judicial decisions (e.g., the Supreme Court's free-speech jurisprudence), or the legal system or body of law of a particular country (e.g., French jurisprudence), but its primary referent is the philosophy of law – theoretical reflection on the nature of law and legal institutions.

Psychoanalytic jurisprudence, therefore, is best distinguished from the evidentiary uses (in court) of psychoanalytic clinical theory and practice. The latter came into the legal establishment in the 1930s and 1940s, because it became a dominant framework among psychologists and psychiatrists, and then left the legal establishment, roughly in the 1960s, because it was no longer dominant. Indirectly, of course, Freudian notions persist in the contemporary practice of psychotherapy, and therefore in law as well – and whether one wants to give Freud credit, or to hold that we would have discovered everything that is true in Freud without him, is beside the point. Direct appeals to Freud as an authority, or even to contemporary neo-Freudian scholarship, are generally speaking not going to work in the courtroom or hearing chamber. When a judge needs medical science, he or she needs either currently accepted (by most scientists in the field) views or scientifically based cutting-edge research, not controversial ideas. If the use of psychoanalytic experts at trial was ever called "psychoanalytic jurisprudence," the label is now available for other purposes.

It is therefore better to think of psychoanalytic jurisprudence as coexisting alongside analytic theory and practice, roughly since the publication in 1930 of Jerome Frank's *Law and the Modern Mind*. Frank integrated psychoanalytic theory into his realist critique of law, for example, by identifying the myth of law's coherence (reinforced unconsciously by lawyers) and the desire for social stability that finds rest in law's authority as a father figure. Such thinking culminated in the 1960s and early 1970s with the appearance of (1) Bienenfeld's lengthy "Prolegomena" (to an unfinished book), which reconsidered the significance of the Oedipus complex in law (Bienenfeld, 1965); (2) Goldstein's article entitled "Psychoanalysis and Jurisprudence" (Goldstein, 1968); and (3) Ehrenzweig's "psychosophy" of criminal law, torts and civil procedure (Ehrenzweig, 1971), but started to decline in confidence with C. G. Schoenfeld's *Psychoanalysis and the Law* (1973), when a certain modesty and defensiveness set in. All of these works are characterized by their use of psychoanalysis (including clinical terms and concepts) to explain how law works – how law gets into people's heads, how authority is projected onto law, how the law functions to create and/ or satisfy demands and desires and, most significantly, how many aspects of law are unconscious, repressed and irrational.

## Psychoanalysis as a legal theory

Rather than viewing the Freudian tradition as a set of concepts that can be borrowed and applied to legal issues, psychoanalysis can also be seen as the very basis for a comprehensive theory of law.

> The legalism of Freudian thought is nowhere more evident than in his interpretations of the origins of the social order in the transgression of the authority or law of the father. This well-known myth is elaborated in the story of Oedipus, the narrative of a son who kills his father and marries his mother. It is also elaborated in terms of the social anthropology of *Totem and Taboo*, the pre-historical story of the murder of a tribal father by jealous sons, which leads to the genesis of law.
>
> *(Goodrich, 1997b, p. 1035)*

A revival in psychoanalytic jurisprudence is nowadays evident, although a certain level of defensiveness persists. Peter Fitzpatrick, in *Modernism and the Grounds of Law* (2001), concedes the extravagance of beginning his study with Freud's "fantastic tale" (in *Totem and Taboo*) of the violent origins of social order in the primal horde and patricide. Freud's own ambiguity about whether his story was allegory or history was never settled, though the "anthropological evidence [he] used was scant and is now considered unsound" (Douzinas, 1998, p. 8). But for Fitzpatrick, historical accounts of the origins of law seem necessarily mythical; the attributes of law – stability and responsiveness to change – are always present before and after the alleged origin. For example, law is everywhere in Freud's story – in the father's power over the horde, in the possibilities that follow from the father's destruction, in the determinate order that becomes modern society and in the unlimited responsiveness of legal order to social change. Law is both constitutive of and constituted by culture.

Jacques Lacan, eschewing the historical controversy, chose "to turn Freud's story fully into a mythical structure and read it, [like] Lévi-Strauss's explanation of the elementary structures of kinship, as an attempt to give narrative epic form to the structure of subjectivity and the operation of desire" (Douzinas, 1998, p. 8). Law is therefore central to Lacan's account of the subject of psychoanalysis:

> The murdered and cannibalized primal father is a symbol of the subject's internalization of law, a necessary prerequisite for the development of socio-cultural identity . . .
>
> [P]sychoanalysis proves itself a legal theory, a discourse obsessed with the creation, internal organization and action of the law.
>
> *(Douzinas, 1998, p. 9)*

For Peter Goodrich, the Oedipal myth is likewise a representation or graphic illustration of (the force of) unconscious desire and violence, "which neither institutions nor subjects can fully understand or control" (Goodrich, 1997b, p. 1040). Psychoanalytic jurisprudence, in Goodrich's estimation,

> is not an external discipline that analysts "apply" to law, but rather it is intrinsic to an understanding of law as a cultural system of symbols, as well as a system of repression and an object of desire, particularly through its rites, ceremonies, and other images . . . [P]sychoanalysis not only suggests another dimension, or unconscious, of law . . . but also . . . implies that law is a species of mythology, an illusion or phantasm that fascinates and binds the subjects of the legal order. For this reason it merits an historical and theoretical analysis that looks beyond its merely surface and manifest authorities and reasons.
>
> *(Goodrich, 1997b, p. 1041)*

Both Goodrich and Costas Douzinas emphasize the emotional aspects of (1) obedience to law as well as (2) practicing law, and both see psychoanalytic theory as an "attempt to address and understand the affective dimensions of legality, in its aim of analyzing the forms of subjective attachment to law" (Douzinas, 1998, p. 1; Goodrich, 1997b, p. 1041). Thus Douzinas announced, in 1998, that psychoanalysis "and in particular its Lacanian revision, are fast becoming the latest great frontier of jurisprudence" (Douzinas, 1998, p. 2).

## Critical legal theory

To be sure, the tradition of appropriating psychoanalysis continues in legal theory, but only in a scattered fashion – there is no identifiable movement, journal, association or annual conference, and the occasional reference to Freud (or to some neo-Freudian school, such as object relations theory or self psychology) is far more common in legal scholarship than sustained reliance on psychoanalytic theory. One recent survey of the many interactions between law and psychology mentioned neither Freud nor psychoanalysis (Satin, 1994, p. 581). While it is not the purpose of this chapter to survey all appropriations of psychoanalysis in recent legal scholarship, examples do appear with regularity, albeit at the margins of mainstream law and psychology scholarship.

Critical legal scholarship, to the extent that it remains an identifiable category (that is, it has synthesized into critical race theory, radical feminist theory, and law and literature), sometimes employs psychoanalytic terminology. That phenomenon is not surprising, given that Frankfurt School neo-Marxism and French critical theory, which have inspired critical scholars in law, each betray psychoanalytic influences.

The "Law and the Post-Modern Mind" conference at Cardozo School of Law (Yeshiva University) in the fall of 1993 became a focal point, of sorts, for critical scholars interested in psychoanalysis. (Indeed, it must be said that Cardozo School of Law has become a de facto center for the study of law and psychoanalysis, with (1) numerous faculty members not merely interested in, but experts in, various psychoanalytic approaches, and (2) sponsorship of numerous "law and psychoanalysis" symposia drawing psychoanalytically oriented scholars from around the world). Derrida gave a keynote address at the conference about Jacques Lacan, and many of the conference papers were Lacanian or simply Freudian in orientation (Conference, 1995). Several of the papers from the conference were published in a volume entitled *Law and the Postmodern Mind: Essays on Psychoanalysis and Jurisprudence* (Carlson & Goodrich, 1998). Contributors included Slavoj Žižek, Renata Salecl, and Drucilla Cornell; and one of the chapters is a translation of an essay by Pierre Legendre ("The Other Dimension of Law"), a legal historian influenced by both Freud and Lacan.

A recent symposium issue of *Legal Studies Forum* on the future of psychoanalytic jurisprudence is also representative of the ongoing discourse about the critical potential of psychoanalysis in law, a discourse that is influenced if not always dominated by the work of Lacan (Symposium, 1997). Contributors to that symposium attempted to create, within the psychoanalytic tradition, a point of leverage for critical legal scholarship. For example, Peter Goodrich's introduction to the work of Pierre Legendre is also an introduction to one style or form of contemporary psychoanalytic jurisprudence. In his contribution to the *Legal Studies Forum* symposium (entitled "The Unconscious is a Jurist: Psychoanalysis and Law in the Work of Pierre Legendre"), Goodrich acknowledged the influence of Pierre Legendre on his own work, and described Legendre's compelling conception of psychoanalytic jurisprudence (Symposium, 1997, pp. 195–228). Legendre reads the institution of law, in its early texts, as if it were a subject – with an unconscious, with a body exhibiting symptoms of madness and, most importantly, with the capacity to capture other subjects.

> [Legendre's] psychoanalytical jurisprudence is a theory of law which seeks to understand the legal order as the structural mechanism or social form of reproduction of subjects. Law, for Legendre, is intrinsic to the formation of the individual subject, and law is both historically and theoretically at the center of the symbolic order in relation to which individual identity is formed.
>
> *(Symposium, 1997, pp. 199–200)*

Goodrich's introduction to Legendre is part of a larger English translation project that culminated in the publication of *Law and the Unconscious: A Legendre Reader* (1997).

Legendre's methodology is exemplified in his own *Legal Studies Forum* article (translated by Peter Goodrich) on the sacraments (entitled "*Id Efficit, Quod Figurat: The Social Constitution of Speech and the Development of the Normative Effect of Images*"), which sends readers to theological discourse in the 12th and 13th centuries in search of the founding images of contemporary law (Symposium, 1997, pp. 247–263). In that era of religious authority (but also lively theological debate), not scientific or secular-legal authority, we can observe the unconscious dimension of representation, figuration, ritual and staging that persists but is nowadays denied – we resist the uncomfortable knowledge of how discursive, indeed religious, the foundations of our social institutions are.

> Understood . . . as a progressively secularized universal symbolic order, the contemporary managerial and rationalist forms of institution of images, the social status of scientific knowledge and the ideology of self-foundation so successfully promoted in the twentieth century, would all be understood as the products of this a-genealogical theology that sprung from the medieval interpretative [r]evolution.
>
> *(Symposium, 1997, p. 263)*

For both Legendre and Goodrich, the contemporary institution-of-law's unconscious – that which has been repressed, denied, exiled or forgotten – is revealed in historical analyses. In Goodrich's assessment, Pierre Legendre

> has resolutely applied a Freudian model of analysis to the history and the theory of law. His project can be depicted most directly in legal historical terms as that of recovering a repressed poetics of law . . . To the [Lacanian] observation that language is the inescapable symbolic structure into which each subject is born, Legendre adds that in the west we are the inhabitants of a very specific material form or body of language, the text or written reason of law. [Legendre] thus refers us to the foundational structure, the symbolic form and scriptural identity of Western institutions.
>
> *(Symposium, 1997, pp. 198, 201–202)*

The notion of law as *text*, establishing legitimate authority, is not new, but in socio-psychoanalytic terms Legendre argues that the text of law

> establishes our social identity and institutional place, [and] provides us with our jurisdiction or right of speech . . . [I]t is the text in which we are born and in which we die, or in classical legal terms, Rome – a Text, a system of law – is our common homeland (*Roma communis nostra patria est*).
>
> *(Symposium, 1997, p. 202)*

For example, Roman law gave absolute power to the father of a *private* household, which reflected the *public* legal power of the emperor, who spoke the law, which in turn reflected (or represented) the power of the *divine* father:

> To legislate or speak the law was to take up a position in relation to a complex, textually-defined order of precedence and of the names of the law. In substantive terms, it was to find a place and role, an identity and image, within the inscribed or textual order of power. To state the law was literally to speak "in the name of the father," whether that father was God, the emperor, the sovereign, the People, or the head of the family. To take up the textually, and so also legally, defined position of the father is to adopt an image or role, to speak "as the law."
>
> *(Symposium, 1997, p. 203)*

As to lawyers, they function, in Legendre's account, *unconsciously* as mere instruments or voices of the law, of an authority (or "paternity") external to themselves – they count "for nothing in the

David Caudill

epiphany of law," and are dependable "precisely because they silence themselves" (Symposium, 1997, p. 221, quoting and translating Legendre, *Paroles poétiques échappées du texte: Leçons sur la communication industrielle* (1982)):

> In Legendre's terms it is the principal symbolic function of law precisely to maintain or keep open the blank space of the social unconscious against which a culture can maintain its myths and preserve its relation to poetry, art and justice, fate or Law. The lawyer deals unwittingly with Law and yet the role of the lawyer is intrinsic to the maintenance of the symbolic structures of social life.
>
> *(Symposium, 1997, p. 221)*

Goodrich's own *Oedipus Lex: Psychoanalysis, History, Law* (1995) also described a psychoanalytic methodology for interpreting the history and texts of legal institutions, which effort was exemplified in *Law in the Courts of Love: Literature and Other Minor Jurisprudences* (1996), where Goodrich identified certain repressed and forgotten episodes, images, and texts of the common law. Specifically, Goodrich shows how early (16th- to 17th-century) images of law as unitary, ancient, and rational eclipsed and exiled other images – the foreign, the feminine, the plural – and therefore other "jurisdictions."

Renata Salecl's article in the *Legal Studies Forum* symposium (entitled "Love Me, Love My Dog") recounts the Russian artist Oleg Kulik's performance as a dog at European art shows, which act included barking at and biting visitors (Symposium, 1997, pp. 266–276). While this may seem an unlikely touchstone for psychoanalytic jurisprudence, Salecl manages to reveal certain assumptions of "deep ecology" with reference to Freudian, and particularly Lacanian, themes concerning human enjoyment of suffering, human losses upon entrance into language, human dilemmas about desire (as in hysteria) and the unique burdens of the human subject in addressing, needing and finding himself or herself in the Other. (That notion in Lacanian theory, the "Other," is only mentioned in passing by Salecl, but deserves attention in any discussion of psychoanalytic jurisprudence conceived as an attempt to reveal law's unconscious. The term is notoriously ambiguous in Lacan's seminars and among his commentators, but variously refers to the unconscious, or the collective unconscious, and to the place where we find ourselves – in the mother, in the law of the father, and in the conventions of language, family, school, workplace, relationships and society, including the institutions and processes of law. To name those things "unconscious" is to interiorize them, in the subject, and to deny any space between identity ("self") and the Other.)

Several more Lacanian notions were explicated in some detail in the contribution to the *Legal Studies Forum* symposium by criminologist Dragan Milovanovic (entitled "'Rebellious Lawyering': Lacan, Chaos, and the Development of Alternative Juridico-Semiotic Forms"), who works within distinctively Lacanian frameworks (e.g., Schema R, the Borromean Knot, and various Lacanian mathemes or algorithms). Milovanovic wrote the first book on Lacan and law, *Postmodern Law and Disorder* (1992), and is known for his synthesis of Lacan's work and chaos theory. In his symposium essay, Milovanovic argues for alternative discourses in law and against dominant discursive structures (Symposium, 1997, pp. 295–319), and offers a complex psychoanalytic justification of Gerald Lopez's *Rebellious Lawyering: One Chicano's Vision of Progressive Law Practice* (1982) with reference to Lacan's three orders of being (Real, Symbolic, Imaginary), legal semiotics, Paulo Freire's dialogical pedagogy, and various chaos diagrams.

The *Legal Studies Forum* symposium concluded with a review essay (entitled "Psychoanalysis Becomes the Law") by Douzinas (Symposium, 1997, pp. 323–336), who reflects on the future of psychoanalytic jurisprudence with reference to Peter Goodrich's *Oedipus Lex: Psychoanalysis, History, Law* (1995), Jeanne Schroeder's *The Vestal and the Fasces: Psychoanalytical and Philosophical Perspective on the Feminine and Property* (1995) and my own *Lacan and the Subject of Law: Toward a Psychoanalytic Critical Legal Theory* (1997). Against a "background of misunderstanding and missed opportunities," Douzinas sees an emerging field of legal scholarship concerned with how the

> unconscious and desire both create and disrupt consciousness and subjectivity and, as a result, [how] the understanding of human experience, action and meaning always involves "another scene" and demands a "double reading" of the causes and effects of "free will."
>
> *(Symposium, 1997, pp. 323, 325)*

The review essay critically categorizes the three books, recognizing one as a prolegomena, a second as developing a "regional" theory with critical potential, and the third as exemplifying the promise of ethical critique in the field of law and psychoanalysis.

Douzinas identifies *Lacan and the Subject of Law* as "the first sustained attempt to bring together psychoanalysis and legal theory," by applying a Lacanian framework to explore such varied topics as contract interpretation disputes and judicial gap-filling measures, false child abuse accusations and their roots in social hysteria, the assumed (autonomous, Cartesian) subject of law, and the controversy over religious influence in politics (Symposium, 1997, pp. 325–328). And while the book presents "the best possible case for a Lacanian legal theory," it is "not yet a psychoanalytic legal theory" (Symposium, 1997, pp. 325–328):

> Undoubtedly, this is the most accomplished attempt to date to present psychoanalytical theory to a legal audience. It draws out and emphasizes its legally relevant aspects and proceeds to apply psychoanalytical themes to an array of legal issues and areas. But . . . is it just a series of engagements between the two fields? . . . In Lacan's terms, it constitutes the "prolegomena" to or the clearing of the ground for the creation of such a theory which is still to come.
>
> *(Symposium, 1997, pp. 327–329)*

Jeanne Schroeder's *The Vestal and the Fasces* is, in contrast, "one such attempt to develop a regional psychoanalytical theory" (Symposium, 1997, p. 329):

> Schroeder [imaginatively] combines Hegelian property theory and Lacanian psychoanalysis and discovers a fundamental homology in their method and ontology. Property (the fasces) and the feminine (the vestal) are objects of exchange between subjects which lead to the constitution of "subjectivity as intersubjectivity through the mediation of objectivity."
>
> *(Symposium, 1997, p. 329)*

Schroeder then transitions from jurisprudence to a critical mode, placing Lacan's "surprising and controversial (many would say misogynistic) statement" that "woman does not exist" at the center of her analysis of the feminine as a metaphor for the phallus (Symposium, 1997, p. 331).

Douzinas acknowledges the power of psychoanalysis for critique, but also identifies the need for reconstruction, "which has always meant putting injustice to work on the passions in order to address the inadequacies of the institution and the traumas of the social bond" (Symposium, 1997, p. 333). That is the goal of Goodrich's *Oedipus Lex*, where the

> whole argument is predicated on the assertion that the body politic or legal can be compared with the human subject and can legitimately, albeit metaphorically, be endowed with a social or legal unconscious. The stories of foundation of Western law are predicated on the banning or destroying of idols, images of other laws, and of different, plural and feminine jurisdictions.
>
> *(Symposium, 1997, p. 334)*

Coming to terms with the unconscious should "signify a return of justice to law and a revitalization of its ethical component" (Symposium, 1997, p. 336). Psychoanalysis, for Douzinas,

> eschews general laws and categorical principles in favour of listening to the voice of the Other and giving her full and uninterrupted attention, which however can only proceed from the affects, emotions and traumas of the listening self. It is in this sense that psychoanalysis is an ethical practice.
>
> *(Symposium, 1997, p. 336)*

The psychoanalytic intervention into critical legal studies is here conceived not as a set of critical, hermeneutical tools, but as offering social therapy, paying attention to the history of law's injustices and the (repressed, unconscious) structures that maintain oppression of the "other" in contemporary culture.

More recently, Jeanne Schroeder published *The Four Lacanian Discourses, Or Turning Law Inside Out* (2008), in which she argues that law includes all four discourses: two discourses of (masculine) power (the Master discourse, exemplified by H.L.A. Hart's positivist concept of law; and the University discourse, reflecting the power to manipulate and coerce subjects to achieve society's ends), and two critical (feminine) discourses (the Analyst's discourse, the inverse of the Master discourse; and the Hysteric's discourse). Schroeder explores the Analyst's discourse in the activities of legal interpretation and counseling clients, wherein the Master discourse is "turned inside out" in acknowledgment of the uncertainty of the symbolic, and she adopts the Hysteric's discourse, submitting positive law to moral critique and locating the feminine *supplement* (characterized by acceptance of contradictions) to the masculine (characterized by denial or attempts to resolve contradictions).

## Interdisciplinary variations: economics and political theory

In 2004, Schroeder published *Triumph of Venus: The Erotics of the Market*, a psychoanalytic critique of the law-and-economics movement, which is dominant in legal academia, but also a critique of its romantic critics. Using Lacan's analytical framework (and Hegelian philosophy), Schroeder challenges the scientific status of law-and-economics, argues that reason and passion are not inalterably opposed, and reveals the deeply repressed, erotic nature of law and markets.

If Schroeder engages law and economics by way of psychoanalytic theory, Juliet Rogers engages law and politics using the same orientation, in order to address the production of the liberal subject (Rogers, 2007). She questions whether psychoanalysis can or should be used to discern "a universal psyche or the psyche of all":

> The psychoanalytic subject, far from being universal, can be seen as [culturally] specific to the West insofar as the concerns of Freud, his peers and inheritors, articulate the political discourse emerging in the 18th century in Europe. Psychoanalysis' fundamental texts mirror

western concerns with the relation of the subject to the sovereign, or the individual to its freedom before an imagined aggressive, decision making, and potentially persecuting Other. Psychoanalytic concerns thus parallel, and arguably contribute to, the production of the liberal subject wrangling with its autonomy qua freedom in the West.

*(Rogers, 2007, pp. 176–177)*

Lacan's notion of the Other is here not the figure of law but "the fantasised sovereign that . . . plagues the liberal subject's desire and thus its capacity to perform as desirable, or, in the terms of the democratic body politic, as free" (Rogers, 2007, pp. 152–154). The subject anxiously seeks freedom of contract, freedom of speech, and other legal rights in the face of "the reality that we do not know what the sovereign will want tomorrow," rendering the law (that is loved) "flighty, fickle and without regular and enduring desire" (Rogers, 2007, pp. 176–177). Rogers offers an example of popular dissent in Australia, in which a "performance as 'free speech' is the fantasy of securing freedom before the castrating, abandoning and sometimes very unloving sovereign" (Rogers, 2007, pp. 152–154).

In the foregoing discussion, a particular model of psychoanalytic jurisprudence is at issue. The recurrent themes include Lacan's revision of Freud; the turn in legal scholarship to hermeneutics, semiotics, linguistics, and narrative/discourse theory; the identification of law's unconscious operations, functions and guiding images, both in the individual and in society, both historically and in contemporary institutions; and, most importantly, the search for a critical position – for ethics, justice, diversity – between the failures of mainstream jurisprudence and the perceived excesses of postmodern theory. That orientation is, for these critical psychoanalytic legal theorists, both theoretical *and* practical, social *and* individual, Freudian *and* (yet) highly revisionist, and legal *and* interdisciplinary.

## Traditional Freudian approaches

There are other models oriented to more traditional Freudian categories or to particular schools of neo-Freudian theory and practice). For example, law professor Anne Dailey recently served as guest editor for *American Imago*, and devoted an issue of that journal to reflection about the relationship between psychoanalysis and law (Special Issue, 2007). Dailey identified the "high water mark" of law and psychoanalysis scholarship in the 1960s, reflecting the influence of Freud on psychiatry and psychology, but also conceded a degree of overreaching because so much legal thought is incompatible with the notion of the unconscious and the legal subject's lack of control (Special Issue, 2007, pp. 291–295). Nevertheless, Dailey anticipates a new generation of scholars employing a more nuanced and modest psychoanalytic orientation, and offers the contributions to the special issue of *American Imago* as exemplary.

Amy Adler's essay, entitled "Symptomatic Cases: Hysteria in the Supreme Court's Nude Dancing Decisions," highlighted the Court's discomfort in analyzing striptease as free speech (Special Issue, 2007, pp. 297–316). The justices' worries were symptomatic of fantasies and anxieties about female sexuality, and their judicial narratives can be seen as (neo-Freudian) case studies on hysteria, thus challenging the presumed rationality and objectivity of law.

Susan Schmeiser's essay, "Punishing Guilt," explores the resistance to psychoanalytic insights in the criminal law – for example, guilt in psychic life and the desire for punishment should be relevant to adjudication of culpability (Special Issue, 2007, pp. 317–337). Such resistance is understandable, however, in light of psychoanalysis's implied challenge to the legitimacy of many established legal practices, including the primacy of punitive regulation of antisocial behavior.

Nomi Maya Stolzenberg, in "Anti-Anxiety Law: Winnicott and the Legal Fiction of Paternity," sees similarities between Winnicott's good-enough mother and the "close-enough" understanding of legal facts, as both acknowledge that perfection is unattainable and that we need to rely on probabilities (Special Issue, 2007, pp. 339–379). A child's stabilizing illusions concerning reality, suppressing anxiety in a matrix of belief, are analogous to legal fictions, such as the fiction of legitimacy when a child is born to a married couple, irrespective of biological facts, to avoid uncertainties.

Adam Sitze reverses the premise that law and psychoanalysis studies concern the application of psychoanalytic insights in legal settings; in "The Question of Law Analysis," Sitze uses law to illumine and overcome a weakness psychoanalysis (Special Issue, 2007, pp. 381–411). Psychoanalysis originates in a juridical form, exemplified by Oedipus, and just as psychoanalysis rejects fantasies of self-mastery, it misses the opportunity to question the structure of sovereign power, leaving the problem of tyranny in silence.

## Practical studies

Despite the appearance of legal terminology (e.g., Oedipal murder and the incest taboo, crime and guilt, and the judicial, even prosecutorial, activities of the superego) and the references to various legal proceedings in Freud's writings,

> he never tried to explain the possible interactions between law and psychoanalysis . . .
>
> [I]t was when he abandoned a legal career to turn his attention to science that Freud, in a letter to his friend Emil Fluss on May 1, 1873 . . ., used the word *Prozess* (trial) for the first time. Rather than getting involved in real trials [*Prozesse*], he will study the "millennial cases of nature" so he can bear witness to its "eternal trials." The use of this legal term is not an isolated occurrence in the Freudian corpus.
>
> *(Trapet, 2005)*

And notwithstanding the contemporary interest in applications of psychoanalysis in practical legal contexts, Freud was cautious concerning the potential of psychoanalysis in law (Zagury, 2005). In his 1906 guest lecture to a jurisprudence seminar at the University of Vienna, Freud noted that his "work is far removed from the practical administration of justice," and warned against amateur and inappropriate uses of psychoanalysis to discern the guilt or innocence of criminal defendants (Freud, 1961b, p. 114). Likewise, when Freud was consulted concerning the use of the Oedipus complex to explain Philipp Halsmann's murder of his father, Freud warned that a bad relationship with one's father (even if it could be established)

> is a far cry from there to the causation of such a deed. Precisely because it is always present [i.e., its "universality"], the Oedipus complex is not suited to provide a decision on the question of guilt.
>
> *(Freud, 1961a, p. 252)*

On the other hand, Freud was happy to write the preface to August Aichhorn's *Wayward Youth* (1935), a psychoanalytic study of juvenile delinquency.

As Goodrich explains, the crime of Denis Lortie who, in 1984, killed three people in an effort to "kill the government in Quebec,"

> is treated by the French psychoanalyst and jurist Pierre Legendre as an exemplary one and becomes the focus of a study of the function or structural place of the father, and of authority or more technically "legitimacy," in psychoanalysis and in law.
>
> *(Goodrich, 1996, p. 197)*

Other examples of practical applications of psychoanalysis in criminology contexts include Steven Morrison's examination of sentencing guidelines; using Lacanian theories of how the "Other" is created through neglect, censorship, error, and speech/language, he argues that US Federal Sentencing Guidelines create the offender as "Criminal" and therefore dehumanize him.

> In any system, be it one that re-bestows upon the federal judiciary great discretion in sentencing, or one that takes us further than the [federal guidelines] ever did into rigid rules and uniform sentences, dehumanization should be recognized and humanization of the offender should become a primary sentencing goal. [D]ehumanization is found not in the structure of the system, but in the psychological relationship that people in power have with offenders.
>
> *(Morrison, 2006, pp. 124–125)*

Although it is difficult to characterize as an example of criminology studies, or even practical psychoanalytic studies, the proceedings of the 2002 symposium on "Lacan and Crime: The Jouissance of Transgression," held at Cardozo School of Law (Yeshiva University) and published in 2004 in the *Cardozo Law Review*, included papers on serial homicide, psychosis and the criminal act, guilt and transgression, infanticide and torture.

Apart from criminology, Helen Stacy, in "Lacan's Split Subjects: Raced and Gendered Transformations," addresses a recent Australian legal controversy in terms of Lacan's four discourses – Master, University, Hysteric and Analyst (Symposium, 1997, pp. 277–293). Stacy is concerned with the potential of discursive structures to destroy and create identity, voice and power in the subject of law. Her appropriation of Lacan to analyze the Hindmarsh Island Affair (wherein Aboriginal women claimed (1) that the island was the site of "secret women's business," which could not be revealed, and (2) that a proposed bridge and marina would destroy their fertility) provides a rare and impressive example of practical-legal analysis in terms of a discourse theory that is usually inaccessible to all but Lacan's disciples.

> The Hindmarsh Island affair is saturated in contested identities and refuted subject positions. The identity of the minority group of Aboriginal women who claim secret spiritual knowledge is organized around a double axis of gender and race that in Lacan's schema is driven below the line of consciousness. The women are caught [and] must choose between quiet abuse in private through not speaking of their spiritual beliefs (Lacan's discourse of the master), or noisy abuse in court proceedings that require them to validate their beliefs in a setting which can neither accommodate their need for secrecy nor translate their authentic identities (Lacan's discourse of the university).
>
> *(Symposium, 1997, p. 290)*

With respect to legal subjectivity, Paula Baron also employed the psychoanalytic theories of Freud and Lacan in her critique of a 2004 Australian family law judgment, *Re: Alex*, permitting gender reassignment medical procedures for a 13-year-old child (biologically a girl). While the court assumed "that gender is somehow 'natural,' dichotomous and inevitable," psychoanalytic theory "provides an explanation of identity that reveals the extent to which gender may be seen as a social construct, the result of the individual's internalisation of desire, language and parental narcissism" (Baron, 2005, p. 31). As an alternative to the court's identification of "gender dysphoria," which pathologized or stigmatized the child, Baron's

> psychoanalytic account would place considerably more weight upon the interaction of Alex and her primary [caretakers] in the determination of her gender identification . . . [I]n

contrast to the conventional analysis presented to the court, a psychoanalytic reading would suggest that gender reassignment might ultimately exacerbate, rather than resolve, Alex's aggression and suicidal ideation.

*(Baron, 2005, p. 31)*

Finally, an example of a traditional Freudian engagement with current legal problems is offered by Hugh Butts's perspective on group-related paranoia in the racial profiling controversy.

Racist practices that exist in several areas of the criminal justice system are motivated unconsciously by a false belief about evil and other negative attributes [projected upon] black individuals. This trend leads to a variety of behaviors that result in a "contrived reality" that supports this [delusional] belief that whites are pure and blacks are evil.

*(Butts, 1999, p. 634)*

It bears mention that even in publications (identifiably from the field of law and psychoanalysis) that focus on practical applications, authors tend to begin with theoretical, descriptive explications of psychoanalytic concepts, due to the fact that psychoanalytic terminology is not part of mainstream legal discourse; therefore familiarity with Freud or (especially) Lacan cannot be assumed (e.g., Lacan's discourse categories are very theoretical). Moreover, even the most theoretical articles and studies (discussed elsewhere in this chapter) are not meant to be impractical or useless, so my own categorization of "practical studies" is somewhat subject to challenge.

## Law and literature: psychoanalytic approaches

Law and literature studies, sometimes called law, culture, and the humanities (referring to the International Association for the Study of Law, Culture and the Humanities, which holds annual conferences) is a movement in legal scholarship concerned with either (1) using literary methodology to analyze legal texts, or (2) using a literary text to illuminate issues in law and legal processes. For example, a judicial opinion might be viewed as a story (or a rhetorical achievement), and a novel like Dickens's *Bleak House* might be studied for its critique of the ethical failures of lawyers (or of the sluggishness of a complex trial). And just as some literary theorists use psychoanalysis (see chapter 20 of this volume), some law and literature scholars, on law school faculties and in literary studies (or rhetoric) departments, also work in the Freudian tradition. With respect to literary interpretation, "psychoanalysis offers a method for reading legal texts in the symptomatic terms of their latent meanings" (Caudill, 1997, pp. 42–65; Goodrich, 1997b, p. 1038) (regarding interpretation of gaps in contractual language); and with respect to great works of literature, *Bleak House* can be understood as the capturing of the subject in terms of Lacan's symbolic order of law and language (Caudill, 1997, pp. 116–128).

For example, law professor Martha Grace Duncan's *Romantic Outlaws, Beloved Prisons: The Unconscious Meanings of Crime and Punishment* (1999) focuses on numerous great works of literature, including *The Grapes of Wrath*, *Heart of Darkness*, *Les Misérables*, *Crime and Punishment*, and *The Great Gatsby*, and reveals how positive fantasies of prison and romantic images of crime, generally repressed and resisted, function to create a partnership, not an adversarial relationship, between criminals and noncriminals in contemporary culture. Professor Martha Merrill Umphrey likewise explores, from a Freudian perspective, the relation between law and violence in Herman Melville's novella, *Billy Budd, Sailor (an inside narrative)*; the execution of Billy Budd, for example, requires repression of the erotic bonds between Captain Vere and Billy (Special Issue, 2007, pp. 413–431). Finally, Professor Ravit Reichman argues that property is allied to trauma, loss, grief, and guilt in Walter Benjamin's "Unpacking My Library" and James Joyce's *Ulysses* (Special Issue, 2007, pp. 433–449). These few examples, and many more could be offered, demonstrate the potential for a hybridized law, literature, and psychoanalysis movement.

## Criticism of psychoanalysis in law

> Psychoanalysis is both obviously relevant and obviously threatening to the discipline or "science" of legal studies.
>
> *(Goodrich, 1997a, p. 208)*

Criticism of psychoanalysis generally is a perennial phenomenon. Consider the recent debate over the planned, postponed, cancelled and finally rescheduled Freud Exhibition at the US Library of Congress. Opponents of Freud and the exhibition (who believe that the "science" of psychoanalysis has been discredited) wondered why they needed another nail in the coffin of psychoanalysis; and the controversy effectively divided the friends of psychoanalysis between those who defend it as science and those who concede it is only hermeneutical.

In *mainstream* legal studies, there is no longer any significant interest in the Freudian tradition, which in Peter Goodrich's view

> has long been perceived as too threatening or too personal a form of knowledge to be addressed directly. Study of the unconscious threatens to disrupt the complacent truths of modernist jurisprudence and so also to question the rationality of legal practice by finally addressing the unconscious of institutions, and correlatively the repetitions and repressions, the drives and desires both of the authors and interpreters of law as well as of its subjects. It is thus perhaps unsurprising that although law is primarily concerned to judge the discourses and the actions of natural and corporate subjects it has studiously avoided the most radical of contemporary theories of the subject.
>
> *(Symposium, 1997, p. 199)*

Indeed, "law has lost the tools for addressing such issues," and in disciplinary terms, the legal academy is willing "to act as if the discoveries of Freud and the writings of Lacan had either never happened or, if sufficiently rigorously ignored, would go away" (Symposium, 1997, p. 207).

Such denial in contemporary legal contexts parallels the history of criticism of psychoanalytic techniques by Freud's own contemporaries; but, as Freud predicted, there is a particular aversion to psychoanalysis in law, which is concerned with the conscious acts of a responsible and autonomous subject:

> With its emphasis upon dreams, sexuality, symbols, and the unconscious, [psychoanalysis] belongs – in a sense like morality and religious belief – to a domain anterior to law, a realm of subjectivity or interiority with which secular law is not and never has been concerned. Although this depiction of law as an objective technology is common both within the profession and in popular perception, claiming that legal governance is exclusively exterior and objective is historically untenable and theoretically absurd.
>
> *(Goodrich, 1997b, p. 1039)*

Nevertheless, there is a vibrant if marginalized interest in the relevance of psychoanalytic studies for law, notwithstanding the criticism that psychoanalysis is outdated or eclipsed by biological and neuroscientific explanations of human behavior. Numerous legal scholars find in the psychoanalytic tradition the tools for critique and reformation of law and its institutions.

## Conclusion: the future of Freud in law

The popular conception of law's relationship to psychological and psychiatric knowledge is that of an institutional process – law – in need of outside guidance. Ideally, scientific "truth" is imported, when necessary, to settle disputes over causation or mental capacity. Of course, legal processes and institutions develop, over time, their own versions of psychology and psychiatry, while scientific institutions and processes are themselves divided and full of controversies over matters psychological, so the ideal falters. Even so, psychoanalysis, once in fashion in the courtroom, is no longer respected as admissible expertise.

In the field of social theory, however, psychoanalytic jurisprudence holds promise, notwithstanding the fears that it would disrupt and discredit established legal presumptions and doctrines – fears that have resulted in a certain "degree of hostility from the legal academy":

> But on closer inspection, these fears seem misplaced. Psychoanalysis interprets the individual psyche and the social bond in terms of inter-subjective investments which are created or animated by basic legal structures. The law is the ground of individuality and sociality and [therefore] analysis is destined to become a privileged domain for legal theory. It seems however that the conservative reflexes of the legal academy are once more resisting the inevitable. Psychoanalysis [nevertheless] does not have a place yet in the legal curriculum, and its contribution to scholarship is not fully recognized.
>
> *(Symposium, 1997, pp. 324–325)*

Despite the pretenses of law as a stabilizing force above culture and politics, and despite its implied claim to doctrinal consistency, law is ideological, embedded in history and subject to hidden cultural biases – and therefore ripe for analysis of its symptomatic language, anxieties, slips, repressions, denials, fantasies and illusions. Legal scholars oriented to psychoanalysis will continue to identify the collective unconscious underlying legal processes and institutions, and to reveal law's pathologies.

## References

Baron, P 2005, 'The web of desire and the Narcissistic trap: A psychoanalytic reading of *Re Alex*', *Griffith Law Review*, vol. 14, pp. 17–33.

Butts, H 1999, 'Psychoanalytic perspectives on racial profiling', *Journal of the American Academy of Psychiatry and the Law*, vol. 27, no. 4, pp. 633–635.

Carlson, D & Peter Goodrich, P (eds), 1998, *Law and the postmodern mind: Essays on psychoanalysis and jurisprudence*, University of Michigan Press, Ann Arbor.

Caudill, D 1997, *Lacan and the subject of law: Toward a psychoanalytic critical legal theory*, Humanities Press, Atlantic Highlands, NJ.

Conference, 1995, 'Law and the post-modern mind', *Cardozo Law Review*, vol. 16, pp. 699–1444.

Douzinas, C 1998, *Law and the emotions: Prolegomena for a psychoanalytic approach to legal study*, EUI Working Paper (Law) No. 98/8, European University Institute, Florence.

Ehrenzweig, A 1971, *Psychoanalytic jurisprudence: On ethics, aesthetics, and law – On crime, tort, and procedure*, Sijthoff, Leiden.

Freud, S 1961a, 'The expert opinion in the Halsmann case', in J Strachey (ed), *Standard edition of the complete psychological works of Sigmund Freud*, vol. 21, Hogarth, London, pp. 251–253.

Freud, S 1961b, 'Psycho-analysis and the establishment of the facts in legal proceedings', in J Strachey (ed), *Standard edition of the complete psychological works of Sigmund Freud*, vol. 9, Hogarth, London, pp. 103–114.

Goldstein, J 1968, 'Psychoanalysis and jurisprudence', *Yale Law Journal*, vol. 77, pp. 1053–1077.

Goodrich, P (ed), 1997a, *Law and the unconscious: A Legendre reader* (P Goodrich, A Pottage & A Schütz, trans), Macmillan, London.

Goodrich, P 1997b, 'Maladies of the legal soul: Psychoanalysis and interpretation in law', *Washington & Lee Law Review*, vol. 54, pp. 1035–1074.

Imwinkelried, E 2003, 'Peer dialogue: The how and what of "appropriate validation" under *Daubert*: Reconsidering the treatment of Einstein and Freud', *Missouri Law Review*, vol. 68, pp. 43–52.

Milovanovic, D 1992, *Postmodern law and disorder*, Deborah Charles, Liverpool.

Morrison, S 2006, 'Dehumanization and re-creation: A Lacanian interpretation of the federal sentencing guidelines', *Dartmouth Law Journal*, vol. 4, pp. 81–126.

Rakoff, J 2008, 'Science and the law: Uncomfortable bedfellows', *Seton Hall Law Review*, vol. 38, pp. 1379–1393.

Rogers, J 2007, ' "Who's your daddy?" A question of sovereignty and the use of psychoanalysis', *Law Text Culture*, vol. 11, pp. 151–182.

Satin, M 1994, 'Law and psychology: A movement whose time has come', *Annual Survey of American Law*, pp. 581–563.

Schroeder, J 2008, *The four Lacanian discourses, or turning law inside-out*, Birkbeck Law Press, Oxford.

Special Issue 2007, 'Legal analysis', *American Imago*, vol. 64, no. 3, pp. 291–411.

Symposium 1997, 'The wake of psychoanalysis', *Legal Studies Forum*, vol. 20, no. 3, pp. 187–343.

Trapet, M 2005, 'Law and psychoanalysis', *International Dictionary of Psychoanalysis*, available at http://www.encyclopedia.com/doc/1G2–3435300802.html

Zagury, D 2005, 'Criminology and psychoanalysis', *International Dictionary of Psychoanalysis*, available at http://www.encyclopedia.com/doc/1G2–3435300317.html

# 22

# Feminism, gender and psychoanalysis

*Janet Sayers*

Many feminists dismiss psychoanalysis as incurably "misogynist, ahistorical, and acultural" and as seeking to rationalize and justify women's social subordination in terms of their anatomy.

Others are committed to reforming, rereading or reinterpreting "psychoanalytic doctrine" as means of furthering understanding and remedying this subordination (Rowley & Grosz, 1990, p. 175).

In this chapter I will recount these and other issues in feminism and psychoanalysis. First, I will recount, at length, the historical and intellectual development of these issues beginning with Freud. Second, again at length, I will focus on claims by contributors to feminist debate about psychoanalysis regarding femininity and masculinity, and regarding symbolism and fantasy.

Third, I will recount briefly some of the principal contributions of feminism and psycho-analysis to each other; fourth, again briefly, I will recount major criticisms of feminism and psychoanalysis. Finally, I will conclude with the continuing importance and future development of feminism and psychoanalysis insofar as it can be envisaged today.

## Historical and intellectual development

Historically and intellectually feminism and psychoanalysis are rooted in what has been described as bourgeois individualist struggles in the 19th century to secure women equal legal rights with men. Contributing to these struggles, John Stuart Mill, as member of parliament for Westminster in London, added to the 1867 Reform Act an amendment granting women the same political rights as men. Following the defeat of this amendment Mill's book, *The Subjection of Women*, was published in 1869 and translated, in 1880, by Freud into German. He was, however, no radical as regards remedying the social wrongs done to women by their traditional social role, about which he wrote as follows to his fiancée, Martha Bernays:

> I believe that all reforming action in law and education would break down in front of the fact that, long before the age at which a man can earn a position in society, Nature has determined woman's destiny through beauty, charm and sweetness. Law and custom have much to give women that has been withheld from them, but the position of women will surely be what it is: in youth an adored darling and in mature years a loved wife.
>
> *(Freud, 1883, p. 193)*

He was nevertheless sympathetic to the plight of young middle-class women's enforced idleness making them liable, in his view and in the view of his medical colleague, Josef Breuer, to daydreaming and thus, they said, to hysteria. He also criticized the sexual repression of young middle-class women contributing, in his view, to their being prone to nervous illness.

Yet in founding psychoanalysis with his books, *The Interpretation of Dreams* and *Three Essays on the Theory of Sexuality*, Freud subordinated the sexuality of girls and women to that of boys and men. "It is self-evident to a male child that a genital like his own is to be attributed to everyone he knows," he wrote. "This conviction is energetically maintained by boys . . . and is only abandoned after several internal struggles (the castration complex)," he added in going on to maintain apropos the childhood origin of women's sexuality:

> Little girls do not resort to denial of this kind when they see that boys' genitals are formed differently from their own. They are ready to recognize them immediately and are overcome by envy for the penis – an envy culminating in the wish, which is so important in its consequences, to be boys themselves.
>
> *(Freud, 1905, p. 195)*

And it was in terms of this theory of envy for the penis that Freud characterized the feminism of one of his young women patients in Vienna following the victory of feminism in securing the vote for women in many countries in Europe, including Austria, in 1919. Writing about this patient, Freud said:

> [She] had brought along with her from her childhood a strongly marked "masculinity complex". A spirited girl, always ready for romping and fighting, she was not at all prepared to be second to her slightly older brother; after inspecting his genital organs she had developed a pronounced envy for the penis, and the thoughts derived from this envy still continued to fill her mind. She was in fact a feminist; she felt it to be unjust that girls should not enjoy the same freedom as boys, and rebelled against the lot of woman in general.
>
> *(Freud, 1920, p. 169)*

Soon after this was published an article by Freud's Berlin-based psychoanalyst colleague, Karl Abraham, diagnosed women's feminist rebellion against not having the same "freedom" as men in choosing "their profession . . . sphere of activity . . . sexual life" as means by which women rationalized and defended against their infantile penis-envy that Abraham described as the female version of the "castration complex" already postulated in boys by Freud (Abraham, 1922, p. 2).

The feminist psychoanalyst, Karen Horney, was appalled. Women's sexuality, she insisted, is not given by high regard for the penis or by feeling they are castrated. Rather, she maintained, their sexuality is rooted in their different and just as intact biology as that of men. If they envy the penis this is primarily due to the advantages it gives boys and men in urinating. This envy might then be used secondarily by girls and women as part of their masculine defense against the disappointment, guilt or anxiety resulting from their biologically given feminine and Oedipal desire to take their mother's place sexually with their father.

Horney's resulting article was published in 1926. Previously Freud had argued that since, he claimed, boys and girls initially only know of one genital – the penis – he had decided to rename the genital stage of psychosexual development the phallic phase of which he said:

> The antithesis here is between having a male genital and being castrated. It is not until development has reached its completion at puberty that the sexual polarity coincides with male

and female. Maleness combines [the factors of] subject, activity and possession of the penis; femaleness takes over [those of] object and passivity. The vagina is now valued as a place of shelter for the penis; it enters into the heritage of the womb.

*(Freud, 1923, p. 145)*

This phase, he also maintained, includes the Oedipal desire of boys to take their father's place sexually with their mother, or their mother's place sexually with their father. Both these heterosexual and homosexual Oedipal desires are brought to an end in the boy, however, by fear that their realization might involve his losing his penis. He resolves this fear by identifying in his superego with the law against incest established by the overthrow of the primal horde that, Freud claimed, was succeeded by the patriarchal organization of society.

What, then, of the girl's psychosexual development? Its phallic phase, Freud maintained, includes the girl's phallic masturbation of her clitoris. After seeing the penis – "strikingly visible and of large proportions" – however she immediately recognizes it as "superior counterpart" of her "small and inconspicuous organ" and, said Freud, "from that time forward fall[s] a victim to envy for the penis" (Freud, 1925, p. 252).

The little girl's penis-envy, also described by Abraham and then by Freud as the girl's castration complex, leads, Freud claimed, to the following possible outcomes. She may develop a "masculinity complex" involving continuing penis-envy, the wish to have a penis, and the longing to become "like a man." She may react against her penis-envy by developing "a sense of inferiority" and share "the contempt felt by men for a sex which is the lesser in so important a respect." This may involve her displacing her penis-envy onto jealousy, which, claimed Freud, "plays a far larger part in the mental life of women than of men." Or she may give up her wish for a penis, substitute for this the desire for a baby, and "with that purpose in view" take "her father as a love-object" (Freud, 1925, pp. 253, 254, 256).

This last response by the girl to her penis-envy or castration complex thus initiates, according to Freud, her Oedipus complex consisting of sexual desire for the father in rivalry with the mother. Since her Oedipus complex is initiated by her castration complex the latter does not bring the former complex to an end through her resolving it by identifying with the law of the father, and with morality more generally, in her superego. As a result the superego in girls and women is, maintained Freud, "never so inexorable, so impersonal, so independent of its emotional origins as we require it to be in men" (Freud, 1925, p. 257).

Again Horney objected. The account by Freud and Abraham of the psychology of women is no different, she argued, from the little boy's assumption that girls possess a penis like him; his attributing the lack of a penis in girls to castration; his regarding girls as inferior to him; and his inability to imagine how girls ever get over their envy of, and lack of a penis. Furthermore, Horney maintained, Freud and Abraham ignored men's envy of women's mothering that she found evident in her men patients' experience of her as a mother. Indeed, she suggested, this envy of women's mothering might be the cause of men's defensive depreciation of women in characterizing them as inferior and suffering with penis-envy. As for women, Horney argued, their defense against their biologically given innate feminine Oedipal desire for the father with "flight into the male role" is reinforced by "the hitherto purely masculine character of our civilization" (Horney, 1926, p. 69).

Whereas Horney was motivated by feminism in criticizing Freud and Abraham, Melanie Klein was motivated in criticizing them by her findings in helping pioneer the extension of psychoanalysis to the treatment of very young children. This led her to argue that the Oedipus complex begins not genitally, as Freud maintained, but in the infant's reaction to the oral and anal deprivations of weaning and potty-training evoking pre-genital fantasies of attacking the mother's sexual coupling with the father. This, in turn, evokes dread in the infant that the mother may retaliate with counterattack against its sexuality. Boys respond to this "femininity complex" by reassuring themselves that their penis is intact and with "excessive protestations of masculinity" and "excessive aggression" while girls, Klein added, respond by identifying with the father as less anxiety-making than the mother (Klein, 1928, pp. 190, 193). This was followed by Klein's psychoanalyst colleague, Joan Riviere, arguing that women use their innately given femininity secondarily as a defensive masquerade to ward off the hostility of men to their competing in their traditional sphere of influence. It was also followed by another London-based psychoanalyst, Ernest Jones, defending Klein's theory of innate femininity against her psychoanalyst detractors in Vienna.

Meanwhile Freud had either rejected or ignored the claims of Horney in Berlin, and of Klein in London, regarding the biologically given innate determinants of femininity and female sexuality. He was more sympathetic and responsive to the claim of women psychoanalysts in Vienna, specifically Jeanne Lampl de Groot and Helene Deutsch, based on their patients' response to them as mother figures, that the female Oedipus complex is preceded by pre-Oedipal desire for the mother. Adopting this claim, Freud argued that the Oedipus complex is preceded in both girls and boys by active and passive, masculine and feminine, aims in the oral, anal and early phallic phase of their psychosexual development. These bisexual – masculine and feminine – aims include, he maintained, the pre-Oedipal girl's phallic masturbation of her clitoris and fantasies of actively impregnating her mother and of being the passive object of her mother's phallic seduction.

This phallic phase in the girl's development is then brought to an end by her "castration complex." It consists, said Freud, in the girl acknowledging "the fact of her castration, and with it, too, the superiority of the male and her own inferiority." Her penis-envy and castration complex then inaugurates, he maintained, the following three possible lines of development.

The first leads to a general revulsion from sexuality. The little girl, frightened by the comparison with boys, grows dissatisfied with her clitoris, and gives up her phallic activity and with it her sexuality in general as well as a good part of her masculinity in other fields. The second line leads her to cling with defiant self-assertiveness to her threatened masculinity. To an incredibly late age she clings to the hope of getting a penis some time. That hope becomes her life's aim; and the phantasy of being a man in spite of everything often persists as a formative factor over long periods. This "masculinity complex" in women can also result in a manifest homosexual choice of object. Only if her development follows the third, very circuitous, path does she reach the final normal female attitude, in which she takes her father as her object and so finds her way to the feminine form of the Oedipus complex (Freud, 1931, pp. 229–230).

Furthermore, according to Freud's 1931 account of female sexuality, the castration and Oedipus complex in little girls determines not only their sexuality but also "the character of females as social beings" (Freud, 1931, p. 230). "It is to be anticipated that men analysts with feminist views, as well as our women analysts, will disagree with what I have said here," he added.

They will hardly fail to object that such notions spring from the "masculinity complex" of the male and are designed to justify on theoretical grounds his innate inclination to disparage and suppress women. But this sort of psychoanalytic argumentation reminds us here, as it so often does, of Dostoevsky's famous "knife that cuts both ways." The opponents of those who argue in this way will on their side think it quite natural that the female sex should refuse to accept a view that appears to contradict their eagerly coveted equality with men. The use of analysis as a weapon of controversy can clearly lead to no decision (Freud, 1931, p. 230, n.1).

Then, taking issue with Karen Horney's claim that "penis-envy" is a defense adopted by the girl to fend off "her feminine attachment to her father," Freud asked, "if the defense against femininity is so energetic, from what other source can it draw its strength than from the masculine trend which found its first expression in the child's penis-envy and therefore deserves to be named after it?" (Freud, 1931, p. 243).

"[P]sycho-analysis does not try to describe what a woman is – that would be a task it could scarcely perform – but sets about enquiring how she comes into being, how a woman develops out of a child with a bisexual disposition," he subsequently wrote in going on, as follows, to anticipate and recount his answer to feminist criticism (Freud, 1933, p. 116).

For the ladies, whenever some comparison seemed to turn out unfavorable to their sex, were able to utter a suspicion that we, the male analysts, had been unable to overcome certain deeply rooted prejudices against what was feminine, and that this was being paid for in the partiality of our researches. We, on the other hand, standing on the ground of bisexuality, had no difficulty in avoiding impoliteness. We had only to say: "This doesn't apply to you. You're the exception; on this point you're more masculine than feminine" (Freud, 1933, pp. 116–117).

That said, Freud reiterated his claim regarding the girl's "discovery that she is castrated"; that this can lead to her becoming sexually inhibited or neurotic or to her developing "a masculinity complex" or, optimally in his view, to her acquiring "normal femininity" through abandoning her pre-Oedipal love of her "phallic mother . . . with the discovery that her mother is castrated" (Freud, 1933, p. 126).

Meanwhile anti-Semitic Fascism was brewing in Europe from where – with the rise of Hitler to power in Germany in 1933, the German annexation of Austria in 1938, and the German invasion of France and the Netherlands in 1940 – many psychoanalysts left for the USA. They included the German émigré, Karen Horney, whose liberal-minded cultural version of psychoanalysis, evident in her 1939 book, *New Ways in Psychoanalysis*, conflicted with the conservative ego psychology version of psychoanalysis developed by the Austrian émigré, Heinz Hartmann, in his 1939 book, *Ego Psychology and the Problem of Adaptation*. More in keeping with Horney's liberal-minded cultural version of psychoanalysis was the German émigré Erich Fromm's 1941 book, *Escape From Freedom*. Their version of psychoanalysis, however, led to their being discriminated against within orthodox ego psychology psychoanalysis in the USA.

Meanwhile the emigration of Anna Freud and other psychoanalysts from Vienna to London led to fierce debate between them and Melanie Klein and her followers in the British Psychoanalytical Society about the nature and function of fantasy and its origins in infant and child psychology. Psychoanalysis was also used by the British psychoanalysts John Bowlby and Donald Winnicott in writing about the ills of separating infants from their mothers. This was used to legitimize the closure of day nurseries following World War II and to reinforce a family ideology consigning women with children to full-time mothering. It also strengthened the mother-centered version of psychoanalysis, known as object relations theory, begun before the war by Klein and by other psychoanalysts in Britain.

Klein's account of the infant's part-object relations with the mother (as breast, feces, penis) and her account, in these terms, of children's drawings, some of which were reproduced in an article published in the 1945 issue of the *International Journal of Psychoanalysis*, was soon after praised, as follows, by the Paris-based psychoanalyst, Jacques Lacan.

Through her [Klein] we know the function of the imaginary primordial enclosure formed by the *imago* of the mother's body; through her we have the cartography, drawn by the children's own hands, of the mother's internal empire, the historical atlas of the intestinal divisions in which the *imagos* of the subject himself, dispute their deleterious dominance over her sacred regions (Lacan, 1948, pp. 20–21).

From these divisions, claimed Lacan, the infant seeks escape through identifying with the whole image of itself reflected by the mirror.

> "Whether or not the mirror actually plays a more or less considerable part, it is certain that
> the child commences towards the age of six months to mimic his parents, and under their

gaze to regard himself as an object," commented the feminist, Simone de Beauvoir, in her book, *The Second Sex*. The little boy, she added, may defensively identify with his penis as "a symbol of autonomy, of transcendence, of power" whereas the little girl is likely to be given a doll as *alter ego* which, unlike the penis, "represents the whole body" and is "a passive object." This, however, does not inevitably determine differences in the destiny of boys and girls since, insisted Beauvoir, "it is within the totality of their lives that each factor – penis or doll – takes on its importance."

*(De Beauvoir, 1949, pp. 297, 306, 307)*

De Beauvoir's existentialist ethics insisting on the equal freedom in principle of boys and girls to realize their transcendence as individuals was contradicted, however, by subsequently developed theories concerning the social structures shaping individuals. Examples included the theory developed by the American sociologists, Talcott Parsons and Robert Bales, in their book, *Family Socialization and Interaction Process*, emphasizing the social structures of girls and boys shaping their individual psychology and thus preparing them for their "expressive" and "instrumental" roles as adults (e.g., Parsons & Bales, 1955, p. 355).

Meanwhile, in France, the structural linguistics of Ferdinand de Saussure (emphasizing the structuring of the meaning of words in terms of the antithesis of the presence and absence of what they signify) and the structural anthropology of Claude Lévi-Strauss (emphasizing that all societies are structured by the patriarchal kinship exchange of women by men in marriage) was adopted by Lacan in reinterpreting Freud's theory of the Oedipus and castration complex in terms of the meaning of the phallus as symbol of the structuring of the different fate of individual women and men in patriarchy.

Freud had argued, as we have seen, that the phallic phase in psychosexual development is given by the antithesis of "having a male genital and being castrated" and that this differentially shapes the boy's and girl's Oedipus and castration complex (Freud, 1923, p. 145). Adding to this Saussure's theory of meaning and Lévi-Strauss's theory of patriarch, Lacan maintained: "We know that the unconscious castration complex has the function of . . . the installation in the subject of an unconscious position without which he would be unable to identify himself with the ideal type of his sex." Then, rejecting Horney's "culturalist" and "feminist" revision of psychoanalysis, Lacan went on to distinguish his version of psychoanalysis from that of Klein.

Whereas she had written about the unconscious fantasy – or phantasy – of the father's penis as part-object inside the mother, Lacan focused on the "phallus" not as "phantasy" nor as "an object (part-, internal, good, bad, etc.)" but as symbol or "signifier" (Lacan, 1958, pp. 281, 284, 285).

His theory of the symbolic role of the phallus in positioning boys and girls as men and women within patriarchy was taken up and promoted by the Marxist philosopher, Louis Althusser, in an article published first in 1964 in the French communist party journal, *La Nouvelle Critique*, and then in revised form in the London-based journal, *New Left Review*. In this article Althusser applauded what he described as Lacan's "Law of the Symbolic" and account of the "Oedipal phase," whereby if all "goes well," said Althusser, the child accepts itself as a boy having "the full right to become one day 'like daddy,' that is, a masculine human being with a wife" or as a girl who will become "like mummy" as "a feminine human being with a husband" (Althusser, 1969, pp. 194, 196).

Becoming a feminine human being with a husband, however, was not a happy lot for many graduate women. Their unhappiness was given central place by Betty Friedan in her 1963 book, *The Feminine Mystique*, in which she criticized psychoanalysts in the US for abandoning Freud's emphasis on liberating sexuality from repression and for using Freud's penis-envy theory as means of characterizing women who rebelled against their allotted housewife role as pathological. Together with other liberal-minded feminists, she helped found, in 1966, the National Organization for Women geared to making the Equal Employment Opportunity Commission enforce its legal mandate to end sex discrimination in the US. The following year, 1967, Shulamith Firestone and Pam Allan started the more confrontational feminist group, New York Radical Women, which became one of the first feminist collectives to start what became known as consciousness-raising – contributing, not surprisingly, to reviving feminist interest in psychoanalysis.

Other contributing factors included the student events of 1968; the start of the Boston Women's Health Collective in 1969; the opening that year at Cornell of the first women's studies program; the 1970 women's liberation conference in Oxford demanding equal pay, education, job opportunities, free contraception and abortion on demand, and 24-hour nurseries. This last demand entailed challenging the psychoanalytic claims of Winnicott and Bowlby regarding the psychological ill-effects of the separation of infants from their mothers entailed by nursery provision.

The year 1970 also saw the publication of a spate of feminist articles and books dealing, more or less explicitly and confrontationally, with psychoanalysis. They included Anne Koedt's article, "The Myth of the Vaginal Orgasm"; Shulamith Firestone's *The Dialectic of Sex*; Kate Millett's *Sexual Politics*; Germaine Greer's *The Female Eunuch*; and Eva Figes's *Patriarchal Attitudes*. The first women's liberation march in Britain was held in London the following year. In 1971 the first refuge for battered women opened in London. Phyllis Chessler's book, *Women and Madness*, was published in 1972, as was Anne Oakley's feminist sociology book, *Sex, Gender and Society*.

This was followed by the publication of a number of books variously criticizing or developing Lacan's version of psychoanalysis. In 1974 these books included *Speculum of the Other Woman* by Luce Irigaray; *Revolution in Poetic Language* by Julia Kristeva; and *Psychoanalysis and Feminism* by Juliet Mitchell. They were followed by the publication in 1975 of Lacanian influenced articles including "The Traffic in Women" by Gayle Rubin and "The Laugh of the Medusa" by Hélène Cixous. Other non-Lacanian versions of psychoanalysis, however, were adopted by Susie Orbach and Luise Eichenbaum in founding the feminist inspired women's therapy clinic in London in 1976; by Dorothy Dinnerstein in her 1967 book, *The Mermaid and the Minotaur*; by Nancy Chodorow in her 1978 book, *The Reproduction of Mothering*; and by Susie Orbach in her 1978 book, *Fat Is a Feminist Issue*.

By then many feminists had become disenchanted with psychoanalysis for theorizing women's psychology without regard to differences between them due to history, ethnicity, social class, disability, sexual orientation and so on. This contributed to feminist enthusiasm for the emphasis on difference in the work of the French literary theorist, Jacques Derrida, and for the emphasis of the French social historian, Michel Foucault, on deconstructing the universalizing theories of Marxism and Freud in favor of emphasizing the host of different theories and discourses producing a multiplicity of different individual subjectivities and sexualities.

Differences between women as regards their sexualities became a major cause of dissension between feminists in a conference held at Barnard College in 1982. The same year saw the start in Baltimore, Maryland, of one of the first incest survivors groups. This in turn led to feminist critique of Freud for rejecting his initial claim that the cause of mental illness in women lies in their having been incestuously or sexually abused as infants, and for instead arguing that mental illness in women is rooted in their own self-generated infantile sexual fantasies.

Further critique or rejection of Freudian together with Marxist theory followed the fall of the Berlin Wall in 1989 and the subsequent dissolution of the Soviet Union. Foucault's post-structuralist critique of Freudian and Marxist theory was increasingly adopted by feminist academics including advocates of what was first described by Teresa de Lauretis as queer theory in a conference on lesbian and gay sexualities held in 1990 at the University of California in Santa Cruz. Queer theory was also boosted by the publication that year of Judith Butler's book, *Gender Trouble*, and by the publication in 1993 of her book, *Bodies that Matter*.

In both books Butler used not only Foucault's post-structuralist critique of Freudian theory. She also used Freudian theory. So did the feminists and psychotherapists Noreen O'Connor and Joanna Ryan, in their 1993 book *Wild Desires and Mistaken Identities*, and the sociologist and psychoanalyst, Nancy Chodorow, in her 1994 book, *Femininities, Masculinities, Sexualities*, in using psychoanalysis to counter the heterosexism of many psychoanalysts and psychiatrists.

Psychoanalytically and non-psychoanalytically minded feminists and others also organized a protest at Regent's Park College in London against a lecture given there in 1995 by the US psychiatrist, Charles Socarides, then well known for his characterization of homosexuality as pathological.

Despite the heterosexism not only of psychiatrists like Socarides but also of psychoanalysts, feminists working in the humanities, social sciences, and in mental health institutions continue to use psychoanalytic ideas. Examples include the sociologist, Jessica Benjamin, in her 1995 book, *Like Subjects, Love Objects*; the literary theorist, Jacqueline Rose, in her 2005 book, *Femininity and its Discontents*; the art historian, Griselda Pollock, in her contribution to the edited 2010 collection, *The Male Gaze*; and the philosopher, Alison Stone, in her 2012 book, *Feminism, Psychoanalysis and Maternal Subjectivity*. What, though, have been some of the major claims, key developments and key contributors to feminism and psychoanalysis since, and including, the claims made many years ago by Freud?

## Major claims, development and key contributors

In considering some of the major claims, developments, and key contributors to feminism and psychoanalysis I will focus first on femininity and masculinity, and second on symbolism and fantasy.

### Femininity and masculinity

"Anatomy is Destiny," claimed Freud, writing of differences in the development of femininity and masculinity in girls and boys (Freud, 1924, p. 178). This has led many feminists to characterize Freud as a biological determinist in his account of femininity and masculinity. And, indeed, he was a biological determinist insofar as he argued that girls and women are castrated, due to their biological lack of a penis, and insofar as he depicted this "fact" as determining their femininity or masculinity. Yet he also claimed that these traits result from the way girls and women construe this "fact" of their biology.

With this latter claim Freud distinguished psychoanalysis from biological determinism and was applauded as such by Simone de Beauvoir, who said of this aspect of psychoanalysis:

> The tremendous advance accomplished by psychoanalysis over psychophysiology lies in the view that no factor becomes involved in the psychic life without having taken on human significance; it is not the body-object described by biologists that actually exists, but the body as lived in by the subject. Woman is a female to the extent that she feels herself as such . . . It is not nature that defines woman; it is she who defines herself by dealing with nature on her own account in her emotional life.
>
> *(De Beauvoir, 1949, p. 69)*

Karen Horney, by contrast, in taking issue with Freud's penis-envy theory argued that femininity in the little girl is biologically determined by "organic vaginal sensations" that cause her Oedipus complex desire for her father and her maternal desire to have a baby by him (Horney, 1926, p. 65).

Nor was she the only psychoanalyst to claim that femininity is determined by biologically given vaginal sensations in girls and women. "The question of early vaginal sensibility is admittedly obscure, but several women analysts, the latest being Dr. Payne and Dr. Brierley, have produced, if not absolutely conclusive, at least highly significant evidence of its occurrence together with breast feeding," reported Ernest Jones in defending this claim (Jones, 1935, p. 489).

Many years later, like Horney, Payne, Brierley, Jones and others before her, the feminist philosopher and psychoanalyst Luce Irigaray argued that femininity is rooted in female biology and does not depend on awareness of the penis to come into being. "Your/my body does not acquire a sex by some operation – You are already a woman," she tells her assumed woman reader. "[W]e are women from the start," she adds. "We are two, long before any representation of us exists," she insists, referring by implication, not only to the pre-Oedipal twoness of women as infants with their mothers but also to the two lips of the female vulva (Irigaray, 1980, pp. 74, 78).

While some Horney, Irigaray and other feminist and nonfeminist psychoanalysts argue that femininity and female sexuality are given by female biology, other feminists have criticized ways in which psychoanalysis has been used to pressurize women into conformity with their socially assigned role as housewife and mother. This was the argument, as I have already indicated, which Betty Friedan pursued in her 1963 book, *The Feminine Mystique*. In it she praised "Freudian psychology with its emphasis on freedom from a repressive morality to achieve sexual fulfilment" as "part of the ideology of women's emancipation." She then went on to criticize its subsequent use as "ideological bulwark of the sexual counter-revolution in America" (Friedan, 1963, p. 92). Writing this during the heyday of the social adaptation and conformist version of ego psychology developed by Hartmann and other psychoanalysts in the USA, she added:

> The concept "penis envy," which Freud coined to describe a phenomenon he observed in women – that is, in the middle-class women who were his patients in Vienna in the Victorian era – was seized in this country in the 1940s as the literal explanation of all that was wrong with American women . . . One needs only to know what Freud was describing, in those Victorian women, to see the fallacy in literally applying his theory of femininity to women today.
>
> *(Friedan, 1963, p. 93)*

Like Betty Friedan, Kate Millett noted that Freud's version of psychoanalysis had initially been welcomed in the US as "a prototype of the liberal urge toward sexual freedom, and a signal contributor toward softening traditional puritanical inhibitions upon sexuality" (Millett, 1970, p. 178). Unlike Friedan, however, she criticized Freud for disregarding social factors that might contribute to penis-envy in girls and women; for making no distinction, in his account of penis-envy and the castration complex, between "fact and feminine fantasy"; and for purportedly describing femininity while actually prescribing it in arguing that girls should overcome their penis-envy, and any masculinity complex to which this might lead, and instead opt for heterosexuality, maternity, and femininity equated with "passivity, masochism, and narcissism." By convincing himself that these three traits of femininity are "constitutional and biologically determined," she maintained Freud "made it possible to prescribe them and for his followers to attempt to enforce them" and thus perpetuate "a condition which originates in oppressive social circumstances" (Millett, 1970, pp. 183, 194, 197).

Millett's critique of Freud for not only describing but also prescribing femininity was negated by Juliet Mitchell. "However it may have been used, psychoanalysis is not a recommendation for a patriarchal society, but an analysis of one." She insisted in going on to denounce Millett's critique of Freud and other "bourgeois and idealist tendencies within, largely, American radical feminism," which she countered by adopting Althusser's Lacan-based version of psychoanalysis that she admired for providing, she said, "an analysis of the place and meaning of sexuality and of gender differences within society" (Mitchell, 1974, pp. xv, xxi, xxii).

Others, not surprisingly, took issue with Mitchell. They included the feminist sociologist Nancy Chodorow. "Mitchell defends uncritically Freud's work, sharply criticizes that of his contemporaries (both supporters, like Deutsch, and opponents, like Horney and Jones), and ignores most later developments in psychoanalytic theory," she objected (Chodorow, 1978, p. 141). It was just such later developments in psychoanalytic theory that she used in theorizing femininity and masculinity. In particular she used the post-Freudian theories of Donald Winnicott regarding the mother's identification with her infant and of Ralph Greenson regarding the mother's subsequent disidentification from her son as means of promoting his male identity. Using these theories Chodorow sought to explain how girls and boys acquire the feminine closeness to others and the masculine separateness from others required of them in their respective adult roles as caring mothers and wage-earning fathers.

Her psychoanalytically based account of women's feminine closeness with others was very much welcomed by many feminists including the poet, Adrienne Rich, who used it in arguing against the intrusion into this closeness by what she described as "compulsory heterosexuality" (Rich, 1980, p. 631). Chodorow's account, however, ignores the ambivalence of women's feminine closeness with their mothers. With her theory that sexual inequality could be ended through getting men to parent equally with women so that girls and boys equally acquire the traits of caring femininity and wage-earning masculinity, Chodorow also proposes a solution to sexual inequality that is pure wish-fulfilling voluntarism in failing to tackle the question of why men would ever want to give up the advantages they gain from not sharing parenting equally with women.

The feminist sociologist Jessica Benjamin adopts another aspect of post-Freudian theory in explaining femininity and masculinity. In particular she uses the psychoanalytic theory of Margaret Mahler and others (1975) about the paradoxical dependence of the toddler on its mother's recognition of its independence, and Donald Winnicott's (1968) theory that it is through the mother surviving her infant's actual and imagined attacks on her that it acquires a sense of itself and its fantasies as separate from her. Women's social subordination, Benjamin argues, results in their not seeming to have the authority to confer recognition on their toddlers' independence, and in their not seeming to survive their infants' actual and imagined attacks on them. Boys look instead to the masculine authority of the father to confer recognition of their independence. Girls, however, are obstructed in doing this by their feminine gender identity.

Benjamin explained in these terms the frequent feminine capitulation of women to men akin to that of the slave in relation to the master in Hegel's account of the dialectic of self-consciousness. Or, as Benjamin also put it, "the mother's lack of subjectivity, as perceived by both male and female children, creates an internal propensity towards feminine masochism and male sadism" (Benjamin, 1988, p. 81).

This was followed by Judith Butler adopting Joan Riviere's psychoanalytic account of women defending against men's envy of their achievement by adopting a masquerade of femininity.

Butler also adopted Freud's psychoanalytic account of melancholia as effect of identification with those the melancholic has loved and lost in arguing that femininity involves identification with the masculinity that is its loss, and vice versa. To this Butler adds the emphasis on psychoanalysis as one of many discursive practices producing the body as sexual. It is through discursive practices that female and male bodies are produced and gendered as feminine and masculine, she claims. This, in turn, has led more recently to criticism of Butler and other feminist theorists – by, for instance, Raewyn Connell (2009) – for paying so much attention to discursive practices that they fail to pay sufficient attention to the female and male bodies in their account of feminine and masculine identity or identities.

## Symbolism and fantasy

While some claims regarding feminism and psychoanalysis focus on femininity and masculinity other claims focus on symbolism and fantasy. In his 1900 book, *The Interpretation of Dreams*, Freud took issue with those who interpreted dreams in terms of preconceived symbols. He likewise took issue with Jung for interpreting dreams and fantasies in these terms in his 1912 book, *Symbols of Transformation*. Feminists have nevertheless argued that Freud's theory of female penis-envy should be understood in terms of the symbol of the penis as phallus.

"The phallus assumes such worth as it does because it symbolizes a dominance that is exercised in other domains," argued Simone de Beauvoir, adding:

> If woman should succeed in establishing herself as subject, she would invent equivalents of the phallus; in fact, the doll, incarnating the promise of the baby that is to come . . . I believe that she has the power to choose between the assertion of her transcendence and her alienation as object.
>
> *(De Beauvoir, 1949, pp. 80, 82)*

De Beauvoir went on to cite psychoanalytic theories about the anxiety of the baby, aged 6 months, on discovering its separateness from the mother and fleeing from this newfound "freedom" in losing itself in "the bosom of the Whole" or in projecting itself in an image of its wholeness as reflected by the mirror. "Whether or not the mirror actually plays a more or less considerable part, it is certain that the child commences towards the age of six months to mimic his parents, and under their gaze to regard himself as an object," she argued, citing as evidence the psychoanalytic observations of Lacan (De Beauvoir, 1949, pp. 296–297).

Then, referring to the masculine protest theory of the psychoanalyst, Alfred Adler, she argued that "it is the valuation established by the parents and associates that lends to the boy the prestige of which the penis becomes the explanation and symbol in the eyes of the little girl." The advantage of the penis as symbol resides in it serving as "an organ that can be seen and grasped," she continued in going on to add:

> Because he has an *alter ego* in whom he sees himself, the little boy can boldly assume an attitude of subjectivity; the very object into which he projects himself becomes a symbol of autonomy, of transcendence, of power . . . But the little girl cannot incarnate herself in any part of herself. To compensate for this and to serve her as *alter ego*, she is given a foreign object: a doll . . . The main difference is that, on the one hand, the doll represents the whole body, and, on the other, it is a passive object. On this account the little girl will be led to identify her whole person and to regard this as an inert given object.
>
> *(De Beauvoir, 1949, pp. 305, 306)*

Whereas De Beauvoir wrote interchangeably about the penis and its symbol, the phallus, Lacan (1958) emphasized the latter in his theory of the Oedipus and castration complex. This was followed by two further Paris-based psychoanalysts, Laplanche and Pontalis (1968), pointing out that the meaning of the phallus in symbolizing castration and its opposite is learnt by children via the myths, legends, stories and other images conveyed to them by relatives, friends and acquaintances in the culture into which they are born.

Shulamith Firestone, by contrast, took a rather different tack. She argued that Freud's theory of the Oedipus and castration complex should be understood symbolically as a metaphor of men's power over women in the patriarchal family. "As for the 'penis envy,' again it is safer to view this as a metaphor," she continued. "Even when an actual preoccupation with genitals does occur it is clear that anything that physically distinguishes the envied male will be envied," she explained (Firestone, 1970, pp. 53–54).

Ironically, although she rejected this rereading by Firestone of Freud's penis-envy theory in terms of the symbolic value of the penis in the patriarchal family, Juliet Mitchell adopted a similar symbolic rereading of Freud's theory of the Oedipus and castration complex in recounting it as follows:

> The girl only acquires her secondary feminine identity within the law of patriarchy in her positive Oedipus complex when she is seduced/ raped by, and/or seduces the father. As the boy becomes heir to the law with his acceptance of symbolic castration from the father, the girl learns her feminine destiny with his symbolic seduction . . . The bisexual disposition of her pre-Oedipal moment remains strong and her Oedipus complex is a poor, secondary affair. An affair in which she learns that her subjugation to the law of the father entails her becoming the representative of "nature" and "sexuality," a chaos of spontaneous, intuitive creativity. As she cannot receive the "touch" of the law, her submission to it must be in establishing herself as its opposite – as all that is loving and irrational.
>
> *(Mitchell, 1974, pp. 404, 405)*

This does not seem very promising for women! Nevertheless Mitchell sought to wrest an optimistic conclusion from her Lacan-influenced version of psychoanalysis. The way forward, she claimed, resides in analyzing the contradiction between "the specifically capitalist ideology of a supposedly natural nuclear family" and "the kinship structure as it is articulated in the Oedipus complex" (Mitchell, 1974, p. 409).

Analyzing this or any other contradiction might be the way forward for feminist and psycho-analytic theory. It is not necessarily the way forward, in and of itself, for feminist politics. The feminist anthropologist, Gayle Rubin, nevertheless adopted Lacan's version of psychoanalysis, together with Marxist theory, in arguing for the isolation of "sex and gender" from the "mode of production" in dreaming of "an androgynous and genderless (though not sexless) society, in which one's sexual anatomy is irrelevant to who one is, what one does, and with whom one makes love" (Rubin, 1974, pp. 203, 204).

Dreaming, like analyzing contradictions, cannot by itself bring about the sexual equality that feminist politics seeks to achieve. Nor can symbolism. How, then, can feminists best counter the centrality accorded by Lacan to the symbol of the phallus that results, says Irigaray, in woman becoming the "more or less complacent facilitator for the working out of man's fantasies" without knowing "what she wants, ready for anything, even asking for more, if only he will "take" her as the "object" of his pleasure" (Irigaray, 1977, p. 100).

So what does woman want? Not the visible penis or phallus, says Irigaray, according to whom woman's sexuality is given not by vision but by touch. "Caressing the breasts, touching the vulva, opening the lips, gently stroking the posterior wall of the vagina, lightly massaging the cervix, etc." That is what women want, she says. It is this that evokes "the most specifically female pleasures." Yet this is overlooked by Lacan, complains Irigaray, with his focus on the "phallically" symbolic trade and kinship exchange of women by men in patriarchy (Irigaray, 1977, pp. 101, 103, 105).

"Get out of their language. Go back through all the names they gave you," Irigaray urges women, alluding to Lacan's claim that women (like men) only find themselves in terms of their fathers' names and in terms of patriarchy's law against incest symbolized by the phallus (Irigaray, 1980, p. 69). "Let them have oneness . . . in which the other is the image of the one, but an image only," Irigaray adds in going on to advocate that women find their sexuality in the two-lipped vulva as symbol of their sexuality (Irigaray, 1980, pp. 69, 71).

But, like Chodorow's shared parenting solution to sexual inequality, Irigaray's solution to the centrality accorded by Lacan to the phallus by advocating an alternative female symbol for women is nothing but wish-fulfilling voluntarism. The centrality accorded to the phallus as symbol of women's as well as men's sexuality in our still patriarchally ruled society cannot be overturned by simply wanting and urging women to adopt a different female symbol of their sexuality. Nevertheless Irigaray's riposte to Lacan in these terms continues to find much support among feminists.

So does the appropriation by the feminist philosopher, Judith Butler, of Lacan's phallus-centered theory for queer theory and lesbianism. Writing about the implications of Lacan's theory for lesbianism she says

> If the phallus is that which is excommunicated from the feminist orthodoxy on lesbian sexuality as well as the "missing part," the sign of an inevitable dissatisfaction that is lesbianism in homophobic and misogynist constructions, then the admission of the phallus into that exchange faces two convergent prohibitions: first, the phallus signifies the persistence of the "straight mind," a masculine or heterosexist identification and, hence, the defilement or betrayal of lesbian specificity; secondly, the phallus signifies the insuperability of heterosexuality and constitutes lesbianism as a vain and/or pathetic effort to mime the real thing. Thus, the phallus enters lesbian sexual discourse in the mode of a transgressive "confession" conditioned and confronted by both the feminist and misogynist forms of repudiation: it's not the real thing (the lesbian thing) or it's not the real thing (the straight thing). What is "unveiled" is precisely the repudiated desire, that which is abjected by heterosexist logic and that which is defensively foreclosed through the effort to circumscribe a specifically feminine morphology for lesbianism. In a sense, what is unveiled or exposed is a desire that is produced through a prohibition.
>
> *(Butler, 1993, pp. 85–86)*

Despite this prohibition, symbolized in Lacan's version of psychoanalysis by the phallus, Butler argues that it raises the possibility of the phallus being re-appropriated for lesbian desire.

If the lesbian "has" the phallus she does not "have" it in the traditional sense. Thus, argues Butler, she throws into question what it means to "have" a phallus at all (Butler, 1993, pp. 88–89). So saying, Butler concludes

> When the phallus is lesbian, then it is and is not a masculinist figure of power; the signifier is significantly split, for it both recalls and displaces the masculinism by which it is impelled. And insofar as it operates at the site of anatomy, the phallus (re)produces the spectre of the penis only to enact its vanishing, to reiterate and exploit its perpetual vanishing as the very

occasion of the phallus. This opens up anatomy – and sexual difference itself – as a site of proliferative resignifications.

*(Butler, 1993, p. 89)*

This lesbian phallus argument is not easy to understand. Some feminists are nevertheless attracted to this argument. Others reject it. They include Judith Gardiner, who complains that this argument wrongly echoes "Freudian notions that women – especially lesbians – envy and wish to appropriate men's penises and that powerful women are by definition phallic" (Gardiner, 2012, p. 607).

A rather different tack is taken by the literary theorist and psychoanalyst, Julia Kristeva. She argues that Lacan emphasizes the phallus as symbol at the expense of paying little attention to its precursors in pre-symbolic fantasy and what he calls the illusory identification of the toddler with its imaginary or virtual image in the mirror. Lacan's emphasis on the phallus also overlooks, or was developed in opposition to, the mother-centered version of psychoanalysis developed by various psychoanalysts, including Winnicott's popular psychoanalytic theory emphasizing the developmental precursors of symbolism in the transitional phenomena of the baby's sucking, self-caressing with fluff, for instance, and in its farting, "mum-mum" babbling and so on (Winnicott, 1953, p. 4).

Freud long ago observed that symbolism can become so abstract and divorced from the "perceptual residues" in which it originates developmentally that it has to be re-enlivened with new perceptual qualities (Kristeva, 1972, p. 217). Kristeva links this with the following observation:

When the means of expression have become so refined, so attenuated that their power of expression wears thin, it is necessary to return to the essential principles which made human language. They are, after all, the principles which "go back to the source," which relive, which give us life. Pictures which have become refinements, subtle gradations, dissolutions without energy, call for beautiful blues, reds, yellows – matters to stir the sensual depths in men.

*(Kristeva, 1972, p. 221)*

From these and other observations Kristeva formulated her theory emphasizing the precursors of symbolism in the "semiotic" constituted by "primary process . . . drives" articulating "a *chora*" preceding "the realm of signification" (Kristeva, 1974).

In contrast to Lacan's emphasis on the symbol of the phallus she emphasizes the fantasy, in men as well as women, of mothering as an idealized lost continent: *un continent perdu* (Kristeva, 1977, p. 30). She links this with the sublime and also with horror of woman as site of abjection in evoking the fantasy of one with the mother again as in the womb and in early post-uterine life prior to birth, as it were, into symbolism and language.

Previously the term *nameless dread* had been used by the psychoanalyst, Wilfred Bion, to describe the horror involved in psychotic states of mind (Bion, 1962, p. 116). Kristeva writes in similar terms in starting her essay on abjection, the subtitle of her book, *Powers of Horror*.

There looms, within abjection, one of those violent, dark revolts of being, directed against a threat that seems to emanate from an exorbitant outside or inside, ejected beyond the scope of the possible, the tolerable, the thinkable . . . When I am beset by abjection, the twisted braid of affects and thoughts I call by such a name does not have, properly speaking, a definable *object*. The abject is not an ob-ject facing me, which I name or imagine. Nor is it an ob-jest, an otherness ceaselessly fleeing in a systematic quest of desire. What is abject is not my correlative, which, providing me with someone or something else as support, would allow me to be more or less detached and autonomous. The abject has only one quality of the object – that of being opposed to *I*.

*(Kristeva, 1980, p. 1)*

Kristeva links this state of mind with melancholia that she characterizes as a sense of being invaded by an "unnamed Thing" (Kristeva, 1987, p. 13).

Kristeva links this with pre-symbolic immersion in the mother prior to emergence from paranoid-schizoid and projective identification fantasy into depressive position recognition of separateness as theorized by the Kleinian psychoanalyst, Hanna Segal. The work of psychoanalysis entails, says Kristeva, putting into words the fantasies, against which things and symbols are used as a deadening defense, so as to bring back to life the patient's capacity for free association.

As illustration Kristeva describes one of her psychoanalytic patients, a painter, Didier. "Even Didier's accounts of his dreams seemed defensive, neutralizing," she writes. He only became psychologically alive, it seemed, in speaking about his paintings. Even then his "specialized" and "technical" account of them kept Kristeva, she says, from imagining what these paintings looked like. So she got him to bring and describe pictures of them whereupon she was struck by their depiction of "mutilated persons, who were primarily female, and who were shown to have a derisive nature and an unsuspected ugliness" (Kristeva, 1993, pp. 15, 18, 19). In keeping with the talking method of psychoanalysis Kristeva put the fantasies evoked by Didier's pictures into words whereupon, it seems, he gave up his dead-seeming account of himself, his life and work with the liveliness of his free associations in accepting, varying, rejecting or adding to Kristeva's interpretations.

The same year as this was published (1993), an exhibition of abject art, inspired by Kristeva's account of symbols as defense against fantasies of woman as site of horror and abjection, was held at the Whitney Museum in New York. That year also saw the publication of a book, *The Monstrous-Feminine*, in which the feminist academic, Barbara Creed, used Kristeva's theory of fantasies of the female body as site of horror and abjection as means of countering depictions of woman as victim in horror films. Other feminists have adopted psychoanalytic theory of abjection and horror and ways these psychodynamic processes and the defense of projection is used to promote fear of others. The feminist academic, Sara Ahmed (2004), for instance, uses psychoanalysis in this sense as means of understanding so as to combat sexist and racist discrimination.

Bracha Ettinger has become influential in using Kristeva's focus on "the feminine site of matrixial co-subjectivity" as counter to Freudian and Lacanian focus on "phallic difference" (Pollock, 2006, p. 166). Others have taken issue with the starting point of Kristeva's psychoanalytic work in literary research into the modernist novels of Louis-Ferdinand Céline using rhythms and slang to convey the chaos of human suffering. From this research it is but a short step to Kristeva going beyond Lacan's theory of the phallus to the pre-symbolic world of suffering, horror, and objection. In doing so, however, complains Imogen Tyler (2010), neither Kristeva nor her followers attend to ways in which the fantasy of woman as site of suffering, horror, and abjection contributes to their becoming the object of sexual abuse, rape, battering and other forms of violence.

More recently, and in quite different vein from Tyler, the feminist theorist, Alison Stone, has written appreciatively about Kristeva's idea of the pre-Oedipal "imaginary father" and Winnicott's idea of the pre-symbolic "potential space" in arguing that the infant's development of an identity separate from that of its mother can be explained without recourse to Lacan's theory of the phallus (Stone, 2012, p. 118). The engagement of these and other feminists with psychoanalysis continues with further claims regarding femininity and masculinity, and regarding symbolism and fantasy.

## Contributions

How, in sum, has feminism contributed to psychoanalysis and vice versa? Feminist contributions to psychoanalysis include persuading at least some psychoanalysts and psychoanalytic psychotherapists to become less prone to heterosexist discrimination and more aware of the social subordination of women contributing to the ills of their patients.

Psychoanalysis, on the other hand, has contributed to feminism's greater awareness of the psychological ramifications of bodily differences between the sexes and the symbols and fantasies – including fantasies of castration and horrifying abjection – which these differences may evoke.

## Criticisms

Feminist criticisms of psychoanalysis include rejection of Freud's seemingly biological determinist account of female psychoanalysis as determined by the lack of a penis in girls and women. They have also criticized Freud's subordination of female psychology to that of boys and men; and for the use of Freud's writing by his ego psychology followers and others to advocate, more or less explicitly, the conformity of girls and women with their socially allotted role as heterosexual wives and mothers. In addition to this feminists have criticized Freud for equating the lack of a penis in girls and women with castration not as fantasy but as fact; and for abandoning his recognition of the fact of sexual abuse as a cause of women's psychological ills in favor of attributing these ills instead to wish-fulfilling sexual fantasy.

Feminists, in turn, have been criticized for their academic elitist and obscurantist use of psychoanalysis, and for their adopting psychoanalysis in developing accounts of women's psychology that overlook ways this is affected by differences of history, culture, social class, disability and sexual orientation.

## Conclusion: continuing importance and future

Feminism and psychoanalysis remain important as means of countering continuing social inequalities between the sexes that feminism seeks to redress, and as means of highlighting the role of femininity and masculinity, and of symbolism and fantasy, in perpetuating these inequalities. Ensuring the continuing value of feminism and psychoanalysis in the social sciences, humanities, the arts, and in psychotherapy depends on this value not being eroded by the greed of individual men and women in power in the name of the selfsame liberal ideology in terms of which the historical and intellectual development of feminism and psychoanalysis began.

## References

Abraham, K 1922, 'Manifestations of the female castration complex', *International Journal of Psychoanalysis*, vol. 3, pp. 1–29.

Ahmed, S 2004, *The cultural politics of emotion*, Routledge, London.

Althusser, L 1969, *Lenin and philosophy and other essays*, New Left Review, London, pp. 177–202.

Benjamin, J 1988, *The bonds of love*, Pantheon, New York.

Bion, WR 1962, *A theory of thinking: Second thoughts*, Heinemann, London, pp. 110–119.

Butler, J 1993, *Bodies that matter*. Routledge, London.

Chodorow, N 1978, *The reproduction of mothering*, University of California Press, Berkeley.

Connell, R 2009, *Gender*, Polity, Cambridge.

De Beauvoir, S 1949, 1972, *The second sex*, Penguin Books, Harmondsworth.

Firestone, S 1970, *The dialectic of sex*, Morrow, New York.

Freud, S 1883, 1972, 'Letter to Martha Bernays, 5 November', in E Jones, 1953, *The Young Freud*, Hogarth, Harmondsworth.

Freud, S 1905, *Three essays on sexuality on the theory of sexuality*, Basic Books, London.

Freud, S 1920, 'The psychogenesis of a case of homosexuality in a woman', in J Strachey (ed), *Standard edition of the complete psychological works of Sigmund Freud*, vol. 18, Hogarth, London, pp. 145–172.

Freud, S 1923, 'The infantile genital organization', in J Strachey (ed), *Standard edition of the complete psychological works of Sigmund Freud*, vol. 19, Hogarth, London, pp. 141–145.

Freud, S 1924, 'The dissolution of the Oedipus complex', in J Strachey (ed), *Standard edition of the complete psychological works of Sigmund Freud*, vol. 19, Hogarth, London, pp. 173–179.

Freud, S 1925, 'Some psychical consequences of the anatomical distinction between the sexes', in J Strachey (ed), *Standard edition of the complete psychological works of Sigmund Freud*, vol. 19, Hogarth, London, pp. 243–258.

Freud, S 1931, 'Female sexuality', in J Strachey (ed), *Standard edition of the complete psychological works of Sigmund Freud*, vol. 21, Hogarth, London, pp. 221–243.

Freud, S 1933, 'Femininity', in J Strachey (ed), *Standard edition of the complete psychological works of Sigmund Freud*, vol. 22, Hogarth, London, pp. 112–135.

Friedan, B 1963, *The feminine mystique*, Penguin Books, London.

Gardiner, J 2012, 'Female masculinity and phallic women', *Feminist Studies*, vol. 38, no. 3, pp. 597–624.

Horney, K 1926, 'The flight from womanhood', in *Feminine psychology*, Norton, New York, pp. 54–70.

Irigaray, L 1977, *This sex which is not one*, Cornell University Press, Ithaca, NY.

Irigaray, L 1980, 'When our lips speak together', *Signs*, vol. 6, no. 1, pp. 69–79.

Jones, E 1935, *Papers on psycho-analysis*, Beacon Press, pp. 485–495.

Klein, K 1928, 'Early stages of the Oedipus complex', in *Love, guilt and reparation*, Hogarth, London, pp. 186–198.

Kristeva, J 1972, 'Giotto's joy', in LS Roudiez (ed), *Desire in language*, Columbia University Press, New York, pp. 210–236.

Kristeva, J 1974, *Revolution in poetic language*, Columbia University Press, New York.

Kristeva, J 1977, 'Hérethique de l'amour', in LS Roudiez (ed), *Tales of love*, Columbia University Press, New York, pp. 234–263.

Kristeva, J 1980, *Powers of horror*, Columbia University Press, New York.

Kristeva, J 1987, *Black sun*, Columbia University Press, New York.

Kristeva, J 1993, *New maladies of the soul*, Columbia University Press, New York.

Lacan, J 1948, 'Aggressivity in psychoanalysis', in *Écrits*, Tavistock, London, pp. 8–29.

Lacan, J 1958, 'The signification of the phallus', in *Écrits*, Tavistock, London, pp. 281–291.

Laplanche, J & Pontalis, J 1968, 'Fantasy and the origins of sexuality', *International Journal of Psychoanalysis*, vol. 49, no. 1, pp. 1–18.

Mahler, M, Pine, F & Bergman, A 1975, *The psychological birth of the human infant: Symbiosis and individuation*, Basic Books, New York.

Millett, K 1970, *Sexual politics*, Doubleday, New York.

Mitchell, J 1974, *Psychoanalysis and feminism*, Allen Lane, London.

Parsons, T & Bales, R 1955, *Family, socialization and interaction process*, Free Press, Glencoe, IL.

Pollock, G 2006, 'Beyond Oedipus: Feminist thought, psychoanalysis, and mythical figurations of the feminine', in V Zajko & M Leonard (eds), *Laughing with Medusa*, Oxford University Press, Oxford, pp. 67–117.

Rich, A 1980, 'Compulsory heterosexuality and lesbian existence', *Signs*, vol. 5, no. 4, pp. 631–660.

Rowley, H & Grosz, E 1990, 'Psychoanalysis and feminism', in S Gunew (ed) *Feminist knowledge: Critique and construct*, Routledge, London, pp. 175–204.

Rubin, J 1974, *A psychoanalysis for our time: Exploring the blindness of the seeing*, New York University Press, New York.

Rubin, G 1975, 'The traffic in women', in R. Reiter (ed) *Towards and anthropology of women*, Monthly Review Press, New York, pp. 157–210.

Stone, A 2012, 'Against matricide: Rethinking subjectivity and the maternal body', *Hypatia*, vol. 27, no. 1, pp. 118–138.

Tyler, I 2010, *Social abjection and resistance in noliberal Britain*, Zed Books, London.

Winnicott, DW 1953, *Playing and reality*, Penguin, Harmondsworth, pp. 1–30.

Winnicott, DW 1968, 'The use of an object and relating through identifications', in *Playing and reality*, Penguin, Harmondsworth, pp. 101–111.

# 23

# Psychoanalysis and sexuality

*Muriel Dimen*

Psychoanalysis is witnessing a return to sex. There at the start, sexuality slipped backstage along with drive theory, as object relations, attachment theory and psychoanalytic gender theory made their way forward. Its contemporary positioning needs to be seen in that context, in relation to psychoanalysis as a whole. Psychosexual theory is imbricated with all the changes psychoanalysis has undergone since its beginnings: the shifts in theory of motivation (from drive theory to attachment theory), model of development (from Oedipal to pre-Oedipal dynamics), structure of mind (from the second topology to the ego and the self) and mode of treatment (from the classical one-person and objectivist to the postclassical, intersubjective and relational). Each of these changes inflects how sexuality is understood, addressed and experienced in clinical psychoanalysis.

In the realm of the sexual as in any other region of mental life, psychoanalysis is a theory alive in practice. The way it conceives of sexuality shadows the consulting room as well as the page. At the same time, psychoanalysis is alive in culture: its intellectual richness means that it both draws and bears on other bodies of thought. Its ideas are inevitably inspired by various disciplines; indeed, Freud's 1920 Preface to the Fourth Edition of his epochal *Three Essays on the Theory of Sexuality* (1905[1953]) pays tribute to philosophy: "For it is some time since Arthur Schopenhauer, the philosopher, showed mankind the extent to which their activities are determined by sexual impulses – in the ordinary sense of the word" (p. 134).

Sexuality is a category whose map, to employ Alfred Korzybski's metaphor, is easily confused with its territory. With this one brilliant, and breathtaking, phrase – "sexual impulses – in the ordinary sense of the word" – Freud starts a new map. What will happen during the course of the following century, however, will be a case of the territory repeatedly correcting the map. For what the 20th century would show – and what Freud already knew – is that what is deemed "ordinary," in sexuality as in any other realm, is largely a result of culture.

"Sexuality" has many meanings – maps – that vary historically and culturally, among disciplines, and among schools of thought. Indeed, in the dialectical process by which changes in the territory force changes in the map, psychoanalysis itself has had a profound influence on what Western culture has come to consider sexual since Freud's day. Two regions of sexuality are at stake here. One is sexuality as lived, the other is sexuality as lynchpin of theory. Given sexuality's centrality to Freud's conceptualization of mind, illness and treatment, these two facets are, classically, intimate neighbors.

However, as Freud's thought has unfolded and as psychoanalysis has evolved, their intimacy can no longer be taken for granted; even where it endures, crucial departures from the classical model of mind and desire have taken place.

Psychoanalysis has not yet replaced that all-encompassing structure of psyche, theory and practice called "psychosexuality," nor is there any inevitability that it can, will or should. For now, at least, multiple models are necessary. Some schools of thought – largely of the object relational and intersubjective sort – tend to sideline sex, assuming or ignoring or subsuming it to attachment. Lacanian and other French theory regard it as coextensive with mind, desire, sanity and language, while eschewing the developmental pathways Freud deemed its spine. Still other psychoanalytic approaches – principally psychoanalytic feminism – address sexuality here and there, but focus mainly on gender. While the term "sexuality" is no less complex than that of gender or object relation or self or desire, the debates about it within psychoanalysis are much less thickly layered, its intellectual history patchier.

## Defining "sexuality"

Excess, in a way, can be said to define psychosexuality and, in any event, it describes how much is and was compacted within the single signifier of "sexuality." By the time Freud wrote his epochal *Three Essays on the Theory of Sexuality* (1953[1905]), the OED (2013) shows many meanings of "sex," "sexuality" and "sexual" dotting the map. "Sex," in the 14th century, denotes the polar categories (male vs. female). During the 18th century, "sexuality" comes to signify a personal capacity: "the quality of being sexual or possessing sex." By 1900, the taxonomy of "sex," in effect coordinate with sexuality as a state of mind, designates activities too. At the start of the 19th century, "sexual" identifies feelings, while at its end, "sexuality" indicates "a person's sexual identity in relation to the gender to which he or she is typically attracted; the fact of being heterosexual, homosexual, or bisexual; sexual orientation" (French notions of sexuality evolved as well [Colombo, 2002, in Widlöcher, pp. 68–69]).

## Libido: from impersonal to personal

With one stroke, Freud at once simplifies and complicates this already teeming conceptual territory. From a single idea, *libido*, he derives a theory of desire that circulates back and out to his theories of mind. Of course, Freud does not think of *libido* as an idea: for him, it is the territory and he is mapping it:

> The fact of the existence of sexual needs in human beings and animals is expressed in biology by the assumption of a "sexual instinct," on the analogy of the instinct of nutrition, that is of hunger. Everyday language possesses no counterpart to the word "hunger" but science makes use of the word "libido" for that purpose.
>
> *(Freud, 1953[1905], p. 135)*

Freud draws on both biology and physics to craft his cardinal concept. If, say Laplanche and Pontalis (1967, p. 239), instinct inhabits "the frontier between the mental and the physical" (Freud, 1953[1905]), libido dwells on the mental side of that line. It consists in a continuous flow of impersonal excitement that underlies psychic process and structure and that seeks discharge. Found among all human beings, it does not observe yet partakes of that natal divide between male and female (about which Freud was sometimes of two minds): although libido is "masculine," it nevertheless manifests in women (if perhaps with a reduced flow).

As a concept, libido does much theoretical work. To condense Person's (1986) admirable summary, it is not only an appetite demanding satisfaction, it has psychological power: it is a force that registers sexual instincts in the mind and thereby partners the emotion of sexual longing. Alternatively conceived, libido is an energy that accumulates to produce a tension Freud calls "unpleasure": it mounts, surges, seeks release. Existing outside awareness, it nevertheless serves to excite consciousness, there to be transformed into something the psyche wishes to get rid of.

This original and very appealing psychoanalytic solution to the problem of defining or mapping that excess called sex nevertheless fell short of its goal. As Karen Horney (1926) would complain in regard to women's desire (a complaint Freud [1923] himself recognized but tendentiously negated), libido, if only masculine, may obscure more than it reveals about women's sexuality. Nor is what is now (but not in Freud's time) termed *gender* the only complication. Some 50 years after the *Three Essays*, libido would be deemed a relational river as well as, or even instead of, a sexual one. If, in classical, "one-person" psychology libido is a force that, drawing on the body but registered in the mind, drives individual developmental process and behavior, in postclassical psychology, which construes mind as both made of relations between subjects and emergent in complex relational networks, libido obtains between individuals.

According to this new map, argues Fairbairn (1954), libido is not an impersonal force. Rather, it is personal, seeking not discharge but objects. Correspondingly, everything changes. Discharge and the decrease of unpleasure can no longer be thought to be the prime constituents of pleasure. If we construe the need for objects – others and relationships to them – at the root of psyche, or self, then we need to reinterpret pleasure. In this view, mind is inherently interpersonal, or, at least, the manifest divide between intrapsychic and interpersonal is no longer self-evident. Mind, in this perspective, develops not within an individual skin but between persons; psychic process and structure emerge out of early object relations. Likewise, pleasure inheres in attachment, issuing not from tension-discharge but from object relationships themselves. To put it more schematically, libido, circulating between, as well as within, persons, is a two-person phenomenon.

## Drive, aim, object: corresponding transformations

The story of the map and territory of sex is a series of what Foucault (1966, p. xii) termed "corresponding transformations." In psychoanalysis, these several transformations take place in our understandings of sexuality; of gender; of mind; of health and illness; and of clinical process, including the roles and relationship of analyst and patient. The argument that sexuality is interpersonal and intersubjective as well as intrapsychic applies also to psychosexual development.

Freud begins his argument by disagreeing with the conventional view. Sexuality, he says, is not born whole, but arrives piecemeal via three innate, but initially disparate elements: drive, aim and object. "Drive," according to Laplanche and Pontalis (1967, p. 214), is a dynamic process in which a pressure pushes an organism toward an "aim." Issuing from a corporeal "source," the drive's goal is to dispel the tension created by this stimulus, while the "object" serves as the means by which this aim may be achieved.

By thus formulating the relations among drive, aim and object as they constitute libido's trajectory, Freud challenged prevailing opinion. Generally, the object – the beloved – had been held to be the stimulus that, at puberty, excites the drive and sets it on its way toward its aim of heterosexual and reproductive intercourse. Freud contended instead that the sexual instinct, albeit innate, precedes the object. Its aim and object are not inherent but acquired, even achieved, and consequently pleasure takes multiple forms. Aims are many and disconnected, and objects are "variable, contingent and only chosen in . . . definitive form in consequence of the vicissitudes of the subject's history" (Laplanche & Pontalis, 1967, p. 215). Significantly, though, the Freudian corpus implicitly anticipates postclassical counterarguments that psychosexuality, among other phenomena, emerges neither at birth nor epigenetically. An innate energy, its particular form nevertheless takes shape and color as a consequence of particular experience, a distinction that the *Three Essays* terms "constitution" versus "accident," or what later would be called "object-relational."

## Component instincts complicated by intersubjectivity

Complications abound. Take, for example, psychosexual development, called by Freud "biphasic." The first phase, infantile sexuality, is "polymorphously perverse." The second, puberty, concludes psychosexual development by using genital heterosexuality to "solder" together drive, aim and object. These "transformations of puberty" also unite what have hitherto been the severally emerging component or partial instincts that sequence sexual development. In turn, each of these has two parts: a bodily source and an energic aim. Even though in Freud's ultimate view, the entire body is an erogenous zone, the mucus membranes, like the mouth or anus, vagina or urethra, are fundamental and originary: "We must regard each individual as possessing an oral erotism [or instinct], an anal erotism, a urethral erotism, etc." (Freud, 1953[1905], p. 205, n. 1). These partial instincts are partnered by partial aims; for example, the scopophilic instinct underlies the voyeuristic and exhibitionistic instincts, the instinct to master anchors the instinct for cruelty and so on (Laplanche & Pontalis, 1967, p. 74).

At the end of the *Three Essays*, however, libido's intricate complications fold neatly into a familiar story. At the end of development, heterosexuality is achieved, partiality settles into wholeness, and all becomes clear. Initially, the component instincts, disconnected from one another, may serve as elements of anarchic foreplay. With the advent of genital erotism, however, a governing principle arrives and links them in linear sequence: each having been involved with its own pleasures, they now line up, the earlier and lesser supporting the later and greater. The emergence of the reproductive aim bestows functional and experiential dominance on the genitals, and all other pleasures into preparation for genital excitement. In sum, then, "a new sexual aim appears, and all the component instincts combine to attain it, while the erotogenic zones become subordinated to the primacy of the genital zone" (Freud, 1905, p. 212).

Much can be said about this oversimplification. Its reification of heterosexuality as the sexuality of record – installed and culturally ratified via the Oedipal crisis (discussed in more detail later) – has been criticized abundantly in feminist and queer literatures; even Freud supplied qualifications in a variety of footnotes. Less familiar, though, are the shifts in psychoanalytic theories of mind and psychoanalytic technique that in turn reveal new portions of the psychosexual territory in need of new maps. For example, the notion that mind forms in the space between self and other (Benjamin, 1988) recasts erogenous zones and component instincts: desire, argues Fairbairn (1954), is fed by connections between people, not just by body chemistry (or epigenesis). Eros may bring forth connection, but connectedness likewise excites passion. Sexual desire is also intersubjective, arising in the space between subjects as well as inside them.

Developmental theory and eros partner differently too. Psychosexual stages, read through two-person psychology, acquire new meanings, their corporeality intensified by interpersonal valence. Sullivan's (1953) example is the most familiar and famous: the mouth is an erogenous zone because nursing makes it a primal site of attachment, not because its mucosity innately situates excitement. The oral pleasure experienced within and by the individual organism has two-person roots and resonances: it is exciting to get together with mother and get fed. Likewise, the anus is excitable because it situates toilet-training power struggles. Out of this phase of parent–child relatedness, which makes matters of control and will primary, anality acquires its close link to the component instincts of sadism and masochism. Indeed, it may be possible to situate at this stage of development the primary, if often disregarded centrality of power to sexual pleasure, unpleasure and relationships.

## Lust, psychoanalysis and the politics of sex

Freud's map of psychosexuality – libido; the independence of drive, aim and object; the component instincts; the gathering of all by and under the banner of heterosexuality identity and intercourse – is the only one that psychoanalysis has. Its potential not yet entirely exploited, it is also out of date. The crafting of a new one is barely nascent. Even Freud knew, however, that, as must be already evident, his preemptively clarifying map of an inherently ambiguous territory made even more complicated by its mappings, was not so simple. As developments beginning a half-century later would show, psychosexual theory benefits from varied and multiple readings.

Indeed, the reduction offered by "libido" was perhaps already causing complications. Explaining on the first page of the *Three Essays* his choice of a Latinate term, Freud (1953[1905]) adds a footnote (the bottom of the page often situating his ambivalence): "The only appropriate word in the German language, *Lust*, is unfortunately ambiguous and is used to denote the experience of a need and of its gratification" (1953[1905], p. 135, n. 2). Freud's map succeeds by omitting part of the territory he is trying to chart. The map mandated by science – and Freud, a medical man, wanted psychoanalysis known as a science – requires precision, not ambiguity. *Lust*, however, does not meet this standard. It is apparently self-contradictory, denoting (Strachey adds as editor) either desire or pleasure.

The meaning of *Lust* is, in other words, excessive: it connotes both the longing for pleasure and pleasure itself, a doubleness unavailable in the English homonym, lust. In rejecting *Lust*'s hybridity, Freud strips sexuality of something vital. Perhaps there is a straight shoot from biological need to biological satisfaction; he has indicated, remember, that hunger is simple (although the convolutions of anorexia and bulimia qualify this suggestion considerably). The sexual way is, however – and it is Freud who teaches this – anything but straight.

Between libido and *Lust* lies a century of controversy, contest and changes in theoretical and clinical practice. If libido marks the ultimately straight and narrow of biology, *Lust* marks the contradictions, the twinned joy and suffering of the psyche. Libido and *Lust* render two competing psychoanalytic accounts of sex, one articulated, the other buried. Libido is the account we know, but *Lust*, a piece of sexuality hiding in plain sight beneath the text, is the account we intuit. Sexuality as territory is riddled with paradoxes and uncertainties to which must be put questions that would have lacked legitimacy within classical thought, but answers to which are potentiated by the idea of *Lust*.

The cardinal feature of libido, its drive toward discharge, is rich with presupposition and implication, with models of body and mind, illness and cure, desire and action, social values and moral dicta. In clinical context, it is the bridge between sex and sanity.

Classically, sex requires release, without which illness ensues; there is a psychic economy, and sex is central to it. It is not far from sex as safety valve to catharsis as psychic cure, an excursus on which will illuminate two corresponding transformations crucial to the understanding of the trajectory of psychosexuality: the method of clinical psychoanalysis and the psychoanalytic feminist critique of gender and sex.

It seems useful here to review a classic psychoanalytic text on the psychoanalytic theories of treatment, illness, and sexuality, "Anna O." The "talking cure," the basis for the fundamental psychoanalytic technique Freud would term *free association*, is what Anna O (Breuer & Freud, 1891) named it, although today she might have said she "just needed to talk." Then she called it "chimney sweeping" – a domestic metaphor appropriate to much of her life at the time and also true to the root meaning of catharsis, "to clean." Although this account of psychoanalytic cure is controversial (whether in fact Bertha Pappenheim, for whom the pseudonym "Anna O" was given, got symptomatic relief but not cure), and although the therapeutic mechanisms are under debate (whether it was the mere act of talking or, rather and as will be further addressed later, talking *to* someone that helped her), still Anna O's strong image of chimney sweeping accorded well with classical psychic economy.

Nowadays, psychoanalysts do not measure their work by catharsis. Indeed, much of psychoanalysis may be regarded as a dialectical development in response to this early formulation. Clinicians think instead of many sorts of transformation – mutual engagement between subjects, between analyst and patient; the integration of vertical splits into a self with a coherent consciousness; the achievement of the depressive position; the registration of lack. This evolved hybridity of theory and technique demands similar shifts in psychosexual theory, such as an overhaul of the discharge model of and for sex.

Discharge and sex do make a suspiciously perfect couple: sexual discharge and psychic discharge, the economics of body and mind, cure and sex. Freud, it is said, derived the sexual discharge model from the economic theory (which he drew from Newton and Darwin). But, to flip map and territory here, it is equally likely that the economic theory drew on the sexual model. Perhaps discharge became the psychoanalytically defining moment of sex because of its physicality: discharge-as-map may have had rather more literal origins. If, in the beginning of *Three Essays*, of sex and of psychological development, all sexual pleasures are equal, in the end only one is said to count: "end pleasure," or orgasm. So goes the argument of *Three Essays*. The desired and psychically necessary completion of the sex act, end–pleasure is defined as discharge of two things – force and, in Freud's (1953[1905], p. 207) phrase, "sexual substances."

The force is familiar: energy, libido. Discharge as substance, however, can refer only, in Freud's time, to seminal emission. Contemporary research on female ejaculate notwithstanding (Ladas, Whipple, & Perry, 1983), only the orgasms of men routinely entail physical discharge – at least in the Euro-American view of these matters; Tantric Buddhism, by way of contrast, teaches a sexual practice in which male orgasm occurs without ejaculation (Odier, 1997). In argument with, especially, Krafft-Ebing, Freud (1953[1905]) recognizes the bias of this formulation: "Having been designed to account for the sexual activity of adult males, it takes too little account of three sets of conditions which it should also be able to explain. These are the conditions in children, in females and in castrated males" (p. 214). However, that he goes on to warn against laying "more weight on the factor of the accumulation of the sexual products than it is able to bear" does not impel him to rethink further the implications of the discharge model. This is a task left to later generations.

Maybe, as Holt (1989, p. 184, n. 7) quite sensibly and perhaps humorously proposes, there was another substance at stake. He suggests that the original model for drive was not hunger but urination – a model that captures the drift but also the insufficiency of discharge theory (see also Ferenczi, 1933). Although the implicitly invidious comparison between seminal discharge and micturition may ill serve the erotics of urination, it does bring out a certain grimness in the classic theory of psychosexuality. Revealed is the astonishing chain implicated by the figure of discharge: urine, semen, symptom, cure. At work here is the hydraulics of sex and psyche: the relief upon excreting urine, the release of ejaculating semen, the cathartic passing of the symptom, the calm after the storm of illness.

Cleanliness and godliness would not seem to be far behind. This often unquestioned imbrication of hygiene, sex, illness, and treatment is worth noting. Semen-as-waste-product reveals a somewhat insalubrious layer to sexuality, at least in its cultural interpretation, which psychoanalysis unknowingly shares. Enter the power or political dimension of sexuality, which the psychoanalytic map does not mark out but which the late 20th century, with its critique of the heteronormatizing drift of psychosexual theory, made known as a central part of the territory.

A Foucauldian perspective unveils a sort of policing function, a moralizing tone that stands out when discharge becomes the exclusive metaphor for sexuality or, for that matter, for sanity. As hygiene, sexuality becomes a moral and medical matter subjected to the authority of doctors, clergy, therapists and other guardians of the contemporary soul. The economic theory of sex, or at least the aim it bestows on sex, embeds sexuality in a model of health and illness, engineering and efficiency. Indeed, one can wonder whether this theorization of sex on a model of dirt and pollution served unconsciously and structurally to push it to the clinical sidelines.

It is possible then to see how the discharge model of psychosexuality exerted a moral force exercised on clinical practice. In the classical mode of treatment, what mattered was the interpretive climax: once the patient had told all, the doctor would know what was wrong and could then tell the patient what caused the illness – an authoritative (if also sometimes authoritarian) telling that was curative. Doubting not only the efficacy of this model of cure, but its veridicality, analysts work very differently now. They entertain a variety of psychic outcomes and sexualities; they notice and value enactments and the indeterminacy they sow (Chused, 1996; Ogden, 1994); they employ a variety of theoretical and clinical practices. They ask whether it is the destination that matters or the journey. They ponder the relative importance of three factors: interpretation, the process of arriving at it, and the relationship between analyst and patient.

## Sexuality and gender

In correspondence with this clinical evolution has been a fundamental transformation toward a multifaceted understanding in psychosexual theory itself. For one thing, much of the territory once designated by the map of libido has been remapped – by political and intellectual forces – as gender. Freud's conventional, undertheorized blurring of sexual difference with sexual desire left a gap where theory ought to have been. Mid-20th-century, this vacuum began to be filled: first the sexologist John Money et al. (1955), then the psychoanalyst Robert Stoller (1965, 1968, 1975), and, following them, feminists of many stripes, began to use "gender" to designate the psychological and social dimensions of the traditional male/female dualism. The new map – perhaps a meta-map – charts a continuum, with gender the psychosocial at one end and sex the biological at the other. This distinction, however, was and is inadequate for the complex thing psychoanalysis is.

This remapping, and the social forces prompting it, fell on ground already prepared for the sociocultural challenges of and to gender and sex confronting psychoanalysis in the late 20th century. One might point to Freud's expressed feelings that one could be a good citizen despite not having followed the *Three Essays'* developmental pathway. Witness his famous and moving letter to the American mother, in which he offers reassurance that homosexuals are among the culturally preeminent, that her son's homosexuality is not an illness, and that, insofar as he is neurotic, he can be helped to resolve his conflicts into peace of mind. Consider the ironic take on the prevalence of sexual variation in the most apparently normal: many become neurotic in order not to be perverse ("neurosis is the negative of perversion"). And, despite the way every fiber of his theory of mind strives toward pathologizing the nonheterosexual, it is indubitable that his insistence on the universal presence of sexual variation in psychic substrate has inclined the heterosexual mainstream, at least in the First World, increasingly, if not yet conclusively, to accept homosexuality, trans phenomena, and perverse sexual practices within the range of human sexual possibility.

Yet, the tension, in Freud's work and in psychoanalysis as a whole, between convention and radicalism is dynamic. The pull toward the former is reassuring, the push toward the latter disturbing and therefore easier to resist. For example, Freud argued that women had desire, just like men, and they suffered especially from its frustration. At the same time, he believed their desire was inferior in strength and significance. Given this underlying ambiguity in psychoanalysis, the delay in its institutional acceptance of gender and sexual variance is perhaps not strange.

The social movements around gender and sex had a large if delayed and not always credited impact on psychoanalytic thought and practice. Only at the end of the 20th century, in the 1990s, as psychoanalysis was becoming feminized in personnel and maternalized in theory and practice (Phillipson, 1993), did it become possible for out gay psychologists to be admitted to psychoanalytic training. Prior to that time, when homosexual identification was diagnosed as an illness – privately if not overtly, since it had been removed from the *Diagnostic and Statistic Manual* (DSM) in 1973 gay analysts would go through training, including their mandatory psychoanalytic treatments, in the closet. How odd that a practice that asks its patients to tell the truth, or at least to come as close to the truth as they are aware, would implicitly have required a special category of analysands to lie.

## The paradigm flip: a matrix of diverse models

Instead of a single narrative, a matrix of diverse models of psychosexuality is now evolving. By the end of the last century, it became clear the classical formulation of psychosexuality had been negated in clinical theory and practice. Classically, drive theory views affective and interpersonal needs as "an overlay upon a more basic template of sexuality and aggression" (Domenici, in Domenici & Lesser, 1995, p. 34). In contrast, a congeries of new theories such as object relations theory, interpersonalism, intersubjectivity theory, self psychology, and American relational psychoanalysis reverse the matter, making sexuality the secondary precipitate of a desire for connection and intimacy (Fonagy, 2008; Stein, 1998).

Yet, at the very moment when this negation was recognized, sexuality had begun to reenter psychoanalytic purview. The watershed year seems to have been 1995. "Has sexuality anything to do with psychoanalysis?" is the sarcastic title of the late André Green's (1996) Freud birthday lecture at the Anna Freud Centre. The same year also saw four new books on psychosexuality. Sheldon Bach (1995) freshly sets a Winnicottian platform under the traditional binary of sex and aggression. Joyce McDougall (1995) finds dilemmas of psychic life and death embedded in sexual desire and practice. Otto Kernberg (1995) couples classic psychosexuality with postclassic object relations.

Finally, the authors in *Disorienting Sexuality*, an anthology edited by Thomas Domenici and Ronnie Lesser (1995), deploy social constructionist, feminist and queer theory to interrogate the way sexual identity is construed in clinical and theoretical psychoanalysis.

The simultaneity begs for explanation. Looking first to the immediate historical context, it is arguable that the presence in the psychoanalytic community of the previously sexually marginalized – women and homosexuality, feminism and queer theory – had revived interest in sexuality altogether. The establishment of a robust and critical psychoanalytic gender theory (Benjamin, Butler, Corbett, Dimen, Goldner, Harris) had challenged and mitigated psychoanalysis' traditionally febrile focus on the putative illness of women's desire. Add the aftereffects of this change to the ongoing force of homosexuality's 1973 removal from the DSM, incomplete and unstable as it may have been (Young-Bruehl, 1996). The harm caused by such stigmatization having been put into question, a welcome void resulted, in which new conversations about identification and preference could commence, an absence that also made room to consider whether sex can once again be theorized without regard to gender (Dimen, 2003; Stein, 1998).

The year 1995 also dates two psychoanalytic anniversaries. The lesser, oddly, is the centenary of Breuer and Freud's *Studies on Hysteria*. Of greater import for the understanding of sexuality is the 50th anniversary of the end of World War II, which had scattered European psychoanalysts to the winds and in so doing forced the break in psychosexual theory that was, paradoxically, to allow its contemporary transformation from a single to a hybrid narrative. There is no doubt that, until this time, many aspects of Freud's view of sexuality had become a sort of dogma on which the existence of the discipline and the movement were thought to depend. Not only was psychoanalysis itself founded on the treatment of hysteria, an illness thought to issue from sexual repression. Its theory and treatment of sexuality and of its sufferings were fused with its theory and treatment of mind and mental illness.

The year 1995 marks the sea change. Before World War II, theoretical difference within psychoanalysis was professionally and personally dangerous. To question psychosexual theory was to question psychoanalytic practice and to question either was to question the movement. Disagreement therefore turned into dissent, and dissent into dismissal: in regard to women's desire, for example, penis-envy and vaginal orgasm became shibboleths to which obeisance had to be paid in order for membership in the psychoanalytic order to be achieved and maintained. As evidence for this faith-based entrance requirement, we need only look to Karen Horney's expulsion from the ranks.

By 1995, however, it would appear that these shackles had rusted away. Difference has become the name of the game. And since then, psychosexuality has once again become a staple of psychoanalytic colloquy. If Françoise Davoine is right to argue that it takes two generations to shake off the trauma of war, then perhaps it makes sense that, 50 years after World War II's end, a new cohort could emerge that no longer had to fight their grandparents' battles. Instead, they could look at old questions from a refreshed vantage point. The map of psychosexuality now shows new territories to be explored, mined, inhabited: the relationship between sexuality and attachment; sexuality as enigmatic and alien; autoerotism and intersubjectivity; sexuality and power; and sexual phenomenology.

## A debate deferred: sex and attachment

Perhaps the region currently drawing the most attention is what Widlöcher (2001b) has artfully mapped as the debate "that did not take place." Arising in the 1930s but interrupted by war, its central bone of contention was whether sexuality is inborn or arises in relationship. A correlative question – which is developmentally originary, sex or attachment? – had marked crucial divides among psychoanalytic schools. Freud and his (particularly American) followers believed that sexual desire begins in primary narcissism and auto-erotism, with object-love acquired secondarily. In contrast, Melanie Klein, Sandor Ferenczi, Michael Balint and others held by primary object love and attachment: first came the relationship, based on inborn needs for attachment, and thence sexual desire.

Enter the French. Perhaps it has taken an encounter with difference to break this stand-off, with its origins in Vienna, Berlin and Budapest, and its continuations in London and the United States. With the ascendancy of British object relations, which substituted issues of attachment for psychosexuality, and North American ego-psychology, which Oedipalized it (e.g., Fenichel, 1945; see Corbett, 2011), psychosexuality had come to take a back seat in the Anglophone psychoanalytic world. However, it had always remained front and center in French psychoanalysis. The work of Jean Laplanche (1976) is crucial at this juncture, because it appears to offer the possibility of resolving the apparent contradiction between sex and attachment that had emerged in psychosexual theory.

In a new map, Laplanche proposes that sexuality is originally and always on a twofold path, both narcissistic and object related (Widlöcher, 2001). Thinking of how sexuality comes to individual psychology, Laplanche follows Winnicott's (1953, p. 39), proclamation: "There is no such thing as an infant," only the mother–infant unit: no baby develops outside object relation. Where, however, Winnicott – who is uninterested in sexuality – goes on to tell us mostly about the infant and some about the mother, Laplanche, in his focus on sexual desire, elaborates on the mother's subjectivity. Her unconscious, he contends, is a sexual unconscious, and it constitutes the psychic amniotic fluid in which the baby comes into its psychological self (see also Kristeva, 1983).

However, the child, who cannot yet understand sexuality, receives this implanted desire as indecipherable, disturbing and enigmatic. It's as though the mother's desire, now transmitted through unconscious communication, is a question that cannot be understood, a bewildering demand the infant experiences and will spend a lifetime trying to decipher.

Laplanche also characterizes sexuality. It always feels foreign, "an alien internal entity" with the lifelong capacity to unsettle and distract. This strange state of affairs is complicated by sexuality's trajectory. Laplanche's version of a developmental theory has the infant, having tasted the milk, longing for it – and not the breast – ever after. In other words, the breast comes to stand in for the substance that the baby needs/wants and that can never be enjoyed again in the way it was in the first place; the hallucinated breast represents primal nourishment. Every displacement afterwards follows the same pattern. Sexual desire, in this view, partakes of the constant deferral core to Lacanian thought.

Here one might think of Freud's characterization of sexuality: "*En attendant toujours quelque chose qui ne venait point*" ("Always waiting for something which never came"; quoted in Green, 1996, p. 872).

Yet, the idea of the generalized seductiveness of the maternal dyadic relation had been anticipated by Ferenczi, at least in principle (1933). In his landmark but shunned and only recently revived "The Confusion of Tongues Between Adults and Children," he attempts to account for patients' accusations of cruelty by their analysts. In exploring these moments, he happens on his patients' recovered memories of trauma, in which an adult had inflicted one version of sexuality – "the language of passion" – on a child who lived a different version – "the language of tenderness." The sexual abuse and its manifestation in transference and countertransference constituted a discovery (which led to Ferenczi's silencing by the International Psychoanalytical Association) were, Widlöcher (2001) points out, local versions of the more general phenomenon Laplanche theorizes.

Conceptualizing infantile sexuality as evolving within the relationship with the mother allows it to be theorized in the context of attachment. Although Laplanche himself did not operationalize this process, others interested in attachment and development are now making the attempt. Inspired by Laplanche, Fonagy (2008), for example, links sexual enjoyment and sexual development. Employing attachment models, he imagines the Laplanchean mother as sexualizing "the infant's arousal, unconsciously seducing him" (or, we should add, "her," although attention to gender would introduce a host of complications that no attachment-sexuality theorist has yet taken up).

Both sides of the debate meet in this formulation: some innate, sexualizable energy is assumed to infuse a relationship in which a formed adult influences the form and structure that energy takes. This process is an opportunity for the mother (or other parent) to promote or discourage or otherwise inform the infant's sexual expression. It takes place via her responses to manifestations of her baby's arousal, responses that could be called "procedural" (Boston Change Process Study Group [BCPSG]). For example, let's say the parent catches sight of what she or he interprets as sexual enjoyment in the baby, who is smiling or entranced while she plays with her genitals. The parent who is comfortable with sexuality both personally and as it manifests in babies can smile in return. Or, unsettled in a variety of ways, he can fail to mirror this proto-sexuality: he may turn away, or frown, or become anxious or angry or embarrassed, or restrain the offending hand. Fonagy adduces research to indicate that, most of the time, mothers fail to mirror. Or, at least, they tell the researcher that they look away. Thus is sexuality instilled, tinged with anxiety, perplexity and loneliness.

## The alien internal entity, and enigma

Perhaps Laplanche's unique contribution is his proposition that strangeness is key to sexuality. Unmirrored, sexuality comes with tension, disrupted self-coherence and feelings of incongruence, as Fonagy puts it. It is thereby always uneasily more than itself, an excess that, in different language, Benjamin (1998) attributes to "failures in affective containment [which] may produce sexual tension rather than reflect some interpersonal transmission of unconscious sexual content" (p. 7). Davies (2001), unearthing yet another effect of the unmetabolizable spillover of parent–child intimacy, argues that parents usually find themselves at a loss when faced with a child's sexual affect. Such empathic failure, while not inherently traumatizing, evokes relative to sex a trauma-like atmosphere of unspeakability. (Of course, such an absence depends on cultural context in societies where parents and children share a sleeping space, children's presence during parental sex may afford mutual sexual empathy. The primal scene's significance is, in other words, culturally relative, not necessarily traumatic or even, as Aron [1995] proposes, generative.)

One of the problems in assimilating a model of attachment to a theory of psychosexuality however, is the gravitational pull toward considerations of health and illness. To think in terms of attachment is to engage developmental theory, which in turn leads to concerns for good and bad outcomes; even to consider the question of mothering prompts assessments of adequacy. Pronouncements of sexual health and illness follow inevitably. Fonagy, for example, proposes a model of sexual enjoyment that he bases in relationship, reciprocity, and "at least the appearance of mutuality in the physical act" (2008, p. 26).

The pull here seems to be a positive model of sexual mental health, birthed in marriage and untroubled by loss. Indeed, the authorization granted by normativity compels Kernberg (1995) to sanction bondage and domination as long as practiced in conjugal intimacy.

However, a normative model of healthy development ill suits the excessiveness of sexuality. It leads away from one of Freud's main and ironic percepts about psychosexual health, which, he contends, is achieved via suffering: intercourse via penis in vagina, with seminal emission uninterrupted – the act and mark of heterosexual identity – comes at the cost of relinquishing many other sorts of pleasures. An ideal of sexual health likewise obscures the main import of Laplanche's perception: psychosexuality is, by its nature, disturbing and unsettling, which means it lies outside the binary of health versus illness: sexual disturbance is routine.

Yet, although sexual passion look like illness, it occupies a different register, that of enigma (Stein, 1998). Sexuality lives psychically in the place where self-understanding stops: at the gap, to use a Lacanian formulation, before which one is dumb, stymied.

Although Stein situates her understanding of the alien-ness and excessiveness of sexuality in relation to the primal (and normative) dyad, her focus is on sex as ineffable, unspeakable, simultaneously traumatic and ecstatic. Sexuality represents a wordless world apart from daily life's logic and care. Governing it are forces toward self-dissolution, the melting of boundaries that feels like the death of self, a pleasure that is suffered (Saketopoulou, 2014), the shattering of the psychic structures necessary to get through the ordinary day. Sex here situates both the sacredness of ecstasy and the profaneness of body and mortality.

Perhaps this dimension of sexuality can illuminate, from another angle, why the transmission of sexuality through the bonds of attachment crackles with anxiety. Laplanche's notion of the disturbance of sex reprises in a different lexicon Freud's (1930) famous observations about its amorality. It is not only that a parent's sexual self-revelation would constitute a sort of incest and therefore be wrong. Consciously, parents want their kids to have beautiful sex, like they want everything beautiful for them – no trauma, pain or abjection. At the same time, they know that the altered state Stein limns is not always beautiful. It is hard to imagine parents revealing, with self-respect, the fact that to achieve ecstasy they willingly risk what, perceptible to a daily frame of mind, would spark embarrassment, shame and humiliation. To imagine them being entirely at ease with their kids' sexual affect and expression is to imagine them being at ease with what Ferenczi (1933, p. 206) called "the hate-impregnated love of adult mating."

## Desire

This way of seeing things leads psychoanalysis in a new direction. To say that psychosexuality is enigmatic – one's unknownness to oneself – is to make a statement about sexual subjectivity, that is, the experience of sex – or as Stein called it, its phenomenology: the unconscious and conscious registry of desire, identity, object-choice and practices. Examining sexual subjectivity becomes crucial to interrogate because sexuality itself can no longer be taken for granted as a self-evident drive, affect, or set of behaviors. It is no longer a unisex model of tension, discharge, relief, of progress from polymorphous perversity to adult procreativity. Not only must femininity as well as masculinity, homosexuality as well as heterosexuality as well as bisexuality, the missionary position as well as versions of bondage and domination, be taken into account when it comes to desire. There may be as many sorts of desire as there are individuals who desire (Chodorow, 1994); indeed, desire itself changes throughout life, to extend a point insisted on by the classical narrative.

"Desire" is a far better mapped region of sex now than in 1905, when it stood under the aegis of "wish." Most simply, desire is about longing, not having. It may be sweet or poignant or terrible, but without it, one is as without appetite. Its ambiguous location both between and within those who feel it generates an irony: it is our "only instinct requiring the stimulation of another person" (Claude Lévi-Strauss, 1949, p. 12). If one takes attachment into account, one could say that desire emerges in relationship but, belonging to the child alone, survives only if lightly held, even benignly neglected, by the authorized caretaker(s). In one-person terms, writes Levenson (1994), desire seems to spring full-blown in intrapsychic process, almost a species characteristic. In the linguistically based Lacanian view, it emerges as a consequence of the failure of speech, of the gap between the Imaginary and the Symbolic. From a two-person vantage point, however, desire turns out to be oddly intersubjective.

In sum, desire eludes the neat binary between one-person and two-person psychologies. Lacan (1966) situates its origin in a relation that is, all the same, not quite a relationship: as the yearning to be the object of the (m)Other's desire, it emerges in (maternal) intimacy, a nexus situated, however, in the presymbolic Imaginary. Levenson would have it both ways, insisting that "desire requires another person" (1994, p. 692) while stressing the "peculiar paradox built into this wish to find one's completion in the regard of the Other." Betwixt and between, desire tends toward the cryptic, an "enigmatic message," as Laplanche sees it, or, as Winnicott (1971) and Khan (1974) view it, located in a private self that, to one's pleasure and regret, no one else can access.

## Models of desire

Certainly, like sexual identity, sexual subjectivity must be built of multiple elements and function as a compromise formation. Chodorow (2003, pp. 12–17) has proposed that individual sexuality comprises several linked, interacting components that are universally occurring, but idiosyncratically combined: erotization, sexual practices, an internal world, affective tonality, sexual object choice, sexual (and, we should add, gender) identity, culture and fantasy, which integrates in highly personal fashion all the preceding elements, marking them with aggression as well as lust.

Taking sexual subjectivity into account demands multiple models of desire. If, for example, libido signifies the drivenness of sex, *Lust* describes the experience during it. *Lust* means not the conclusion of discharge but the penultimate moment of peak excitement when being excited is both enough and not enough, when each rise in excitement is, paradoxically, satisfying. The pleasure of *Lust* is as central as the catharsis of orgasm. In this state of sustained excitement, opposites meet. A need calling for satisfaction, a satisfaction becoming a thrilling need. In this excitement whose gratification is simultaneously exciting, one is both "lost to the world" and in the world at once (Bach, 1995). *Lust* stands for the extraordinary poignancy marking the moment before the climax: libido puts a distance between tension and release, *Lust* posits their simultaneity. The line between them is therefore always on the verge of disappearing. As Freud himself notes later in the *Three Essays*, "The concepts of 'sexual excitation' and satisfaction' can to a great extent be used without distinction" (p. 210; see Dimen, 2003).

This doubleness in sexual subjectivity may also be theorized in object relational terms. Davies (2006, pp. 672–673) proposes the interaction of two distinct erotic subsystems that are related to two opposing psychic configurations. In this interaction, the building and plateauing and rebuilding of *Lust* play a role in the creation of a sexual state of mind.

Davies links two sorts of sexual experience, "the times we sizzle and the times we sigh," to two internal structures. The experience "of sexual arousal and yearning" arises in relation to a desired other who excites the unconscious fantasy of a tantalizing, "bad" other. The experience of "satisfaction, pleasure, and release" is for its part linked to a desired other who taps into the internal good, caring object. The ability to achieve sexual gratification rests in the capacity to bridge these two sexual states. Bearing eroticized frustration consists in the ability "to sustain a state of increasingly intense sexual excitement (essentially a form of frustration) along with the equally pleasurable anticipation of its ultimate satisfaction."

## Toward a new Oedipus

It is striking that these newer accounts omit what might be considered cardinal to the classical theory of psychosexuality: the Oedipal story. However, the place of this iconic narrative in psychosexual theory is complicated. There is no question that the whole meta–concept denoting the Oedipal crisis, complex and resolution is lacking in regard to variance in gender identity, sexual orientation and sexual practice. It is, after all, not an account of desire per se. Rather it accounts for the development of desire once it reaches the phallic stage (see Abraham, 1924; Meltzer, 1979). Serving as Freud's attempt to formulate how the object relations of sexual desire emerge, it parallels very well his theory of the normative development of heterosexuality. In its narrative of a child's (boy's) love, it shows how the members of the normative nuclear triangle become positioned in a sexual imagination. Loving and hating his father, loving his mother and fearing his father, submitting to his father's power to avoid castration, he defers his desire for his mother in return for a future woman of his own.

The Oedipal crisis and its resolution could almost be described as an ideal and normatizing account of how frustration is eroticized. Through a series of reversals of desire – passive then active then inhibited in relation to father, inhibited then lustful toward mother – the child becomes a sexual being in the context of a set of relationships that are a model for mind: The Oedipal triangle embodies a psychic, mythic, and cultural crisis in which the tripartite structure (id, ego, superego) of mind is formed, a family stabilized by a hierarchy of gender difference, and a culture reinforced by a psychically meaningful power structure (Mitchell, 1974).

As a story of psychosexuality, however, the Oedipal account leaves something to be desired. Certainly it needs an overhaul in regard to gender difference: we know nothing satisfactory about the equivalent psychic passage for girls. Nor do we know much about the relation between Oedipality and the multiple manifestations of desire. That this is also a story of patriarchy and its reproduction; that female subjectivity receives short shrift; that homoerotic desire, however elaborated in the story's nooks and crannies, appears only as a wrong turn; that a blank stands where the mother ought to be – this is old news (see Dimen & Goldner, 2005). If it is possible to make some inferences about the origins of sexual desire by looking into the pre-Oedipal relation – the mother-infant dyad – it would be interesting to have some studies of the transmission of desire in triangular context. The effect of parents' sexual activity, intimacy, and attitudes, of sexual preference, of practices of monogamy and non-monogamy, just to mention a view variables – all these flavor the sexual atmosphere in which a mind comes to be.

An equally compelling question would be why psychoanalysis cannot seem to do without the classical recounting of the nuclear family triangle and its transformations. In addressing this puzzle, it is possible and perhaps even desirable to put on hold the necessary gender critique in order to understand the relation of Oedipus to incestuousness. A clue lies in the clinical dimension. The transformations undergone by psychosexual theory since Freud's day – and in part as a result of that day – have been concurrent with elemental changes in how psychoanalysis is conducted. Classically, the analyst, doctor of the mind, treated the mentally troubled patient the way the doctor of the body might have treated the physically ill patient. In his omniscience, the doctor knew the patient's desire, especially hers for him, for which he would be on the lookout. In a well-conducted analysis, this desire was thought to manifest as one or another permutation of the Oedipal crisis: the female patient's desire for her analyst, in particular, would bump up against the impossibility of sex with him. The psychoanalytic incest taboo would be the means for her frustration, which would occasion a crisis that the patient had to pass through on her way to cure.

Here, then, is one reason the Oedipal narrative lasts: it narrates how the incest prohibition – for Freud (1913), the foundation of civilization – is reinstantiated with each generation (Mitchell, 1974). And it tells why this reinstantiation is necessary: to order a mind, preserve the family, and shore up civilization. At issue, therefore, is the taboo's transgression. Before 1897, Freud argued that the violation of the taboo by a parent – usually father with daughter – and the repression that ensued caused in the child the illness called hysteria. After 1897, he elected to attribute hysteria's etiology to the child's repression of fantasies of sex with her parent (or father, maternal incest not being covered by the general theory, although it has come under discussion recently [Shapiro, 1999, pp. 288–290]). At the same time, the Oedipal account claims that obedience to the taboo is socially and morally necessary, and reiterates that the required loss is worth the benefit bestowed by civilization as enforced by subordination to what Lacanians refer to as the Law of the Father.

When it comes to the incest prohibition and its Oedipal frame, an irresistible parallel obtains between the family and the analysis. As the child and his/her father, or mother, are enjoined by the taboo, so are analyst and analysand. The taboo, issued by the paternal function, keeps them from getting out of sexual line, thereby safeguarding both social continuity and sanity.

At the same time, the Oedipal account lacks a crucial story: that of the parent's desire, and this absence creates a problem for the fate of sex in the consulting room. If sexuality begins in the maternal relation, then perhaps civilization begins when parents (not, *pace* Freud [1913], the siblings in the primal horde) recant their incestuous desire. By tradition, the incest taboo is read through the Oedipal drama, which stars a unique subject of desire, a child who must single-handedly manage triangulated love and hate (Freud, 1913, 1923). To be sure, the father has a supporting role, for he disrupts the (incestuous) mother–son merger so as to redirect the boy's desire away from his mother (and father) toward a future mate.

Newly mapped in the territory of sex is the desire of the adult: costarring in these emergent Oedipal narratives are the parents and their sexual desire. In the classical account, the parental objects lack subjectivity. Postclassical revision, in contrast, thickens the Oedipal plot, recognizing that insofar as the play is only internal, it tells but part of the story. Fairbairn (1954) and, to a lesser extent, Kohut (1977) cue the dyad: the child is not onstage alone. Front and center are the parents as subjects, their pleasure, inherent as it is in object relation, influencing if not generating the child's. This underexplored and possibly even buried psychoanalytic history contains a puzzle or two.

As proposed by Dimen (2011), some light might be shed on parental subjectivity and hence on that of analysts, if a heuristic binary were to be created – divide the Oedipus from the incest taboo so as to provide two views of the same drama. In concurrent and interpenetrating processes, the Oedipus speaks to children, while the incest taboo addresses adults (even as, of course, the Oedipus continues to evoke childhood dramas and dilemmas). The Oedipus, a developmental crucible, infuses a nascent psyche with a particular genre of desire in a triangular space. At the same time, the ban on incest embargoes the materialization of adults' desire in dyadic relation to their children (and, in the background, to the other parent). The incest prohibition addresses substantially formed beings, the adults in charge who, adept at personal and intersubjective multitasking, can hold the other(s) in mind without self-erasure; tend relationships (dyadic, triadic, multiple) without self-sacrifice and the ensuing resentments, from which children need protection; and, in fact, find this juggling act self-enhancing (a partial job description for analyst and parent alike; see Cooper, 2003).

These twin injunctions on desire's realization are interimplicated, their accomplishment is interdependent. The Oedipal fiat demands that the child abjure the fantasy of sexual and personal completion with the parent(s). This loss cannot be achieved without the parental willingness to endure the complementary loss (Davies, 2003), that is, to tolerate and grow from the suffering caused by the ban on materializing one's sexual desire for one's child (a submission implicit in Loewald, 1980). This intersubjective context, in which adults can reap the bittersweet power and pleasure of helping children toward their own sexuality, resonates in the analytic dyad, where it requires reflection as well as (in)action.

Such a reconstrual may be what clinicians need in order to address the ubiquitous problem of the analyst's desire and its not infrequent indulgence in sexual transgression with patients (Celenza, 2007; Gabbard, 1989). In the classical understanding of the clinical treatment of sexual suffering, nothing was said of the doctor's desire. In fact, they doctor was thought to be free of it, or at least was supposed to free himself from it. Between doctor and patient obtained a divide: the doctor knew; the patient came to be known. Consequently, what counted, classically, was the analyst's theory of the patient's sexual feelings: the map mattered more than the territory, and it did not chart the analyst's feelings, sexual or otherwise. Within the treatment, the focus was on the patient's transference to the analyst, whose own feelings in turn were generally considered irrelevant to the therapeutic proceedings. Erotic feelings, like any emotion, were to be erased, taken elsewhere, deemed the residue of incomplete analysis.

During the second half of the 20th century, however, the analyst came to be recognized as a presence in the room. Not just the neutral and objective knower, the analyst is a person with character and particularities and gifts and failings. The concepts that permitted mapping and clinical use of this territory were that of, first, countertransference, and, later, of subjectivity/ intersubjectivity. As uniquely as any other individual, the analyst's idiosyncratic reactions to the patient were seen to influence the treatment, and so had to be taken into account as part of it. Reciprocally, the patient notices the analyst's state of mind, including sexual feeling, and the analyst needs to be trained to recognize all sorts of countertransference (or co-transference or, for some, just plain transference), including the sexual.

The absence of psychosexual theory has probably limited the use clinical psychoanalysis can make of this admission of sexual countertransference to the map. The systematic inclusion of the analyst's subjectivity represents a total transformation of psychoanalytic technique. It is unprecedented in classical psychoanalysis, a genuine paradigm shift, an unthought-known of clinical psychoanalysis whose theorization revolutionized the field. However, as Mary Target (2007) has argued, the more that transference and, later, countertransference became central to clinical interest, the more sexuality faded from clinical attention. Uneasy with the challenge to their own psychic comfort, analysts began to ignore sexuality so as to reduce their anxiety; anyway, they and their patients had much else to focus on as the complexities of object relations were elaborated.

Perhaps, though, it would be better to say that what psychoanalysis lacks is a theory of sexuality that can help analysts think about their own sexual feelings as they arise in treatment. For most people, sexuality inhabits the realm of doing, not that of contemplation or reflection: a desire – a sexual impulse – is felt and a psychic struggle ensues about whether to act on it or not. Rules abound about when action is appropriate or not, their origins being diverse but tending to cluster in the Oedipal crisis, that meeting point of unconscious impulse, gender difference and hierarchy, and social regulation.

As goes Oedipal resolution, so goes the adult incest taboo: neither is ever fully accepted or resolved. The relation is likely causal: to the degree that adults' own Oedipal closure is always only partial (Meltzer, 1979) and precarious (Freud, 1923), their observation of the prohibition becomes as difficult as it is necessary. Lingering Oedipal regrets, stirred in adult fantasies of revitalized fulfillment, haunt analysts too (Twemlow & Gabbard, 1989). However intersubjectively carried such ecstatic fantasies of repair, still their disposition belongs finally to the person in charge – parent, analyst – who must register their presence but forego their realization. Achieving this surrender – tolerating the permanence of sexual melancholy – is no small task. It requires support from various sources, what Benjamin (2006) calls the moral third but also all that is denoted by *le nom du père* – community, culture, morality, the Law. This accomplishment is crucial: the negotiation of desire that constitutes one's life flourishes when tended by another's restraint.

If psychoanalysis were to offer a theory of adult incestuousness to partner its theory of Oedipal longing, perhaps analysts could find a way to speak and not act on their desire and so to leave room for their patients'. As is well known, if perhaps infrequently articulated, analysts' ability to contain their own desire with self-awareness equates to parents' observance of the incest prohibition. Such self-conscious containment creates and protects a gap in which the patient's subjectivity can come into its own (Bernstein, 2006). Bound to the mast of professionalism and care, analysts, like Odysseus (Wilner, 1998), ought to hear but not dance to the music of patients' desire. Their holding back depends on their cultivated capacity to recognize and contemplate their own desire (hence the required training analysis).

Recursively, in fact, the two abilities, to reflect on desire and to contain it, enhance each other. One may read Odysseus's mast as phallic and paternal. Or, with Benjamin (1998), one may theorize the labor of holding and reflecting as a (traditionally) maternal practice: revising the active/passive binary, she argues that passivity is not just activity's opposite, but also signifies containment. Others (e.g., Cooper, 2003) style this work as an analytic capacity, technique and obligation. They argue that, by detecting and analyzing adult sexuality, analysts can decode and manage sexual countertransference.

Conceived thus, the taboo on adult incest causes a rupture – the parent says "no" – that allows one to know one's own desire. By making room for child or, mutatis mutandis, the patient, the two-person materialization of the incest prohibition cultures a one-person experience. The ban, observed, opens a space that is at once full and empty (which might be as good a description as any to capture the feeling of desire). This opening is replete with potential: the option of sex between parent and child or analyst and patient, ruled out, transmutes into the child's/patient's potency and fantasy (see Samuels, 1996, p. 310). The parent/doctor who slips desire's leash leaves the child/patient at once famished and overfull. By contrast, analysts who contemplate their passion for their patients can exchange stolen pleasure for the sense of a job well done. They can savor a subtle, privileged view of dependents becoming what they need and will: autonomous. Or, to be more realistic, analysts may get to survive the equally delicate pain of watching patients make their own errors and discover that they no longer want what they once (thought they) did – which may, indeed, be one way to capsule the Oedipal resolution.

In revising the psychoanalysis of incestuous desire, it is important to render desire as neither wholly discharge-driven nor solely object-seeking. What matters is that, insofar as the ban on incest is observed, childhood's bolus of longing and loss, of disappointment, shame and anger, is part of growing up. Parents cannot save their children from it, just as analysts cannot save patients. Indeed, they foster it and, with it, an interior space for imagination, wish and fantasy. One of those predictable life wounds that Freud warns about, the suffering of unrequited love, is also key to a certain freedom: having endured it, one both gains oneself and is spared the unbelievable confusion attendant on one's desires being granted by the very other from whose desires one is trying to free oneself. One is granted the room to create oneself as if one were autonomous.

This map of a new Oedipus also demands that the analyst relinquish power. Or, rather, suffer a transformation of the familiar power over another to the power to contain self and other in an emergent process. If you can reflect on it, unrequited love permits you to sense your desire *as distinct* from, other to, the desire of the other who matters to you as much as your own life. But, like Anna O, you need someone else to help you do it. This growth takes place via the experience – or maybe even a fantasy – of being held by a parent or analyst or teacher or other like person. Symbolizing the previously unsymbolized, the abjection (Kristeva, 1982) that, survived, results from such restrained containment, constitutes a painful, profoundly personal corner for self-knowledge and self-containment. This trial by fire, a passage in every successful analysis, grows the analyst too (Cooper, 2003).

This yielding of power correlates with another sort of power that must not only show up on the map of sex, but transform itself so that new mapping can be done. There is no question that the whole concept of the Oedipal crisis, complex, and resolution needs a thoroughgoing revision. The more psychoanalysis can take this project seriously, the more it will alter the scope and rootedness of patriarchy, and the more patriarchy comes into reflective space, the more that analysts of whatever desire and gender/sexual identity will question how they deploy their clinical power. The territory is large, and ever-changing, and new maps are in the making as this writing happens.

# References

Abraham, K 1924, 'A short study of the development of the libido, viewed in the light of mental disorders', in E Jones (eds), *Selected papers on psycho-analysis*, Brunner & Mazel, New York, pp. 418–502.

Bach, S 1995, *The language of perversion and the language of love*, Aronson, New York.

Benjamin, J 1988, *The bonds of love: Psychoanalysis, feminism, and the problem of domination*, Pantheon, New York.

Benjamin, J 1998, *Shadow of the other: Intersubjectivity and gender in psychoanalysis*, Routledge, New York.

Bernstein, J 2006, 'Love, desire, jouissance: Two out of three ain't bad', *Psychoanalytic Dialogues*, vol. 16, pp. 711–724.

Breuer, J & Freud, S 1891, *Studies on hysteria*, Basic Books, New York.

Celenza, A 2007, *Sexual boundary violations: Therapeutic, academic, and supervisory contexts.* Aronson, New York.

Chodorow, N 1994, *Femininities, masculinities, sexualities: Freud and beyond*, University Press of Kentucky, Lexington.

Chodorow, N 2003, 'From behind the couch: Uncertainty and indeterminacy in psychoanalytic theory and practice', *Common Knowledge*, vol. 9, pp. 463–487.

Chused, J 1996, 'The therapeutic action of psychoanalysis: Abstinence and informative experience', *Journal of the American Psychoanalytic Association*, vol. 44, no. 4, pp. 1047–1071.

Colombo, E 2002, 'Sexuality and erotism: Fromsexuality to fantasy', in D Widlocher (ed), *Infantile sexuality and attachment*, Karnac Books, London, pp. 68–69.

Cooper, S 2003, 'You say Oedipal, I say post-Oedipal: A consideration of desire and hostility in the analytic relationship', *Psychoanalytic Dialogues*, vol. 13, no. 1, pp. 41–61.

Corbett, K 2011, *Boyhoods: Rethinking masculinities*, Yale University Press, New Haven.

Davies JM 2001, 'Erotic overstimulation and the co-construction of sexual meanings in transference and countertransference experience', *Psychoanalytic Quarterly*, vol. 70, pp. 757–788.

Davies JM 2003, 'Falling in love with love', *Psychoanalytic Dialogues*, vol. 13, pp. 1–27.

Davies JM 2006, 'The times we sizzle, and the times we sigh: The multiple erotics of arousal, anticipation, and release', *Psychoanalytic Dialogues*, vol. 16, pp. 665–686.

Dimen, M 2003, *Sexuality, intimacy, power*, Analytic Press, Hillsdale, NJ.

Dimen, M 2011, '*Lapsus linguae*, Or a slip of the tongue? A sexual violation in an analytic treatment and its personal and theoretical aftermath', *Contemporary Psychoanalysis*, vol. 47, pp. 36–79.

Dimen, M & Goldner, V 2005, 'Gender and sexuality', in E Person, A Cooper & G Gabbard (eds), *Textbook of psychoanalysis*, American Psychiatric, Washington, DC, pp. 96–113.

Domenici, T 1995, 'Exploding the myth of sexual psychopathology: A deconstruction of Fairbairn's anti-homosexual theory', T Domenici & R Lesser (eds), *Disorienting sexuality: Psychoanalytic reappraisals of sexual identities*, Routledge, New York, pp. 33–64.

Fairbairn, R 1954, 'Observations on the nature of hysterical states', *British Journal of Medical Psychology*, vol. 27, pp. 105–125.

Fenichel, O 1945, *The psychoanalytic theory of neurosis*, Norton, New York.

Ferenczi, S 1933, 'The confusion of tongues between adults and the child', *Contemporary Psychoanalysis*, vol. 24, pp. 196–206.

Fonagy, P 2008, 'A genuinely developmental theory of sexual enjoyment and its implications for psychoanalytic technique', *Journal of the American Psychoanalytic Association*, vol. 56, pp. 11–36.

Freud S 1905, 1953, 'Three essays on the theory of sexuality', in J Strachey (ed), *Standard edition of the complete psychological works of Sigmund Freud*, vol. 7, Hogarth, London, pp. 125–245.

Freud, S 1913, 1955, 'Totem and taboo', in J Strachey (ed), *Standard edition of the complete psychological works of Sigmund Freud*, vol. 13, Hogarth, London, pp. 1–155.

Freud, S 1923, 1961, 'The ego and the id', in J Strachey (ed), *Standard edition of the complete psychological works of Sigmund Freud*, vol. 19, Hogarth, London, pp. 1–66.

Foucault, M 1966, *The order of things*, Tavistock, London.

Gabbard, G (ed), 1989. *Sexual exploitation in professional relationships*, American Psychiatric Press, Washington, DC.

Green, A 1996, 'Has sexuality anything to do with psychoanalysis?', *International Journal of Psychoanalysis*, vol. 76, pp. 871–883.

Holt, R 1989, *Freud reappraised: A fresh look at psychoanalytic theory.* Guilford Press, New York.

Horney, K 1926, 'The flight from womanhood: the masculinity-complex in women, as viewed by men and by women', *International Journal of Psychoanalysis*, vol. 7, pp. 324–339.

Kernberg, O 1995, *Love relations: Normality and pathology*, Yale University Press, New Haven.

Kohut, H 1977, *The restoration of the self*, International Universities Press, Madison, CT.

Kristeva, J 1982, *Powers of horror* (L Roudiez, trans), Columbia University Press, New York.

Kristeva, J 1983, *Tales of love* (LS Roudiez, trans), Columbia University Press, New York.

Ladas, A, Whipple, B & Perry, J 1983, *The G spot and other recent discoveries about human sexuality*, Henry Holt, New York.

Laplanche, J 1976, *Life and death in psychoanalysis*, Johns Hopkins University Press, London.

Laplanche, J & Pontalis, J 1967, *The language of psychoanalysis*, W.W. Norton, New York.

Levenson, E 1994, 'Beyond countertransference', *Contemporary Psychoanalysis*, vol. 30, pp. 691–707.

Lévi-Strauss, C 1949, *Les structures élémentaires de la parenté*, Walter de Gruyter, Berlin.

Loewald, HW 1980, *Papers on psychoanalysis/Hans W. Loewald*, Yale University Press, New Haven.

McDougall, J 1995, *The many faces of Eros: A psychoanalytic exploration of human sexuality*, W.W. Norton, New York.

Meltzer, D 1979, *Sexual states of mind*, Clunie Press, Perthshire, Scotland.

Mitchell, J 1974, *Psychoanalysis and feminism: Freud, Reich, Laing, and women*, Pantheon Books, New York.

Money, J, Hampson, JG, and Hampson, J 1955, 'An examination of some basic sexual concepts: The evidence of human hermaphroditism', *Bulletin of the Johns Hopkins Hospital*, vol. 97, no. 4, pp. 301–319.

Odier, D 1997, *Tantric quest: An encounter with absolute love*, Inner Traditions/Bear, Rochester, VT.

Ogden, T 1994, *Subjects of analysis*, Karnac Books, London.

Oxford English Dictionary Online Third Edition, 2008, s.v. 'Sex', 'Sexual', 'Sexuality', accessed April 28, 2013.

Person, E 1986, 'A psychoanalytic approach', in J Geer & W O'Donohue (eds), *Theories of sexuality*, Plenum, New York, pp. 385–410.

Phillipson, I 1993, *On the shoulders of women: The feminization of psychoanalysis*. Guilford, New York.

Saketopoulou, A 2014, 'To suffer pleasure: The shattering of the ego as the psychic labor of perverse sexuality', *Studies in Gender and Sexuality*, vol. 15, pp. 254–268.

Samuels, A 1996, 'Jung's return from banishment', *Psychoanalytic Review*, vol. 83, pp. 469–489.

Shapiro, S 1999, 'Gender issues in transference and countertransference work with male survivors of childhood sexual abuse', in R Gartner (ed), *Psychoanalytic treatment of male survivors of childhood sexual abuse*, Jason Aronson, Northvale, NJ, pp. 266–294.

Stein, R 1998, 'The poignant, the excessive and the enigmatic in sexuality', *International Journal of Psychoanalysis*, vol. 79, no. 2, pp. 253–268.

Sullivan, H 1953, *The interpersonal theory of psychiatry*, Norton, New York.

Target, M (2007). 'Is our sexuality our own? A developmental model of sexuality based on early affect mirroring', *British Journal of Psychotherapy*, vol. 23, pp. 517–530.

Twemlow, S & Gabbard, G 1989, 'The lovesick therapist', in G Gabbard (ed), *Sexual exploitation in professional relationships*, American Psychiatric Press, Washington, DC, pp. 71–87.

Widlöcher, D (ed.) 2001a, *Infantile Sexuality and Attachment*, Karnac Books, London.

Widlöcher, D 2001b, 'The treatment of affects: an interdisciplinary issue', *The Psychoanalytic Quarterly*, vol. 70, no. 1, pp. 243–264.

Wilner, W 1998, 'Working experientially in psychoanalysis', *Contemporary Psychoanalysis*, vol. 34, pp. 591–596.

Winnicott, DW 1953, 'Transitional objects and transitional phenomena', *International Journal of Psychoanalysis*, vol. 34, pp. 89–97.

Young-Bruehl, E 1996, *The anatomy of prejudice*. Harvard University Press, Cambridge.

# 24

# Psychoanalysis and reconciliation

*Pumla Gobodo-Madikizela*

> Tonight I am reaching out to every single South African, black and white, from the very depths of my being. A white man, full of prejudice and hate, came to our country and committed a deed so foul that our whole nation now teeters on the brink of disaster. A white woman, of Afrikaner origin, risked her life so that we may know, and bring to justice, this assassin [. . .] This is a watershed moment for all of us. Our decisions and actions will determine whether we use our pain, our grief, and our outrage to move forward to what is the only lasting solution for our country.
>
> —Nelson Mandela, 10 April 1993

In April 1993, the former commander of the armed wing of the African National Congress (ANC), Chris Hani, was gunned down in the driveway of his home in a multiracial suburb in Boksburg, a city in the Gauteng province of South Africa. One of Hani's neighbors, a white woman, took the registration number of the assassin's car as he fled from the scene of the crime. She called the police, and Hani's killer was arrested shortly after the incident. Amidst fears that the country would erupt into waves of violence, Nelson Mandela's address calling for calm was televised in prime time on national television on the same day as Hani's assassination. In the minds of many black South Africans, Chris Hani epitomized the ultimate fighter for the struggle for freedom against the oppressive rule of the white apartheid government. If Nelson Mandela in prison was the embodiment of the vision for freedom, Chris Hani, as the commander of the military wing of the ANC, U-Mkhonto Wesizwe (literally "the Spear of the Nation"), kept that vision alive with its concrete expression. Hani returned to South Africa after the unbanning of the ANC when all exiled antiapartheid activists were granted indemnity shortly after the release of Nelson Mandela in February 1990. In 1993, the political negotiations for a multiparty democracy were in progress, and the killing of Hani was seen as a ploy by the white right wing to derail the negotiations process. In the end, however, Hani's assassination was a historical turning point, because the negotiations, which were experiencing some setbacks, moved forward with greater resolve, leading to a decision to hold South Africa's first all-race elections in April the following year.

Nelson Mandela was not yet president when he addressed the nation to calm emotions that were threatening to explode. Yet he was already being presidential, setting the tone for the kind of leadership that South Africa needed. For Mandela, the critical moment of Hani's death was at once a moment of grief and a siren call reminding the nation of the vision of peaceful freedom, an opportunity for dialogue and transformation. South Africans heeded the call and moved forward to embrace the horizon of hope that was Mandela's quest for the birth of a new country. The foundation for this quest was his vision that connection between former enemies was better than rekindling old hatreds. Throughout his journey to restore peace in South Africa, Mandela used moments of rupture as opportunity to break open the possibility for collective reflection, connection and restoration. He introduced a new language that transformed the narrative of violence in South Africa, and for the first time, there was a strong sense of social solidarity that united South Africans across racial lines and instilled national pride.

After the passing of Nelson Mandela in December 2013, the need to return to his vision remains clear. The killings of striking mineworkers by the South African police, the ongoing strike by labor unions demanding better pay from platinum mining companies, violent demonstrations against poor service delivery in black township communities across South Africa, and the massive corruption at the highest level of government, are all examples of the kind of "watershed moment" that Nelson Mandela refers to in the quote at the beginning of this chapter. As I write this introduction, I have been conducting interviews with residents of one of the black townships near Cape Town, and have presented testimony to a special commission set up to investigate the state of violence in townships where crowd violence has become a regular occurrence. South Africa is a troubled country. As some of us respond with outrage to the events around the country that are threatening to shatter Mandela's legacy, we remember his call "to use our pain, our grief, and our outrage" to reconnect with our common humanity, and instead of becoming stuck in despair, "to move forward" and find meaning and inspiration in the richness of the lessons he left behind.

The hope that Nelson Mandela inspired was grounded in the quest for South Africans to establish a richer sense of their identity as human beings, connected to others in the human community. He expanded the horizons of what is possible in human relationships by spearheading, as part of the political negotiations, a process of dialogue, fostering the capacity for connecting with others – even others who are former enemies – in order to confront and heal a past characterized by moral corruption and widespread violations of human rights. The Truth and Reconciliation Commission (TRC) of South Africa broke new ground not because it was the first, but because it was unique in many ways, not least because of the public expressions of remorse by perpetrators of gross human rights violations, and the scenes of victims forgiving perpetrators. This chapter is concerned with this unique dimension of the South African story. I explore remorse, forgiveness and the related concept of reconciliation in the aftermath of mass trauma and violence, using as context the public hearings of the South African TRC.

Some may be quick to suggest that the subjects of forgiveness and reconciliation have received "enough" attention in psychology and related fields, as well as in other disciplines. Yet I would counter this claim and assert that with few exceptions (see, e.g., Gobodo-Madikizela, 2008a; Prager, 2006, 2008), the analysis of these concepts from a psychoanalytic perspective has received less attention than studies in the experimental realm have. Therefore, I approach this project with the image of peeling off layers of the proverbial onion in mind. In the illustrative examples that I use in the chapter, I engaged survivors in dialogue about their experiences, probing deeper in order to gain new insights about the conditions that bring about expressions of forgiveness for perpetrators of gross human rights violations, and how reconciliation unfolds from this outcome.

My aim in the chapter is threefold. First, I will argue that the TRC was a unique dialogic space that enabled the emergence of new subjectivities in the encounter between survivors and perpetrators. The prosecutorial procedures of a courtroom impede the emergent outcomes that have characterized the work of the South African TRC. Second, the discussion will draw on the concepts of intersubjectivity and explore how a psychoanalytic perspective might contribute to understanding the process of trauma testimony, and examine the different ways in which empathy plays out in survivors and perpetrators' responses as witnesses to trauma testimonies. The final section of the chapter will examine remorse and its relationship to forgiveness. Contextually rich case study material from my research on forgiveness will provide illustrative examples for the discussion in the last section of the chapter.

## The Truth and Reconciliation Commission as emotional container

In his exploration of the legacy of collective trauma, and the contribution of truth commissions in efforts to overcome this legacy, Prager (2008) remarks on how truth commissions help members of a community "to move beyond memory and to enable . . . a hopeful world of possibility for everyone" (p. 418). Prager's consideration of the question of how individual and social healing after mass trauma might be achieved provides the impetus for the points raised in this chapter in order to elucidate the context and the interactive processes that give rise to forgiveness and reconciliation.

The TRC was established through an Act of Parliament, the Promotion of National Unity and Reconciliation Act of 1995. This was a culmination of a series of debates during the negotiations process following the release of Nelson Mandela from prison. At the heart of these debates was the question of how to deal with human rights abuses committed in the past under the apartheid regime, and whether to prosecute perpetrators of these crimes or grant them blanket amnesty. There was consensus among the negotiators that prosecutions would undermine the already fragile peaceful transition to democracy. Signs that the country was "teetering on the brink of violence," to paraphrase Mandela,[1] were beginning to emerge. Furthermore, the outgoing apartheid government, the National Party, wanted assurance that those who carried out its policies of human rights abuses would not be prosecuted. As one of two main parties in the negotiation process, the National Party refused to support the transition to democracy and the holding of all-race elections without the constitutional guarantee of amnesty for security police, members of the South African Defence Force, and other perpetrators of gross human rights violations who were part of the apartheid machinery of violence. The negotiating political parties agreed to establish a mechanism for granting amnesty under specific conditions. The amnesty conditions included the requirement that amnesty applicants testify in public about the crimes they committed, and giving full disclosure about the nature of these crimes and those who ordered them. The reasons for the provision of amnesty were outlined at the end of the Interim Constitution of 1993 in a section entitled "National Unity and Reconciliation" as follows: The past violations of human rights

> [should be] addressed on the basis that there is a need for understanding but not for vengeance, a need for reparation but not for retaliation, a need for *ubuntu* but not for victimisation. In order to advance such reconciliation and reconstruction, amnesty *shall* be granted in respect of acts, omissions and offenses associated with political objectives and committed in the course of the conflicts of the past
> *(South African Interim Constitution, 1993, [located after chapter 15, subsection 251])*

From the very onset then, national unity and reconciliation dialogue were central elements of the political negotiations and democratic transition. The pursuit of reconciliation was crucial, because in South Africa victims and perpetrators live in the same country. After the genocide of the Tutsi in Rwanda, similar processes were established, such as the National Reconciliation Commission and the *gacaca* "courts," a traditional process of dealing with conflict between people and within communities. In the majority of cases in Rwanda, after the genocide survivors continued to live as neighbors with perpetrators, or, in cases where the perpetrators are serving long-term prison sentences, with their families. The Promotion of National Unity and Reconciliation Act was passed in 1995 after South Africa's first democratic elections. Commissioners were appointed through a rigorous public process that was chaired by Nelson Mandela. Every effort was made to appoint individuals with unquestionable moral stature, who were respected citizens and who represented the diverse South African population in terms of race, religion and gender. The TRC was formally established under the leadership of Archbishop Desmond Tutu in December 1995.

Concern about victims was central in debates about the TRC, and the negotiating parties clearly recognized the significance of public testimony as an important step in the restoration of victims' dignity, as well as the potential of public testimony to bring about healing and recovery for survivors of the trauma of political violence.

The TRC's public hearings were held in large halls as well as in small town hall meeting types of settings. Its iconic banner, visible at every public hearing and inscribed with the words "Truth, the Road to Healing," positioned the TRC as the "healer of the nation." Thus, presented with a task of such great magnitude and critical significance, the TRC had to function as a container for the memories and emotions that cried out for expression (or disavowal, in the case of those struggling to face the past). The encounters between survivors and perpetrators and their respective family members at TRC public hearings, the overlapping of a matrix of emotions and memories, the exchange of identifications that played out in such an intense public setting, created an extraordinary social context pregnant with a range of unique and unexpected outcomes.

By its very nature, then, and as a quasi-judicial process, the TRC was a dialogic space with the potential to create emergent forms of subjectivity and transformation. Glimpses of this role of the TRC were evident in the responses of some of the witnesses who testified. For example, Lucas Baba Skwepere was one of the witnesses shot by a police officer who was known as "the Rambo of the Cape Peninsula," a title he earned for his notoriety as the police shooter who deliberately aimed for the eyes of antiapartheid demonstrators during confrontations between police and protesters with the intention of blinding them. Skwepere lost sight in both his eyes from "the Rambo's" blinding violence. At the end of his witness testimony to the TRC, Skwepere told the commission that he felt as if he no longer carried "the weight of heavy bricks" on his shoulders, "it is as if I got my sight back" (Human Rights Violations TRC hearings, Cape Town, April 1997).

Another witness, Owen McGregor, wrote his testimony in his dead brother's "voice," and explained that the words were what he thought his brother would have said had he, Owen, been the one who died. His brother, Wallace, was killed when he served as a conscript under the South African Defence Force fighting the forces of liberation in Namibia before its independence in 1989. In the testimony, Wallace, speaking through his brother Owen's voice, accused the apartheid government leaders of lying to the young white men who were forced to serve in the army, and he asked: "Why did I die?" Giving a dead person a voice – entering the silence of the grave – is quite profound in symbolism. It is a kind of sacrificial act: trading places with one's brother and "dying" in his place. Owen McGregor's testimony was as much about maintaining a sense of attachment to his brother's memory, as it was an attempt at working through his own loss. His mother Anne-Marie McGregor's testimony, about her anguish at not being able to see her son's face for the last time when his body was brought home for burial in a body bag, was presented at the end of the first TRC session of the day before morning tea break. During the tea break, a group of black women who had testified earlier about the brutal killing of their sons by security police took turns in reaching out and embracing Anne-Marie McGregor. I asked one of the women what motivated their show of compassion for McGregor, and she replied, "None of us ever had reason to embrace a White person before, but this was an instinctive act, you know, a mother-to-mother feeling." Another woman explained: "We know what losing a loved one means. She seemed so alone – we just couldn't help it."

This illustrates the power and spontaneity of human relating – a bonding, despite decades of apartheid's racial divisions, between black mothers' pain and a white mother who lost her son in the violence of apartheid's war. The unfolding of this process will be explained later in the chapter; suffice to point out at this stage that the example illustrates how the TRC opened up what Prager (2008) has referred to as a "hopeful world of possibility."

An important factor that contributes to these emotional possibilities is the complex field of relational encounters that unfold at public hearings of the TRC. Whether it was encounters happening on the actual stage of TRC hearings, among the audience present at public hearings, or through encounters that occurred vicariously on the "national stage" far beyond the audience present, the power of the relational context paved the way for a range of identifications and reciprocal influences that are difficult to imagine in prosecutorial responses to historical trauma, such as, for example, the Nuremberg trials in the aftermath of the Holocaust. The TRC approach was totally unique in that by adopting an invitational stance – rather than an adversarial one – perpetrators were asked to "give full disclosure" of the crimes they committed in exchange for amnesty. Without the threat of punishment, and with the promise of amnesty for truth telling, perpetrators were inspired to admit rather than eschew guilt. Thus, it was possible to face, and for some of them to *feel*, their guilt. This is an important distinction, because one can simply "face up" to what one has done only through acknowledgment at an intellectual level, without taking responsibility for horrific deeds committed, but rather continuing to externalize blame. It is as if the person is saying, "I give you what you want, full disclosure. Here is my list of evil deeds in which I participated under orders."

In contrast, feeling the burden of guilt goes beyond acknowledgment to recognize that one's actions have caused injury and led to a rupture in one's human community, and that by the very fact of one's participation in those acts, one excluded oneself from the realm of humanness. It is this recognition of alienation from the bonds of human community, and a deep sense of guilt about it – a feeling of brokenness at one's inner core of humanness – that makes remorse possible. Perpetrators' subject position of guilt for the crimes they committed – rather than the position of innocence "until proven guilty" – is the context within which a new perpetrator subjectivity unfolds, one that seeks integration of the uncomfortable reality within the self at a deeper, internal level. Remorse can be a painful affect (Gobodo-Madikizela, 2002), because it involves facing the past and its uncomfortable and internally unsettling truths. Remorse is also an important moment of recognition of the self in relation to the "other," which is a crucial step in working through trauma and the mourning process. All this leads me to conclude that engagement with TRC testimonies of perpetrators in dialogue with testimonies of survivors offers unique analytical possibilities.

An important observation from the TRC process concerns how the dialogue between survivors and perpetrators testifying before the TRC, facilitated by TRC Commissioners, sometimes created a desire, either in the survivor or perpetrator, for closer and more direct dialogue between the parties. In these dialogue encounters between survivors and perpetrators, the nature of the interaction that unfolds has a significant impact on the outcome, particularly expressions of remorse by perpetrators and forgiveness by survivors. The dynamic at play in this dialogic space is similar to the one that develops in the collaborative relationships of therapeutic alliances. Thus, the capacity to enter into the other's feeling state – in other words, the capacity for empathy – profoundly influences the emergence of remorse and forgiveness.

Remorse is itself a sign that a perpetrator is reflecting empathetically on his deeds and that he *feels*, if not at least appreciates, the pain of the survivor. The perpetrator's remorse then opens the route toward the survivor's overcoming the past and its dehumanizing legacy. I therefore take the relational perspective in this chapter to explore remorse and forgiveness of gross human rights abuses, acts that, arguably not until the TRC's began its hearings, were considered "unpardonable" and "unforgiveable" in the canons of political theory (see, e.g., Arendt, 1998). The relational perspective is a view that sees relationships, connecting and interacting with others as fundamental. This perspective has influenced contemporary psychoanalytic work, leading to a paradigm shift and recasting phenomena that emerge from therapeutic interaction in terms of intersubjectivity.

Since publication of their first volume in 1991, Jordan and her colleagues at the Wellesley Stone Centre concede – and increasingly so following the 1991 volume – that the need and proclivity for "connection" is central to human – and therefore also male – development. They are correct in arguing for the primacy of interconnectedness, a concept of development of self in interaction with others. In debunking the "separate self" model of human development Jordan (2003) writes:

> Freud (1920/1955) once wrote, "Protection against stimuli is an almost more important function for the living organism than reception of stimuli." [. . .] Yet from a relational perspective, a "boundary" could be conceived of as a place of meeting and exchange with the surrounding milieu rather than as a place of protection from it.
>
> *(Jordan, 2003, p. 93)*

Jordan provides a crucial counter-position for a problematical bias that has dominated too long, and I'd suggest (although with some reserve) that the reconception of "boundary" as "a place of meeting and exchange" recognizes certain ethical potentialities and draws attention to Martin Buber's notion of the "vital reciprocity" of human relationships (Agassi, 1999, p. 84). I would certainly agree with Abram (1997) that "the boundaries of a living body are open and indeterminate; more like membranes than barriers, they define a surface of metamorphosis and exchange" (1997, p. 46).

## On witnessing, TRC testimonies and their transformative possibilities

In cases of political trauma, where the trauma has a collective or shared aspect, individual trauma testimonies transcend the individual – they extend beyond the personal to the collective and cultural. Exposure to psychologically traumatic events leads to a profound disruption in the capacity to organize aspects of one's experiences into a narrative. Narrative and storytelling are an important means by which individuals and communities make sense out of their experiences. Traumatic events are too painful to be integrated into the overall landscape of one's life. They cannot be contained within the normal linguistic and narrative structures. Instead of assimilation into narrative memory, traumatic experiences often take on a timelessness (Langer, 1993), living on, being relived and acted out in various ways that reflect fragmented temporality, or "time out of synchrony [where] the present is without end," to appropriate Blanchot's (1992, p. 44) analysis. Narrating traumatic memory may be one way that victims and survivors attempt to reconstruct a shattered self, transcend the passivity of victimhood, and find a voice to construct meaning from their traumatic experience. By making their wounds public through trauma testimonies, recording the atrocities done to them, and identifying the perpetrators, these testimonies were the first step toward survivors' reclaiming a sense of agency. The testimonies served to recreate temporal boundaries that placed brutalities in the past, in order to achieve what Prager (2008) has referred to as "jump-starting timeliness." The assertion of agency took various forms.

One antiapartheid activist, who had been raped multiple times and tortured during detention, described her unbearable experiences, and said that in order to shut out the pain and shame she would "remove" her soul from her body and put it in a corner so that the rape was "only" on her body. Appealing to the restorative possibilities of the TRC, she expressed a wish that the commission would help her to get her soul back.

Nomonde Calata, the wife of an antiapartheid activist whose body was found burned by the security police, charred beyond recognition, confronted her husband's killers and told them that they had robbed her of a loving husband and her children of a loving father. At the end of her testimony to the TRC, she let out a piercing scream that shattered the stillness of the large city hall where the hearing was held. She "dared" to wail her pain and suffering into the large hall, giving voice to her pain, bearing witness for all those who were inside it and beyond its walls to hear.

In these and other testimonies, survivors who suffered under apartheid want to lay to rest the memory of the pain and abuse of the past, not in order to forget the past, but rather to heal their and the brokenness of one's community, to reclaim the dignity of the living and the dignity and respect of their loved ones who suffered dehumanization in life and in death. In this sense then, the testimonies are not just to get the listeners' "affirmation and validation," as I have suggested elsewhere (Gobodo-Madikizela, 2012, p. 253). Felman and Laub (1992) have also applied a similar interpretation in their discussion of testimonies. They suggest that the testimonies are deployed "essentially in order to *address* another, to impress upon a listener, to *appeal* to a community" (p. 204). This formulation of the purpose of trauma testimonies gives power to the listener as the one to bestow recognition upon the survivor and her/his suffering. This, too, happens. Viewed as assertion of agency and assertion of the dignity of one's community, however, trauma testimonies seek a response from the witness, but in order to wrest away from perpetrators and from the dominant culture the fiat power to destroy. It is part of ridding oneself and the collective memory of one's community of the subject position of the dehumanized other.

Although Holocaust testimonies still occupy center stage in the literature on testimony, scholarly debates on testimony cover a range of historical traumas globally (in Latin America, American slavery, and in stories of "the stolen generation" in Australia). Since publication of works by Felman and Laub (1992), Langer (1993) and Caruth (1995, 1996), and especially since 9/11, discussions on trauma testimonies in the United States have gained great prominence. Some of the insights from this literature are, however, not compatible with, or generalizable to other contexts. Felman and Laub (1992) for example, in their discussion of the relationship between trauma testimonies and the listener, describe the role of the listener:

> The listener, therefore, is a party to the creation of knowledge *de novo*. The testimony to the trauma thus includes its hearer, who is, so to speak, the blank screen on which the event comes to be inscribed for the first time.
>
> *(Felman & Laub, 1992, p. 57)*

The notion that a listener, or "secondary witness," to use Laub's term, participates as a "blank screen," requires critical examination. In countries such as South Africa and Rwanda, where victims, perpetrators and beneficiaries of oppressive regimes are present in the audience as "secondary witnesses," survivor testimonies confront not only perpetrators with their guilt, but also stir up the conscience of beneficiaries about their complicity. In the case of beneficiaries of oppressive regimes, survivors' testimonies cannot be regarded as falling on a "blank screen," because beneficiaries know about the traumas suffered by survivors under the repressive regimes in which they led a life of privilege and from which they benefitted.

LaCapra's (2009) reflections on secondary witnessing, and the distinction he makes between identification, empathy or compassion, and "empathic unsettlement" raises important questions regarding the unavoidably problematical nature of witnessing and also pointing to the limits of understanding the experience of an Other: "I would argue that there may well, perhaps even should, be a form of empathic unsettlement in the commentator who addresses the traumatic experiences of others" (LaCapra, 2009, p. 65).

LaCapra (2004) distinguishes between two forms of impact of traumatic testimonies on the listener. The first is when the listener is affected in a vicarious way by the trauma testimony. The problem with vicarious traumatic impact, argues LaCapra, is that the listener identifies so strongly with the witness that she/he takes on the role of "surrogate victim," that this blurs the line between the trauma of the witness, and the secondary witness' vicarious experience of this trauma (LaCapra, 2004, p. 125). The second way in which the secondary witness may be affected is the "virtual" experience of trauma in which the secondary witness puts herself/himself in the victim's shoes "while respecting the difference between self and other" (LaCapra, 2004, p. 125). LaCapra then refers to this "virtual" experience of trauma as "empathic unsettlement," which he considers to be the desirable kind of empathy because it recognizes "that one cannot take the victim's place" (p. 125). It is respectful of the other and "does not mean identification . . . appropriation or incorporation" (LaCapra, 2009, p. 66).

On the one hand, Felman and Laub's (1992) concept of the "blank screen" suggests a blank slate on which the story of the victim's trauma becomes inscribed on the listener without the listener's agency. On the other hand, LaCapra's "empathic unsettlement" suggests that the listener responds empathically to the victim's trauma testimony while at the same time engaging reflectively with her/his response in order to distinguish between the witness' trauma and the listener's *virtual* traumatic experience. Yet there is something in both Laub's and LaCapra's formulations that falls short of an adequate explanatory framework for the transformative possibilities witnessed at TRC public hearings. The "empathic unsettlement" that emerges goes beyond the notion of "virtual" experience, a term that is problematic because it suggests an event that manifests only in the brain, rather than through shifts in the intrapsychic and intersubjective relational realms. It is a response that, to borrow a phrase from Stern (1985) arises from the affective attunement with the other. In the TRC encounters that are the subject of discussion in this chapter, this process takes at least two forms. The first involves responses that become manifest when the historical trauma is shared by the listener/s, and the second form concerns emotional responses by the perpetrators responsible for the horrific deeds about which witnesses are testifying.

## Survivors' responses to witnesses' testimony

The first form of response occurs when the listener shares a similar traumatic experience with the witness. In this case, the empathic resonance leads to an alignment of the inner subjectivities of witness and listener in a way that creates a sense of community between survivors and listeners. The story presented earlier in the chapter of the group of black mothers embracing a white woman who testified about the loss of her son is an example of this kind of affective resonance. The statement by one of the women that their embrace was "an instinctive act" can be linked to Stern's (1985) observation that attunement behaviors occur automatically and without conscious awareness. This captures the intrapsychic dimension of the process, an intersubjective dynamic that leads not only to a shared memory of the loss, but also to shared mourning. In the case of the example of the black women's embrace of the white mother, the connection through shared pain is an extraordinary moment of restoration for the women, because the moment serves to confirm their identity *as mothers*. We can see how reconciliation can be mediated through this intersubjective relational context of mothers reaching out to another mother in a spontaneous act simply because, as they pointed out, "we couldn't help it." According to Stern and his colleagues (1998, 2004), such spontaneous relational acts fall into the category of what he terms "implicit relational knowing." Stern is correct in suggesting that the capacity to engage and to connect with others exists implicitly, outside of our awareness. The TRC introduced conscious intention to this by creating a relational space where the starting point of the dialogue was that of openness to receiving the Other and allowing the *felt* terrain of affective resonance – beyond the words being communicated – to play out. This then propelled the intersubjective narrative and the TRC became a potential catalyst of subjective and intersubjective transformation.

The image of women from opposite sides of historical trauma connecting through their shared pain is a powerful symbol of solidarity. In my research work in Rwanda, I have witnessed similar acts of solidarity between widows of the genocide of the Tutsi and the wives of perpetrators who are serving long prison terms. What forces enable compassion and care for others, even an "other" who is a former enemy? What has been most striking about the women who forge links with one another, despite coming from opposite sides of past violent conflict, is that the reason for their connection is sometimes given as something as simple as "I am a mother too."

The experience of human empathy, however, traverses gender boundaries. During a recent research visit to Rwanda in Bugasera, one of the villages most affected by the genocide, a young Tutsi man who was born during the genocide sat across from the man who killed his father explaining, through an interpreter, what his forgiveness of the man who killed his father means for him as a survivor. He explained to our small group of researchers that forgiving made him realize how lucky he is "that my father was not a Hutu." Asked by a colleague to comment on the view held by some that survivors cannot forgive on behalf of the dead, he replied that he knows his father would support his decision.

> Firstly, we should try not to carry the burden of hatred on and on. In my case, it would be passing it on to my children, and then they to theirs. Secondly, if I cannot have compassion for a man who has expressed remorse for his crime, I am casting darkness on his quest to becoming human, then that burden will be mine, another layer of burden, you see. I know my father would wish for me to be an agent of peace in my community.
>
> *(Interview, April 2014)*

The TRC, the Rwandan *gacaca* process, and other similar restorative justice processes – all these are strategies meant to create a space for testimony, a space for confrontation and listening, and for initiating the difficult process of healing. These sites of testimony, of individual and shared experience provided points of identification, entryways into the experiences of others, which enable comparison across critical registers of difference. Appeal to the familiar and the familial creates a context in which it is possible to engage empathetic questions, such as "How old was your daughter/son when . . .?" By grounding themselves in what is shared, they create mutual intelligibility. The shared experience of loss, for example, cuts across the distinction of "black" or "white," "Tutsi" or "Hutu." On the terrain of a horrific past, certain statements resonate deeply:

> My son was eighteen years old when he was conscripted into the South African Defence Force during apartheid; he was brought back in a body bag and I wasn't allowed to see him.

My son was eighteen when he joined the anti-apartheid struggle. He was abducted, tortured and killed by apartheid security police.

It is ironic that the same factors that can ignite and perpetuate animosity, fear and hatred – the love for those killed or maimed by "the other" – might also suspend those negative sentiments. By providing a way into the experience of the "enemy," love and loss may provide a way out of violence. Ultimately, love and loss are what is common and thus in a sense is shared. Love and loss enable healing that opens new possibilities in the aftermath of violence. The loss is placed in the past where it belongs, and its finality accepted.

For families who have not found the remains of their loved ones, however, it is particularly difficult to confront loss, to situate it in the past, to construct narrative memory, and to accept its finality. When what happened remains intangible and elusive, the process of working through and healing trauma is deferred, replaced by a haunting and an unfillable chasm of sorrow. Such trauma cannot be assimilated, not only because of its overwhelming quality, but also because of the void created by an experience that by its very nature is inarticulable. A void separates the possibility of knowing from not knowing, an unspeakable emptiness that cannot be grasped. The survivor's mournful lament is suspended between acting out the trauma and an attempt to work through it, a situation that invites comparison with what Maclear (2003) calls the "unstitched terror of remembering and witnessing [. . .] the vexed impossibility of memory" (p. 238).

## Perpetrators' (and beneficiaries') responses to witness testimonies

The second form of listener responses to trauma testimonies are those of perpetrators responsible for the traumatic experiences recounted by survivors. Earlier in the chapter, I discussed the significance of facing and feeling guilt, and pointed out that confronting guilt lays the ground for authentic expression of remorse. Some perpetrators are either incapable of feeling remorse – they lack the capacity for the kind of empathic resonance that leads to remorse. Alternatively, they understand the moral implications of their actions, but in order to protect themselves from an inner shattering of the self, they try to hide from their shame. Instead of facing the truth about their actions, they pervert the truth, claiming righteousness of their actions. This is a manifestation of the mechanism of "splitting." Contradictory aspects of the self – the part that committed, or was complicit in evil acts, and the part that is a good father, mother, lover, Christian and so forth – are kept apart, split off, and only one of these conflicting polarities (usually the good part) is embraced or acknowledged. Clive Derby-Lewis, for example, who is responsible for the assassination of Chris Hani,[2] told the TRC that the killing of Hani could be justified because of his Christian faith: "[W]e as Christians are told that it is our duty to fight the anti-Christ in whichever way we can."[3] Expressions of accountability are inverted by simultaneously turning the spotlight of blame away from the self in order to project blame externally, including shifting blame to the victim or survivor. Remorse is unlikely to emerge under these conditions.

The kind of splitting described in the earlier section has also been observed among white South Africans. Acknowledgment of complicity with apartheid is rare (see Steyn & Foster, 2008; Theissen & Hamber, 1998). Even when a window opens to acknowledge complicity, another one may close to shut out the rising tide of shame and guilt that confronts the subject. The constant confrontation with one's complicity exerts an intolerable toll intrapsychically. To deal with the force of these emotions, a more subtle form of denial emerges. Speech acts similar to the "we Christians" statement quoted earlier, where expressions of accountability are inverted by simultaneously turning the spotlight of blame away from the subject are deployed in order to "efface" the feeling of personal responsibility. This is dramatically illustrated in the statement heard repeatedly from white South Africans: "The ANC government's policies of affirmative action are more racist than apartheid." The perversion of the meaning of the term "racist" is familiar discourse that one finds in post-apartheid South Africa. I have referred to this narrative strategy as "reformative narratives" (Safier & Gobodo-Madikizela, 2014), because they are deployed to hide from the inevitable reality and to soften the intrapsychic blow triggered by the feelings of shame and guilt. "White denial" of apartheid makes it difficult to achieve reconciliation. The denial reflects underlying fear of a rupture in one's sense of identity. Overwhelmed by shame because of one's association, either as a beneficiary of apartheid policies or voter who kept a system that was declared a crime against humanity alive, the confrontation with the past is too much to bear. This leaves little room for acknowledgment of the "other's" pain and experiencing guilt and empathic concern for her/him.

Yet the dialogic space of the TRC can also engender in the perpetrator affective attunement (Stern, 1985) with the survivor's pain and suffering. Such a context opens up the possibility for perpetrators to feel guilt for the harm they have caused. Instead of a foreboding feeling of disintegration, there is a feeling of containment that allows a deeper awareness of the wounding the perpetrator has caused, and that his actions are responsible for the survivor's pain and suffering. Understanding how one outcome and not the other – the disconnection created by shame on the one hand, and the affective bonds that lead to remorse on the other – requires delving into the complexity of these encounters, and is not an examination that can be undertaken in the limited space allowed for this chapter.

The image of people, one a parent and the other the killer of her/his child, is something from which some might want to avert their gaze. It is not a straightforward encounter: people have had damage done to them; they hurt and are still hurting. The complexity of this meeting is something that has rarely been fully explored, and my own examination in this chapter must necessarily fall short of an adequate explanation. For the most part, the literature that one draws on speaks to psychotherapists' consulting rooms and a world where intersubjective mutuality of reciprocal interaction reigns. It is a world of therapists and/or researchers (see, e.g., Finlay & Evans, 2009) that is fine-tuned (or at least aims to be) and responsive to the client/research participant, and of encounters that are ultimately ones of mutuality, responsiveness, connection and empathy. Yet these are settings where participants are not accountable to each other (and to society) for atrocities committed against each other (and greater society). Nevertheless, one draws insights from these therapeutic encounters and from the literature on relational encounters, taking as a starting point the fact that those encountering each other will be *affected*; whether they will necessarily be affected in a way that will move them to not only a new relationship, but also one that is desirable is another matter.

In encounters between adversaries, these relational encounters may not be defined by reciprocity. Innumerable possibilities – both destructive and restorative and all that cannot be reduced to these oversimplified categories – arise, both within and between bodies. The potential for the unexpected, unforeseen and thoroughly creative, endemic to the human condition is always present. Cromby (2007) for instance, writes of feelings:

> So feelings have no intrinsic capacity for progressive action, but their ontological status and concomitant irreducibility to the linguistic, the formally symbolic, gives them the continuous potential to be spatio-temporally disjunctive with any given "rationality." And it is these disjunctions, rather than their intrinsic qualities, that generate feelings' potential for creative disruption – just as their conjunctions generate their normative potentials.
>
> *(Cromby, 2007, p. 113)*

But how might we deepen our understanding of the need to *face* the wronged or offending Other, or to search him or her out? Granted, sometimes there are clearly stated motivations (to elicit "the truth," to ask for forgiveness, etc.). Yet there seems to be more at play (Simon Wiesenthal searches out the mother of the SS officer;[4] a mother requests to face her son's murderer; the murderer requests to meet with the widow of the man he killed . . .). It is a tacit recognition that healing must involve the Other, is dependent on the Other. Thus, the encounter is approached with a certain level of conscious (and unconscious) intentionality. While survivor and perpetrator are separated by their historical pasts, at the same time, their past also connects them, opening up a potential space for the emergence of unexpected human moments. The dialogic context that is established then becomes a facilitative environment in which a perpetrator feels less threatened, inspiring in him an ethical impulse that may obviate the need to hide from his shame and guilt, and instead open a window for expression of acknowledgment and remorse. Elsewhere I have referred to the "paradox of remorse" (Gobodo-Madikizela, 2002), because while the perpetrator's actions create a chasm between him and the world of survivors, his expression of remorse changes the intersubjective context and tries to bring closeness between survivor and perpetrator.

## Remorse and forgiveness: "making reparations"

Melanie Klein's term, "making reparations," is a fitting expression for the unconscious internal dialogue that unfolds when perpetrators of gross human rights violations face up to guilt for their crimes. Earlier I referred to the mechanism of splitting as a strategy for hiding from guilt and from shame. "Making reparations" requires confronting the internal split headlong, and integrating the disparate split-off parts of the self. In her discussion of shame and guilt, Klein (1975) argues that the grievances we harbor against our parents for the wrongs they have committed, and for having frustrated us with their denial of these wrongs, give rise to feelings of hate and revenge against them. These feelings are internalized, and they become internal representations of the problematic relationships with parents. At the same time, these feelings of hate and revenge lead to guilt and despair for the injury that they have caused the parents we love. Klein suggests that the process of undoing this labyrinth of conflicting emotions requires making reparation with the internal objects: "by playing at the same time the parts of loving parents and loving children [. . .] we make good the injuries which we did in phantasy, and for which we still unconsciously feel very guilty" (Klein, 1975, pp. 312–313). Durham (2000) then explains that the capacity for making reparations in the internal object world is the basis upon which the capacity and concern for others is established. I consider empathy to be central in both remorse and forgiveness, because both involve processes of "repair," which, in the Kleinian sense of the term suggest the unfolding of a mourning process or "working through" and integration of the complexities of a subject's past.

Kohut defined empathy as "the capacity to think and feel oneself into the inner life of another person." Other definitions of empathy are aligned with this view of empathic responsiveness – for example, "affect attunement" in Stern's (1985) turn of phrase. Neuroscientific insights on empathy have largely been about the biological roots of this resonant connection in the worlds of self, objects and others. Yet an aspect of empathy that has received scant scholarly attention is the component of care for the other that sometimes emerges in the context of empathic responsiveness. Caring goes beyond "mirroring" or feeling into the mental state of an Other. It arises from the moment-by-moment negotiation of the intersubjective relationship between actors, introspection and ongoing reciprocal mutual reflection, and it involves making sense of the intersubjective experience of the empathic resonance. In this desire-to-care-for-the-other aspect of empathy, the empathic response of the survivor is imbued with a quality of wishing to "rescue" the remorseful perpetrator as if in order to affirm his identity as a member of the human community (instead of the identity of "monster" or "evil one"). The desire to rescue the perpetrator, I argue, constitutes the fundamental moment, a pivotal point in the intersubjective context in which forgiving feelings emerge.

The word forgiveness, I argue further, is "the wrong word" for describing the phenomenon that unfolds in these survivor–perpetrator encounters. Forgiveness seems to suggest a coming to an end – "I offer you forgiveness so that I can move on." There is a subtext that seems to signify an act of leaving something *behind*, moving on without looking back. This is evocative of the notion of "letting go" of the stage theory of forgiveness advocated by Enright and his colleagues (see Enright & North, 1998). A more appropriate phrase that might meaningfully describe what unfolds in victim–perpetrator encounters is to think about forgiveness as "the emergence of the unexpected." It is a process that unfolds from being witnesses to each other's pain – the "witnessing dance" (Gobodo-Madikizela, 2008b) of trauma on the one hand, and of guilt on the other. It is a dance that brings the survivor and the perpetrator in step with each other into the spiral movement of a new intersubjective context that edges them toward the center of possibility, and then upwards toward the apex of reconciliation. The new intersubjective context that emerges allows for integration, rather than "letting go." Acknowledgment that bears the responsibility, which is prepared to go into the pain of the other, is crucial for this transformative process to unfold, because it is the kind of acknowledgment that conveys compassion and care for the other, opening the door for the expressions of apology and remorse.

The development of the capacity for empathy is deeply embedded in early childhood development, and Fonagy and Target (1996) refer to this developmental process as *mentalization*, the capacity to reflect on one's mental state and the mental state of others. Mentalization might also be considered as the capacity to *engage imaginatively* with the mental state of an Other. While I would hesitate to reduce empathy to an imaginative act, there does seem to be something in considering the part that the human capacity for imagination plays in the desire to understand the experiences of others. More extraordinary is the idea that the imagination is even necessary to recognize the existence of the other – her/his "human beingness." This is what seems to be suggested by Benjamin's (1990) conceptualization of "mutual recognition" as the core of intersubjectivity through which "the subject gradually becomes able to recognize the other person's subjectivity." The idea of a "gradual" process that leads to recognition is suggestive of an ongoing dialogue with self and with the Other (as well as with internal "others") in a way that continuously allows one to test, through multiple levels of reflective engagement, one's perceptions of the Other. The process occurs at an internal as well as external level through language and other more subtle forms of nonverbal dialogue.

Let me now illustrate with an example the notion of empathy as *caring for*, as indicative of a desire to "rescue" a perpetrator. Eugene de Kock was the head of covert operations of the apartheid security police. Among the crimes he committed is the murder of four black police officers who had threatened to expose de Kock's colleagues for killing the "Cradock Four," a group of well-known antiapartheid activists in the Eastern Cape. When de Kock offered a heartfelt apology to two of the widows of his victims, the widows were visibly moved. In an interview with them after their meeting with de Kock, one of them said that she hoped "to be there" for de Kock. She explained:

> I hope that when de Kock sees our tears, he knows that they are not only tears for our husbands, but tears for him as well . . . I would like to hold him by the hand, and show him that there is a future, and that he can still change.
>
> *(Interview with widows of the "Motherwell Bombing," 1997)*

Linda and the late Peter Biehl's work with the killers of their daughter Amy Biehl is another example that illustrates the expression of care beyond empathic resonance. Amy Biehl was a Stanford University student on a Fulbright Scholarship in South Africa. She was stabbed to death when, as part of her work with a nongovernmental organization (NGO), she visited Gugulethu Township in Cape Town. The Biehls supported the amnesty application of their daughter's killers, and when the men were released, they arranged skills training for them and offered them positions in the foundation established in memory of their daughter, the Amy Biehl Foundation. "I have no hatred in my heart," Linda said when I asked her to explain why she sought connection with the men who murdered her daughter. "All I am concerned about is how these young men can re-enter their community and rebuild their lives" (Interview with Linda Biehl, June 2000).

This kind of response to the intersubjective experience of the dialogue between survivor and perpetrator transcends empathic resonance and seems to be concerned with the affirmation of the Other's identity as a member of the human community, the recognition of the complex reality of the Other's experience and his human beingness. The understanding of empathy as resonance makes visible only the perpetrator's actions and his struggle with his past. For a deeper relationship and understanding, the *caring for* aspect of the empathic response is important. This provides much-needed "holding" for the perpetrator, which serves to mitigate potential rupture, protect him from disintegration, and to reinforce the possibility of connection instead of a rupture. When I asked one of Amy Biehl's killers what it was like to work with Linda Biehl, he described the first months of his affiliation with the Amy Biehl Foundation as having been "pure torture." "To see Linda's warm and grand-motherly face every morning seemed like an unbridgeable burden at first," he said. So intense was the "burden" of memory for what he had done in the face of the kindness of the mother of his victim that he left the Foundation to join the life of violence – cash heists and carjackings – with his former comrades. This life offered him continuity; he did not have "to think" about what he had done, he said. Linda Biehl, however, sought him out again and he returned to his position at the Amy Biehl Foundation. When I interviewed him, he had married, had a daughter, and was waiting for his daughter to grow up before he could tell her about his past. "I want her to witness my relationship with Linda, to know my good deeds in society and to experience me as a good father before telling her about my shameful past" (Interview, March 2007).

Therefore, the "caring for" element in empathy is a result of a deeper level of imagination and seeking understanding of the Other's experience. This deeper level of imagination takes "feeling into" the mental state of the Other to another level, and asks the question: what should I do about it? Caring, whether demonstrated in words, nonverbally, or in actions, helps to prevent the disintegration that may shatter the self after the experience of remorse. Thus, rather than a focus on empathy only as "resonance," the notion of "empathic repair" (Gobodo-Madikizela, 2008c) might be usefully applied to capture the healing and reconciliation that emerge from the dialogic encounters between survivors and perpetrators. (I have come to view the experience of empathic repair as the "royal road" to reconciliation.) The perpetrator's transformation stands as a symbol of the survivor's capacity (and more generally, of the human capacity) for imagination and understanding, and of the power of empathic care that is inherent – always a potentiality – in the dialogue encounters between survivors and perpetrators. The transformative possibilities may also be seen as a metaphor pointing to a more general horizon of an ethics of care and responsibility for the Other in the context of "dealing with the past."

For Kearney (1993), "imagination is indispensable to ethics," a claim resting on what he regards as imagination's "*empathic* powers of receptivity to the other" (p. 224). Kearney explains: "While the role of imagination in understanding pertains to its productive and projective powers, its role in sensible intuition expresses its ability *to remain open to what is given from beyond itself* (my italics)[. . .]. Imagination is ethical to the extent that it suffers the other to be other while suffering with (*com-patire*) the other as other" (Kearney, 1993, p. 225).

One might be hesitant to impute empathy and the imaginative capacity with too many ethical potentialities (and at best, that is what they are: potentialities). Nevertheless, regardless of the breadth of one's conceptualization of empathy, what might one *reasonably* expect empathy to "do" at the very least? Stein's (1964) phenomenological analysis of empathy provides us with a possible entryway:

> We could proceed from the complete, concrete phenomenon before us in our experiential world, the phenomenon of the psycho-physical individual [. . .]. This individual is not given as a physical body, but as a sensitive, living body belonging to an "I," an "I" that senses, thinks, feels, and wills. The living body of this "I" not only fits into my phenomenal world but is itself the centre of orientation of such a phenomenal world. It faces this world and communicates with me.
>
> *(Stein, 1964, p. 6)*

Stein (1964) here is pointing us to the importance of a deeper level of recognition, one that goes beyond acknowledgment (which may at times simply recognize the Other as a mere object) – for it is possible to empathize while failing to recognize the Other's humanity. Reciprocal mutual recognition of the Other's humanity, acknowledging the reality of their pain and suffering, whatever its source, is the kind of empathy that creates pathways to caring for the Other as a fellow human being, which in turn establishes the conditions for meaningful reconciliation to take place. The following words by a mother whose son was killed by apartheid security police illustrate this point. Cynthia Ngewu, whose son Christopher Piet was lured to a death trap by a black police collaborator with six others, was responding to a question I asked her about the meaning of her forgiveness for the police collaborator at a public dialogue event on reconciliation that I had organized in Cape Town:

> This thing called reconciliation – if I am understanding it correctly – if it means that this man who killed Christopher has a chance to become human again, so that I, so that all of us . . . so that our humanity can be restored, then I agree with it. I support it.
>
> *(Rotberg & Thompson, 2000, p. 241)*

This brings us to the discussion of the point I made earlier in this section of the chapter about forgiveness being "the wrong word." The example I will present is from the meeting between Cynthia Ngewu and other mothers of the victims of the Gugulethu Seven killing with the man who lured their sons to death. The meeting with the families of the victims was requested by the black police collaborator, Thapelo Mbelo.[5] Mbelo was a beleaguered man, tormented by the knowledge that he betrayed his black brothers, that he was the one who lured them into a death trap. In an act of desperation as he experienced his life as unraveling, he requested a meeting with the mothers of the victims whose killing he orchestrated. When he sat facing the mothers, he was visibly shaking, his face muscles twitching. "I apologise from the bottom of my heart," he told them. The women's pain and anger was palpable as they took turns confronting him with his betrayal, telling him that he was a wolf dressed in sheep's skin, and each of them taking turns telling him about the disruption his actions caused in their lives.

Cynthia Ngewu was the most visibly emotional, and the most expressive of the group of family members gathered for the meeting with Mbelo. At some point, she asked Mbelo tearfully: "How do you feel about what you did? What does your conscience say to you?" After this pouring out of the women's feelings had gone on for some time, with Mbelo shaken, but seemingly holding up despite the verbal blows, Ngewu was now watching Mbelo quietly. It was as if she was searching for something, reading between the lines, searching deep within his eyes, perhaps for signs of malice, or signs of something that might redeem him from the identity of the wolf in a sheep's skin that they said he was. She waited for the force of the other women's voices to subside. Then, as Mbelo was about to say something, she said, "Just a minute my son – I don't know whether I can say you have followed your name [his name, Thapelo, means prayer] – I don't think you have followed the name that your mother gave you."

Earlier on during the meeting, Mbelo had addressed the mothers of his victims as follows: "I would like to ask you to forgive me, my parents . . . I ask your forgiveness from the bottom of my heart . . . I ask your forgiveness my parents." It might seem strange, perhaps presumptuous, that the man responsible for the killing of their sons should refer to the mothers as "my parents." In any other context, this would have been inappropriate. Mbelo's choice of language illustrates the multidimensionality of social relationships within the African cultural context. This context seeks to preserve a sense of human connectedness in social discourse. Thus, when Mbelo asked for the mother's forgiveness, "*Ndicela uxolo bazali bam*" ("I ask your forgiveness my parents"), his appeal to them went beyond the words themselves. It is important to note that Mbelo was positioning himself here as an obedient and remorseful "child": "*Bazali bam*" – my parents – a child who has gone astray and is now begging to be reintegrated back into the family circle of care, compassion and love. By addressing the mothers in this way, Mbelo draws on the relational bonds in the African cultural context, and reclaims his own sense of belonging within a wider community of others.

Now Ngewu had interrupted him from speaking further, and after quietly looking at him searchingly, she said: "My son, you are the same age as my son, Christopher. I want to tell you that I as Christopher's mother, I have forgiven you. I forgive you my son . . . Yes, I have forgiven you. I am at peace. Go well my child."

She repeated her forgiving words as if to convey the unconditionality of her forgiveness, "Yes, I have forgiven" (*Ewe, ndixolile*, which also means, "I am at peace"). Cynthia's final words to Mbelo, "Go well my child," may be seen as an affirmation, and as expression of hope – an affirmation of the humanity that binds Mbelo to her and to the other women's collective humanity, and hope that he will live up to the promise of his remorse. After a few other exchanges with Mbelo, the meeting ended with all except one of the mothers embracing him. The embrace of Mbelo – the physical touching that went round the room – gestures toward a reparative humanism and seems to communicate the message: "we are connected."

Over the years since that meeting, I have interviewed the mothers of the Gugulethu Seven, and some of the children of the slain men, who are now young adults. In my retrospective interviews with Mrs. Ngewu, and trying to understand how the dialogue with Mbelo moved from anger to forgiveness without the kind of direct facilitation that is often in "forgiveness counseling," I asked her what triggered her change of heart. "I don't know what it is like to be a murderer," she said,

> I could see that he felt his regret very deeply, his shame for his actions written all over his face. It occurred to me then, that this is another woman's child. Not knowing the darkness in his heart, I know the pain of a mother when your child has done something that cuts at the core of your motherhood, the womb of a mother [in Xhosa "*inimba yomzalikazi*"]. My feelings were for his mother, not so much for him.
>
> *(Interview with Cynthia Ngewu, June 2009)*

Here she describes again how she was drawn to feeling sorry for Mbelo through connection with his mother:

> I looked at this poor woman's child and thought to myself, "his mother did not bring him to this world to commit evil deeds. She had dreams for him." That was the moment for me,

and when I looked at his sorrowful face, something pulled at the very depths of my stomach. That was *inimba*. [. . .] You see, we are all human. It is better to release him, let him do what he has to do among other human beings.

(Interview with Cynthia Ngewu, 2009)

The closest literal translation for the word *inimba* is "umbilical cord" and perhaps "placenta." *Inimba* is a descriptive noun that denotes the feeling of empathic care that mothers feel naturally for their children. Some women speak of *inimba* for one's own child as a visceral feeling inside the womb when, for example, their children are in trouble or experiencing pain, despite physical distance from them (on discussion of "inimba" see also Gobodo-Madikizela, 2011). Not being able to connect empathically with the perpetrator, at least initially, Ngewu appeals to the closest comparable experience at her disposal: motherhood. I think that forgiveness emerges within this context *unexpectedly*, as something unthought-of until "now." This "knowledge" of how to connect with the other, this symbolic connection with the perpetrator's mother is an emergent part of the self that becomes manifest within the unpredictable intersubjective matrix of the encounter between survivors and perpetrators. While the perpetrator has committed an evil deed, remorse cannot be evil; it is a moment in the context of the intersubjective relatedness when the survivor experiences a human moment with the perpetrator. An expression in Xhosa gives meaning to this experience: shame makes you human (*iintloni zikwenz'umntu*). Thus, the survivor experiences the perpetrator's remorse as something authentically human that changes not only the survivor's perception of the perpetrator, but also as something that transforms the survivor's sense of self. Regardless of the extent of Mrs. Ngewu's take on Mbelo's motives for betraying her and the other women's sons, her *desire* to connect with him on a human level is what seems significant here. Also significant is the fact that the path of empathic care comes not through the words between them, but rather through an embodied connection with a third person not physically present. This transformation can best be understood in relation to the concepts outlined by Stern and his colleagues (1998) to explain therapeutic change.

Forgiveness then implies the beginning of something new, rather than an end or a closure of the chapter. For example, Ngewu and other survivors I have interviewed regarding their expressions of forgiveness for perpetrators admit to sometimes experiencing a degree of anger and resentment toward the men they have forgiven during family gatherings and anniversaries such as for their children's death or their birthdays. What sustains the connection with the perpetrator is the memory of his remorse and the feelings it evoked in the survivor. As one survivor said, "You re-engage with that original dialogue every time you feel overwhelmed by sadness for your loss, and somehow it is reassuring – it brings you to a peaceful place and restores your sanity."

The quite obvious observation I am making here is that engaging in dialogue about the past is a multifaceted terrain. In considering encounters between survivors and perpetrators of gross human rights violations, what is perhaps necessary is shifting the lens from a focus on forgiveness and reconciliation (as concepts that imply a goal) to "experience" (complicated, enigmatic, muddy, elusive and unpredictable), because I think that much of what happens in these encounters remains implicit.

## Conclusion

This chapter takes the importance of empathic care as its starting point for understanding the emergence of forgiveness and reconciliation in survivor–perpetrator dialogue. I consider remorse the most important and yet under-researched topic in scholarly debates on forgiveness, reconciliation and transformation in the aftermath of mass trauma and violence. In his work on the evolutionary basis of empathy (and the connection between the empathic capacity and ethics), primatologist de Waal et al. (2006) refers to the "ought" of human behavior "that we recognize so clearly in the moral domain" (p. 45). The "ought," I would argue, is that part of us that wants to hear, see and *feel* remorse from the person who has wronged us – the recognition that he/she *ought* to feel and communicate some remorse. Remorse answers an expectation – it makes fellow-feeling and empathic care (feeling-for) possible; it recognizes the perpetrator as a human being capable of the "ought." For instance, I interpret the question posed by Mrs. Ngewu, one of the Gugulethu Seven mothers' questions to Mbelo – "What does your conscience say to you?" – precisely as a concern with, and acknowledgment of, an ethical dimension of human relations.

Should perpetrators of violent atrocities against humanity be forgiven? Do they even have the capability to receive forgiveness? I believe that perpetrators who are remorseful should be given a chance to change. Whether a perpetrator rises to the call or not may depend on a range of circumstances and opportunities for such change to take place. In much of the world's great literature, and much of its past and current history as well, the idea of vengeance has carried with it a certain noble air, as if motivated by a force of good that somehow enables it to transcend the original violence that gave birth to it. Vengeance, sometimes thinly cloaked under the euphemism of "justice-seeking," or "defending" one's country, has an attraction and logic that have come to hold a central position in the thinking and values of powerful states, and of the mainstream legal-moral culture. But the roots of the revenge response lie closer to primal feelings engendered by the trauma of violence. Violence shatters the integrity of the self, and those victimized by it struggle to find words to describe it, or feelings to address the trauma to the self that it brings. The desire for revenge is sometimes mobilized as a way of dealing with the wordlessness of traumatic pasts. The tragic outcome of this is the transformation of victims into perpetrators, and the continuing cycles of repetition that it breeds. Processes such as the TRC can help break the cycles of violence and trauma that so often repeat themselves historically. The principle of reconciliation, although not a panacea for all the problems facing post-conflict societies, or countries in the throes of ongoing violence, is an important strategy that can help build social solidarity and establish a foundation for a shared humanity.

## Notes

1  See commentary on "The Root of Afrikaner Rage" by Pumla Gobodo-Madikizela in *New Times,* January 10, 2003.
2  See Nelson Mandela quote at the beginning of the chapter.
3  TRC Amnesty hearing, August 1997.
4  See S. Wiesenthal (1998). *The Sunflower: On the Possibilities and Limits of Forgiveness.* Tel Aviv, Israel: Schocken.
5  I facilitated this meeting at the request of Mbelo. Although it was not meant to be filmed, a TRC counselor arranged access into the room for the producer of Iris Films. Fortunately, they kept a respectful distance during filming. Some of the footage from this meeting appears in the award-winning film, *Long Night's Journey into Day.*

## References

Abram, D 1997, *The spell of the sensuous: Perception and language in a more-than-human world*, Vintage Books, New York.
Agassi, JB 1999, *Martin Buber on psychology and psychotherapy: Essays, letters, and dialogue*, Syracuse University Press, Syracuse.
Arendt, H 1998, *The human condition* (2nd ed), University of Chicago Press, Chicago.
Benjamin, J 1990, 'An outline of intersubjectivity: The development of recognition', *Psychoanalytic Psychology*, vol. 7(S), p. 33.
Blanchot, M 1992, *The infinite conversation* (Susan Hanson, trans), University of Minnesota Press, Minneapolis.
Caruth, C 1995, *Trauma: Explorations in memory*, Johns Hopkins University Press, Baltimore.

Caruth, C 1996, *Unclaimed experience: Trauma, narrative, and history*, Johns Hopkins University Press, Baltimore.

Cromby, J 2007, 'Toward a psychology of feeling', *International Journal of Critical Psychology*, vol. 21, pp. 94–118.

de Waal, F, Wright, R, Korsgaard, C, Kitcher, P & Singer, P 2006, *Primates and philosophers: How morality evolved*, Princeton University Press, Princeton, NJ.

Durham, M 2000, *The therapist's encounters with revenge and forgiveness*, Jessica Kingsley, Philadelphia.

Enright, R & North, J 1998, *Exploring forgiveness*, University of Wisconsin Press, Madison.

Felman, S & Laub, D 1992, *Testimony: Crises of witnessing in literature, psychoanalysis, and history*, Routledge, New York.

Finlay, L & Evans, K 2009, *Relational-centred research for psychotherapists: Exploring meanings and experience*, Wiley-Blackwell, Chichester.

Fonagy, P and Target, M 1996, Playing with reality: I. Theory of mind and the normal development of psychic reality, *International Journal of Psychoanalysis*, 77, 217–233.

Gobodo-Madikizela, P 2002, Remorse, forgiveness, and rehumanization: Stories from South Africa, *Journal of Humanistic Psychology*, vol. 42, no. 1, pp. 7–32.

Gobodo-Madikizela, P 2008a, 'Transforming trauma in the aftermath of gross human rights abuses: Making public spaces intimate', in A Nadler, J Fisher & T Malloy (eds), *Social psychology of inter-group reconciliation: From violent conflict to peaceful co-existence*, Oxford, London, pp. 57–76.

Gobodo-Madikizela, P 2008b, 'Trauma, forgiveness and the witnessing dance: Making public spaces intimate', *Journal of Analytical Psychology*, vol. 53, pp. 169–188.

Gobodo-Madikizela, P 2008c, 'Empathic repair after mass trauma: When vengeance is arrested', *European Journal of Social Theory*, vol. 11, no. 3, pp. 331–350.

Gobodo-Madikizela, P 2011, 'Intersubjectivity and embodiment: Exploring the role of the maternal in the language of forgiveness and reconciliation', *Signs: Journal of Women in Culture and Society*, vol. 36, no. 3, pp. 541–551.

Gobodo-Madikizela, P 2012, "Remembering the past: Nostalgia, traumatic memory, and the legacy of apartheid," *Peace and Conflict: Journal of Peace Psychology*, vol. 18, no. 3, p. 252.

Jordan, JV 2003, 'The relational-cultural model', in M Kopala & M Keitel (eds), *The handbook of counseling women*, Sage, Thousand Oaks, CA, pp. 22–30.

Kearney, R 1993, *Poetics of imagination: From Husserl to Lyotard*, Routledge, London.

Klein, M 1975, *Love, guilt and reparation and other works 1921–1945 (The writings of Melanie Klein, volume 1)*, Free Press, New York.

LaCapra, D 2004, *Representing history, representing trauma*, Cornell University Press, Ithaca, NY.

LaCapra, D 2009, *History and its limits: Human, animal, violence*, Cornell University Press, Ithaca, NY.

Langer, L 1993, *Holocaust testimonies: The ruins of memory*, Yale University Press, New Haven.

Maclear, K 2003, 'The limits of vision: *Hiroshima Mon Amour* and the subversion of representation', in A Douglass & T Vogler (eds), *Witness and memory: The discourse of trauma*, Routledge, London, pp. 233–248.

Prager, J 2006, 'Jump-starting timeliness: Trauma, temporality and the redressive community', in J Parker, M Crawford & P Harris (eds), *Time and memory: The study of time XII*, Koninklijke Brill, Amsterdam, pp. 229–245.

Prager, J 2008, 'Healing from history psychoanalytic considerations on traumatic pasts and social repair', *European Journal of Social Theory*, vol. 11, no. 3, pp. 405–419.

Republic of South Africa 1993, *South African Interim Constitution*, viewed 15 February 2016 at http://www1.chr.up.ac.za/chr_old/indigenous/documents/South%20Africa/Legislation/Constitution%20of%20South%20Africa%201993.pdf

Rotberg, R & Thompson, D 2000, *Truth v. Justice: The Morality of Truth Commissions*, Princeton University Press, Princeton.

Safier, R & Gobodo-Madikizela, P 2014, 'Conversation between Ruth Safier and Pumla Gobodo-Madikizela on "Remembering the past: Nostalgia, traumatic memory, and the legacy of apartheid"', *Peace and Conflict: Journal of Peace Psychology*, vol. 20, no. 1, pp. 95–99.

Stein, E 1964, *On the problem of empathy* (W Stein, trans), The Hague, Nijhoff.

Stern, D 1985, *The interpersonal world of the infant*, Basic Books, New York.

Stern, D 2004, *The present moment in psychotherapy and everyday life*, Norton, New York.

Stern, D, Sander, L, Nahun, J, Harrison, A, Lyons-Ruth, K, Morgan, A, Bruschweilerstern, N & Tronick, E 1998, 'Non-interpretive mechanisms in psychoanalytic therapy: The "something more" than interpretation', *International Journal of Psychoanalysis*, vol. 79, pp. 903–921.

Steyn, M & Foster, D 2008, 'Repertoires for talking white: Resistant whiteness in post-apartheid South Africa', *Ethnic and Racial Studies*, vol. 31, pp. 25–51.

Theissen, G & Hamber, B 1998, 'A state of denial: White South Africans' attitudes to the truth and reconciliation commission', *Indicator South Africa*, vol. 15, pp. 8–12.

Wiesenthal, S 1998, *The sunflower: On the possibilities and limits of forgiveness*, Schocken, Tel Aviv.

# 25

# Psychoanalysis and political repression

*Max Hernández*

The first attempt of the application of psychoanalysis to "some unsolved problems of social psychology," *Totem and Taboo* (Freud, 1913), took place, as stated in "The Claims of Psycho-Analysis to Scientific Interest" by "a similar application[1] of its points of view, its hypotheses and its findings" to the study of the origins of the great cultural institutions.

Such early interest of Freud and his disciples Otto Rank and Theodor Reik would serve to clear the way for a fruitful dialogue between psychoanalysis and anthropology, which has consolidated over time. As regards the application of psychoanalysis to political phenomena, the inaugural test was *Group Psychology and the Analysis of the Ego* (Freud, 1921). Additionally, Freud often resorted to political and military images when it comes to mental organization: territory, laws, *fueros* (the Spanish word for a special type of jurisdiction), borders, censorship, defenses and attacks. That is, he expresses as if speaking of a state organization. The use of such metaphors led some to force comparisons between substantively different elements and, therefore, proposing "wild" readings of political events.

Unlike what happens when psychoanalysis is "applied" – transferred? – to so-called anthropological material, the tensions between the disciplinary domains of psychoanalysis and politics are obvious. Beyond the disagreements brought about by its proposals, the contributions of the Frankfurt School were instrumental in establishing important methodological precautions. In any case, psychoanalysis can open avenues for a better understanding of "politics" and of "the political." That is, both set of practices that are deployed in political institutions, and in which a government is instituted in society, and provide the essential matter of the "political". The relationship continues to be problematic: as soon as the words "psychoanalysis" and "politics" are put side by side, the existence of a gap becomes evident. It is in this sort of no man's land that, in what follows, the concepts "political oppression" and "psychic repression" will be put in question.[2] Political oppression refers to the set of dispositions implemented by sociopolitical structures organized as systems of domination aimed at enforcing the reasonable, commonsense behaviors attuned to the objectives of a group in power. Psychic repression which refers to the defense mechanism that acts to keep out of awareness what is unacceptable to the conscious mind, yet nonetheless affects the behavior, will be examined.

## An Andean example

I have chosen as starting point a foundational moment of the Andean civilizations in which the relationship between political oppression and psychic repression appears with special clarity, with all the caution that this word awakens in an audience of psychoanalysts. Then I will proceed to explore some circumstances in which the exercise of power involves oppression at the political level and repression in the subjective realm.

Before beginning with the first point, it is worth remembering that 3 years before publishing *Totem and Taboo* (1913), Freud had published an essay about a childhood memory of Leonardo da Vinci. In connection with a fantasy that the artist fused with memories, Freud refers to some ancient deities to highlight how the genitals had become "through a long series of generations . . . the *pudenda*," that is object of shame, and even disgust, and draws attention to the fact that data collected by civilization researchers "provide convincing evidence that originally the genitals were the pride and hope of living beings" (1910, p. 92). The now devalued pudenda were once worshiped and transferred their divinity to all human activities.

What happened in the central Andes during the last millennium before our era seems to sum up the history of "a long series of generations," a long sequence in which a tempo of accelerated change processes took place – population increase, multiple and continuous contacts between the coast, the highlands and the lowland, the development of pottery, the domestication and spread of maize farming, the invention of the hand loom, the advancement in construction techniques, metallurgical development – led to a differentiation in the social structure that, until then, had been fairly homogeneous. It was the beginning of a state order and a system of social classes. A great social organization allowed a first integration in the central Andes that overflowed the narrow limits of a difficult territory.

The aforementioned processes were contemporaneous with a marked stylistic unification, inferring that a group of communities shared the same religious universe. The Chavín de Huántar temple, which brings together a rich collection of artistic and architectural expressions, illustrates the cultural uniformity at that time. Being its most accomplished representative, the name Chavín Horizon has been given to this period of Andean history. The remains of this ceremonial center, a maze of stone ruins, render the key role of religion in structuring the political, the social and the economic. From the profusion of images that seem to dominate the universe of mythological creatures made of ceramic, stone, fabric, bone and gold, it has been possible to infer what, in Marcel Gauss's terms, would have been a total social phenomenon.

Falcons, snakes, tiger-like bird-men or feathered felines mix the human and the animal evoking a genealogy of sacred predators. Some features that play a central role in the iconographic design of Chavín art are present in the Raimondi Stela: linearity, symmetry, repetition and the use of patterns define a figurative style that includes abstract and decorative elements. Incisions and reliefs seem to betray traces of an ideo-affective belief system linked to a mythical-religious cult. Meanwhile, the Lanzón, stone embodiment of an anthropomorphic god, spellbinds and frightens. Like a mammoth tusk, it penetrates into the earth and appears willing to open its voracious jaws. Female, masculine and hermaphrodite divinities have in common the reference to the alliance, parentage and kinship systems and to sexual relations. All these images are integral to the world of beliefs and fears of the period in question.

It is worth stopping at the two cylindrical columns that currently flank the access to the temple's portal. Being architecturally functional parts it is unlikely that they have served as objects of worship; rather, they could represent minor deities, "angels" or guardians of the gods, as proposed by John H. Rowe. One of the images has two rows of teeth facing each other in the zone corresponding to the genitals in the manner of a toothed vagina. The other has a single row of teeth with a single-canine – or beak of a bird of prey – which seems a phallic attribute.

If intercourse is represented in the Tello Obelisk as an exuberant and labyrinthine entanglement, these columns anticipate it as a fierce encounter. The sexual jaws and the menacing fang stand for the genitals. Substitution has created an equivalence effect that evokes and confounds the relationship between theocratic oppression and sexual prohibition. The intimate and familiar yet strange reference offers a glimpse of the signs of the renunciation of sexual satisfaction and the control of aggressive tendencies that the civilizing process has demanded from the masses. This seems to have taken place on par with the assertion of domination imposed by the coalition of priests and artisans. The fierce genitals account for the presence of supernatural powers in the depths of man and the sequestering of the naturalness of sex by the mechanisms of repression and idealization.

Freud's essay on Leonardo (1910) seeks to clarify the role of the unconscious fantasy of the phallic mother in the artist's childhood memory. By referring to the primitive deities of the Egyptian pantheon and the cults associated with Dionysus and Aphrodite in ancient Greece, Freud emphasizes the androgynous condition of their representations that expressed the union of male and female attributes. In them, the images from the world of nature were mingled to produce strange forms that were presented as existing realities. The addition of the phallus to the female figures of these deities gave them a divine character as they gathered the creative forces of nature. When the connection of the official religions with sexual activity became hidden from general awareness, secret cults practiced by a small number of initiates emerged.

In the theocratic kingdoms and seigniories of the Chavín period, an elite consisting of priests of terrible deities represented in society their supernatural power and cast on heaven and earth the symbols of their earthly power. Gathered in the ceremonial center, it displayed knowledge and power and administered terror on behalf of the gods of the pantheon whose depictions in stone presided over the rituals. The agrarian borders were defended by an active amalgam of religion and technology.

The tangle of extensions of the images of the deities that seem replicated ad infinitum externalizes the subtle dialectic that unfolds from the restricted possession of propitiation and fertility rituals and the secret management of knowledge. It is thus that the "'imaginary' monopoly of the monopoly 'of the imaginary'" that Maurice Godelier has explained so clearly in his anthropological writings (1989, 2000) is consolidated. Monopoly "squared" that made possible to control the means of reproduction of nature, of goods and services, and of society. In the relations between men and of these with nature, even in regard to material aspects, there are ideal aspects that are part of their internal armor.

So far, we have followed, according to some clues, a possible itinerary of the trajectory by which the genitals became "pudenda," objects of shame. Now, Freud had held very early, as recorded in the letters to Wilhelm Fliess, the relationship between the development of civilization and the suppression of instincts. The "striking correspondence" between the two totemic commands (not to kill the totem and not to have intercourse with the women of the clan) and the two impulses of the Oedipus complex (get rid of the father and possess the mother) was investigated in *Totem and Taboo* (1913). The ideas of Charles Darwin and J. J. Atkinson on the primal horde subjected to a powerful male and of William Robertson Smith on the totemic meal were the basis for the Freudian conception about the despotic father of the primal horde that had all the women for himself and who was murdered by his sons and devoured by them in the totemic meal.

Now, the subjugation of women, the totemic order or the building of a State and social differentiation did not arise ex nihilo. Anthropological research on the Baruya society by the same Godelier (2000) can clarify what could have happened in previous circumstances. The power that governs this pre-State human society does not derive from an order based on an accumulation of goods and wealth or social class stratification: it is based on the domination of women by men. The conception of power as exercised in social relations of the Baruya society, where there is no State or social classes, is not based on material appropriation, but in dominance at a "symbolic" level. Or, to be more precise, beyond the merely symbolic for ritual practices are integrated to the body.

It is through the sexed human body, anatomy, sexuality, semen and blood that order is established and power prevailing in society is transmitted. Anatomical differences serve to determine the fate of each. The social order is, at the same time, the sexual order. Ideas shared by men and women – semen is power, menstrual blood is poison – are transmitted by the body. It is a kind of silent speech: the appropriate place in society corresponding to everyone is foreshadowed in their sex. The power of men over women is stated in the explicit denigration of female powers – barely implicitly acknowledged – to keep them alienated from their own powers without the possibility of protest.

In Chavín society, once a State and a system of social stratification was configured, concrete and monopolistic power was "officiated" in a magic-religious manner by the priestly caste, that segment linked to administrative and "ideological" activities. The new situation created by the revolution in agricultural production and increasing specialization demanded more work and a more complex administration of community affairs. Under the new conditions power exerted on the body and by the body was inserted into the social imperative imposed by the theocratic domination arranged in a terrible imagery that weighted on individuals that composed a society dependent on agriculture.

The sexual had been sequestered with regard to the new demands: it was the necessary renunciation to carry out the civilizing project. This renunciation had a cost: it generated inner urges that, in turn, encouraged the terrifying imagery. Social oppression and sexual repression became tied, outside the community's knowledge, by a bond of cross-linked fibers. The rituals that regulated the social imaginary remitted sexual representations to psychic depths with the help of the impressive power of images and myths. In the depths of the psyche, the phallic tusk could defeat the *vagina dentata*.

The changes in the social system would have required an "ideology" to explain the new situation. It was a necessary form of justification for the domination of one group over the social whole that stretched over disparate communities and regions, a sanction of the established power and a redefinition of the cultural identity of the extended group. The members of the theocratic class, identified with predator gods, were the first and most fervent believers. Fixed in and by a belief system that made the privileges granted by power to be exercised in the "imaginary" context of the public interest, they suffered their vocation with awe and reverence.

Deities and officiants, priests and believers, were conjoined by a fabric of emotional adhesions. Recourse to the imposition of a rigid magical-religious structure allowed social groups with diverse and even conflicting interests, and different communities to share the same representations. A cult that appealed to the mechanisms of reciprocity and functioned using the structures of kinship had spread incorporating the elements of an ancient tradition as witnessed by some Chavín images whose distant precursors are seen in the textiles corresponding to the Pre-ceramic period.

The idea that through successive historical sediment there remained a system of power based on the domination of women by men, and not on the accumulation of property and wealth or class stratification, seems suggestive. The correspondence between representations of ancient androgynous deities and some infantile sexual theories, on the one hand, and between the established social order and power transmitted to society by virtue of the sexed human body and sexuality, on the other, somewhat clarify the role of repressive processes in the relationship between sex, gender and power. Likewise, the emergence of a priestly caste bolstered by a belief system that granted privileges allows one to understand and elucidate the complex weave of intrapsychic repression, intersubjective domination and subjugation, and oppression exerted through social systems.

In that sense, it is possible to state that Chavín's lithic representations, those wordless images that remain in a sort "of pictographic state" – to use Roland Barthes's expression (1977, p. 38) – are the tangible sign of a foundational event previously befallen. The "free of words" images arouse emotions that reverberate in the most intimate areas of each inhabitant. The incisions of the temple columns show the trace of that instant where the link binding social oppression and sexual repression was instituted in the same act that withdrew it from the consciousness of the community group.

This first part of the presentation can be considered an "application" of psychoanalysis to an anthropological "material" in the manner of Freud's *Totem and Taboo* (1913). In what follows the "applicability" of psychoanalysis to today's prevailing sociopolitical conditions will be explored in terms of the tensions between the disciplinary domains of psychoanalysis and of politics. To navigate this sort of no man's land will require to initiate a movement driven by a constant inquiring, that is, "a conversation" in the line of David Tracy (1989).

Thus we will try to overcome the conceptual hiatus successively threading some Freudian texts and concepts to different proposals made about society from sociology and political theory.[3] It goes without saying that this invites adopting a bifocal gaze.

## A subject of our times

Approaching the current sociopolitical conditions implies attempting a threefold millennial leap and situating ourselves at the dawn of the modern era. The idea of an unchanging, orderly and hierarchical cosmos had yielded to the incursions of sailors who widened the boundaries of their world and to scientific and philosophical assaults. Chavín culture had disappeared and the Inca culture that occupied the Andean territory many centuries later had been submitted to the Spanish Empire. The nature of government, sovereignty, rights and participation in public affairs were matter of reflection and debate.

By the mid-17th century Thomas Hobbes had argued the need of the sovereign State to end a situation of anarchy. The State has the monopoly of violence under a covenant of men submitting to the authority of an absolute, undivided and unlimited sovereign power. Thus becomes consolidated a relationship of control sustained by coercion – accepted as legitimate – that enables life in society. Plautus's dictum, *Homo homini lupus*, used by Hobbes in *Leviathan*, illustrates the state of war of all against all (*Bellum omnium contra omnes*) that would have been the natural state of human groups.

Before a half-century had passed, Hobbes's work was questioned. John Locke called into question absolutism and proposed a theory both of political society and of civil society based on the natural rights of men prior to the formation of society that proposed a social contract in which sovereignty emanates from the people. The natural state of human groups is not necessarily good or bad; it is chaotic. From this derives the convenience of a society capable of bringing order, a civilized society. In the *Two Treatises of Government*, a State acting in an atmosphere of diversity and tolerance is put forward.

In the mid-18th century Jean-Jacques Rousseau published his *Discourse on the Origins of Inequality Among Men*, later elaborated in *The Social Contract* (1952). Rousseau maintained that men in their natural state are free and equal. Man in a State of Nature had a sort of "innate repugnance" to see others of his kind suffer, a trait that was vitiated in the process of civilization. When the natural state presents obstacles, men coordinated by a "general will" seek to achieve the "social contract." Might does not make right and, therefore, only legitimate powers must be obeyed. Freedom and equality of men should be preserved by a State established by the social contract. The new conditions that called into question the premises of a mentality that justified a long history of exclusion, were reflected in the realm of ideas. The desire for freedom, the exigencies of equality and the demands for recognition made way for democracy.

G. W. F. Hegel published *The Phenomenology of Spirit* in 1807 when the thunder of the French Revolution rumbled in Europe. Several authors have read it with contemporary eyes either to establish a comparison between these various versions of the big events that would be at the origin of the great institutions of culture or to obtain a better understanding of bourgeois society and modernity. These approaches allow demarcating a meeting space for the domains of psychoanalysis and politics. For the latter purpose it is particularly valuable to consider matters relating to the passage from the individual subjective spirit, which tends to the consciousness of its independence and freedom, to the objective spirit, realized as right and ethics and which finds in the State the conjunction of the objectivity of the legal and the subjective singularity of morality.

In the famous passage of the master and slave (or lord and bondsman) dialectic, Hegel proposed the tendency of consciousness to disregard other consciousness, and to engage in a fight to the death with the consciousness it faces, and to ignore external reality. When two consciousnesses clash in a fight to the death, one of them, called "noble consciousness," does not hesitate at the prospect of its death; the other, which feels invaded by fear, is called "servile consciousness." In the development of the process comes the need of the noble consciousness of being recognized by another consciousness. The other is necessary to affirm self-recognition. The noble consciousness, which wants to feel free and indifferent, and impose its own truth, stumbles upon the need of obtaining recognition of another consciousness. The master needs the servant and therefore spares his life; he contents himself with dialectically suppressing his existence.

The master and slave dialectic does not only refer to the social positions of each individual, but also to two attitudes: one that denies and one that recognizes the other. Recognition consists in assigning value and, therefore, only recognition by a peer is relevant. Therefore, if the value of the servant as a person has been dialectically suppressed, the recognition that comes from him is worthless. All this leads to a trap that only can be escaped through mutual recognition, the full acceptance of the other. This implies a decisive transformation in the relationship between consciousnesses.

Enlightenment's winds of universalism had unleashed the revolutionary hurricanes. Romanticism and nationalist passions had turned them around. In the realm of ideas, certainties dissolved in Hegelian negativity and in suspicions sown by Karl Marx and Friedrich Nietzsche. In the early 20th century the West was a field of forces tensioned by a partly industrial economy, a society in which the dominant order remained aristocratic, a technology whose impact was just beginning to be felt and an open and uncertain political horizon in which many hoped for or feared an onslaught against the hegemonic order. In this field psychoanalysis emerged.

The first attempt of application of psychoanalysis was, as stated, *Totem and Taboo* (1913). The versions of Hobbes, Locke and Rousseau about the "natural state" differ from Freud's proposal about origins. There is no reference in them to a horde submitted by a despotic male. The "hypothesis, or, . . . rather . . . vision," if we stick to what was said by Freud in his autobiography, states that after the totemic meal there was no individual who by his power or superiority could have assumed the role of father. The paternal horde had been replaced at the beginning by the fraternal clan, whose guarantee was given by the ties of kinship. If each of the members of the fraternal clan had wanted for himself the prerogatives of the primal father, that would have resulted in a general struggle and in the downfall of the new organization. However, as Freud observes, the primitive democratic equality of all members of the tribe could not be maintained. Deep consequential changes to the state of civilization gave rise to a tendency to resurrect the old ideal of the father and even to elevate to the status of gods men who had shown to be superior to others.

Shortly after the end of World War I, in 1921, *Group Psychology and the Analysis of the Ego* appeared. In the aforementioned essay Freud proposed a new interpretation of the changes affecting the individual when it becomes part of a group. The individual psychology/social or collective psychology dilemma, "which at a first glance may seem to be full of significance," is questioned. In the text Freud glosses, comments, complements and criticizes the work of Gustave Le Bon and proceeds to explain group psychology from the analysis of the individual ego. A double bond links individuals when they are part of a group. They are simultaneously attracted to their peers and to a leader whose prestige and speech exert fascination over others. The group exacerbates impulsivity, the instinct of self-preservation disappears, gullibility increases, and critical thinking and logic are suspended; at the same time, the member of the group succumbs to the need to be dominated and subdued.

The essay was written when the active model of domination from the late 17th century had reached its climax. Michel Foucault called disciplinary society the one governed by this form of surveillance and discipline and that had superseded a model that prevailed in social formations based on the principle of sovereignty. In disciplinary societies, the great spaces of confinement were instituted: the family, school, the barracks, the factory and occasionally the hospital or prison. At the end of World War II conditions no longer responded to the model of the disciplinary society; it was being eroded by a crisis affecting family, schools, barracks, factory, hospital and prison. Now, societies of control that employ "freely floating" forms of subjection are in the process of replacing disciplinary societies.

Unprecedented changes developed from the Industrial Revolution have resulted in all economic, political and social changes worldwide that are grouped under the concept of globalization. In the realm of ideas, the values of freedom are highlighted. As regards the political arena, it is said there must be no repression by a State that must have the characteristics of the rule of law and regarding the economic sphere it is said that the free market and free competition optimize the ability to produce wealth, work and social welfare. Put simply, the rule of law and capital would be the centers from which power is exercised.

To examine how power is exerted from the centers formed by the rule of law and capital, we should refer briefly to some ideas developed by two French authors of the second half of the 20th century: Louis Althusser and Michel Foucault. Althusser believes that alongside the regulatory, administrative and repressive elements – the state apparatuses, using the term coined by Marx – there are institutions, not necessarily public, with training functions such as religion, education, family, and scientific and artistic associations he calls "ideological state apparatuses" aimed at reproducing the people's subjugation to the dominant ideology. In his perspective, ideology is understood not so much as false consciousness but as the imaginary relationship of individuals to their real conditions of existence and it mediates between systems of power and individuals.

Althusser (1971) distinguishes between the State apparatus and State power. By analyzing the organization of the State we know today, he finds that even though its repressive apparatus is quite similar to those of earlier times, the quantity, quality and autonomy of its ideological apparatuses was much smaller back then. These institutions exert their power through attenuated, symbolic modes of repression. They play the role of reproducing ideological and valuational elements. "Virtues" such as modesty, humility, resignation (if not submission) or as pride, confidence, leadership skills, eloquence and dexterity (if not cynicism and contempt) are taught "even at stadiums" and incorporated into the everyday repertoire. Unlike Hegel, for whom recognition of the subject by the other is essential, Althusser proposes that the subject is constructed by ideology, when interpellated by power in a process that is not of cause-and-effect, but simultaneous.

Michel Foucault (1980), studying the realities of power in today's society, has placed special attention on those unwritten restrictions and constraints to which the subject is exposed. This approach is particularly interesting in that it provides an insight into private areas of the individual beyond the reach of political control exercised by the State and its ideological apparatuses of power or by a privileged class on society as a whole. For Foucault, power relations are in the warp and woof of the social fabric and do not govern from above. Hence, a notion that accommodates the multiplicity of powers that are exercised in the social sphere is needed. A set of minor powers and of institutions positioned in a subsidiary level configure a network of microscopic, capillary power, a grid-like organization in which the multiple relations of authority located at different levels of society, support each other and manifest subtly.

From this perspective, the analysis of the phenomenon of power makes it necessary to transcend both the legal context in which the contract – oppression relationship is inscribed in terms of the legitimacy or illegitimacy of power and the limits bounded by the terms struggle – submission within which the domination – repression dialectic is often proposed. Foucault's considerations on relations of authority between man and woman, student and teacher and within families led him to propose that these are less the direct effects of a sovereign power than the terrain on which it rests. That is, its conditions of possibility.

Sovereign power can work the way it works only because there are specific relations of domination that have their own configuration and relative autonomy.

This social power, which is constructed and operates from other powers and their effects thereof, independent of the economic process, must be analyzed in its microscopic levels if we are to understand it and to prevent its coercive power from enduring. As a result of the intimate intertwining of relationships, they play a conditioning and conditioned role, as product and as tool. A power that works in chain, which is not localized, and is never in the hands of a few, has to be analyzed following an ascending path, from its "infinitesimal mechanisms," which, having its own historical and technical features, have been co-opted by more general mechanisms and forms of global domination. By confronting the visions of power of Althusser and Foucault, we see that the two planes in which they are located belong to the same area of inquiry. Without denying the differences between their approaches, it is not unreasonable to propose a complementary and antagonistic relationship between the two perspectives.

True, Althusser attempts to understand situations of exploitation, while Foucault seeks to clarify the conditions of domination. Gavatri Spivak (1988) notes that Foucault ignores the fact that power "produces" ideology. This bias is probably due to his attention to the diffuse and heterogeneous nature of power that leads him to appeal to culture. The notion of ideology, as Althusser develops it, is necessary to understand collective interests, hence pointing out that this generalization blurs the role played by economics and class conflict in resistance, insurgency and rebellion. This notion of ideology given by Althusser is important in that the hegemony of dominant groups broke up the relationship between interests, desires and knowledge.

Freud used the same quotation from Plautus, *Homo homini lupus*, in *Civilization and Its Discontents* (1930), an essay that argues that repression of aggressive impulses is necessary to live in society. This, he says, has a cost: repressed aggression corrodes the ties that bind the individual to the group. This dissonance present in the inner world determines that the group is always on the verge of disintegration. If this occurs at the individual level, at the same time, the State introduces the laws and regulations needed for public control and the maintenance of social order. These have objective existence but are internalized by individuals. Following these processes, the transgression of those objective laws causes, at the subjective level, the mutual feedback between fear of punishment, often referred to authority, and feelings of guilt, whose empire is limited to the internal realm. Even in many circumstances the unconscious need for punishment and unconscious guilt seem amalgamated.

We have mentioned references to the fascination and power that the leader exerts under his prestige and the magical value of his words in *Group Psychology and the Analysis of the Ego* (1921). Earlier we also mentioned that full acceptance of the other implies a decisive transformation in the relationship between consciousnesses. Wilfrid Bion would describe it as a catastrophic change, that is, the transformation that enables the subject to accept the need to break mind-sets that prevent overcoming prejudices and assumptions that thwart learning from experience and that work as a resistance to change.

The *habitus* is a notion put forward by Pierre Bourdieu (1994) to overcome the pitfalls of "sociologism" and "methodological individualism." This concept, which does not entail a short circuit between the individual and collective levels, allows him to build bridges between objectified aspects and internalized aspects of the social, that is, between external structures (demographic, social, political, economic, etc.) and mental structures incorporated into the subject as categories of social representation (ideologies, mentalities, etc.) governing perception, thought and social action. The *habitus* operates from within the individual and establishes nonconscious relations of meaning between the two realities. If Bion's idea is taken up again we can say that full acceptance of the other demands catastrophic change of the habitus as it governs behaviors acted regularly and simultaneously supports the regularity of conduct.

Regarding the serious difficulties involved in bringing about catastrophic change, it is worth making a brief reference to two experiments conducted by two social psychologists: one by Stanley Milgram at Yale University, and the other by Philip Zimbardo at Stanford University. The results of both experiments showed that very few participants were able to resist the instructions leading them to mistreat and abuse the other. Although both experiments and their conclusions have been subjected to strong criticism, there is no doubt that they dramatically highlight the propensity to obey authority, institutional or scientific. The average person tends to give in to the temptations of power and abuse as long as a minimum semblance of correctness and decency is maintained and finds it difficult to act on his good intentions, even when he feels that not doing it calls into question his moral principles. Environmental pressures and complacency with authority may exert an unusual degree of influence on people's behavior. Milgram emphasizes that the definition of "reality" made by the authority is accepted as valid and thus the difficulty of questioning it.

Earlier, in the *Three Essays on the Theory of Sexuality* (1905), Freud had referred to an instinct for mastery or domination – a term whose use, according to Jean Laplanche and J.-B. Pontalis, cannot be "accurately codified," whose definition, it goes without saying, is not axiomatic and whose translation indicates the oscillation between two meanings: to seize or take possession by force. This is a nonsexual instinct that would only secondarily join sexuality in order to master an external object by force and whose support is the musculature. In its first moments, Freudian theorizing is referred to power and possession. In its origin, infantile cruelty would not tend to inflict suffering on the object, but rather it would not take it into account. That is, to cause suffering is not part of its first aim. In "Instincts and their Vicissitudes," Freud introduces his first thesis about sadomasochism, that, unlike the first formulation that, as we have seen, located the instinct to master at a stage prior to the appearance of both caring for the other and sadism, states that the first aim of sadism is the humiliation and domination of the object by violence.

The role played by the instinct to master in psychoanalytic theory and clinical practice was quite limited though Freud made reference to it at different times. It is interesting to mention since this concept could open a space of importance with regard to the psychoanalytic understanding of political phenomena. *Beyond the Pleasure Principle* (1920), conceived with World War I and the difficult postwar years as background, introduced the concept of the "death drive." This reformulation of the theory of drives subordinated and subsumed the tendency to seize the object to the death drive when it merges with the sexual instinct. The search for mastery is inevitable because without it the death instinct would remain within the psyche and would end one's own life. The emphasis had shifted from mastery to the destruction of the object.

It is perhaps more than anecdotal that it was Ives Hendrick, a prominent member of the group that gained hegemonic power in American psychiatry in the 1930s, who returned to the ideas of the early Freudian writings on the instinct to master. This would be an innate disposition to do and learn to do that when successfully performed would produce a specific pleasure. The instinct to master would have as its aim to master the environment. The proposal, made in the early 1940s, is part of a conception of psychoanalysis markedly influenced by ego psychology and learning theories. Hendrick was part of the generation of young psychoanalysts trained in Europe with the pioneers that led the deployment of psychoanalytic ego psychology and paved the way for the extraordinary professional expansion of psychoanalysis in the United States in the years after World War II.

Paul Denis makes an interesting proposal regarding the instinct to master, which avoids what he considers the meta-biological bias introduced by the death drive. He considers that in the sexual drive two complementary currents of libidinal investiture converge: the component of mastery and of satisfaction. In one of its "two sides" there is an organized register around the erogenous zones and in the other a register in terms of mastery organized around motor and sensory skills. The part of the energy that has separated from the register of representations to invest the motor and the sensorial through which the libido is to link to the objects of the external world converges with that which remains tied to representations. The mastery component would be expressed through a kind of "narcissistic vector" and the satisfaction component, related to the experience, through the "object vector." The convergence of both currents causes the libidinal investment of the erogenous zones to associate with the motor and the sensorial, means by which the libido is to link to the objects of the external world.

In the two versions proposed by Freud and in the ones by Hendrick and by Denis, the instinct to master goes from subject to object. A different view is proposed by Jessica Benjamin in *The Bonds of Love* (1998), an exploration of the possible reasons leading to the acceptance and perpetuation of relations of mastery and submission in spite of protests for freedom and equality. Sadomasochistic relationships would be the clearest expression of a "culture" of mastery that organizes both mastery and submission. Both are part of a complex system of recursive processes involving both those who exert power and those who subject to it.

A review of the classic Freudian theories on early childhood drawing on the ideas of D. W. Winnicott, Daniel Stern and Louis Sander about a condition prior to the establishment of the inner world/outer world, representation/object, self/other polarities, is the starting point to proceed to a reading of the Hegelian master and slave dialectic that questions the assumption of a consciousness of a subject who has himself as absolute to propose a model that transcends Freud's binary model, which places mastery and sadism on the active masculine side and masochism and submission in the passive feminine side to explain the relationship between gender and domination and the complicated network that traverses sexual and social domination.

What has been said is an attempt to answer Sandor Ferenczi's question about which part of sadomasochism is conditioned by culture and which part is autonomous and develops as an organization phase of its own. Now let's go back to the power concentrated in the State and exerted by it both directly and through its ideological apparatuses and which is rooted in a microscopic weave of multiple powers, connected by a capillary network, that circulate through a two-way street. In the first case the main references were the great cultural texts of Freud. In the second, we have resorted to some psychoanalytic concepts. In both cases a weave has been presented where the warp consists of texts on politics and the woof of texts and psychoanalytic concepts. By focusing on the relationships between individuals, we have privileged those aspects that could fall under the "instinct to master." Whether we accept it as a mental construction rooted in and subsumed by the death or destruction drive, or as a component of the sexual drive, both approaches limit to the intrapsychic aspects. If we consider it as the force that puts in play and organizes both mastery and submission, we are either following the logic of object relations or in a relational perspective.

It is true that face-to-face interactions have been studied from the perspective of social psychology as well as of microsociology when entering certain spatiality referred to the intimate realms where issues of friendship, family or chance encounters are unfolded. It has been sought from both perspectives to fill in the details that abstract representations of social phenomena leave out to understand reciprocal relations between these interactions and social facts and thereby explain the social organization of personal experiences, even those that are unknown to the actors themselves. Many of these studies can illuminate the social dimension of interpersonal relationships and allow articulating the intimate universe of gestures, words and actions with social structures accounted for by more abstract theories. It is not necessary to emphasize that to enter the dimensions of the intrapsychic, of object relations and of intersubjective relations requires psychoanalysis.

## Final comments

A crucial issue revolves in the background of what was presented: the possibility of a discipline focused on the problem of the subject of being extrapolated to social issues or even to collective subjects. The relationship between repressive processes, the established social order and power transmitted to society and its representatives structured around the sexed human body and sexuality, as it happened in Baruya society and as it was implemented in Chavín civilization by a theocratic caste, can be extrapolated to currently prevailing conditions. This, provided that the view of history inscribed in an absolute linear time is put in question, and taking into account Siegfried Kracauer's caveat: not to overload chronology with excessive meaning, and also bearing in mind Jürgen Habermas's suggestion about the polygenetic origin of modernity.

Fernand Braudel formulated the idea of the existence of long-term historical realities when he proposed that history unfolds at different times: a short-term in which events occur, a medium-term proper of junctures and long-term through which structures extend. The latter refer to historical realities that persist despite fluctuations in events and circumstantial changes. The permanence in time of political, economic, social and mental structures is obvious. While all of them correspond to long-term historical realities, each one of them is successively slower in its evolution. Thus, political structures are less durable than economic ones; these, less than social ones, and these, in turn, less than mental ones.

Mental structures refer to the ways of interpreting and understanding the world and life, and have deep unconscious roots, which is why they resist wear and tear and their rate of change is very slow.

An unsubtle thread seems to connect the tendency of closed groups of seizing the State and of organizations from which power is exercised to configure secular replicas of Chavín's theocracy. Any historical period, Kracauer argues, should be thought of as a mixture of events that emerge at different times of their own times. It is not anachronistic to say that this archaic trend is repeated in these times when the desire for freedom, the exigencies of equality and the demands for recognition have been collected in democratic creeds. This persistence seems to question the democratic meaning that Robert Dahl assigns to the notion of polyarchy and confirm Robert Michels's idea of the existence of an iron law of oligarchy. Even the idea, so prevalent today, of meritocracy can be seen as a "parody of democracy" ultimately serving to justify the privileges of the elite, if the distances between the points of departure and the reduced opportunities of promotion it offers are not taken into account.

The analysis of the relationship between sex, gender and power at the dawn of civilization may clarify some aspects of the oppression of women in the 21st century, an issue that is by no account confined to some Islamic sectors. Unfortunately what Greek, Latin, Celtic, Saxon, Nordic, Gaul, Hispanic, Arabic or Quechua historical and literary sources record, where stories of women – girls, young, old and elderly, celibate and married, virgins and mothers – sacrificed to some god or raped by a victorious soldier abound, acquire a "stench of presentness" in the very frequent cases of gender-based violence.

Violence whose role as a mechanism for the control of women is far from negligible within a system driven by values associated with the masculine. A quote from Dorothy Smith seems to summarize what has been said: "A man's body gives credibility to his utterance; a woman's body takes it away from her" (Smith, 2000, p. 1148).

Increasing democracy requires mutual recognition, that is, for relationships between men and women to be relationships between equals. Otherwise biopower is being exerted, not in the sense that Foucault has given the term but in the sense constructed and maintained by the Baruya: a hierarchy of sexual basis rooted in biology consecrating oppression by identifying the "inferiority" of women with sexual differences. Some feminist scholars argue that the allocation of housework to women reveals the persistence of a mentality and of a way of subjection of feudal lineage in the conditions of late capitalism. Moreover, the growing capacity of the media to transform the attempts to break the repressive structures of sex into a mere degradation and marketing of the erotic, is but another form of repression exerted by a system of mass commodification of sexuality that treats women as one more object.

Psychoanalytic insights have contributed to a better understanding of social identity, group behavior, leadership styles and personality traits susceptible to authoritarian temptation, the internal dynamics of political options and the consequences of traumatic historical events. In this chapter I have tried to contextualize psychoanalytic proposals in the space of political notions while placing political concepts within the theoretical coordinates of psychoanalysis. I have respected as far as possible the autonomy of the political to circulate some concerns through this attempt at a conversation that may be of interest precisely because of the diversity of theoretical itineraries and intellectual traditions in play.

## Notes

1 Übertragung in the German original.
2 It goes without saying that we must not lose sight of the specificity of each concept.
3 We should not dismiss the possibility, strongly raised by Lyotard, that translation from one to another mode of discourse may be inaccessible.

## References

Althusser, L 1971, *Lenin and philosophy, and other essays*, New Left Review, London.
Barthes, R 1977, 'Rhetoric of the image', in Stephen Heath (ed and trans), *Image, music, text*, Hill and Wang, New York.
Benjamin, J 1998, *The bonds of love*, Pantheon, New York.

Bourdieu, P 1994, 'Structures, habitus, power: Basis for a theory for symbolic power', in NB Dirks, G Eley & SB Ortner (eds), *Culture/power/history: A reader in contemporary social theory*, Princeton University Press, Princeton, NJ, pp. 155–199.

Foucault, M 1980, *Power/knowledge: Selected interviews and other writings 1972–1977* (C Gordon, ed), New York: Vintage Books.

Freud, S 1905, 'Three essays on the theory of sexuality', in J Strachey (ed), *Standard edition of the complete psychological works of Sigmund Freud*, vol. 7, Hogarth, London, pp. 125–171.

Freud, S 1910, 'Leonardo da Vinci and a memory of his childhood', in J Strachey (ed), *Standard edition of the complete psychological works of Sigmund Freud*, vol. 9, Hogarth, London, pp. 63–139.

Freud, S 1913, 'Totem and taboo', in J Strachey (ed), *Standard edition of the complete psychological works of Sigmund Freud*, vol. 13, Hogarth, London, pp. 1–255.

Freud, S 1913, ''The claims of psycho-analysis to scientific interest', in J Strachey (ed), *Standard edition of the complete psychological works of Sigmund Freud*, vol. 13, Hogarth, London, pp. 165–193.

Freud, S 1920, 'Beyond the pleasure principle', in J Strachey (ed), *Standard edition of the complete psychological works of Sigmund Freud*, vol. 18, Hogarth, London, pp. 1–64.

Freud, S 1921, 'Group psychology and the analysis of the ego', in J Strachey (ed), *Standard edition of the complete psychological works of Sigmund Freud*, vol. 13, Hogarth, London, pp. 65–145.

Freud, S 1930, 'Civilization and its discontents', in J Strachey (ed), *Standard edition of the complete psychological works of Sigmund Freud*, vol. 21, Hogarth, London, pp. 64–149.

Godelier, M 1989, *Lo ideal y lo material*, Taurus, Madrid.

Godelier, M 2000, *Cuerpo parentesco y poder. Perspectivas antropológicas y críticas*, Abya–Yala, Ecuador.

Hegel, G 1977, 1807, *Phenomenology of spirit* (A Miller, trans), Clarendon Press, Oxford.

Rousseau, J 1952, 'The social contract', in R. Maynard Hutchins (ed), *Great books of the western world*, vol. 38, Encyclopaedia Britannica, Chicago.

Smith, D 2000, 'Schooling for inequality', *Signs*, vol. 25, no. 4, pp. 1147–1151.

Spivak, G 1988, 'Can the subaltern speak?', in C Nelson & L Grossberg (eds), *Marxism and the interpretation of culture*, Macmillan, London, pp. 271–315.

Tracy, D 1989, *Plurality and ambiguity*. Harper and Row, New York.

# 26

# Psychoanalysis and trauma

*Sverre Varvin*

Trauma, or better, traumatization, places the relation between external reality and psychic reality in focus. This has been a conflictual theme for psychoanalysis throughout its history (e.g., which role to assign to external events and early environment in the causation and maintenance of psychic distress and illness). How is experience represented in the psyche, how is it "personalized," and what role does fantasy derived from drive conflicts play in the shaping of the perception of personal experience? How is the internal world of wishes, conflicts and deficits (resulting from trauma) negotiated in human interaction?

Furthermore, what is a trauma or a traumatizing experience? Is it everything that impinges on the psyche and causes developmental problems or arrests, or is it possible to distinguish between developmental disturbance and traumatization proper? Do specific characteristics of an event make it traumatic, and do specific psychic qualities (or quantities) exist that characterize an experience and make it traumatic? Is there a specific interaction between the environment and the psyche in specific developmental phases that makes an experience traumatic?

The loose and imprecise use of the trauma concept in clinical dialogues has obviously obscured theoretical discourse. One may also argue that the phenomenon of traumatization itself is so difficult to grasp and is an experience so inherently impossible to empathize with, that our countertransference as well our theorizing suffers from the anxiety and wordlessness of the traumatic experience. This aspect is demonstrated in the phenomenon "conspiracy of silence" observed in populations where massive traumatization has occurred. The victim or survivor has few words and feels too much shame, making it impossible to relate what happened, and others, including professional health workers, turn a blind eye to the traumatized person, who then becomes isolated with his/her suffering.

The victim, or survivor, of extreme experiences suffers, however, and there is convincing clinical and empirical evidence that changes and adaptations after such overwhelming experiences are of long duration, complex and far-reaching, involving effects in biological, psychological and relational dimensions (Krystal, 1978).

In medicine and psychiatry controversies have focused on the relative influence of biology/heredity and external influences in causing mental illness. This was a central question when Charcot, Janet, Breuer and Freud revolutionized the concept of mental illness. The dominant view at that time was that mental illness was grounded in heredity and degeneration (connected with theories of race and degeneration in medicine). It was in this context that Freud and Breuer developed their theories of the social cause of hysteria (Breuer & Freud, 1895).

Discussions have revolved not only around etiology, but perhaps more importantly around the mediating forces or processes between the "inner" (the internal world or the genes) and the "outer" reality: for example, what is an outer reality for a child or an adult? When does this reality become associated with clinical trauma? What is mediating between inner and outer reality? What is the relation between conflict and trauma?

Understanding trauma involves thus basic questions related to psychoanalysis as a theory and science at the same time as the traumatized patient poses clinical challenges with no easy answers.

The early debate and controversies between Freud and Janet are reflected in today's controversies in the trauma field. Janet held that the traumatized mind suffered a "feebleness" (*la feblesse de l'ame*) of hereditary origin (Janet, 1907), while Freud argued that defense against the traumatizing influence was motivated, that is, that the dynamics of the mind were at work even when the core-helplessness of traumatization was present, reflecting a cognitive and psychoanalytic perspective respectively.

## The historical and intellectual development of the understanding of trauma and traumatization

In the following I will present a genealogical approach where concepts and theories on trauma are seen in the light of historical, social and cultural contexts rather than seeing them as a linear development of a growing knowledge base. The understanding and acknowledgment of trauma during the last century is an eloquent example on how theories and concepts are influenced by social forces and represents in itself a critique of the belief in a progressive development in science.

## Ambivalence toward the victim

Psychic trauma and the consequences of traumatization have been problematic and characterized by ambivalence both within psychiatry and psychoanalysis, as well as in society at large. After the pioneering confrontation with the effects of trauma of Freud and Janet, the tide has come and gone with periods of denial and ignorance followed by periods of confrontation, often with accompanying feelings of helplessness and horror. "Blame the victim" and the "Conspiracy of silence" have been two "rejecting" strategies throughout the last century. The first was notably seen during and after World War I. In the aftermath of the insane fighting with casualties in the hundreds of thousands on both sides, those who reacted with "hysterical symptoms" were often executed for cowardice or treated as malingerers and subjected to inhuman and torture-like treatments that often scared them back to the battlefields. The same accusation of malingering was met with when they afterwards sought compensations for the damages done to them by the war. The term "Renten Neurose" (pension neurosis) was coined by psychiatry as a derogatory claim about the "real" motivation for being sick after being in the trenches. On the other hand, dynamic approaches seeking to understand shell-shock as a complex dynamic reaction were presented by psychoanalysts.

Wars and crises regularly brought trauma into focus in psychiatry in the last century but subsequently the interest diminished. Kardiner's seminal book on the traumatic neurosis of war, published in 1941 and based on his work with World War I veterans, explained clearly the connection between war traumas and illnesses and described all symptoms of what is now called posttraumatic stress disorder (PTSD). The immediate effects of his work after World War II were, however, poorly reflected in the diagnostic systems. The diagnosis "gross stress reaction," seen as a psychoneurotic disorder and a transitory reaction to an experience of intolerable stress, with vague descriptions of symptomatology, was soon left out. The veterans of World War II were for a long time largely neglected in most countries by psychiatry, psychoanalysis and also by politicians and the public. For example, in Norway many traumatized war sailors led a miserable alcoholic life on the streets; in Israel the survivors of the Holocaust were not acknowledged as suffering from their terrible experiences in the concentration camps; in Germany, it took a long time before their own trauma after World War II was recognized.

The ambivalence toward and the neglect of traumatized persons is still a major problem and it is not only in the consulting room that the encounter with traumatization is filled with gross countertransference problems – the societal neglect impedes the necessary support and assignment of meaning to traumatizing experiences so crucial for rehabilitation of the traumatized person.

The tension between recognition and rejection reflects on a theoretical level the understanding of the traumatized as either victim or participant survivor. The first implies seeing the traumatized as subjected to an external event that causes effects for which the victim has no responsibility. The latter implies a relational view stressing the involvement of the subject in a scenario where motives and wishes causing reaction patterns are central.

The apparent contradiction between these points of view may have to do with different stress laid on the traumatic moment or the later reactions to this respectively or with a confusion of these two moments in the traumatizing process. While the definition of trauma as the state of helplessness certainly expresses a moment where the victim is laid bare to external forces, the involvement with the traumatic *situation or the perpetrators* and the later reaction to the trauma expresses secondary work with the experience. The subject is either involved in the situation expressing what Breuer called a "hypnoid state" (Breuer & Freud, 1895) *or* attributes "Nachträglich" personal agency to the event. The last may be clarified by the differentiation between primary and secondary intentionality. Primary intentionality implies self-representations that have been constituted as a responsible center for the person's own impulses, feelings and actions, while secondary intentionality refers to the situation where the subject initially had no intentional participation in the trauma, but as an act of later organization transferred, for example, bad intentions from other conflictual relationships to the trauma in order to supply an otherwise confusing or terrifying experience with meaning. This distinction refers to conflict pathology and deficit pathology respectively and posttraumatic conditions may be seen as a combination of both.

## The development of the trauma concept in psychoanalysis and related fields

When Freud in 1896 coined the idea of sexual seduction as *the* cause of hysteria, he related primarily to the two current conceptions of etiology in the medical community: the degeneration theory, which he rejected (he was also quite worried about its use in anti-Semitic propaganda), and the "germ theory" derived from Koch's postulates for isolating specific infectious agents. The latter he endorsed during the short period he entertained the specific seduction theory (the affect-trauma model).

The popular history has been that Freud in 1887 supposedly dismissed the conception of an outer force or external incident causing the illness in favor of a purely intrapsychic conception of the neurosis based on unconscious fantasy and conflicting sexual wishes. Behind this reasoning lies a misconception that Freud first believed in this outer event as causative and that he later stressed instinctual conflict as the causative factor(s) in neurosis. His position, as it developed, was, however, in accordance with later research on how memory is distorted and reworked by fantasy and later experiences, assuring the relative influence of external and internal dynamics, as I will show later.

It was thus a case of demonstrating that the effect of an event was dependent on inner psychic experiences and how the child or the adult dealt with them when the peculiarity of time and cause in psychic life are taken into account. The discovery of infant sexuality, and the agency or activity of the child, was of significance in that it could demonstrate that precisely because of the immature sexual drives and wishes of the child, a real seduction could have a serious effect on the mind's functioning.

Both the traumatic origin of neurosis and the traumatic neuroses proper continued to occupy Freud in the following years, and the question in these years became how to reconcile the two apparently distinct, if not contradictory, perspectives: trauma and conflict. In 1919, Freud stated that in the traumatic war neuroses the ego defended itself against outer dangers, while in the transference neuroses the ego had its own libido as its enemy. The theoretical difficulty this implied could, however, be resolved when one could see repression as a reaction to a trauma, that is, all neuroses could be seen as elementary traumatic neuroses.

Freud was thus through his work concerned with time and causation in the psyche and in the relation between experience and mental processes. Already in the 1980s the concept Nachträglichkeit and the adjective *nachträglich* were introduced to explain a causative chain of events. A process with a biphasic causation of trauma was conceptualized where the meaning of, for example, sexual abuse was first understood in a second event reminding of the first and then causing the traumatic reaction.

This points to a complex interaction between outer reality and psychic processes and was taken up by several authors later to explain the late effect of certain traumas and the accentuating effect of new traumas on earlier traumatic or potentially traumatic events (Varvin, 2003).

A summary of Freud's contribution to the understanding of the traumatic neuroses and to their causation could be the following:

1   Freud and Breuer were pioneers in the establishment of the external causation of hysteria and mental illness in general.
2   Freud always distinguished between the event and the psychic trauma.
3   He never denied the existence of incest or child abuse. He denounced the theory that all neuroses had a single cause, sexual abuse. Neurosis had a complex etiology.
4   He established that there is no one-to-one relationship between the event and memory. Retrieval of memory is looked upon as reconstruction and is motivated, that is, dependent on the context, both internal and external.
5   The conceptions of transference and repetition compulsion implied that experiences could be stored and repeated nonverbally (foreshadowing modern theories on procedural memory).
6   His distinction between anxiety, fear (of something) and fright showed that trauma is a state of fright in response to a danger, that the experience produces a primitive anxiety state, automatic anxiety, and that experiences that are endured without the appropriate affect cannot be processed and will return in intrusions and traumatic dreams and so forth.
7   He perceived the mind as inherently symbolizing. First, this was expressed mostly in economic terms as binding (Bindung) of energy. Later this was understood in a symbolization context as the mind's attempt to bind, to connect, on a symbolic level thus giving meaning to the traumatizing experience.
8   Freud developed several etiological models. One was the biphasic model of trauma in which the second event, where the experience was understood (symbolized), brought

about the traumatic reaction. Another not contradictory conceptualization was the theory of complementary series: an inverse relationship between the ego's strength and the strength and seriousness of the event underlining a complex dynamics between external and internal forces.

9    Freud's concept of trauma and traumatization was mainly economic. An important precursor to an object-relational view was, however, present. The concept of stimulus barrier (Reizschutz) was formulated on a quasi-biological level, but can be seen as contained in later relational concepts such as holding.

Even though it is fair to say that traumatizing experiences occupied psychoanalysts continuously, the ground was laid for the study of the inner psychic world, the drives and the dreams. The focus on actual incest lost its grounding both in psychoanalysis and psychiatry. A notable exception was Sandor Ferenczi.

## Sandor Ferenczi's contribution

Ferenczi felt that traumatized patients needed a more direct and intimate approach and this made him aware of the interpersonal aspect of traumatization and how the child represented the traumatizing *relationship* in the psyche. He developed an object-relational perspective of trauma in addition to the psycho-economical model.

Harold Blum summarizes Ferenczi's position in the following way:

> Ferenczi, though naive about the evidence of actual seduction, noted the hypocrisy, pathological lies, evasions, and silent collusion of the traumatising adults. He was concerned with the revival of trauma and its repetition, though not simply in the transference. The analyst might traumatise the patient because of countertransference impediments and enactments of the analyst. Ferenczi stressed the object-relations aspects of trauma and the child's relationship to the traumatising caregivers, which continues after the traumatic experience. He explicitly recorded sequelae of identification with the aggressor: dissociation, fragmentation, and the split in the child's personality between the observing and comforting self and the dissociated, traumatised self. The child is relatively helpless, desperate for the love and approval of the parent, or surrogates who are abusive. The child cannot protest, and silently submits to authority. "Tongue-tied," during and after the trauma, the child also introjects or identifies with the parents' unspoken shame and guilt. He recognised the parents' tendency to project blame and guilt on to the child, and that the child is often punished for the parents' misdeeds. He noted the conspiracy of silence, the censorship, blame of the child, and child's self-blame which so often surrounds and follows child abuse. Ferenczi's work anticipated later concepts of strain and cumulative trauma and contemporary concepts of child abuse.
>
> *(Blum, 1994, pp. 874–875)*

The guilt feelings and shame that Ferenczi describes as both the result of identification with the parent's misdeeds and a result of the blaming of the child and projection of guilt are features easily observable in other victims of interpersonal trauma. Ferenczi introduced the concept "identification with the aggressor," which has become an indispensable tool for understanding certain aggressive and self-destructive behavior of victims. Ferenczi was concerned with the parent's empathic failures, the real traumas and the social and psychological context of traumatization. He described with genuine clarity the experience of being traumatized from the victim's perspective. From the child's perspective, the words of the adult (the language of passion) became part of the trauma. His paper "Confusion of Tongues Between Adult and the Child – The Language of Tenderness and of Passion" (Ferenczi, 1933) anticipates several of the major themes of modern trauma research.

Ferenczi thus strengthened and laid ground for the development of the object relation perspective on traumatization in that he developed an interactional perspective on traumatization.

## The war neuroses

Several leading psychoanalysts had served as army doctors during World War I. At the international psychoanalytic congress in Budapest in 1918, a symposium was held where Freud developed the conception of an ego conflict (*Ich-konflikt*) between the peace ego and the new war ego. Ernst Simmel developed this perspective, in the frame of the new ego-psychological approach and underlined the importance of the *type* of traumatic situation and distinguished between traumatic neurosis in peacetime and in wartime (Simmel, 1944). The significant difference was bound to the fact that the soldier developed a "military ego" as a consequence of functioning in a military unit. This demanded a change in his civilian superego and the development of a kind of child–parent relationship to his superiors. This implied regression. His superiors would guarantee him protection and guidance in a situation that was both unknown and dangerous. If this was accompanied by disappointment, the soldier would feel abandoned in the same way as a child when abandoned by his parents. This then became a precipitating cause for a traumatic reaction due to loss of an inner protective agent. The outer, dangerous situation became overwhelming.

Simmel placed thus significance to the other in the traumatizing process and foreshadowed modern object relational perspectives on traumatization (Laub & Podell, 1995). It should be noted that even though the war neuroses were understood in a frame of an ego conflict between the civilian and military ego taking drive conflicts into consideration, this theory was nevertheless social-psychological in its perspective.

Abraham Kardiner's 1941 book *The Traumatic Neurosis of War* describes the chronic vigilance and sensitivity to environmental stress that characterized the posttraumatic state. There seemed to be a lowering of the threshold for stimulation and, on the psychological side, a "readiness for fright reactions." He described a fixation to the trauma, ego inhibitions and altered relation of the self to the world, chronic irritability and a tendency toward aggressive reactions. The nucleus of the war neurosis was viewed as a "physioneurosis," a condition involving both the body and the mind. Not only did traumatic experiences repeat themselves in dreams and thoughts/images, but the survivor also acted as though the original traumatic situation were still in existence, and behaved accordingly, and also suffered a multitude of bodily reactions foreshadowing the symptoms described in the PTSD diagnosis.

## Trauma after World War II: mourning and exile

A remarkable ignorance of the consequences of traumatization set in after World War II, and research and reflection on trauma and the traumatizing process did not occur to any noticeable extent in psychiatry until the 1980s.

Psychoanalysts had, although apparently with some reluctance, begun to treat Holocaust victims in the 1950s and 1960s, and several important works appeared at the 1967 International Psychoanalytical Congress in Copenhagen. Jaffe described dissociative phenomena and also discussed the psychotic-like phenomena in these conditions (Jaffe, 1969). Simenauer remarked, "the disorganization of the personality structure may be a very rapid process. Restitutional processes are also remarkably independent of duration and kind of injury" (Simenauer, 1968, p. 306), in line with Freud's reasoning on complementary series. What was perhaps most important was establishing how later influences (war, extreme conditions in concentration camps, flight, etc.), had a decisive influence on personality development. These reflections had, however, relatively little influence on mainstream observation of psychical trauma in the following years.

By then, in the 1960s and early 1970s, important epidemiological research had demonstrated the relation between the traumas of war (concentration camps, wartime sailing) and later mental and physical disability. This research also demonstrated the latency between trauma and the development of symptoms and increased psychic and somatic morbidity, in addition to increased mortality among the survivors (Eitinger, 1965).

Martin Bergmann, one of the pioneers in the treatment of Holocaust survivors, summarized the psychoanalytic work with these patients in the first decades after the war as following the model of the war neurosis. The psychoanalyst tried to get in contact with the pre-traumatic personality of the patient in the hope that then the effects of the Holocaust would be diminished (Bergmann, 1998). This turned out to be inadequate, as most of the survivors came to the conclusion that it was too difficult for the psychoanalyst to deal with their Holocaust experience, became silent, withdrew and discontinued their treatment. He noted further that they came to the conclusion that to survive, one must keep silent and that this coincided with their experiences and survival strategies from the camps. When his group (with Jucovy and Kestenberg) started their work, they decided to make it possible for the survivors to live through their traumatic experiences anew: "We did not aim at a cathartic release, but instead to help a process of mourning to enfold which had not been possible in the camps" (Bergmann, 1998, p. 124, my translation).[1]

Grief had two aspects: the grief over lost family members and the grief over the loss of one's own developmental possibilities, which the patients had suffered in their years of imprisonment. For this purpose, Freud's "Mourning and Melancholia" (Freud, 1917) served as a model. This represented a significant development in the understanding of trauma and its context and in the understanding of the treatment of PTSD.

Although it is now mostly acknowledged that loss and mourning are important aspects of the lives of many traumatized people, they are often set up as additional factors to be considered (e.g., in the form of taking care of mourning rituals) or, when the mourning process is halted, in the form of an additional diagnosis of depression.

The importance of working with loss, grief and mourning in psychotherapy with survivors became central. According to Laub and Podell (1995), trauma implies a loss of trust in an external empathic dyad. This results in a loss of communication with "the other" in the internal world, and this loss leads to a loss of representations and self-observing reflective capacity. They claim that

> the feelings of absence, of rupture, and of the loss of representation that essentially constitute the traumatic experience all emerge from the real failure of the empathic dyad at the time of traumatisation and the resulting failure to preserve an empathic tie even with oneself.
>
> *(Laub & Podell, 1995, p. 992)*

Representation and capacity for reflection are, in their view, dependent on the link to an internal empathic other, and therapy must accordingly aim at reestablishing this link.

The work with Holocaust survivors resulted thus in strengthening of the relational perspective and brought loss and mourning to the center stage of the treatment of survivors. This represented a major advancement and laid ground for what today distinguishes psychoanalytic treatment of traumatized patients from many so-called exposure therapies.

Another major contribution came, however, also from Niederland and his conceptualization of the survivor's syndrome (Niederland, 1981), which foreshadows what is now called *complex trauma*.

1  *Chronic or recurrent states of depression.* These depressions are mixed and carry a somatic "mask" that includes "neuralgic rheumatic pains, headaches, backache, gastrointestinal disturbances, muscular weakness, and 'general asthenia'" (Niederland, 1981, p. 414). He also noticed a tendency to isolation, withdrawal and a wordless sadness with occasional outbursts of rage.

2  *Anhedonia* was closely related to unresolved grief, and manifested itself in an incapacity for feeling any pleasure, including sexual pleasure.

3  *Anxiety*, a dominating symptom associated with the fear of renewed persecution and transparent phobic fears, anxiety dreams and what he calls "re-run" nightmares, which reflect the persecution experiences.

4  *Hyperamnesia concerning the persecution events.* This is described as one of the most tormenting manifestations. It concerns the "the survivors' overly sharp, distinct, and virtually indelible memories as far as persecution events are concerned" (Niederland, 1981, p. 416). It concerns both the events and the atmosphere in the concentration camps.

5  *Alterations in the sense of identity.* This affects the body image and self-image as well as the sense of space and time, and is subjectively felt as a lasting impairment of the self. He noted that many survivors expressed a feeling of being a different person, and in severe cases the feeling of not being a person anymore (Niederland, 1981, p. 417). These features may take on psychosis-like proportions with blunt delusions, which now can be understood as having roots in dissociated states of mind.

6  *Psychosomatic conditions.* The increased frequency of psychosomatic conditions such as peptic ulcers, vascular diseases and asthma among survivors.

7  *Survivor guilt and unresolved grief.* Niederland found survivor guilt and unresolved grief in almost all survivors of the Holocaust (he studied about 2,000 survivors). He did not accept the explanation that the guilt was based on early hostility toward parents or siblings. The survival itself was at the core of the inner conflict, and living meant betrayal of the lost loved ones.

8  *Psychic vulnerability in Holocaust survivors.* He described the propensity for having negative emotional reactions to reminders of the traumatic experience and, interestingly, also pointed to possible positive effects in that the alerting impact of such events may counteract the lameness and numbing of emotion.

Hoppe's work on the relation between affect, regression and sublimation is important in relation to Niederland's work. His empirical psychoanalytic study on Holocaust survivors showed the ubiquitous presence of psychosomatic reactions (e.g., tension headache, insomnia, gastrointestinal disturbances). and psychosomatic disorders (e.g., asthma, ulcer, hypertension). He related this to "resomatisation" of negative affect and hypothesized that: "the enforced regression to pre-Oedipal stages during persecution resulted in a revival of the body-self and of an archaic body-image" (Hoppe, 1968, p. 326). The survivors' withdrawal pointed to the lack of basic trust, indicating the preponderance of negatively valued inner representations of self in relation to others. Later research on affect regulation and the importance of internal object relations for regulating affect confirms this view.

The findings and theorization of Niederland and Hoppe is based on encounters with patients who has experiences of prolonged and/or repeated suppression, aggression and traumatization that repeatedly placed them in a situation where the inner supporting structures fail and a situation where object loss may occur. The inner representation of the persecutor may serve as the only "object resource." The attachment to the torturer and repeated hallucinations of them may be conceptualized as secondary to the loss of the inner empathic object and the consequence may be impaired relation to this inner supporting structure. This may be contrasted to the healthy infant's omnipotence with a conviction of invulnerability that is related to a harmonious symbiotic mother–child relationship. When this area in the mind is preserved, even during very harsh conditions, it becomes possible to seek nurturing relationships.

Krystal distinguishes between infantile and adult trauma (Krystal, 1978). While infantile trauma is characterized by the development of automatic anxiety, a condition in which the ego is incapable of dealing with impulses and excitations, and is thus rendered helpless, adult trauma of the massive kind is characterized more by a surrender reaction. The infant becomes overwhelmed by affects without possessing the adult's possibility of making use of defensive mechanisms and coping strategies, and experiences a state of deadly anxiety – not so much a fear of death but rather a mortal bio-traumatic terror. Krystal asserts that the adult, in contrast, owing to the existence of some integrity in ego functions, is unable to feel the almost complete regression and terror an infant may feel. The adult ego may then maintain a stimulus barrier to some degree and maintain what Krystal observed as the most important distinction between adult and infant trauma, namely an observing ego.

These contributions related to extreme traumatization represented important advances in the trauma field. They showed that this kind of traumatization may produce prolonged regressive situations that have devastating effects on the personality in the form of nonintegrated traumatic selves and foreshadows many of the central themes in today's discussion on traumatization.

An important psychosocial dimension needs to mentioned demonstrated in Hans Keilson's seminal research (Keilson & Sarpathie, 1979). He studied Jewish children orphaned after World War II. He described a sequential traumatization that he divided into three sequences: (1) the persecution, beginning with the occupation of Holland in 1940, ending with a separation from mother; (2) the time in hiding or in concentration camps until liberation and the return to Holland; and (3) the post-liberation period, in which some children remained with their wartime foster parents and others returned to the Jewish community. Not only loyalty and identity conflicts, but also the problems of mourning their deceased parents beset the children.

He found that children who had been more traumatized in phase two, but had had good support after the war, had a better course of adjustment than those who experienced unfavorable circumstances in phase three. If the wartime foster family had been unable to provide favorable support, it reinforced the effects of the traumatic events.

There has thus been an important development in the understanding of traumatized patients after Freud. The main perspectives developed were the following:

1   The object relational dimension of traumatization and posttraumatic conditions was developed, first by Ferenczi and then Bergman and others.
2   Affect and affect regulation in relation to extreme traumatization and the role of the body in the regressive states was developed.
3   The devastating consequences for adaptation to family and social life was highlighted.
4   The understanding of the importance of the developmental phase and the difference between childhood and adult traumatization was better understood.

## Trauma: an elastic concept?

Trauma has not had a clear and well-defined meaning in psychoanalysis or psychiatric theory. In the clinic the concept is applied to a variety of experiences and is often loosely used as shorthand for experiences that are burdening, abrupt, distressing and so forth. This reflects basic conceptual problems but might also be related to the subject itself in that trauma, in essence, is a failure of symbolization and evades meaning.

Different types of trauma have been suggested, including shock trauma, cumulative trauma, seduction trauma, strain trauma, extreme trauma, war trauma, incest trauma and so forth. This typology refers both to different situations (war, family), different types of exposure (strain, cumulative, etc.) and different types of reactions (shock). There is often a blurring of the distinctions between the traumatic situation, the traumatizing process (understood as the process whereby the situation influences the subject), the immediate reaction to the external influence, the later reaction and the end result in the form of a specific condition (e.g., acute or chronic PTSD, personality disorder). There is, furthermore, often confusion as to what constitutes an experience that is traumatic. The term extreme traumatization usually refers to situations that would have been traumatic for (almost) everyone. Other experiences will be traumatic only under certain conditions (e.g., loss of a close relative).

A key concept in trauma research is memory, and the diagnosis of PTSD may be seen as a way of structuring the "traumatic memory. Freud's original idea was that it was not the event per se that was traumatic, but the fact that the recollections of them took on the character of pathogenic memories ("Hysterics suffer mainly from reminiscences"; Breuer & Freud, 1895, p. 7). What was traumatic was then constructed post hoc based on the effects, and it needed a second factor in order to become traumatic. The memories appeared in a new internal and external context and then achieved their significance as traumatic.

A distinction was made between the immediate overwhelming of the ego and the subsequent psychic trauma. That is, a shock may later become a psychic trauma when experienced as memories in context. It is the *handling* of the mental impact or later memories that fails. The first phase may then be silent for the trauma to appear later, or the two elements may collapse into one, and the immediate effect of the impact may be traumatic. The first may happen when the subject is able to dissociate at the time of the extreme experience, only to be overwhelmed later when the significance of the event poses a threat.

This, then, points to the problem of *what* these memories consist of and how trauma is represented, and further, what is the nature of the handling or processing of representations and memories of trauma.

Several, for example Anna Freud (Freud, 1967), argued for a restricted definition of trauma. Trauma should be distinguished from other ego-damaging circumstances such as developmental disturbances as the intrapsychic processes are different. A distinction was made between the immediate effect on the ego and the later effects of the posttraumatic condition consisting in further adaptation to an internal environment where ego capacities have been impaired and continue to be so in the face of circumstances provoking traumatic memories. This often results in major inhibitions of ego functioning, anhedonia and general lack of vitality. Developmental interference results also in inhibitions in ego functioning, but more often as adaptations to accumulated environmental failures.

The concepts of cumulative trauma, strain trauma and silent trauma refer to events that in themselves do not constitute trauma but which in sum may exceed a threshold, thus breaking the ego's protective shield (stimulus barrier) and resulting in a traumatic situation, conceptualizations that may have contributed to confusion between developmental interference and trauma.

Some clarifications and several problems follow from this:

## Clarifications

1   Psychic trauma is a complex event involving an individual's personal reaction to an event that is for the individual outside the normal range of experience or outside the average expectable environment.

2. It is not the event itself but the experience of the event, the personal apprehension, which determines whether it is traumatic.

3 Trauma concerns the ego's inability to deal with the stimuli and the affects aroused because of the impact of the event and later because of the memories of it.

4 Trauma refers thus to something prior that has the status of a basis of something meaningful (expectable environment, personal apprehension) (Bohleber, 2000).

5 Trauma is always defined retrospectively. It is the effect on the personality that leads one to look for the traumatic origin.

6 Trauma has an effect on development and is in itself a developmental disturbance. Trauma must, however, be distinguished from other developmental interference that does not have the quality of trauma.

## Problems

1 Is trauma a situation imposed exclusively from without, or does the situation become traumatic only when it arouses internal stimuli and affects that are impossible for the ego to deal with? I have in the foregoing opted for the second alternative, but it still is an area of controversy and confusion in the literature.

2 What characterizes the memories of traumatization, and process of remembering traumatizing experiences? Is there a specific "traumatic memory"? Do these memories undergo later elaborations?

3 What is the character of the failure of the ego's integrating and synthesizing functions?

4 Should the posttraumatic condition be seen as a defense against or as an adaptation to a traumatized internal reality?

5 What is the nature of the posttraumatic process? Are there self-healing processes (posttraumatic growth) and/or posttraumatic destructive processes? Which role does environment play (e.g., psychosocial aid, psychotherapy) in determining outcome? Under what circumstances do the posttraumatic condition lead to further deterioration?

## The trauma field is dominated by a diagnostic approach: a critique

The DSM system resulted in a multitude of illnesses. It represents a neo-Kräpelinian descriptive approach and was established as a reaction to the dominating psychodynamic trend in American psychiatry. According to Nemiah this approach succeeded in throwing the baby out with the bathwater (Nemiah, 1998). Years of empirical clinical research and observation were discarded in the process of reaggregating symptoms according to the Kräpelinian model. Hysteria, which was seen as a disorder with both sensimotor and mental manifestations, was split apart by

> assigning the mental symptoms of hysteria, including amnesia, fugue states, and multiple personality disorder to the major diagnostic category of dissociative disorder and by allocating the sensimotor symptoms (designated as conversion disorder) to the entirely different major category of somatoform disorder.
>
> *(Nemiah, 1998, p. 16)*

The major drawback of such surface descriptions is that disorders that clinically belong to the same complex are treated as distinct and totally unrelated disorders. When they appear in the same person, the clinician has to deal diagnostically with a patient with two illnesses, while he/she hopefully in his clinical work is dealing with one person with one disease. What seemed in the 1980s to be an advantage concerning the reliability of diagnostic practice has thus proven to be a major obstacle in clinical practice.

The advantage of establishing the relation between the traumatic event and the later sequel, a relation Freud and Breuer established more than a century ago, is in the DSM system counteracted by dissociation and disaggregation of clinical manifestations and may lead to the development of problematic clinical technologies by concentrating on single symptoms or a single disease instead of the whole person whose problems and symptoms are viewed in the context of the individual's entire life and personality.

## Influences from developmental research, cognitive- and neuroscience

Freud's (1920) conceptualization of trauma as the breaking of the stimulus barrier, implying a deterioration of the perceptual apparatus' ability to sort out and differentiate stimuli, entails an overwhelming experience where impressions can not be dealt with by the ego-processes, such as thinking and dream work. Torture and concentration camp experiences are maliciously designed to make these "impressions" not only overwhelming and incoherent, but also dehumanizing and thus "playing on" primitive and violent aspects of the mind (perverse and psychotic).

These man–made disasters have the effect of destroying the process of construction of meaning creating a situation of shock and unexpectedness. To be able to experience something as shocking and unexpected, however, there must be a background of the expected, the normal. The expected is the basis of the common, preconscious, symbolic mediated world or, in the words of Hartmann, the "average expectable environment" (Hartmann, 1939). The symbolic mediation concerns symbols on all levels, from verbal high level to bodily signs and gestures that constitute the environment of the mother and child. The devastating effects of extreme traumatization, and perhaps what distinguishes it from the more circumscribed single-shock trauma, may be that this background of the average expectable environment or the background of safety is destroyed.

This view has important consequences. The common symbolically mediated world that we presuppose in all interactions is a construction, the force or effectiveness of which is based on belief and trust. Developmental psychology tells us that this basic trust is constructed by and contained in early established attachment patterns and structures. These function as templates for the continuous construction of emotionally validated meaning in a dialogic process with internal objects or real persons especially concerning negative emotional states. This is also the basis for meaning construction in therapeutic work. This is, from an existential perspective, an act of faith and involves both trust in oneself and in the other. The internal organization of these meaning-producing structures may be conceptualized as attachment styles, internal object relations, emotional schemas and so forth, and is a continuous activity of the mind. The background safety feeling is based on a set of presupposed structures of meaning, which may not, or at least not excessively, be questioned if breakdown is to be avoided. This background structure may become defective after extreme traumatization a view based on developmental research and on internal object relations as basically dialogic.

Infant research has demonstrated that well-functioning mother–infant dyads give room for "time-outs" where the baby can "process" experiences (Brazelton et al., 1974). This "processing" is the moment where meaning is established (Muller, 1996). The semiotic universe of the mother–infant dyad is in this process internalized by the infant, and lays the groundwork for the establishment a background of safety.

Attachment research holds that the need for protection is a basic motive. Based on experienced and assumed responses from the caregivers, the infant establishes age-specific ways of securing basic needs. Three differences in parents' response to infant behavior are envisaged:

1   Sensitively, by transforming infant distress into comfort through positive reinforcement of affective communication and by transforming experiencing into meaningful constructs in an age- and context-specific way. This lays the groundwork for a secure and flexible attachment (type B).
2   Insensitively, by increasing the infant's distress in a predictable way, that is, by using predictable punishment for negative affect and thus signaling/teaching the infant that negative affect is dangerous and should be avoided. This has the effect of making the infant rely on cognitive information to enhance security and to suppress affect. This is the basis for the dismissing attachment style (type A).
3   Inconsistent response by unpredictable, intermittent reinforcement of negative affect and by teaching the infant that there is no information that in a reliable way can change the caregiver's behavior. This reinforces attachment strategies that rely on maintaining negative arousal and display of affect in attempts at eliciting protection from caregivers, that is, the preoccupied attachment style (type C).

When confronted with overwhelming danger it may be useful to be able to apply all the different strategies depending on the danger and the circumstances. In situations of extreme traumatization, avoiding affective display may help survival, while returning to circumstances of possible comfort, such as the possibility of being taken care of by others or, later, in therapy gain empathy from the therapist, type C behavior may yield comfort and protection. The uses of different strategies are context dependent and, not surprisingly, sleep and relaxed situations prepare for intrusion while daytime may promote more avoidant behavior. The dilemma for many survivors is that no strategy gives rest and comfort, and they consequently often experience lack of safety and protection. Central in this line of reasoning is that secure attachment behavior relies on the use of higher brain functions, especially the integrative function of the prefrontal cortex. Type A and type C strategies preclude or hinder the integration of emotional and cognitive information, and the person is not able to be flexible in evaluating new situations and securing comfort and protection when needed. Both tend to evaluate new situations as if they were replicas of past dangerous events. Thus, when one has had the experience of having been betrayed or felt let down, all interpersonal relationships seem unpredictable (type C) or unreliable (type A) (Crittenden, 2011).

Therapy under such internal circumstances is felt as a dangerous prospect. The reliving of past traumatic experiences may yield some comfort and security but will, on the other hand, often result in new disappointments because the ability to symbolize (use higher brain functions) and thereby integrate, is unstable or often almost not present. The alternative strategy of avoiding affect leaves the subject alone and in isolated despair. Overly displaying affect in relationships may, however, lead to confusion.

Central here is how traumatizing experiences are represented in the mind and body and thus remembered. This brings us to the expanding field of memory research.

## Memory and trauma

Memory reflects experience. The reminiscences of their traumatic experiences haunt extremely traumatized persons. They appear in modes that are insistent and that feel real (e.g., "flashbacks") and as bodily memories in the form of feelings and sensations, pains and reactions in the autonomic nervous system. They may be reflected in repetitive behavioral patterns (repetition compulsion), which in therapy is understood as acting in lieu of remembering. These experiences are difficult to reach by verbal reorganization, often felt as a "hole in the mind" separated from the integrating function of the mind. The memories exist in a mental format that may not be repressed, and thus not forgotten in the way we normally forget shameful and unpleasant experiences.

The central question is how traumatic memories are encoded and possibly reworked by the mind and how traces of these experiences appear in therapy, what the conditions are for working with these experiences in therapy.

Memory research gives no evidence for the storehouse metaphor of memory described in Freud's archaeological metaphor implying an archaeological search for stored, hidden memories. Perception and encoding are active reconstructive processes using data from different sources to make a picture with a background. Memory retrieval is likewise reconstructive. Linking impressions from experiences to make a more or less coherent picture is made "on the spot" (Pally, 1997) and is not a direct replica of what happened in the past implying constant alteration in memory recall, where the context will influence and change the memories. Later recall will contain these changes. A traumatic memory, as far as it is expressed as verbal/conscious memory, may then undergo several changes related to each time it is recalled. This is one of the mechanisms of change during therapy. Pally expresses this in the following way:

> In fact, the more often an event is recalled the more memory traces there will be for that event, and the more opportunity for alteration of that memory, since each new retrieval event is a reconstructed phenomenon and not an exact duplicate of the original. The repeated re-telling of painful childhood events or conflicts during an analysis alter the memory of those events as more modified memory traces are laid down that include aspects of the therapeutic situation, and therefore they are somewhat less painful and conflicted, it is hoped.
>
> (Pally, 1997, p. 1228)

Explicit memory (e.g., autobiographical memory) is conscious when it is encoded and may later be retrieved more or less easily. In contrast, implicit memory is the memory for those aspects of experience that are nonconsciously processed at the time. Certain information may be stored in memory without us having been conscious of its occurrence, and it can influence current functioning without being experienced as conscious remembering. This concerns memory for shape and form (primed memory), emotion (emotional memory), and skills, habits and routines (procedural memory) each of which is processed in different brain systems. Procedural memory has been central in the discussion on trauma and have been incorporated in psychoanalytic theorizing as it concerns how internal object relations are constructed and affected by hardship or traumas. Clinical experience show that interpersonal trauma involving regression affect basic ways of relating to others and disturb the ability to maintain a sense of basic trust and the ability to establish trustful relationships to others and to preserve a trusting attitude as a capacity that can be held in the mind and used when appropriate. The problem for the traumatized person is at least twofold: there is impairment in the encoding and later mental working through of the experience, and as a consequence, the non-symbolized mental content is forgotten in a less stable way than repressed material. The mental defenses against the unwanted mental content are thus weaker in that they are "put away," dissociated and may easily be triggered by external or internal circumstances.

There seem to be little evidence for the claim that traumatic memories are of a totally different kind, but the question remains whether memories of traumatizing experiences are kept largely unchanged or are worked on and changed later. Dream research seems to confirm the hypothesis that these memories are worked on in a motivated way and modified by unconscious fantasy processes (Lansky & Bley, 1995). This is also in accordance with dynamic assumptions of psychoanalysis, especially the proposition of deferred action (*nachträglich*, *après coup*) in working through of traumatic experiences.

Based on these views, therapeutic action for traumatized patients must rely on promoting memorizing trauma in a way that activates the integrative forces of the mind. Central in the discussion within psychoanalysis in this connection is the focus on symbolization.

## Symbolization and trauma

There have been several attempts in psychoanalysis to arrive at a more comprehensive understanding of the process leading from "raw" unmediated experience to mental representation and then to the establishment of emotional meaning. Central for Freud was the "representation" concept, which referred to the representation of the drive, the psychic expression of the endosomatic impulses, which specify the drive as a border between the somatic and the psychic. Representation has preserved its colloquial meaning as a mental representation of the somatic in the psyche. This conceptualization was broadened and further developed toward a general theory of mental representation and symbolization.

Freud distinguished between the thing-representation (Sachvorstellungen/Dingvorstellungen) of the unconscious, the word-representation (Wortvorstellungen) of the preconscious and object-representations (Objektvorstellungen) of the conscious (Freud, 1975).[2] He dealt here with the body-mind problem: how affective-somatic experiences are transformed into psychic experiences. This model of the mind portrays how *binding* is a basic process whereby drive excitation, being a source of anxiety, is bound to mental representation. In this way, automatic (overwhelming) anxiety may be transformed into anxiety that may function as a signal (signal-anxiety; Freud, 1926). Defensive measures may then be taken to avoid catastrophic anxiety, implying that the anxiety-provoking situation is interpreted and understood in a way that makes a differentiated action possible.

Mentalization may be seen as a linking function connecting bodily excitations with endopsychic representations, a process of psychic transformation whereby "unmentalized" experiences are changed into mental contents within a human interpersonal and intersubjective matrix (Lecour & Bouchard, 1997). This is a precondition if these experiences are to play any endopsychic role. There are levels of mentalization and all psychic content may be placed on a continuum of increasing mental quality between the poles of somatization and insight. This is an ongoing process in which somatic excitation, and thus psychic content, are constantly reorganized on different levels of mentalization, including bodily excitation, acting, dreaming and higher levels of abstraction. Meaning is, however, not only attached to representation in language but is also inherent in the preverbal organization of emotions (embodied meaning).

What concerns us here is this ongoing process of binding excitation and reorganizing experience, bodily and psychic, and how experience is organized and acquire meaning. Mute suffering of the body, for example, in the form of somatic symptoms of psychic origin, is a central concern for the study of trauma. The body may become the scene for the wordless drama of the traumatizing experience. Words do not reach the wordless representation of experience. Semiosis, the study of sign processes as a dynamic and dialogic process where meaning is established is thus central for understanding of how traumatic experiences can be worked with.

In the philosopher Peirce's semiotic and interpersonal model for the ongoing symbolizing process a sign has a symbolic relation to the object only insofar as there is someone who interprets it as such; another sign functions as an interpreter (interpretant) of the first sign, depicting how this sign is a symbol for the object. The interpretant needs yet another sign (as interpretant) to function as a symbol, and semiosis, symbolization and meaning creation, is thus in principle a perpetual process. The symptom may be seen as a frozen sign, where the interpretant is lacking or not available. Therapy may set the process of semiosis in motion. The interpretant may be a thought, a word, but also an action or affect. Its is an ongoing process in all dialogues and lays at the heart of the psychotherapeutic process (Muller, 1996).

In psychoanalytical treatments, repetition compulsion provides an example of the dynamics of a coercive relationship that tends to force the other into the position of a mirror image or projection, a situation that precludes recognition of the other. This enactive and iconic mirroring lacks a third position (the logical interpretants in Peirce's system), impedes the other's (e.g., the therapist) ability to reflect, and he/she become less available for the traumatized person's need to symbolize traumatic experiences. The traumatized person gets locked in a dependence with diminished capacity to understand the other's and their own motives and ways of thinking (lack of mentalization).

The ongoing process of binding or linking described by Freud may be understood as a process of semiosis. This meaning-making represents the process whereby the individual is connected to culture and where experience is mediated by cultural symbols or signs, that is, given a shared culturally determined meaning. Coerced mirroring is a process by which this link to culture and the social aspect is cut off.

Traumatized people act as if they were partly outside the cultural realm of common meaning and their experiences are often short-circuited by the process of cutting off the cultural mediation by signs; in Peirce's thinking, the interpretants of "logic" are not available in the traumatized part of the personality, which is another way of saying that traumatic experiences may be mediated by dissociated representations in implicit memory, and lead to derealization as the culturally based meaning of experiences becomes less accessible.

According to this viewpoint, trauma is pathological precisely because of this damage to the link to the cultural and social mediation of experience, damage that curtails the process of transformation of bodily excitation to mental content and also reduces the further reorganization of levels of mental representation.

Culturally symbolic expressions, including language, provide protection against "raw experience," and are the medium through which we construct our reality. Traumatized individuals have had experiences that are "beyond the imaginable" and not signified (leading to confusion), badly signified (e.g., only as images or bodily sensations (signs) or action-tendencies (e.g., fight-flight or freeze), that is, stored in the "traumatic, implicit memory") or only partly signified.

The severely traumatized person may experience this uncertainty as a mental state with a lack of ability to comprehend what is happening and doubt whether there can be any meaning assigned to his symptoms and sufferings.

Traumatization results in a dedifferentiation of affects, a loss of ability to identify specific emotions that can serve as guide for taking appropriate actions resulting in further dedifferentiation of emotional meaning toward increasingly primitive emotion-meaning schemas.

In man-made traumas such as torture, body and mind are attacked. The possibility for meaning-making and healing is affected both because of the tendency toward withdrawal and the subsequent disturbance in the ability to use others in a culturally based symbolizing process and because of the ostracizing of the politically traumatized individual that alienates him/her from the cultural context. The bodily pain inflicted may be the least devastating part of the experience. The "automatic" anxiety produced by the mortal danger and the unpredictability of the situation becomes devastating, because it cannot be linked to representations other than very primitive images or fantasies. Being humiliated and dehumanized often produces a profound feeling of loss of hope and belief in oneself and others. Furthermore, meaning and values are attacked, which makes orientation in time and space very difficult and reorientation through the use of culturally defined symbols impossible for many.

What is seen in the aftermath of extreme experiences is the person's adaptation to a changed inner reality and a modified perception of external reality. (One would also have to include real changes of external reality such as rejection, "the conspiracy of silence," which are always a part of the traumatized individual's experience.) The affect pathology implies a disturbance in the transformative capacity of the mind, and dedifferentiation involves a reversal of the ability to work through emotional experiences.

The understanding of extreme traumatization is here placed in relation to the other, both internal and external, and to the categories of memory, representation, symbolization and mentalization. These are seen as different dimensions of the same process, namely the process of reestablishing a personal history and identity through the restoration of the inner empathic relationship. This process represents, in other words, a possibility of historization through a relationship with the other. The other is, in a developmental perspective, not only nurturing and safety providing, but also the one who can structure the world, make it meaningful and predictable through representing a symbolizing function that is then internalized.

Mentalization is thus a relational process. In the mother–infant dyad, and later between the child and other significant others, there is a sign-mediated dialogue, which is essential in the process of making meaning of experience. This will later be established as a part of an internal dialogue that goes hand in hand with exchanges with others. I have shown how this dialogue, both external and internal, tends to be hampered in persons who are in a posttraumatic condition.

## Summary and future development

The scientific understanding of trauma was until Janet's and Freud's pioneering work dominated by theories of disposition and inherited weakness of the soul causing psychic illness. Both opened science for understanding the complicated relation between social conditions and mental illness, and especially Freud opened for understanding of the structure and the dynamics of the mind and the understanding of the human mind as meaning-producing and that behavior, including illness, is the result of attempts to survive psychic pain and to create meaning.

In light of the fact that Freud opened our understanding of the relation between social conditions and mental illness, it is striking that present-day psychoanalysis is immersed in a intersubjective, constructivist and narrative understanding of psychoanalytic therapy often at the expense of seeing mental phenomena, especially trauma, in its historical context. The emphasis on the transference–countertransference relationship and on technique as a means to help the patient reassemble or integrate warded off self-aspects has marginalized the connection between mental disease and real social occurrences. On the other hand, the foundation of psychoanalysis in biology and the understanding of bodily processes as part of the psychological domain have also suffered in the narrative approach. This development has, in my opinion, made necessary a reconsideration of psychoanalytic theory of psychic trauma and to investigate whether present clinical theory is suitable for the treatment of psychic trauma. Bohleber has emphasized the need to adapt both a psychoeconomical and an object relational perspective on trauma (Bohleber, 2000). The first concerns the "too much" of the traumatic experience (the overwhelming of the ego), while the second stresses the experience of loss of the link, or rather dialogue, with the internal empathic other. As I have shown, notably Freud developed the first perspective while the latter is an achievement of later years' psychoanalysis. I see the structural perspective in psychoanalysis as related to the psycho-economic perspective. The "too much" relates to the ability of the psychic apparatus to organize experience and concerns perception, cognition and memory systems and the more or less stable psychic structures that develop in the maturing personality. Extreme traumatization has as its effect a destruction of the personality. In this field, there is therefore a need to understand psychic structure and the mental processes that underlies and upholds it.

The relational problems associated with the posttraumatic state are equally important and are seen as reflecting basic disturbances in mental processing of experience. I have emphasized how relational needs and relational regulatory processes may become deeply disturbed in the post-traumatic state. Under normal circumstances, internal good or empathic objects are mediators between self and environment. The clinically observed mistrust and lack of empathy and ability to understand others in terms of mental states may, accordingly, be seen as reflecting disturbances in these inner relationships or dialogues.

There is, however, a need to bridge the psycho-economic/structural perspective and the interpersonal perspective on trauma and traumatization. I have introduced theories from semiotics as tools to understand symbolization and there are arguments that a structural-semiotic approach may represent such a bridge (Varvin, 2003). The object relational and the psychoeconomic/structural are different perspectives on the same processes. It is difficult to conceive an object relation without an ego structuring the link to the other as mental representations, and it is likewise also impossible to understand the state of being overwhelmed without taking into consideration the concomitant loss of the link to the other both externally and in psychic reality. Further, it is clear the mental processing associated with relational problems is an ego-activity and belongs thus to the structural domain. One may say that the two perspectives more represent difference in emphasis than qualitatively different perspectives. The scientific understanding of trauma has been highly influenced by social and political issues and conflicting perspectives have thus not only been connected with disputes in the scientific field. One may argue that these are tensions that are inherent to the subject of trauma itself.

Psychoanalysis has been occupied with the unbearable of psychic trauma and the state of affairs can summarized as follows:

1   Trauma has been difficult to situate both in psychoanalytic theory and cognitive theory. Social and political conditions have influenced the acceptance and understanding of the traumatized patient as well as the scientific investigation of psychological trauma.
2   Freud's early formulations, especially in relation to his reformulation of the theory of anxiety from 1926, have proved useful for understanding the dynamics and structure of the traumatic situation, especially in focusing the possibility for symbolization and mentalization.
3   The development in cognitive science and neuroscience has proved useful for understanding emotions, emotion schemas and mental processing of experience. This has been important both in relation to the understanding of what happens during overwhelming experiences as well as afterward.
4   The semiotic perspective has helped basic psychoanalytic formulations regarding understanding symbolization, mentalization and the process of meaning-formation as well as the interactional and dialogic aspects of traumatization and posttraumatic conditions.
5   The organization in schemas and scenarios related to traumas may be seen as reflecting mental survival strategies with the double purpose of defending against unbearable memories and coping with the stresses of daily life.
6   The distinction in present trauma theory between the psychoeconomic/structural and the object relational perspective on trauma are seen as aspects of the same model. That is, the object relational perspective is present in the psychoeconomic model and structural theory is presupposed in the object relational model. There are still conceptual and theoretical problems concerned with the integration of these aspects.

Trauma thus affects the individual on several levels (body, identity, social adaptation, etc.) and man-made intentional traumatization also has effects on a social level (disturbing family structures, group-cohesion and even the stability of whole societies).

Following this, I will argue that further research on psychic trauma and traumatization must take the following into consideration:

1   The person's relation to others on a *bodily level*. This concerns the emotional interaction with others as well as basic somatic processes influenced by and influencing the basic somato-emotional level of relating to others (e.g., neuro-vegetative processes). A symptom at this level would be the disturbance in the ability to regulate negative emotion in intimate relationships.

2   The person's relation to others on a *group level*. This concerns the formation of identity by being a member of a group, family, clan and so forth. A symptom at this level would be the grave identity disturbances seen in refugees who have been dehumanized in torture. Being in exile often aggravates this situation.

3   The person's relation to culture and cultural discourses. This concerns the role played by the store of cultural praxis, literature, folktales and ways of thinking about and solving conflict and problems. This is the level where the individual can acquire meaning from personal experience by relating to cultural modes and values. Disturbance on this level is seen in the tendency to isolate/dissociate traumatic experiences in the psyche and in the traumatized person's tendency to isolate him/herself from dialogues with others and with cultural praxis.

There are important gaps in our understanding of traumatic experiences and responses, and it follows from the foregoing that interdisciplinary approaches are needed. The present psychoanalytic literature in trauma has concentrated to a large degree on symbolization. There is, however, obvious deficiencies in that often not only the interdisciplinary approach is lacking but even reference to other psychoanalytic colleagues and schools, leaving the impression of a scattered scientific field. This has resulted in conceptual confusion and disturbed development. For a development to occur it is obvious that clinical, empirical and conceptual research has to go hand in hand.

## Notes

1   "Wir zielten auf keine kathartische Abfuhr, sondern darauf, zu helfen, eine Trauerprozess in Gang zu setzen, der im Lager oder später nicht hatte stattfinden können."
2   Freud combines thus an analogue and a symbolic (digital) representational model, and places the different types of representations in a spatial model of the mind.

## References

Bergmann, MS 1998, 'Die Interaktion zwischen Trauma und intrapsychischem Konflikt in der Geschichte der Psychoanalyse', in A-M Schlösser & K Höhfeld (eds), *Trauma und Konflikt*. Psychosozial-Verlag, Giessen, pp. 113–130.

Blum, HP 1994, 'The confusion of tongues and psychic trauma', *International Journal of Psychoanalysis*, vol. 75, pp. 871–882.

Bohleber, W 2000, 'Die Entwicklung der Traumatheorie in der Psychoanalyse', *Psyche (Stuttg)*, vol. 54, pp. 797–839.

Brazelton, T, Koslowski, B & Main, M 1974, 'The origins of reciprocity', in M Lewis & L Rosenblum (eds), *The effect of the infant on its caregiver*, Wiley, New York, pp. 49–75.

Breuer, J & Freud, S 1895, *Studies on hysteria*, Penguin Books, London.

Crittenden, PM 2011, *Attachment. A dynamic-maturational approach to discourse analysis*, W.W. Norton, New York.

Eitinger, L 1965, 'Concentration camp survivors in Norway and Israel', *Israel Journal of Medical Science*, vol. 1, pp. 883–895.

Ferenczi, S 1933, 'Confusion of tongues between the adult and the child (The language of tenderness and of passion)', *International Journal of Psychoanalysis*, vol. 30, pp. 225–230.

Freud, A 1967, 'Comments on trauma', in SS Furst (ed), *Psychic Trauma*, Basic Books, New York, pp. 235–245.

Freud, S 1915, 'The unconscious', in J Strachey (ed), *Standard edition of the complete psychological works of Sigmund Freud*, vol. 14, Hogarth, London.

Freud, S 1917, 'Mourning and melancholia', in J Strachey (ed), *Standard edition of the complete psychological works of Sigmund Freud*, vol. 14, Hogarth, London.

Freud, S 1920. 'Beyond the pleasure principle', in J Strachey (ed), *Standard edition of the complete psychological works of Sigmund Freud*, vol. 18, Hogarth, London.

Freud, S 1926, 'Inhibitions, symptoms and anxiety', in J Strachey (ed), *Standard edition of the complete psychological works of Sigmund Freud*, vol. 20, Hogarth, London.

Hartmann, H 1939, 'Psycho-analysis and the concept of health', *International Journal of Psychoanalysis*, vol. 20, pp. 308–321.

Hoppe, K 1968, 'Re-somatization of affects in survivors of persecution', *International Journal of Psychoanalysis*, vol. 49, pp. 324–326.

Jaffe, W 1969, *Towards a basic psychoanalytic model*, Basic Books, New York.

Janet, P 1907, *The major symptoms of hysteria*, Hafner, New York.

Kardiner, A 1941, *The traumatic neurosis of war*, Hoeber, New York.

Keilson, H & Sarpathie, R 1979, *Sequentieller Traumatisierung bei Kindern*, Ferdinand Enke, Stuttgart.

Krystal, H 1978, 'Trauma and affects', *Psychoanalytic Study of the Child*, vol. 33, pp. 81–116.

Lansky, M & Bley, CR 1995, *Posttraumatic nightmares, psychodynamic explorations*, Analytic Press, Hillsdale, NJ.

Laub, D & Podell, D 1995, 'Art and trauma'. *International Journal of Psychoanalytic Analysis*, vol. 76, pp. 991–1005.

Lecour, S & Bouchard, M 1997, 'Dimensions of mentalisation: Outlining levels of psychic transformation', *International Journal of Psychoanalysis*, vol. 78, pp. 855–876.

Muller, J 1996, *Beyond the psychoanalytic dyad*. Routledge, New York.

Nemiah, JC 1998, 'Early concepts of trauma, dissociation, and the unconscious: Their history and current implications', in JD Bremer & CR Marmar (eds), *Trauma, memory and dissociation*. American Psychiatric Press, Washington, DC, pp. 1–26.

Niederland, WG 1981, 'The survivor syndrome: further observations and dimensions', *Journal of American Psychoanalysis Association*, vol. 29, pp. 413–425.

Pally, R 1997, 'Memory: Brain systems that link past, present and future', *International Journal of Psychoanalysis*, vol. 78, pp. 1223–1234.

Simenauer, E 1968, 'Late psychic sequelae of man-made disasters', *International Journal of Psychoanalysis*, vol. 49, pp. 306–309.

Simmel, E 1944, 'Kriegsneurosen', in *Psychoanalyse und ihre Anwendungen. Ausgewählte Schriften*, Fisher Verlag, Frankfurt, pp. 204–226.

Varvin, S 2003, *Mental survival strategies after extreme traumatisation*, Multivers, Copenhagen.

# Index

Index

talk–therapy 3
Target, Mary 412, 428
Tavistock Clinic 44, 47, 50, 116, 119, 235, 237
Tavistock Institute of Human Relations (TIHR)
    235–6, 272
Taylor, Barbara 255
Terragni, Giusseppe 322
theism *vs.* atheism 281, 284–6
thinking: Bion 81–3
Third: idea of 158–60; intersubjective recognition
    theory 160–3
Thom, René 95–6n14
Thompson, Clara 185–6, 193, 201, 203
Tolstoy, Leo 354
totalitarianism: attack on creative thinking 72–4;
    democratic political work 62–7
transcendentalism *vs.* immanentism 281, 289
transference 140; enactment and 230–2; Freud
    306–7; Joseph 231–2; Klein, 228–9; Sandler 231;
    unconscious 19–20
transformation: dreaming 139–40
transitional space: Winnicott 67–8, 70–3, 75, 344
trauma: ambivalence toward victim 449–52;
    concept 450–2, 456–8; developmental research
    cognitive- and neuroscience 459–60; diagnostic
    approach 458–9; Ferenczi's contribution to
    452–3; future development 464–6; historical
    and intellectual development 449; memory and
    460–2; psychanalysis and 448–9, 464–6; symbol-
    ization and 462–4; types of 457; war neuroses
    453; after World War II 453–6
trauma theory 306–9, 465
Trilling, Lionel 21, 257n14
Trist, Eric 272
Trotsky, Leon 207, 217–20, 222–3
true self: Winnicott 60, 68, 70, 73–4, 199
Truffaut, François 334, 336
Truth and Reconciliation Commission (TRC) 417;
    as emotional container 418–21; perpetrators'
    responses to witness testimonies 425–7; survi-
    vors' responses to witnesses' testimony 423–5;
    testimonies 421–7; *see also* reconciliation
Tutter, Adele 320–1

Umphrey, Martha Merrill 376
unconscious, 1; concept 13–16; contemporary
    Freudian 21–4; other side of humanities 28–9;
    radicalism of 26–7; structured like a language
    99–100; structure of 16–19; subject of the
    100–102; term 17; transference 19–20
"unconscious defenses against anxiety" thesis 272–3

van der Rohe, Ludwig Mies 320, 322
Varvin, Sverre 9, 448–67
Vasconcelos, José 215
Veterans Community Park and Pavilion Project
    Studio 328–9
Vicedo, Marga 123

victims: trauma and ambivalence toward
    449–52
Vidler, Anthony 316–17, 319
Vietnam War 302, 308, 350–1
visual arts: from art history to psychoanalysis
    348–9; ego psychology 355–9; framing themes
    350–2; Freud's contributions 353–5; object
    relations theory 359–60; psychoanalysis and
    360–1; Rembrandt's *Artist in His Studio* 356;
    Rembrandt's *Polish Rider*, 348, 349, 351, 357,
    361; three-part paradigm 352–3
voice: Lacan 102–3

Wajcman, Gérard 322
Wallerstein, Robert 191
Wallon, Henri 99
Walzer, Michael 72–3
Weber, Max 197, 259–61, 269, 275n20, 275n7
Western philosophy 278–82, 289
White, Hayden 254
Wigglesworth, Sarah 321–2
Wigley, Mark 321
Wilde, Oscar 208, 356
Winer, Jerome 323
Winnicott, Donald 4, 8, 23, 31, 50, 52; aliveness
    59–60, 68; case report of Yuzhen 62–7;
    cinematic approach 344; false self 335; "good-
    enough mother" 361, 373; idea of third
    158–60; mothers and infants 384, 386, 389,
    393–4; object relations theory 229–30, 352, 354,
    359–60, 384, 444; place of illusion in world
    order 67–72; playfulness 60, 69–70; psychic
    space 59–61, 67–8; psychoanalytic vision
    59–62; psychological totalitarianism 62–7;
    psychosexuality 404, 406; three-dimensional
    relationship 60–1, 71; transitional space 67–8,
    70–3, 75, 344; true self 60, 68, 70, 73–4, 199
Wittgenstein, Ludwig 232, 279
working group: Bion 77–9
world order: place of illusion in 67–72
World War I 44, 69, 221, 264, 307, 317, 441, 444,
    449, 453
World War II 20, 60, 69, 77, 230, 233–5, 253,
    260–1, 268, 273, 302, 355, 384, 405, 441, 444,
    449–50; trauma after 453–6
Wright, Elizabeth 23
Wright, Frank Lloyd 315, 326

Yates, Candida 239
Yeshiva University 368, 375
Young, James 318–19
Yuzhen: report of 62–7, 70, 74–5

Zimbardo, Philip 443
Žižek, Slavoj 7, 69–70, 103, 106, 108, 112, 274,
    280, 283, 288, 291, 342, 368
Zumthor, Peter 324, 327
Zweig, Stephan 353, 362n7

478

Printed in Great Britain
by Amazon